FROM THE LIBRARY OF

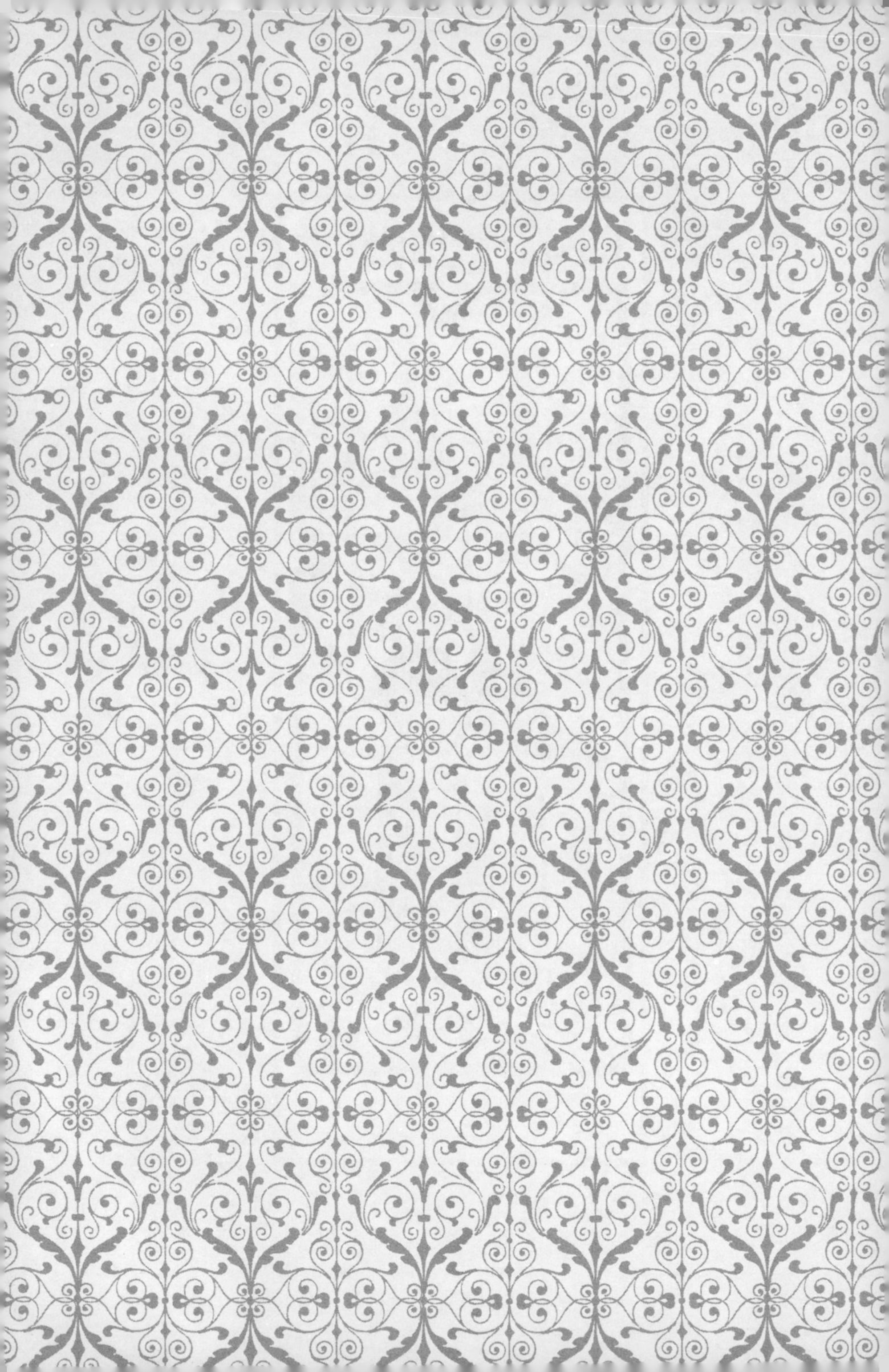

Castle Waiting

VOLUME II · BY LINDA MEDLEY

SANCTUM OMNIUM-GATHERUM

FANTAGRAPHICS BOOKS

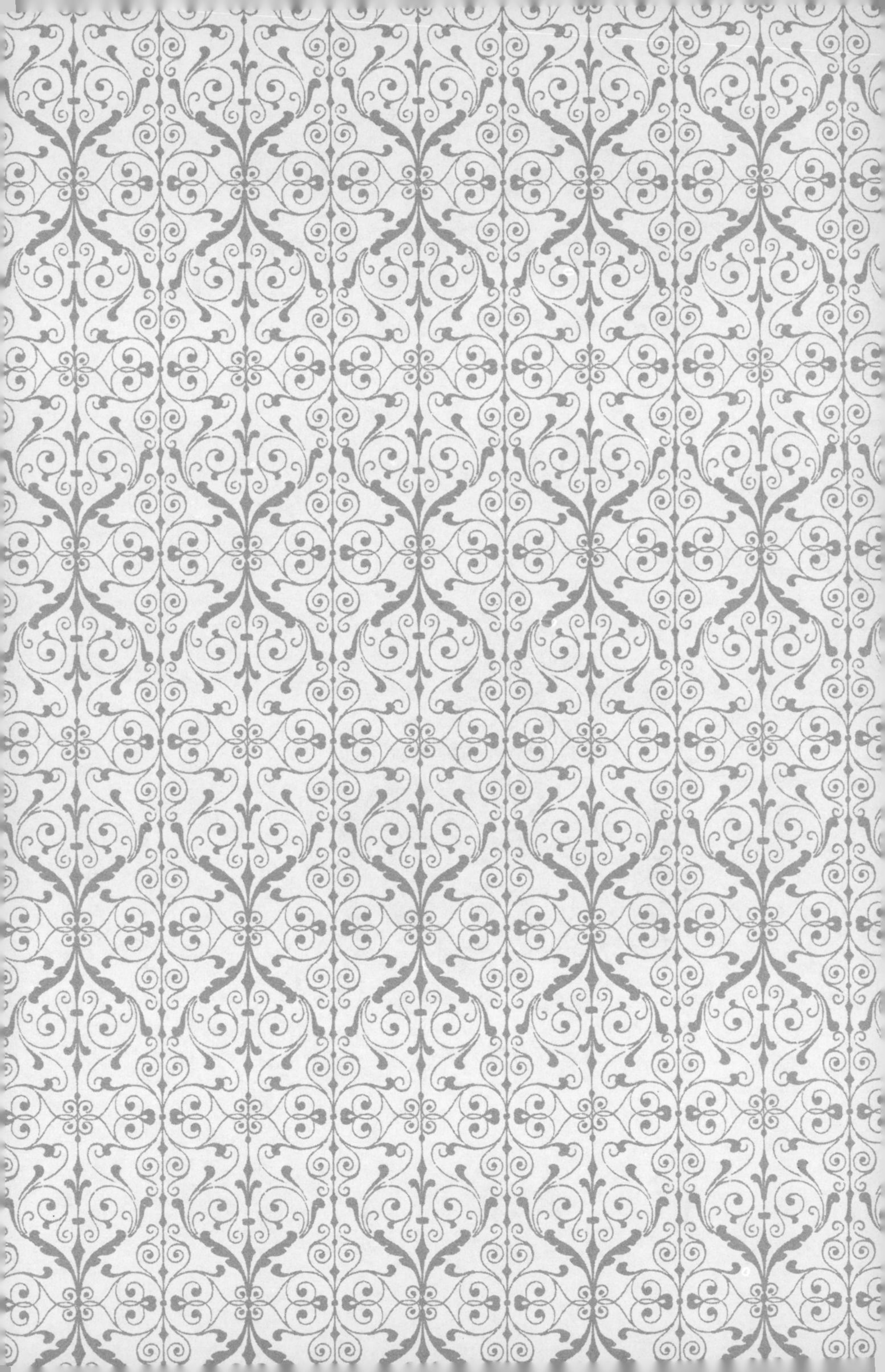

Chapter 1.

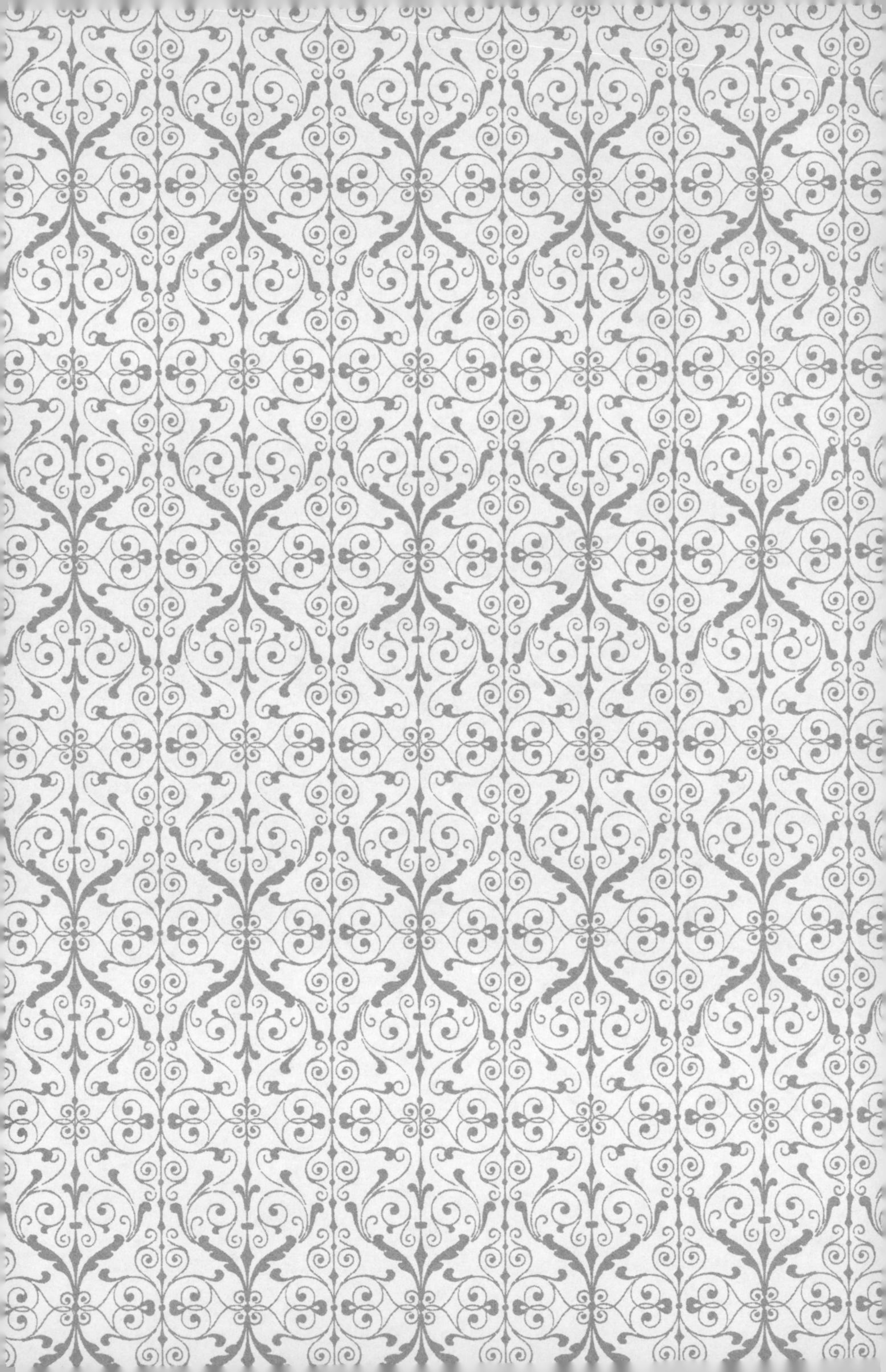

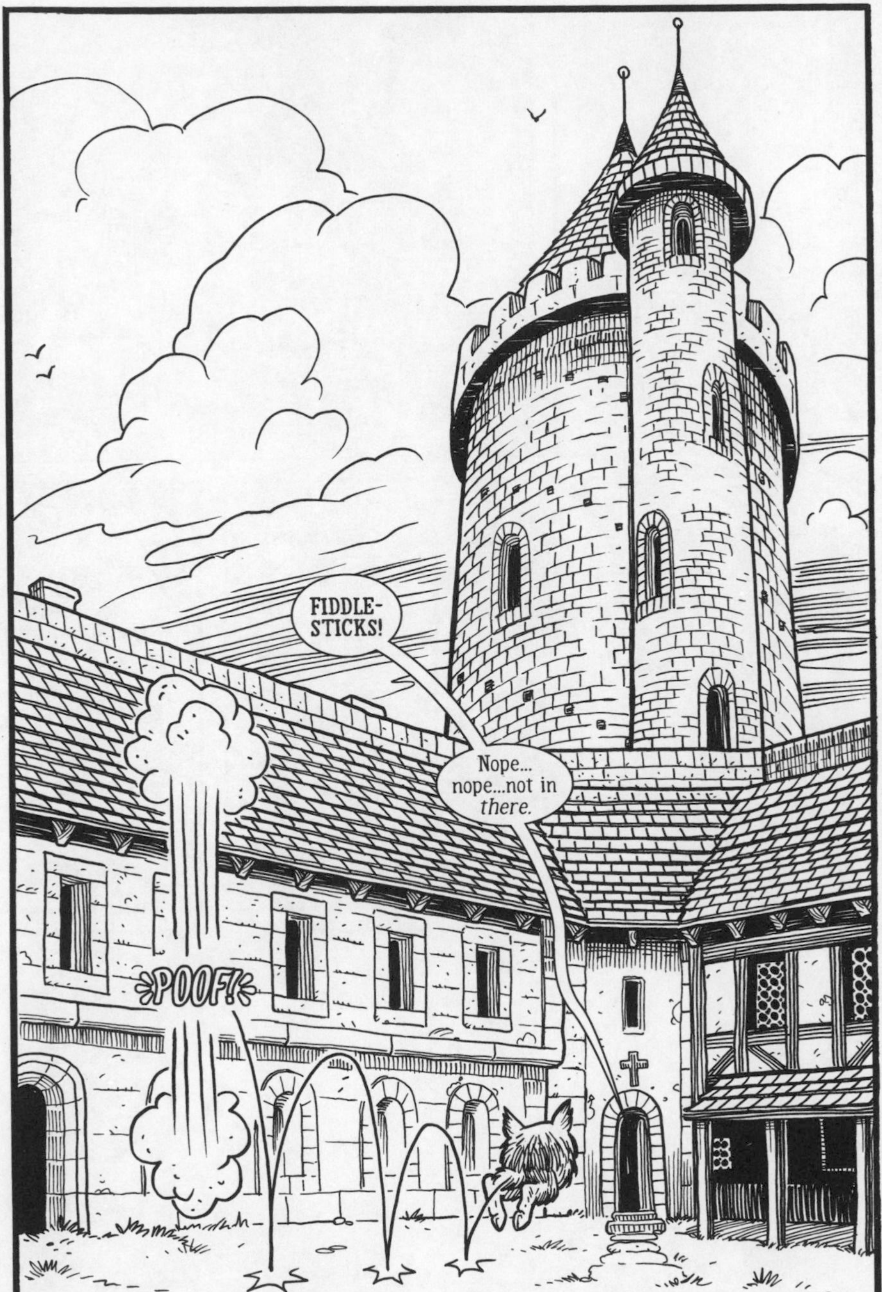
FIDDLE-
STICKS!
Nope... nope...not in *there.*
POOF!

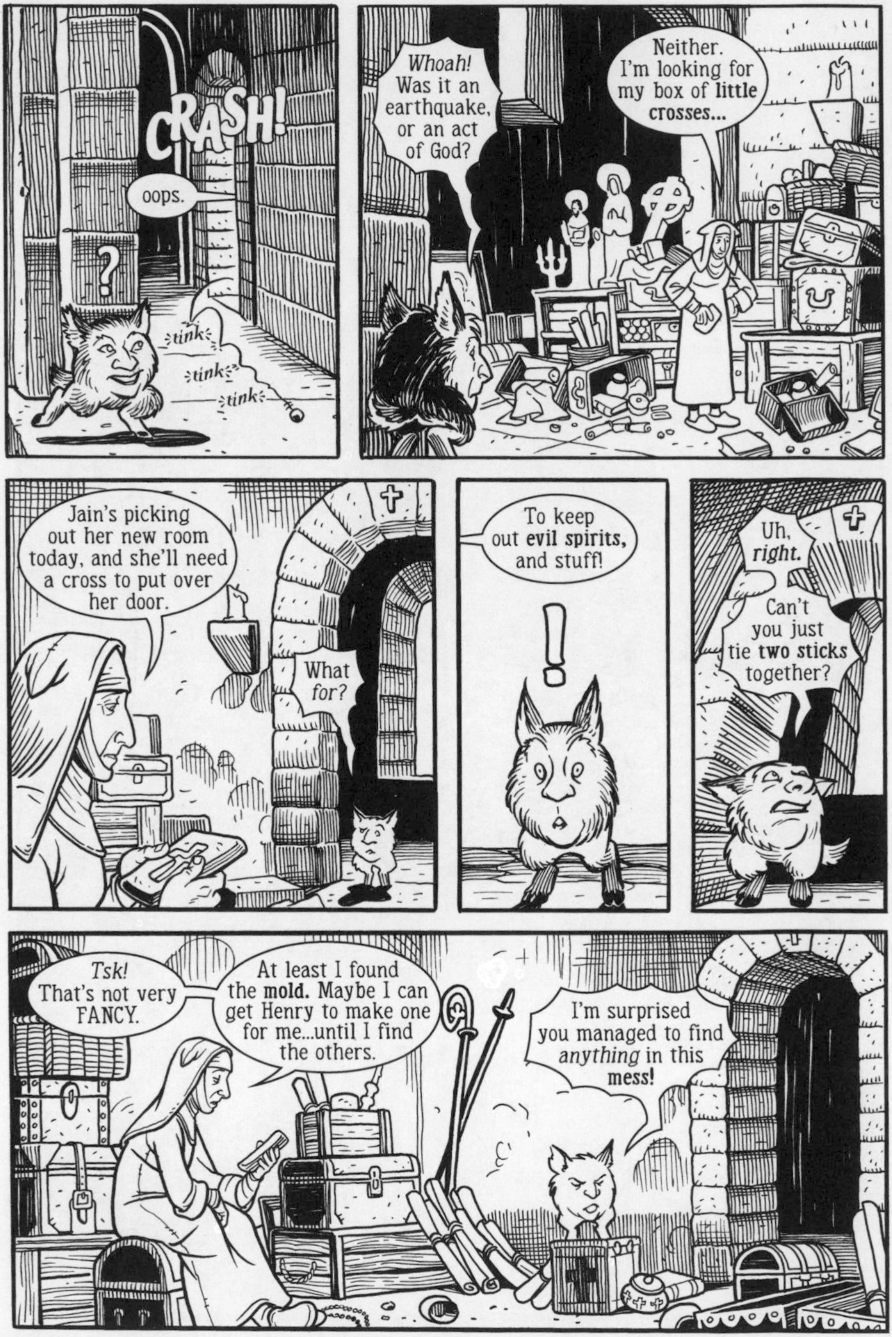
CRASH!
oops.
?
tink
tink
tink
Whoah! Was it an earthquake, or an act of God?
Neither. I'm looking for my box of **little crosses...**
Jain's picking out her new room today, and she'll need a cross to put over her door.
What *for?*
To keep out **evil spirits,** and stuff!
!
Uh, *right.*
Can't you just tie **two sticks** together?
Tsk! That's not very FANCY.
At least I found the **mold.** Maybe I can get Henry to make one for me...until I find the others.
I'm surprised you managed to find *anything* in this **mess!**

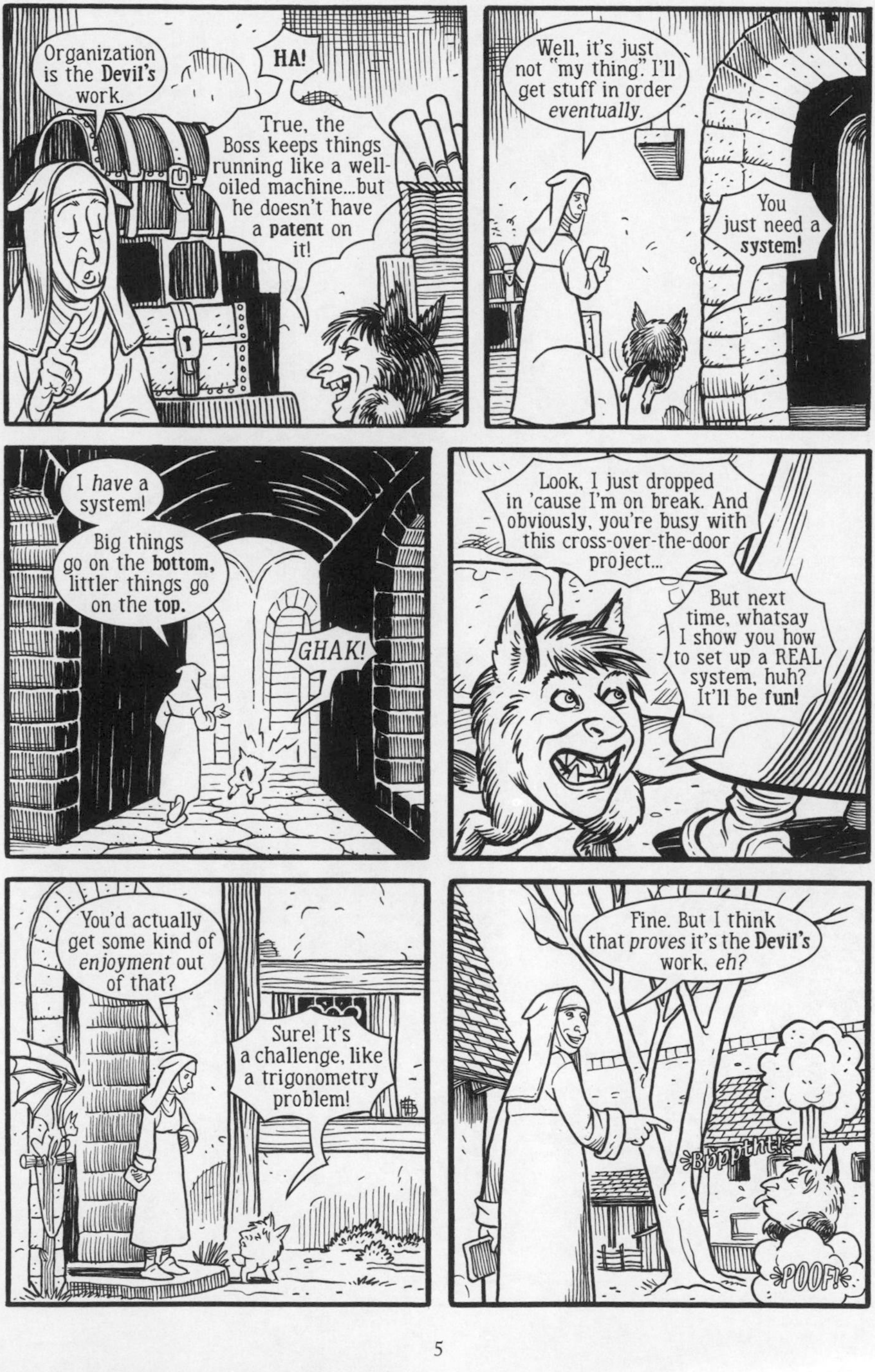
Organization is the **Devil's** work.
HA!
True, the Boss keeps things running like a well-oiled machine...but he doesn't have a **patent** on it!
Well, it's just not "my thing." I'll get stuff in order *eventually.*
You just need a **system!**
I *have* a system!
Big things go on the **bottom,** littler things go on the **top.**
GHAK!
Look, I just dropped in 'cause I'm on break. And obviously, you're busy with this cross-over-the-door project...
But next time, whatsay I show you how to set up a REAL system, huh? It'll be **fun!**
You'd actually get some kind of *enjoyment* out of that?
Sure! It's a challenge, like a trigonometry problem!
Fine. But I think that *proves* it's the **Devil's** work, *eh?*
Bpppthht!
POOF!

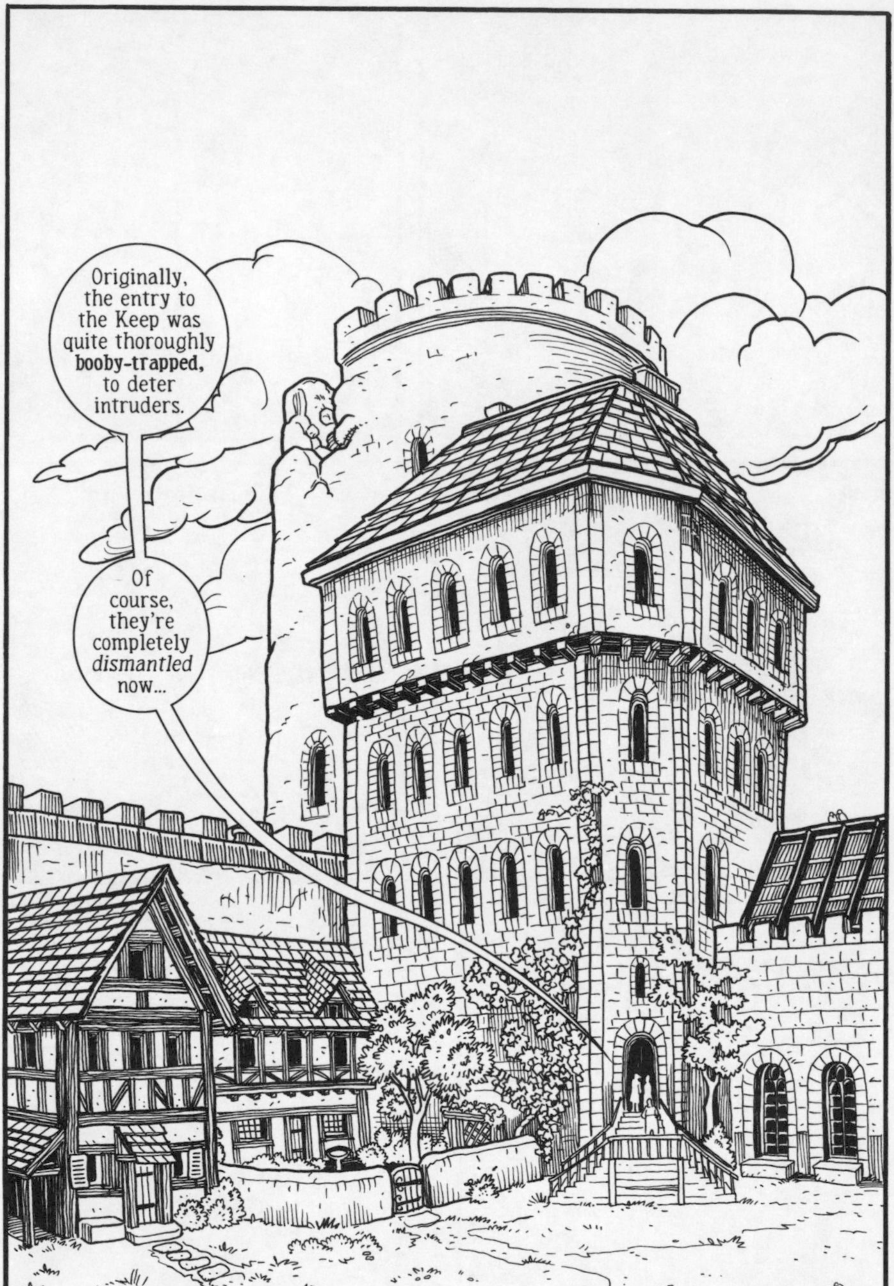
Originally, the entry to the Keep was quite thoroughly **booby-trapped,** to deter intruders.
Of course, they're completely *dismantled* now...

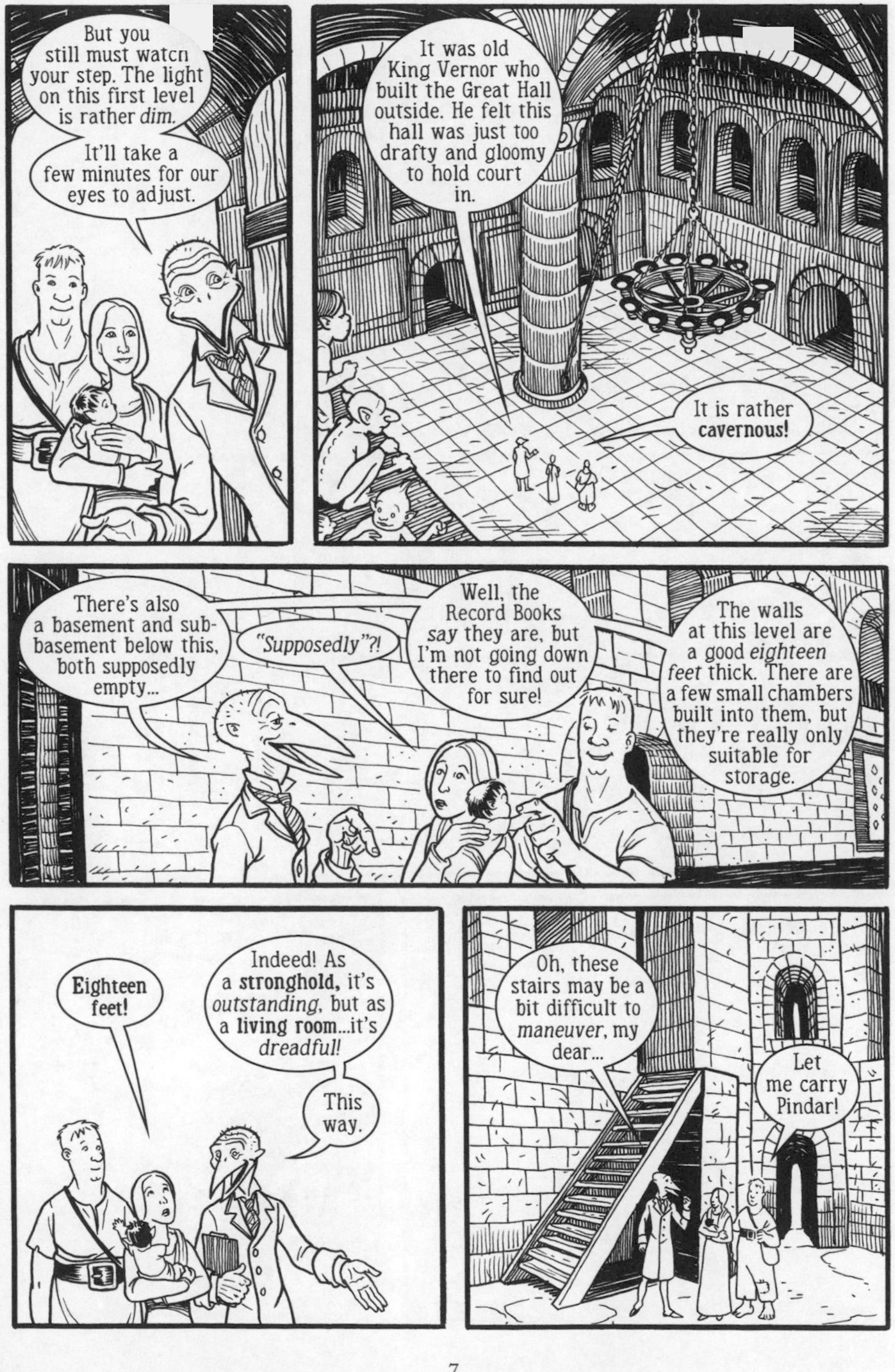
But you still must watch your step. The light on this first level is rather *dim.*
It'll take a few minutes for our eyes to adjust.
It was old King Vernor who built the Great Hall outside. He felt this hall was just too drafty and gloomy to hold court in.
It is rather **cavernous!**
There's also a basement and sub-basement below this, both supposedly empty...
"Supposedly"?!
Well, the Record Books *say* they are, but I'm not going down there to find out for sure!
The walls at this level are a good *eighteen feet* thick. There are a few small chambers built into them, but they're really only suitable for storage.
Eighteen feet!
Indeed! As a **stronghold,** it's *outstanding,* but as a **living room**...it's *dreadful!*
This way.
Oh, these stairs may be a bit difficult to *maneuver*, my dear...
Let me carry Pindar!

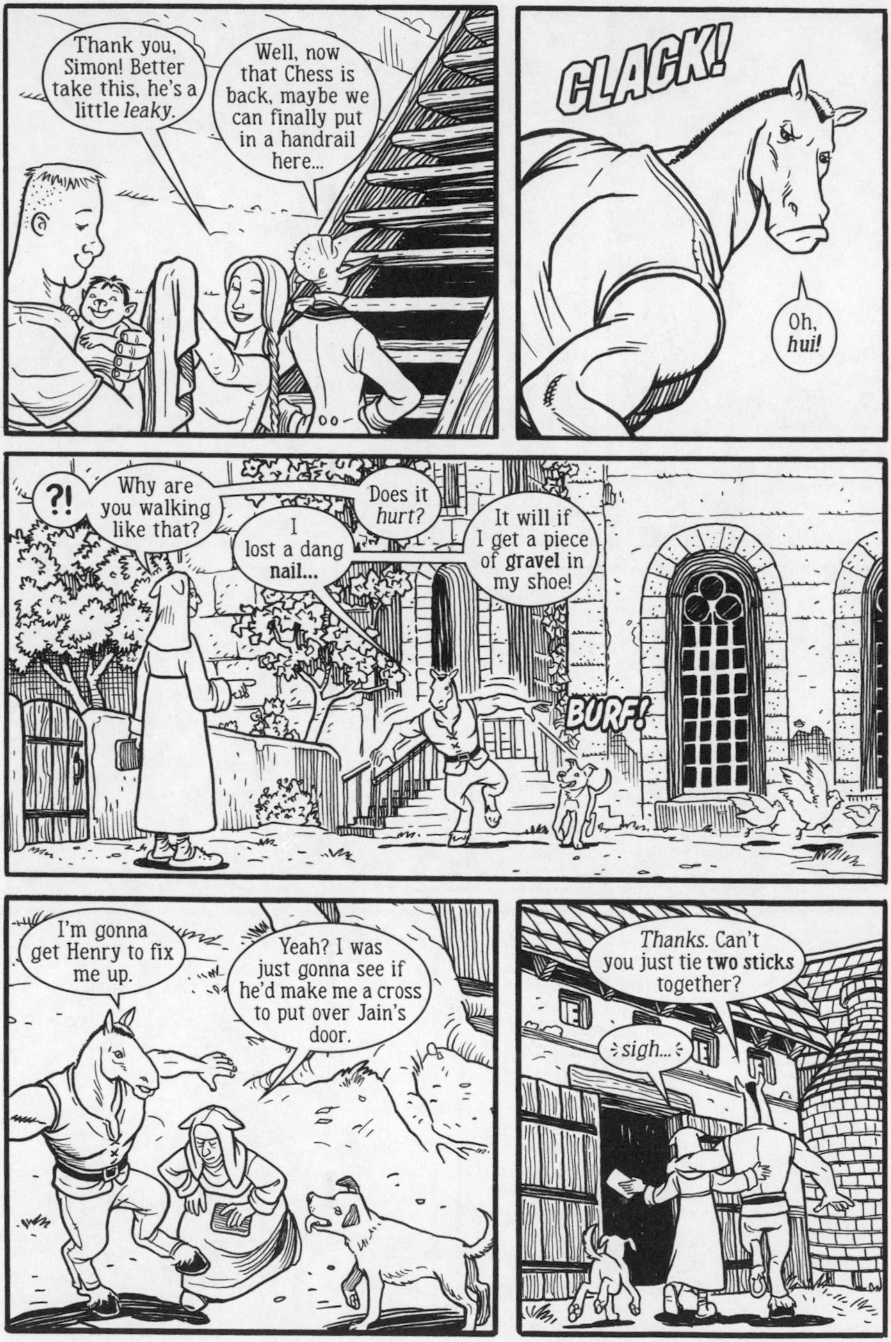
Thank you, Simon! Better take this, he's a little *leaky.*
Well, now that Chess is back, maybe we can finally put in a handrail here...
CLACK!
Oh, *hui!*
?!
Why are you walking like that?
Does it *hurt?*
I lost a dang **nail...**
It will if I get a piece of **gravel** in my shoe!
BURF!
I'm gonna get Henry to fix me up.
Yeah? I was just gonna see if he'd make me a cross to put over Jain's door.
Thanks. Can't you just tie **two sticks** together?
sigh...

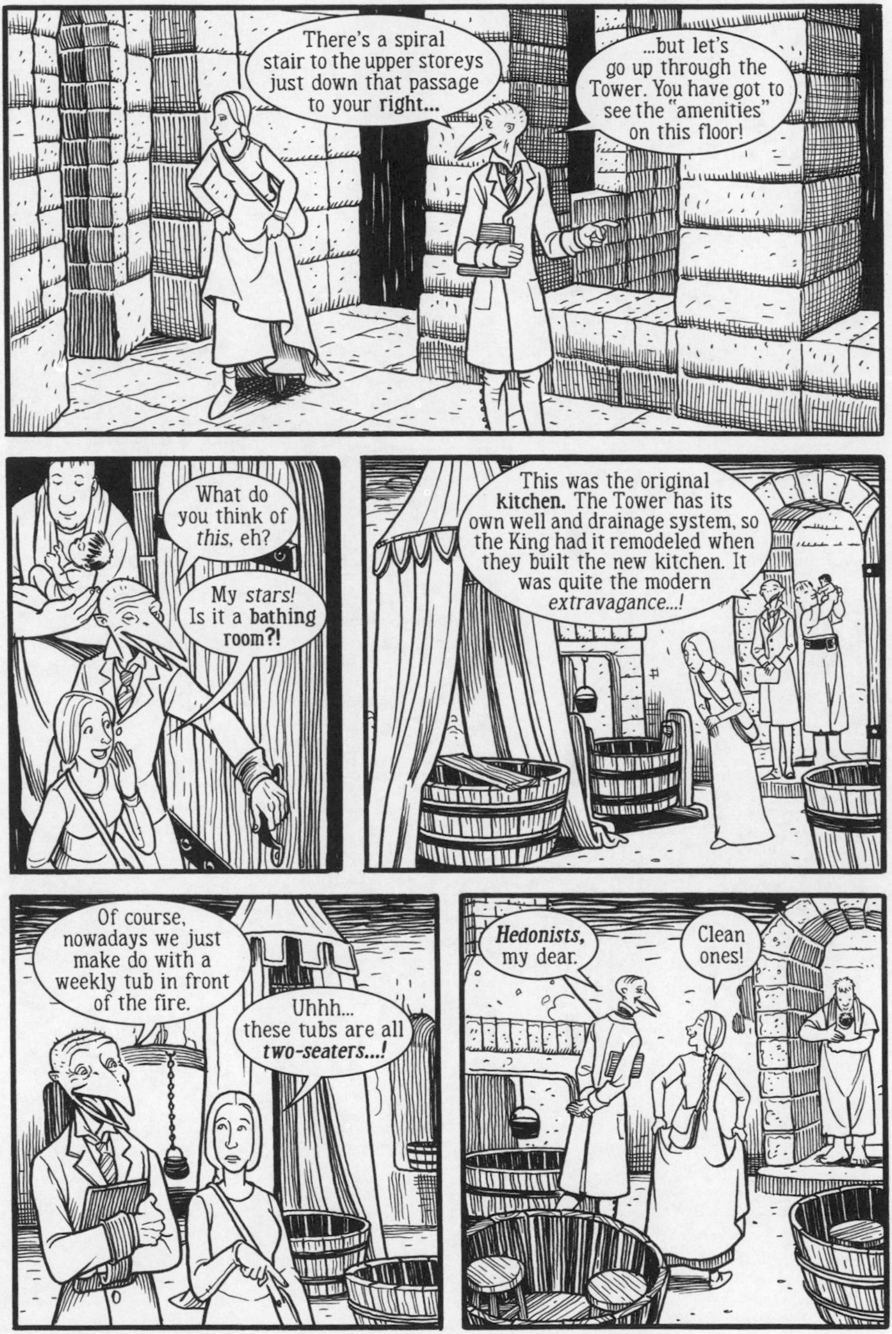
There's a spiral stair to the upper storeys just down that passage to your **right...**
...but let's go up through the Tower. You have got to see the "amenities" on this floor!
What do you think of *this*, eh?
My *stars!* Is it a **bathing room?!**
This was the original **kitchen.** The Tower has its own well and drainage system, so the King had it remodeled when they built the new kitchen. It was quite the modern *extravagance...!*
Of course, nowadays we just make do with a weekly tub in front of the fire.
Uhhh... these tubs are all ***two-seaters...!***
Hedonists, my dear.
Clean ones!

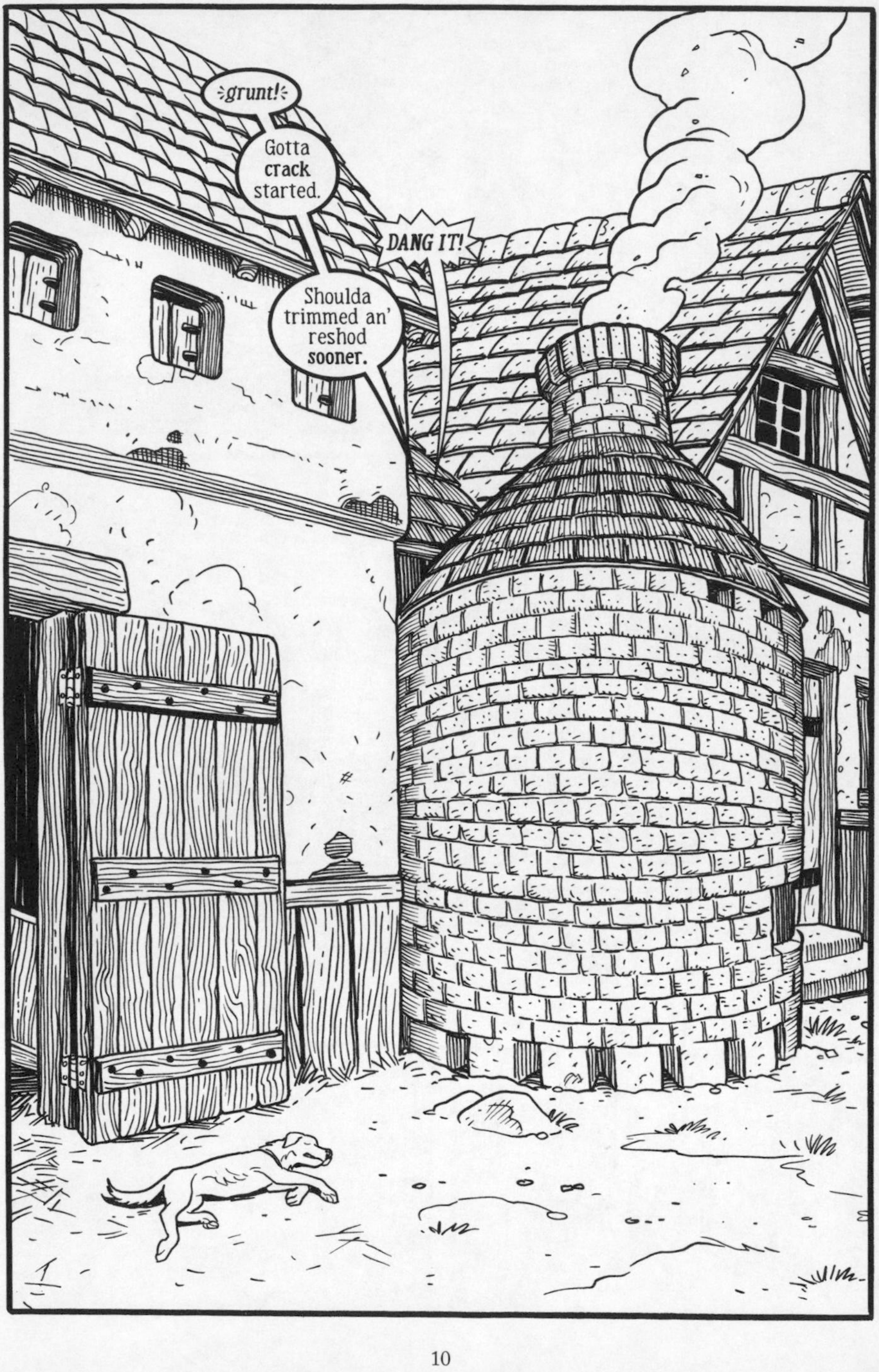
grunt!
Gotta crack started.
DANG IT!
Shoulda trimmed an' reshod sooner.

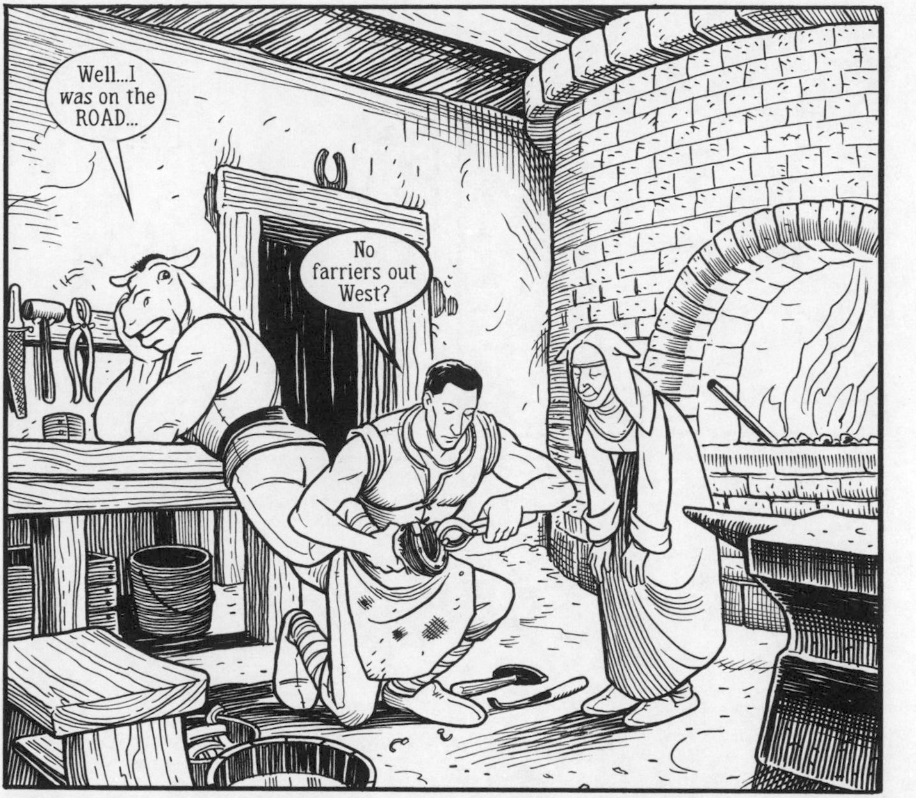
Well...I was on the ROAD...
No farriers out West?

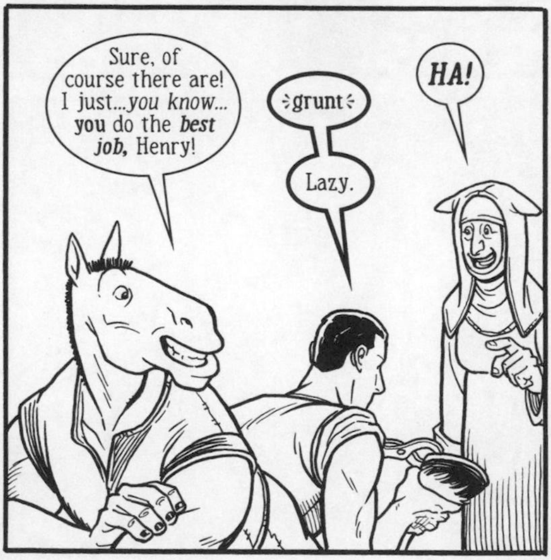
Sure, of course there are! I just...*you know*... **you** do the ***best job,*** Henry!
grunt
Lazy.
HA!

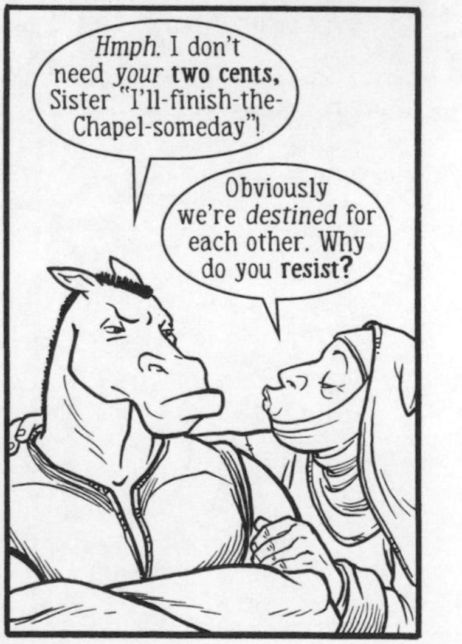
Hmph. I don't need *your* **two cents,** Sister "I'll-finish-the-Chapel-someday"!
Obviously we're *destined* for each other. Why do you **resist?**

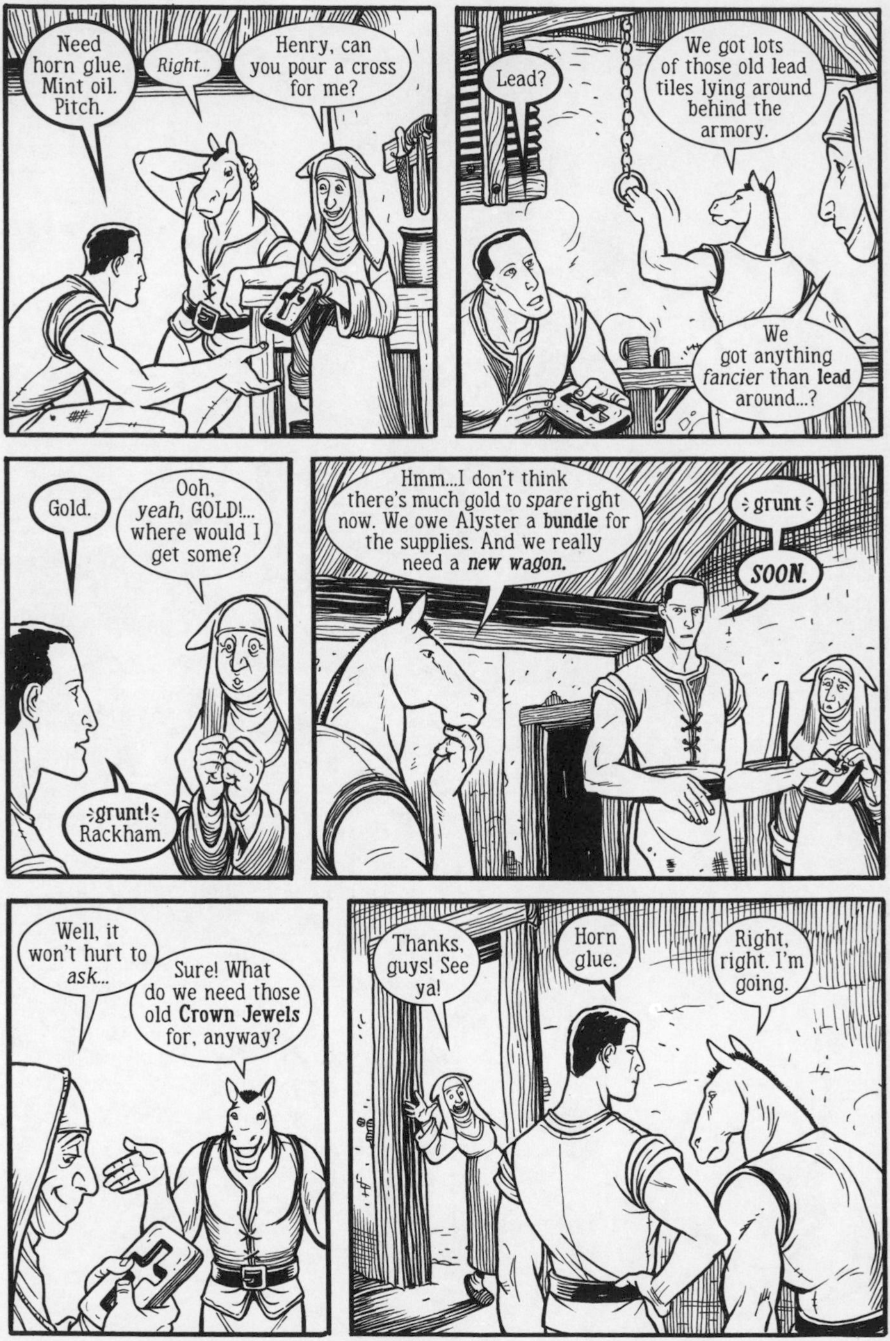
Need horn glue. Mint oil. Pitch.
Right...
Henry, can you pour a cross for me?
Lead?
We got lots of those old lead tiles lying around behind the armory.
We got anything fancier than lead around...?
Gold.
Ooh, yeah, GOLD!... where would I get some?
grunt! Rackham.
Hmm...I don't think there's much gold to spare right now. We owe Alyster a bundle for the supplies. And we really need a new wagon.
grunt
SOON.
Well, it won't hurt to ask...
Sure! What do we need those old Crown Jewels for, anyway?
Thanks, guys! See ya!
Horn glue.
Right, right. I'm going.

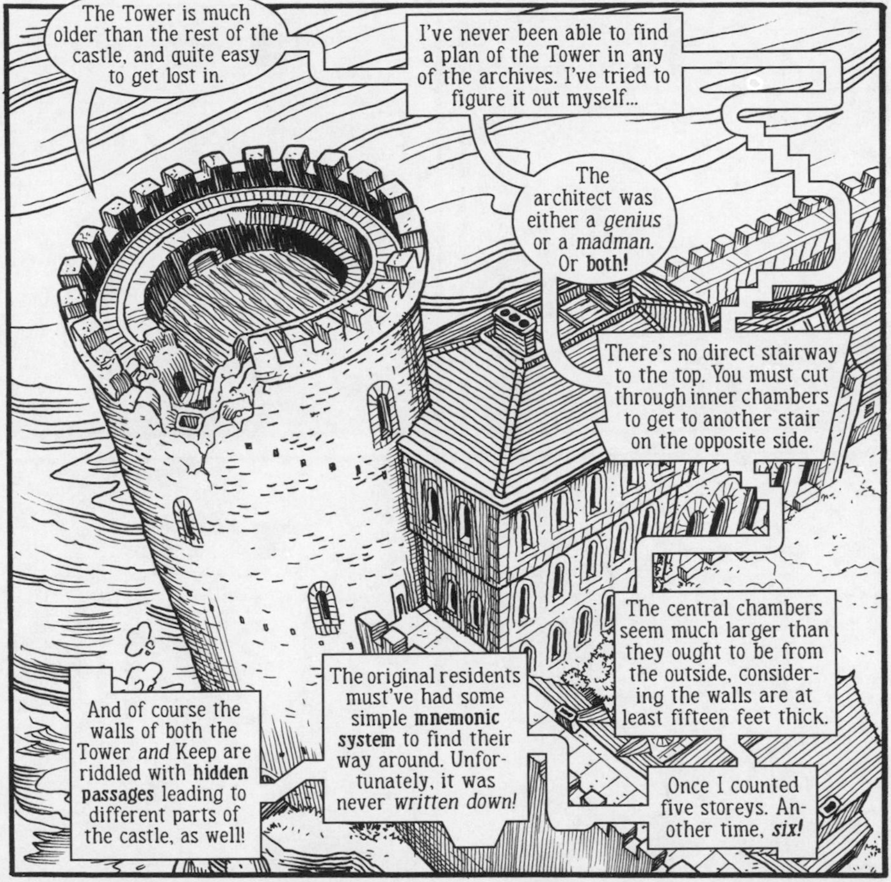
The Tower is much older than the rest of the castle, and quite easy to get lost in.
I've never been able to find a plan of the Tower in any of the archives. I've tried to figure it out myself...
The architect was either a *genius* or a *madman*. Or **both!**
There's no direct stairway to the top. You must cut through inner chambers to get to another stair on the opposite side.
The central chambers seem much larger than they ought to be from the outside, considering the walls are at least fifteen feet thick.
Once I counted five storeys. Another time, ***six!***
The original residents must've had some simple **mnemonic system** to find their way around. Unfortunately, it was never *written down!*
And of course the walls of both the Tower *and* Keep are riddled with **hidden passages** leading to different parts of the castle, as well!

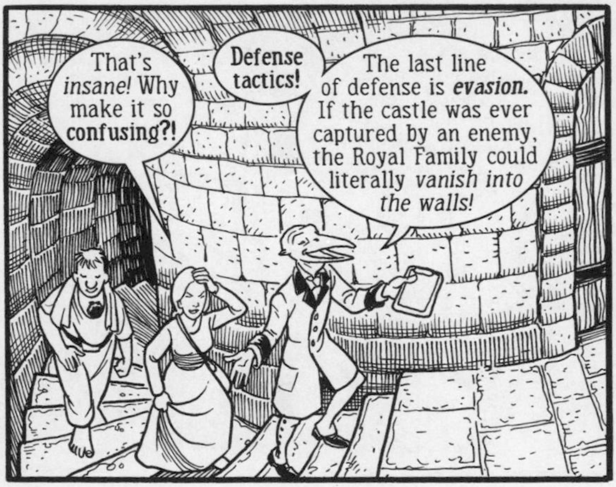
That's *insane!* Why make it so **confusing?!**
Defense tactics!
The last line of defense is ***evasion.*** If the castle was ever captured by an enemy, the Royal Family could literally *vanish into the walls!*

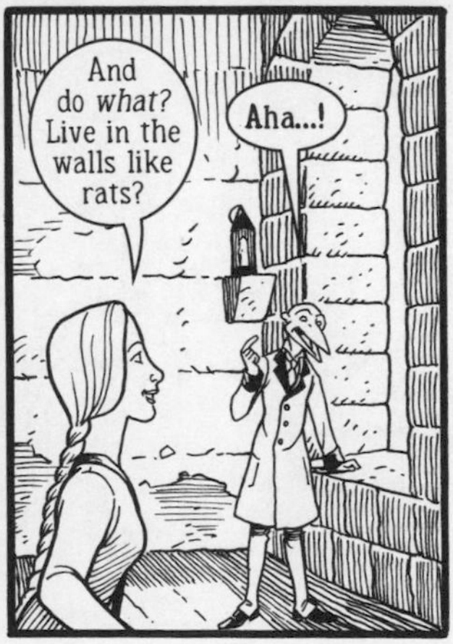
And do *what?* Live in the walls like rats?
Aha...!

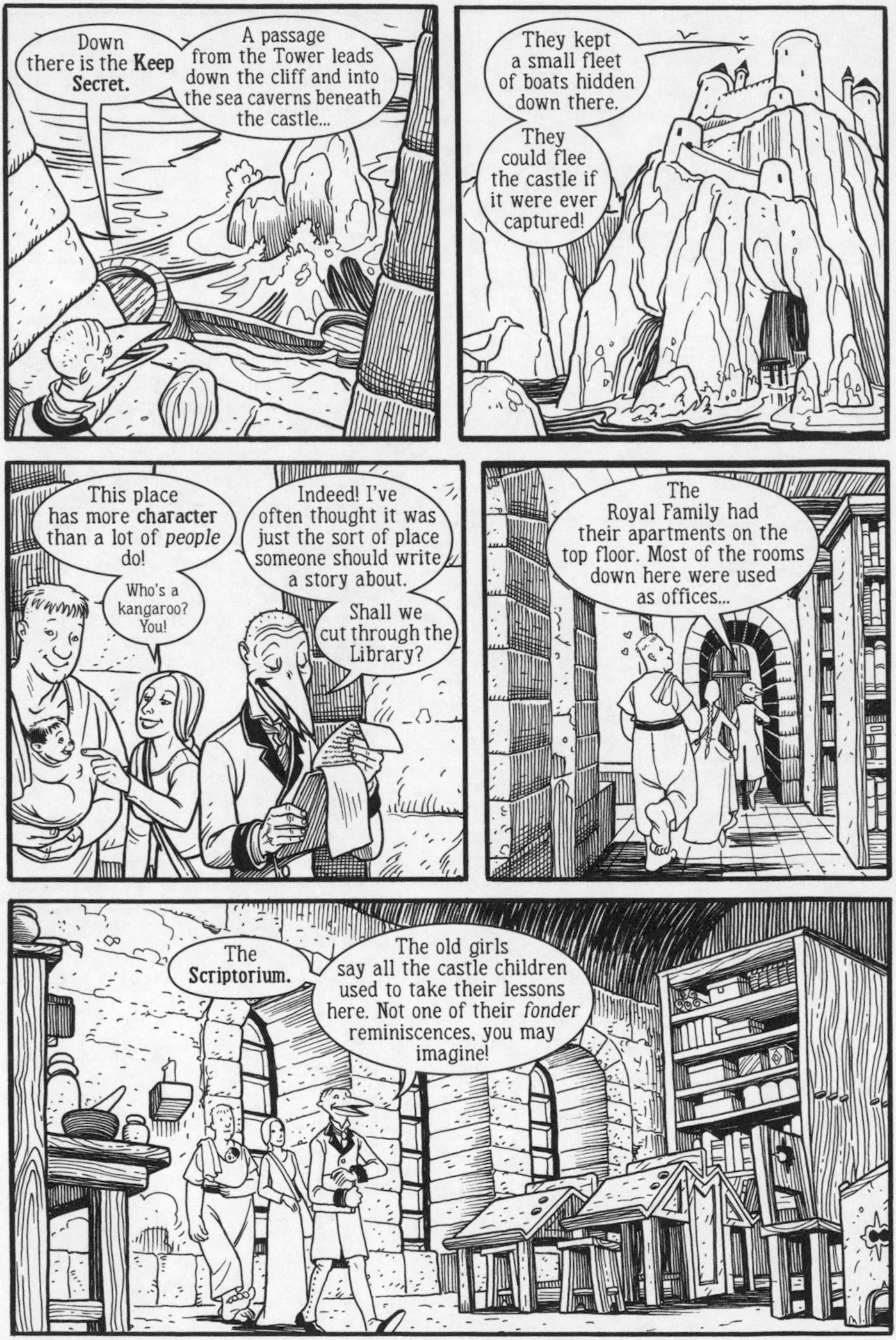
Down there is the **Keep Secret.**
A passage from the Tower leads down the cliff and into the sea caverns beneath the castle...
They kept a small fleet of boats hidden down there.
They could flee the castle if it were ever captured!
This place has more **character** than a lot of *people* do!
Who's a kangaroo? You!
Indeed! I've often thought it was just the sort of place someone should write a story about.
Shall we cut through the Library?
The Royal Family had their apartments on the top floor. Most of the rooms down here were used as offices...
The **Scriptorium.**
The old girls say all the castle children used to take their lessons here. Not one of their *fonder* reminiscences, you may imagine!

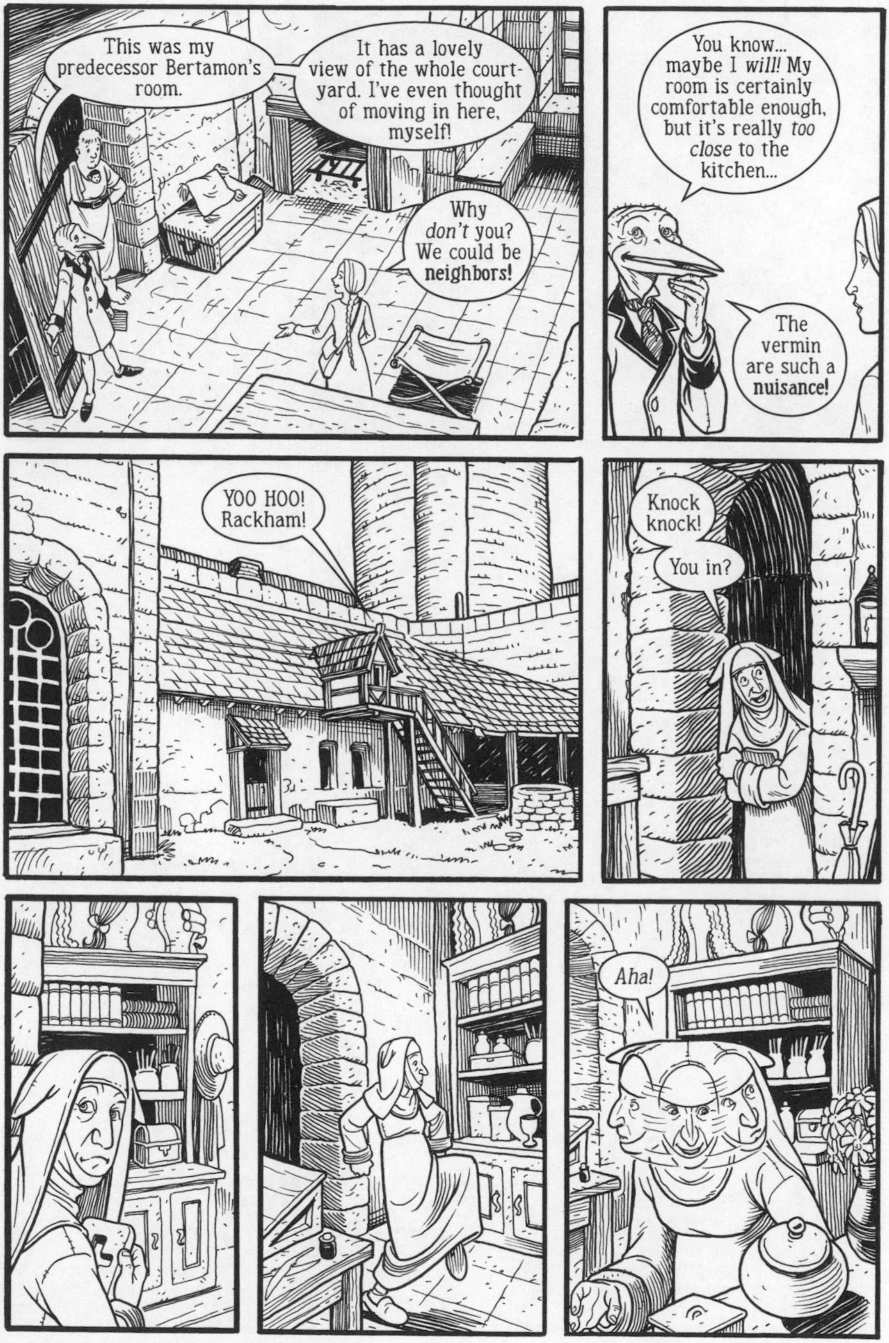
This was my predecessor Bertamon's room.
It has a lovely view of the whole courtyard. I've even thought of moving in here, myself!
Why *don't* you? We could be **neighbors!**
You know... maybe I *will!* My room is certainly comfortable enough, but it's really *too close* to the kitchen...
The vermin are such a **nuisance!**
YOO HOO! Rackham!
Knock knock!
You in?
Aha!

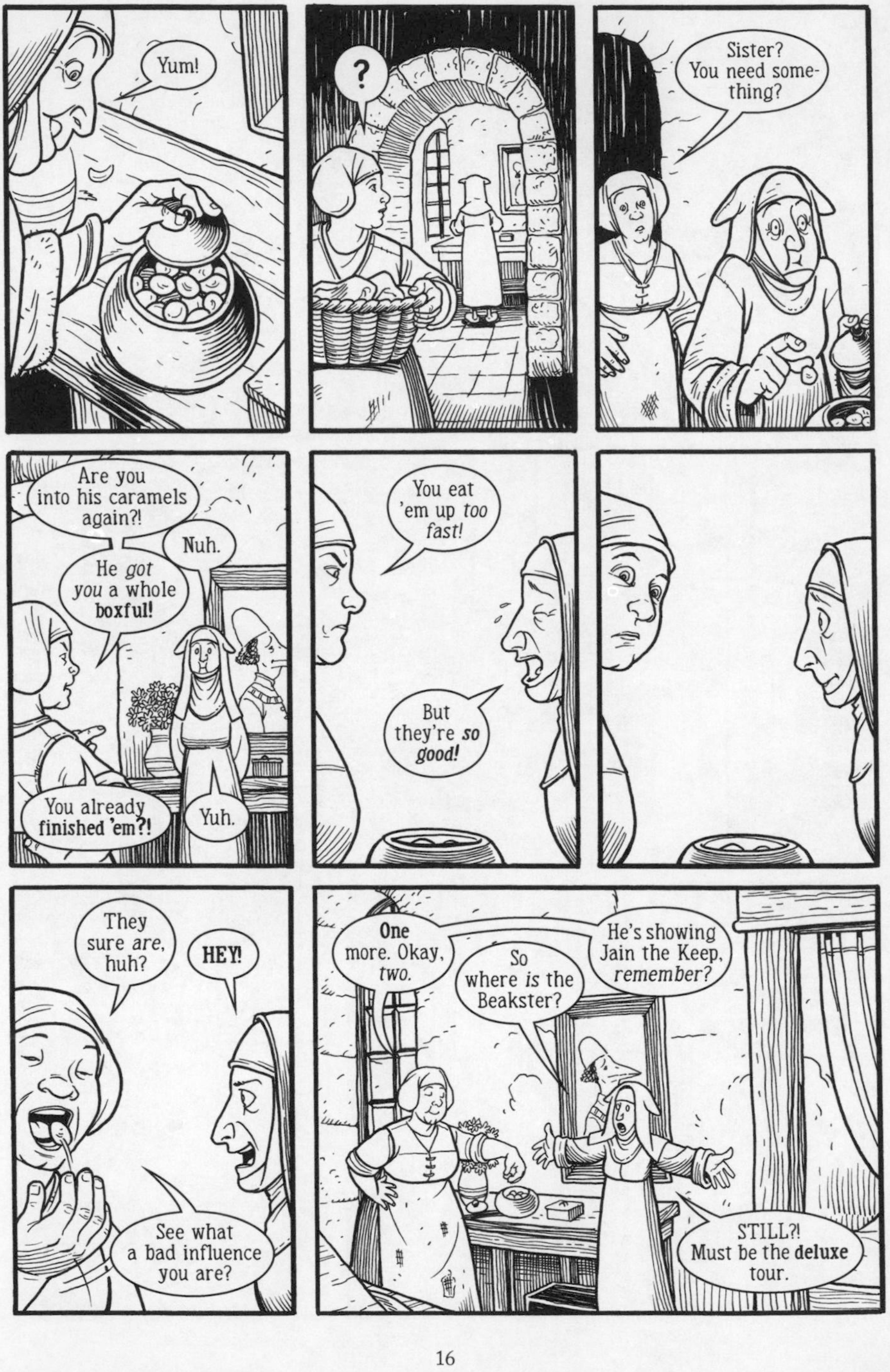
Yum!
?
Sister? You need something?
Are you into his caramels again?!
Nuh.
He *got you* a whole **boxful!**
You already **finished 'em?!**
Yuh.
You eat 'em up *too fast!*
But they're *so good!*
They sure *are*, huh?
HEY!
See what a bad influence you are?
One more. Okay, *two.*
So where *is* the Beakster?
He's showing Jain the Keep, *remember?*
STILL?! Must be the **deluxe** tour.

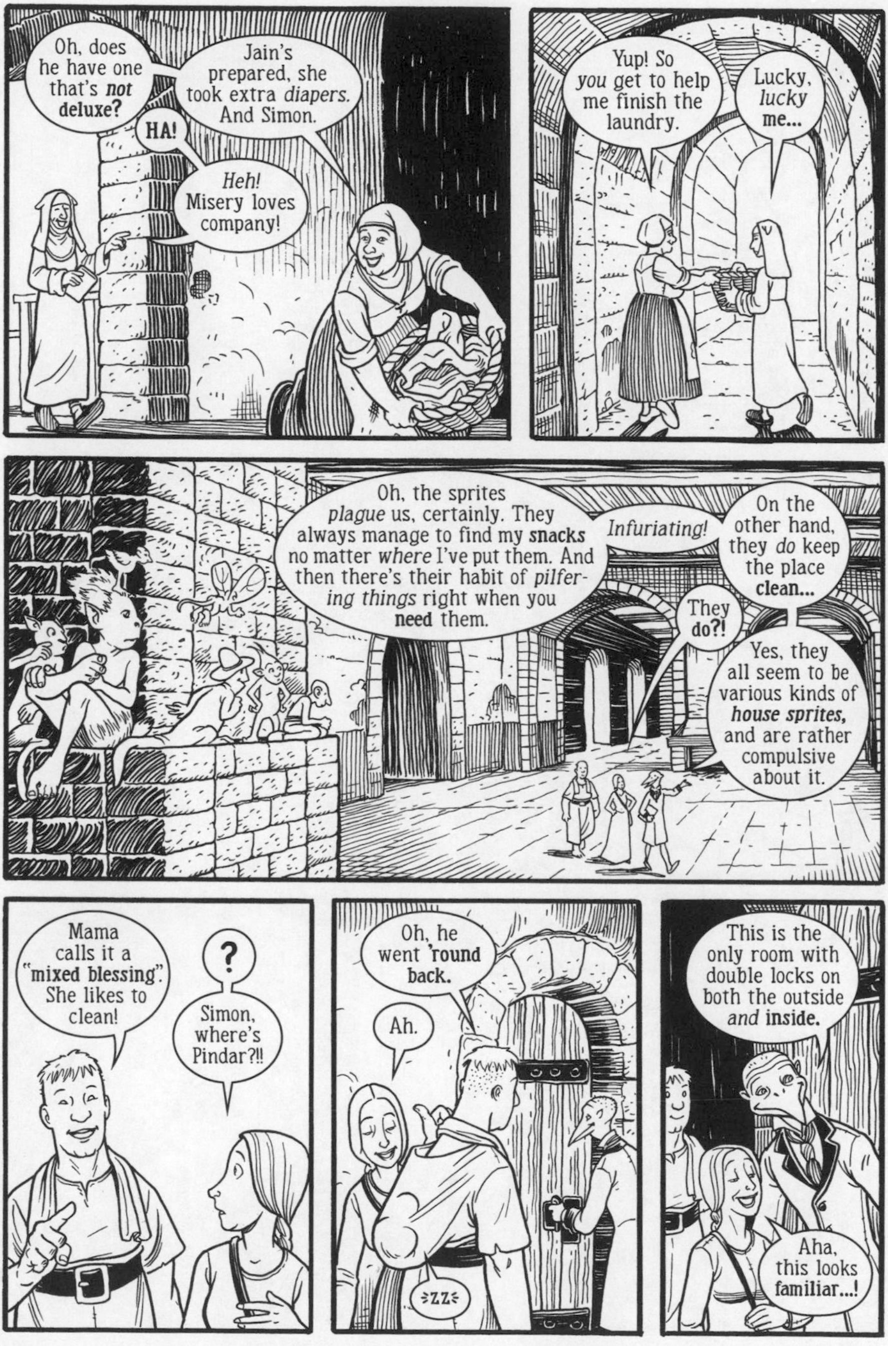
Oh, does he have one that's *not* **deluxe?**
Jain's prepared, she took extra *diapers.* And Simon.
HA!
Heh! Misery loves company!
Yup! So *you* get to help me finish the laundry.
Lucky, *lucky* **me...**
Oh, the sprites *plague* us, certainly. They always manage to find my **snacks** no matter *where* I've put them. And then there's their habit of *pilfering things* right when you **need** them.
Infuriating!
On the other hand, they *do* keep the place **clean...**
They **do?!**
Yes, they all seem to be various kinds of ***house sprites,*** and are rather compulsive about it.
Mama calls it a "**mixed blessing**". She likes to clean!
?
Simon, where's Pindar?!!
Oh, he went **'round back.**
Ah.
ZZ
This is the only room with double locks on both the outside *and* **inside.**
Aha, this looks **familiar...!**

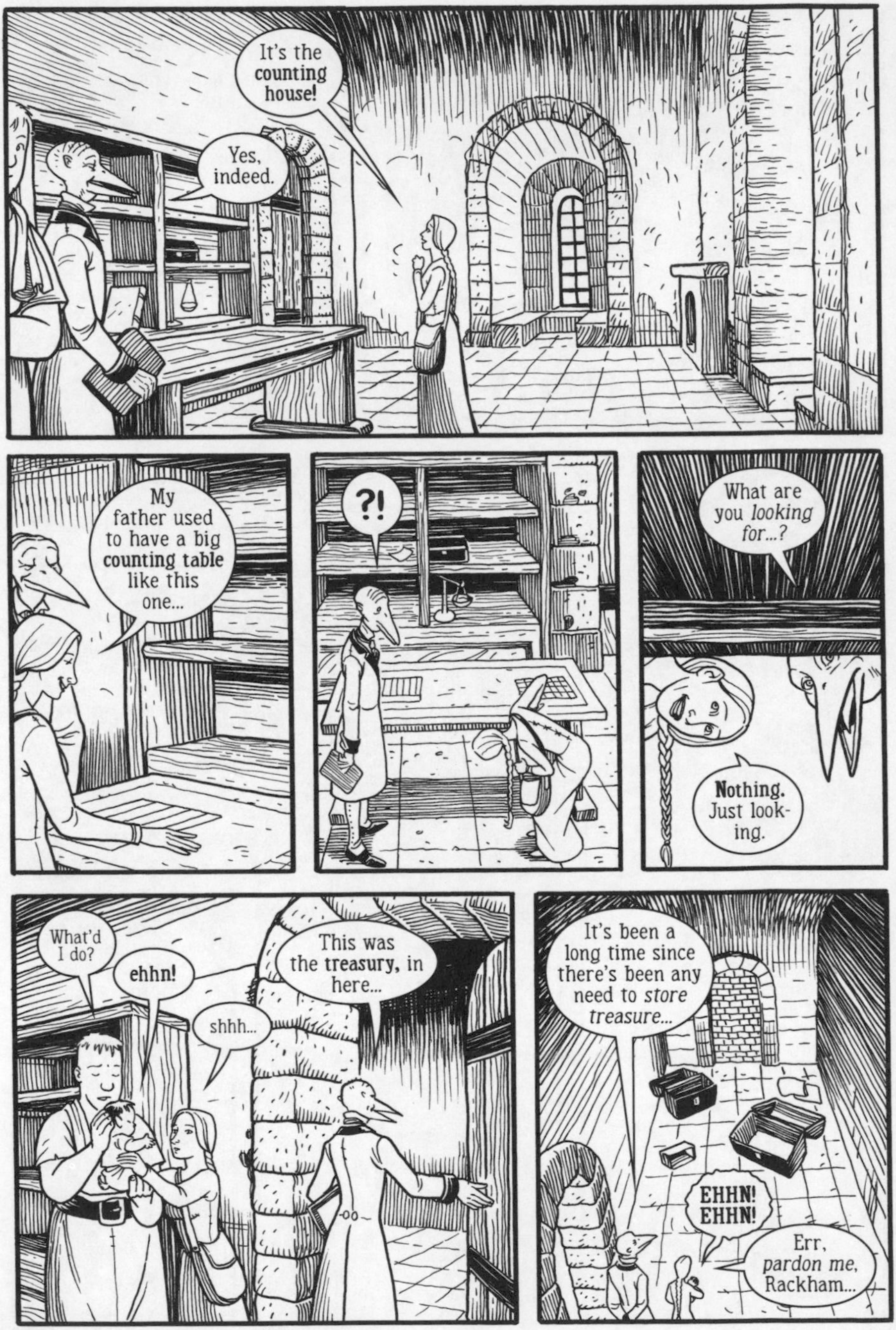
It's the **counting house!**
Yes, indeed.
My father used to have a big **counting table** like this one...
?!
What are you *looking for...?*
Nothing. Just look-ing.
What'd I do?
ehhn!
shhh...
This was the **treasury,** in here...
It's been a long time since there's been any need to *store treasure...*
EHHN! EHHN!
Err, *pardon me,* Rackham...

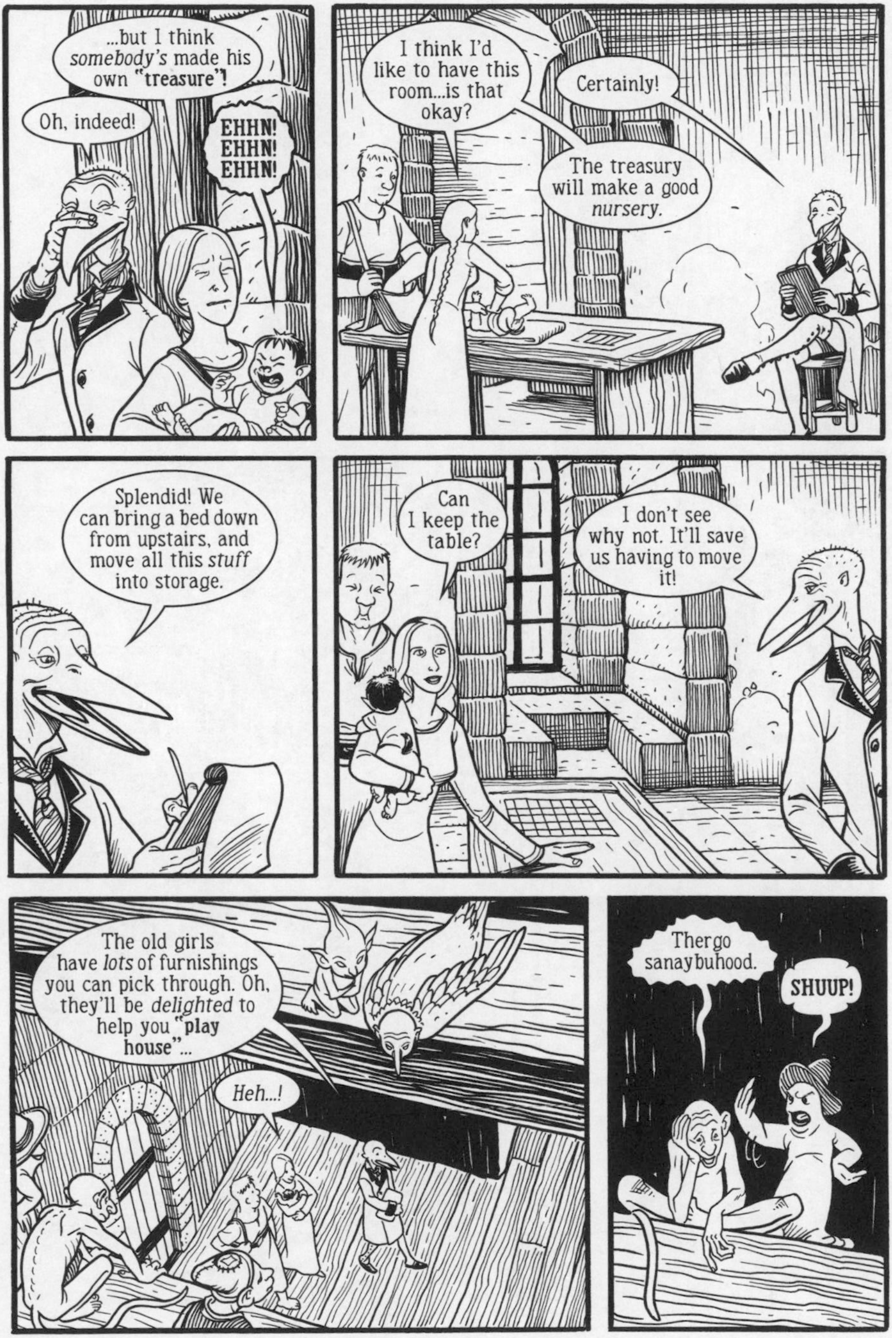
...but I think *somebody's* made his own "**treasure**"!
Oh, indeed!
EHHN! EHHN! EHHN!
I think I'd like to have this room...is that okay?
Certainly!
The treasury will make a good *nursery*.
Splendid! We can bring a bed down from upstairs, and move all this *stuff* into storage.
Can I keep the table?
I don't see why not. It'll save us having to move it!
The old girls have *lots* of furnishings you can pick through. Oh, they'll be *delighted* to help you "**play house**"...
Heh...!
Thergo sanaybuhood.
SHUUP!

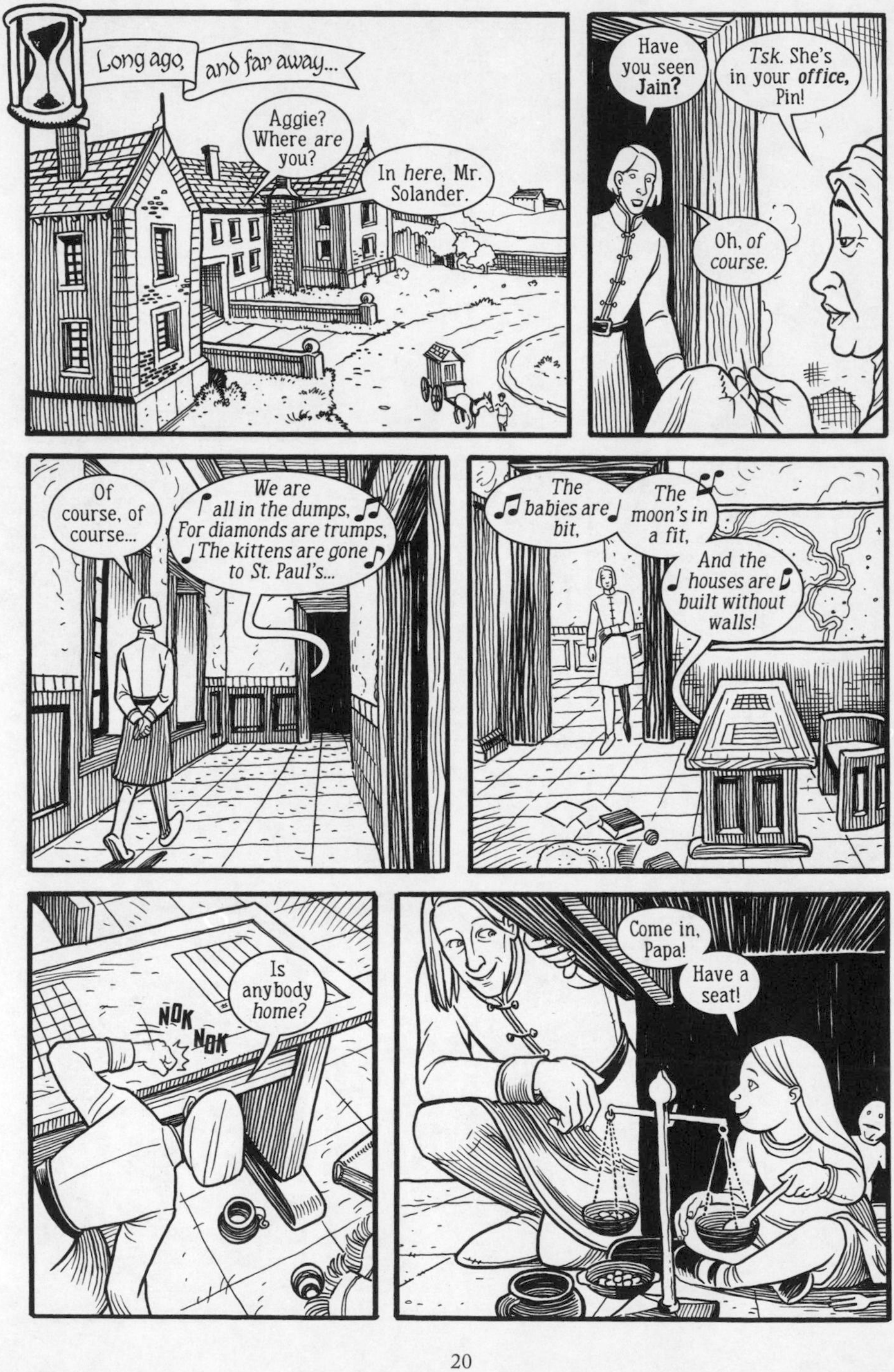
Long ago,
and far away...
Aggie? Where are you?
In here, Mr. Solander.
Have you seen Jain?
Tsk. She's in your office, Pin!
Oh, of course.
Of course, of course...
We are all in the dumps, For diamonds are trumps, The kittens are gone to St. Paul's...
The babies are bit,
The moon's in a fit,
And the houses are built without walls!
NOK NOK
Is anybody home?
Come in, Papa!
Have a seat!

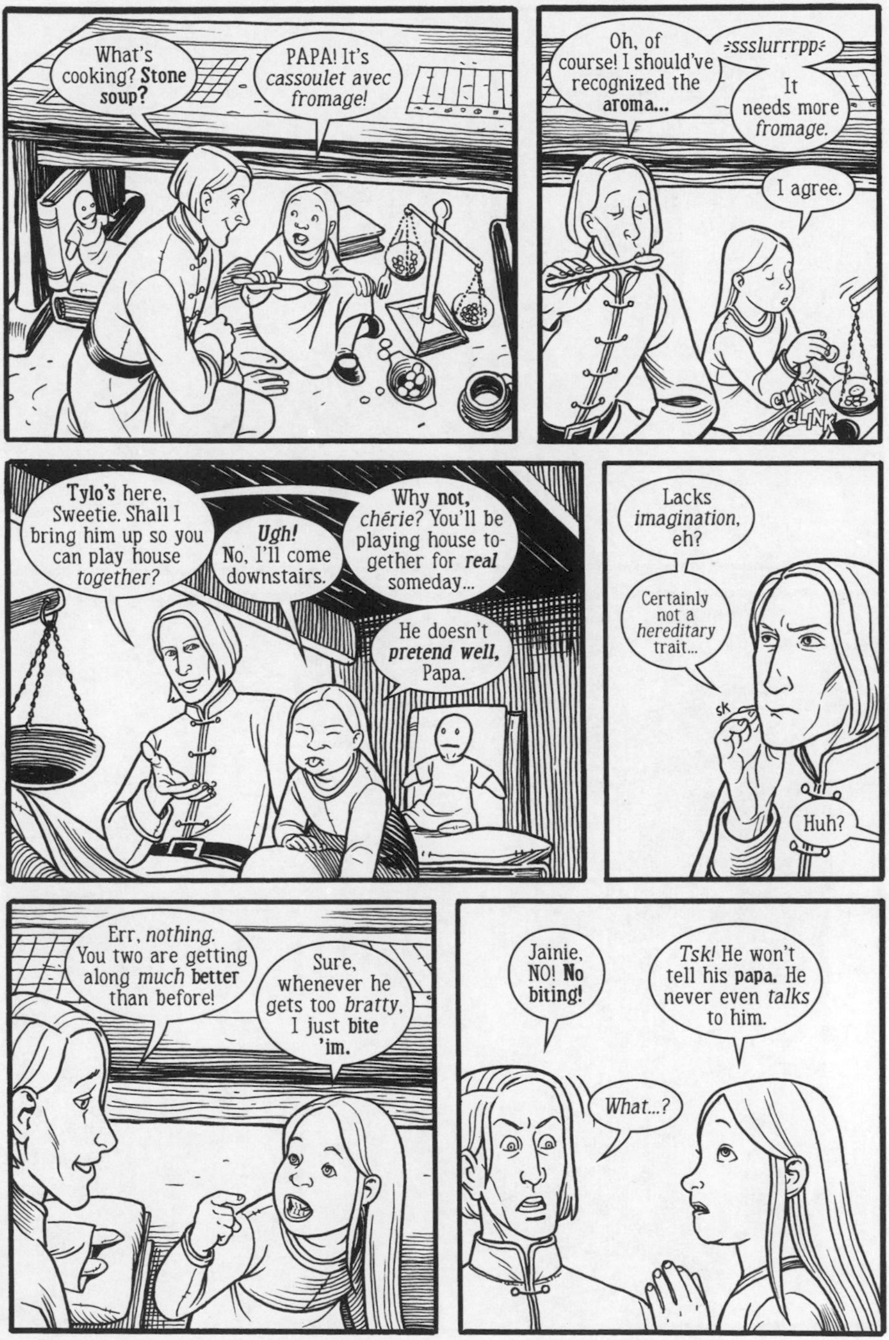
What's cooking? **Stone soup?**
PAPA! It's *cassoulet avec fromage!*
Oh, of course! I should've recognized the **aroma...**
ssslurrrpp
It needs more *fromage.*
I agree.
CLINK
CLINK
Tylo's here, Sweetie. Shall I bring him up so you can play house *together?*
Ugh! No, I'll come downstairs.
Why **not,** *chérie?* You'll be playing house together for ***real*** someday...
He doesn't ***pretend well,*** Papa.
Lacks *imagination,* eh?
Certainly not a *hereditary* trait...
SK
Huh?
Err, *nothing.* You two are getting along *much* **better** than before!
Sure, whenever he gets too *bratty,* I just **bite 'im.**
Jainie, NO! **No biting!**
Tsk! He won't tell his **papa.** He never even *talks* to him.
What...?

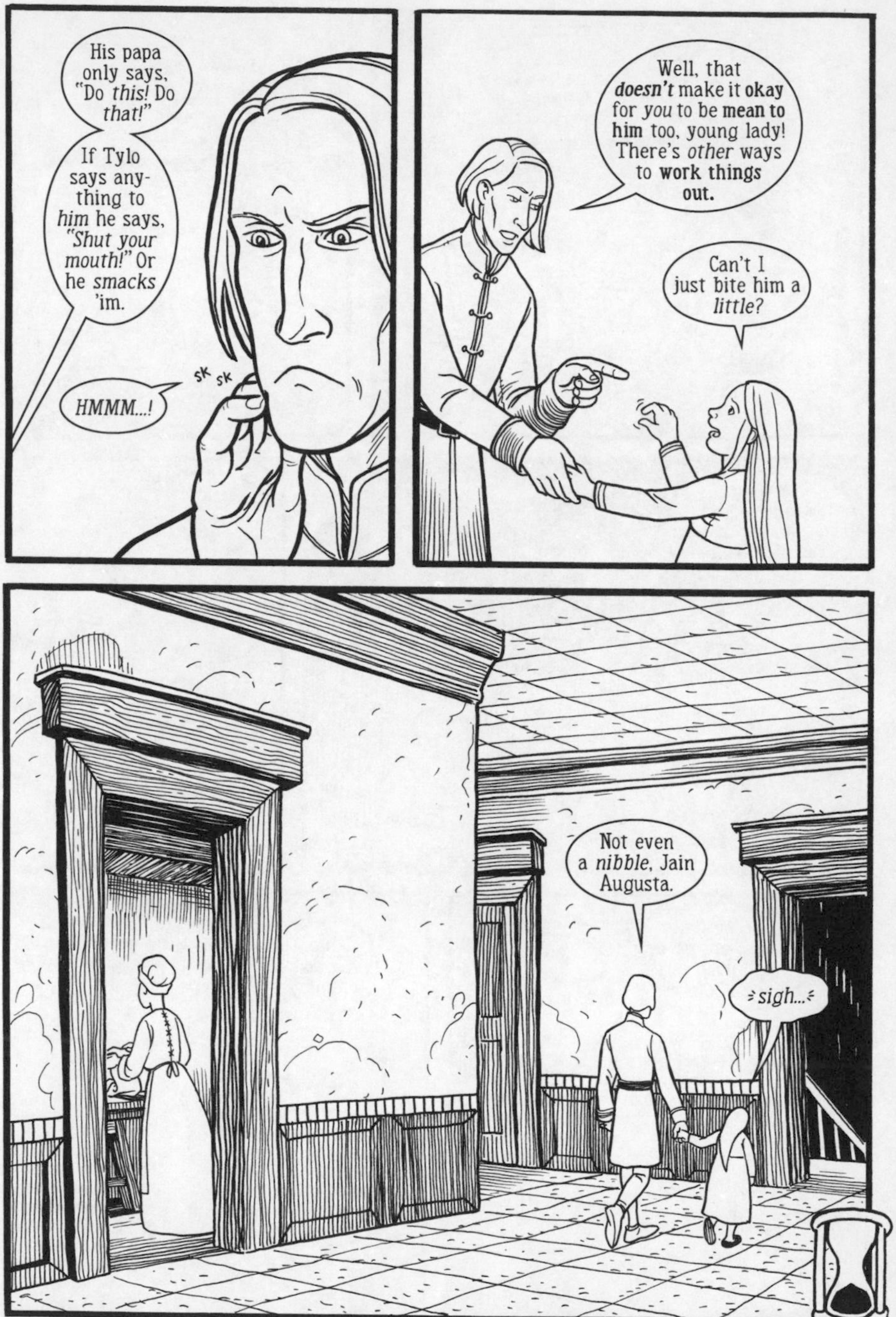

His papa only says, "Do *this!* Do *that!*"
If Tylo says anything to *him* he says, *"Shut your mouth!"* Or he *smacks* 'im.
SK SK
HMMM...!
Well, that ***doesn't*** make it **okay** for *you* to be **mean to him** too, young lady! There's *other* ways to **work things out.**
Can't I just bite him a *little?*
Not even a *nibble,* Jain Augusta.
sigh...

Chapter 2.

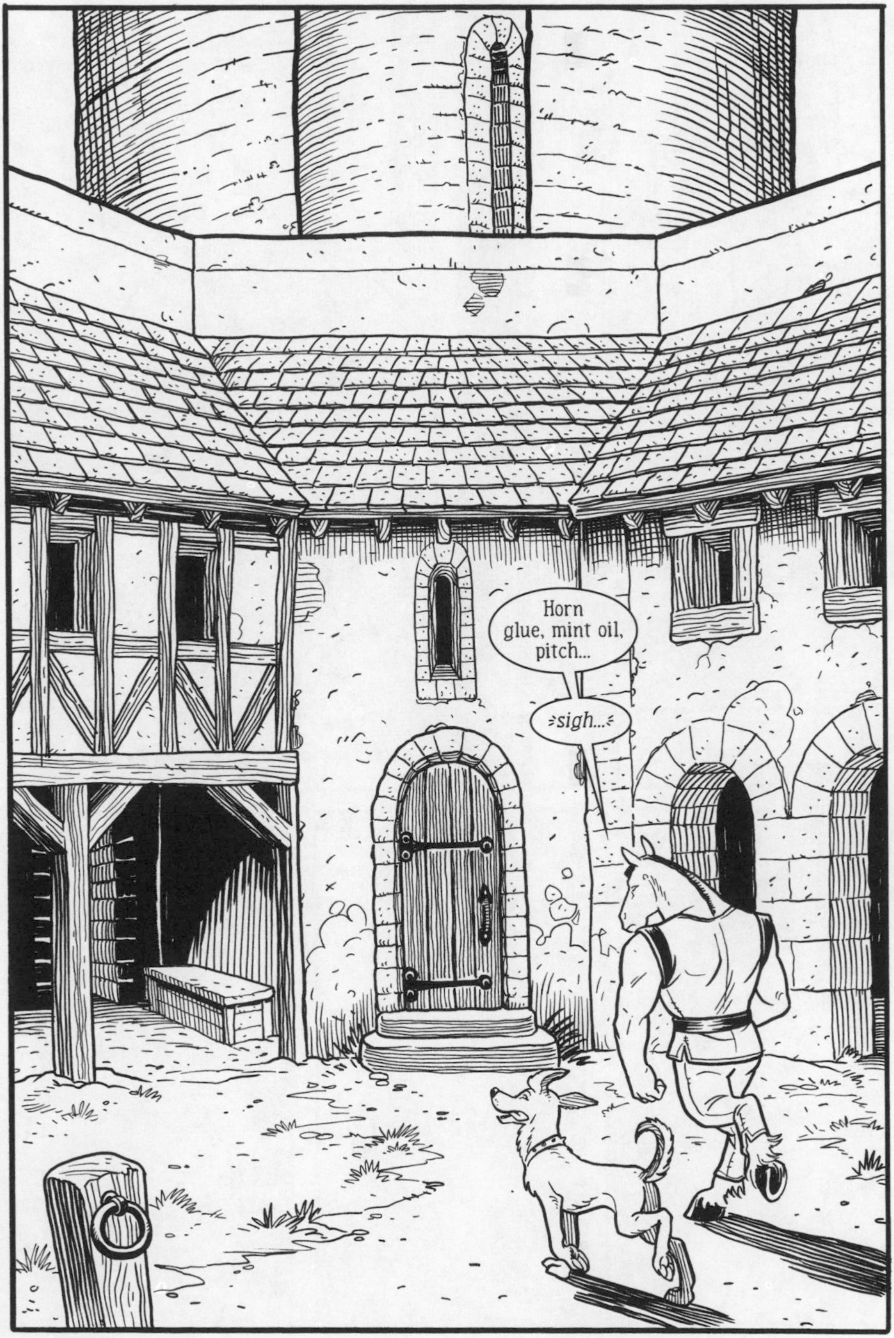
Horn glue, mint oil, pitch...
sigh...

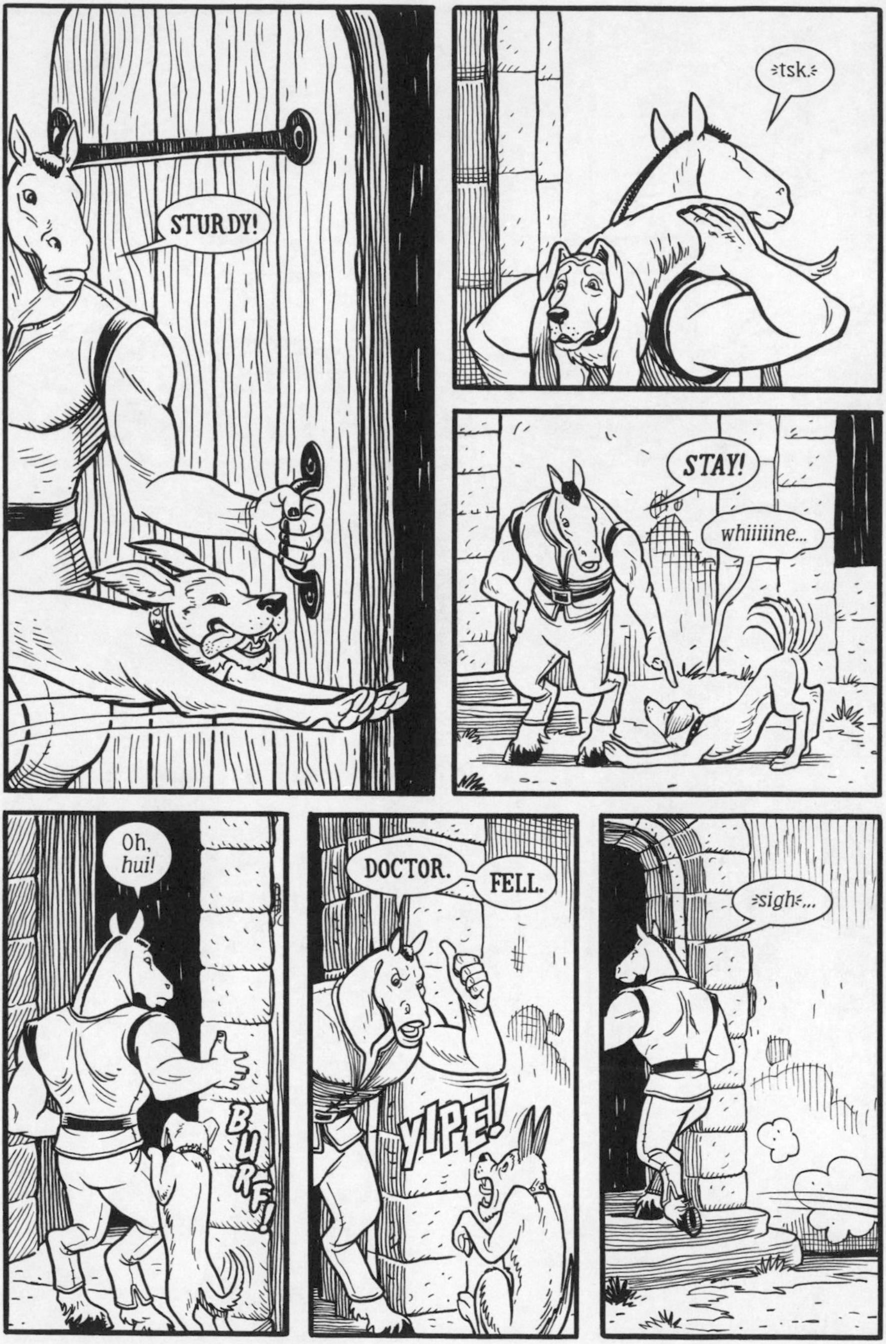

STURDY!
tsk.
STAY!
whiiiiine...
Oh, hui!
BURF!
DOCTOR.
FELL.
YIPE!
sigh...

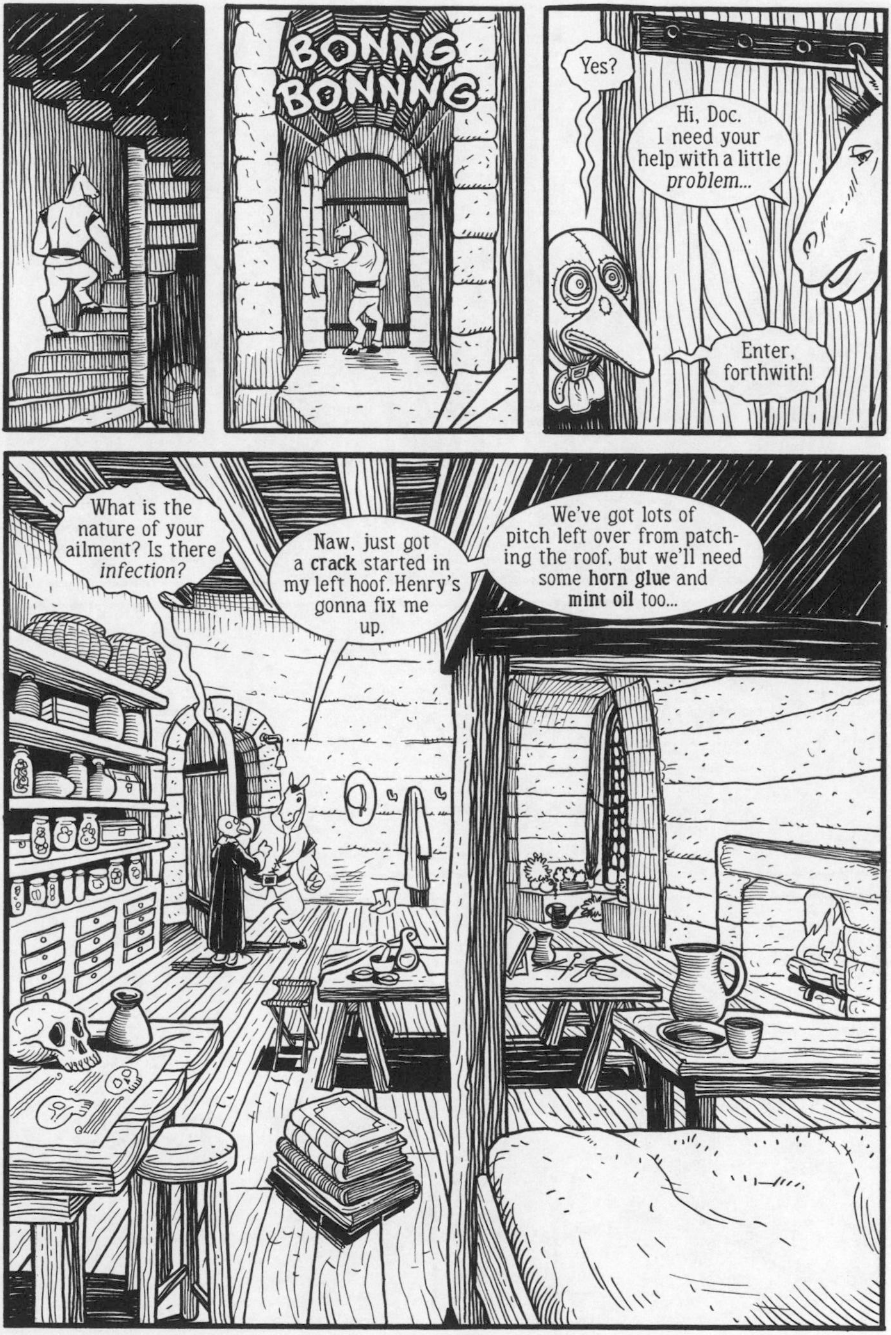
BONNG
BONNNG
Yes?
Hi, Doc. I need your help with a little *problem*...
Enter, forthwith!
What is the nature of your ailment? Is there *infection?*
Naw, just got a **crack** started in my left hoof. Henry's gonna fix me up.
We've got lots of pitch left over from patching the roof, but we'll need some **horn glue** and **mint oil** too...

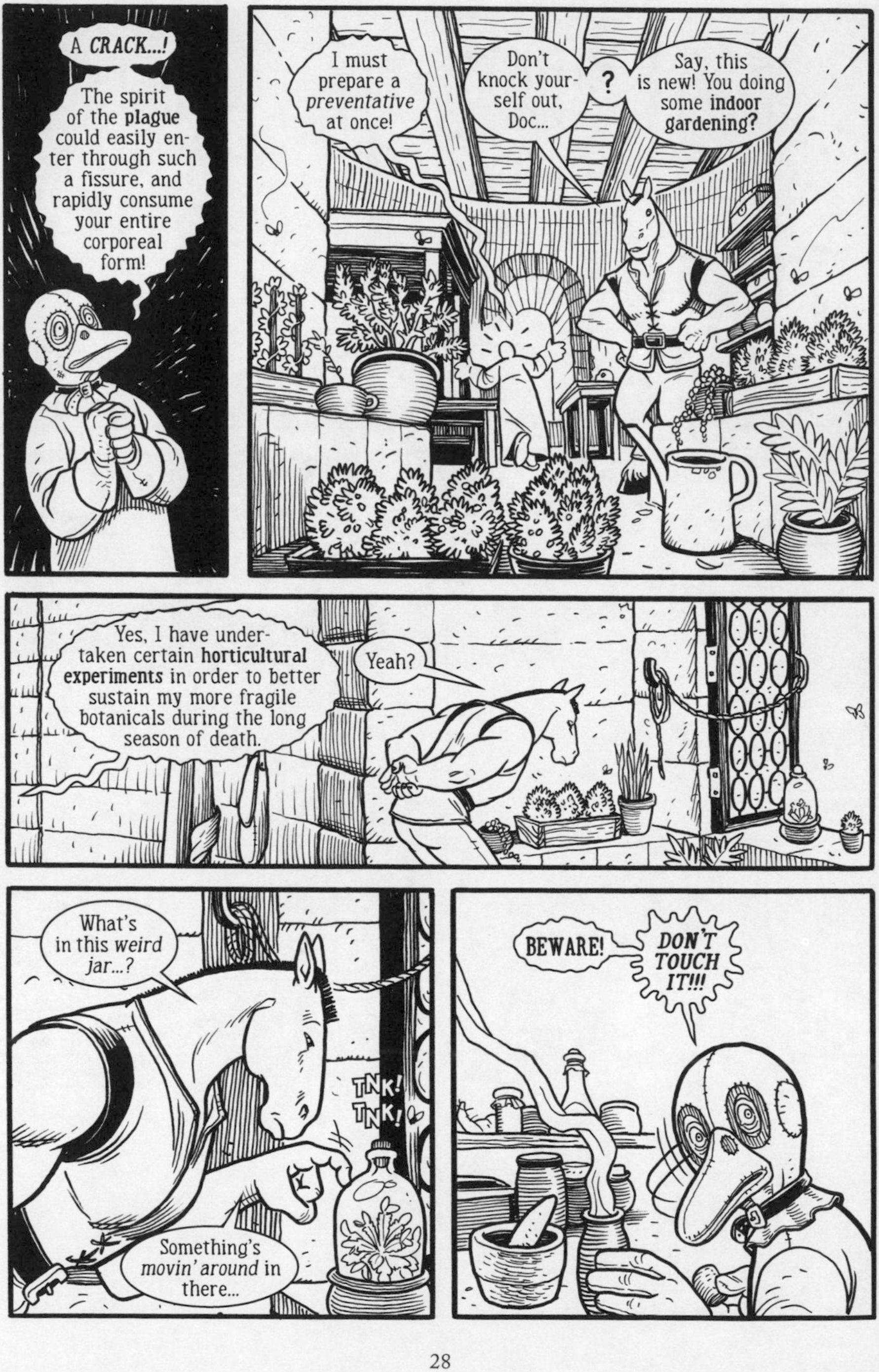
A *CRACK...!*
The spirit of the **plague** could easily enter through such a fissure, and rapidly consume your entire corporeal form!
I must prepare a *preventative* at once!
Don't knock yourself out, Doc...
?
Say, this is new! You doing some **indoor gardening?**
Yes, I have undertaken certain **horticultural experiments** in order to better sustain my more fragile botanicals during the long season of death.
Yeah?
What's in this *weird* jar...?
TNK! TNK!
Something's *movin' around* in there...
BEWARE!
DON'T TOUCH IT!!!

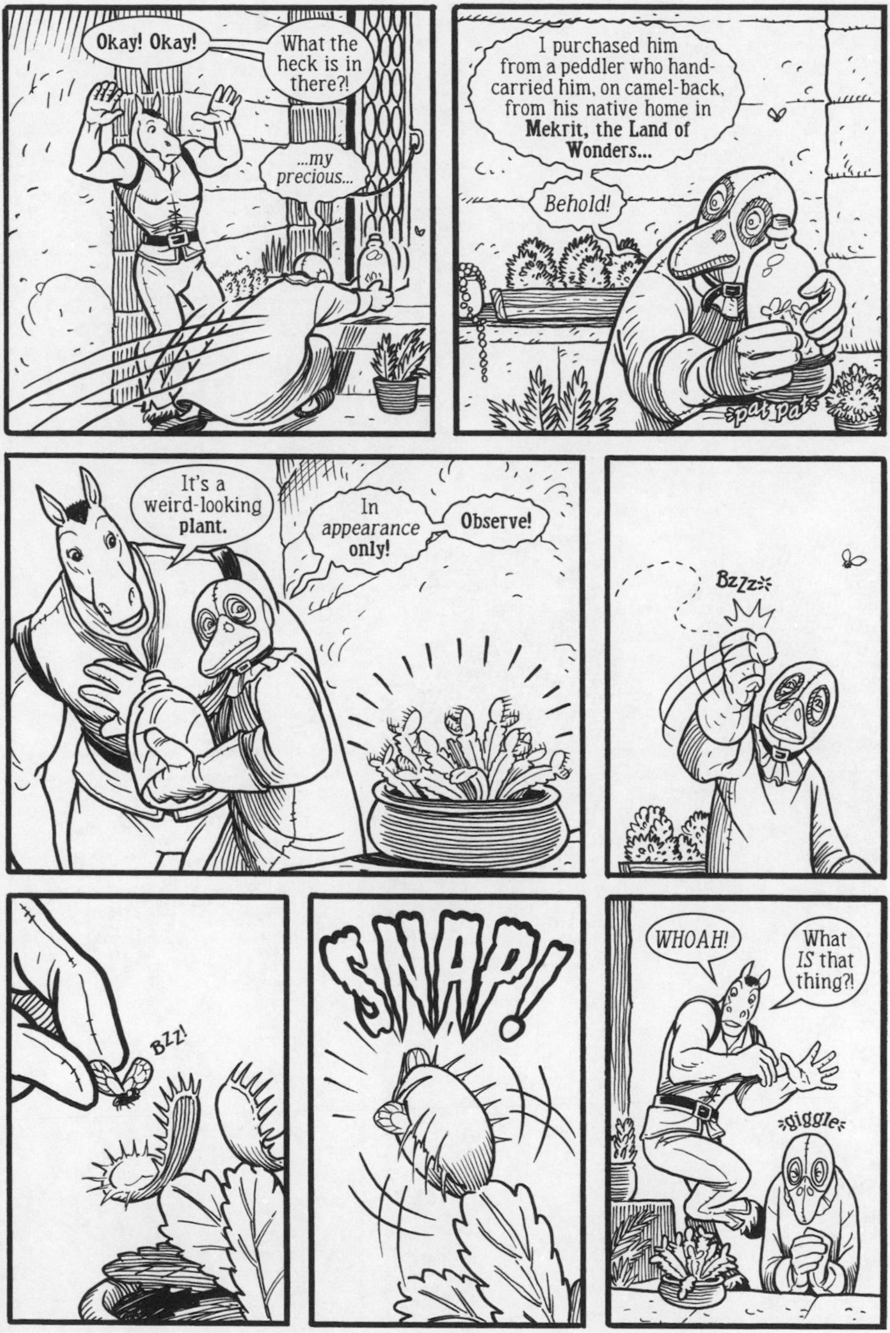
Okay! Okay!
What the heck is in there?!
...my precious...
I purchased him from a peddler who hand-carried him, on camel-back, from his native home in Mekrit, the Land of Wonders...
Behold!
pat pat
It's a weird-looking plant.
In appearance only!
Observe!
Bzzz
BZZ!
SNAP!
WHOAH!
What IS that thing?!
giggle

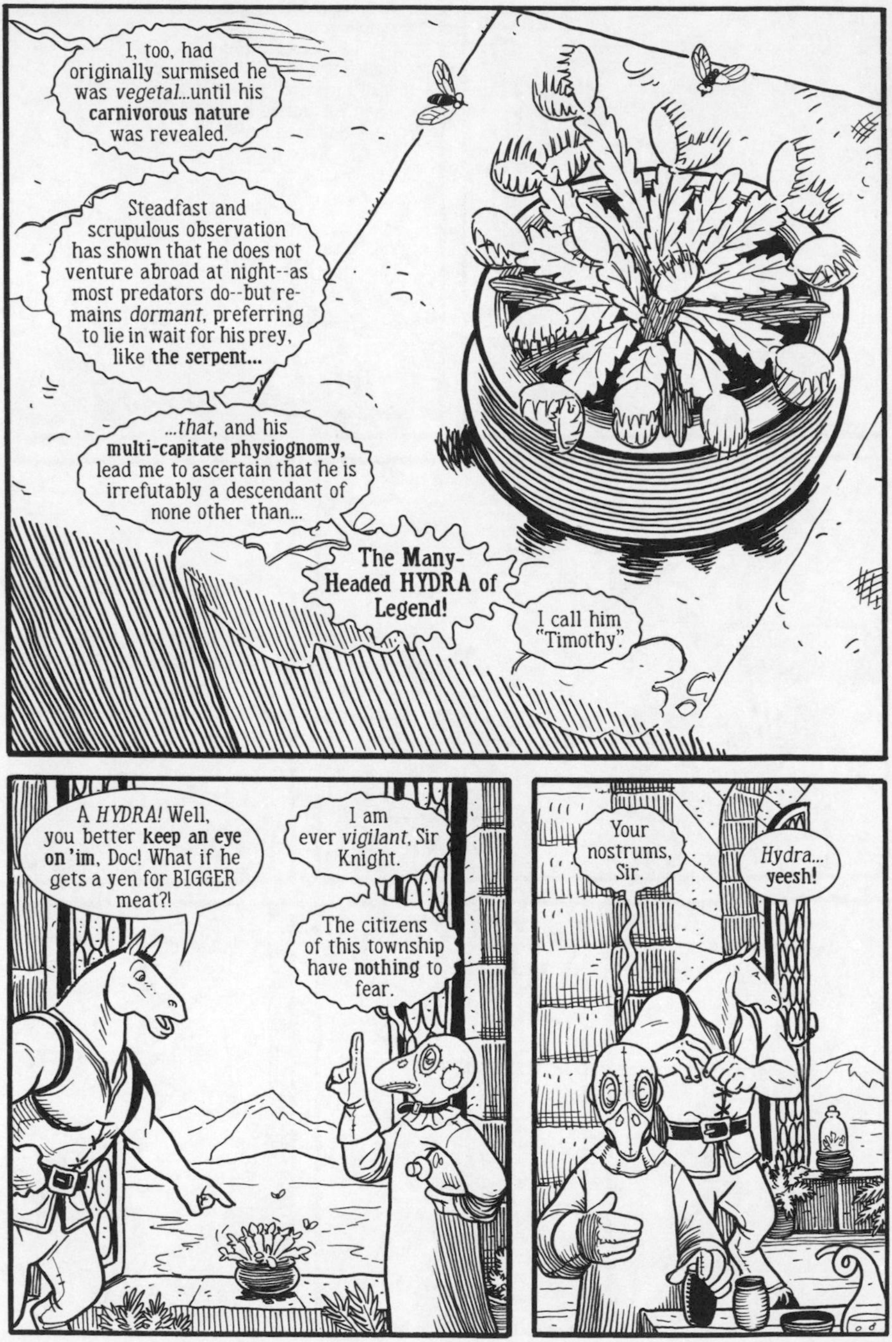
I, too, had originally surmised he was *vegetal*...until his **carnivorous nature** was revealed.
Steadfast and scrupulous observation has shown that he does not venture abroad at night--as most predators do--but remains *dormant*, preferring to lie in wait for his prey, like **the serpent...**
...that, and his **multi-capitate physiognomy,** lead me to ascertain that he is irrefutably a descendant of none other than...
The Many-Headed HYDRA of Legend!
I call him "Timothy".
A *HYDRA!* Well, you better **keep an eye on'im**, Doc! What if he gets a yen for BIGGER meat?!
I am ever *vigilant*, Sir Knight.
The citizens of this township have **nothing** to fear.
Your nostrums, Sir.
Hydra... **yeesh!**

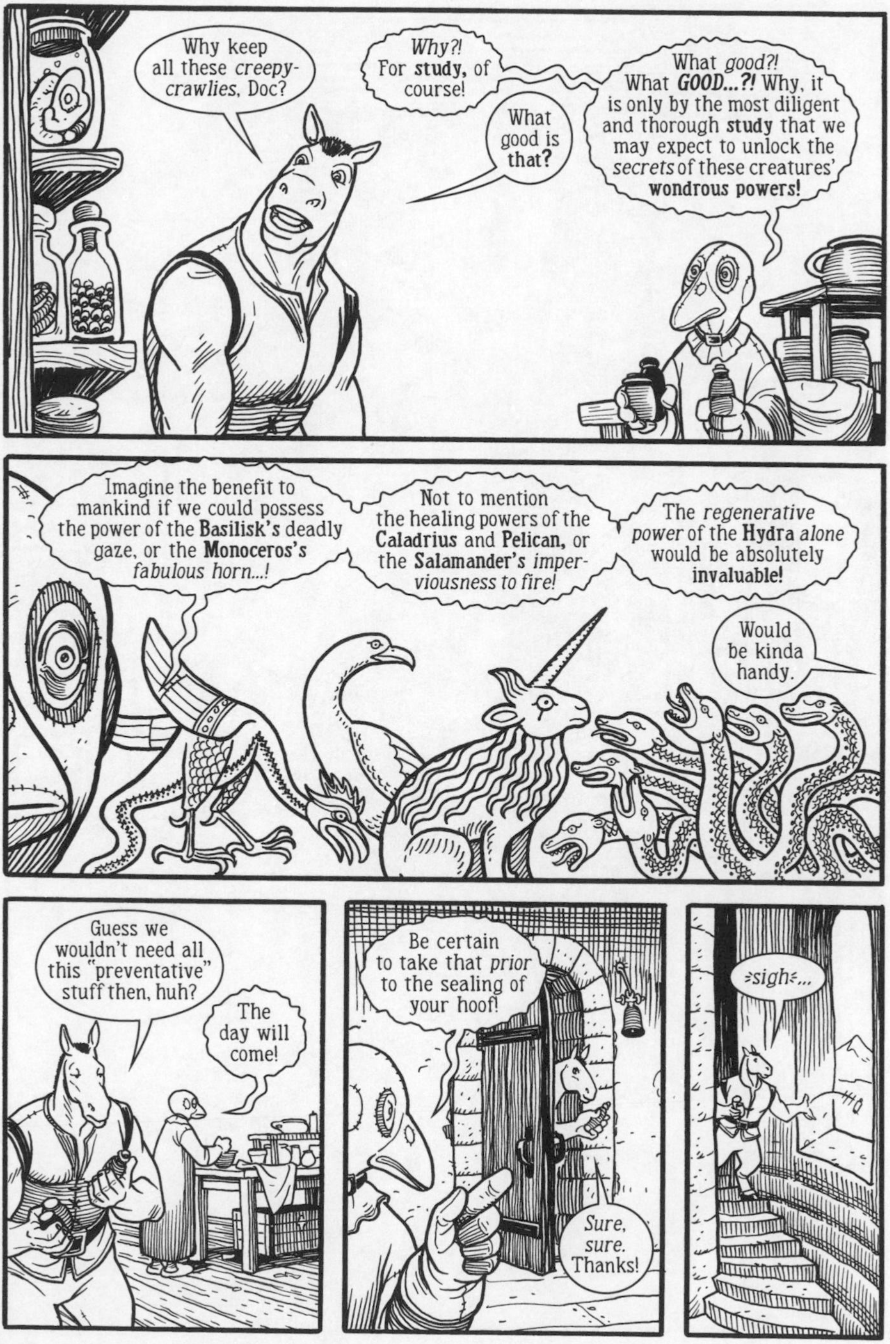
Why keep all these *creepy-crawlies*, Doc?
Why?! For **study,** of course!
What good is **that?**
What *good?!* What ***GOOD...?!*** Why, it is only by the most diligent and thorough **study** that we may expect to unlock the *secrets* of these creatures' **wondrous powers!**
Imagine the benefit to mankind if we could possess the power of the **Basilisk's** deadly gaze, or the **Monoceros's** *fabulous horn...!*
Not to mention the healing powers of the **Caladrius** and **Pelican,** or the **Salamander's** *imperviousness to fire!*
The *regenerative power* of the **Hydra** *alone* would be absolutely **invaluable!**
Would be kinda handy.
Guess we wouldn't need all this "preventative" stuff then, huh?
The day will come!
Be certain to take that *prior* to the sealing of your hoof!
Sure, sure. Thanks!
sigh...

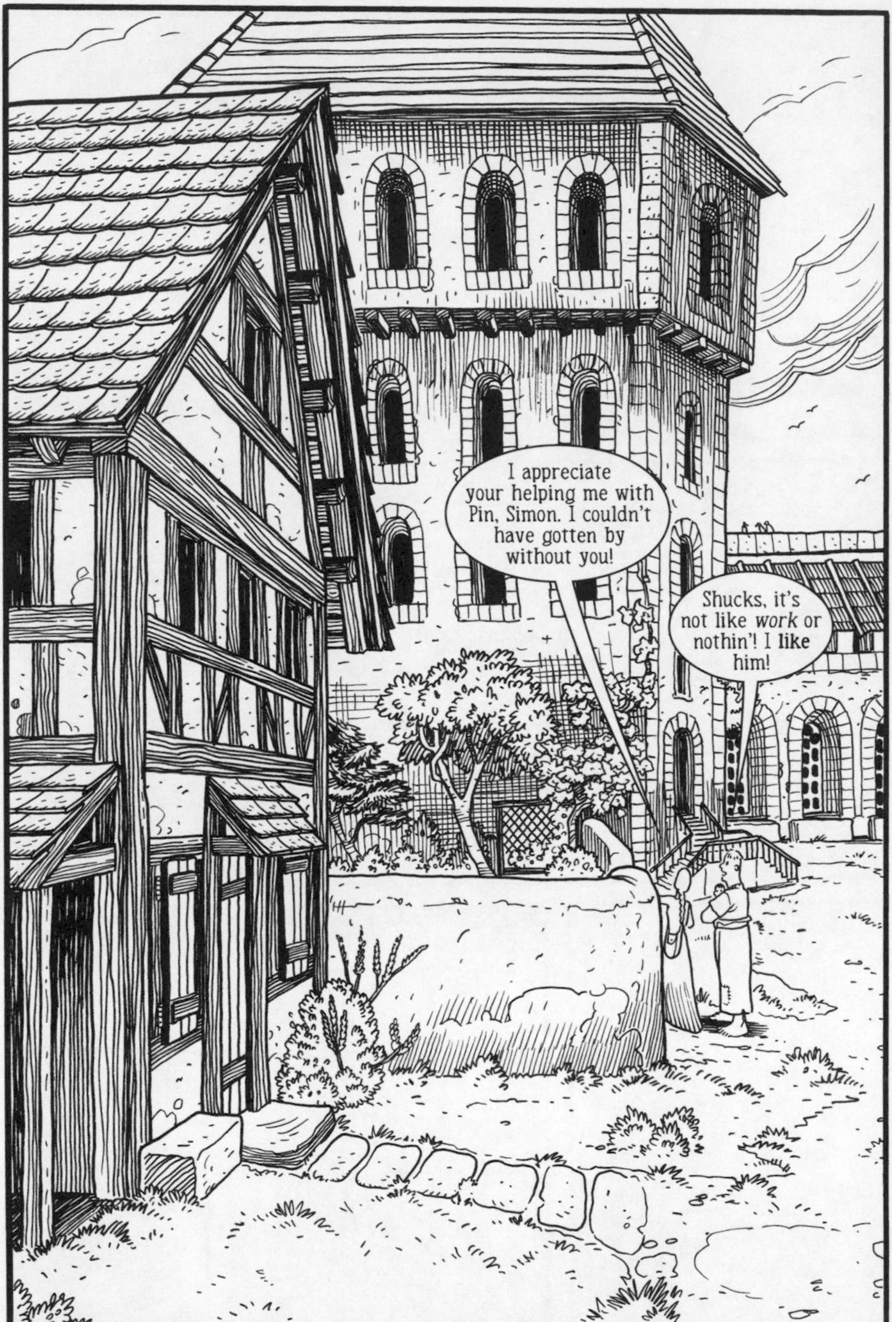
I appreciate your helping me with Pin, Simon. I couldn't have gotten by without you!
Shucks, it's not like *work* or nothin'! I **like** him!

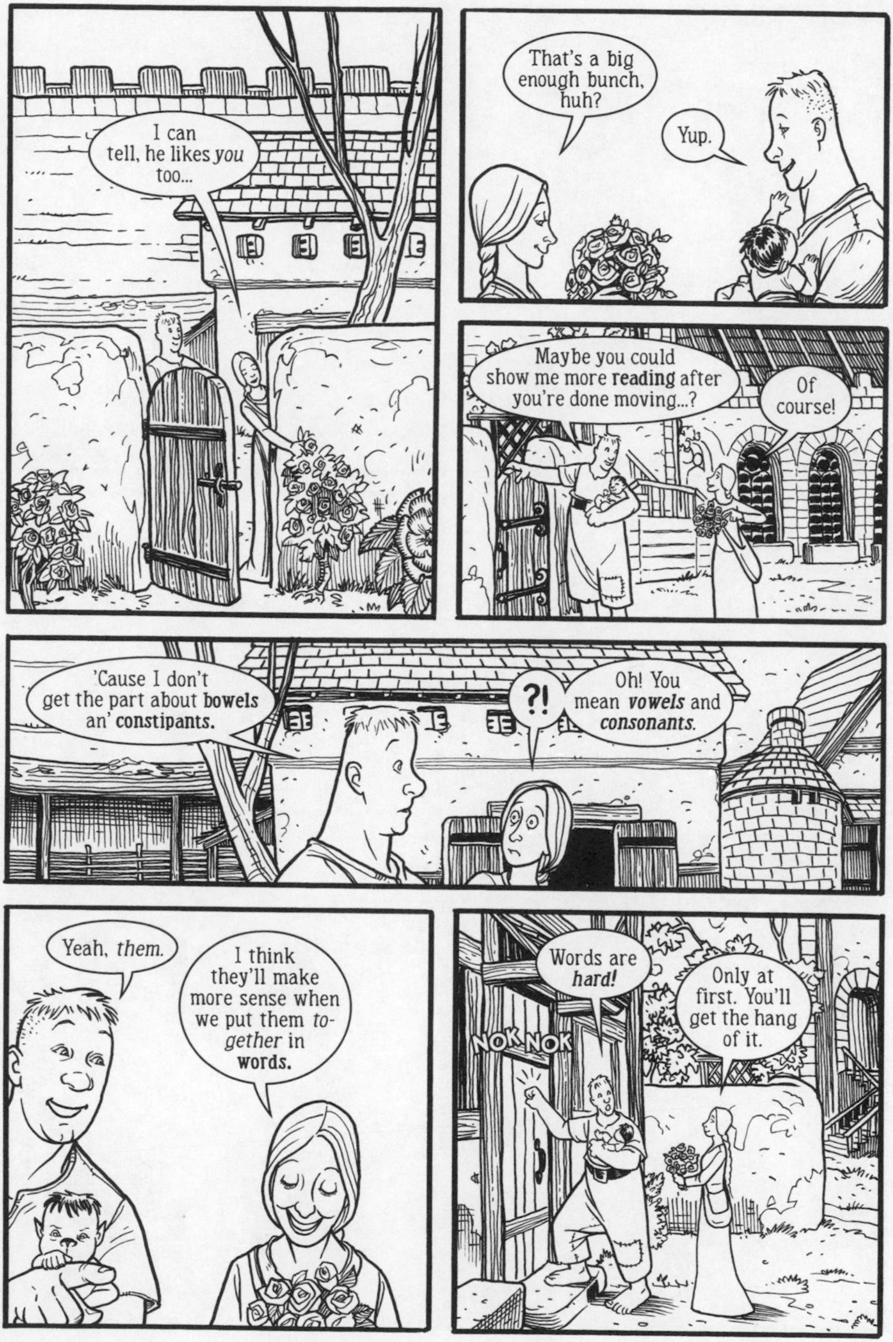
I can tell, he likes *you* too...
That's a big enough bunch, huh?
Yup.
Maybe you could show me more **reading** after you're done moving...?
Of course!
'Cause I don't get the part about **bowels** an' **constipants.**
?!
Oh! You mean ***vowels*** and ***consonants.***
Yeah, *them.*
I think they'll make more sense when we put them *together* in **words.**
NOK NOK
Words are ***hard!***
Only at first. You'll get the hang of it.

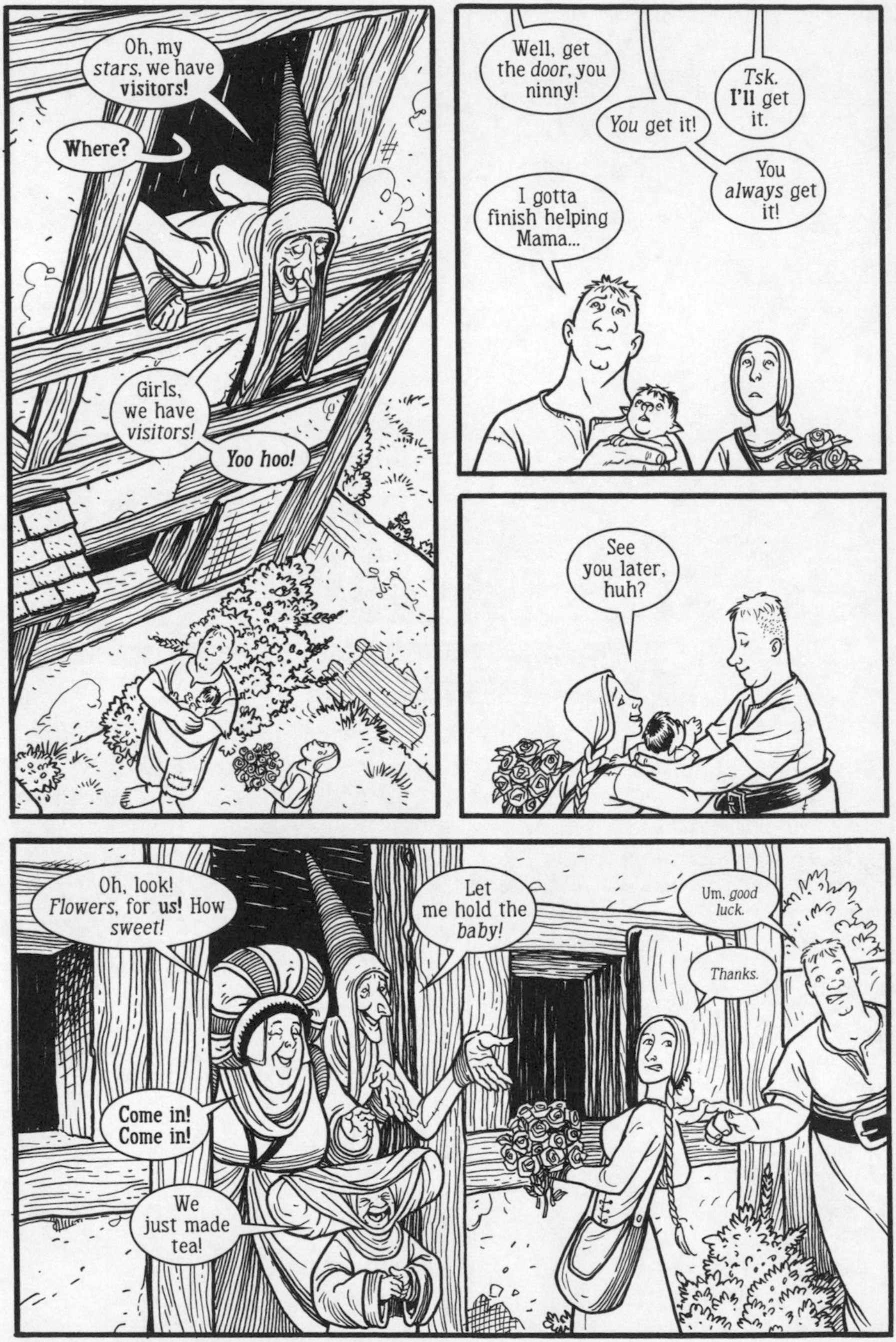
Oh, my *stars*, we have **visitors!**
Where?
Girls, we have *visitors!*
Yoo hoo!
Well, get the *door*, you ninny!
You get it!
Tsk. **I'll** get it.
You *always* get it!
I gotta finish helping Mama...
See you later, huh?
Oh, look! *Flowers*, for **us!** How *sweet!*
Let me hold the *baby!*
Come in! Come in!
We just made tea!
Um, *good luck.*
Thanks.

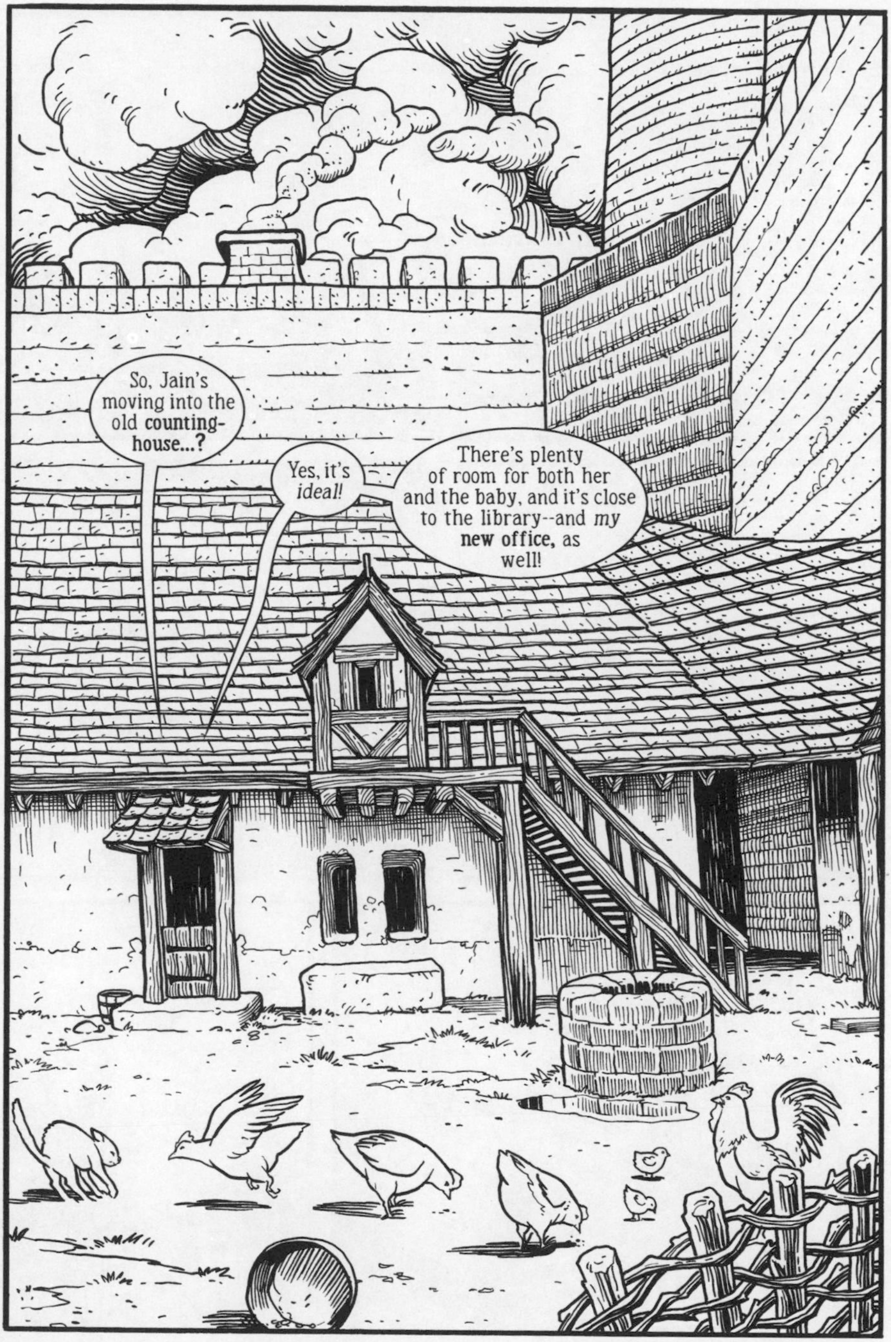
So, Jain's moving into the old **counting-house...?**
Yes, it's *ideal!*
There's plenty of room for both her and the baby, and it's close to the library--and *my* **new office,** as well!

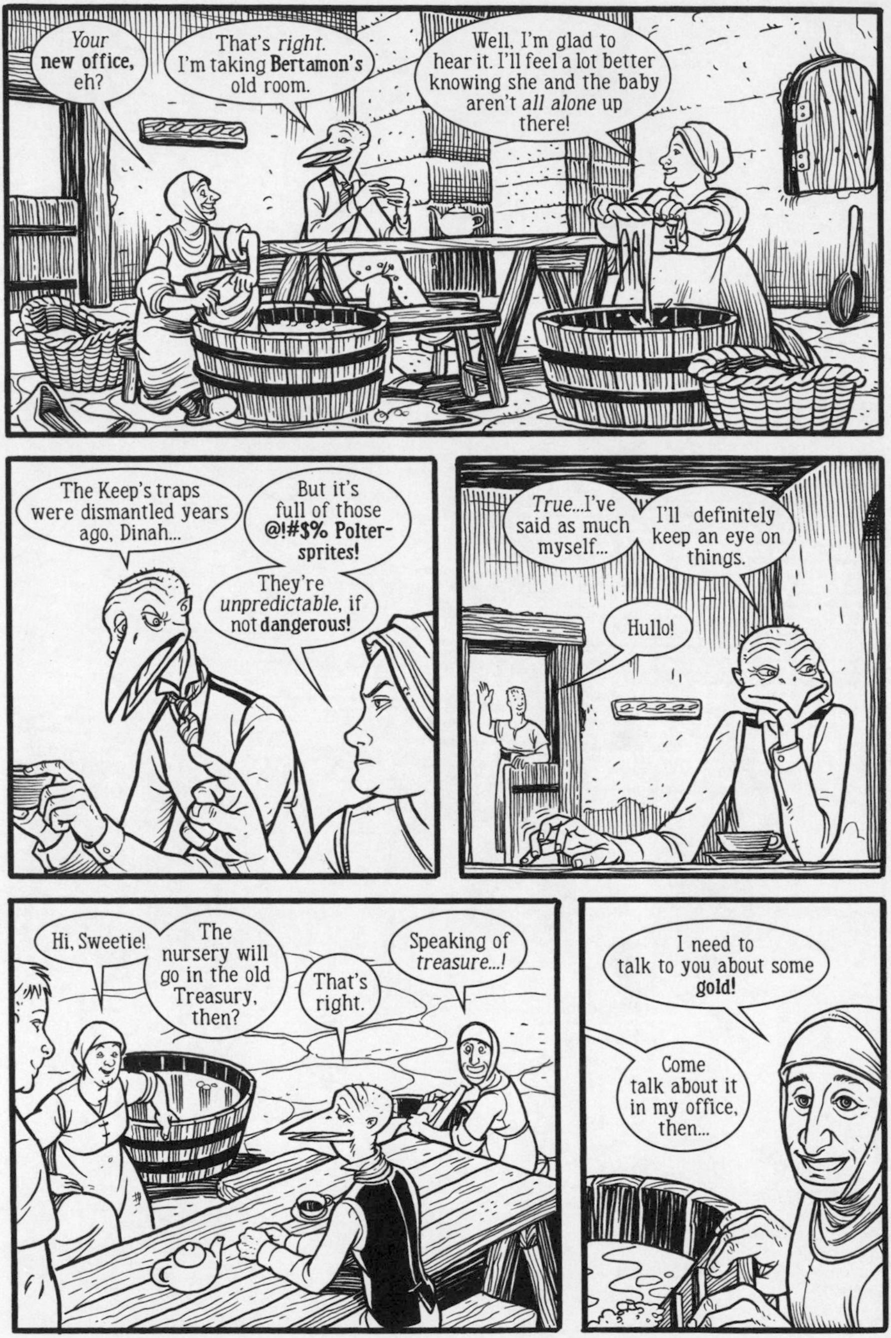
Your **new office,** eh?
That's *right.* I'm taking **Bertamon's** old room.
Well, I'm glad to hear it. I'll feel a lot better knowing she and the baby aren't *all alone* up there!
The Keep's traps were dismantled years ago, Dinah...
But it's full of those **@!#$% Polter-sprites!**
They're *unpredictable,* if not **dangerous!**
True...I've said as much myself...
I'll definitely keep an eye on things.
Hullo!
Hi, Sweetie!
The nursery will go in the old Treasury, then?
That's right.
Speaking of *treasure*...!
I need to talk to you about some **gold!**
Come talk about it in my office, then...

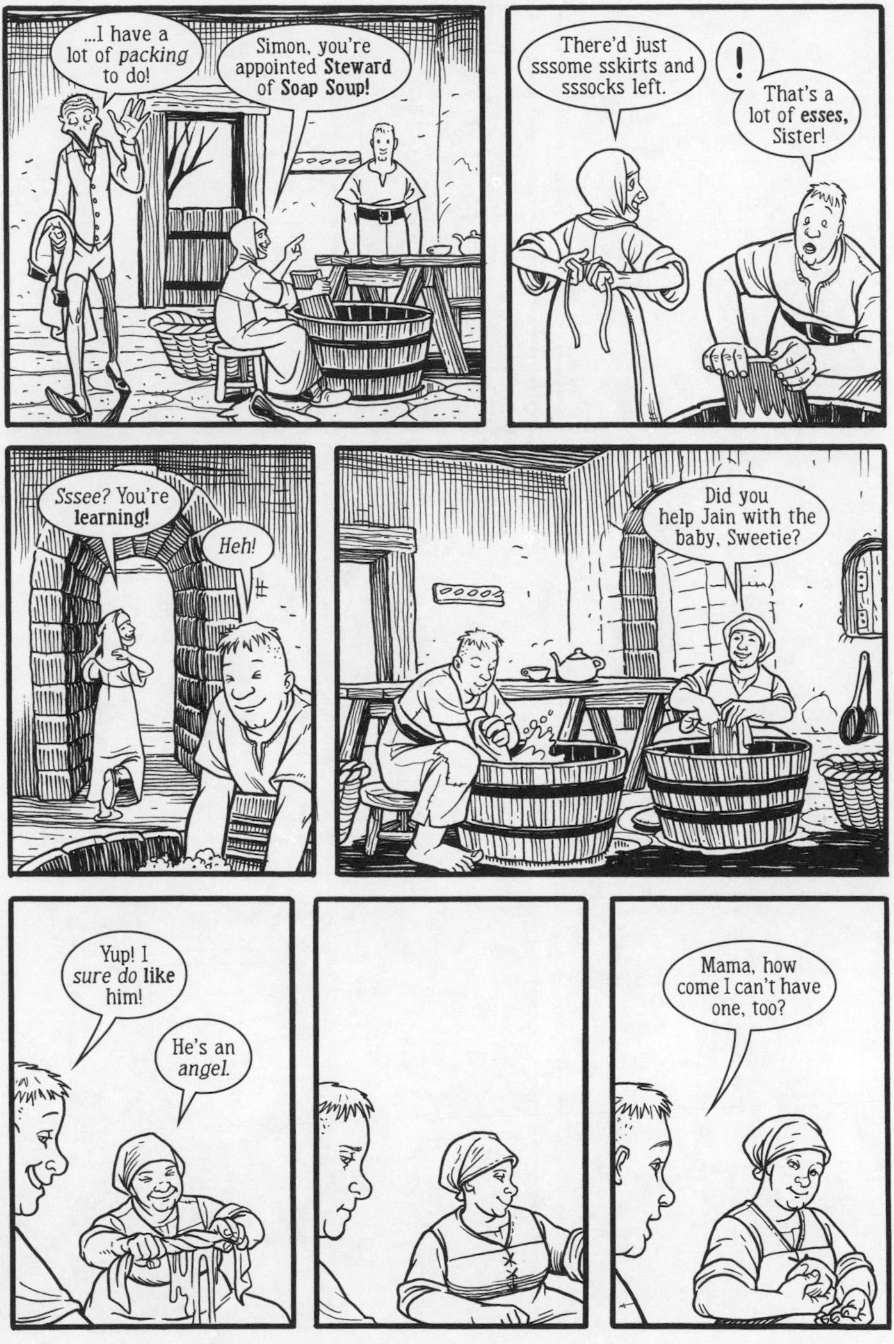
...I have a lot of *packing* to do!
Simon, you're appointed **Steward** of **Soap Soup!**
There'd just sssome sskirts and sssocks left.
!
That's a lot of **esses,** Sister!
Sssee? You're **learning!**
Heh!
Did you help Jain with the baby, Sweetie?
Yup! I *sure do* **like** him!
He's an *angel.*
Mama, how come I can't have one, too?

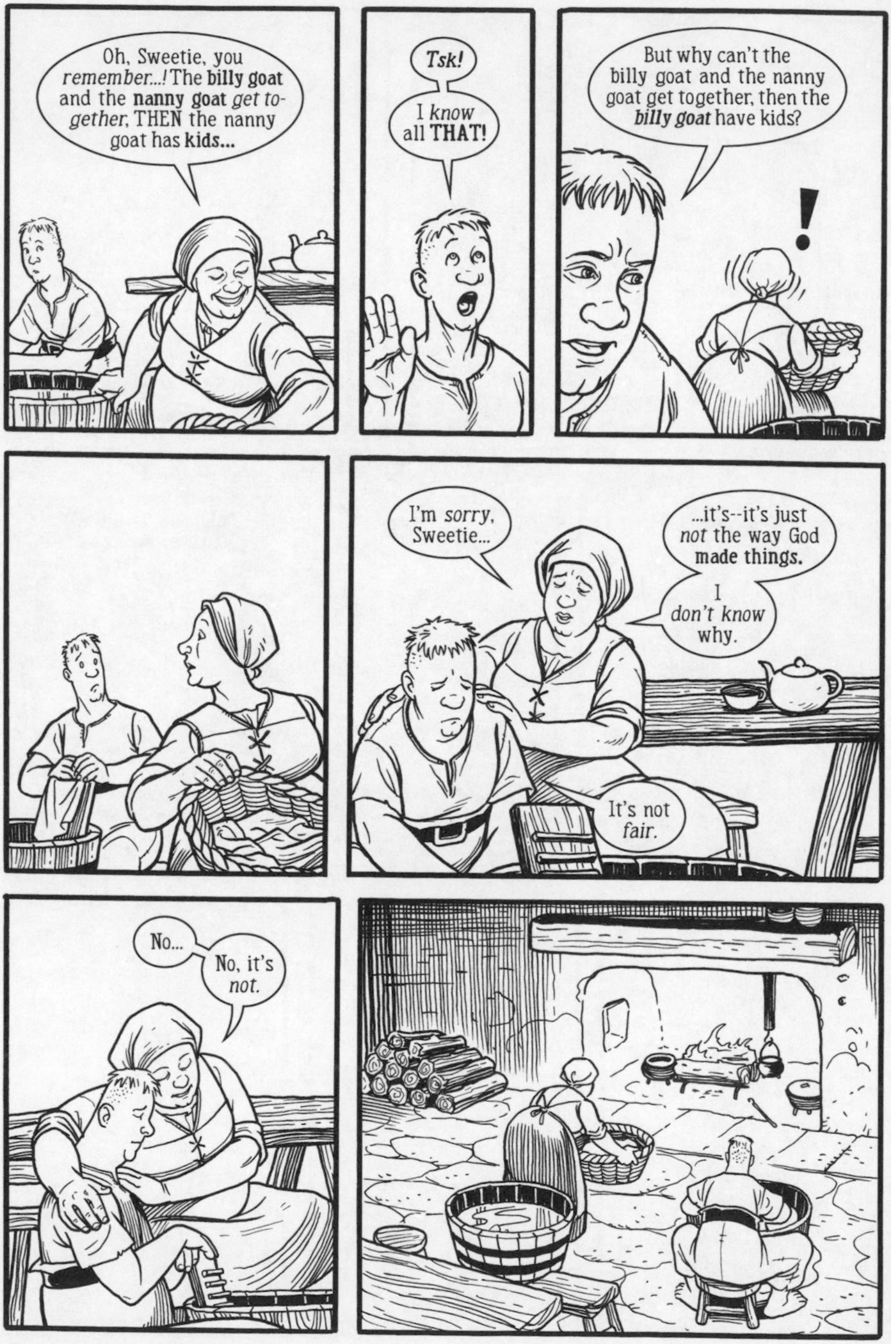
Oh, Sweetie, you *remember...!* The **billy goat** and the **nanny goat** *get together*, THEN the nanny goat has **kids...**
Tsk!
I *know* all **THAT!**
But why can't the billy goat and the nanny goat get together, then the ***billy goat*** have kids?
!
I'm *sorry*, Sweetie...
...it's--it's just *not* the way God **made things.**
I *don't know* why.
It's not *fair.*
No...
No, it's *not.*

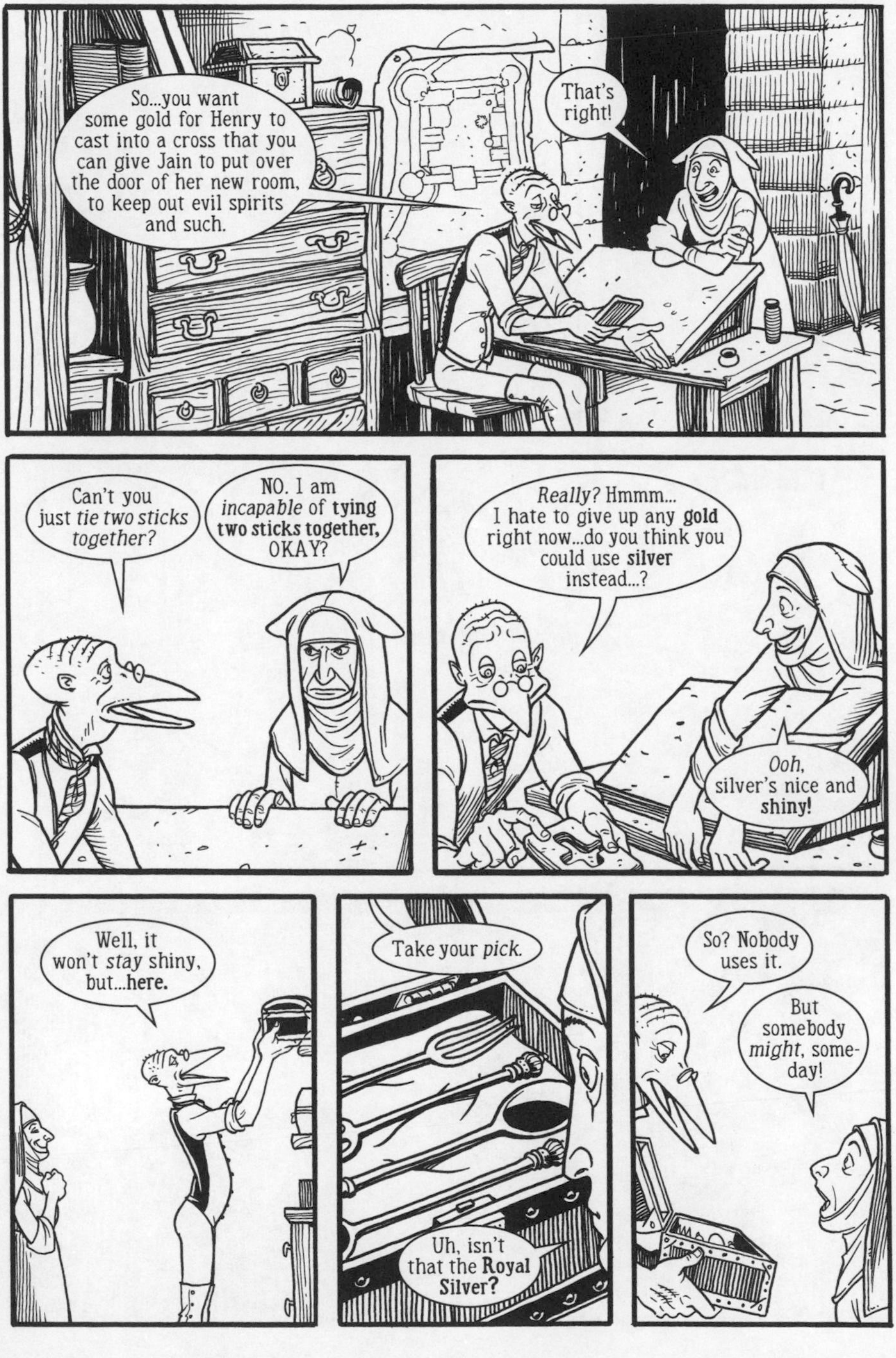
So...you want some gold for Henry to cast into a cross that you can give Jain to put over the door of her new room, to keep out evil spirits and such.
That's right!
Can't you just *tie two sticks together?*
NO. I am *incapable* of **tying two sticks together,** OKAY?
Really? Hmmm... I hate to give up any **gold** right now...do you think you could use **silver** instead...?
Ooh, silver's nice and **shiny!**
Well, it won't *stay* shiny, but...**here.**
Take your *pick.*
Uh, isn't that the **Royal Silver?**
So? Nobody uses it.
But somebody *might,* someday!

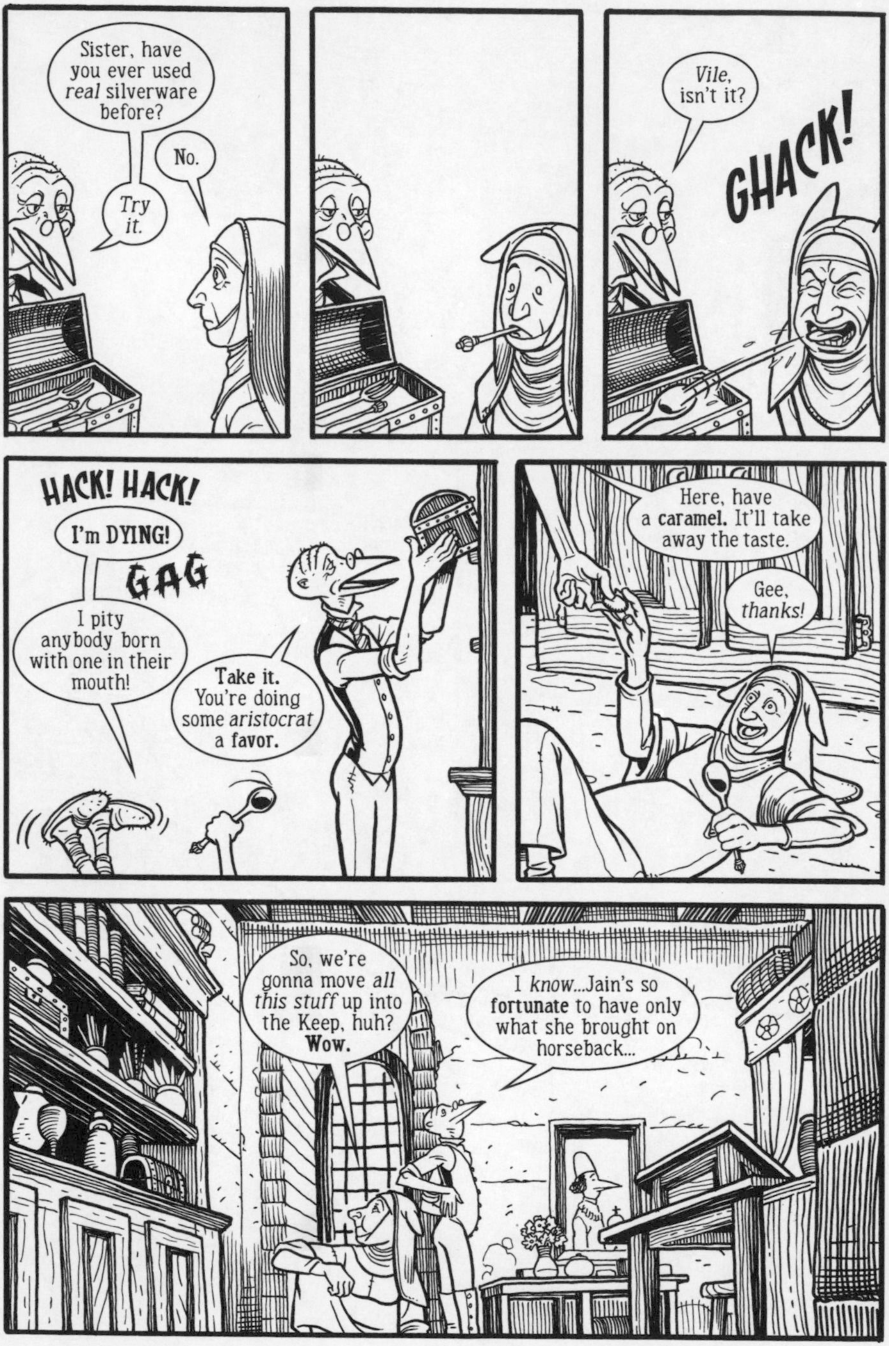
Sister, have you ever used *real* silverware before?
No.
Try it.
Vile, isn't it?
GHACK!
HACK! HACK!
I'm DYING!
GAG
I pity anybody born with one in their mouth!
Take it. You're doing some *aristocrat* a **favor.**
Here, have a **caramel.** It'll take away the taste.
Gee, *thanks!*
So, we're gonna move *all this stuff* up into the Keep, huh? **Wow.**
I *know*...Jain's so **fortunate** to have only what she brought on horseback...

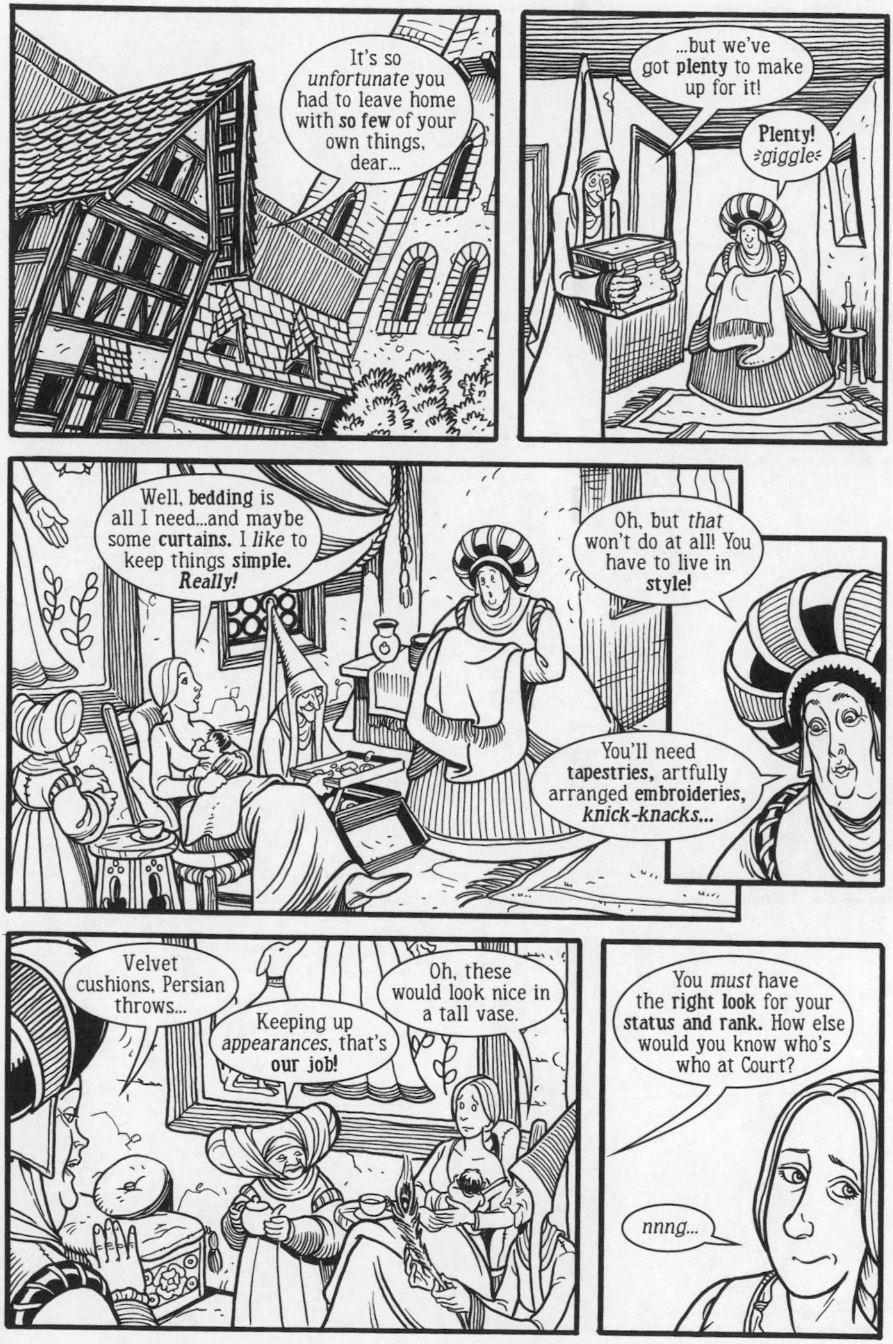
It's so *unfortunate* you had to leave home with **so few** of your own things, dear...
...but we've got **plenty** to make up for it!
Plenty! *giggle*
Well, **bedding** is all I need...and maybe some **curtains.** I *like* to keep things **simple.** ***Really!***
Oh, but *that* won't do at all! You have to live in **style!**
You'll need **tapestries,** artfully arranged **embroideries,** ***knick-knacks...***
Velvet cushions, Persian throws...
Keeping up *appearances*, that's **our job!**
Oh, these would look nice in a tall vase.
You *must* have the **right look** for your **status and rank.** How else would you know who's who at Court?
nnng...

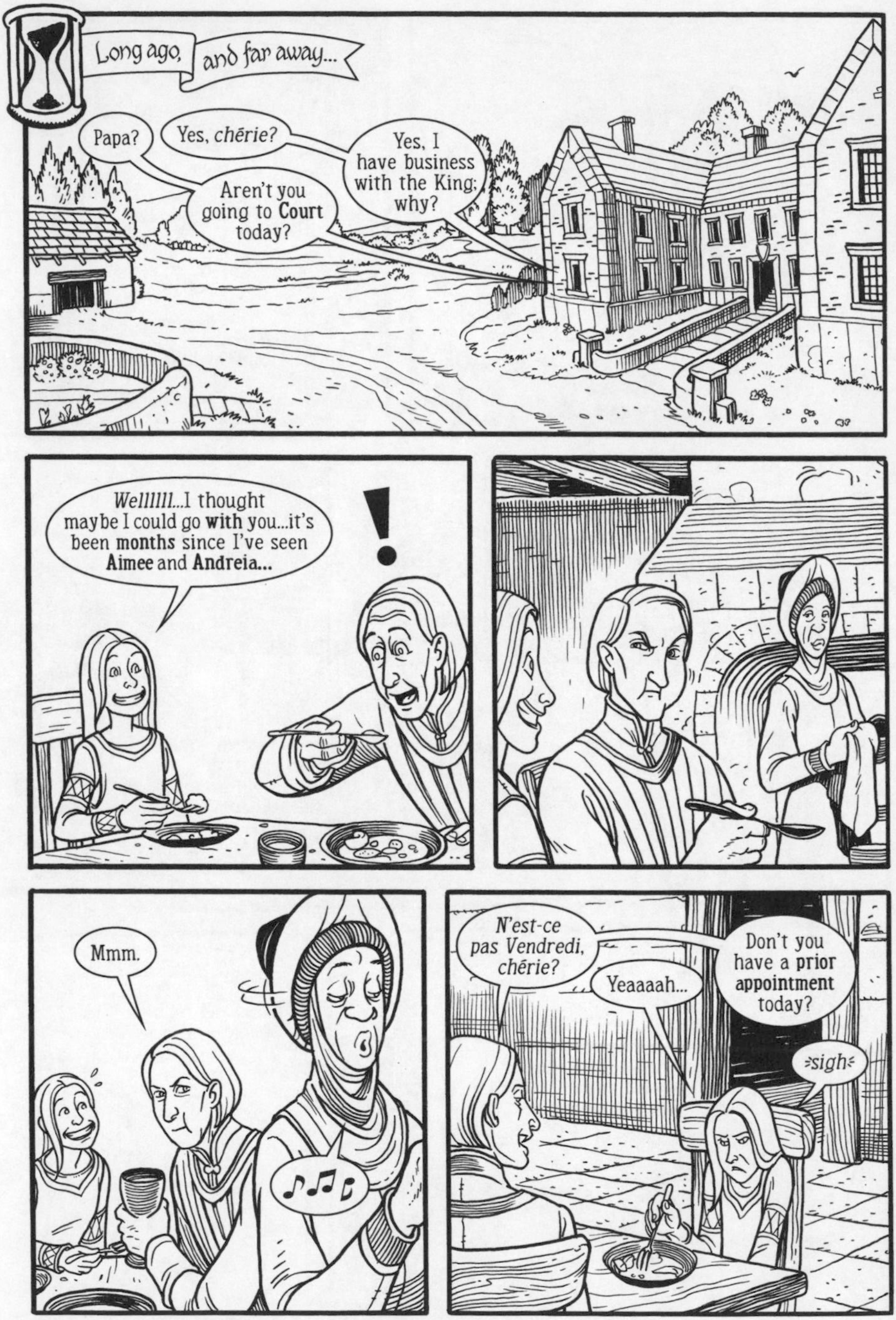
Long ago,
and far away...
Papa?
Yes, *chérie?*
Aren't you going to **Court** today?
Yes, I have business with the King; why?
*Welllllll...*I thought maybe I could go **with** you...it's been **months** since I've seen **Aimee** and **Andreia...**
!
Mmm.
N'est-ce pas Vendredi, chérie?
Yeaaaah...
Don't you have a **prior appointment** today?
sigh

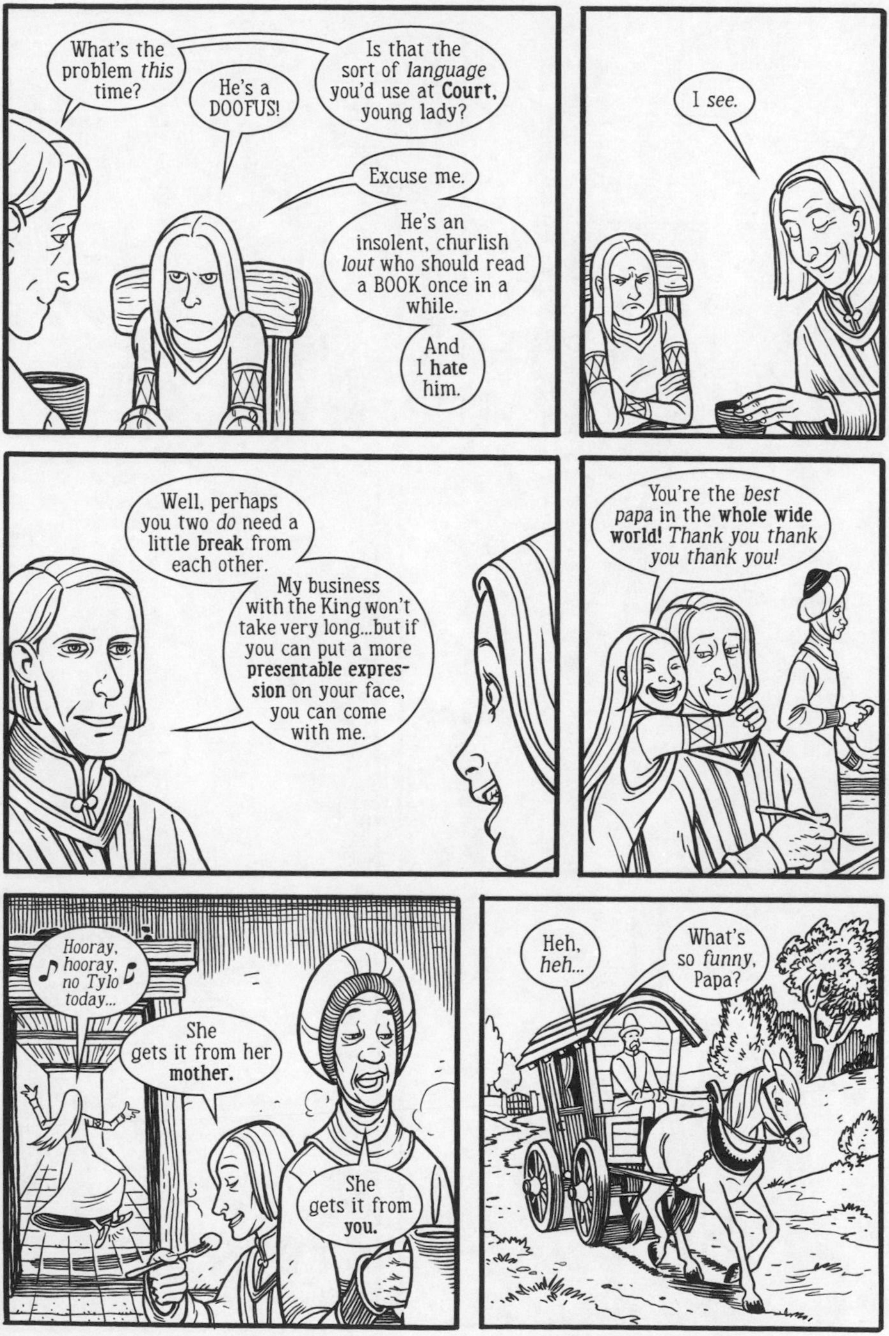
What's the problem *this* time?
He's a DOOFUS!
Is that the sort of *language* you'd use at **Court**, young lady?
Excuse me.
He's an insolent, churlish *lout* who should read a BOOK once in a while.
And I **hate** him.
I *see.*
Well, perhaps you two *do* need a little **break** from each other.
My business with the King won't take very long...but if you can put a more **presentable expression** on your face, you can come with me.
You're the *best papa* in the **whole wide world!** *Thank you thank you thank you!*
Hooray, hooray, no Tylo today...
She gets it from her **mother.**
She gets it from **you.**
Heh, *heh...*
What's so *funny*, Papa?

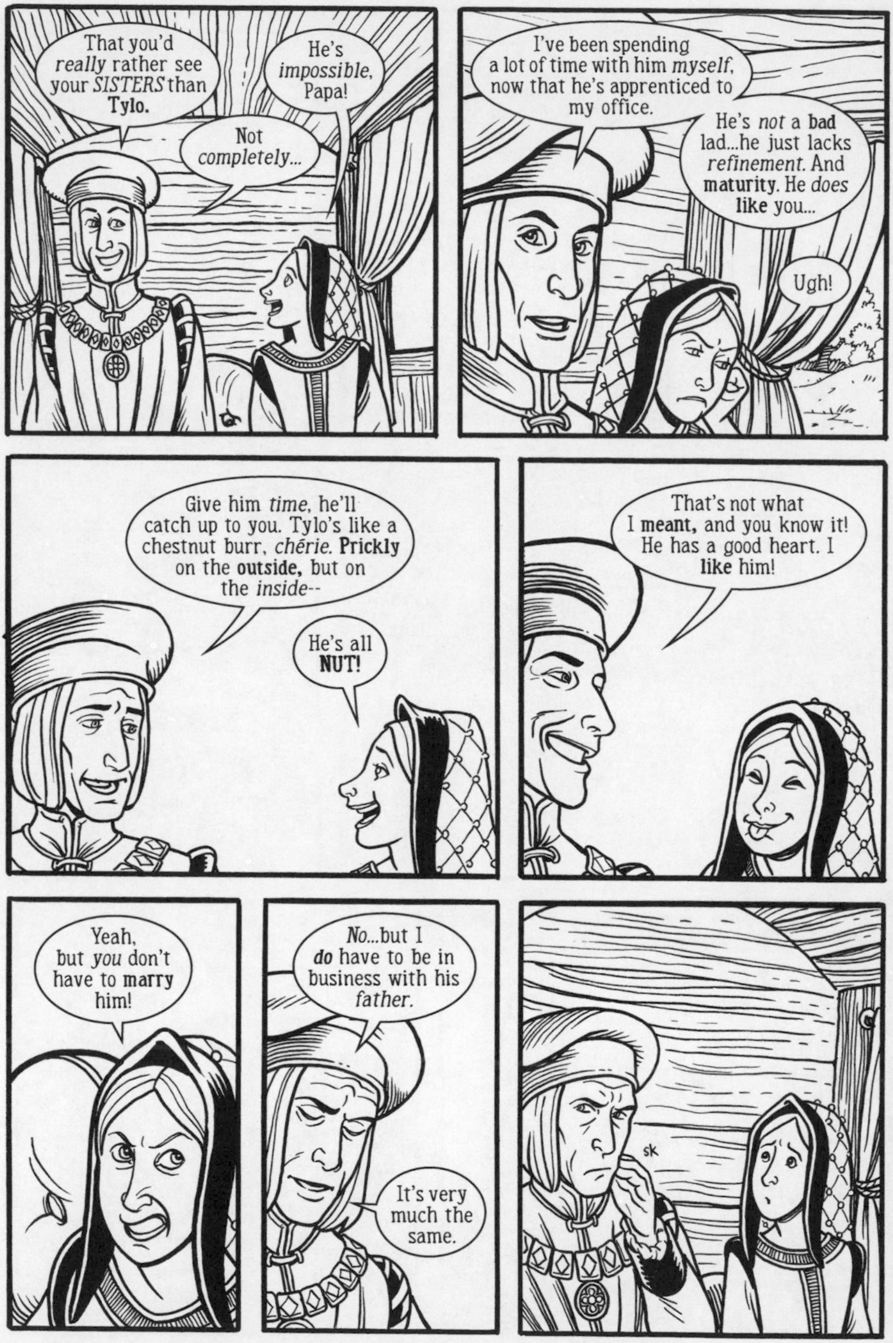
That you'd *really* rather see your *SISTERS* than **Tylo.**
He's *impossible,* Papa!
Not *completely...*
I've been spending a lot of time with him *myself,* now that he's apprenticed to my office.
He's *not* a **bad** lad...he just lacks *refinement.* And **maturity.** He *does* **like** you...
Ugh!
Give him *time,* he'll catch up to you. Tylo's like a chestnut burr, *chérie.* **Prickly** on the **outside,** but on the *inside*--
He's all **NUT!**
That's not what I **meant,** and you know it! He has a good heart. I **like** him!
Yeah, but *you* don't have to **marry** him!
No...but I **do** have to be in business with his *father.*
It's very much the same.
SK

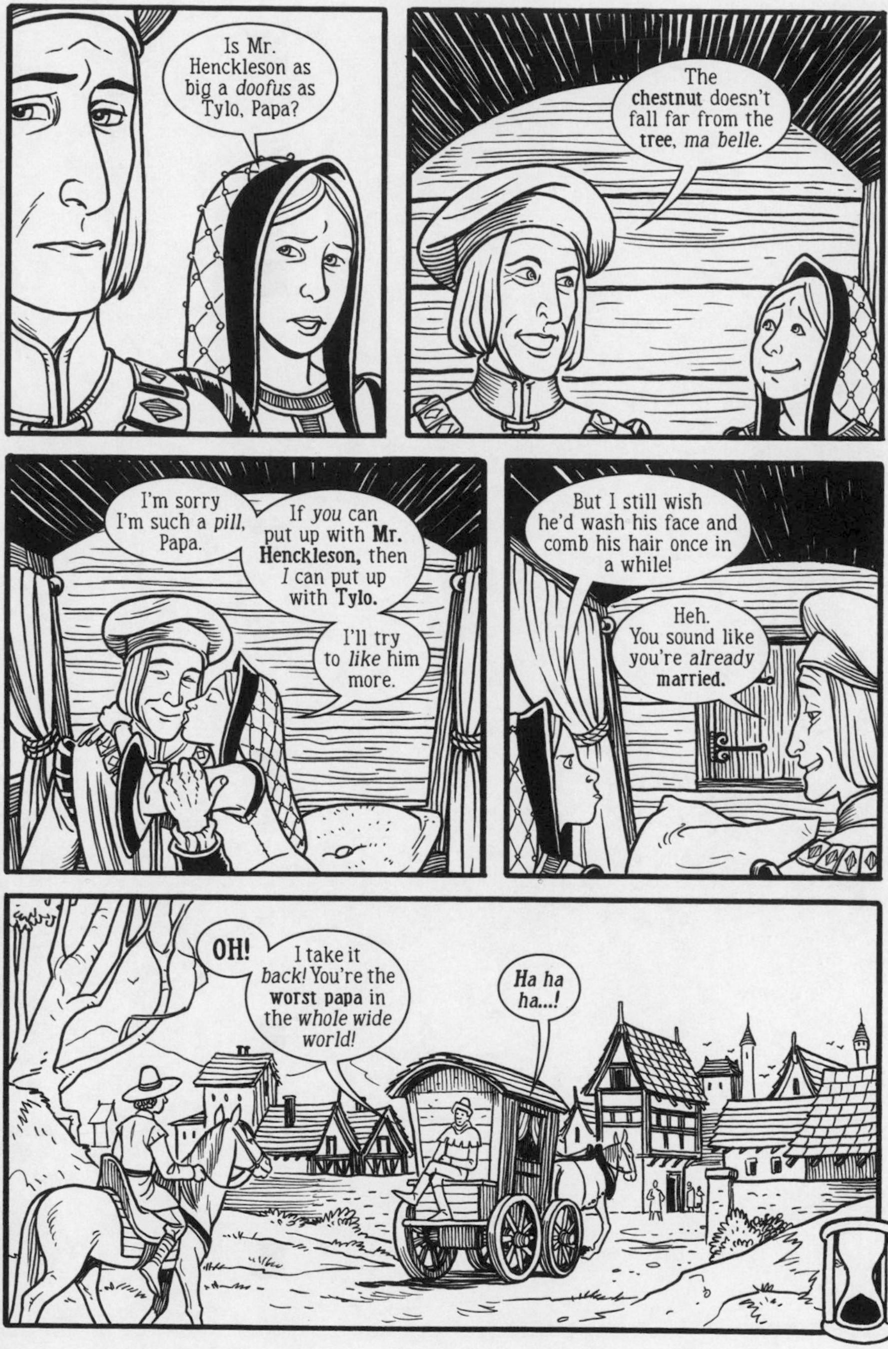
Is Mr. Henckleson as big a *doofus* as Tylo, Papa?
The **chestnut** doesn't fall far from the **tree**, *ma belle.*
I'm sorry I'm such a *pill*, Papa.
If *you* can put up with **Mr. Henckleson,** then *I* can put up with **Tylo.**
I'll try to *like* him more.
But I still wish he'd wash his face and comb his hair once in a while!
Heh. You sound like you're *already* **married.**
OH!
I take it *back!* You're the **worst papa** in the *whole wide world!*
Ha ha ha...!

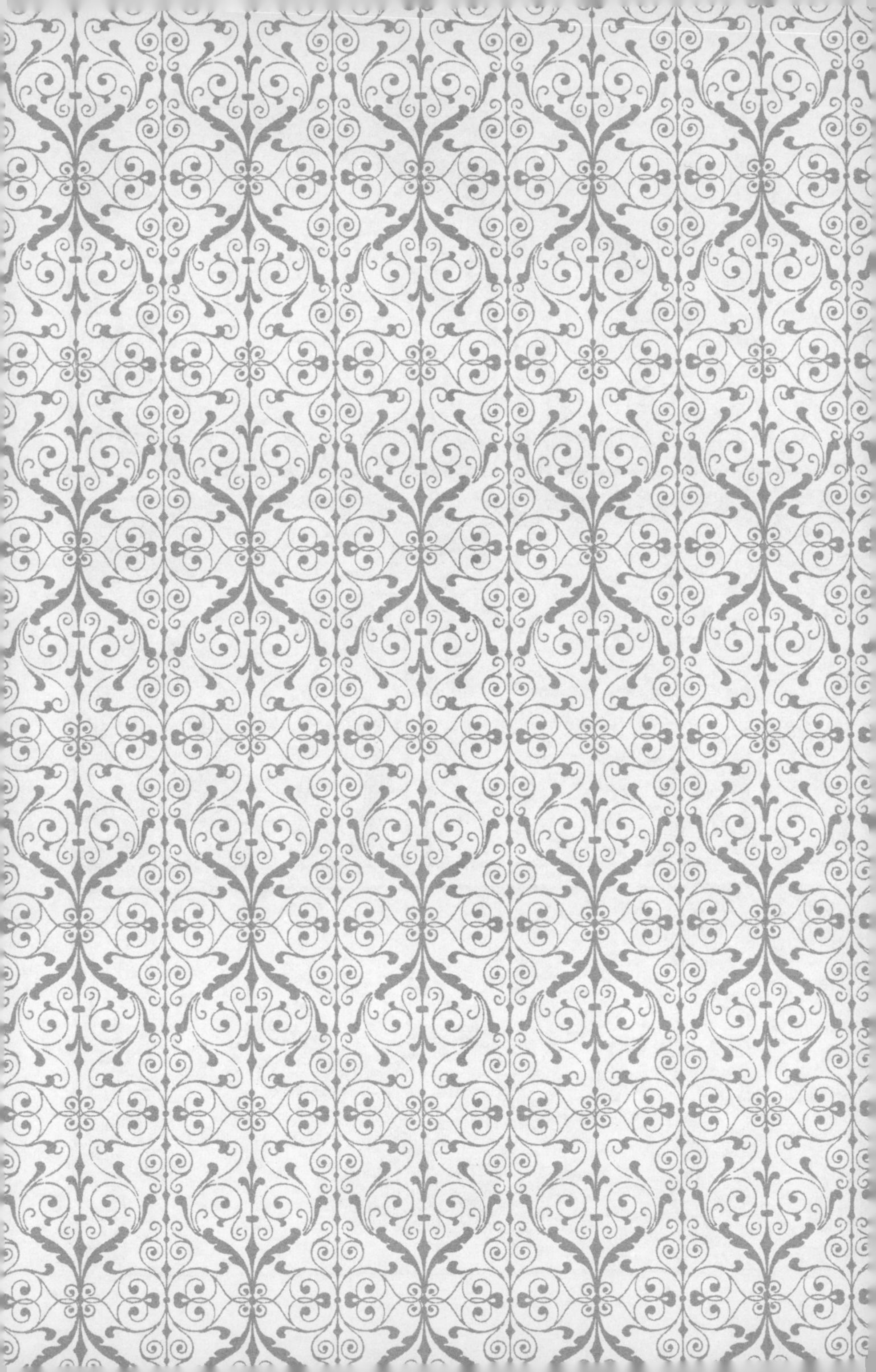

Chapter 3.

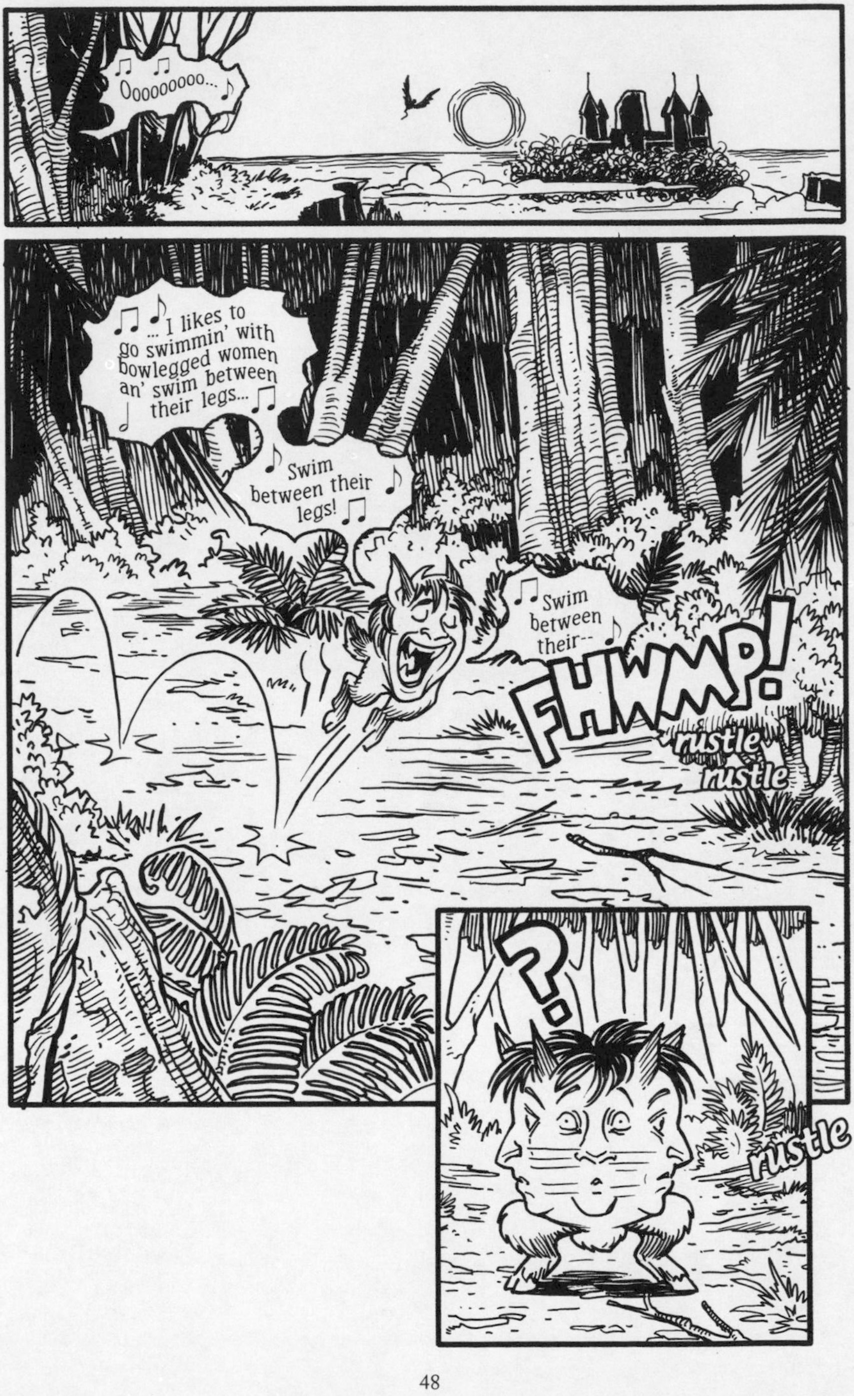
Ooooooooo...
... I likes to go swimmin' with bowlegged women an' swim between their legs...
Swim between their legs!
Swim between their--
FHWMP!
rustle rustle
?
rustle

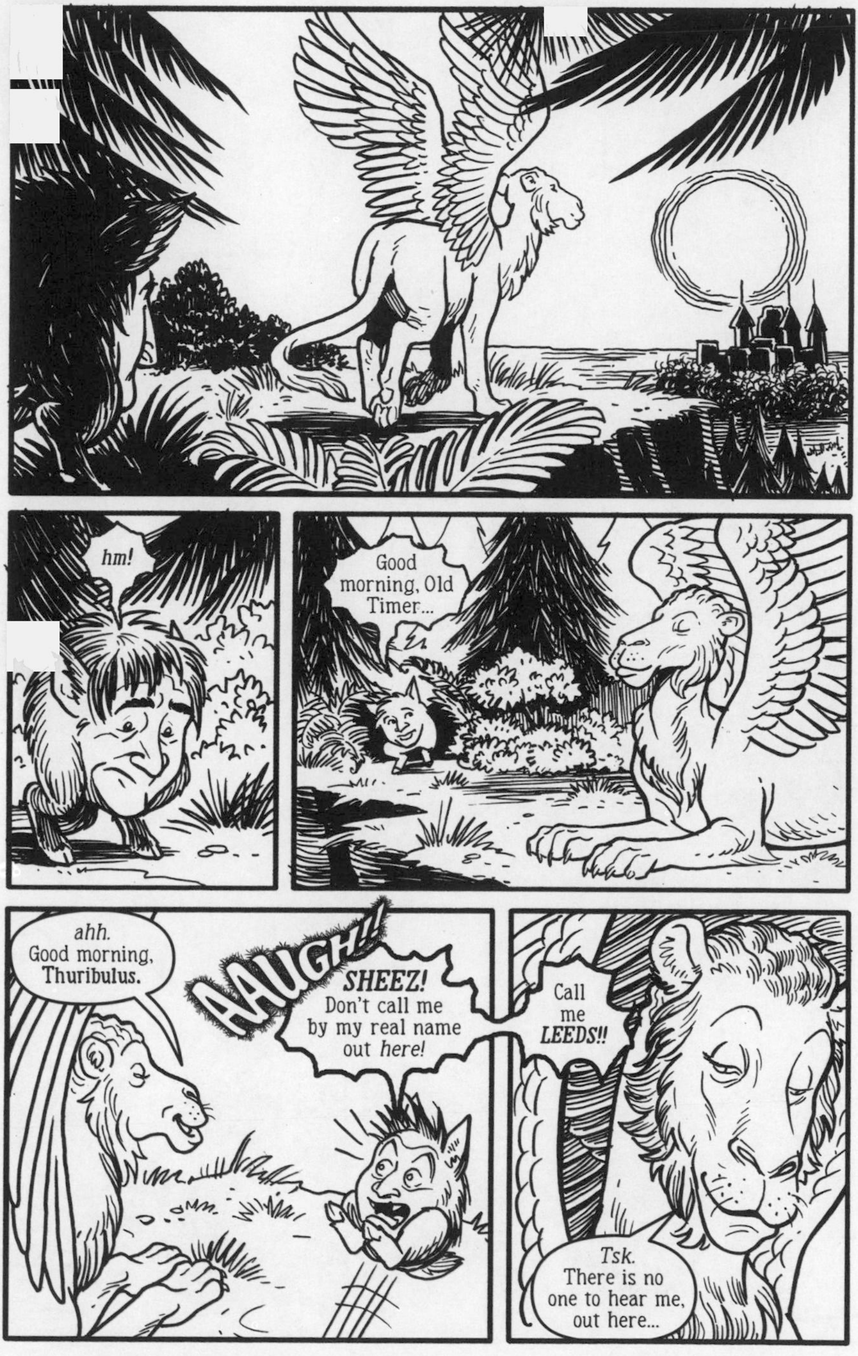
hm!
Good morning, Old Timer...
ahh. Good morning, Thuribulus.
AAUGH!!
SHEEZ! Don't call me by my real name out here!
Call me LEEDS!!
Tsk. There is no one to hear me, out here...

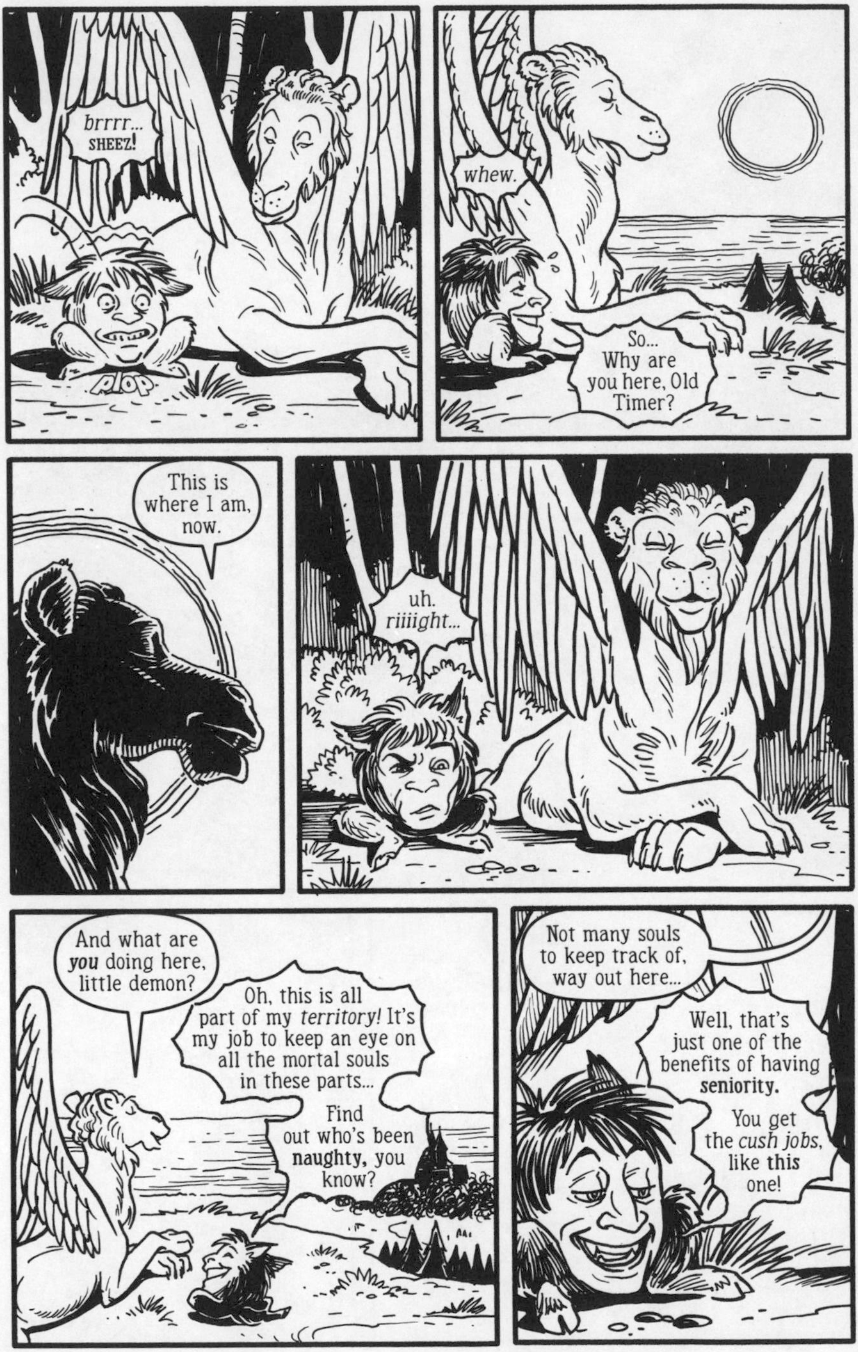
brrrr... SHEEZ!
PLOP
whew.
So... Why are you here, Old Timer?
This is where I am, now.
uh. riiiight...
And what are you doing here, little demon?
Oh, this is all part of my territory! It's my job to keep an eye on all the mortal souls in these parts...
Find out who's been naughty, you know?
Not many souls to keep track of, way out here...
Well, that's just one of the benefits of having seniority.
You get the cush jobs, like this one!

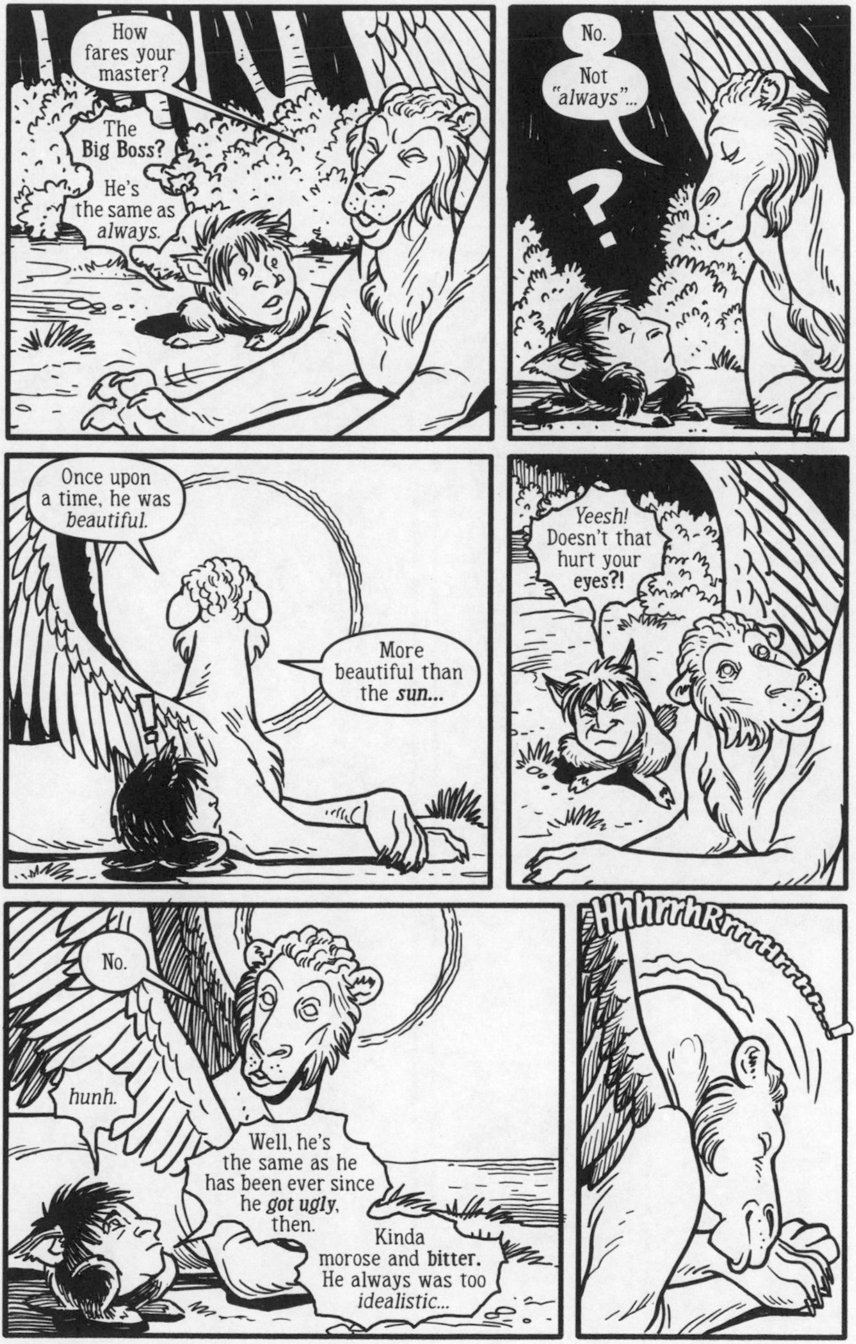
How fares your master?
The **Big Boss?** He's the same as *always.*
No.
Not "*always*"...
?
Once upon a time, he was *beautiful.*
More beautiful than the ***sun...***
!
Yeesh! Doesn't that hurt your **eyes?!**
No.
hunh.
Well, he's the same as he has been ever since he ***got ugly***, then.
Kinda morose and **bitter.** He always was too *idealistic...*
HhhrrhRrrrHrrrrrr

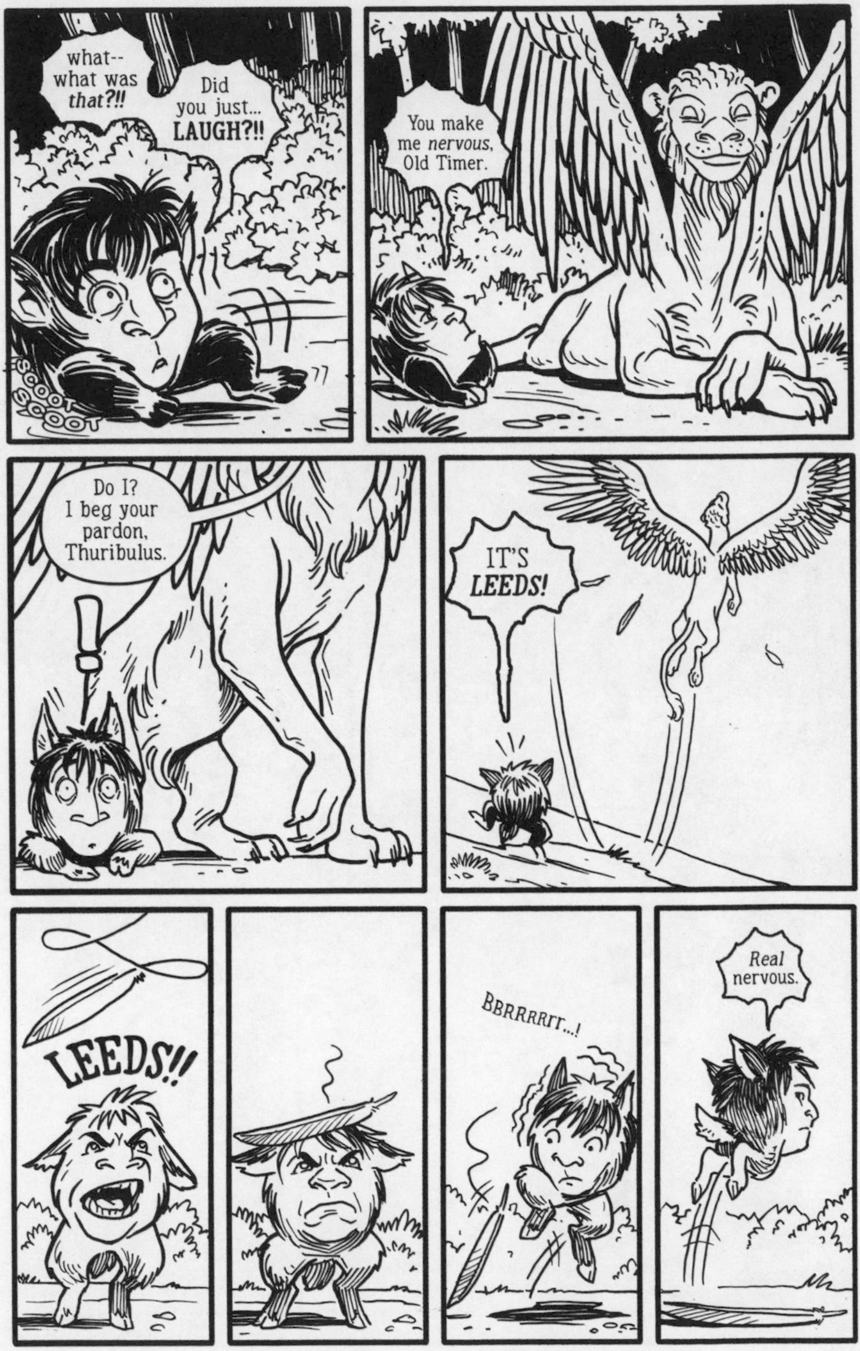
what--
what was
that?!!
Did
you just...
LAUGH?!!
SCOOT
SCOOT
You make
me *nervous,*
Old Timer.
Do I?
I beg your
pardon,
Thuribulus.
IT'S
LEEDS!
LEEDS!!
BRRRRRrr...!
Real
nervous.

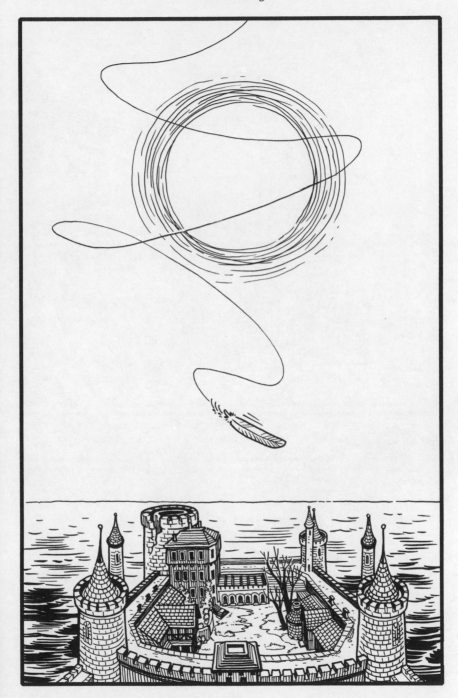

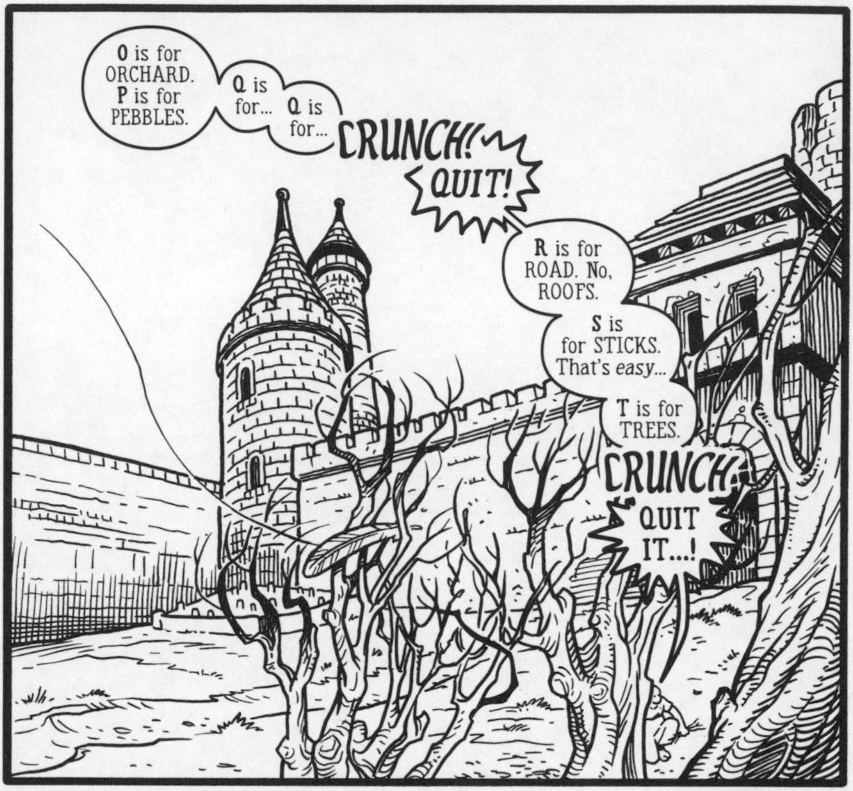
O is for ORCHARD. P is for PEBBLES.
Q is for... Q is for...
CRUNCH!
QUIT!
R is for ROAD. No, ROOFS.
S is for STICKS. That's *easy*...
T is for TREES.
CRUNCH
QUIT IT...!

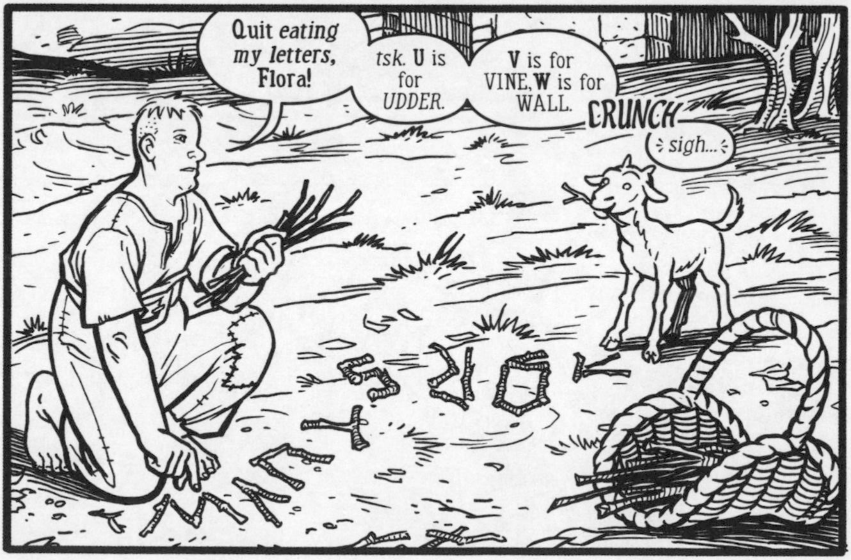
Quit *eating my letters,* Flora!
tsk. U is for *UDDER.*
V is for VINE, W is for WALL.
CRUNCH
sigh...

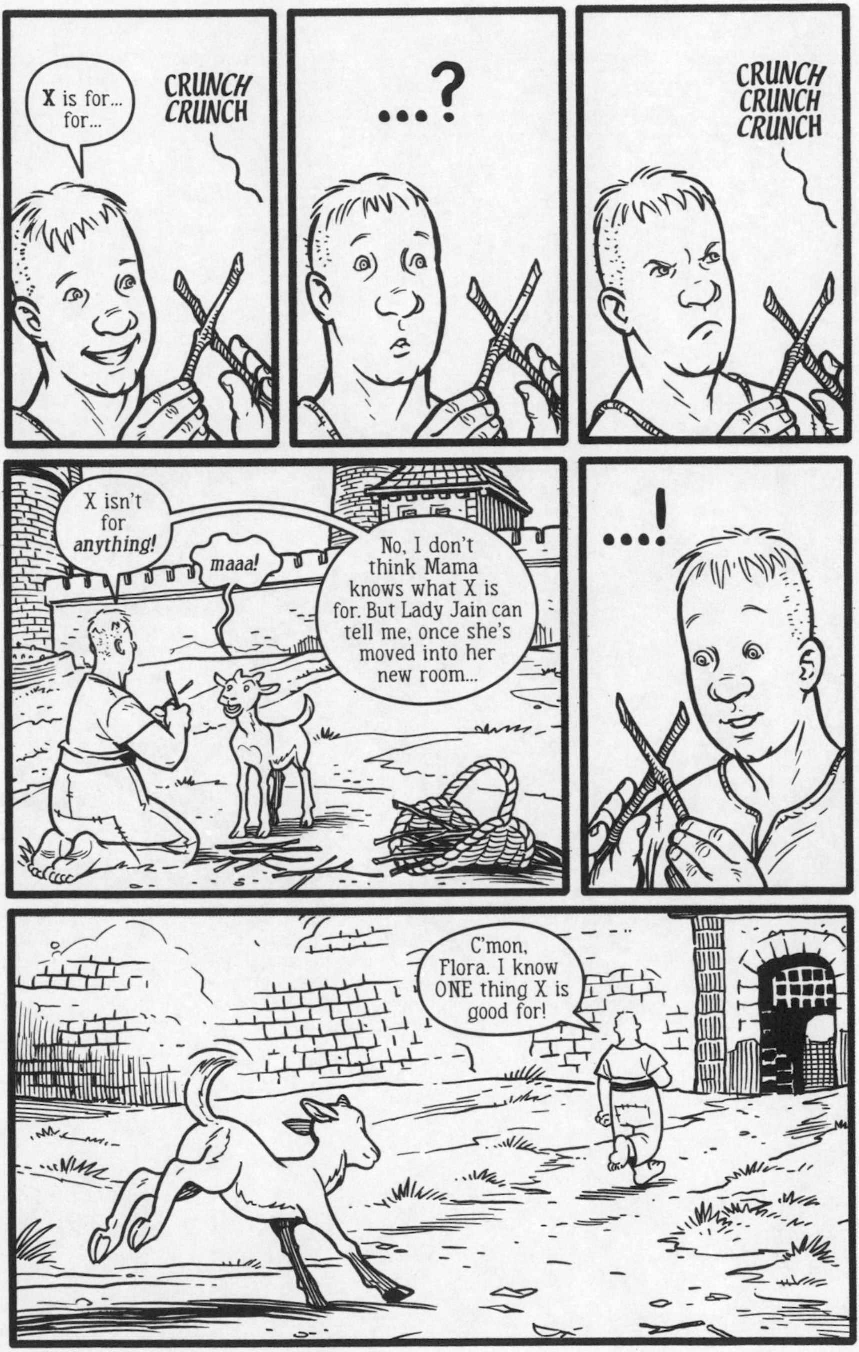
X is for... for...
CRUNCH CRUNCH
...?
CRUNCH CRUNCH CRUNCH
X isn't for *anything!*
maaa!
No, I don't think Mama knows what X is for. But Lady Jain can tell me, once she's moved into her new room...
...!
C'mon, Flora. I know ONE thing X is good for!

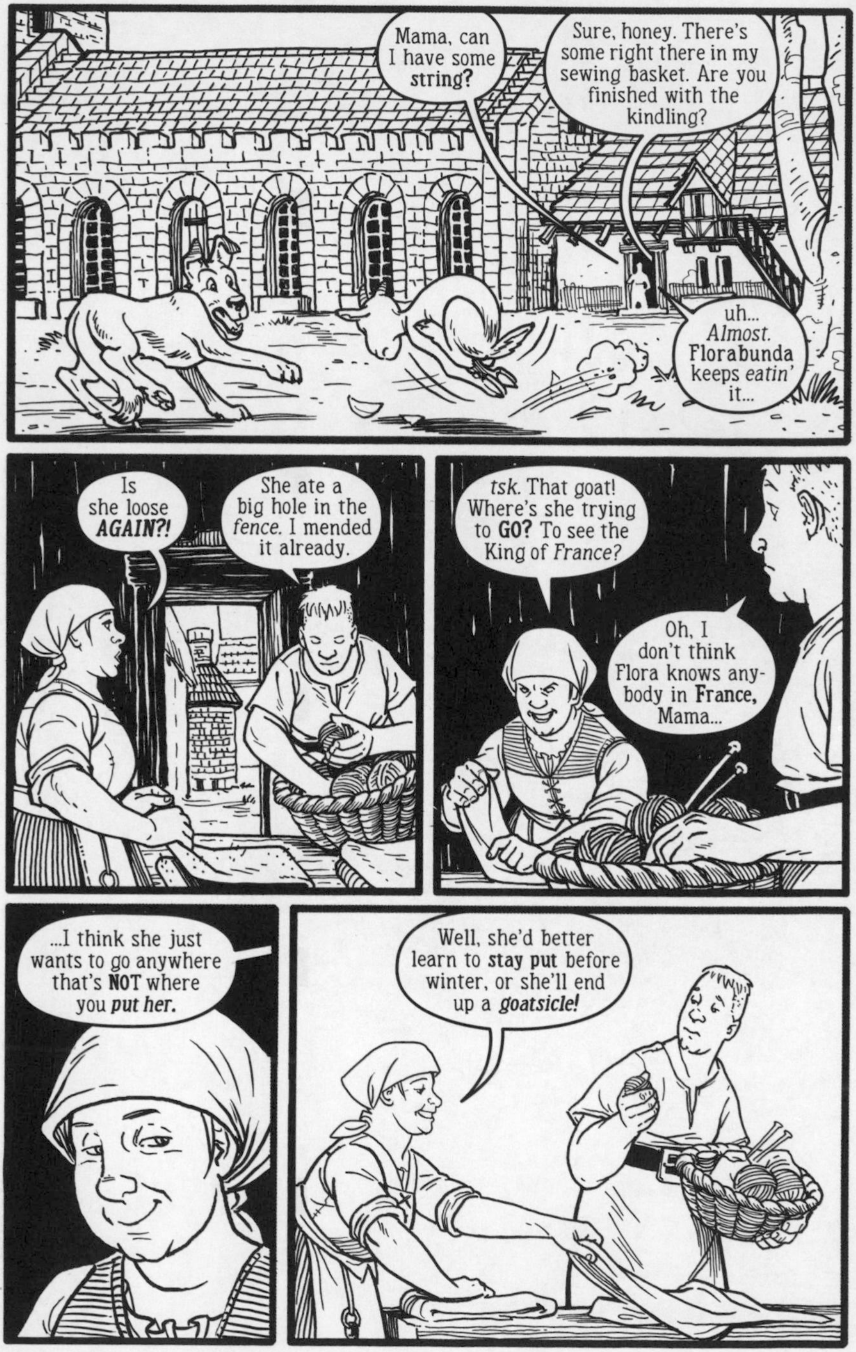
Mama, can I have some **string?**
Sure, honey. There's some right there in my sewing basket. Are you finished with the kindling?
uh... *Almost.* **Florabunda** keeps *eatin'* it...
Is she loose ***AGAIN?!***
She ate a big hole in the *fence.* I mended it already.
tsk. That goat! Where's she trying to **GO?** To see the King of *France?*
Oh, I don't think Flora knows any-body in **France,** Mama...
...I think she just wants to go anywhere that's **NOT** where you ***put her.***
Well, she'd better learn to **stay put** before winter, or she'll end up a ***goatsicle!***

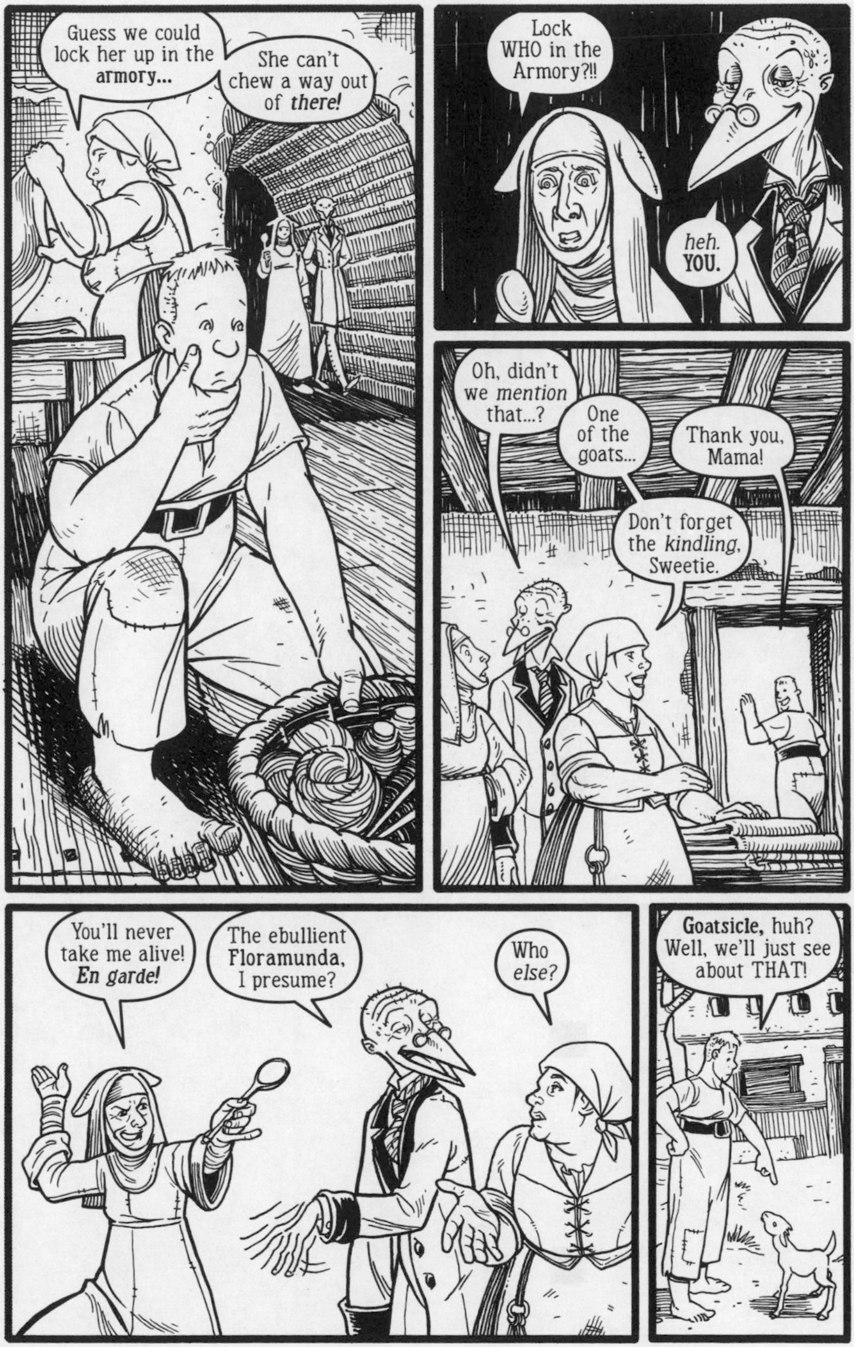
Guess we could lock her up in the **armory...**
She can't chew a way out of ***there!***
Lock WHO in the Armory?!!
heh. **YOU.**
Oh, didn't we *mention* that...?
One of the goats...
Thank you, Mama!
Don't forget the *kindling,* Sweetie.
You'll never take me alive! ***En garde!***
The ebullient **Floramunda,** I presume?
Who *else?*
Goatsicle, huh? Well, we'll just see about THAT!

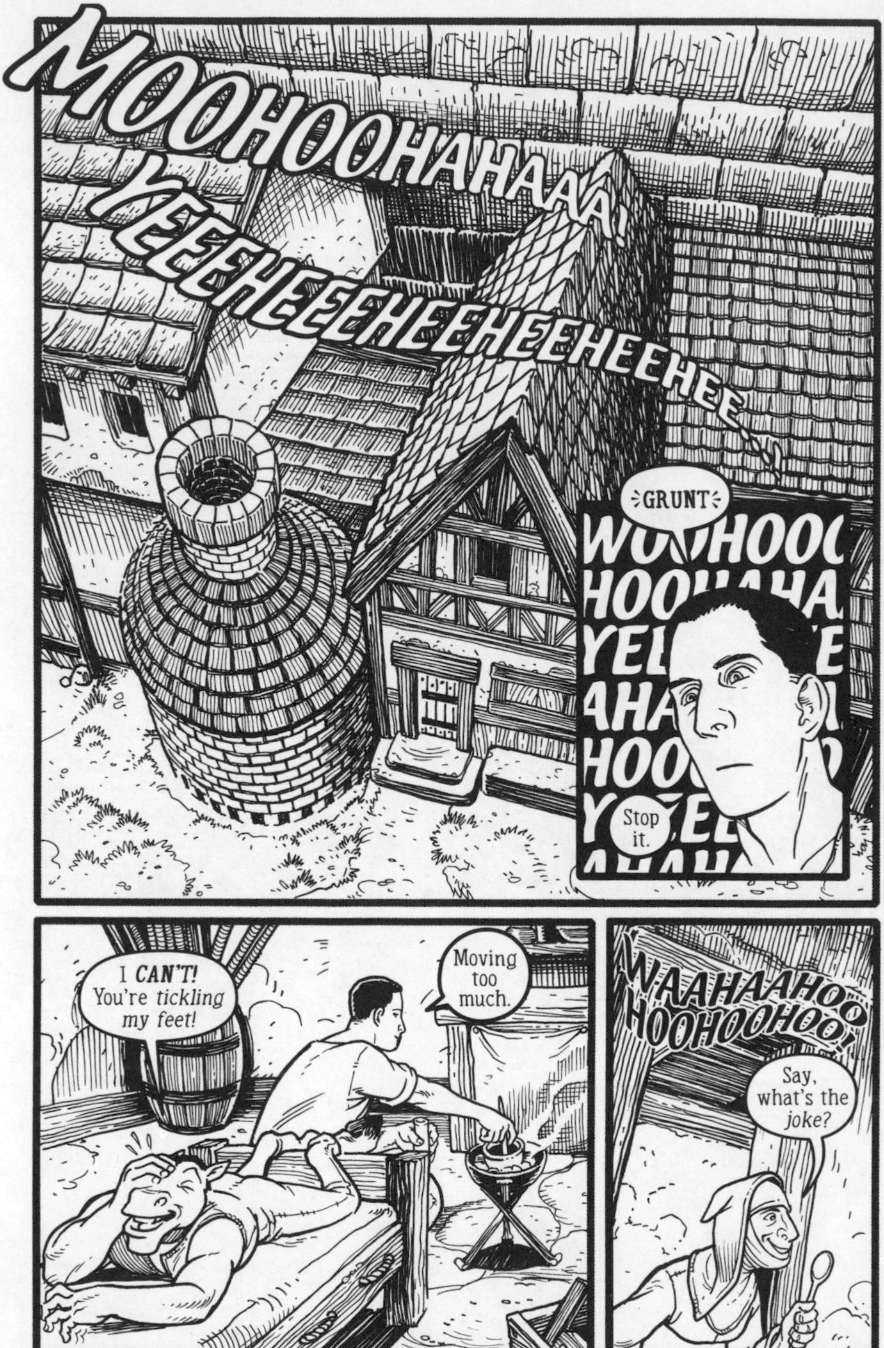
MOOHOOHAHAAA!
YEEEHEEEEHEEHEEHEEHEE
GRUNT
Stop it.
I CAN'T! You're tickling my feet!
Moving too much.
WAAHAAHOO HOOHOOHOO!
Say, what's the joke?

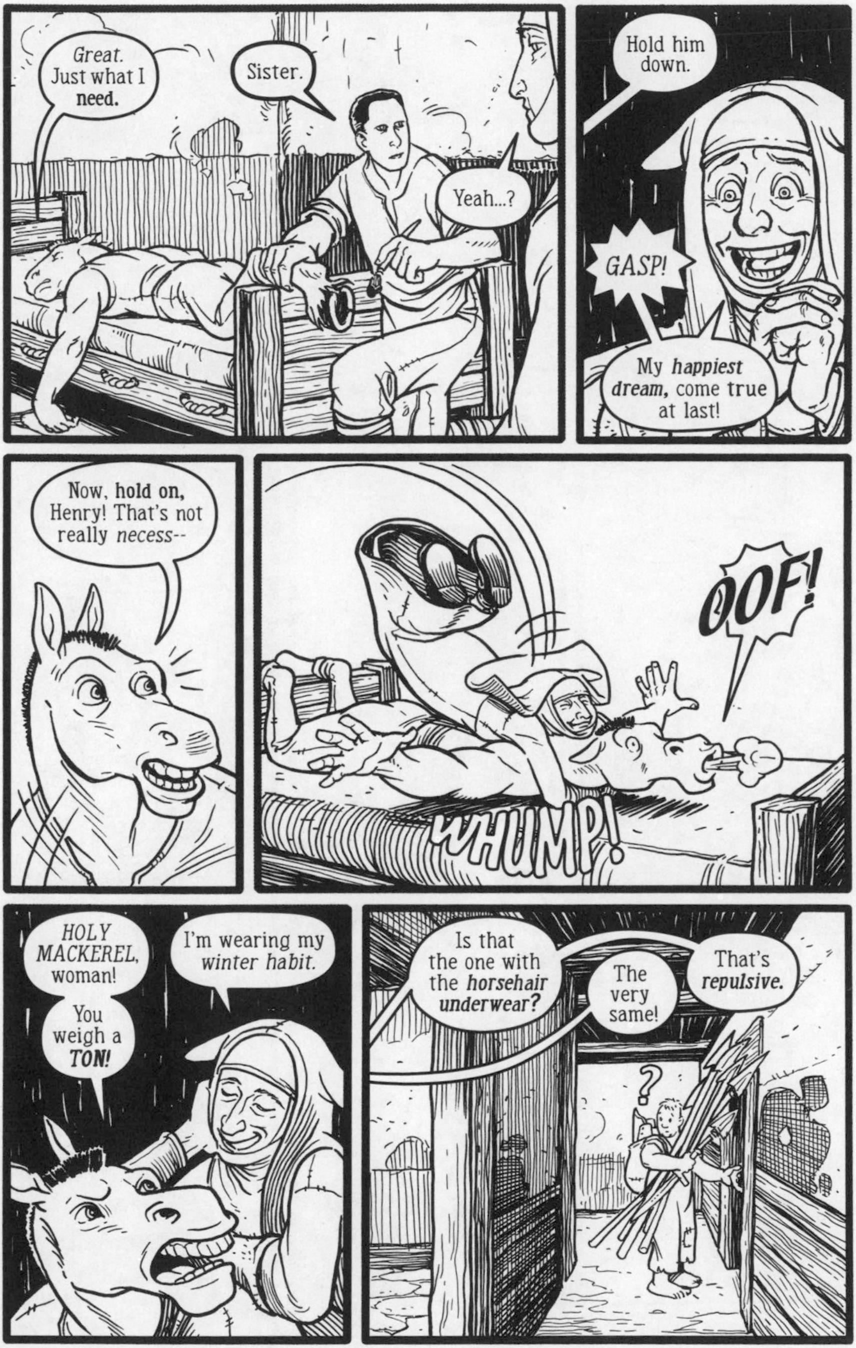
Great. Just what I need.
Sister.
Yeah...?
Hold him down.
GASP!
My happiest dream, come true at last!
Now, hold on, Henry! That's not really necess--
OOF!
WHUMP!
HOLY MACKEREL, woman!
You weigh a TON!
I'm wearing my winter habit.
Is that the one with the horsehair underwear?
The very same!
That's repulsive.
?

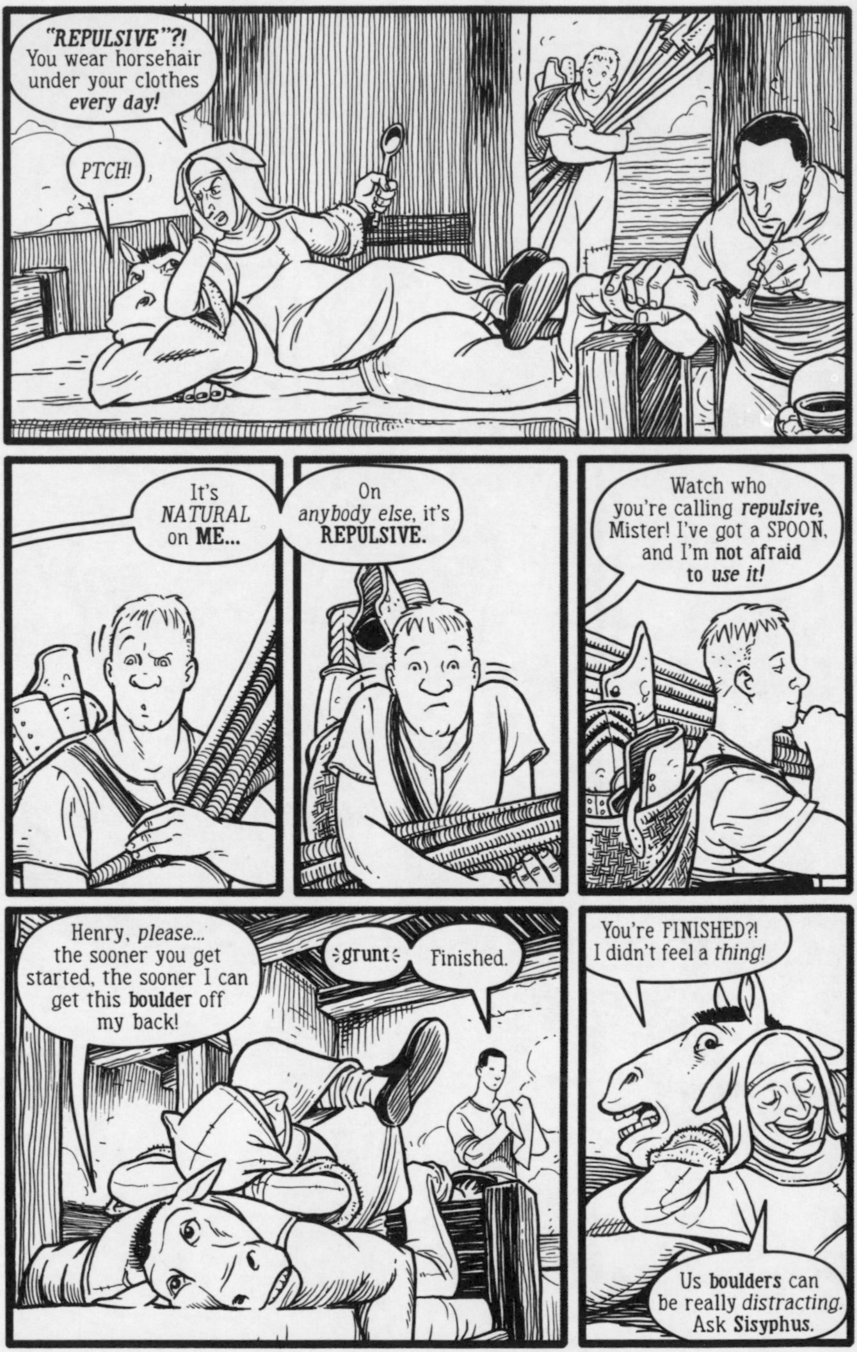
"REPULSIVE"?! You wear horsehair under your clothes every day!
PTCH!
It's NATURAL on ME...
On anybody else, it's REPULSIVE.
Watch who you're calling repulsive, Mister! I've got a SPOON, and I'm not afraid to use it!
Henry, please... the sooner you get started, the sooner I can get this boulder off my back!
grunt
Finished.
You're FINISHED?! I didn't feel a thing!
Us boulders can be really distracting. Ask Sisyphus.

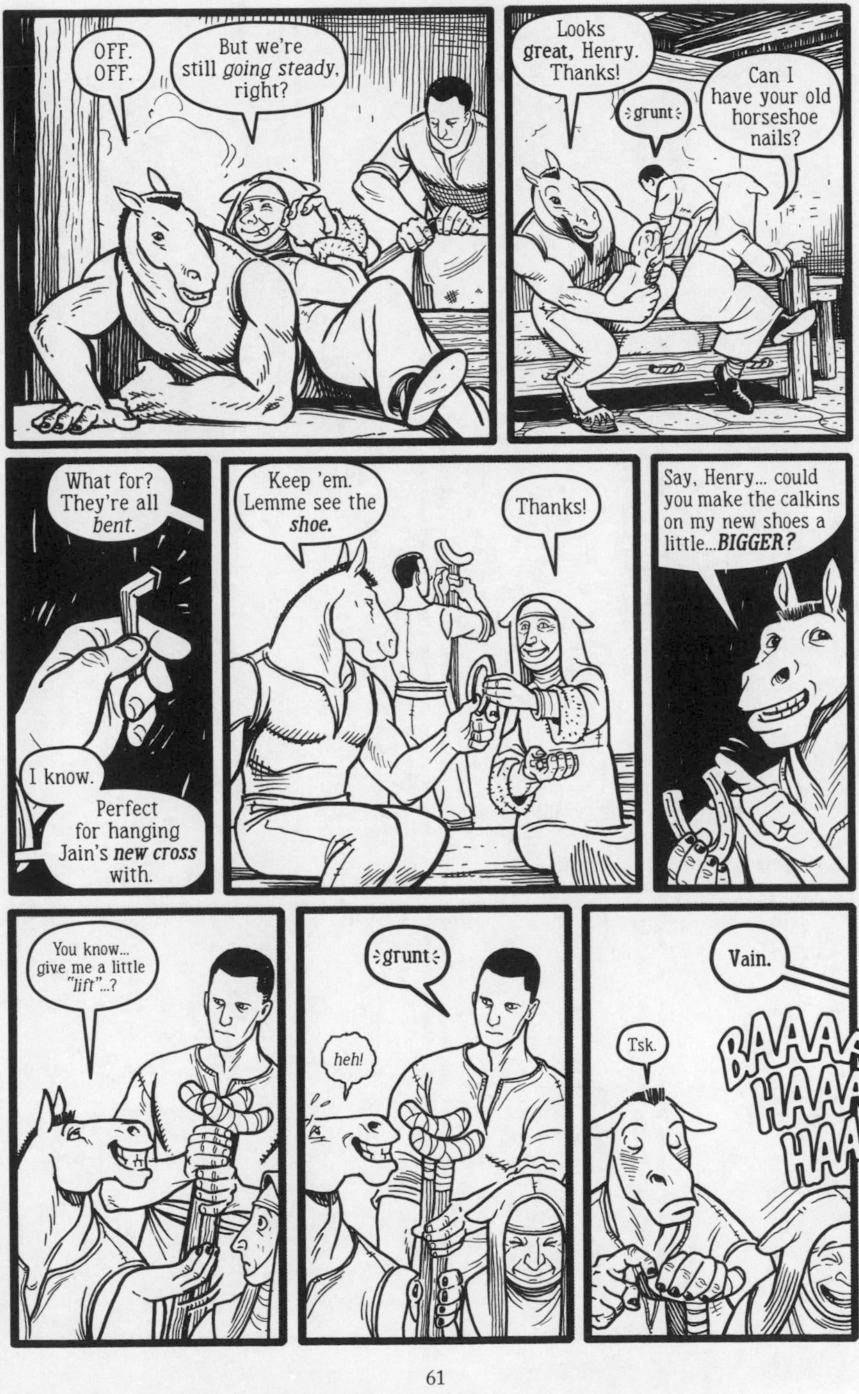
OFF. OFF.
But we're still *going steady,* right?
Looks **great,** Henry. Thanks!
grunt
Can I have your old horseshoe nails?
What for? They're all *bent.*
I know.
Perfect for hanging Jain's ***new cross*** with.
Keep 'em. Lemme see the ***shoe.***
Thanks!
Say, Henry... could you make the calkins on my new shoes a little...***BIGGER?***
You know... give me a little *"lift"*...?
grunt
heh!
Vain.
Tsk.
BAAAA HAAAA HAA

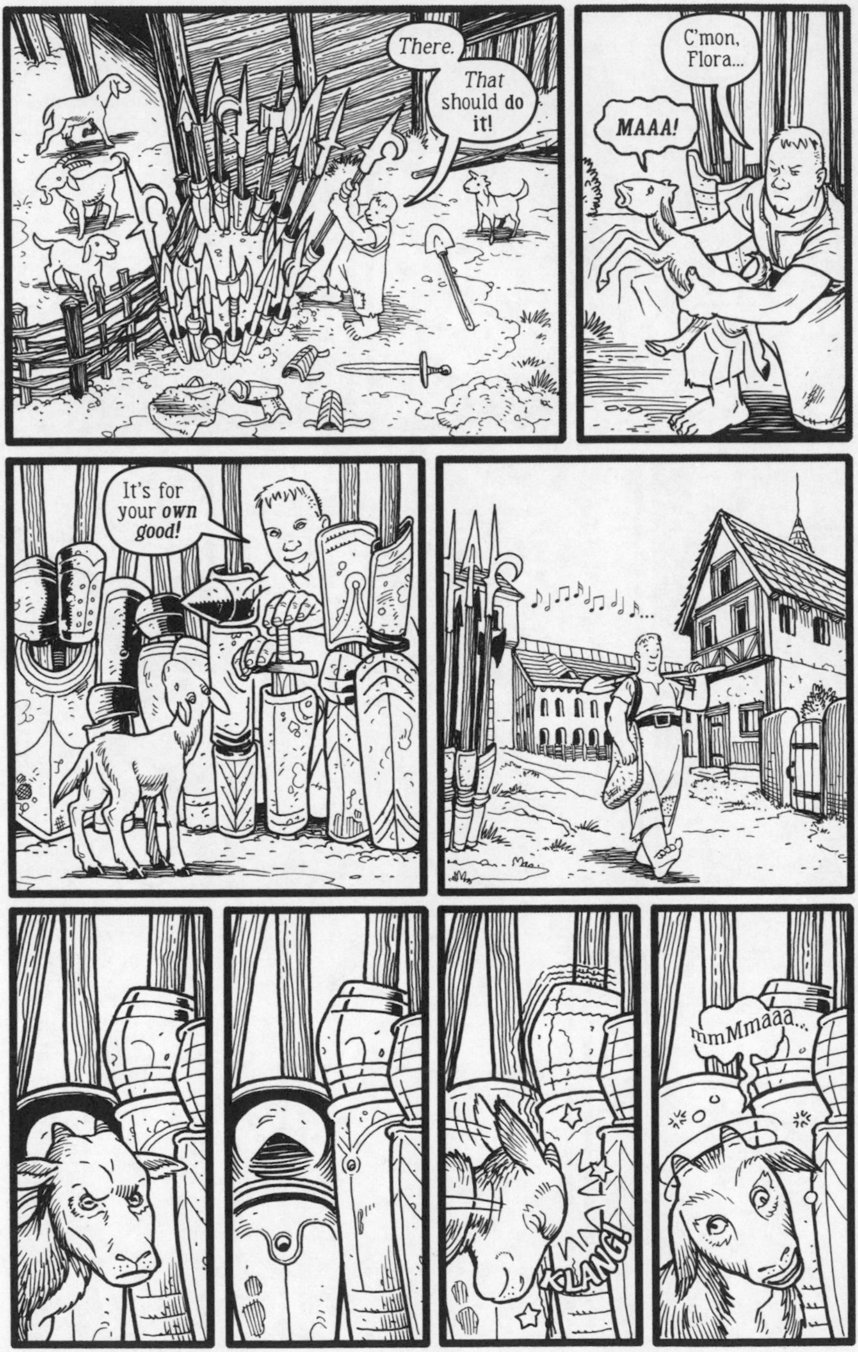
There.
That should do it!
C'mon, Flora...
MAAA!
It's for your own good!
♪♩♫♪♫♩♩♪...
KLANG!
mmMmaaa...

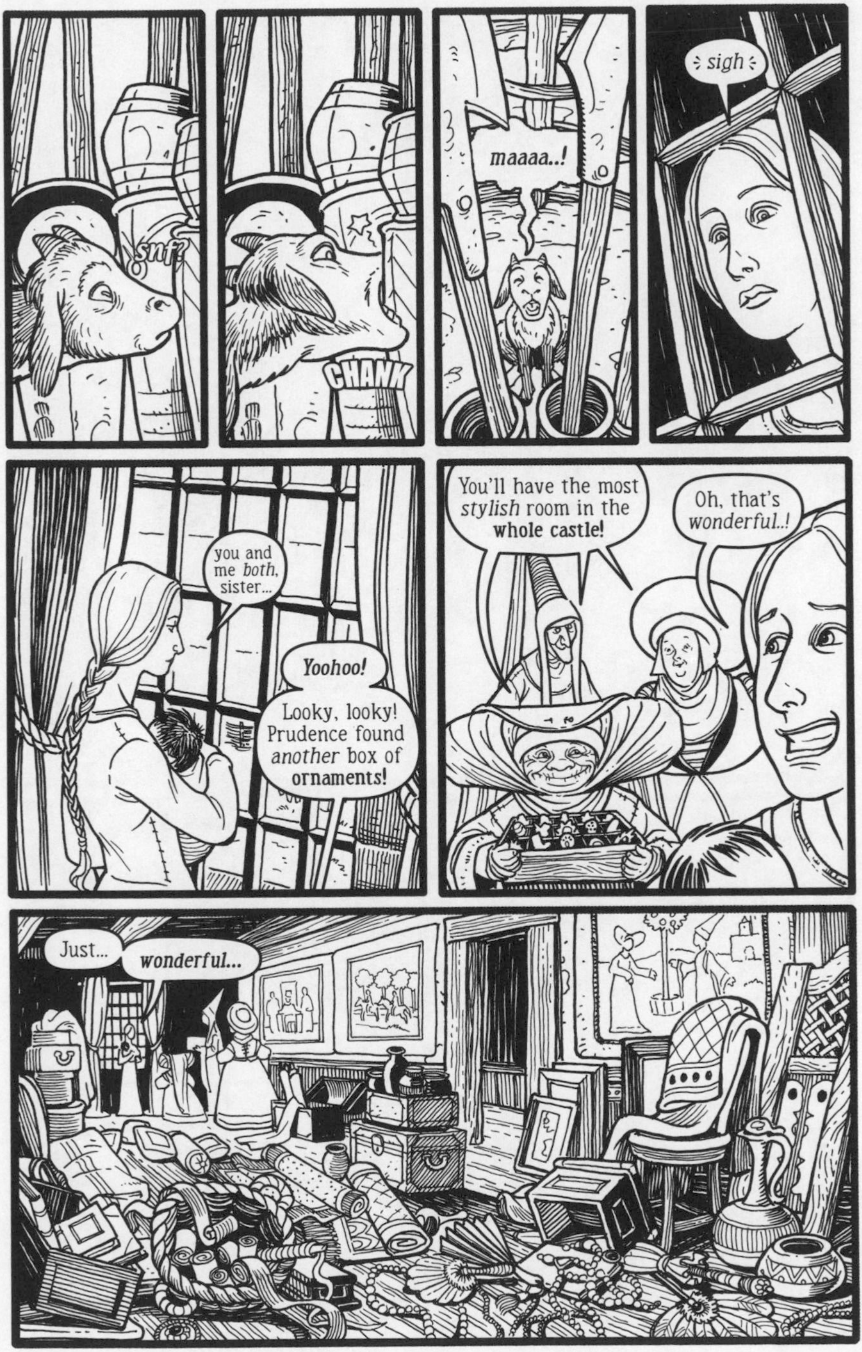
snf?
CHANK
maaaa..!
sigh
you and me *both*, sister...
Yoohoo!
Looky, looky! Prudence found *another* box of **ornaments!**
You'll have the most *stylish* room in the **whole castle!**
Oh, that's *wonderful..!*
Just...
wonderful...

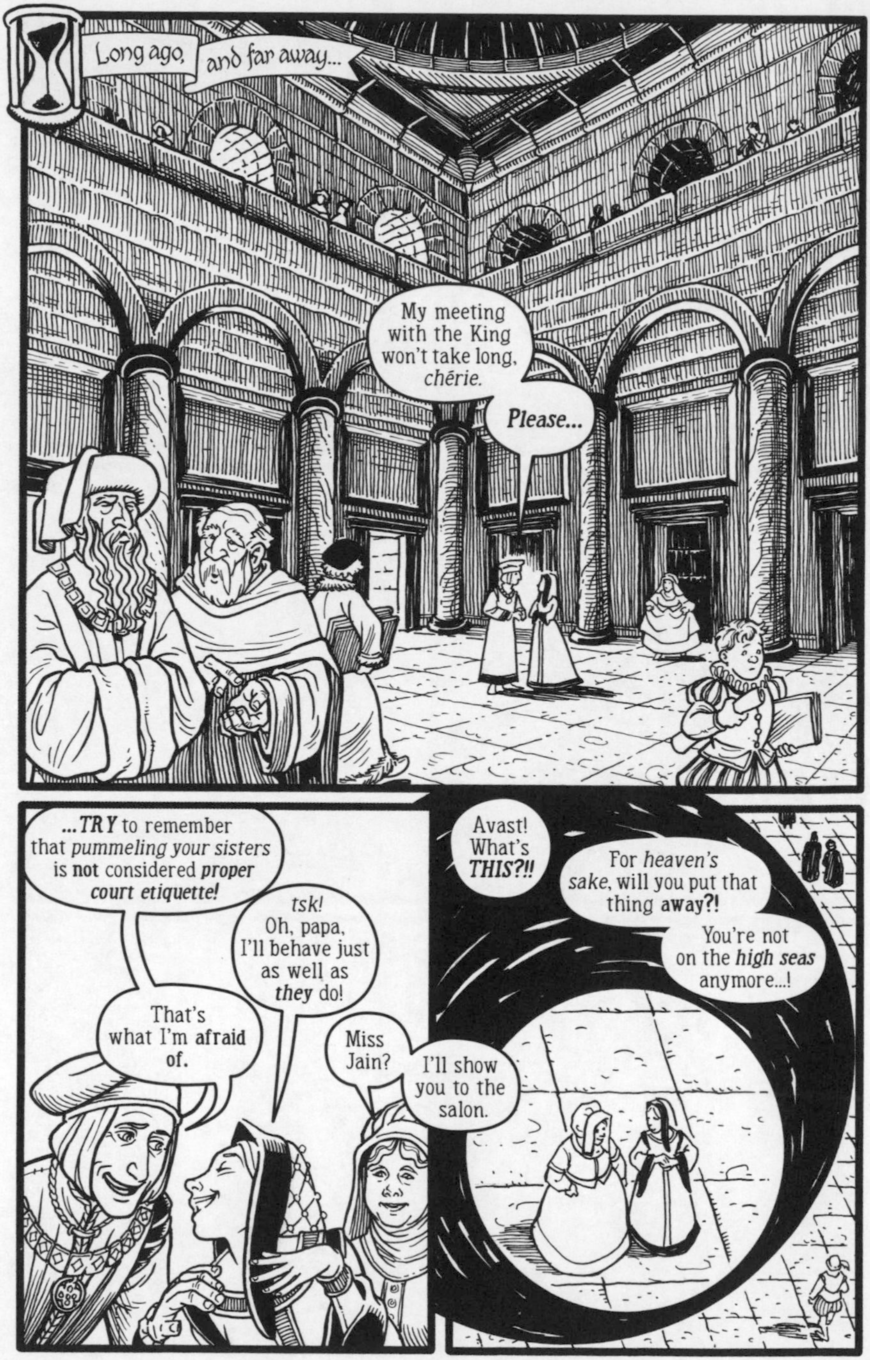
Long ago,
and far away...
My meeting with the King won't take long, *chérie.*
Please...
*...**TRY** to remember that pummeling your sisters* is **not** considered ***proper court etiquette!***
tsk! Oh, papa, I'll behave just as well as ***they*** do!
That's what I'm **afraid of.**
Miss Jain?
I'll show you to the salon.
Avast! What's ***THIS?!!***
For *heaven's sake*, will you put that thing **away?!**
You're not on the ***high seas*** anymore...!

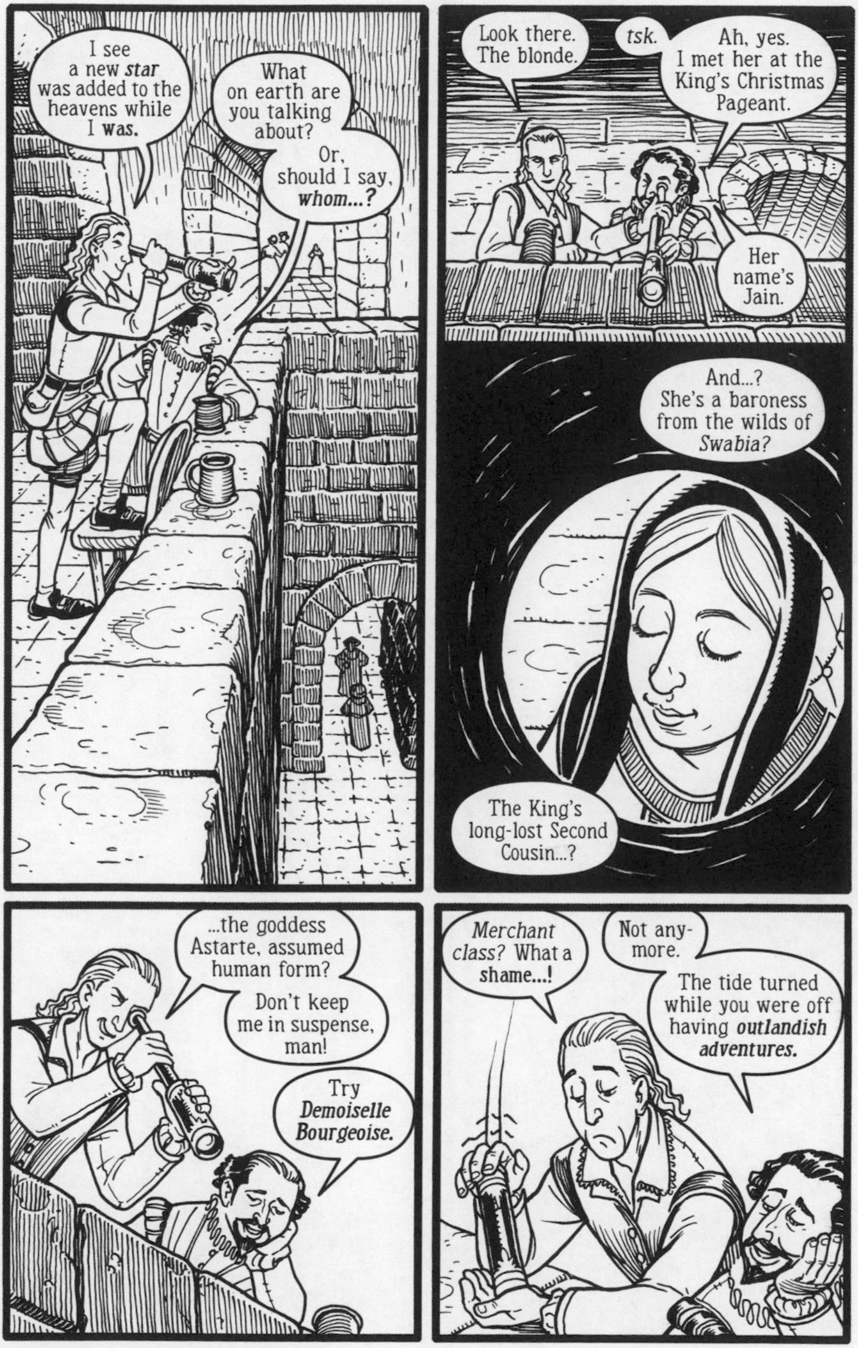
I see a new *star* was added to the heavens while I **was.**
What on earth are you talking about?
Or, should I say, ***whom...?***
Look there. The blonde.
tsk.
Ah, yes. I met her at the King's Christmas Pageant.
Her name's Jain.
And...? She's a baroness from the wilds of *Swabia?*
The King's long-lost Second Cousin...?
...the goddess Astarte, assumed human form?
Don't keep me in suspense, man!
Try ***Demoiselle Bourgeoise.***
Merchant class? What a **shame...!**
Not any-more.
The tide turned while you were off having ***outlandish adventures.***

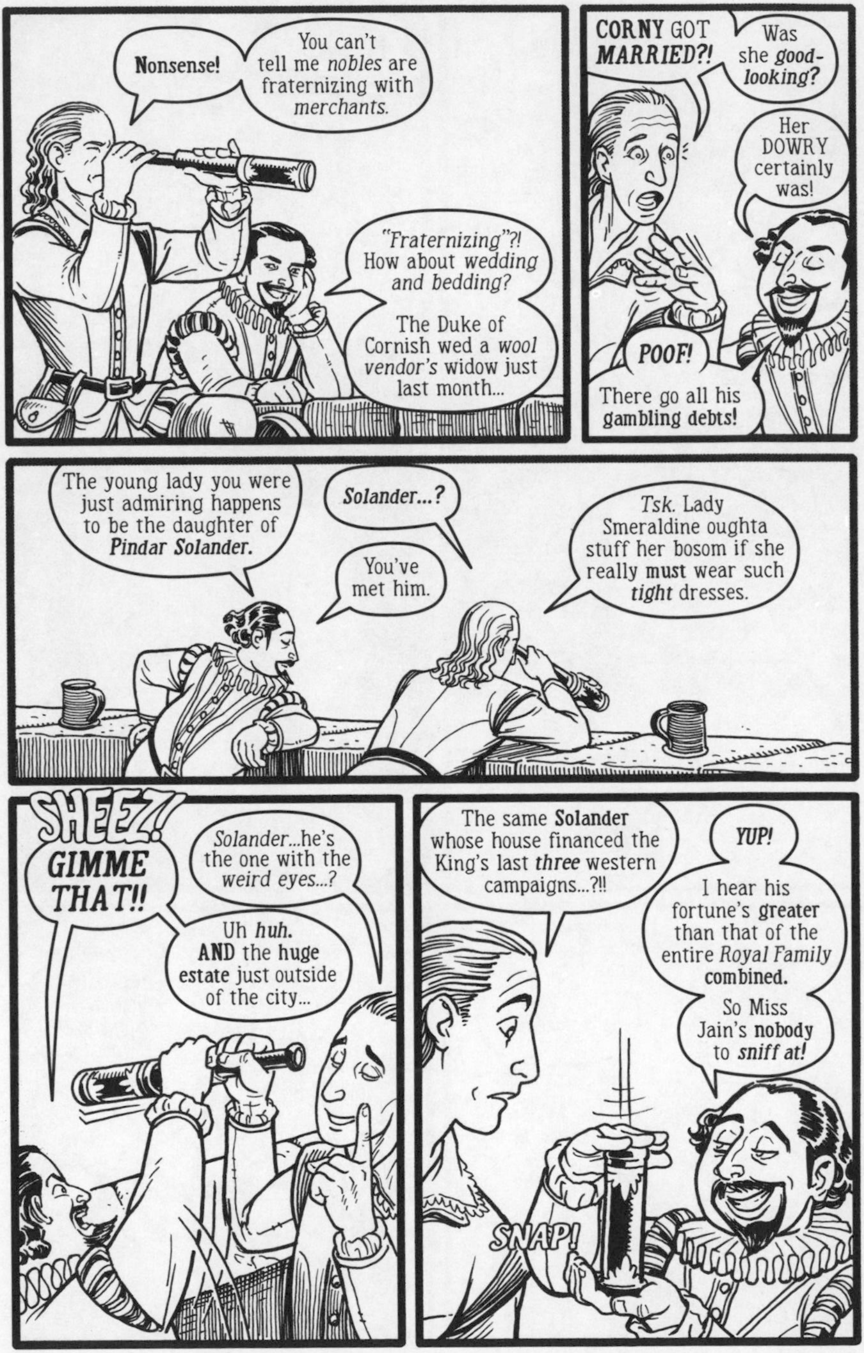
Nonsense!
You can't tell me *nobles* are fraternizing with *merchants.*
"*Fraternizing*"?! How about *wedding* and *bedding?*
The Duke of Cornish wed a *wool vendor's* widow just last month...
CORNY GOT ***MARRIED?!***
Was she ***good-looking?***
Her DOWRY certainly was!
POOF!
There go all his **gambling debts!**
The young lady you were just admiring happens to be the daughter of ***Pindar Solander.***
Solander...?
You've met him.
Tsk. Lady Smeraldine oughta stuff her bosom if she really **must** wear such ***tight*** dresses.
SHEEZ!
GIMME THAT!!
Solander...he's the one with the *weird eyes...?*
Uh ***huh.*** **AND** the **huge estate** just outside of the city...
The same **Solander** whose house financed the King's last ***three*** western campaigns...?!!
YUP!
I hear his fortune's **greater** than that of the entire *Royal Family* **combined.**
So Miss Jain's **nobody** to ***sniff at!***
SNAP!

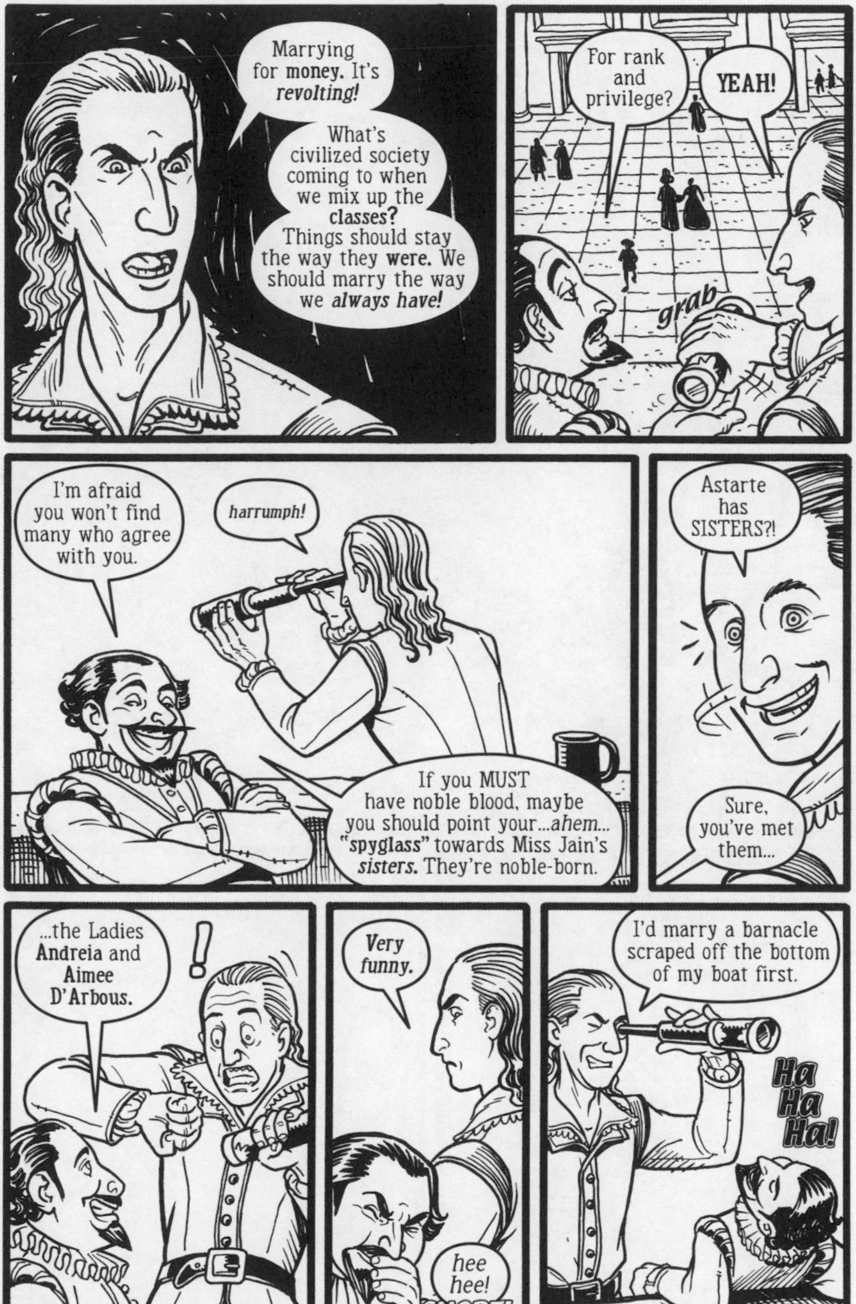
Marrying for **money.** It's ***revolting!***
What's civilized society coming to when we mix up the **classes?** Things should stay the way they **were.** We should marry the way we ***always have!***
For rank and privilege?
YEAH!
grab
I'm afraid you won't find many who agree with you.
harrumph!
If you MUST have noble blood, maybe you should point your...*ahem...* **"spyglass"** towards Miss Jain's ***sisters.*** They're noble-born.
Astarte has SISTERS?!
Sure, you've met them...
...the Ladies **Andreia** and **Aimee D'Arbous.**
!
Very ***funny.***
hee hee!
SNORT!
I'd marry a barnacle scraped off the bottom of my boat first.
Ha Ha Ha!

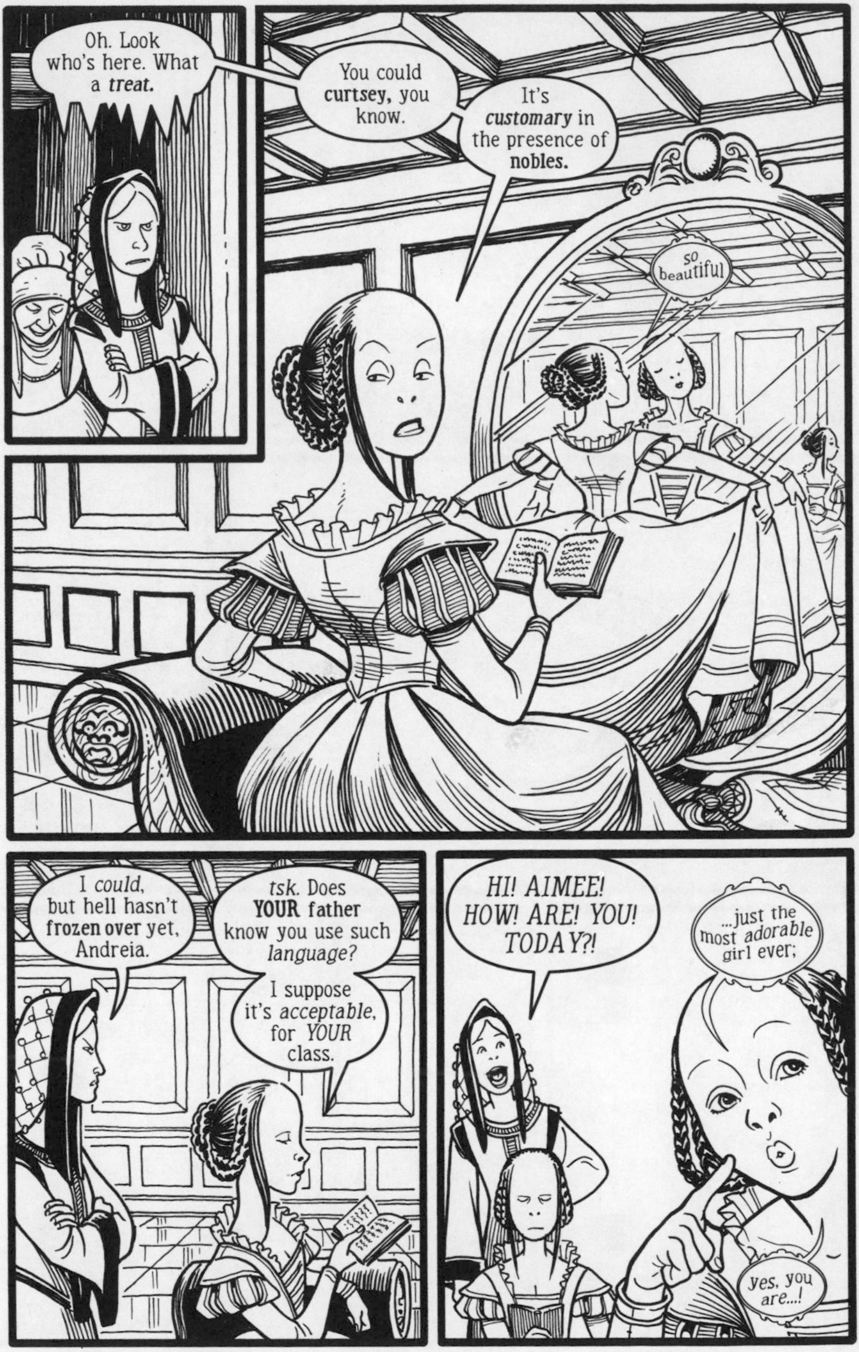
Oh. Look who's here. What a *treat.*
You could **curtsey,** you know.
It's *customary* in the presence of **nobles.**
so beautiful
I *could,* but hell hasn't **frozen over** yet, Andreia.
tsk. Does **YOUR** father know you use such *language?*
I suppose it's *acceptable,* for *YOUR* class.
HI! AIMEE! HOW! ARE! YOU! TODAY?!
...just the most *adorable* girl ever;
yes, you are...!

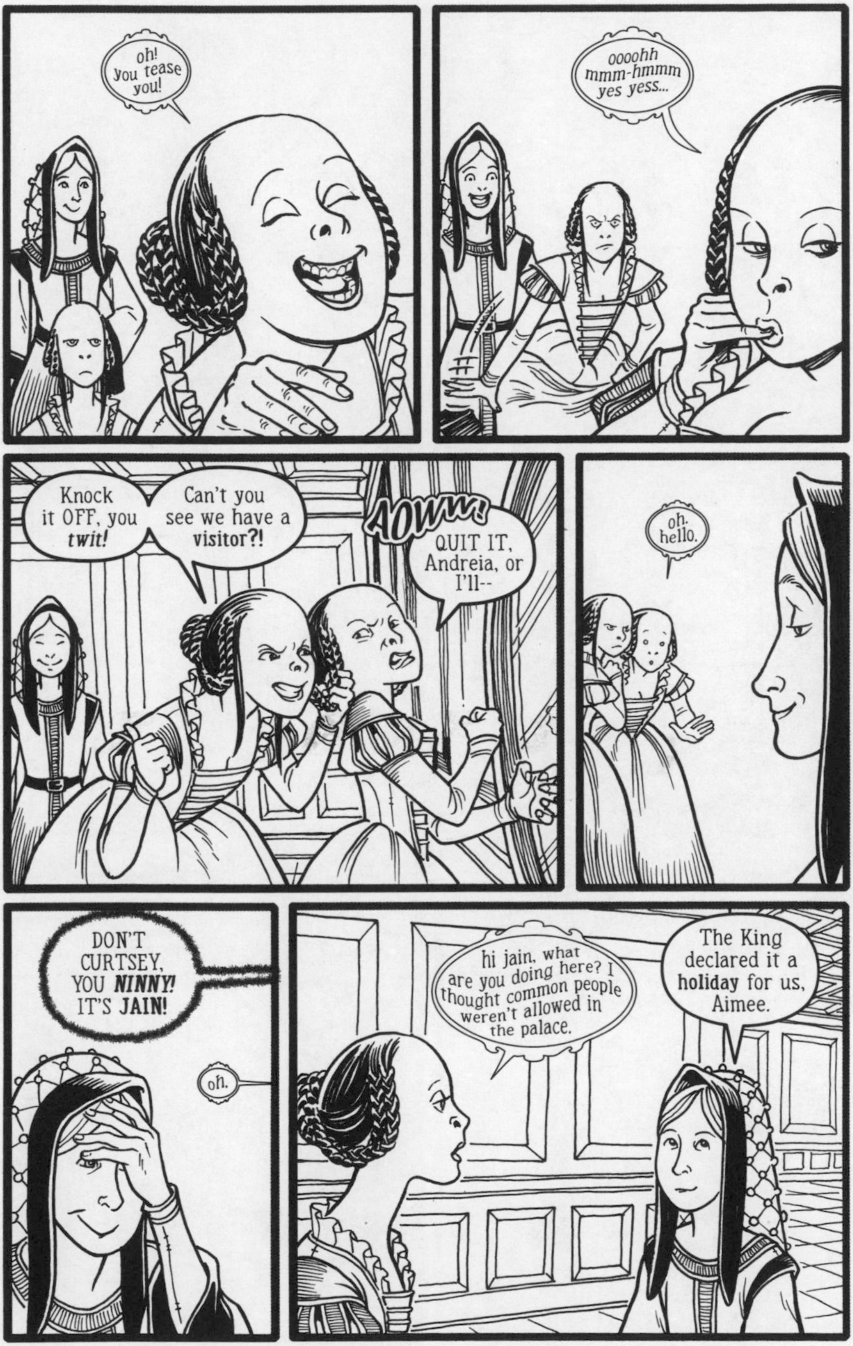
oh! you tease you!
oooohh mmm-hmmm yes yess...
Knock it OFF, you *twit!*
Can't you see we have a **visitor?!**
AOWW!
QUIT IT, Andreia, or I'll--
oh. hello.
DON'T CURTSEY, YOU ***NINNY!*** IT'S **JAIN!**
oh.
hi jain, what are you doing here? I thought common people weren't allowed in the palace.
The King declared it a **holiday** for us, Aimee.

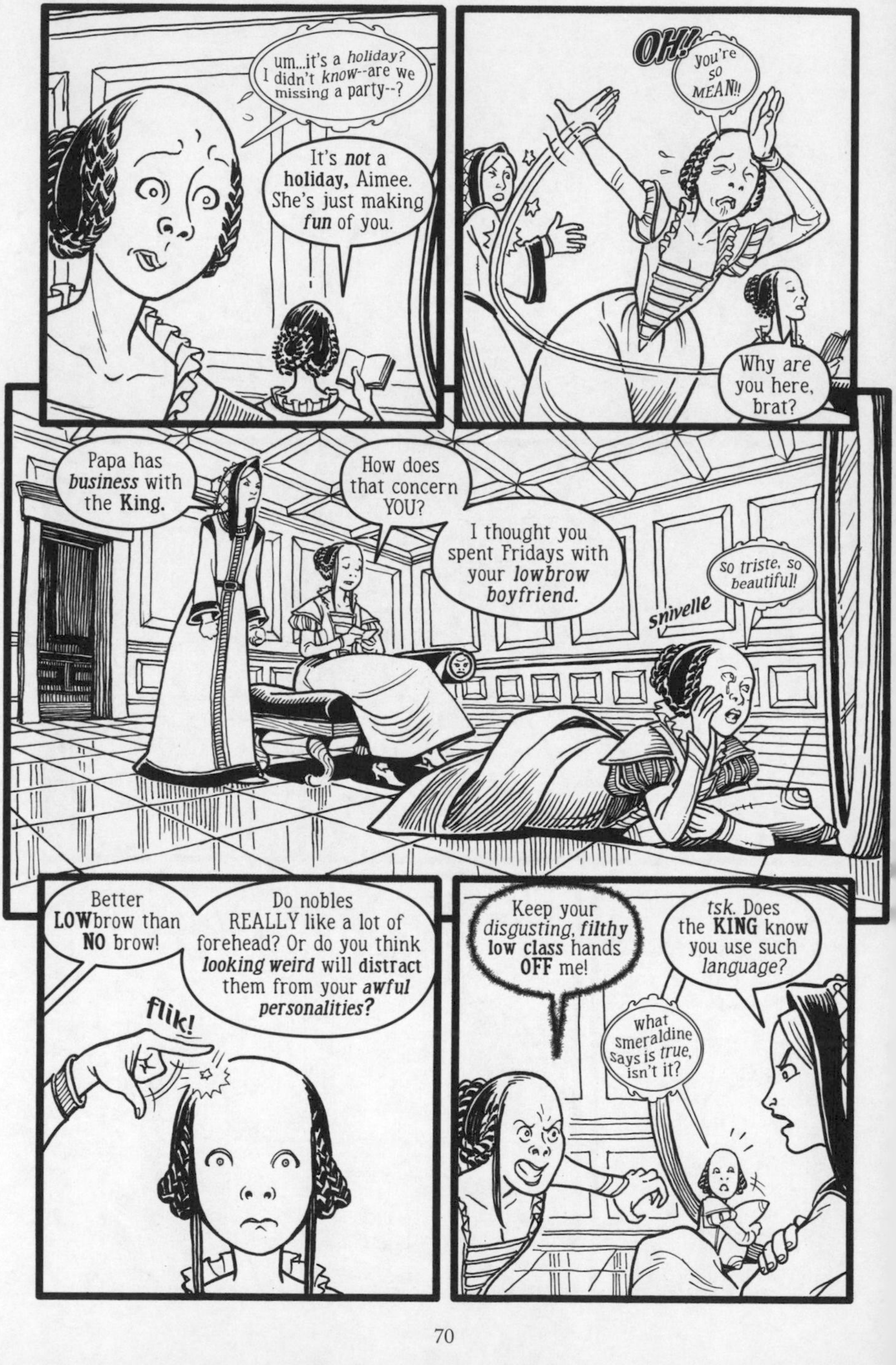
um...it's a *holiday?* I didn't *know*--are we missing a party--?
It's **not** a **holiday,** Aimee. She's just making **fun** of you.
OH!
you're so MEAN!!
Why are you here, brat?
Papa has **business** with the **King.**
How does that concern YOU?
I thought you spent Fridays with your **lowbrow boyfriend.**
snivelle
so triste, so beautiful!
Better **LOW**brow than **NO** brow!
Do nobles REALLY like a lot of forehead? Or do you think **looking weird** will **distract** them from your **awful personalities?**
flik!
Keep your *disgusting,* **filthy low class** hands **OFF** me!
tsk. Does the **KING** know you use such *language?*
what Smeraldine says is *true,* isn't it?

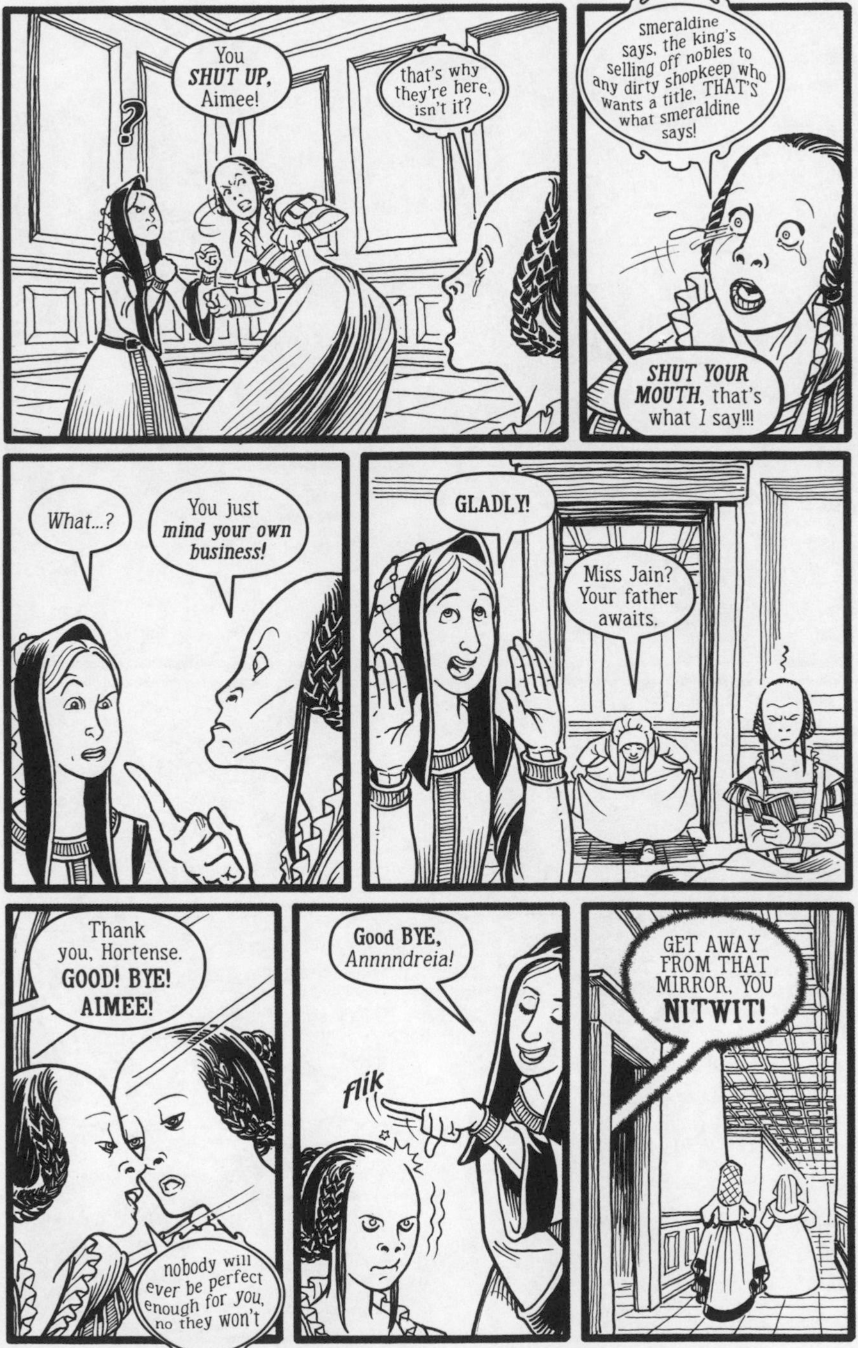
You SHUT UP, Aimee!
?
that's why they're here, isn't it?
smeraldine says, the king's selling off nobles to any dirty shopkeep who wants a title, THAT'S what smeraldine says!
SHUT YOUR MOUTH, that's what I say!!!
What...?
You just mind your own business!
GLADLY!
Miss Jain? Your father awaits.
Thank you, Hortense. GOOD! BYE! AIMEE!
nobody will ever be perfect enough for you, no they won't
Good BYE, Annnndreia!
flik
GET AWAY FROM THAT MIRROR, YOU NITWIT!

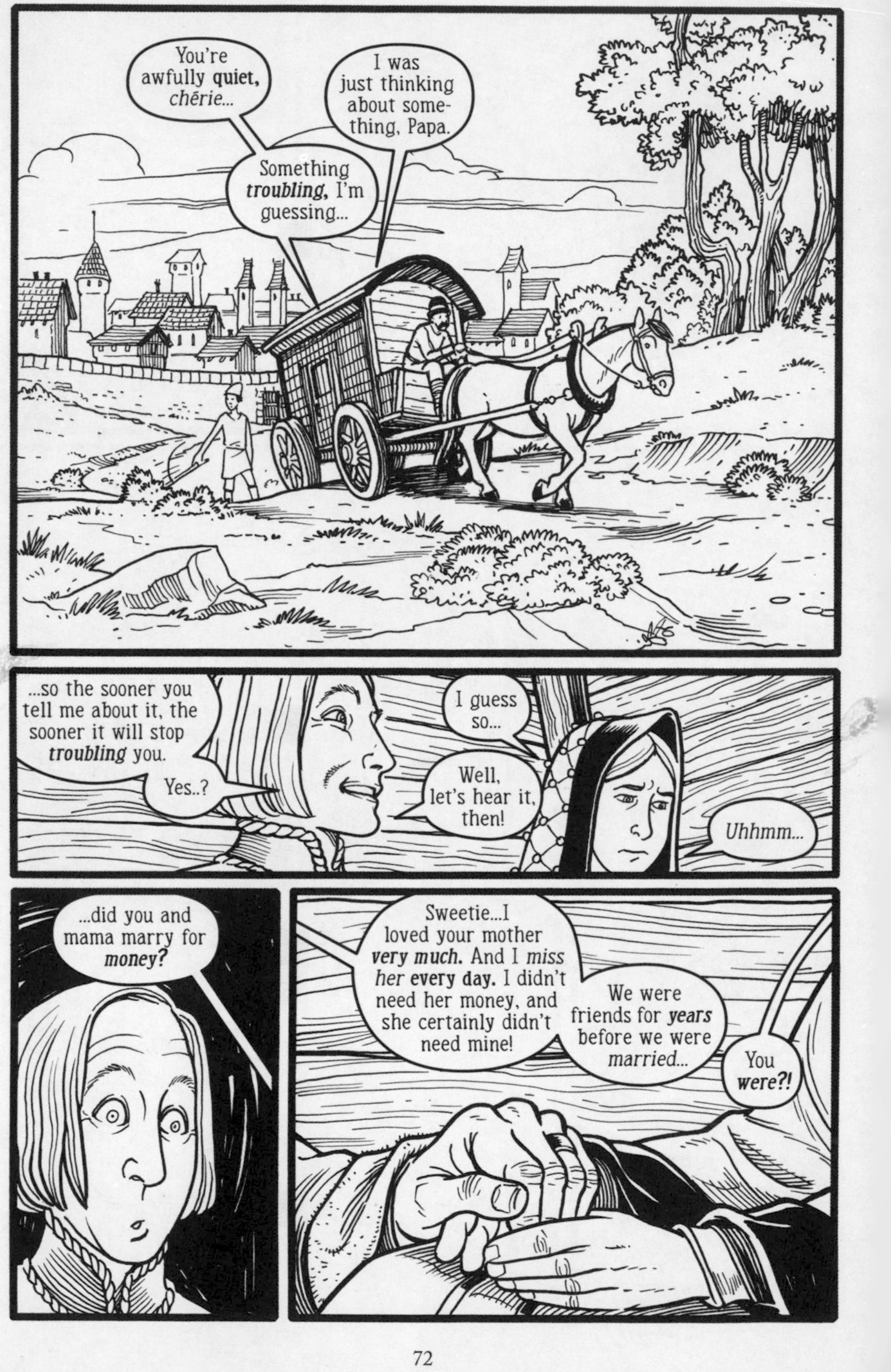
You're awfully **quiet,** *chérie...*
I was just thinking about some-thing, Papa.
Something ***troubling,*** I'm guessing...
...so the sooner you tell me about it, the sooner it will stop ***troubling*** you.
Yes..?
I guess so...
Well, let's hear it, then!
Uhhmm...
...did you and mama marry for ***money?***
Sweetie...I loved your mother ***very much.*** And I *miss her* **every day.** I didn't need her money, and she certainly didn't need mine!
We were friends for ***years*** before we were *married...*
You ***were?!***

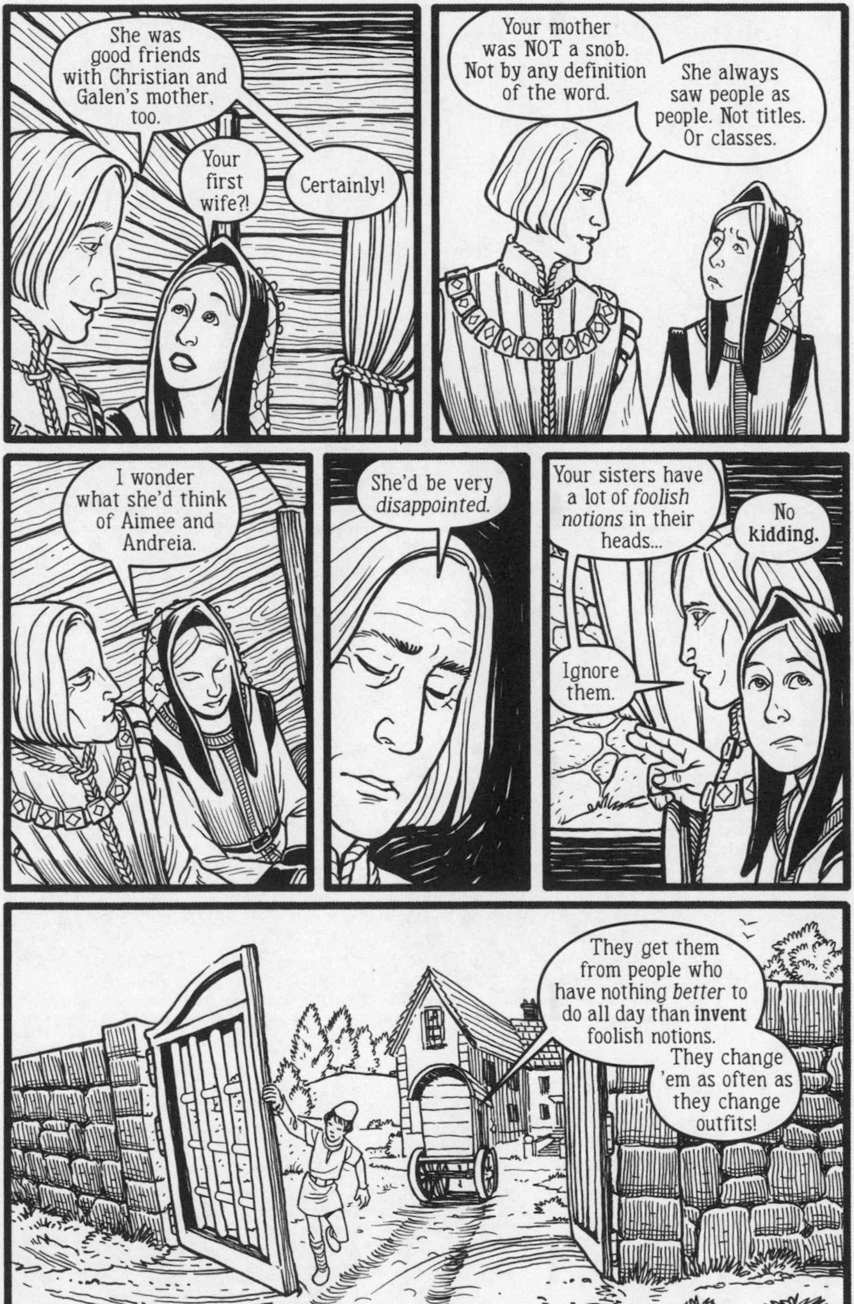
She was good friends with Christian and Galen's mother, too.
Your first wife?!
Certainly!
Your mother was NOT a snob. Not by any definition of the word.
She always saw people as people. Not titles. Or classes.
I wonder what she'd think of Aimee and Andreia.
She'd be very *disappointed.*
Your sisters have a lot of *foolish notions* in their heads...
No **kidding.**
Ignore them.
They get them from people who have nothing *better* to do all day than **invent** foolish notions.
They change 'em as often as they change outfits!

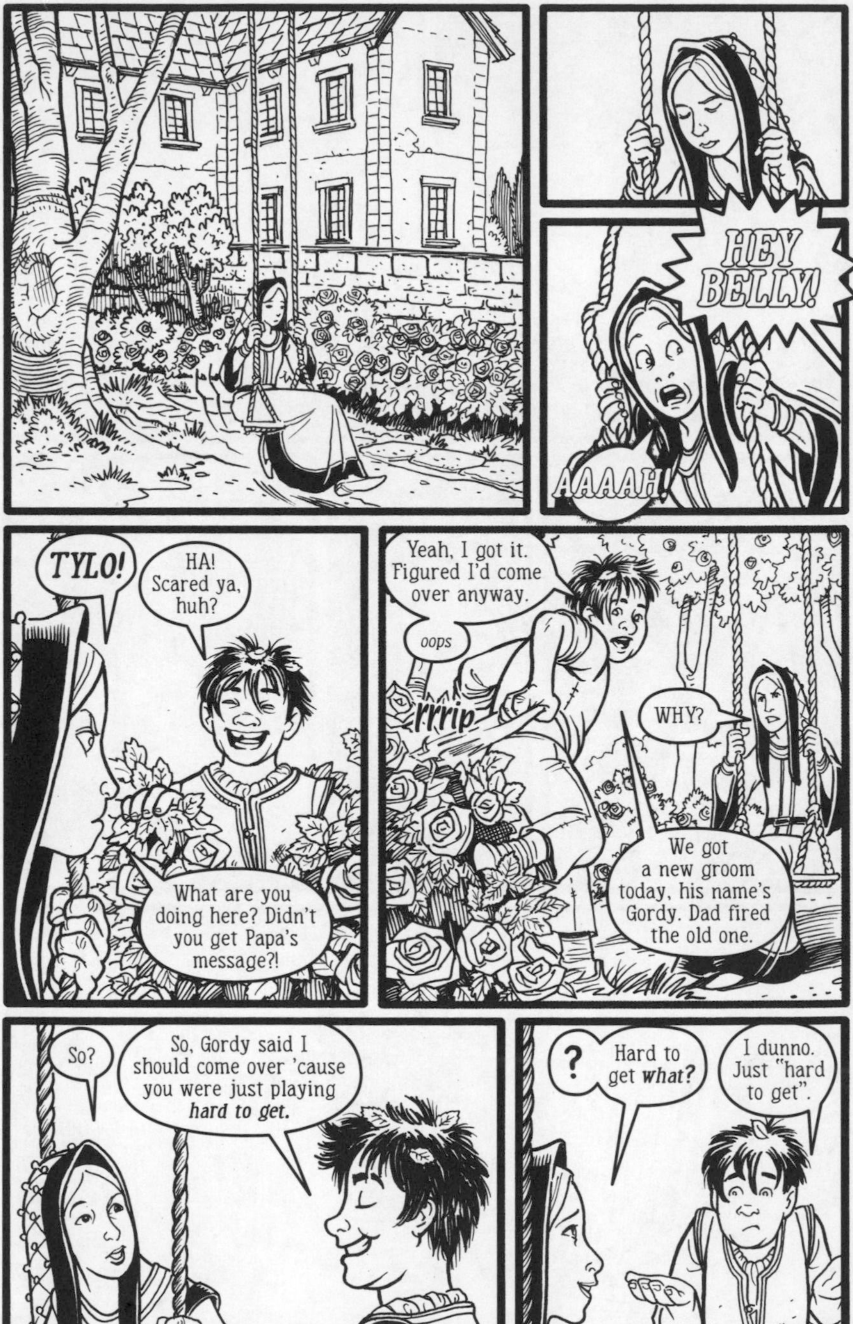
HEY BELLY!
AAAAH!
TYLO!
HA! Scared ya, huh?
What are you doing here? Didn't you get Papa's message?!
Yeah, I got it. Figured I'd come over anyway.
oops
rrrip
WHY?
We got a new groom today, his name's Gordy. Dad fired the old one.
So?
So, Gordy said I should come over 'cause you were just playing *hard to get.*
?
Hard to get *what?*
I dunno. Just "hard to get".

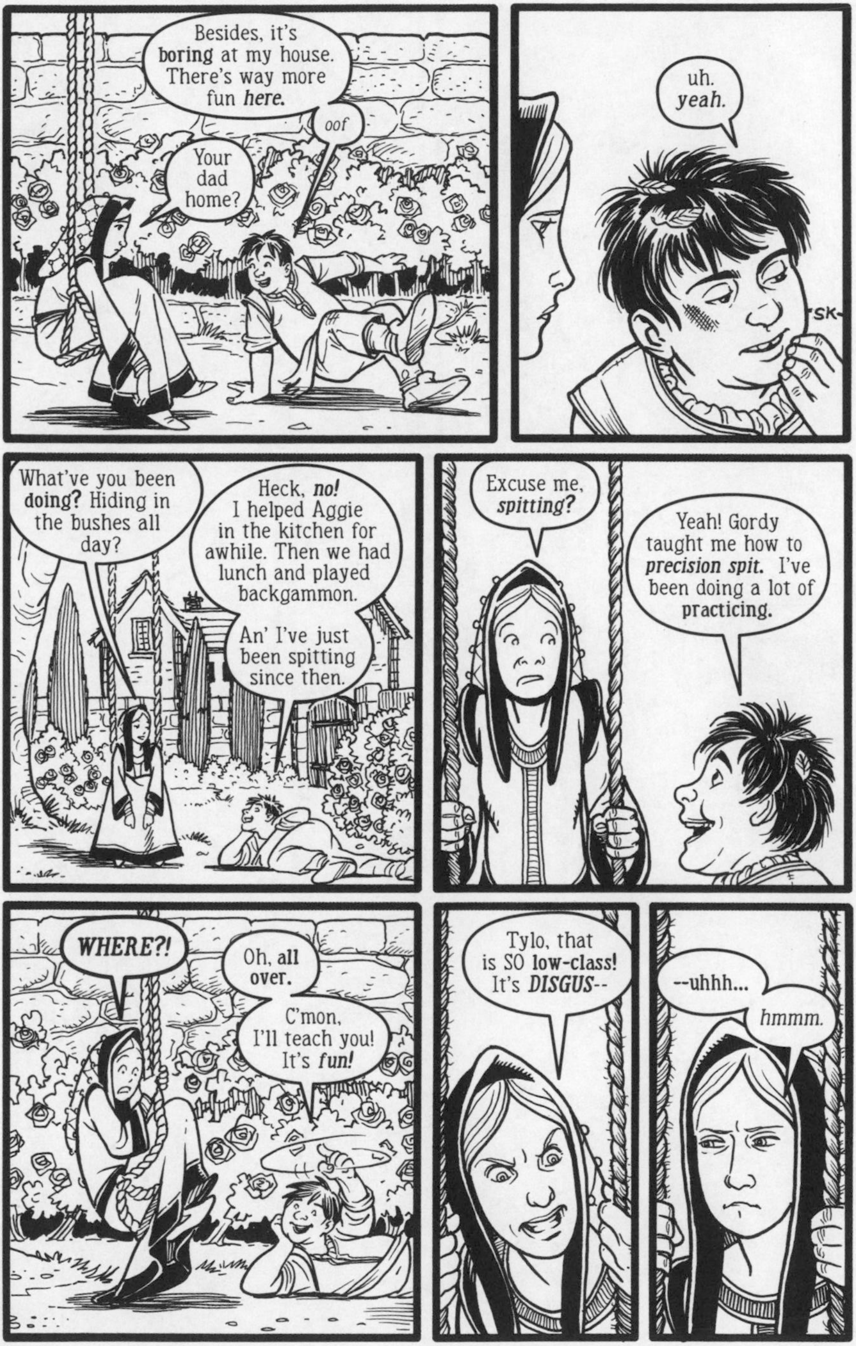
Besides, it's boring at my house. There's way more fun here.
oof
Your dad home?
uh. yeah.
SK-
What've you been doing? Hiding in the bushes all day?
Heck, no! I helped Aggie in the kitchen for awhile. Then we had lunch and played backgammon.
An' I've just been spitting since then.
Excuse me, spitting?
Yeah! Gordy taught me how to precision spit. I've been doing a lot of practicing.
WHERE?!
Oh, all over.
C'mon, I'll teach you! It's fun!
Tylo, that is SO low-class! It's DISGUS--
--uhhh...
hmmm.

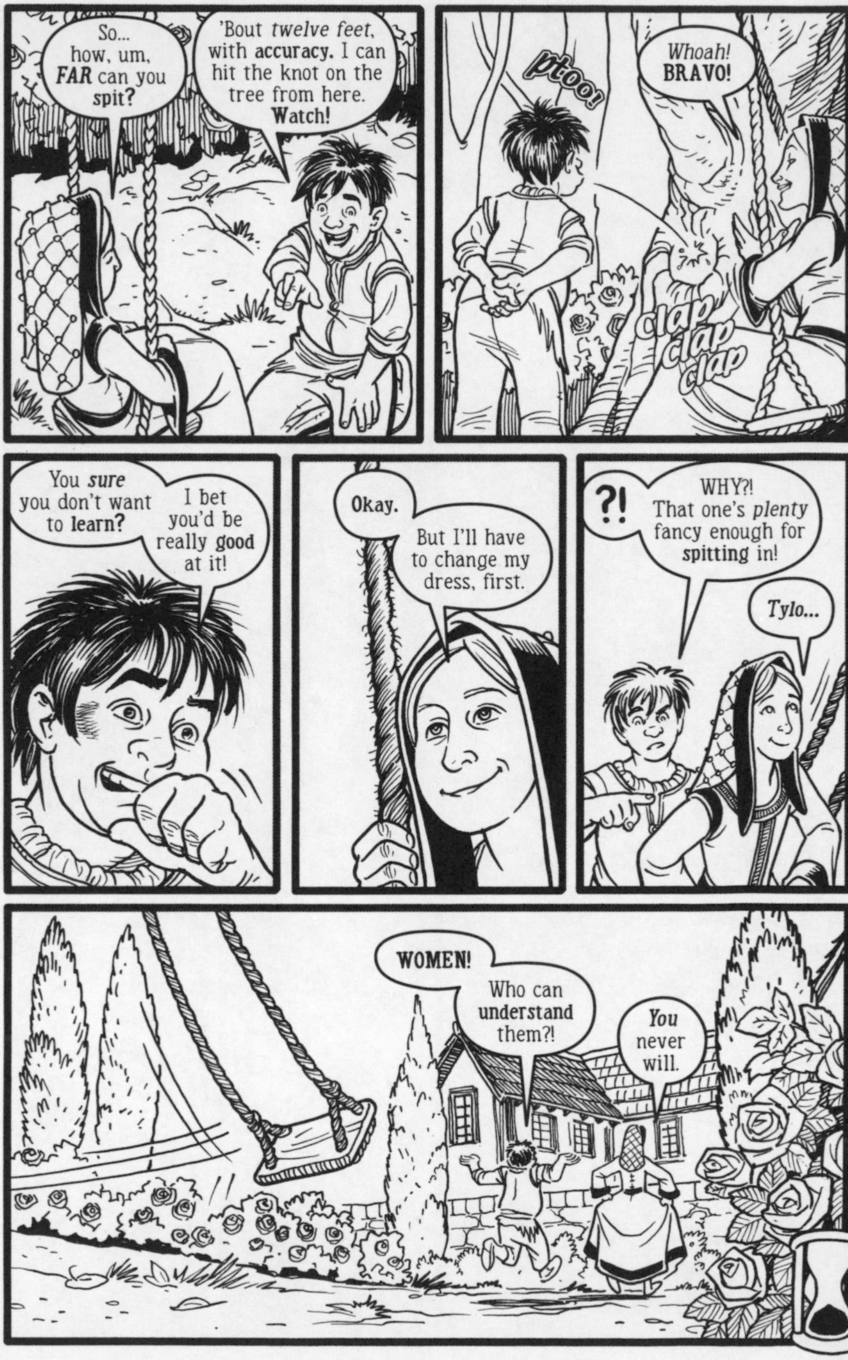

So... how, um, FAR can you spit?
'Bout twelve feet, with accuracy. I can hit the knot on the tree from here. Watch!
ptoo!
Whoah! BRAVO!
clap clap clap
You sure you don't want to learn?
I bet you'd be really good at it!
Okay.
But I'll have to change my dress, first.
?!
WHY?! That one's plenty fancy enough for spitting in!
Tylo...
WOMEN!
Who can understand them?!
You never will.

Chapter 4.

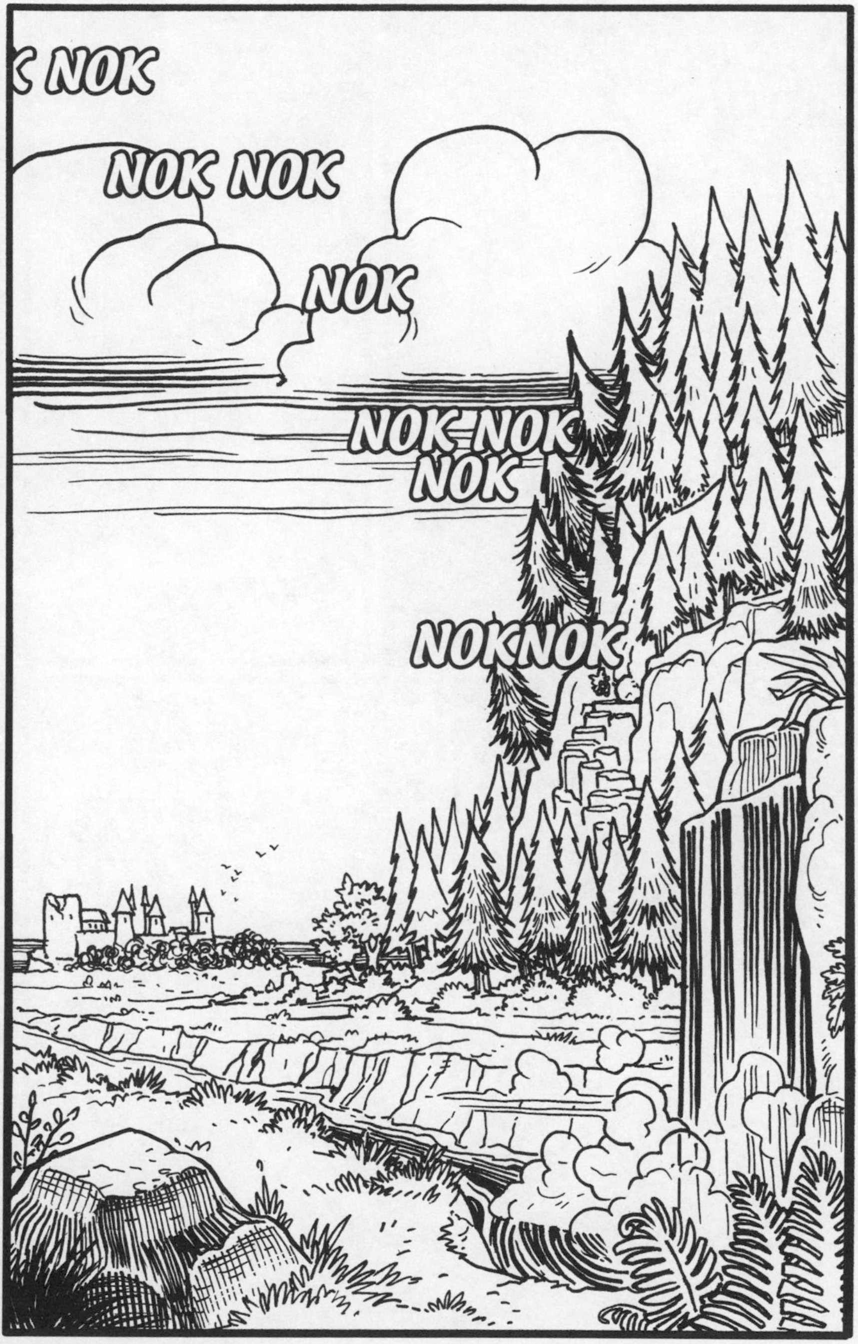
K NOK
NOK NOK
NOK
NOK NOK
NOK
NOKNOK

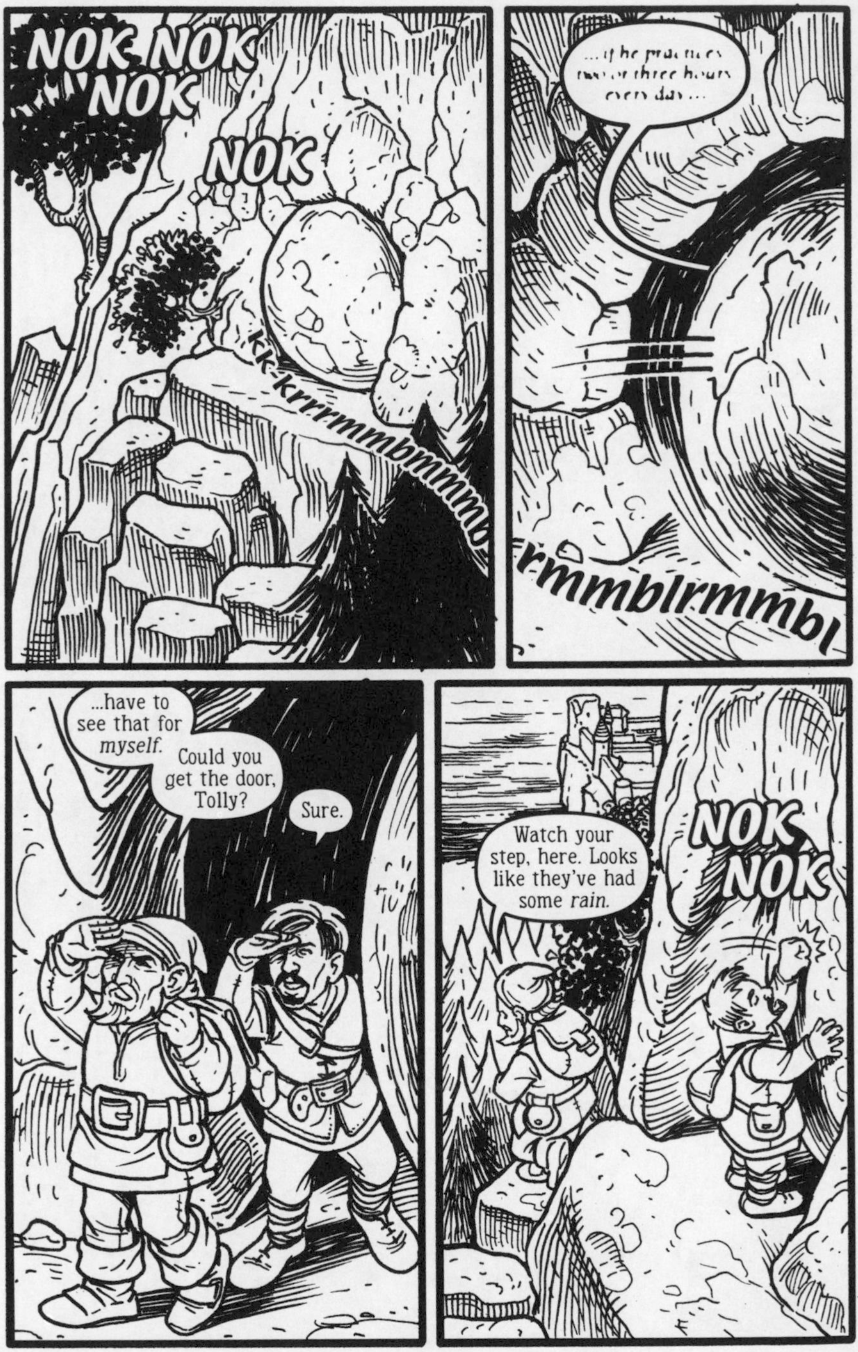
NOK NOK NOK
NOK
kk-krrrrmmbmmmmbl
...if he practices two or three hours every day...
rmmblrmmmbl
...have to see that for *myself.*
Could you get the door, Tolly?
Sure.
Watch your step, here. Looks like they've had some *rain.*
NOK NOK

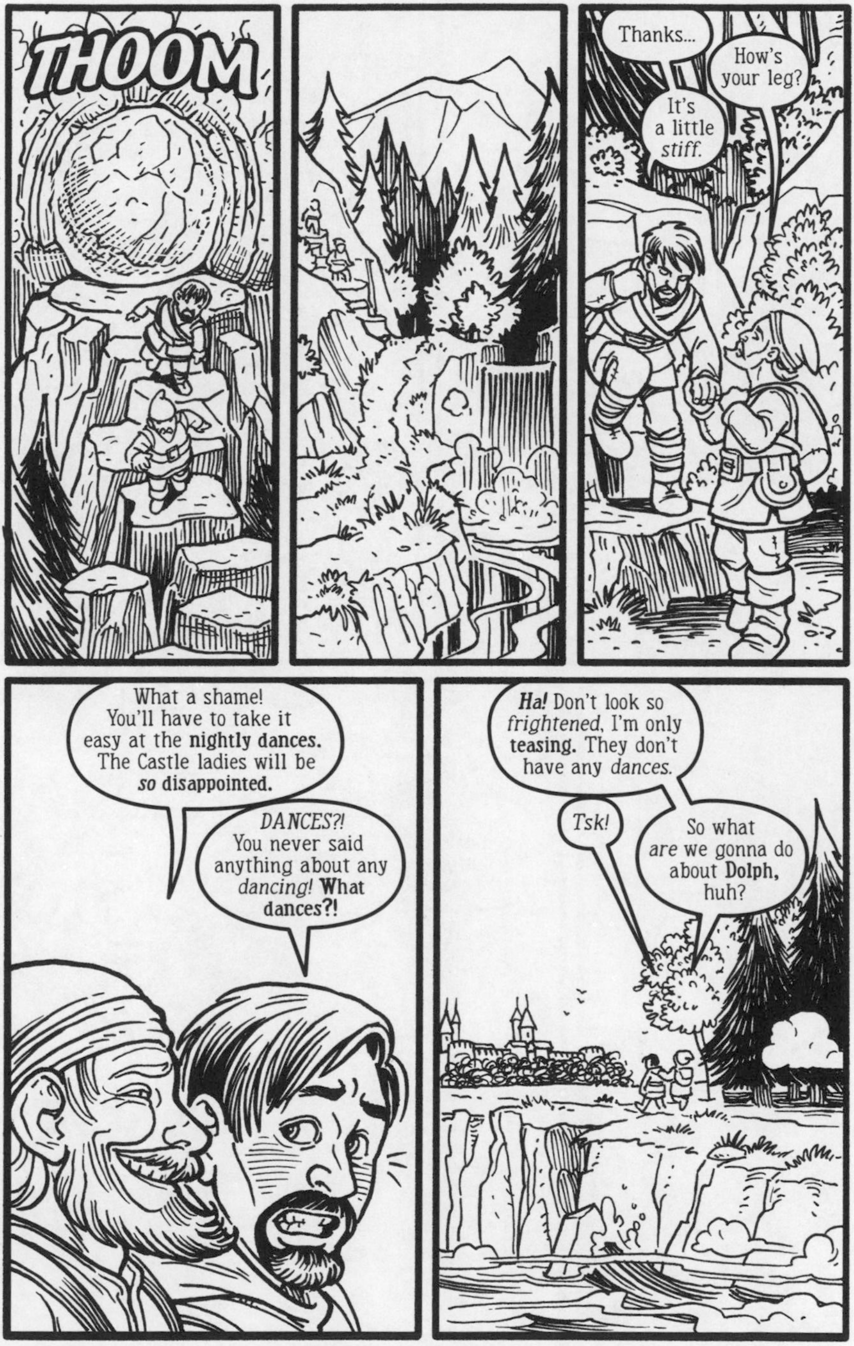
THOOM
Thanks...
How's your leg?
It's a little *stiff.*
What a shame! You'll have to take it easy at the **nightly dances.** The Castle ladies will be *so* **disappointed.**
DANCES?! You never said anything about any *dancing!* **What dances?!**
Ha! Don't look so *frightened,* I'm only **teasing.** They don't have any *dances.*
Tsk!
So what *are* we gonna do about **Dolph,** huh?

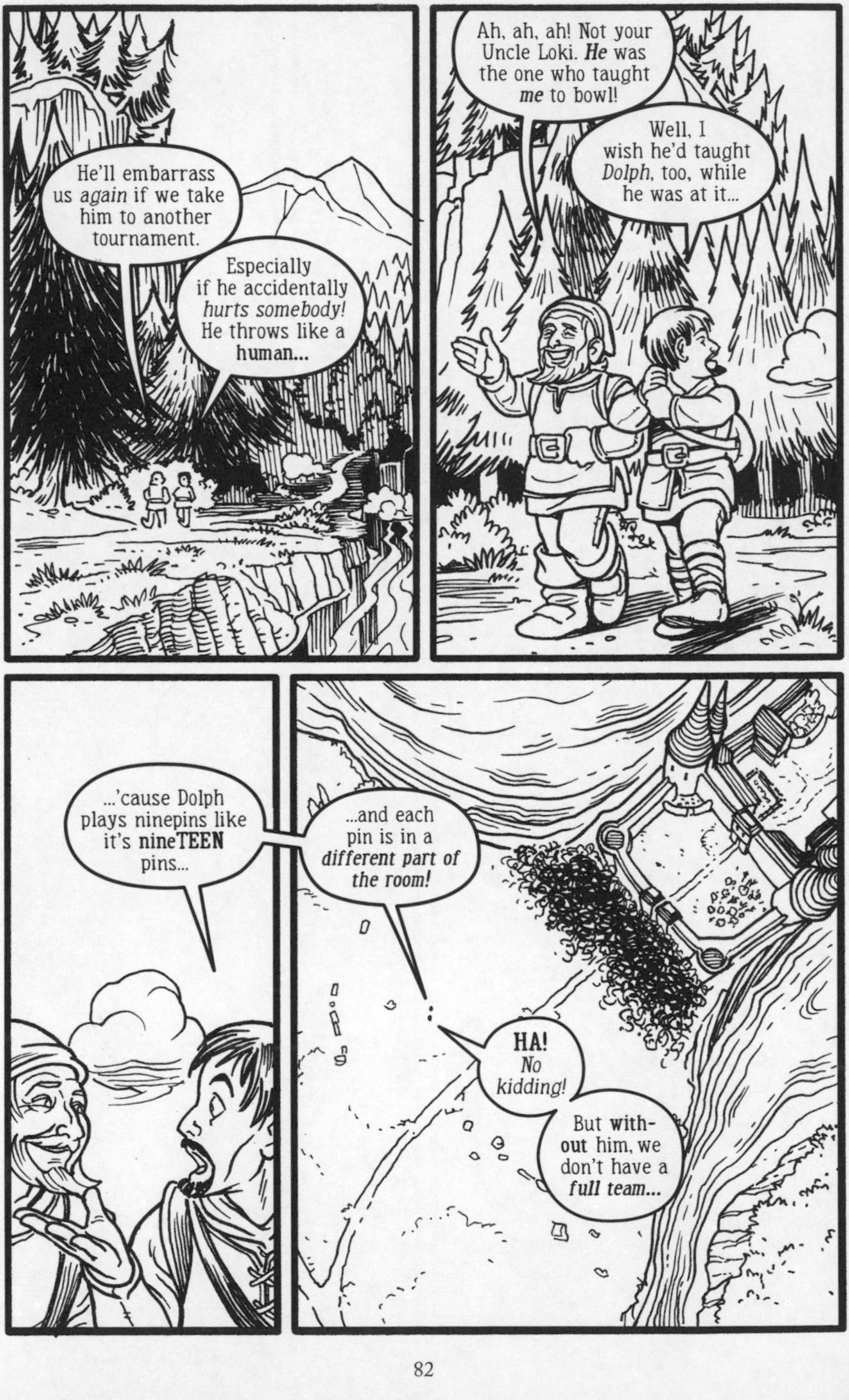
He'll embarrass us *again* if we take him to another tournament.
Especially if he accidentally *hurts somebody!* He throws like a **human...**
Ah, ah, ah! Not your Uncle Loki. ***He*** was the one who taught ***me*** to bowl!
Well, I wish he'd taught *Dolph*, too, while he was at it...
...'cause Dolph plays ninepins like it's **nineTEEN** pins...
...and each pin is in a ***different part of the room!***
HA! *No kidding!*
But **with-out** him, we don't have a ***full team...***

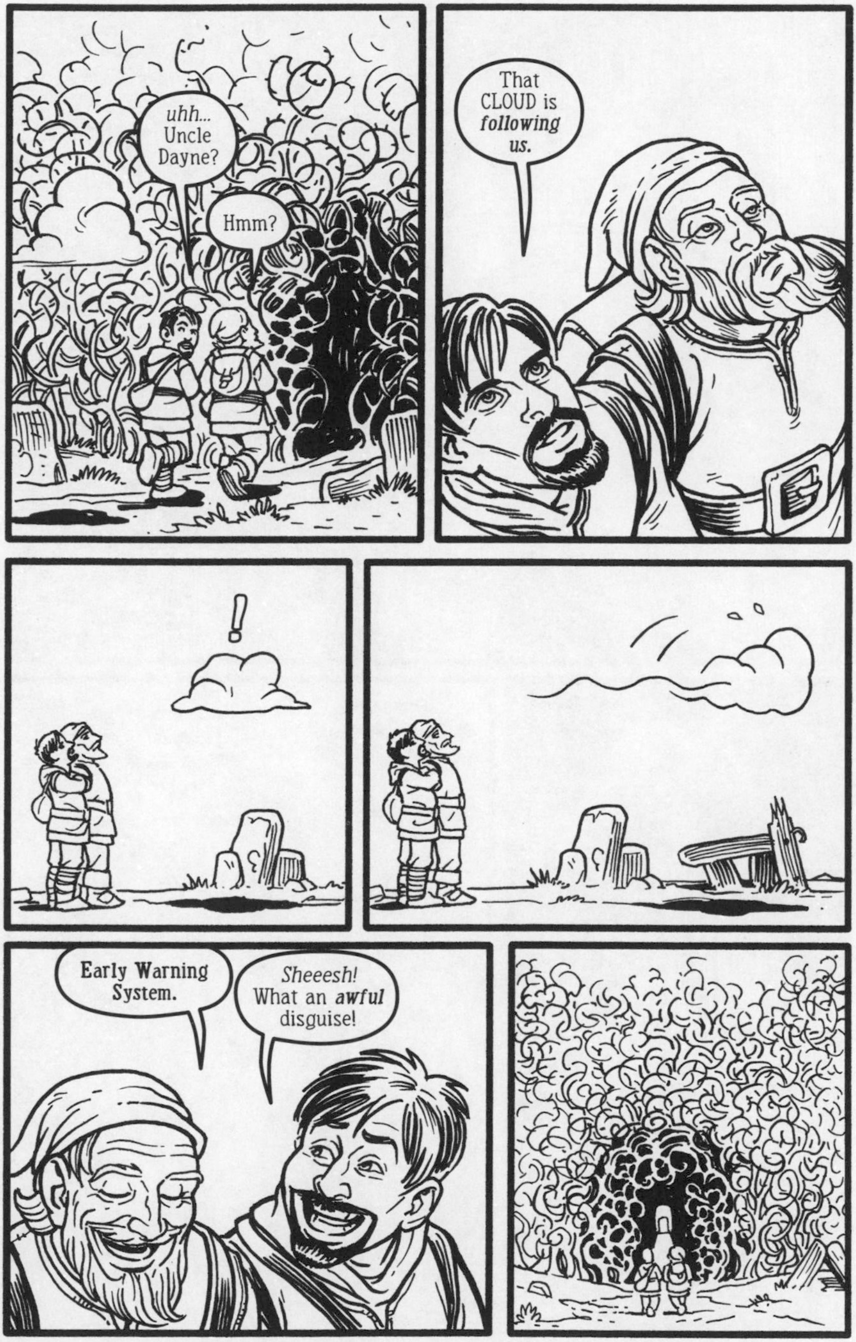
uhh... Uncle Dayne?
Hmm?
That CLOUD is *following* *us.*
!
Early Warning System.
Sheeesh! What an *awful* disguise!

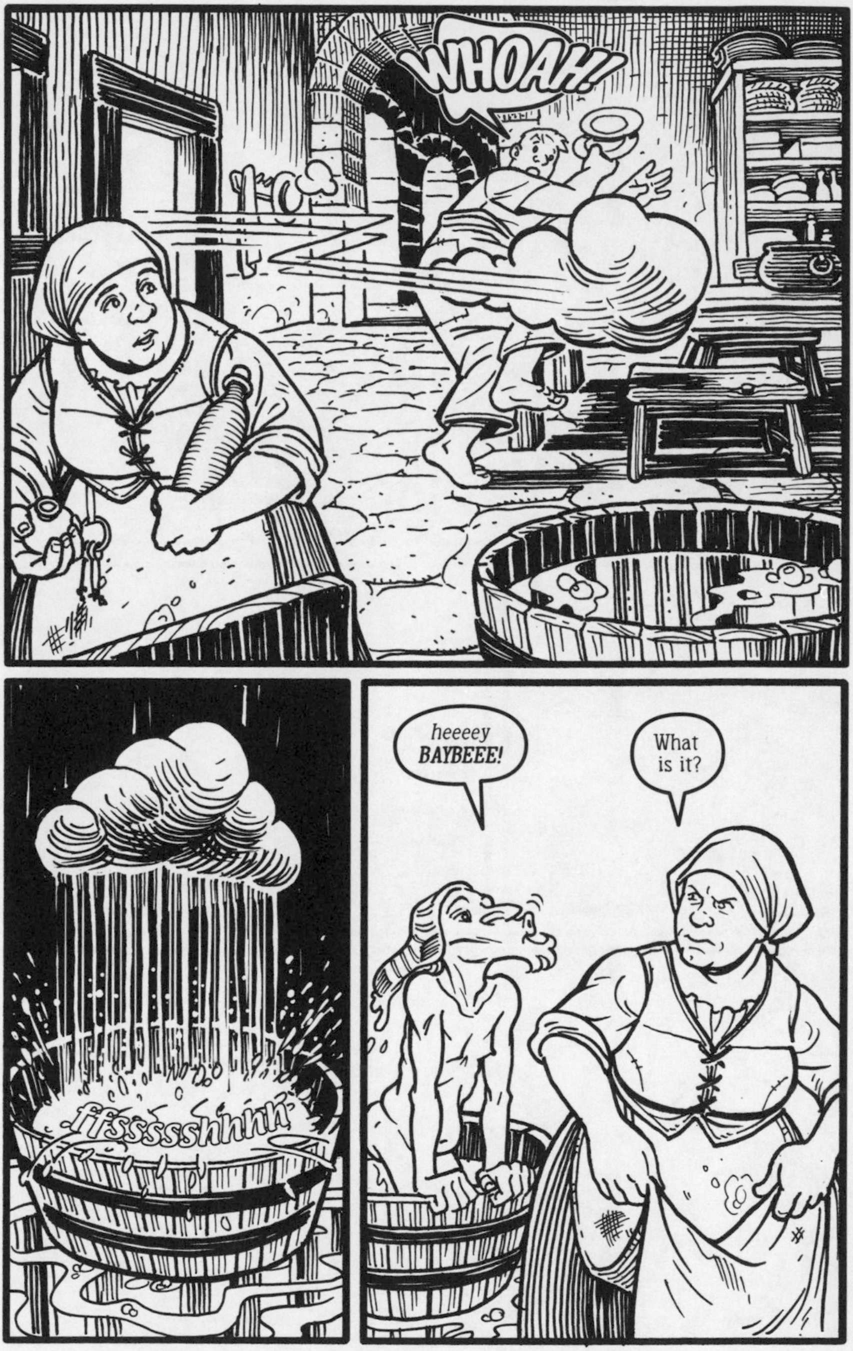
WHOAH!
ffsssssshhhh
heeeey BAYBEEE!
What is it?

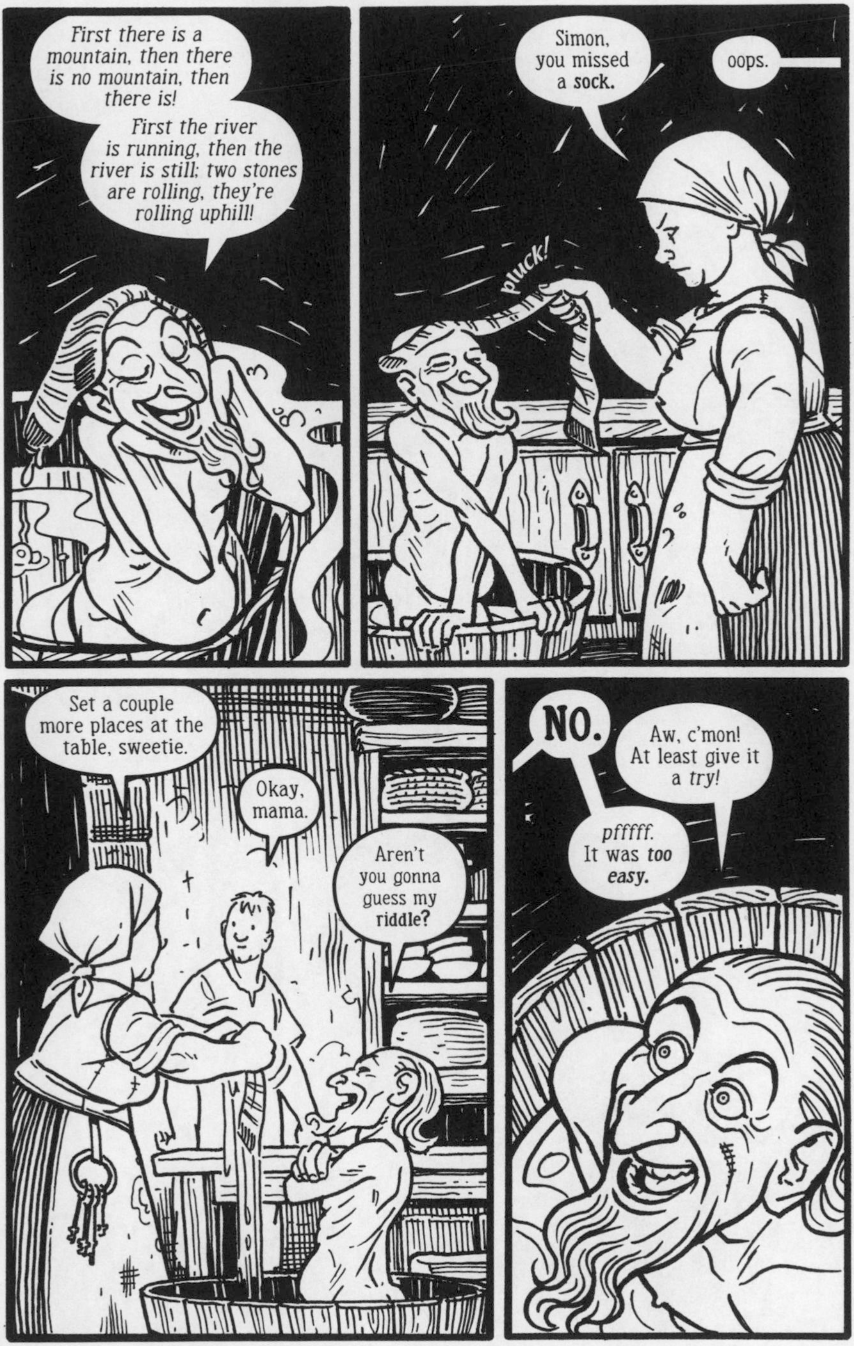
First there is a mountain, then there is no mountain, then there is!
First the river is running, then the river is still; two stones are rolling, they're rolling uphill!
Simon, you missed a sock.
oops.
pluck!
Set a couple more places at the table, sweetie.
Okay, mama.
Aren't you gonna guess my riddle?
NO.
Aw, c'mon! At least give it a try!
pffffff. It was too easy.

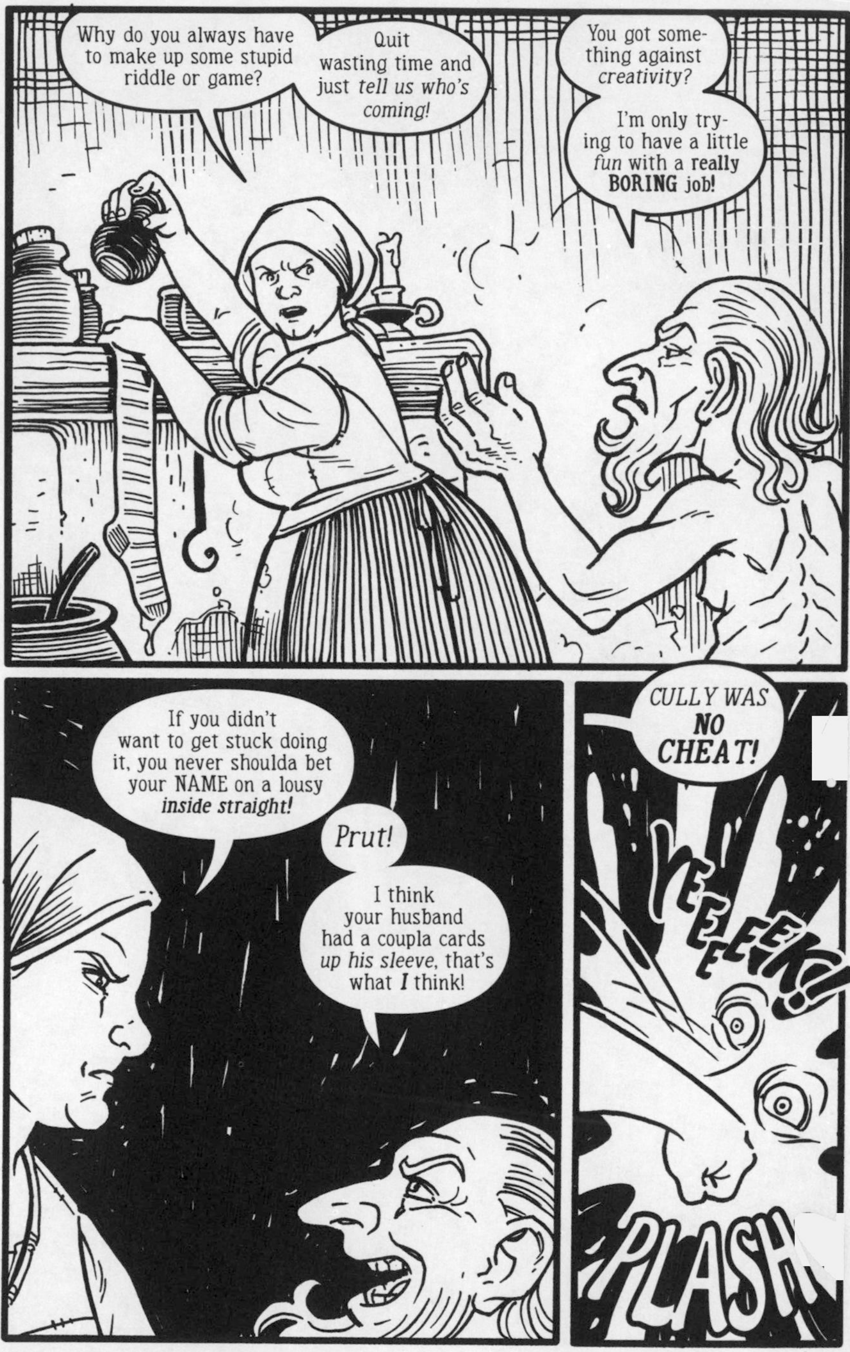
Why do you always have to make up some stupid riddle or game?
Quit wasting time and just *tell us who's coming!*
You got something against *creativity?*
I'm only trying to have a little *fun* with a **really BORING job!**
If you didn't want to get stuck doing it, you never shoulda bet your NAME on a lousy ***inside straight!***
Prut!
I think your husband had a coupla cards *up his sleeve*, that's what ***I*** think!
CULLY WAS ***NO CHEAT!***
YEEEEEK!!
PLASH

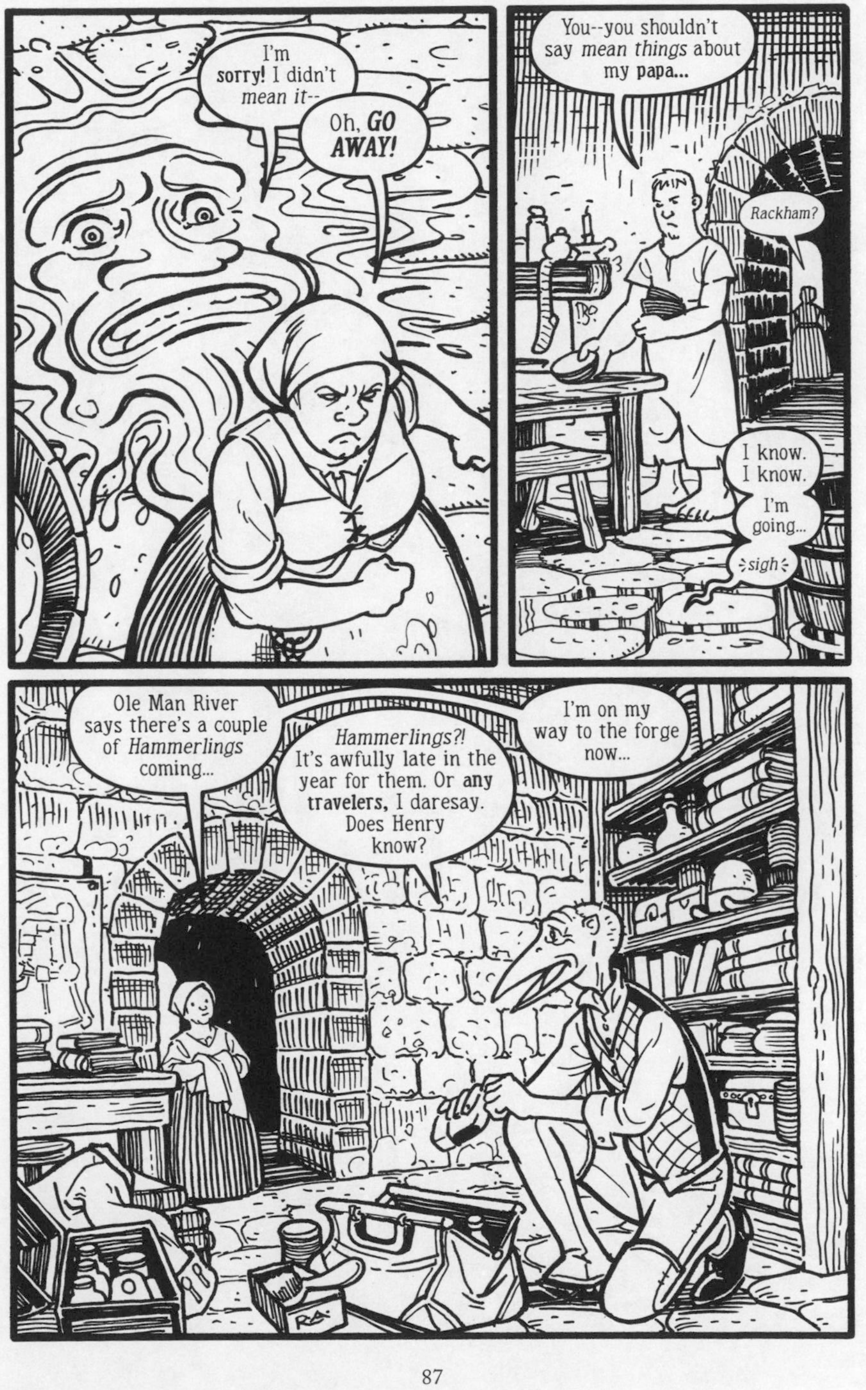
I'm **sorry!** I didn't *mean it--*
Oh, **GO AWAY!**
You--you shouldn't say *mean things* about my **papa...**
Rackham?
I know. I know.
I'm going...
sigh
Ole Man River says there's a couple of *Hammerlings* coming...
Hammerlings?! It's awfully late in the year for them. Or **any travelers,** I daresay. Does Henry know?
I'm on my way to the forge now...

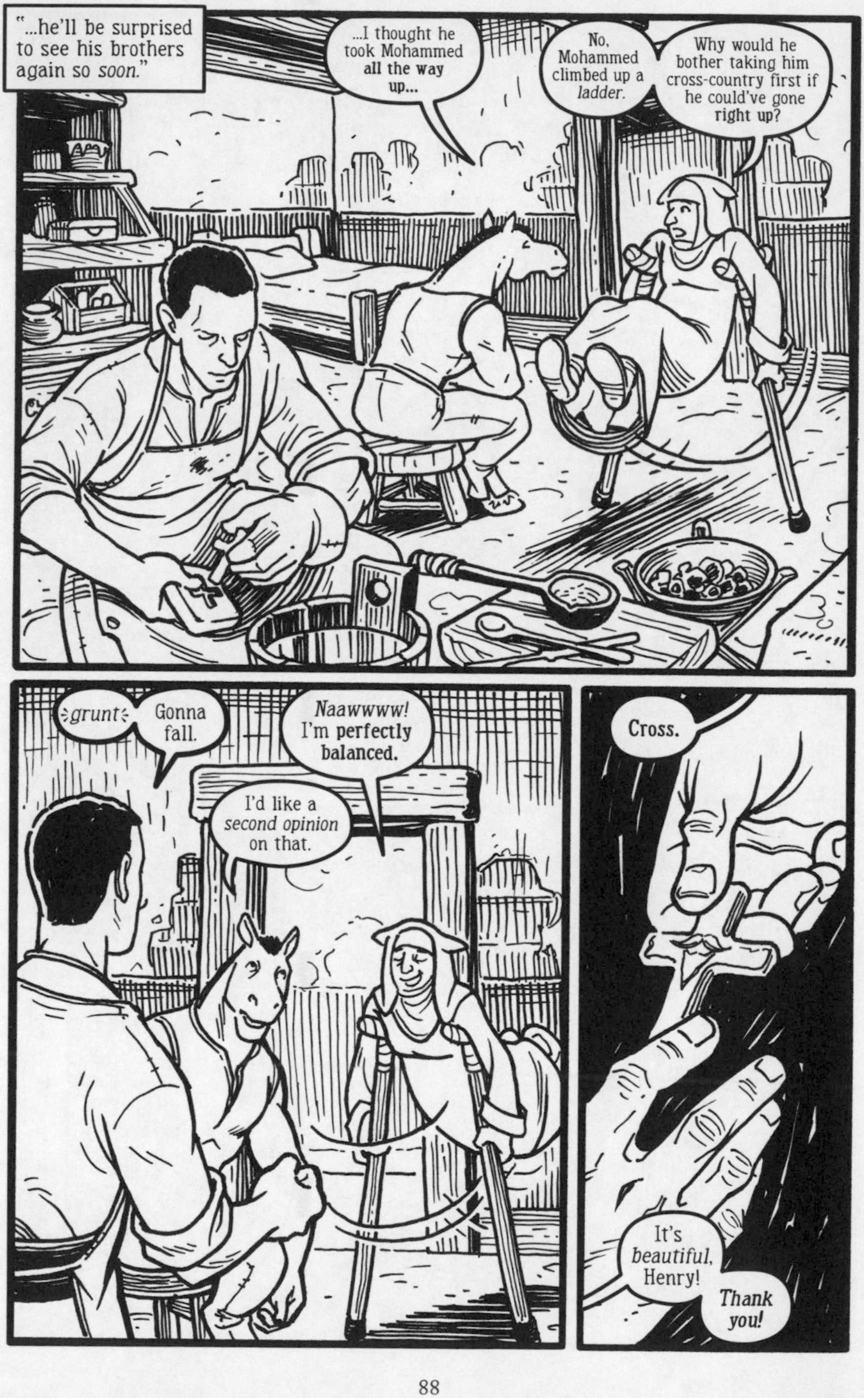
"...he'll be surprised to see his brothers again so *soon.*"
...I thought he took Mohammed **all the way up...**
No, Mohammed climbed up a *ladder.*
Why would he bother taking him cross-country first if he could've gone **right up?**
grunt
Gonna fall.
Naawwww! I'm **perfectly balanced.**
I'd like a *second opinion* on that.
Cross.
It's *beautiful,* Henry!
Thank you!

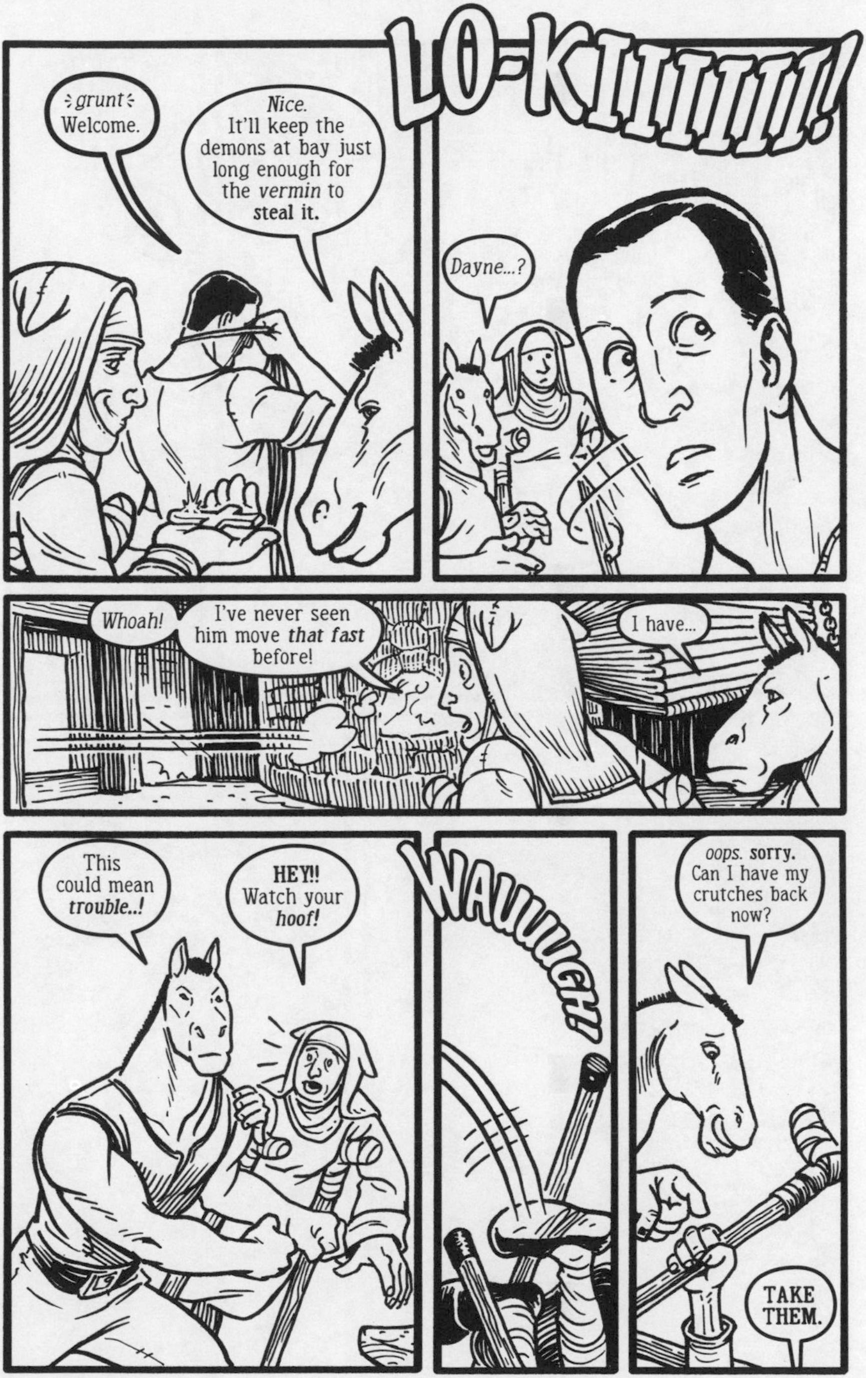
grunt
Welcome.
Nice.
It'll keep the demons at bay just long enough for the vermin to steal it.
LO-KIIIIIII!
Dayne...?
Whoah!
I've never seen him move that fast before!
I have...
This could mean trouble..!
HEY!!
Watch your hoof!
WAUUUGH!
oops. sorry.
Can I have my crutches back now?
TAKE THEM.

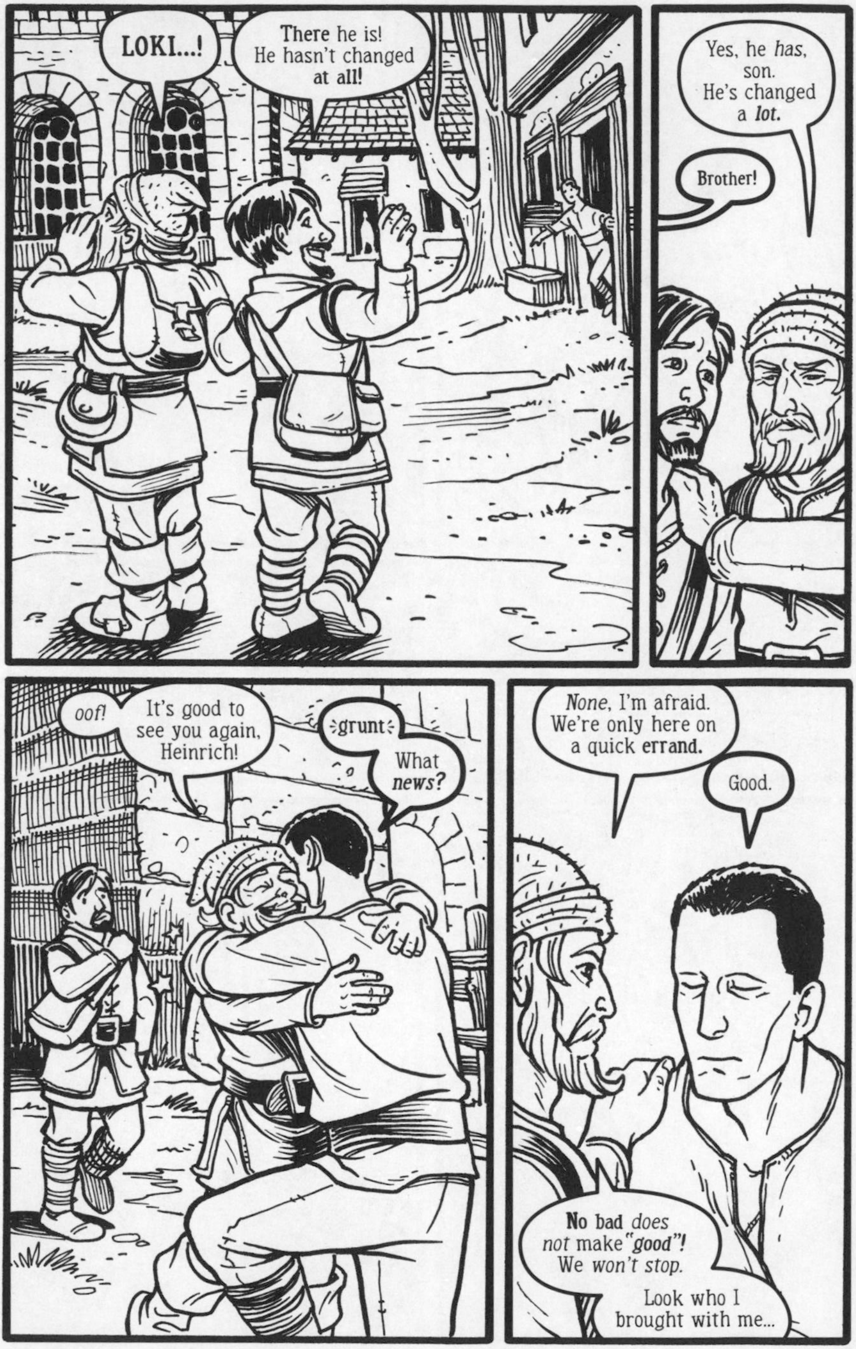
LOKI...!
There he is! He hasn't changed at all!
Yes, he has, son. He's changed a lot.
Brother!
oof!
It's good to see you again, Heinrich!
grunt
What news?
None, I'm afraid. We're only here on a quick errand.
Good.
No bad does not make "good"! We won't stop.
Look who I brought with me...

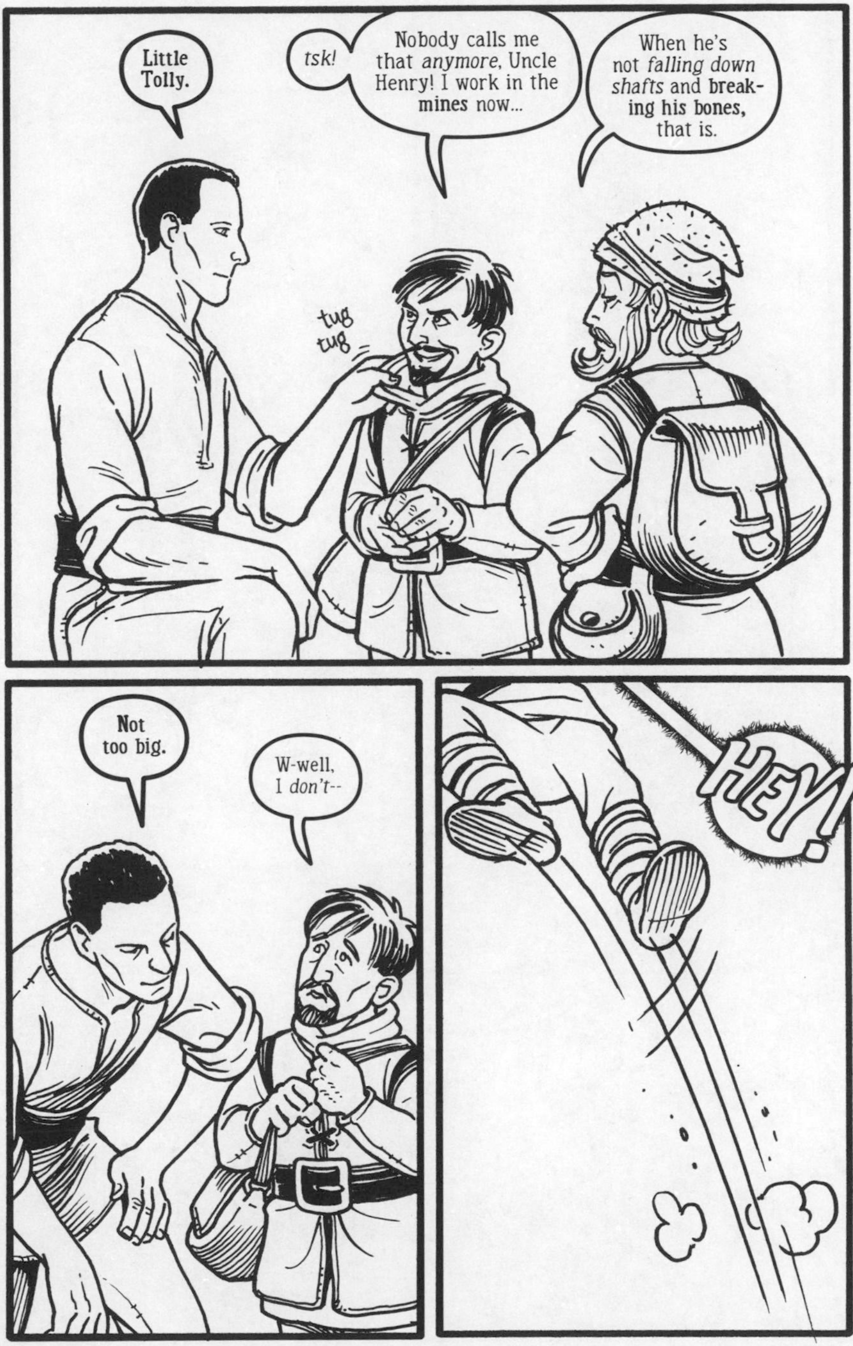
Little Tolly.
tsk!
Nobody calls me that *anymore*, Uncle Henry! I work in the **mines** now...
When he's not *falling down shafts* and **breaking his bones,** that is.
tug tug
Not too big.
W-well, I *don't*--
HEY!

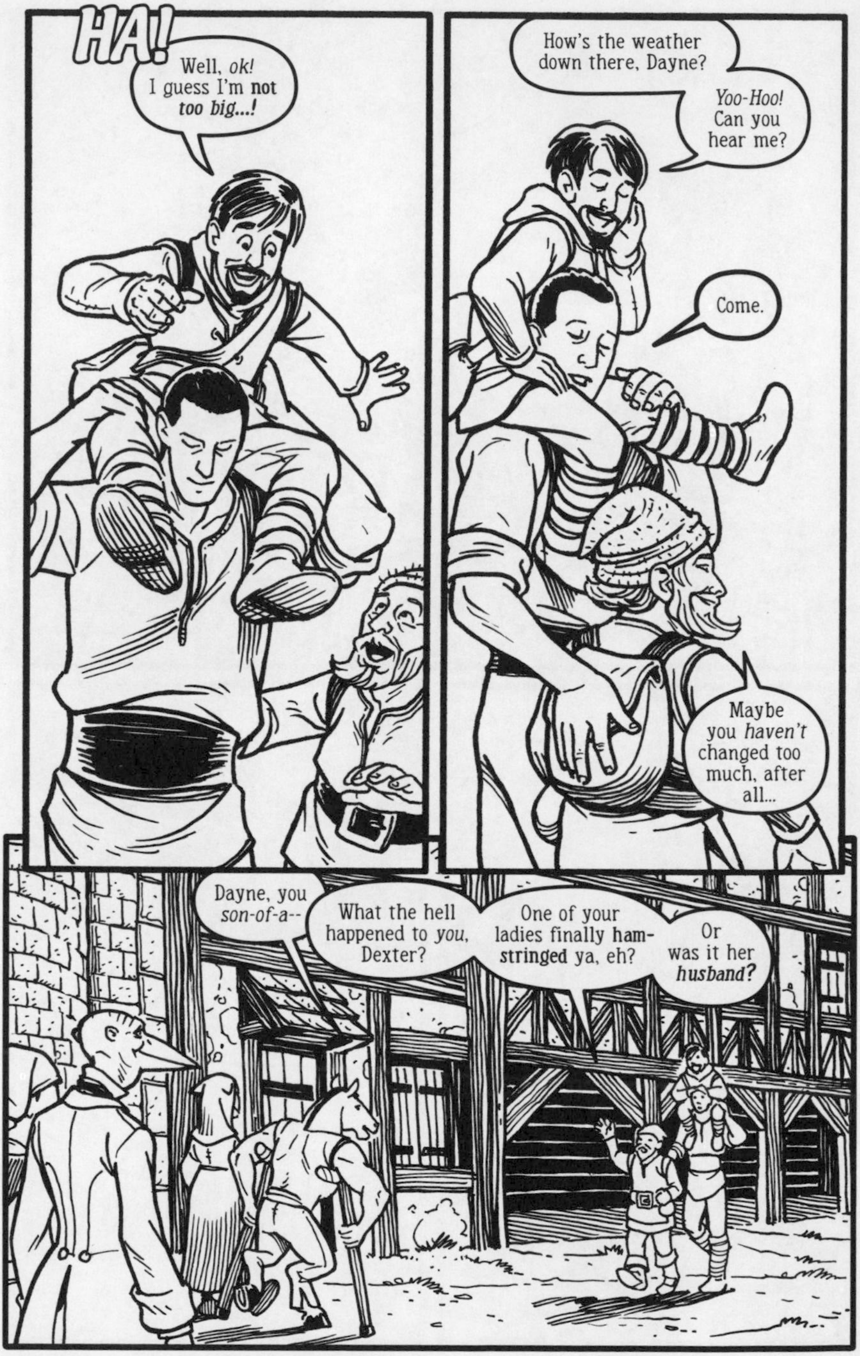
HA!
Well, *ok!* I guess I'm **not** ***too big...!***
How's the weather down there, Dayne?
Yoo-Hoo! Can you hear me?
Come.
Maybe you *haven't* changed too much, after all...
Dayne, you *son-of-a--*
What the hell happened to *you*, Dexter?
One of your ladies finally **ham-stringed** ya, eh?
Or was it her ***husband?***

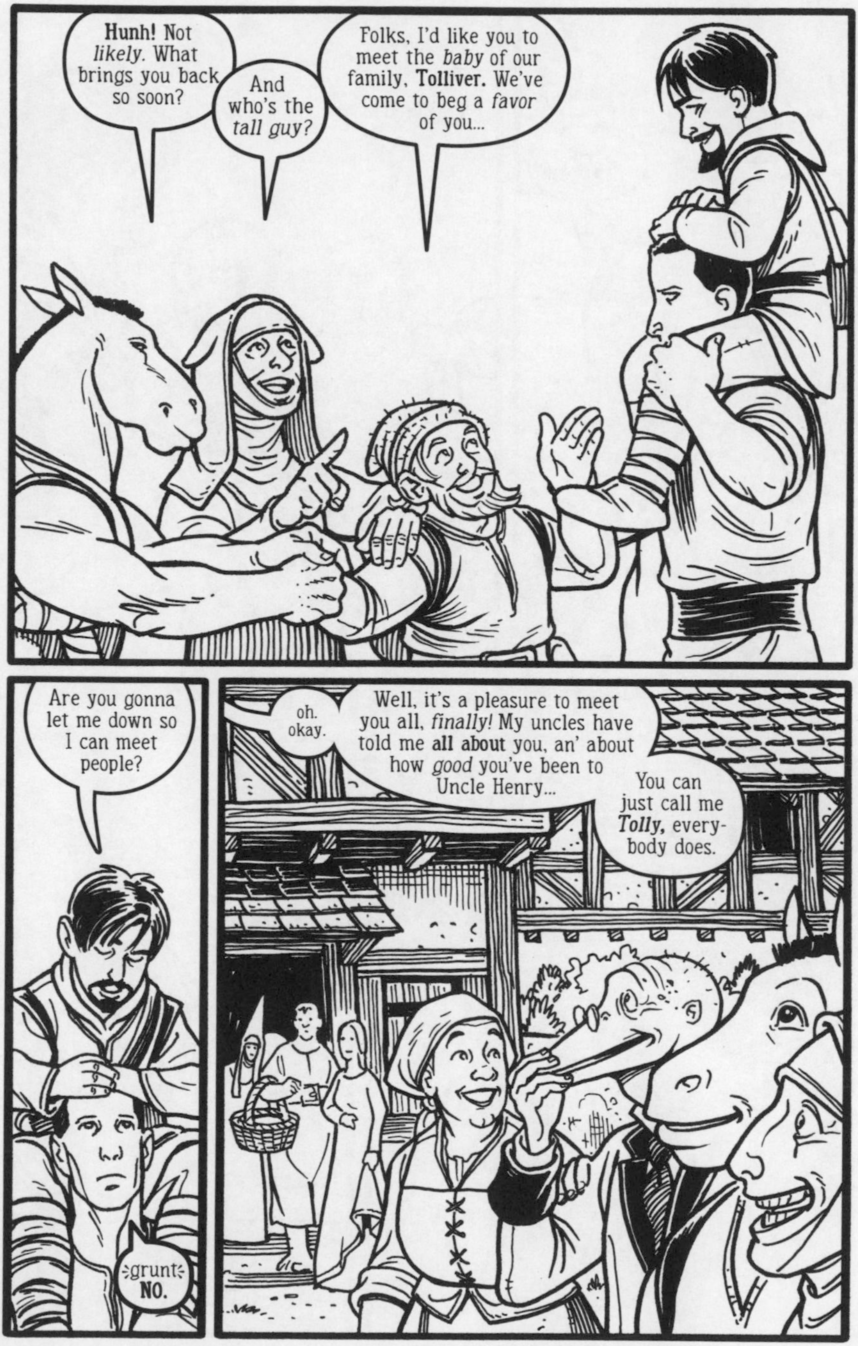
Hunh! Not *likely.* What brings you back so soon?
And who's the *tall guy?*
Folks, I'd like you to meet the *baby* of our family, **Tolliver.** We've come to beg a *favor* of you...
Are you gonna let me down so I can meet people?
grunt **NO.**
oh. okay.
Well, it's a pleasure to meet you all, *finally!* My uncles have told me **all about** you, an' about how *good* you've been to Uncle Henry...
You can just call me ***Tolly,*** every-body does.

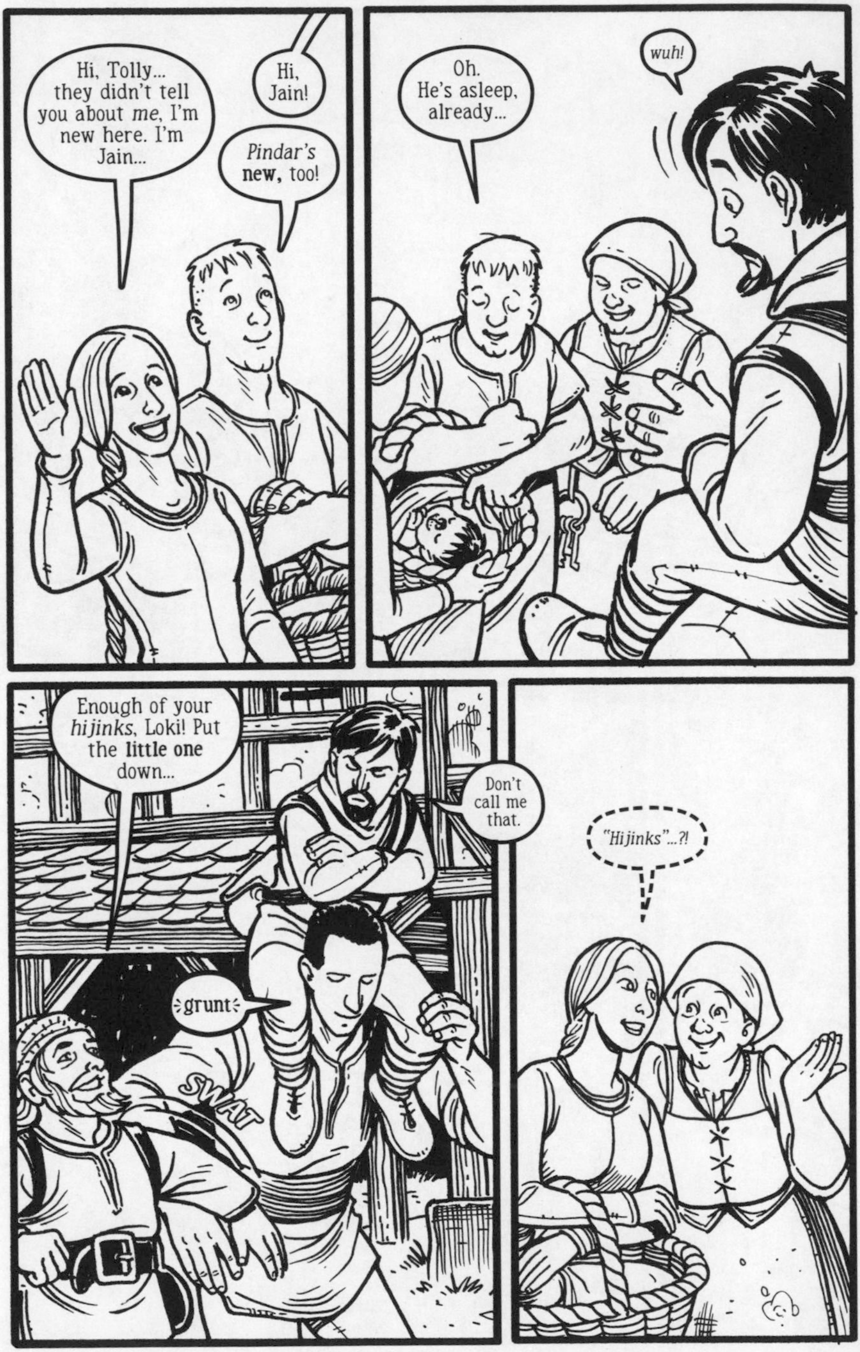
Hi, Tolly... they didn't tell you about *me*, I'm new here. I'm Jain...
Hi, Jain!
Pindar's **new,** too!
Oh. He's asleep, already...
wuh!
Enough of your *hijinks*, Loki! Put the **little one** down...
Don't call me that.
grunt
SWAT
"Hijinks"...?!

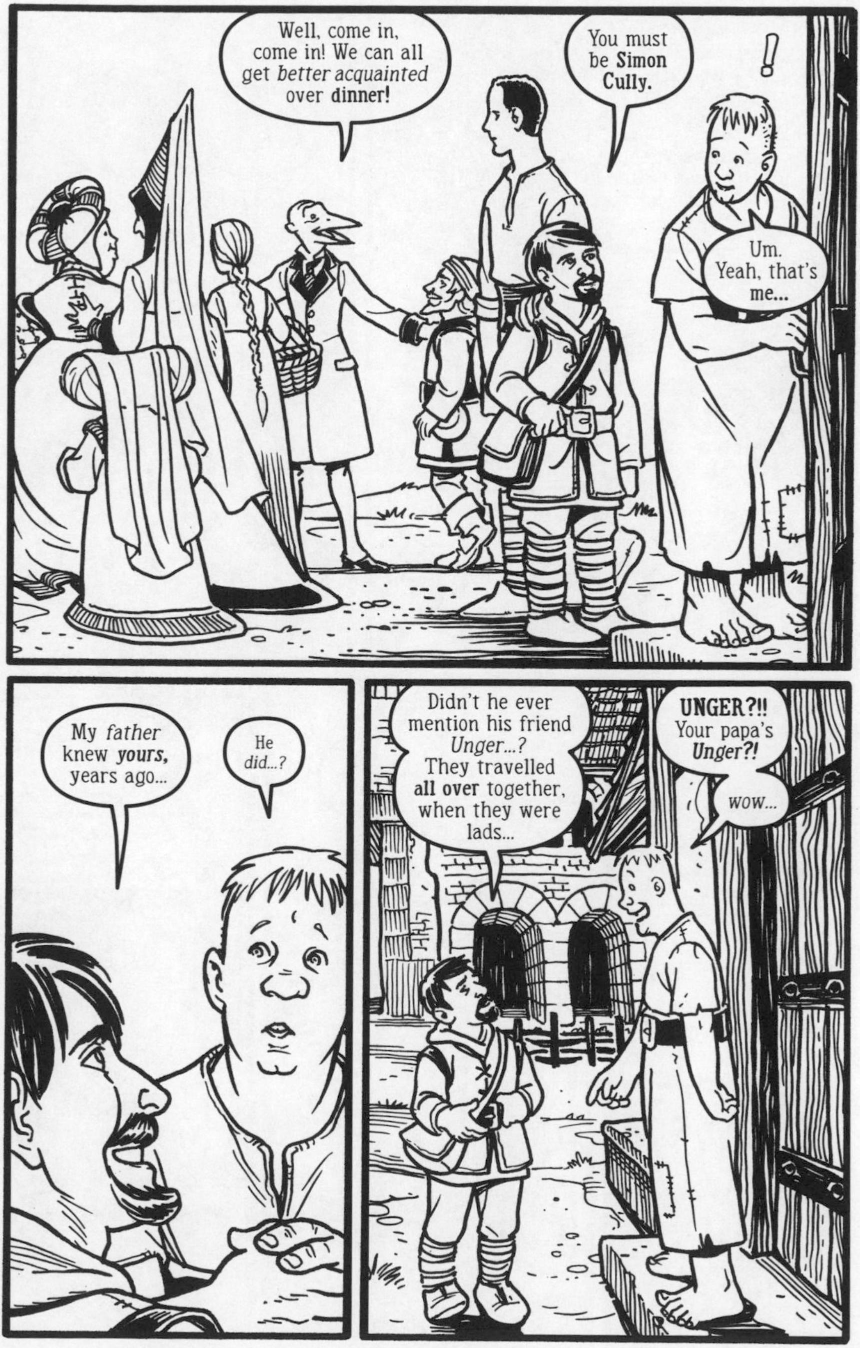
Well, come in, come in! We can all get *better acquainted* over **dinner!**
You must be **Simon Cully.**
!
Um. Yeah, that's **me...**
My *father* knew **yours,** years ago...
He *did...?*
Didn't he ever mention his friend *Unger...?* They travelled **all over** together, when they were lads...
UNGER?!! Your papa's ***Unger?!***
wow...

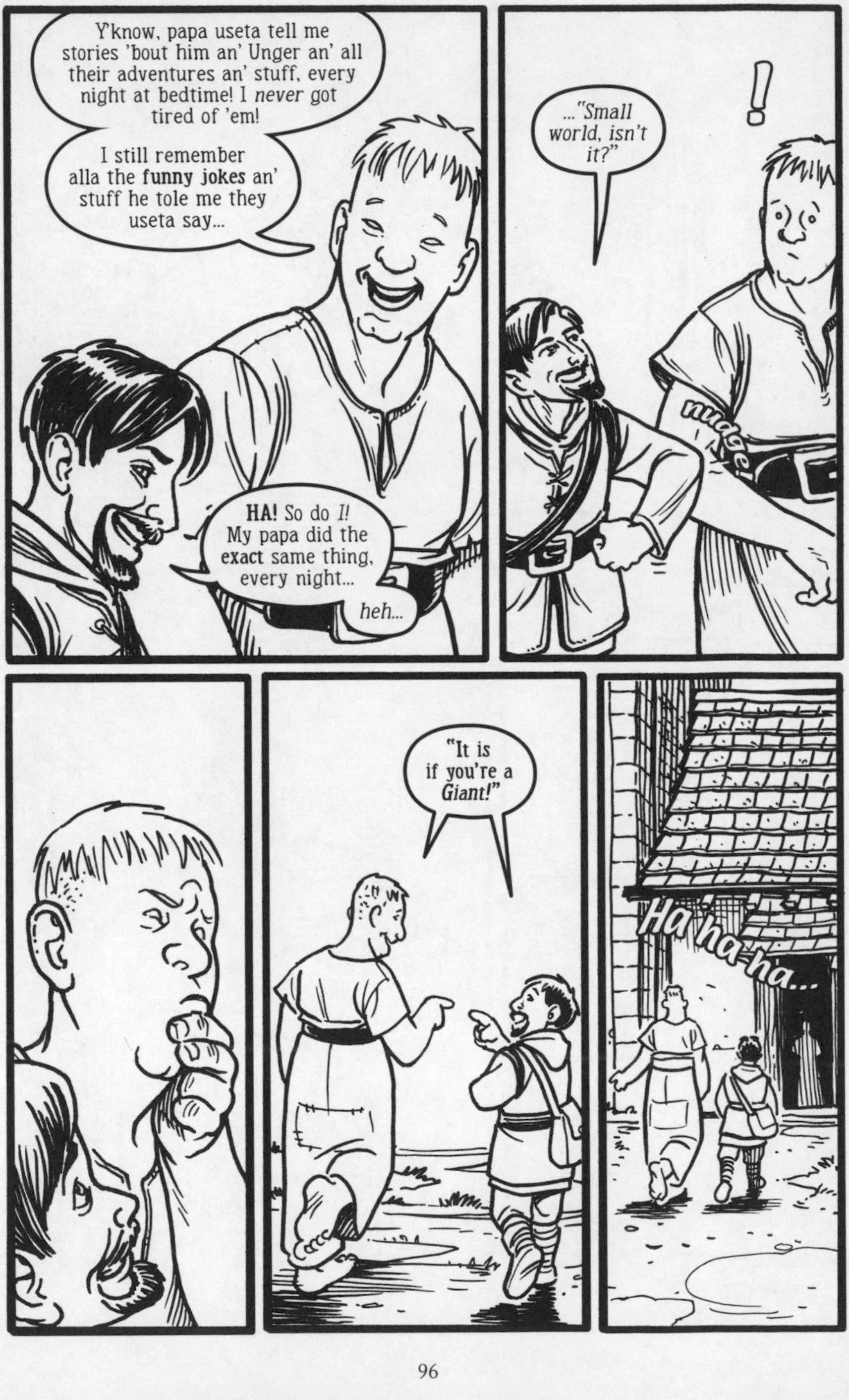
Y'know, papa useta tell me stories 'bout him an' Unger an' all their adventures an' stuff, every night at bedtime! I *never* got tired of 'em!
I still remember alla the **funny jokes** an' stuff he tole me they useta say...
HA! So do *I!* My papa did the **exact** same thing, every night...
heh...
...*"Small world, isn't it?"*
!
nudge
"It is if you're a *Giant!*"
Ha ha ha...

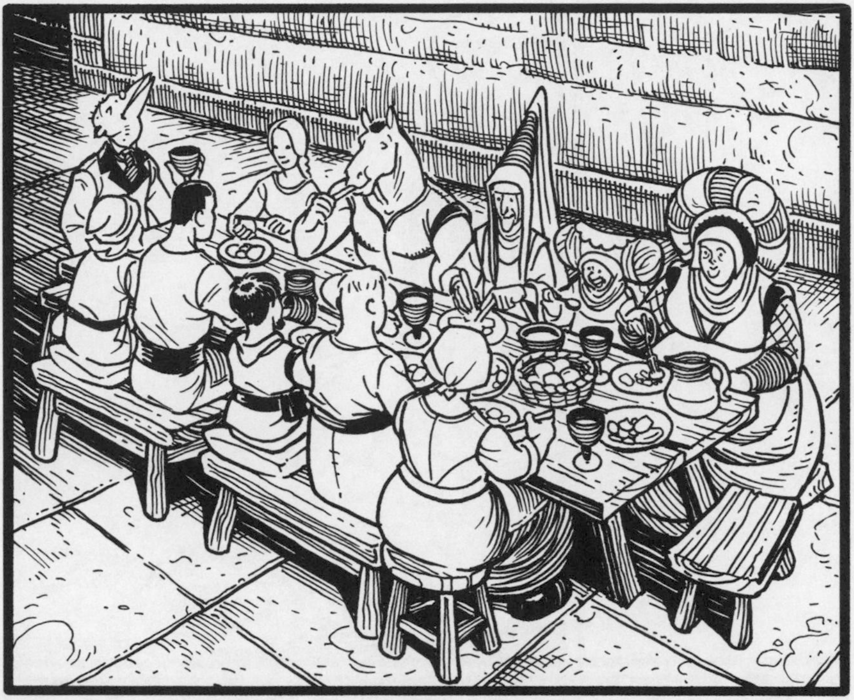

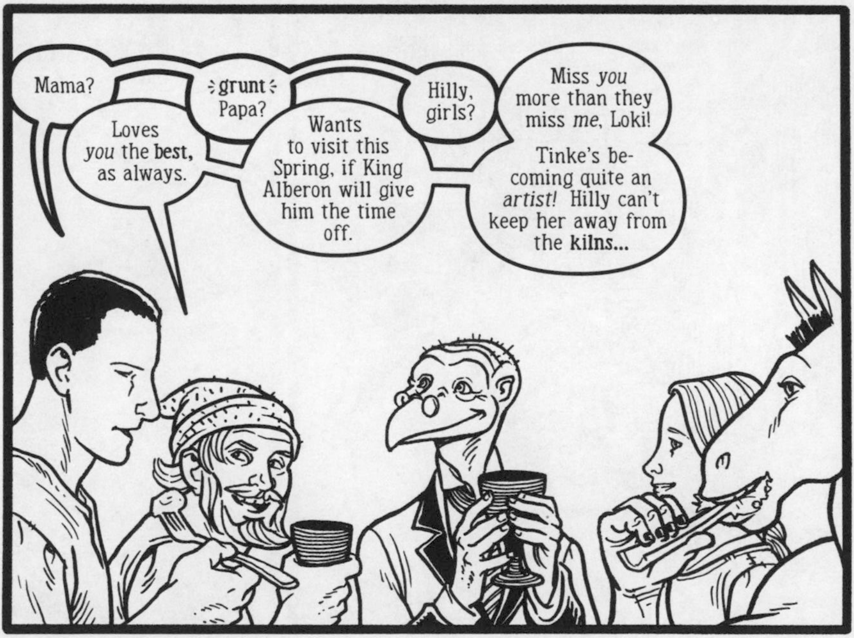
Mama?
Loves *you* the **best,** as always.
grunt Papa?
Wants to visit this Spring, if King Alberon will give him the time off.
Hilly, girls?
Miss *you* more than they miss *me*, Loki!
Tinke's becoming quite an *artist!* Hilly can't keep her away from the **kilns...**

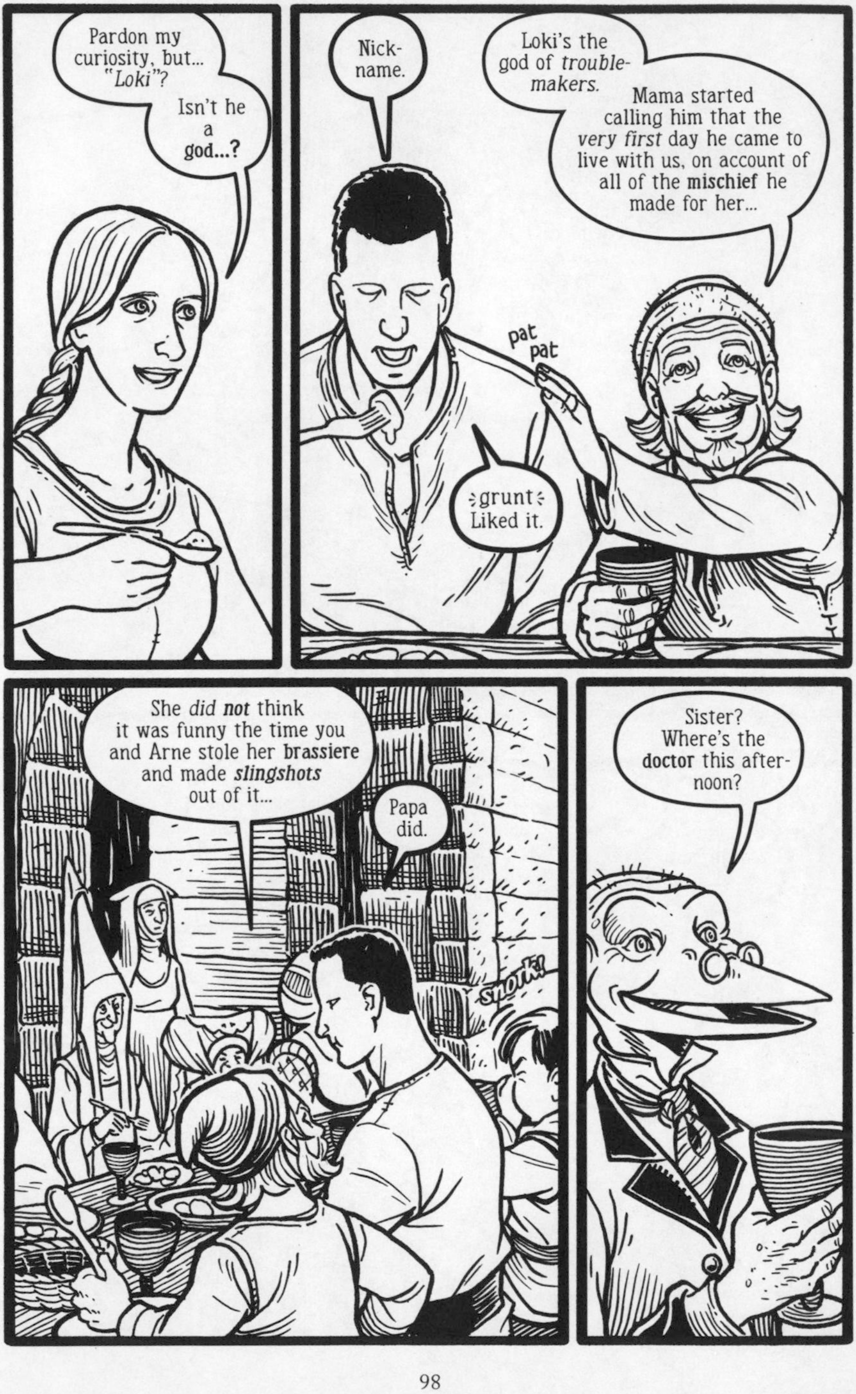
Pardon my curiosity, but... "*Loki*"?
Isn't he a **god...?**
Nick-name.
Loki's the god of *trouble-makers.*
Mama started calling him that the *very first* day he came to live with us, on account of all of the **mischief** he made for her...
pat pat
grunt
Liked it.
She *did* ***not*** think it was funny the time you and Arne stole her **brassiere** and made ***slingshots*** out of it...
Papa did.
SNORK!
Sister? Where's the **doctor** this after-noon?

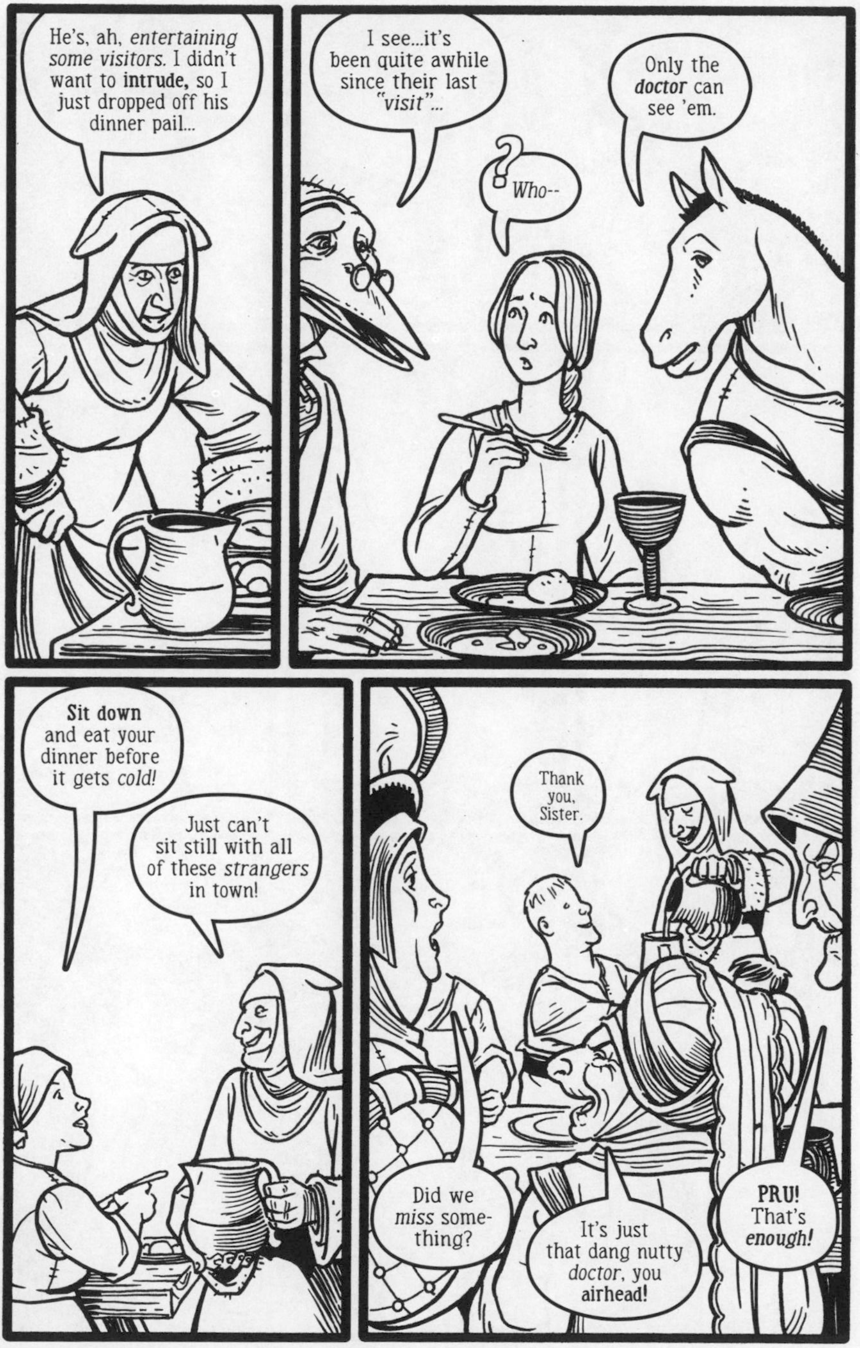
He's, ah, *entertaining some visitors.* I didn't want to **intrude,** so I just dropped off his dinner pail...
I see...it's been quite awhile since their last *"visit"*...
Who--
Only the ***doctor*** can see 'em.
Sit down and eat your dinner before it gets *cold!*
Just can't sit still with all of these *strangers* in town!
Thank you, Sister.
Did we *miss* some-thing?
It's just that dang nutty *doctor*, you **airhead!**
PRU! That's ***enough!***

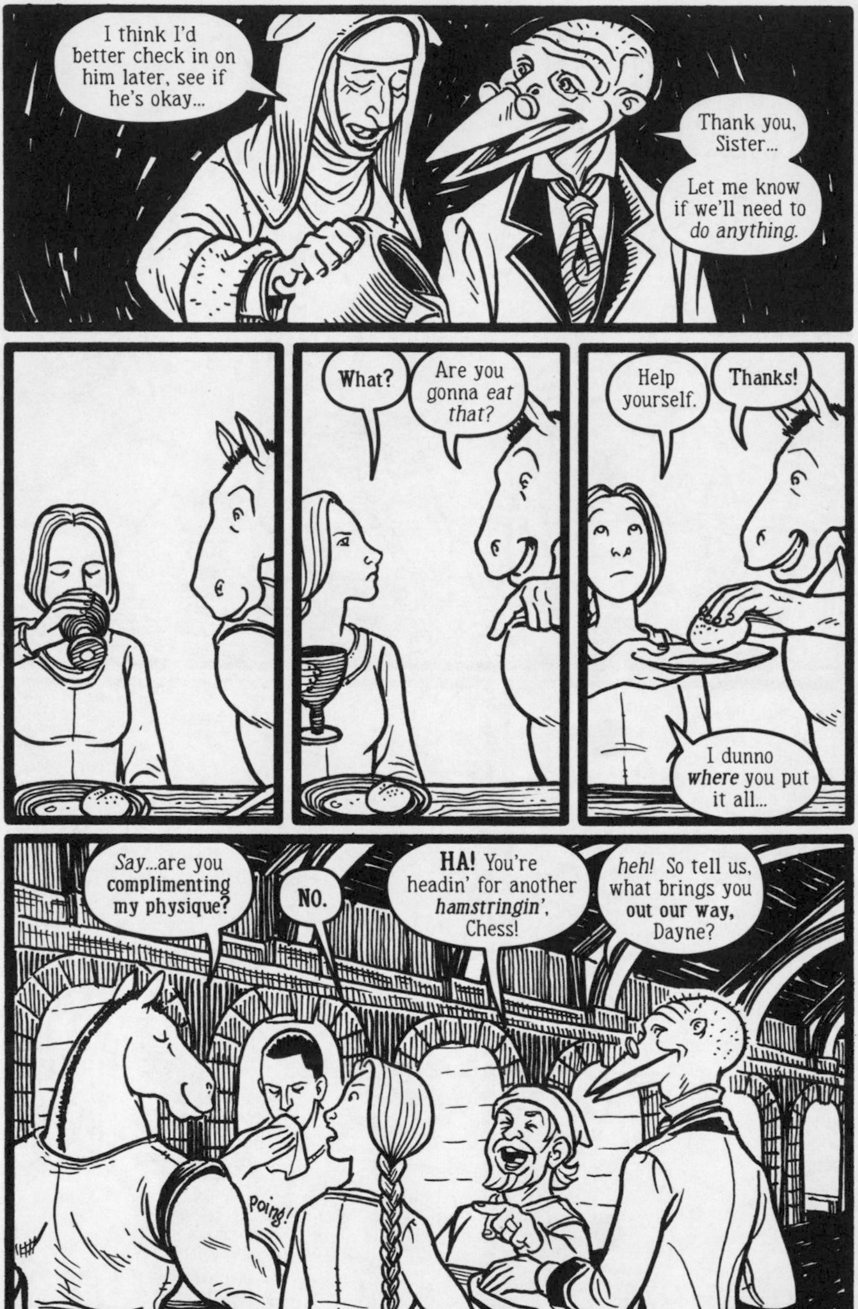
I think I'd better check in on him later, see if he's okay...
Thank you, Sister...
Let me know if we'll need to *do anything.*
What?
Are you gonna *eat that?*
Help yourself.
Thanks!
I dunno **where** you put it all...
Say...are you **complimenting my physique?**
NO.
HA! You're headin' for another ***hamstringin'***, Chess!
heh! So tell us, what brings you **out our way,** Dayne?
poing!

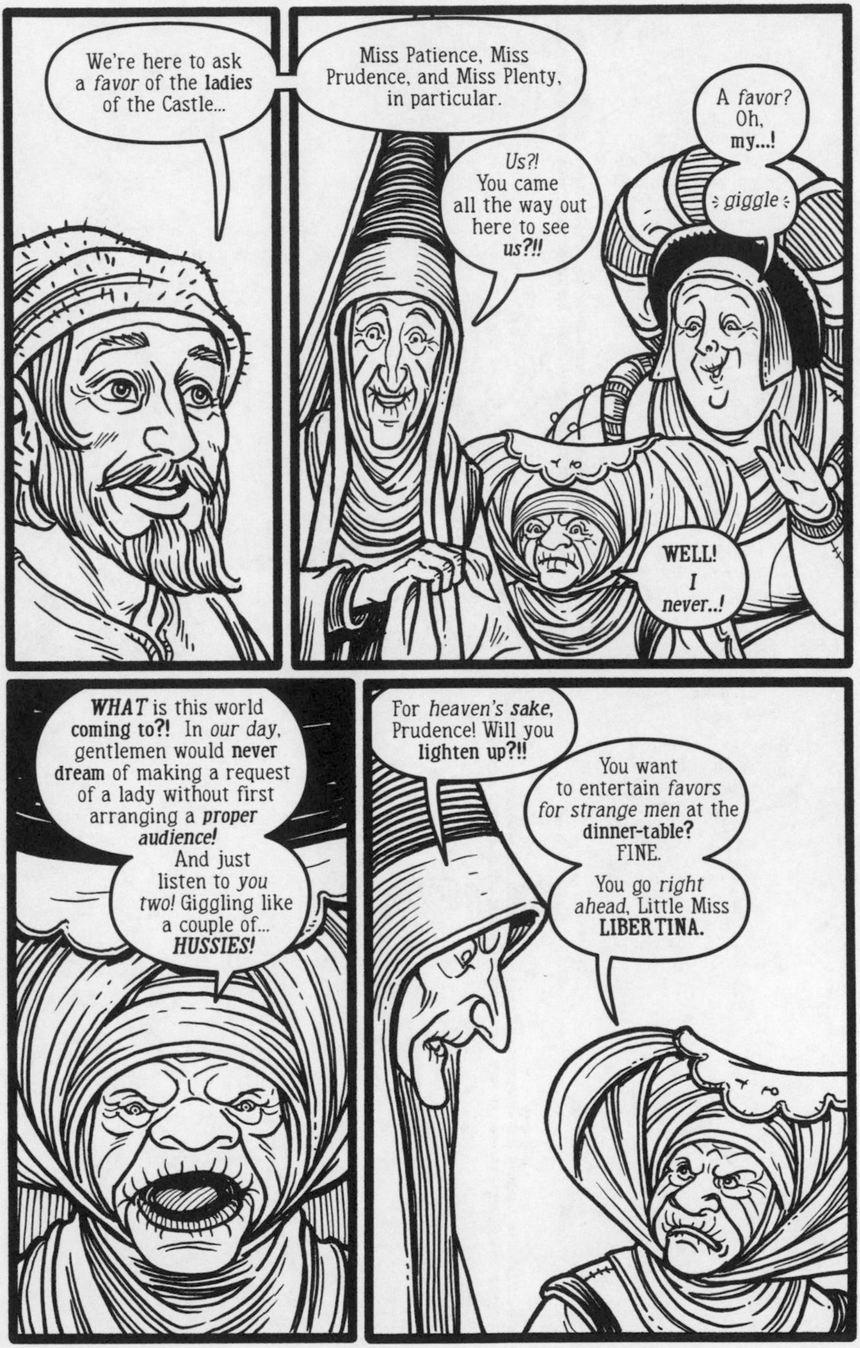
We're here to ask a *favor* of the **ladies** of the Castle...
Miss Patience, Miss Prudence, and Miss Plenty, in particular.
Us?! You came all the way out here to see ***us?!!***
A *favor?* Oh, **my...!**
giggle
WELL! *I never..!*
WHAT is this world **coming to?!** In *our day*, gentlemen would **never dream** of making a request of a lady without first arranging a ***proper audience!***
And just listen to *you two!* Giggling like a couple of... ***HUSSIES!***
For *heaven's* ***sake***, Prudence! Will you **lighten up?!!**
You want to entertain *favors for strange men* at the **dinner-table?** FINE.
You go *right ahead*, Little Miss **LIBERTINA.**

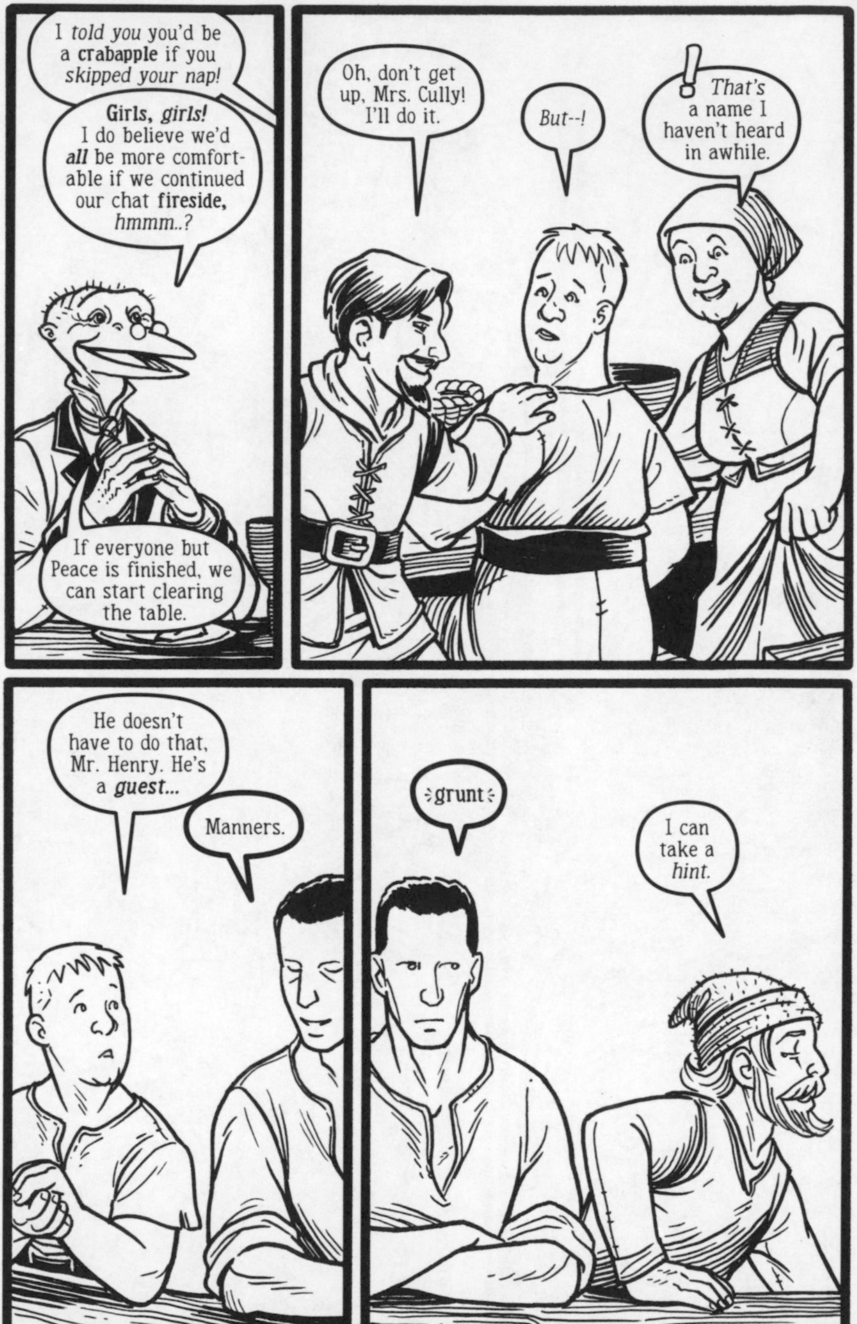
I *told you* you'd be a **crabapple** if you *skipped your nap!*
Girls, *girls!* I do believe we'd ***all*** be more comfortable if we continued our chat **fireside,** *hmmm..?*
If everyone but Peace is finished, we can start clearing the table.
Oh, don't get up, Mrs. Cully! I'll do it.
But--!
! *That's* a name I haven't heard in awhile.
He doesn't have to do that, Mr. Henry. He's a ***guest...***
Manners.
grunt
I can take a *hint.*

Chapter 5.

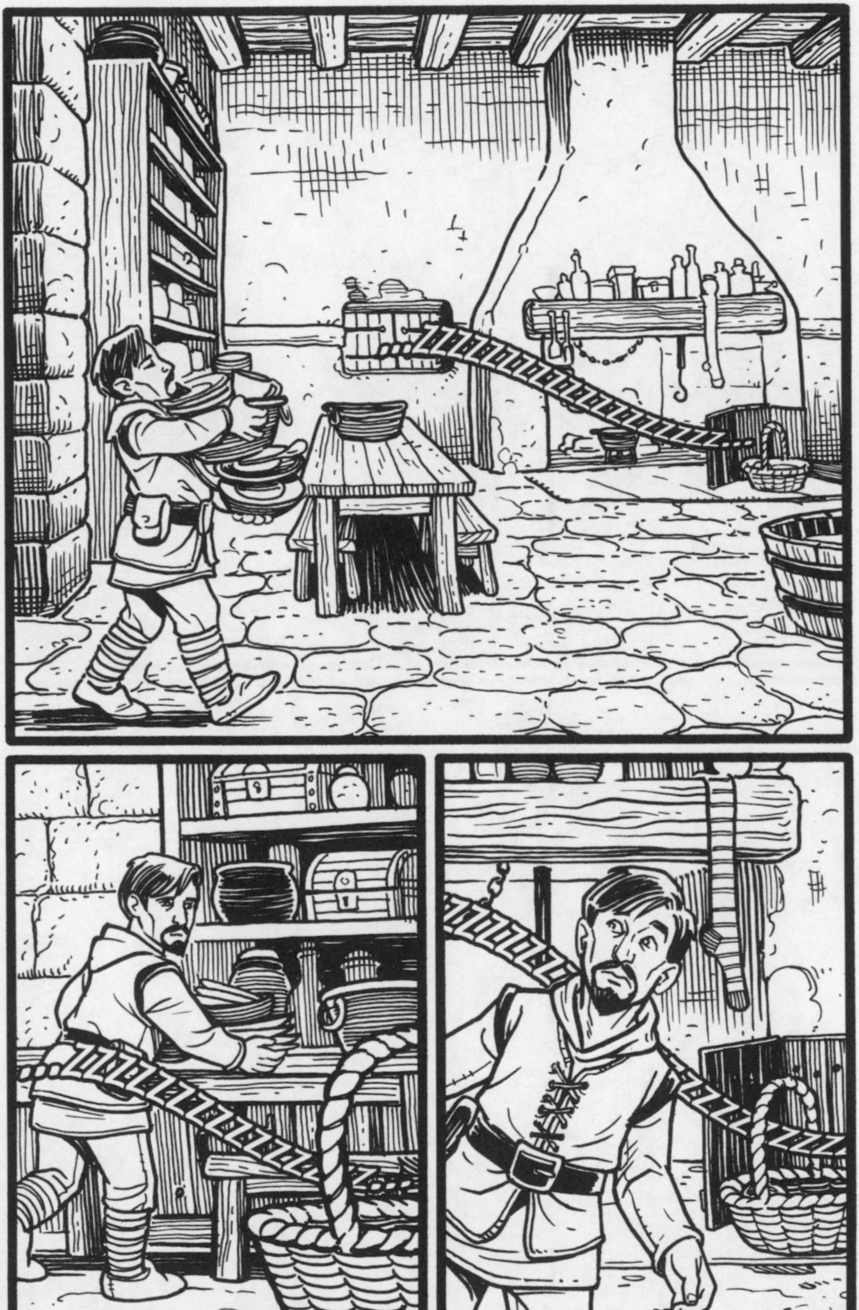

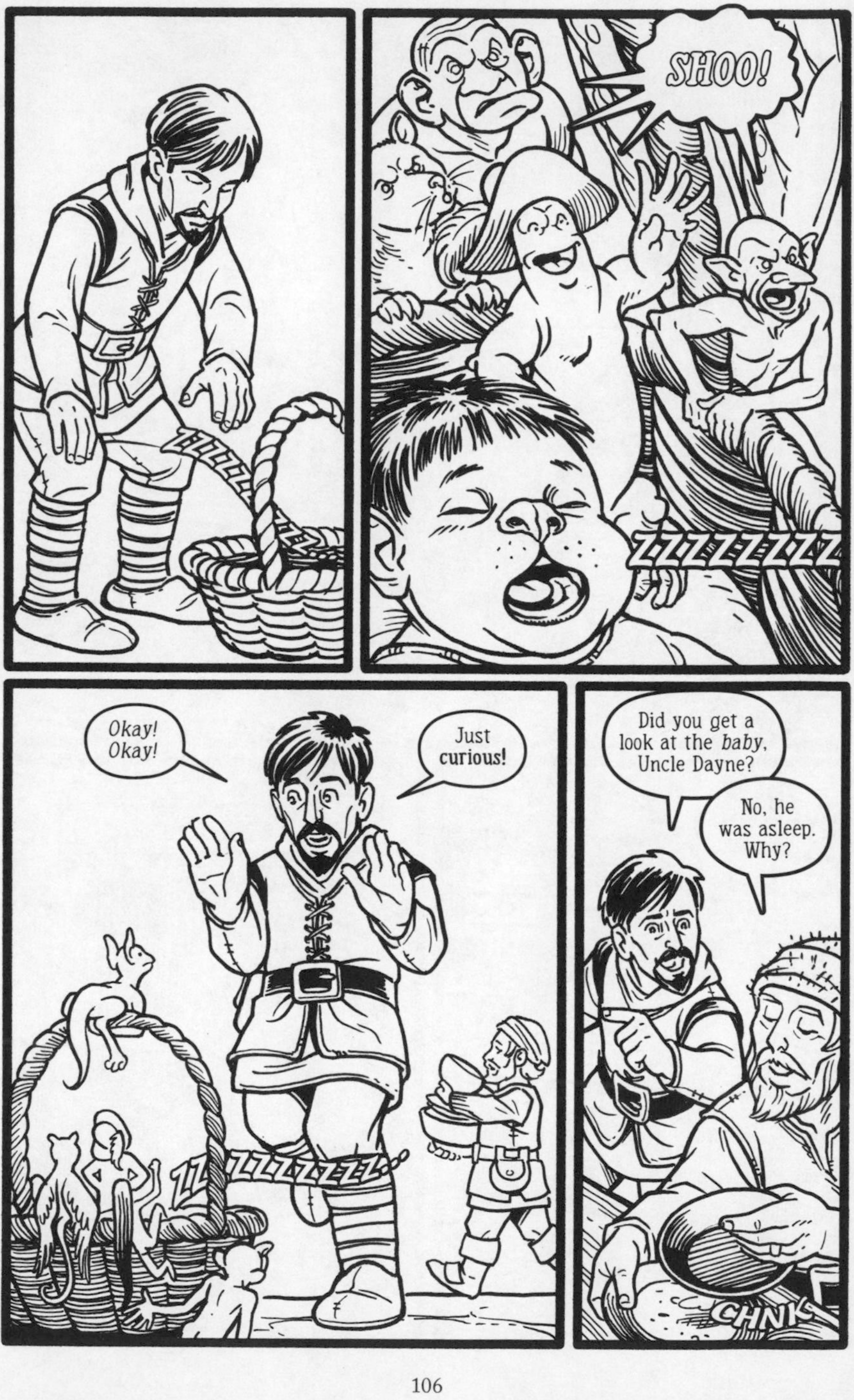
SHOO!
ZZZZZZZZZ
Okay!
Okay!
Just
curious!
ZZZZZZZZZZ
Did you get a look at the *baby*, Uncle Dayne?
No, he was asleep. Why?
CHNK

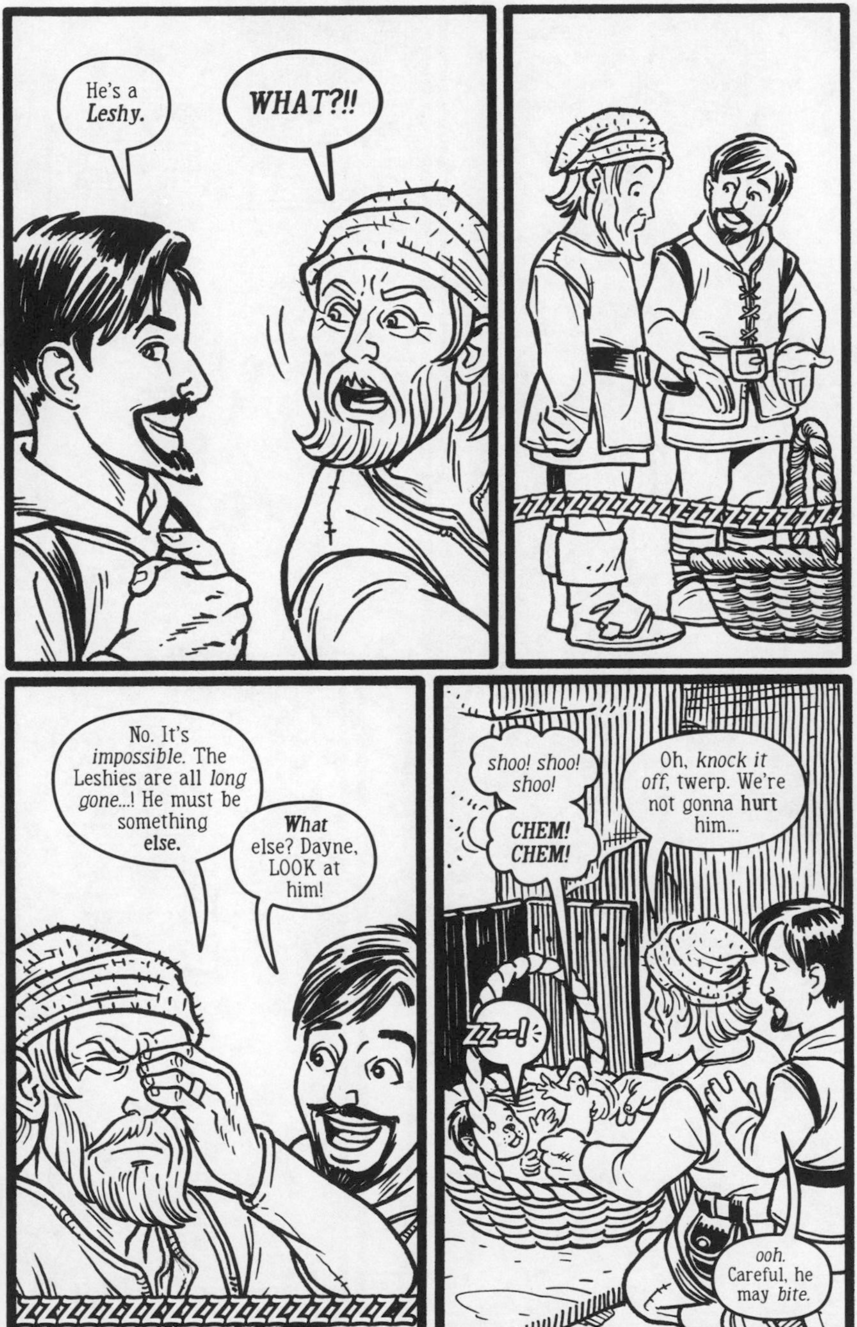
He's a *Leshy.*
WHAT?!!
ZZZZZZZZZZZZZZZZZZZZZ
No. It's *impossible.* The Leshies are all *long gone*...! He must be something **else.**
What else? Dayne, LOOK at him!
ZZZZZZZZZZZZZZZZZZZZZZZZZZ
shoo! shoo! shoo!
CHEM! CHEM!
Oh, *knock it off,* twerp. We're not gonna **hurt** him...
ZZ--!
ooh. Careful, he may *bite.*

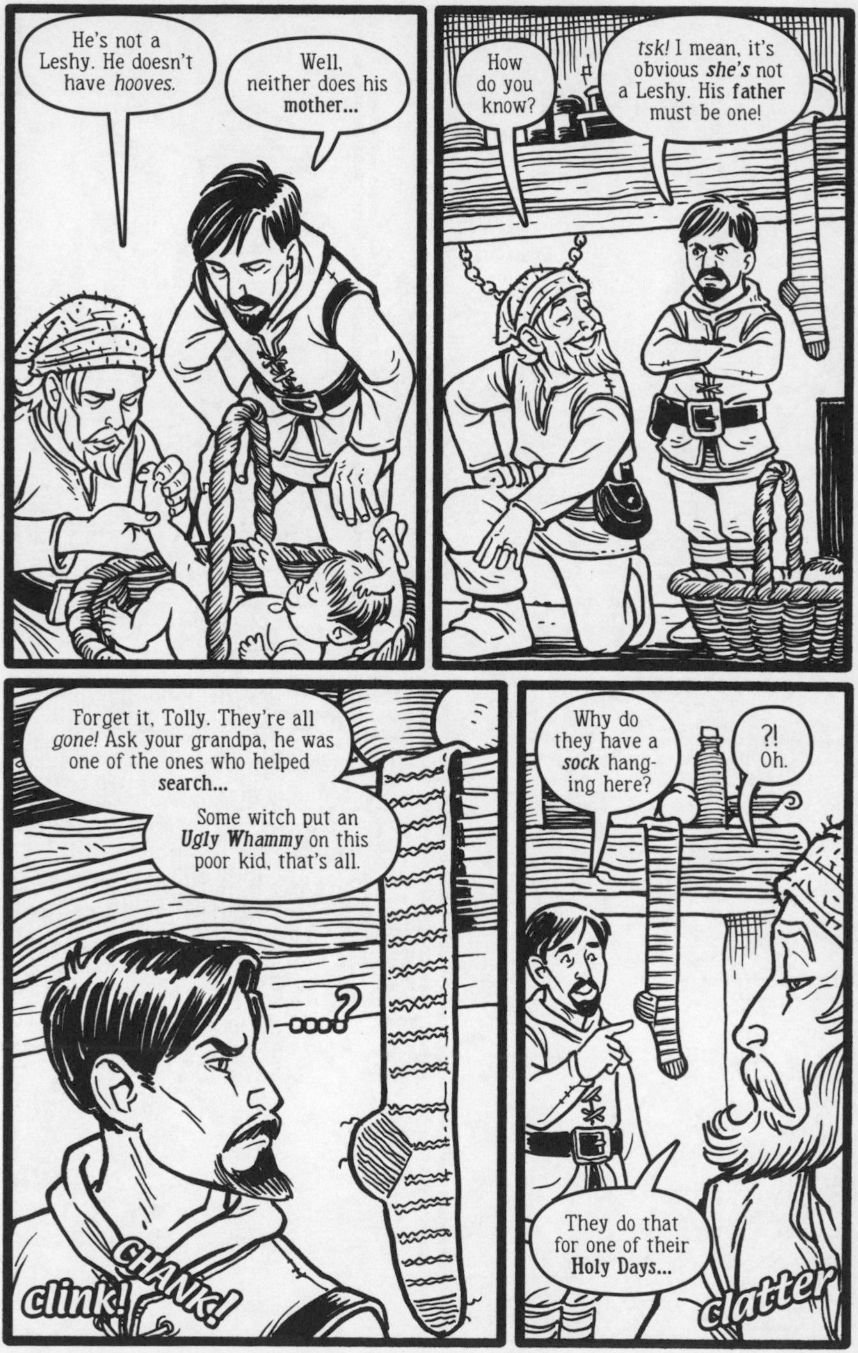
He's not a Leshy. He doesn't have *hooves.*
Well, neither does his **mother...**
How do you know?
tsk! I mean, it's obvious ***she's*** not a Leshy. His **father** must be one!
Forget it, Tolly. They're all *gone!* Ask your grandpa, he was one of the ones who helped **search...**
Some witch put an ***Ugly Whammy*** on this poor kid, that's all.
?
CHANK!
clink!
Why do they have a ***sock*** hang-ing here?
?! Oh.
They do that for one of their **Holy Days...**
clatter

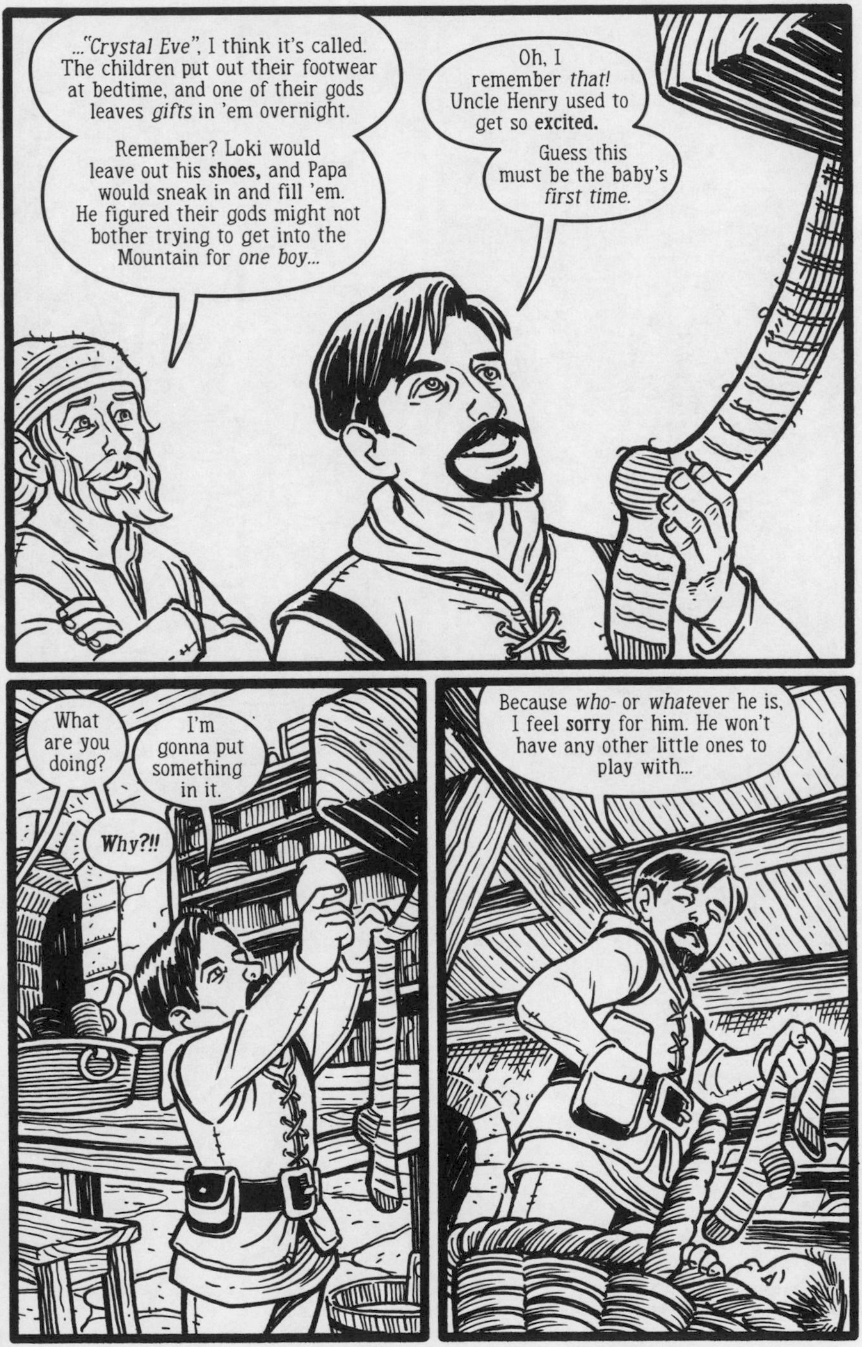
..."*Crystal Eve*", I think it's called. The children put out their footwear at bedtime, and one of their gods leaves *gifts* in 'em overnight.
Remember? Loki would leave out his **shoes,** and Papa would sneak in and fill 'em. He figured their gods might not bother trying to get into the Mountain for *one boy*...
Oh, I remember *that!* Uncle Henry used to get so **excited.**
Guess this must be the baby's *first time.*
What are you doing?
I'm gonna put something in it.
Why?!!
Because *who-* or *what*ever he is, I feel **sorry** for him. He won't have any other little ones to play with...

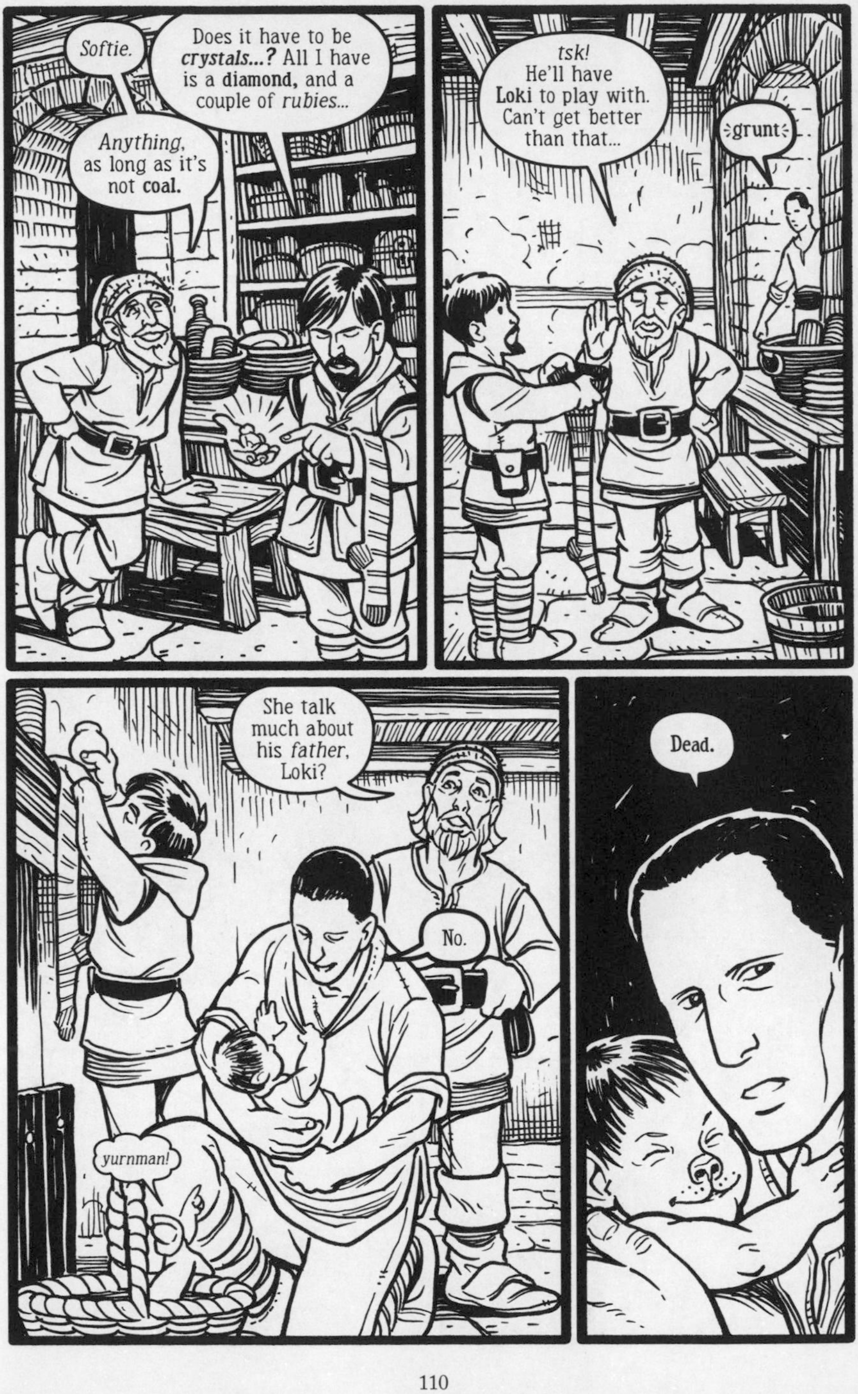
Softie.
Does it have to be *crystals...?* All I have is a **diamond,** and a couple of *rubies...*
Anything, as long as it's not **coal.**
tsk! He'll have **Loki** to play with. Can't get better than that...
grunt
She talk much about his *father,* Loki?
No.
yurnman!
Dead.

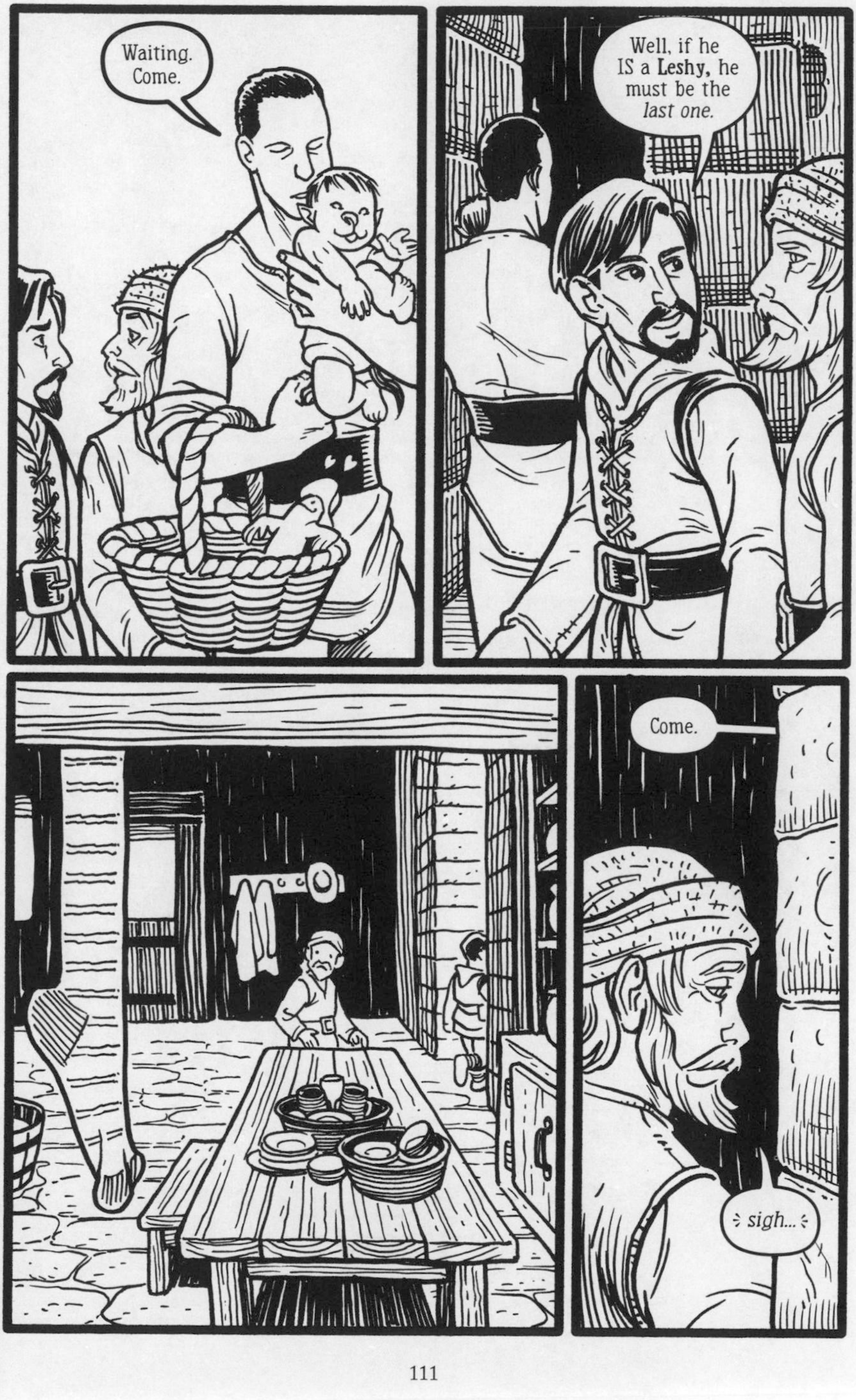
Waiting. Come.
Well, if he IS a Leshy, he must be the last one.
Come.
sigh...

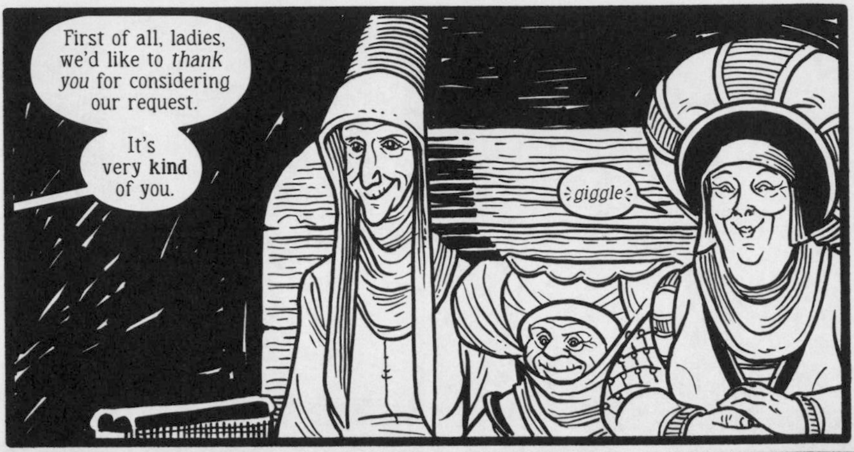
First of all, ladies, we'd like to *thank you* for considering our request.
It's very **kind** of you.
giggle

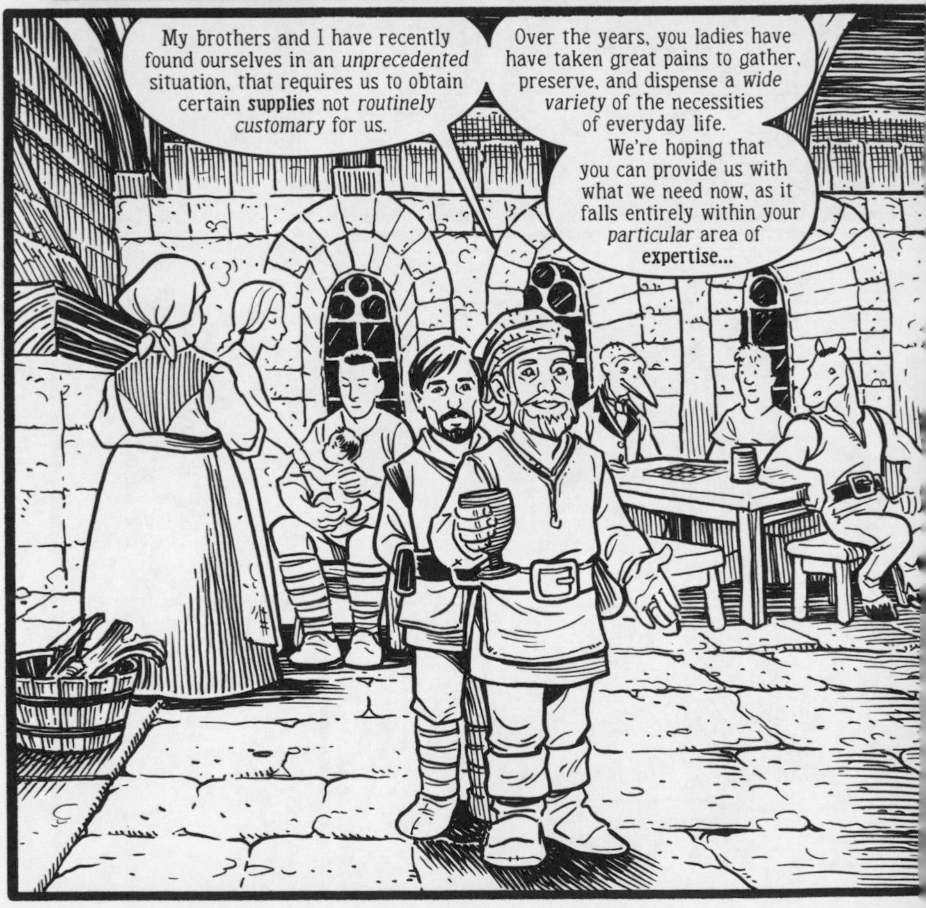
My brothers and I have recently found ourselves in an *unprecedented* situation, that requires us to obtain certain **supplies** not *routinely customary* for us.
Over the years, you ladies have have taken great pains to gather, preserve, and dispense a *wide variety* of the necessities of everyday life.
We're hoping that you can provide us with what we need now, as it falls entirely within your *particular* area of **expertise...**

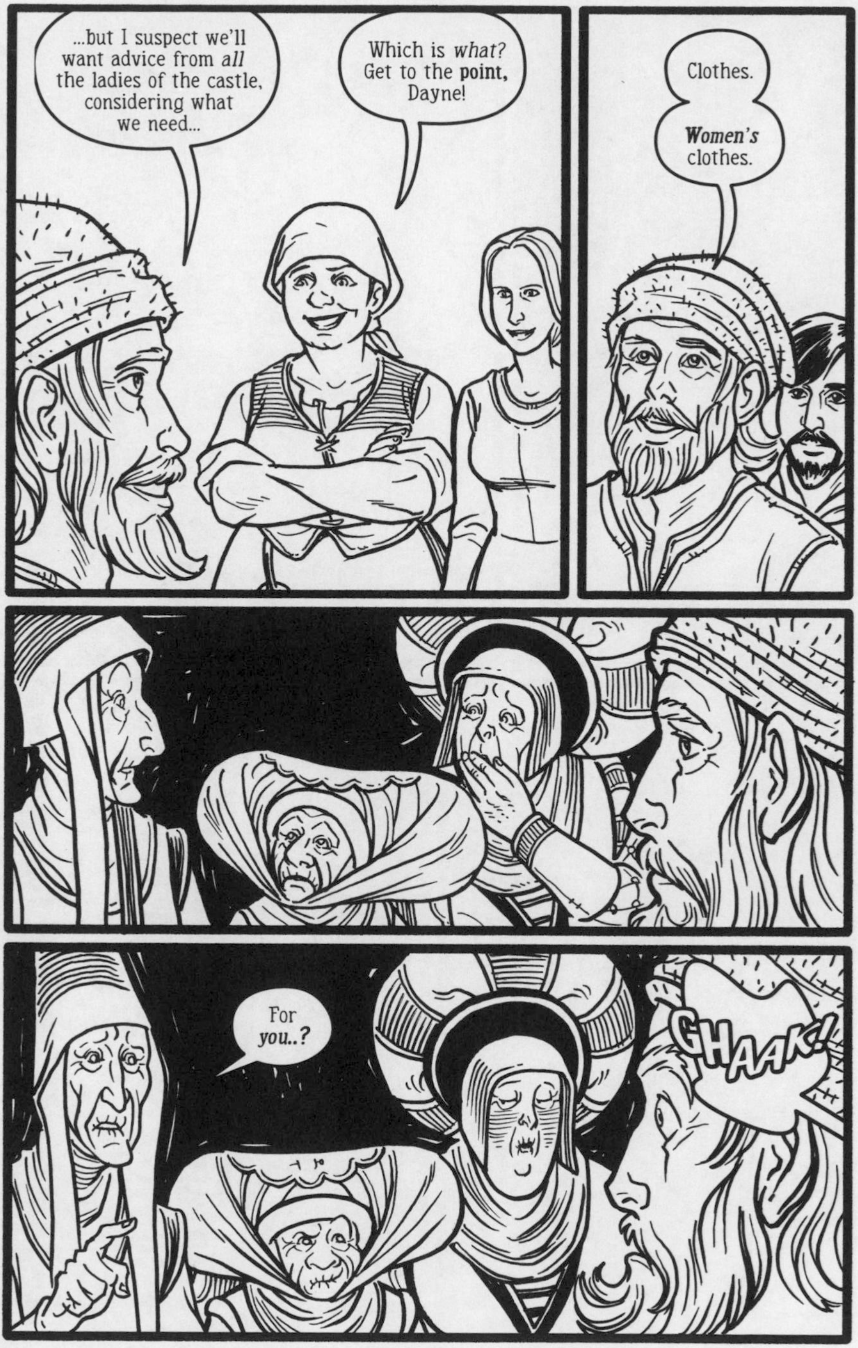
...but I suspect we'll want advice from *all* the ladies of the castle, considering what we need...
Which is *what*? Get to the **point,** Dayne!
Clothes.
Women's clothes.
For *you..?*
GHAAK!

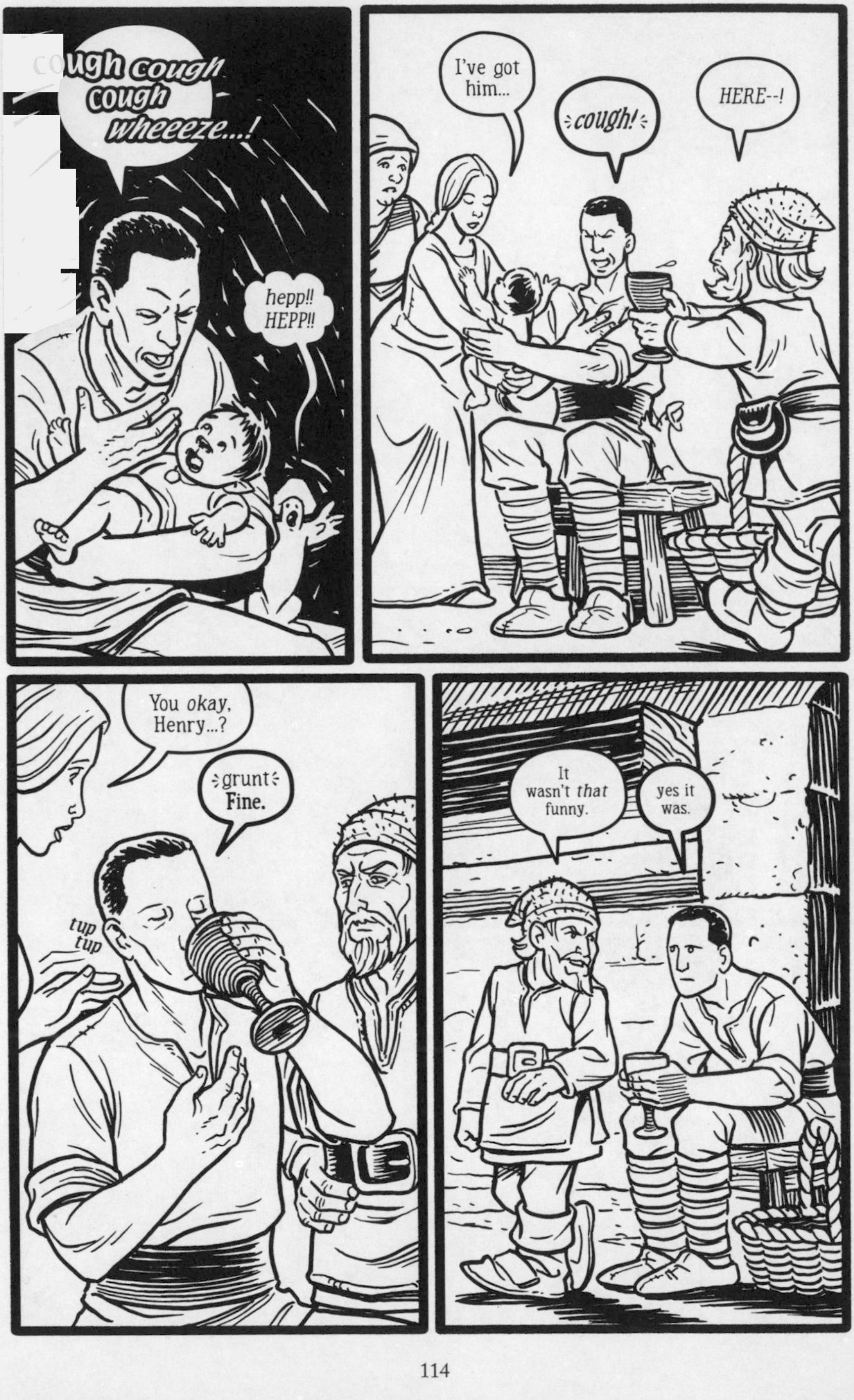
cough cough
cough
wheeeze...!
hepp!!
HEPP!!
I've got him...
cough!
HERE--!
You *okay*, Henry...?
grunt
Fine.
tup tup
It wasn't *that* funny.
yes it was.

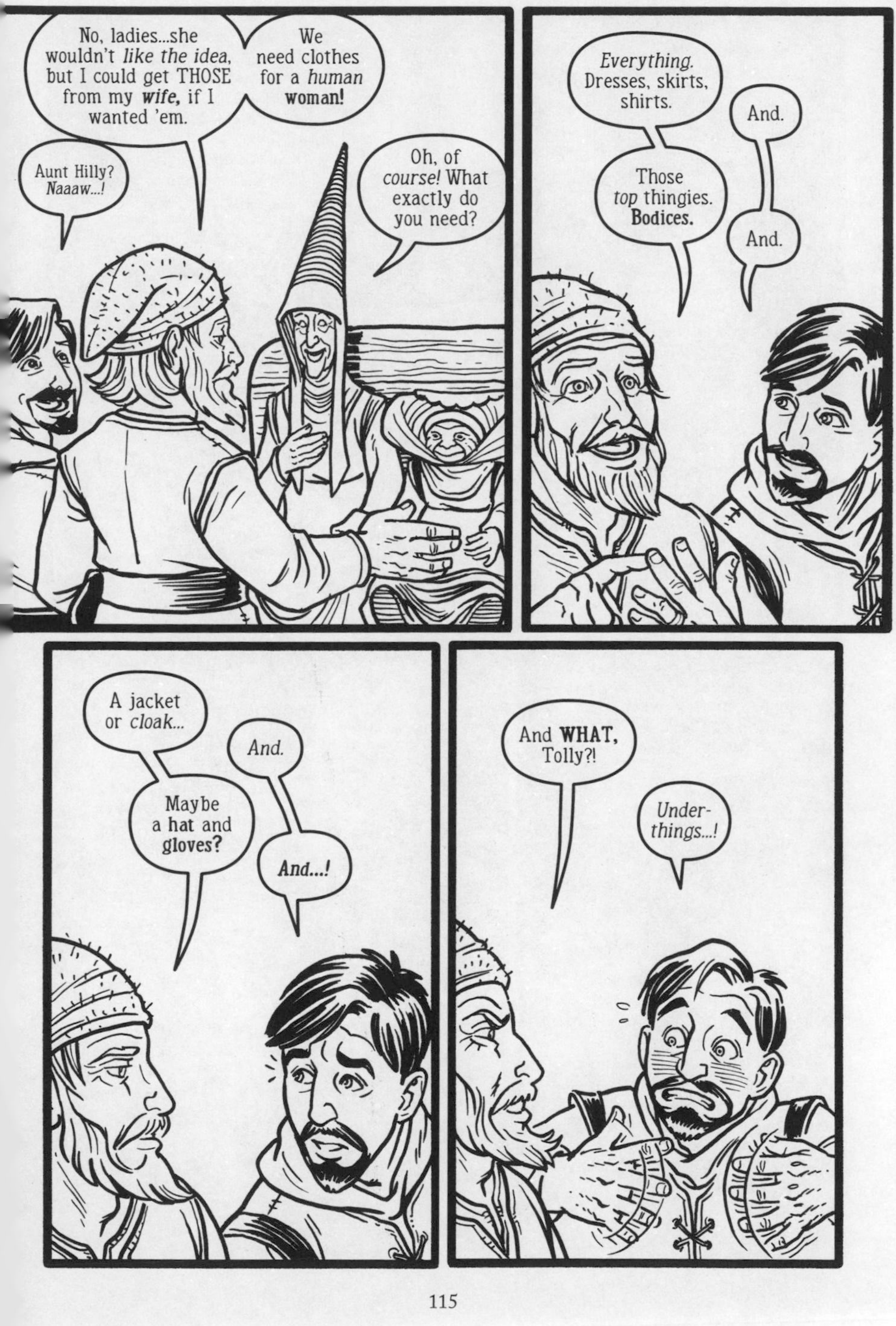
No, ladies...she wouldn't *like the idea*, but I could get THOSE from my ***wife***, if I wanted 'em.
We need clothes for a *human* **woman!**
Aunt Hilly? *Naaaw...!*
Oh, of *course!* What exactly do you need?
Everything. Dresses, skirts, shirts.
And.
Those *top* thingies. **Bodices.**
And.
A jacket or *cloak...*
And.
Maybe a **hat** and **gloves?**
And...!
And **WHAT,** Tolly?!
Under-things...!

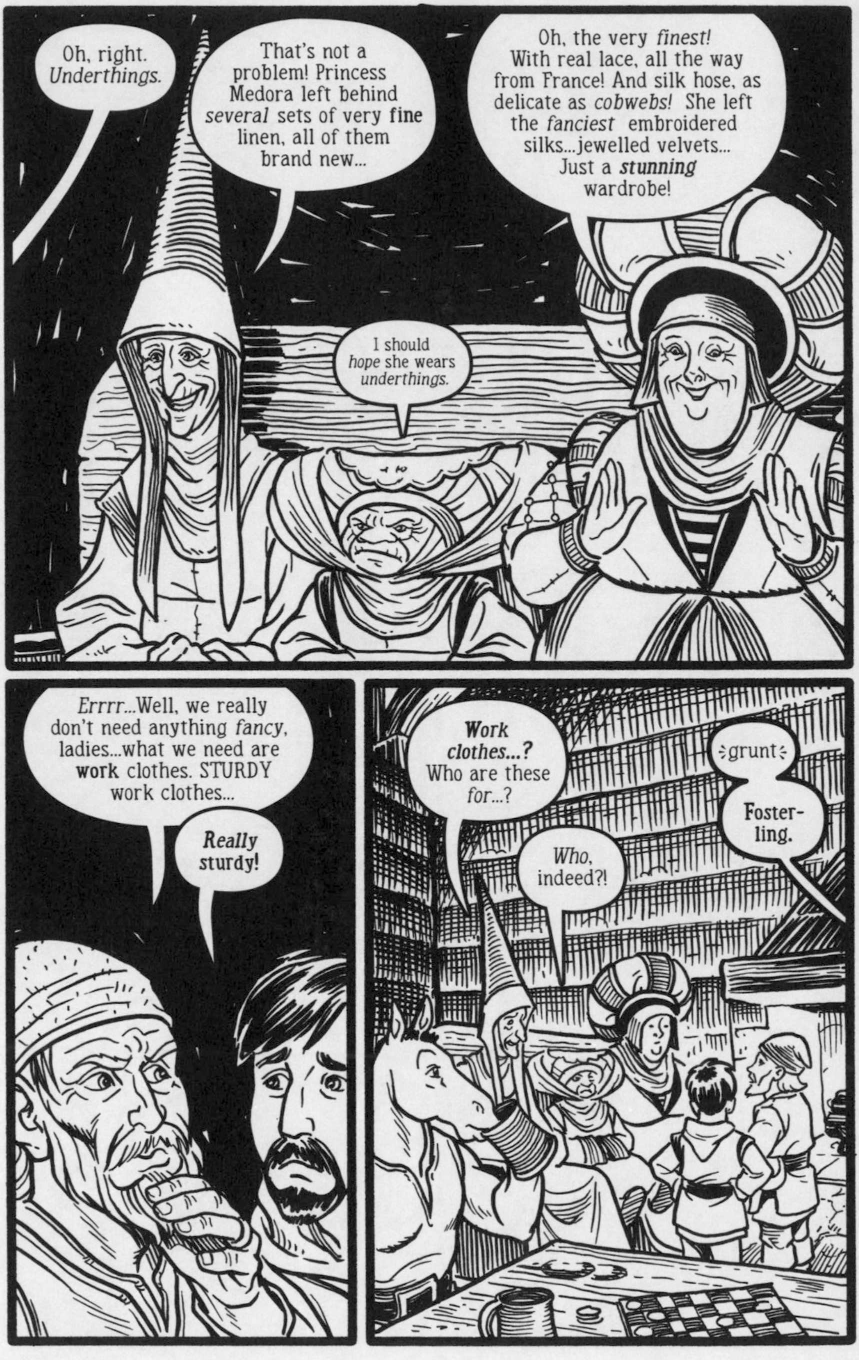
Oh, right. *Underthings.*
That's not a problem! Princess Medora left behind *several* sets of very **fine** linen, all of them brand new...
Oh, the very *finest!* With real lace, all the way from France! And silk hose, as delicate as *cobwebs!* She left the *fanciest* embroidered silks...jewelled velvets... Just a ***stunning*** wardrobe!
I should *hope* she wears *underthings.*
Errrr...Well, we really don't need anything *fancy*, ladies...what we need are **work** clothes. STURDY work clothes...
***Really* sturdy!**
Work clothes...? Who are these *for*...?
Who, indeed?!
grunt
Foster-ling.

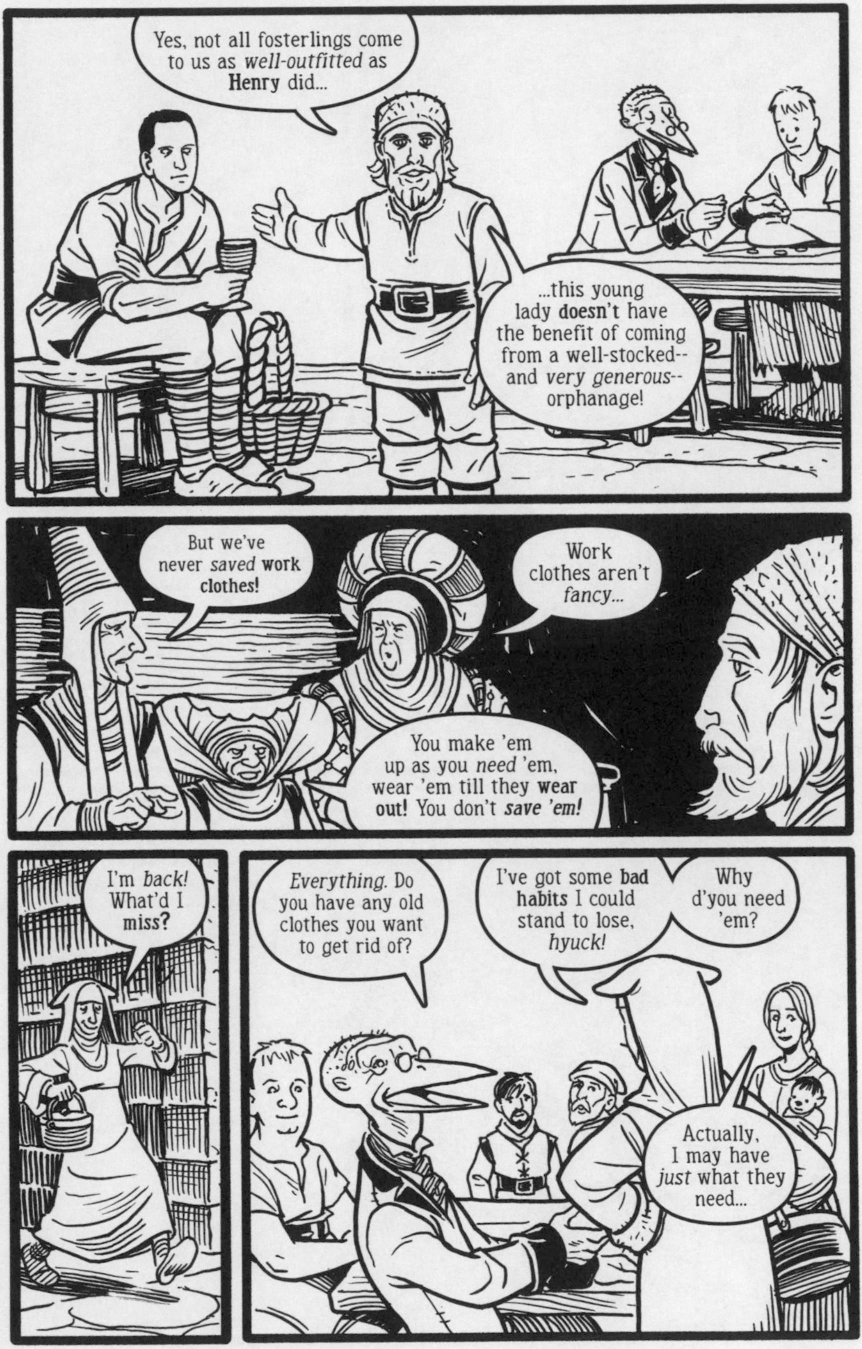
Yes, not all fosterlings come to us as *well-outfitted* as **Henry** did...
...this young lady **doesn't** have the benefit of coming from a well-stocked-- and *very generous*-- orphanage!
But we've never *saved* **work clothes!**
Work clothes aren't *fancy...*
You make 'em up as you *need* 'em, wear 'em till they **wear out!** You don't *save 'em!*
I'm *back!* What'd I **miss?**
Everything. Do you have any old clothes you want to get rid of?
I've got some **bad habits** I could stand to lose, *hyuck!*
Why d'you need 'em?
Actually, I may have *just* what they need...

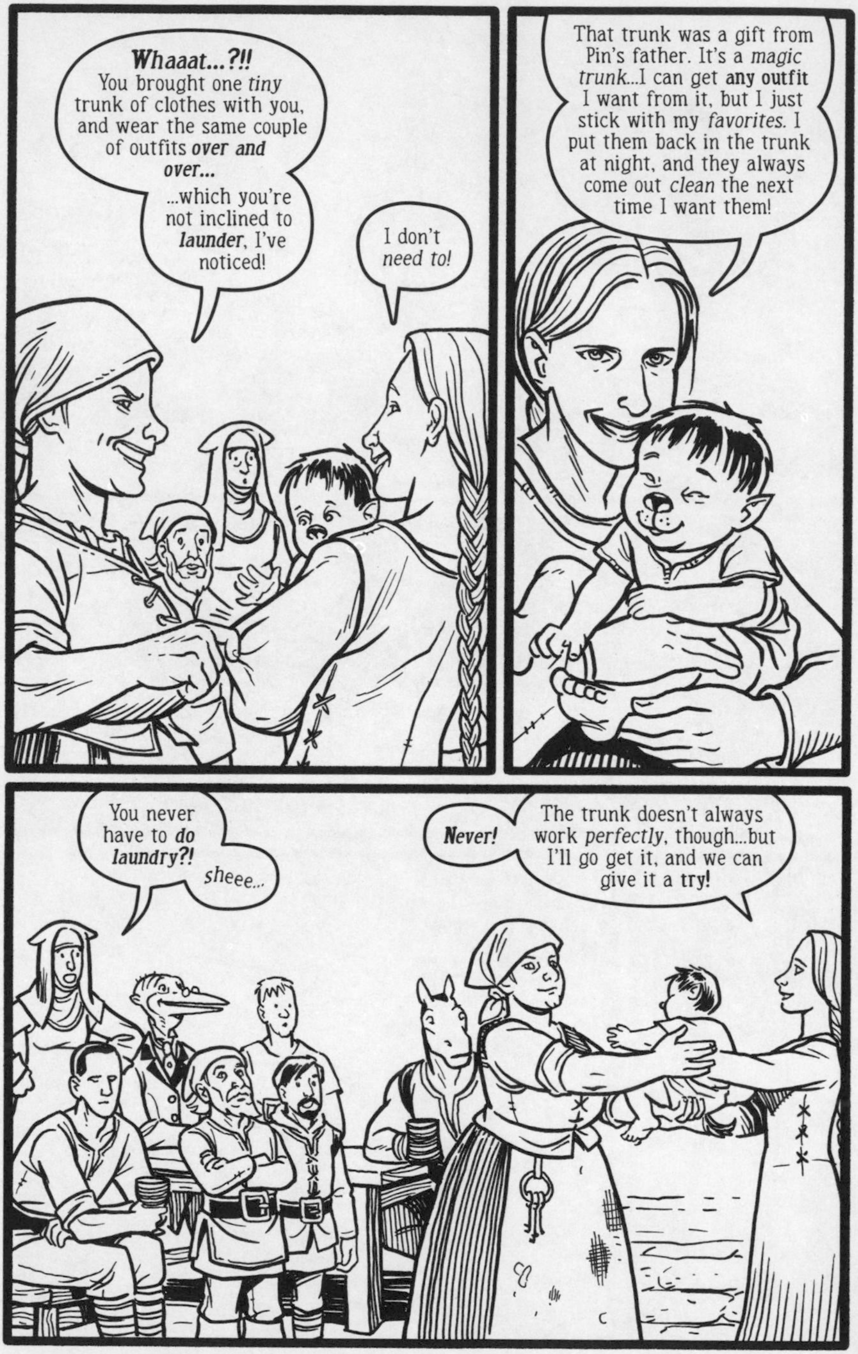
Whaaat...?!! You brought one tiny trunk of clothes with you, and wear the same couple of outfits over and over...
...which you're not inclined to launder, I've noticed!
I don't need to!
That trunk was a gift from Pin's father. It's a magic trunk...I can get any outfit I want from it, but I just stick with my favorites. I put them back in the trunk at night, and they always come out clean the next time I want them!
You never have to do laundry?!
sheee...
Never!
The trunk doesn't always work perfectly, though...but I'll go get it, and we can give it a try!

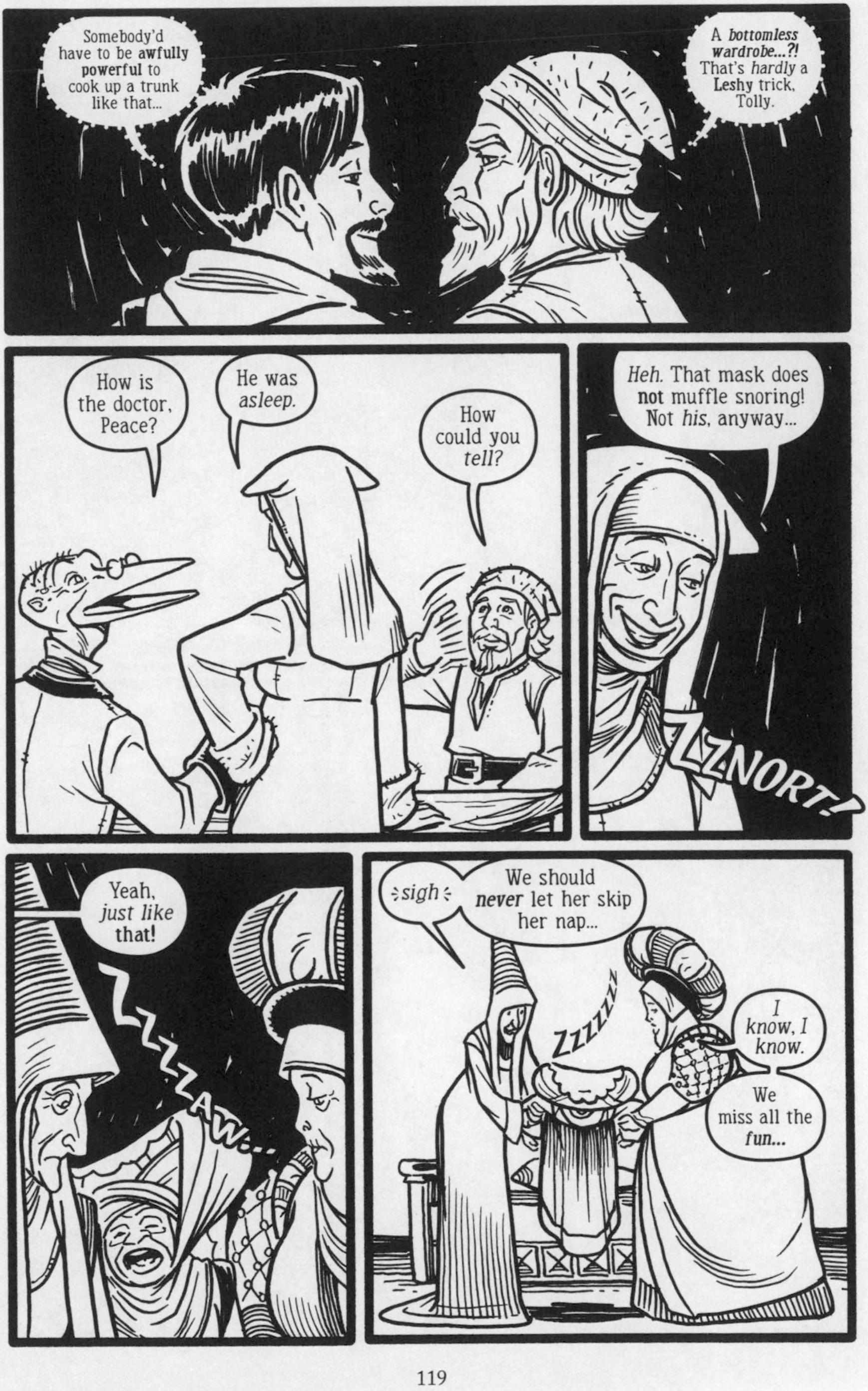
Somebody'd have to be **awfully powerful** to cook up a trunk like that...
A ***bottomless wardrobe...?!*** That's *hardly* a **Leshy** trick, Tolly.
How is the doctor, Peace?
He was *asleep.*
How could you *tell?*
Heh. That mask does **not** muffle snoring! Not *his*, anyway...
ZZNORT!
Yeah, *just like* **that!**
ZZZZZAW...
sigh
We should ***never*** let her skip her nap...
Zzzzzz
I know, I know.
We miss all the ***fun...***

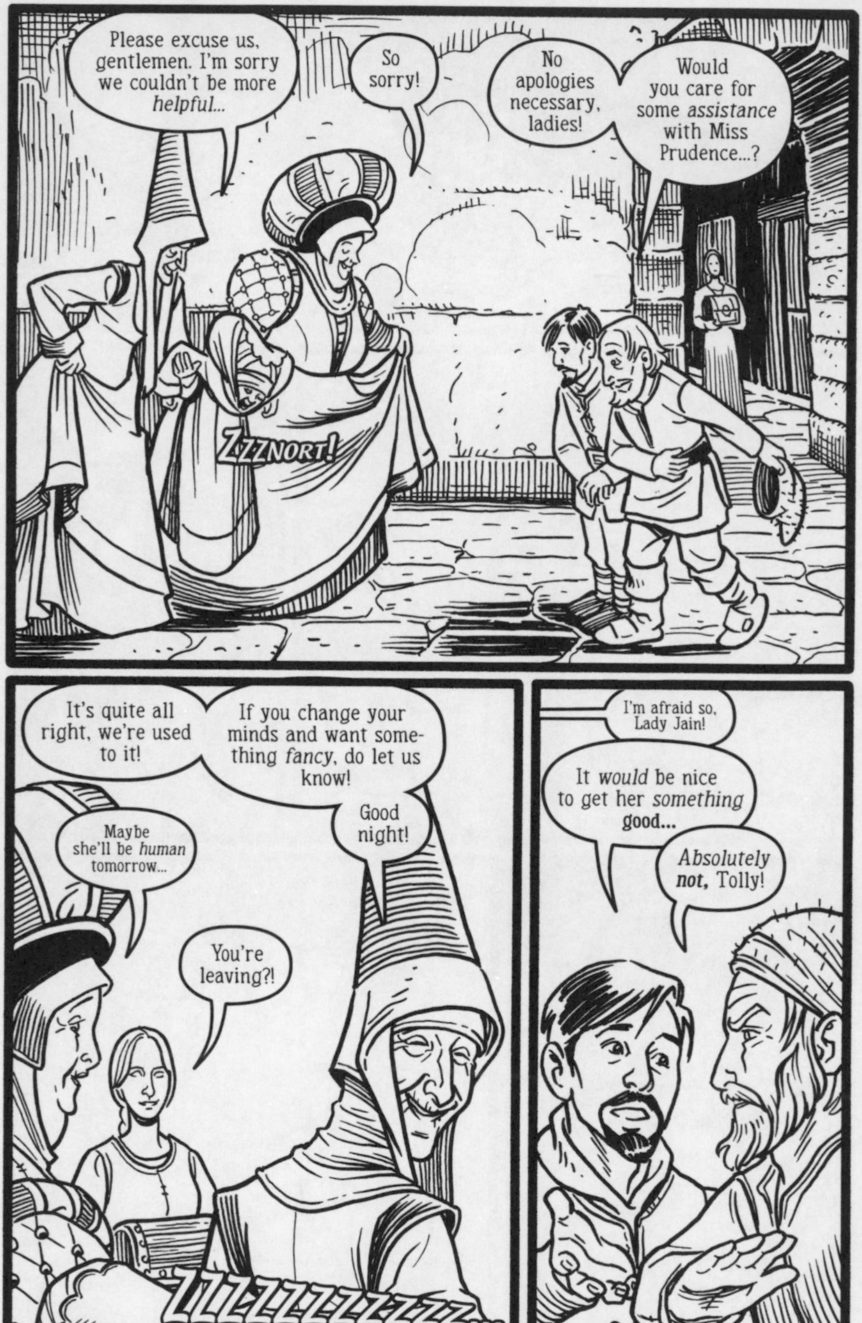
Please excuse us, gentlemen. I'm sorry we couldn't be more *helpful*...
So sorry!
No apologies necessary, ladies!
Would you care for some *assistance* with Miss Prudence...?
ZZZNORT!
It's quite all right, we're used to it!
If you change your minds and want something *fancy*, do let us know!
Good night!
Maybe she'll be *human* tomorrow...
You're leaving?!
ZZZZZZZZZZZZZZ...
I'm afraid so, Lady Jain!
It *would* be nice to get her *something* **good...**
Absolutely ***not,*** Tolly!

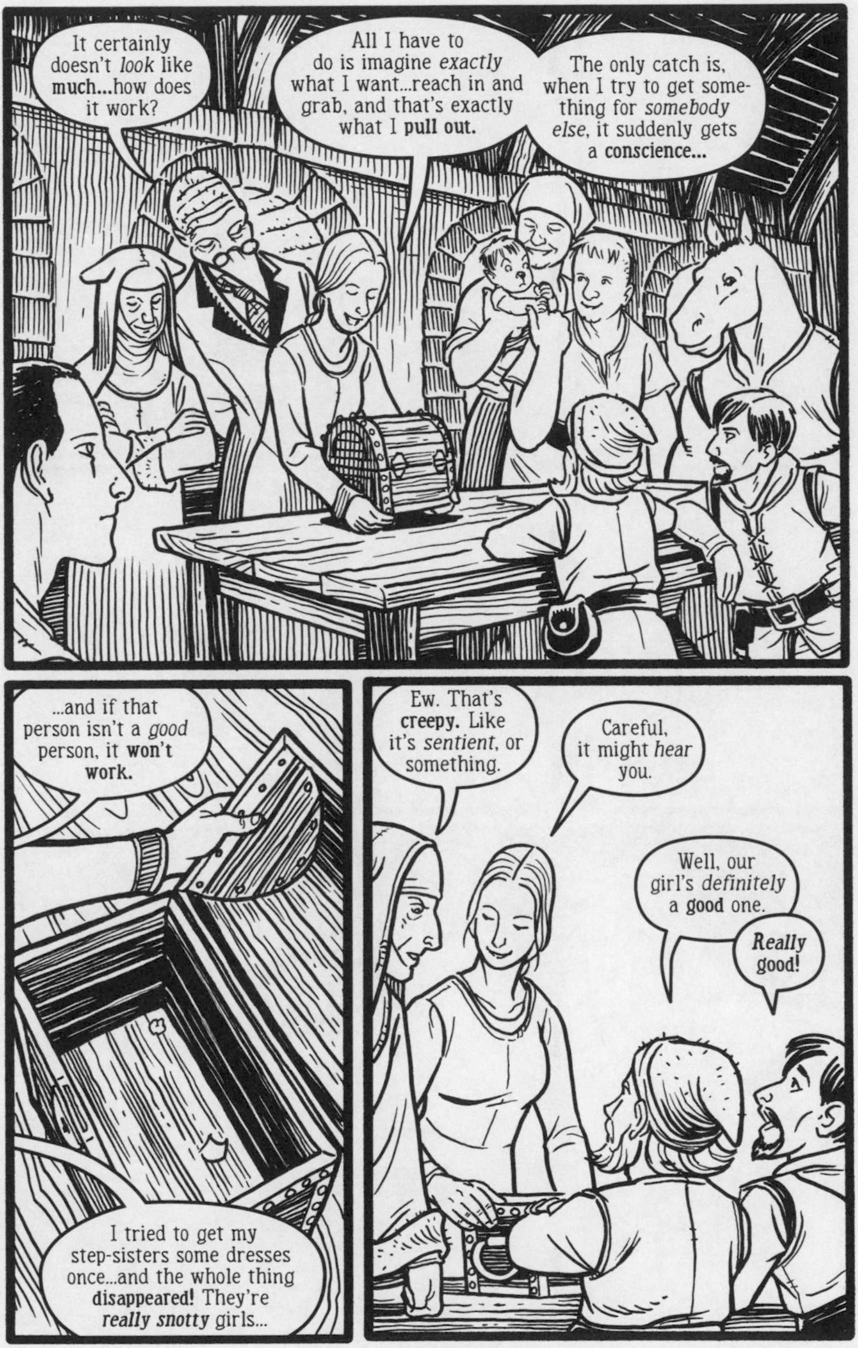
It certainly doesn't *look* like **much...**how does it work?
All I have to do is imagine *exactly* what I want...reach in and grab, and that's exactly what I **pull out.**
The only catch is, when I try to get something for *somebody else*, it suddenly gets a **conscience...**
...and if that person isn't a *good* person, it **won't work.**
I tried to get my step-sisters some dresses once...and the whole thing **disappeared!** They're ***really snotty*** girls...
Ew. That's **creepy.** Like it's *sentient*, or something.
Careful, it might *hear* you.
Well, our girl's *definitely* a **good** one.
***Really* good!**

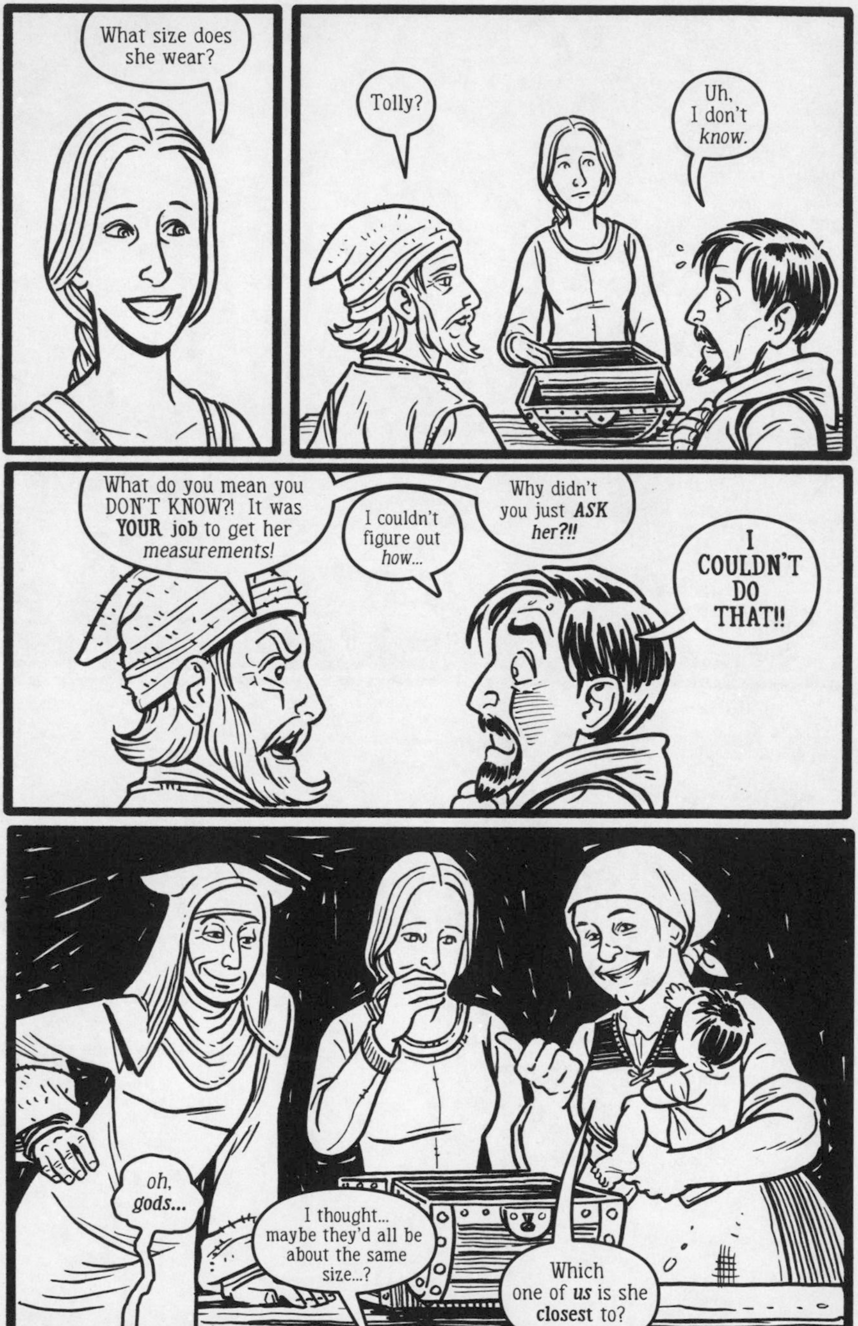
What size does she wear?
Tolly?
Uh, I don't *know.*
What do you mean you DON'T KNOW?! It was **YOUR job** to get her *measurements!*
I couldn't figure out *how...*
Why didn't you just ***ASK her?!!***
I COULDN'T DO THAT!!
oh, ***gods...***
I thought... maybe they'd all be about the same size...?
Which one of **us** is she **closest** to?

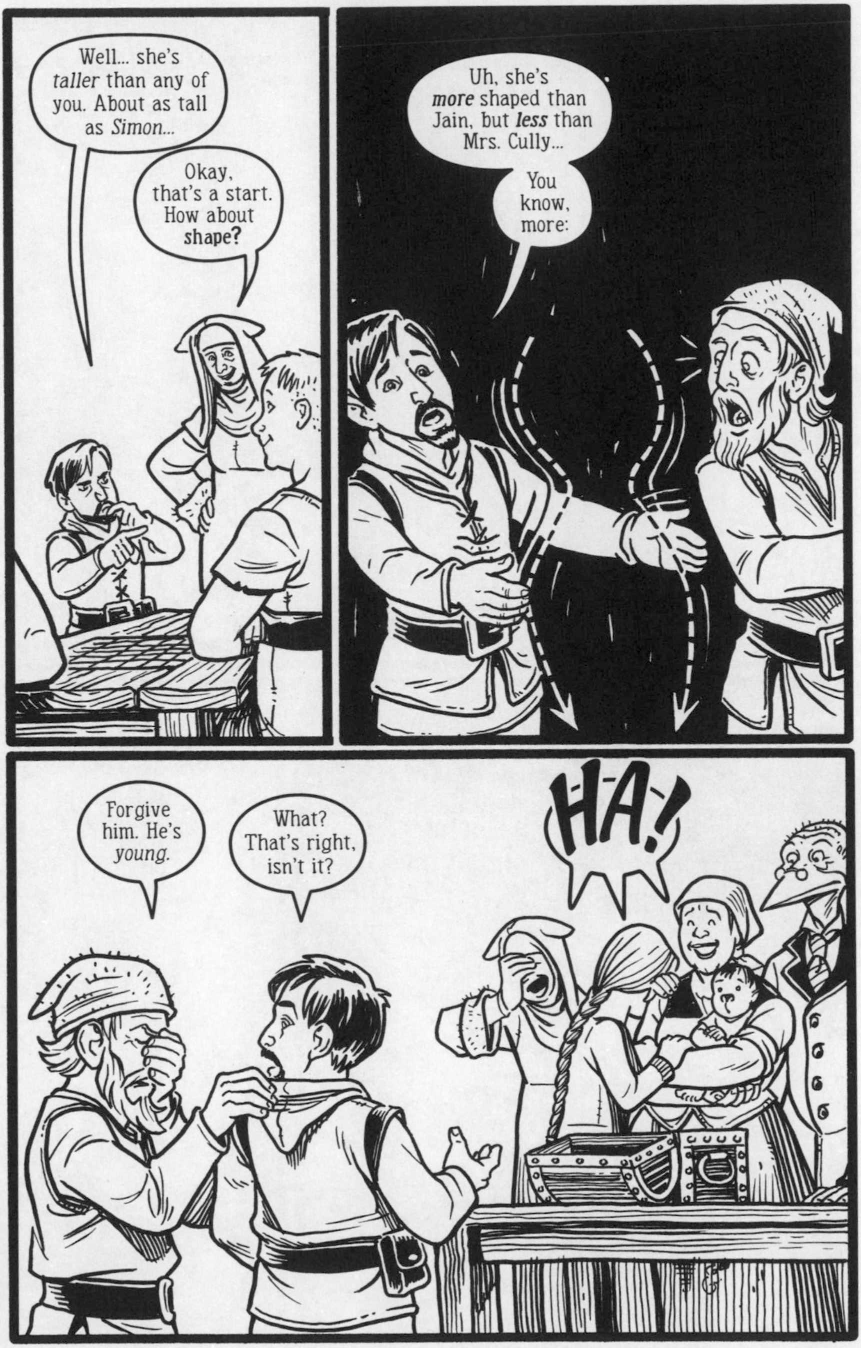
Well... she's *taller* than any of you. About as tall as *Simon*...
Okay, that's a start. How about **shape?**
Uh, she's ***more*** shaped than Jain, but ***less*** than Mrs. Cully...
You know, more:
Forgive him. He's *young.*
What? That's right, isn't it?
HA!

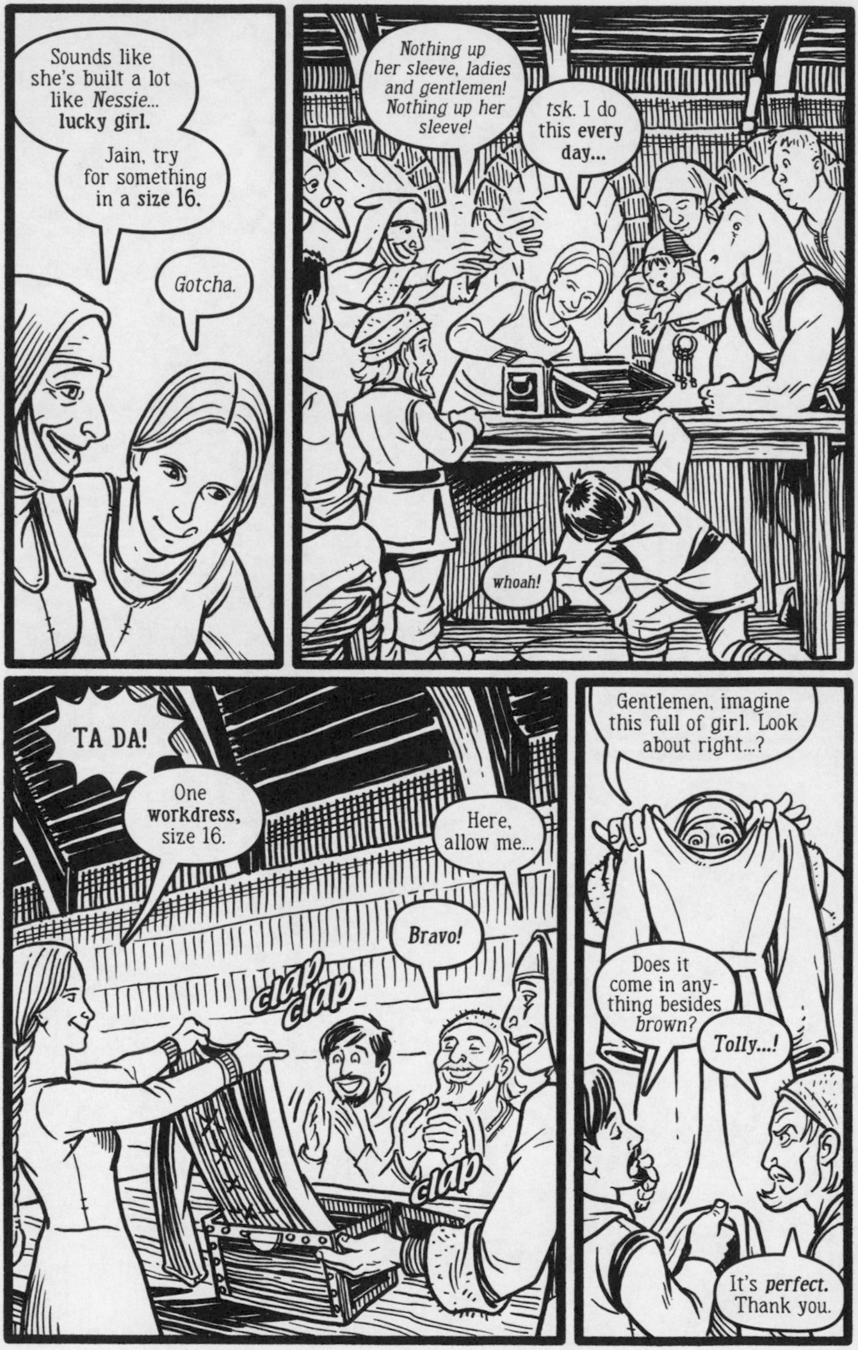
Sounds like she's built a lot like *Nessie*... **lucky girl.**
Jain, try for something in a **size 16.**
Gotcha.
Nothing up her sleeve, ladies and gentlemen! Nothing up her sleeve!
tsk. I do this **every day...**
!
whoah!
TA DA!
One **workdress,** size 16.
Here, allow me...
Bravo!
clap clap
clap
Gentlemen, imagine this full of girl. Look about right...?
Does it come in any-thing besides *brown?*
Tolly...!
It's *perfect.* Thank you.

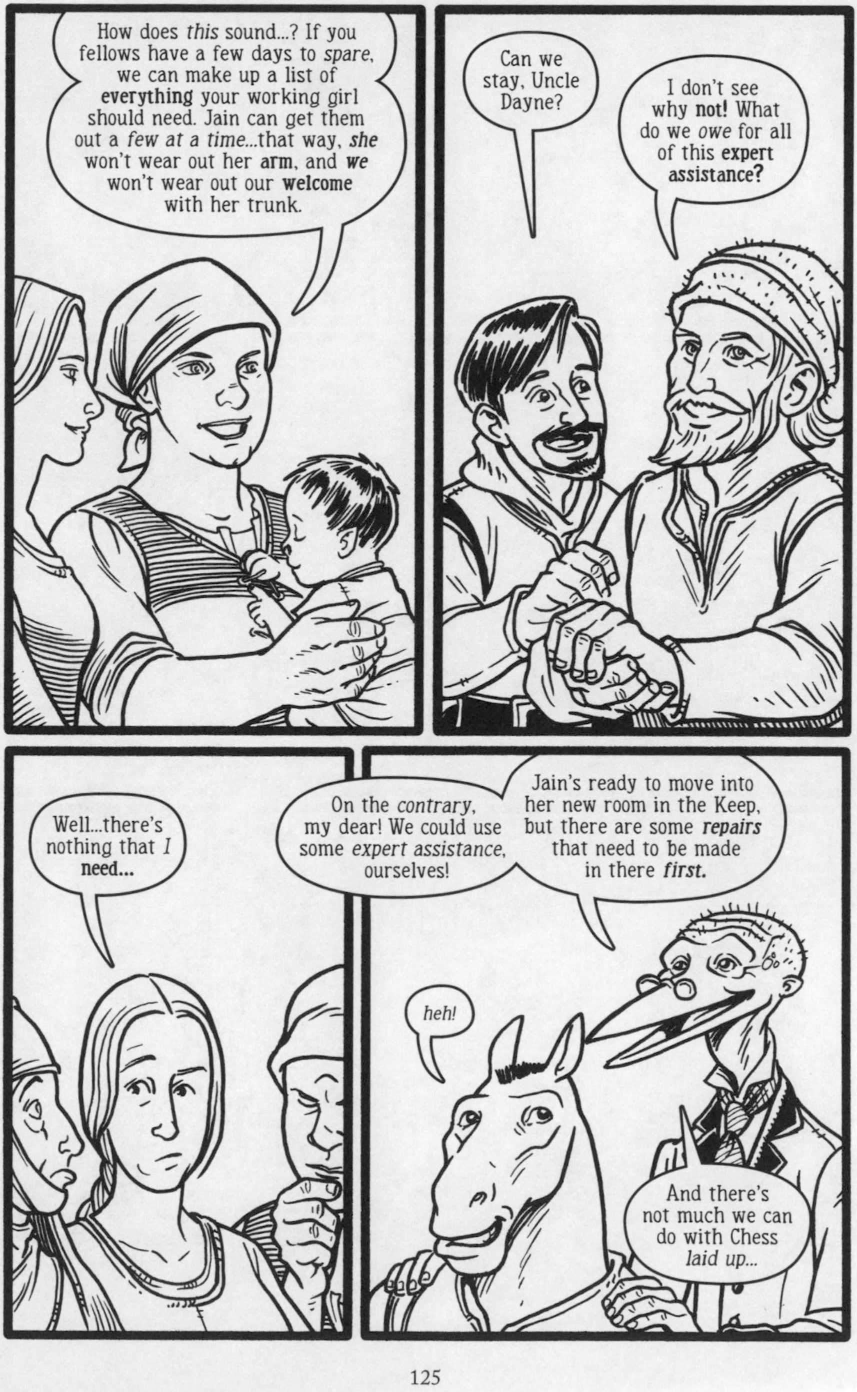
How does *this* sound...? If you fellows have a few days to *spare*, we can make up a list of **everything** your working girl should need. Jain can get them out a *few at a time*...that way, ***she*** won't wear out her **arm**, and ***we*** won't wear out our **welcome** with her trunk.
Can we stay, Uncle Dayne?
I don't see why **not!** What do we *owe* for all of this **expert assistance?**
Well...there's nothing that *I* **need...**
On the *contrary*, my dear! We could use some *expert assistance*, ourselves!
Jain's ready to move into her new room in the Keep, but there are some ***repairs*** that need to be made in there ***first.***
heh!
And there's not much we can do with Chess *laid up*...

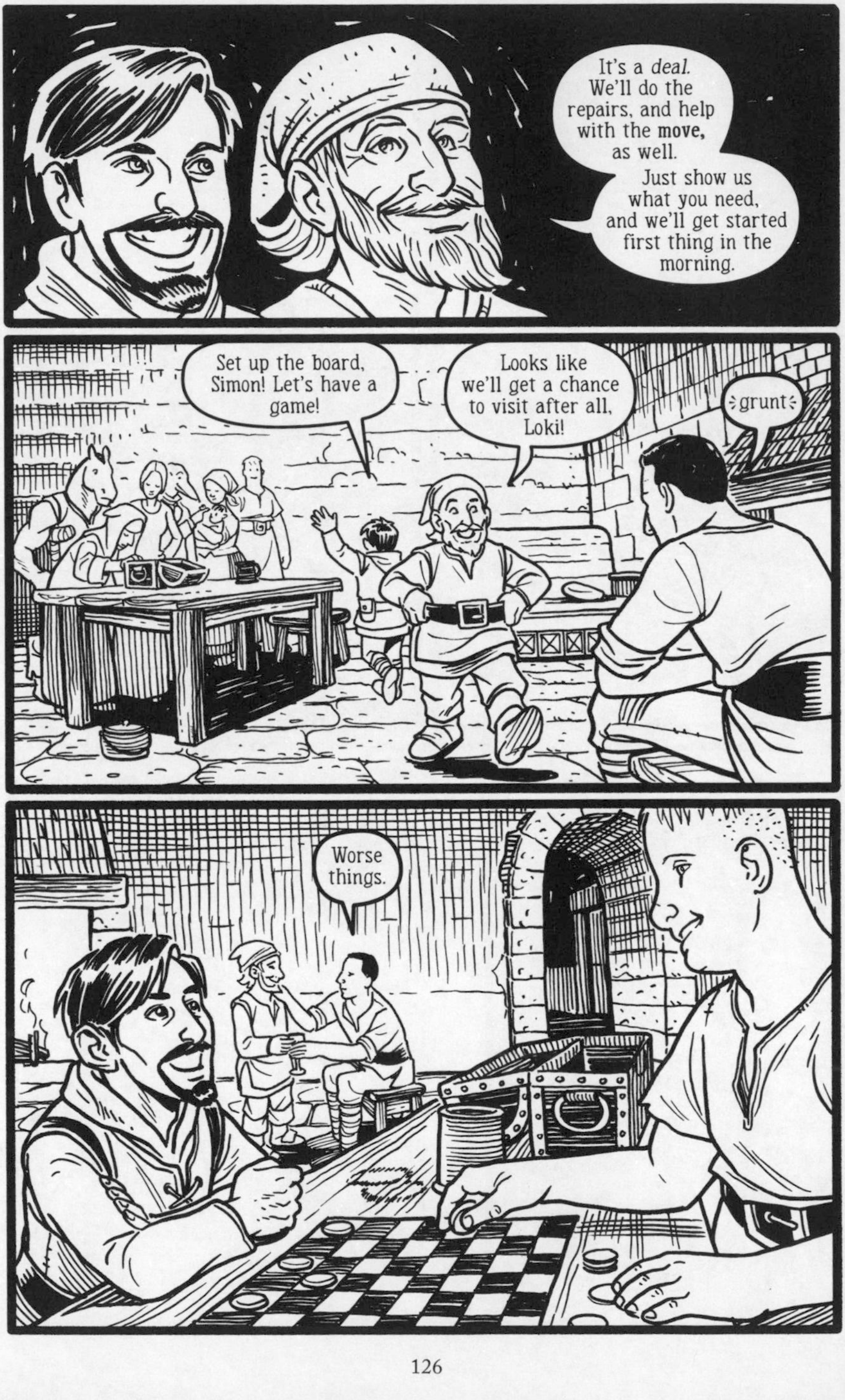
It's a *deal.* We'll do the repairs, and help with the **move,** as well.
Just show us what you need, and we'll get started first thing in the morning.
Set up the board, Simon! Let's have a game!
Looks like we'll get a chance to visit after all, Loki!
grunt
Worse things.

Chapter 6.

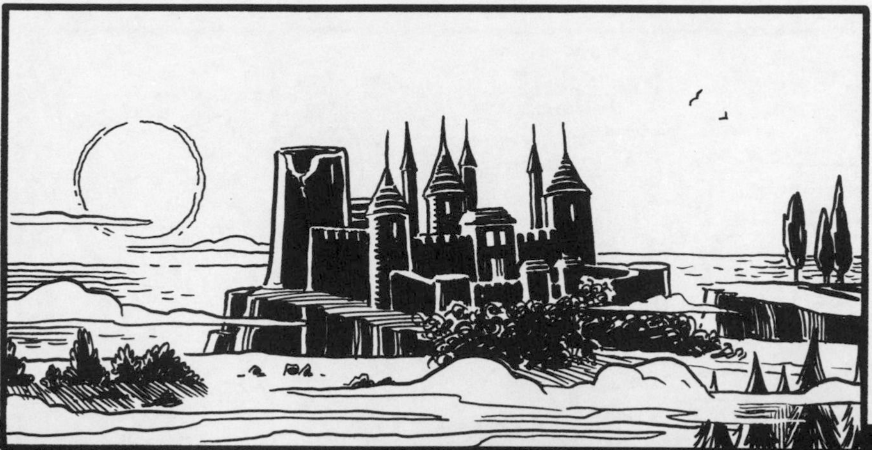

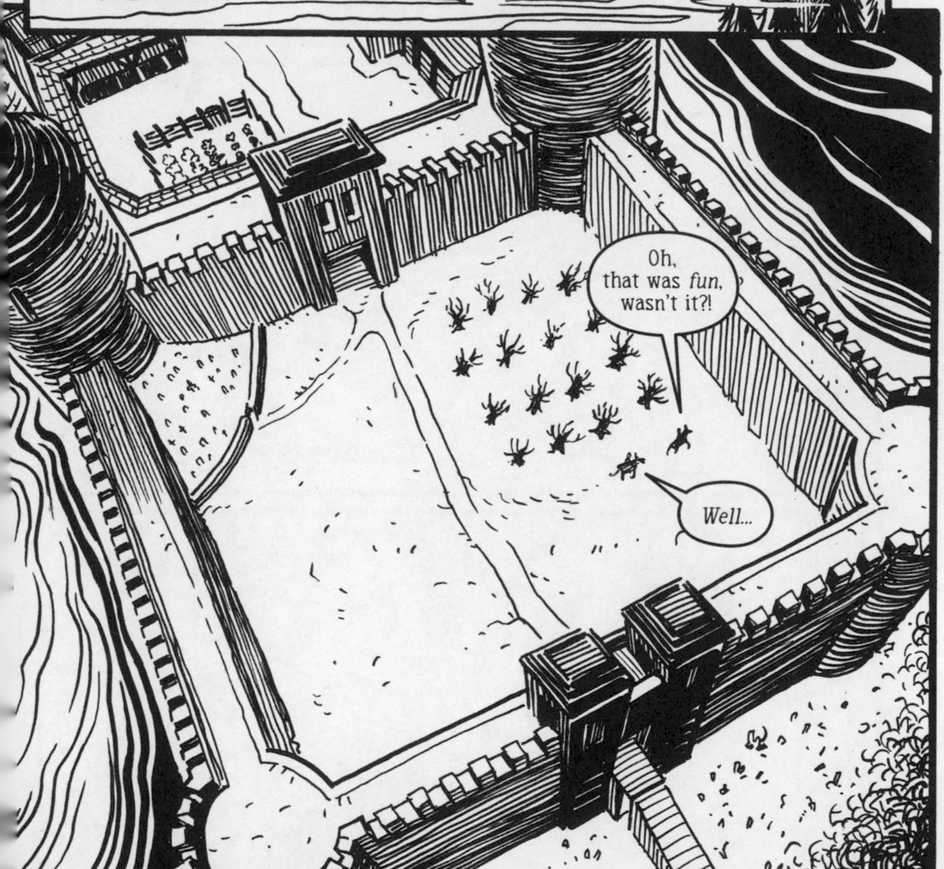
Oh, that was *fun*, wasn't it?!
Well...

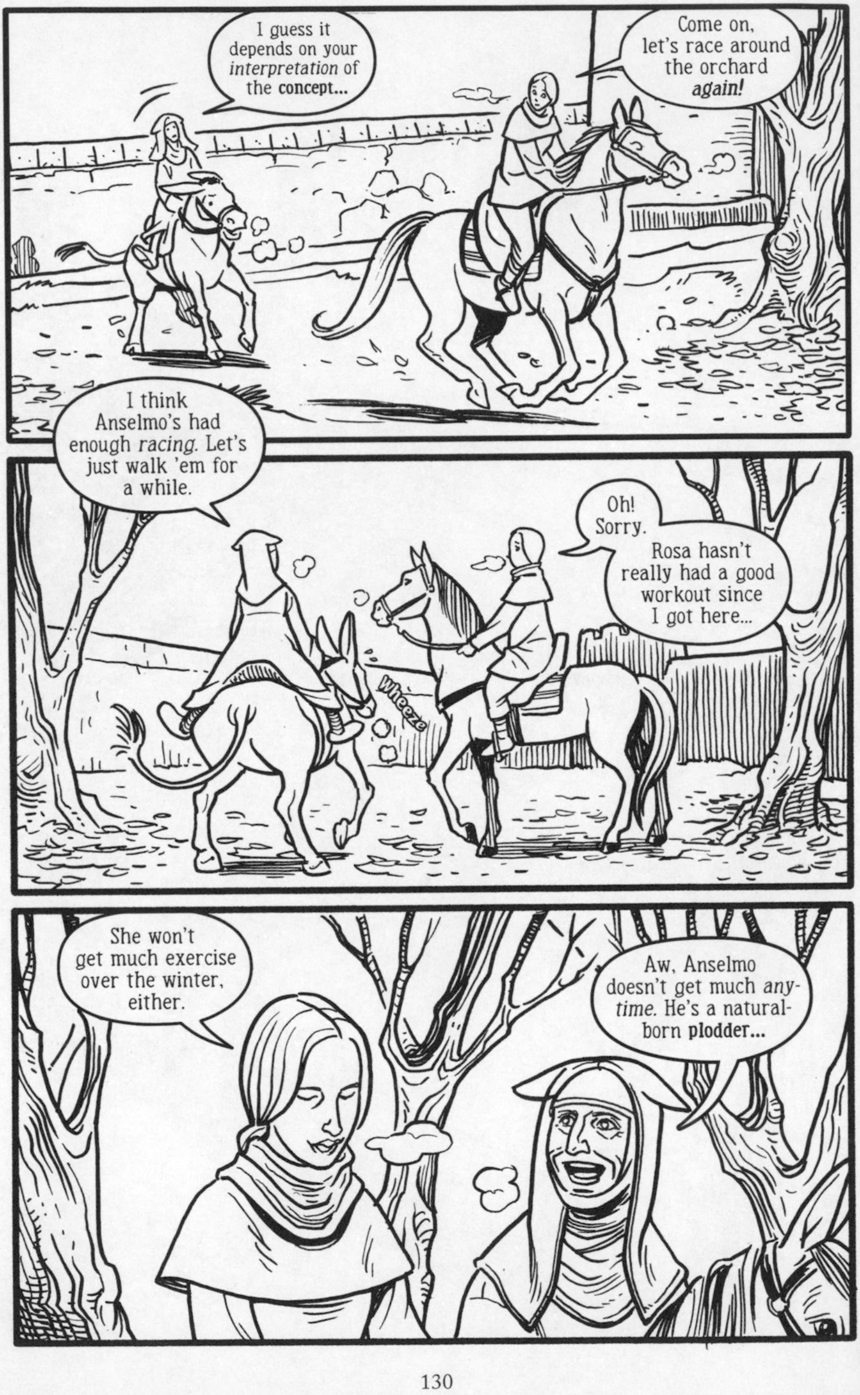
I guess it depends on your *interpretation* of the **concept...**
Come on, let's race around the orchard ***again!***
I think Anselmo's had enough *racing.* Let's just walk 'em for a while.
Oh! Sorry.
Rosa hasn't really had a good workout since I got here...
Wheeze
She won't get much exercise over the winter, either.
Aw, Anselmo doesn't get much *any-time.* He's a natural-born **plodder...**

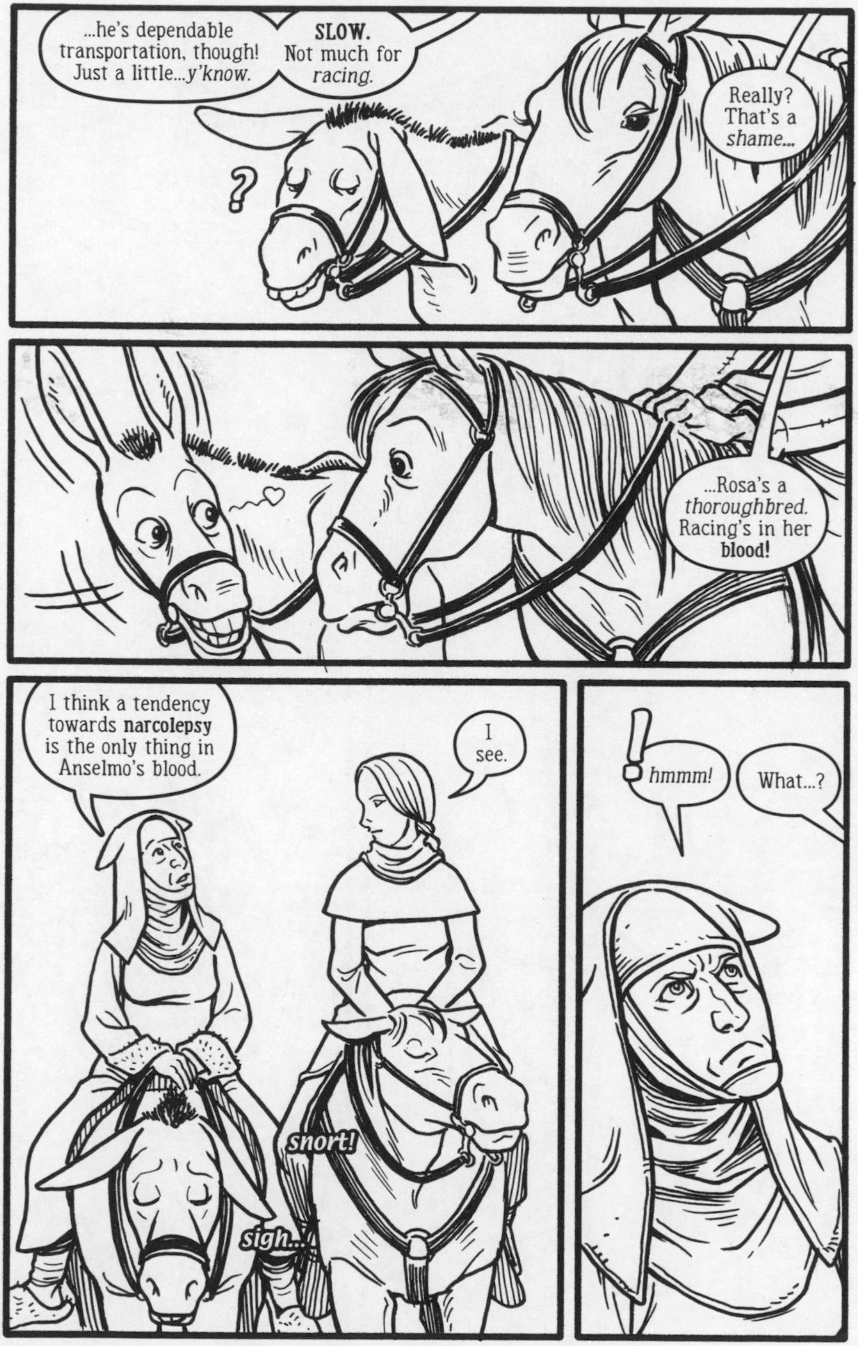
...he's dependable transportation, though! Just a little...*y'know.*
SLOW. Not much for *racing.*
Really? That's a *shame...*
...Rosa's a *thoroughbred.* Racing's in her **blood!**
I think a tendency towards **narcolepsy** is the only thing in Anselmo's blood.
I see.
snort!
sigh...
!
hmmm!
What...?

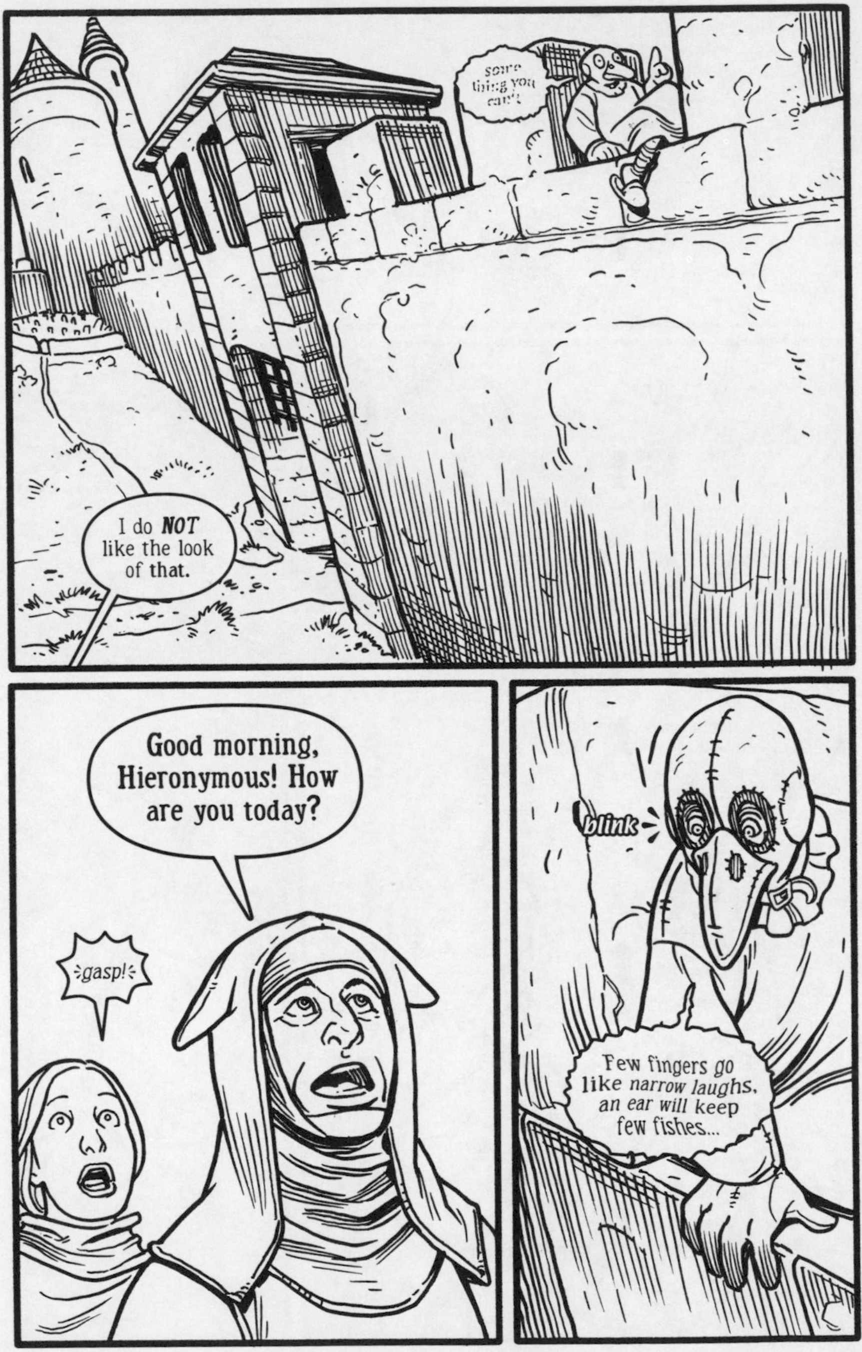
some thing you can't
I do ***NOT*** like the look of that.
Good morning, Hieronymous! How are you today?
gasp!
blink
Few fingers go like *narrow laughs*, *an ear will keep* few fishes...

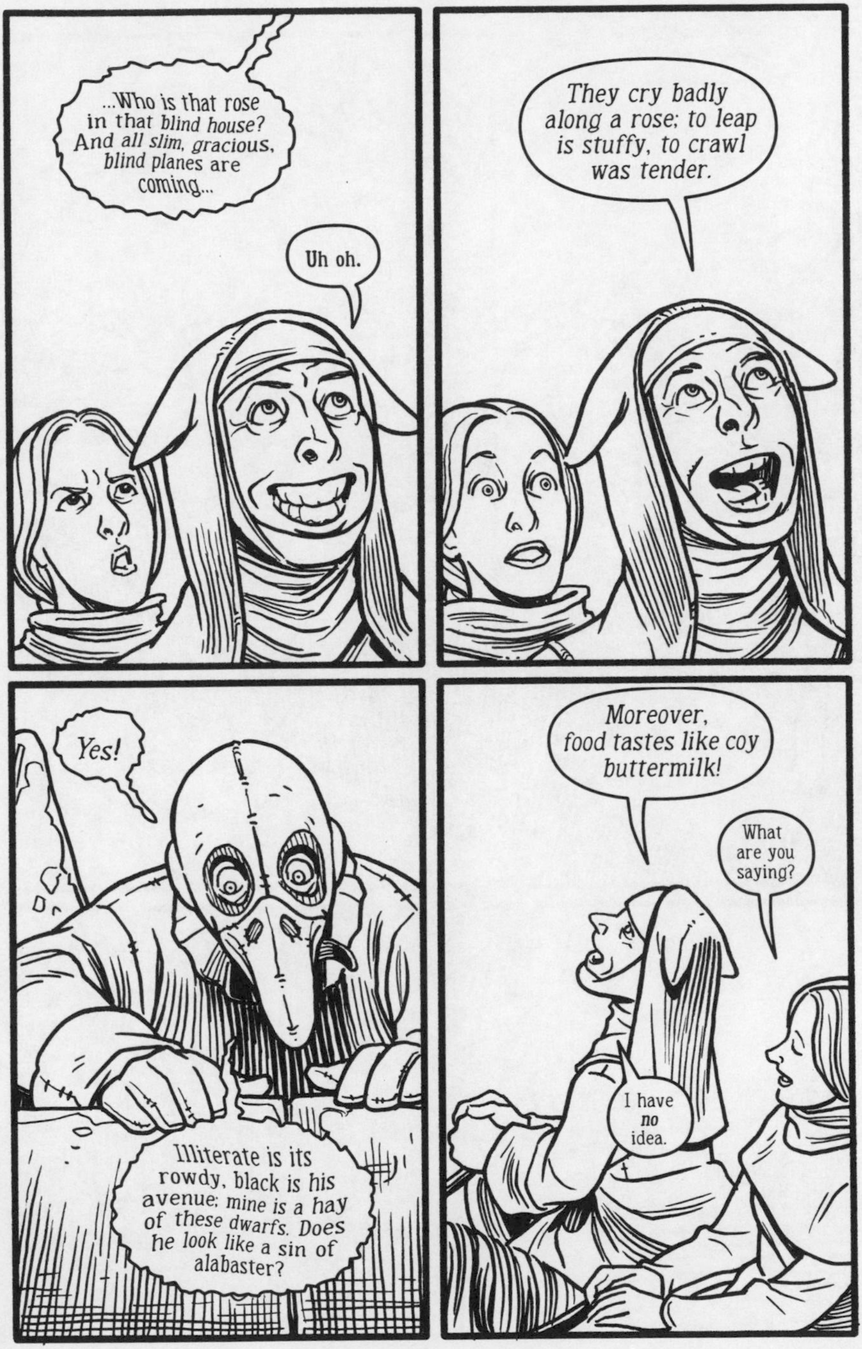
...Who is that rose in that blind house? And all slim, gracious, blind planes are coming...
Uh oh.
They cry badly along a rose; to leap is stuffy, to crawl was tender.
Yes!
Illiterate is its rowdy, black is his avenue: mine is a hay of these dwarfs. Does he look like a sin of alabaster?
Moreover, food tastes like coy buttermilk!
What are you saying?
I have no idea.

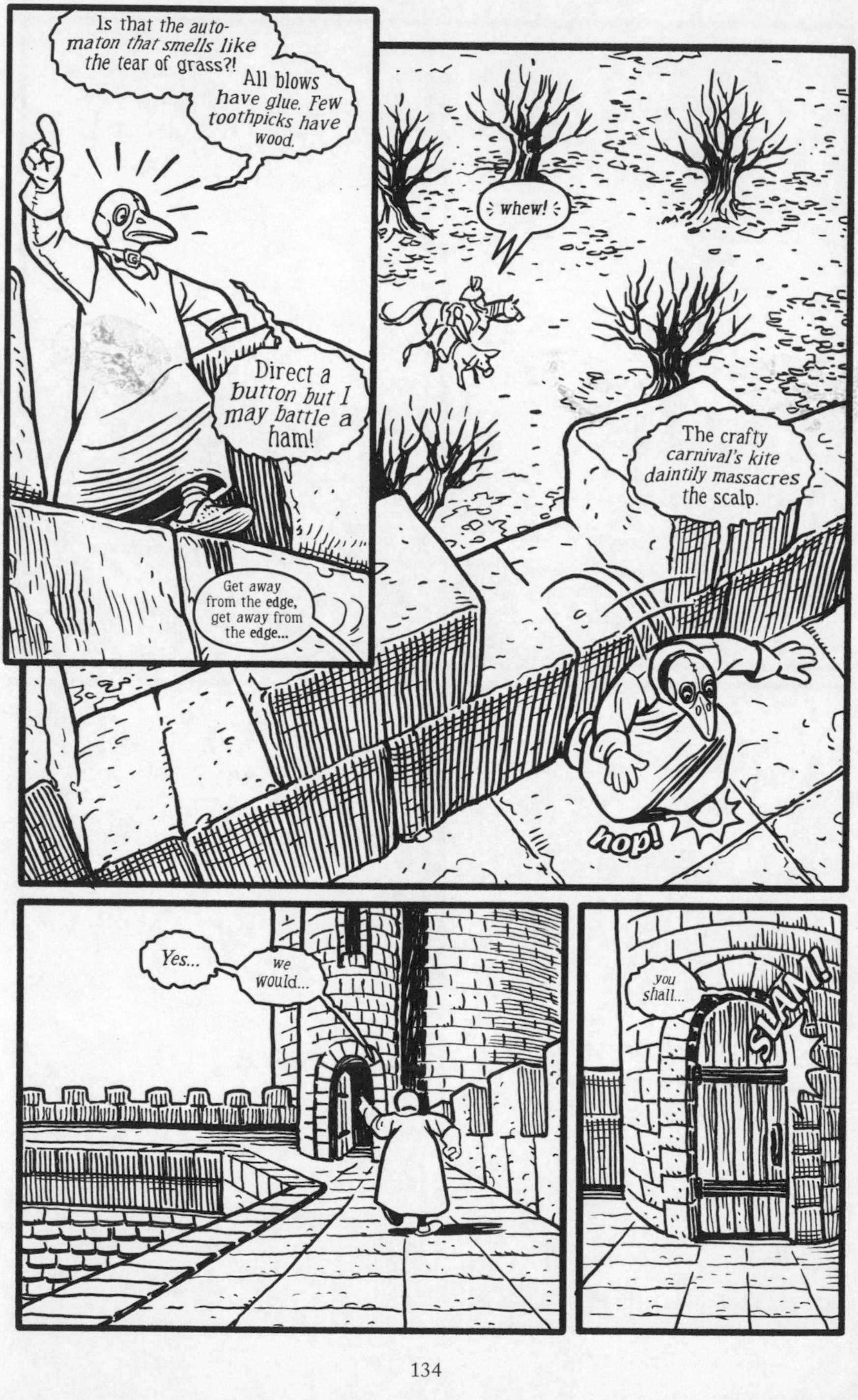
Is that the automaton that smells like the tear of grass?!
All blows have glue. Few toothpicks have wood.
Direct a button but I may battle a ham!
Get away from the edge, get away from the edge...
whew!
The crafty carnival's kite daintily massacres the scalp.
hop!
Yes...
we would...
you shall...
SLAM!

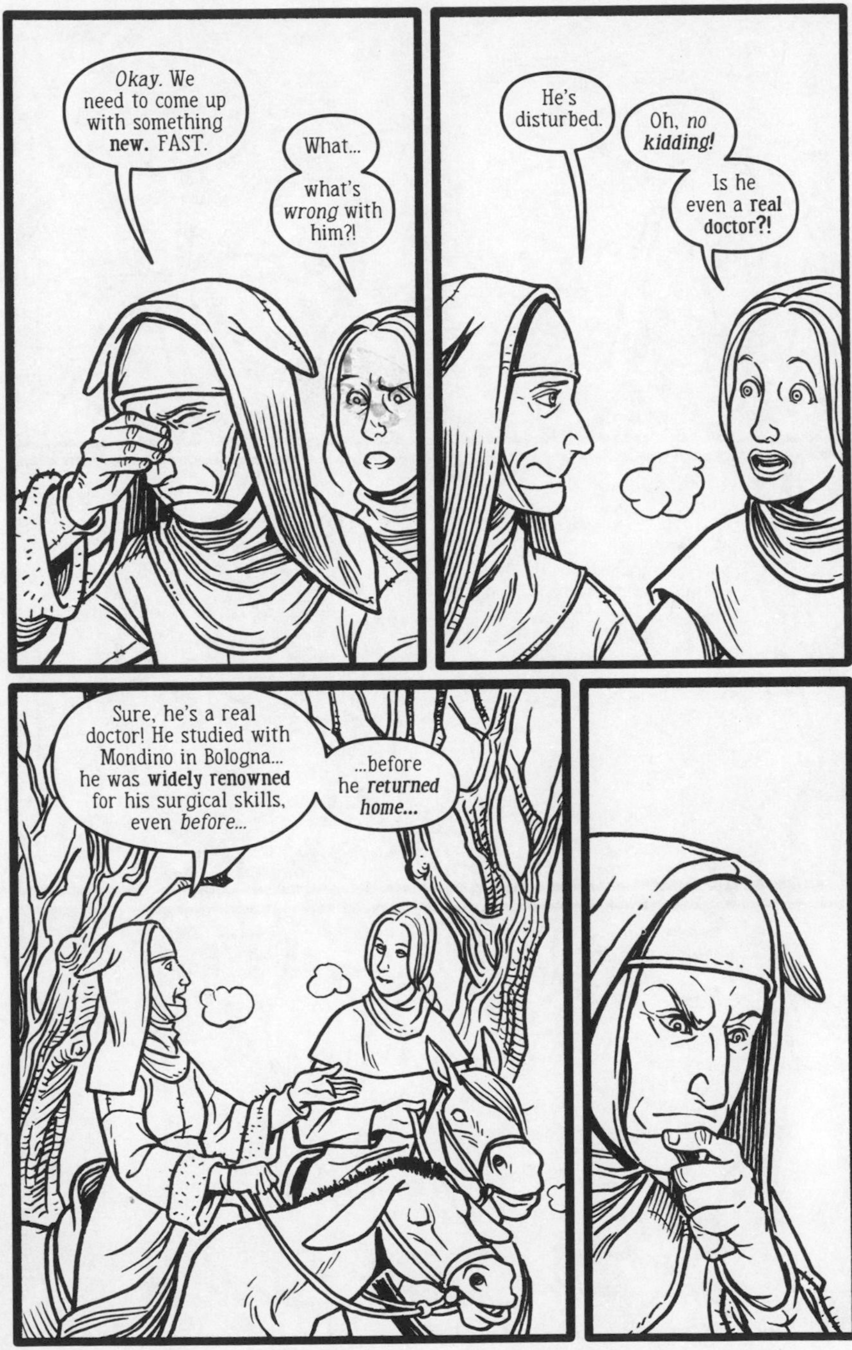
Okay. We need to come up with something **new.** FAST.
What... what's *wrong* with him?!
He's disturbed.
Oh, *no* ***kidding!***
Is he even a **real doctor?!**
Sure, he's a real doctor! He studied with Mondino in Bologna... he was **widely renowned** for his surgical skills, even *before*...
...before he ***returned home...***

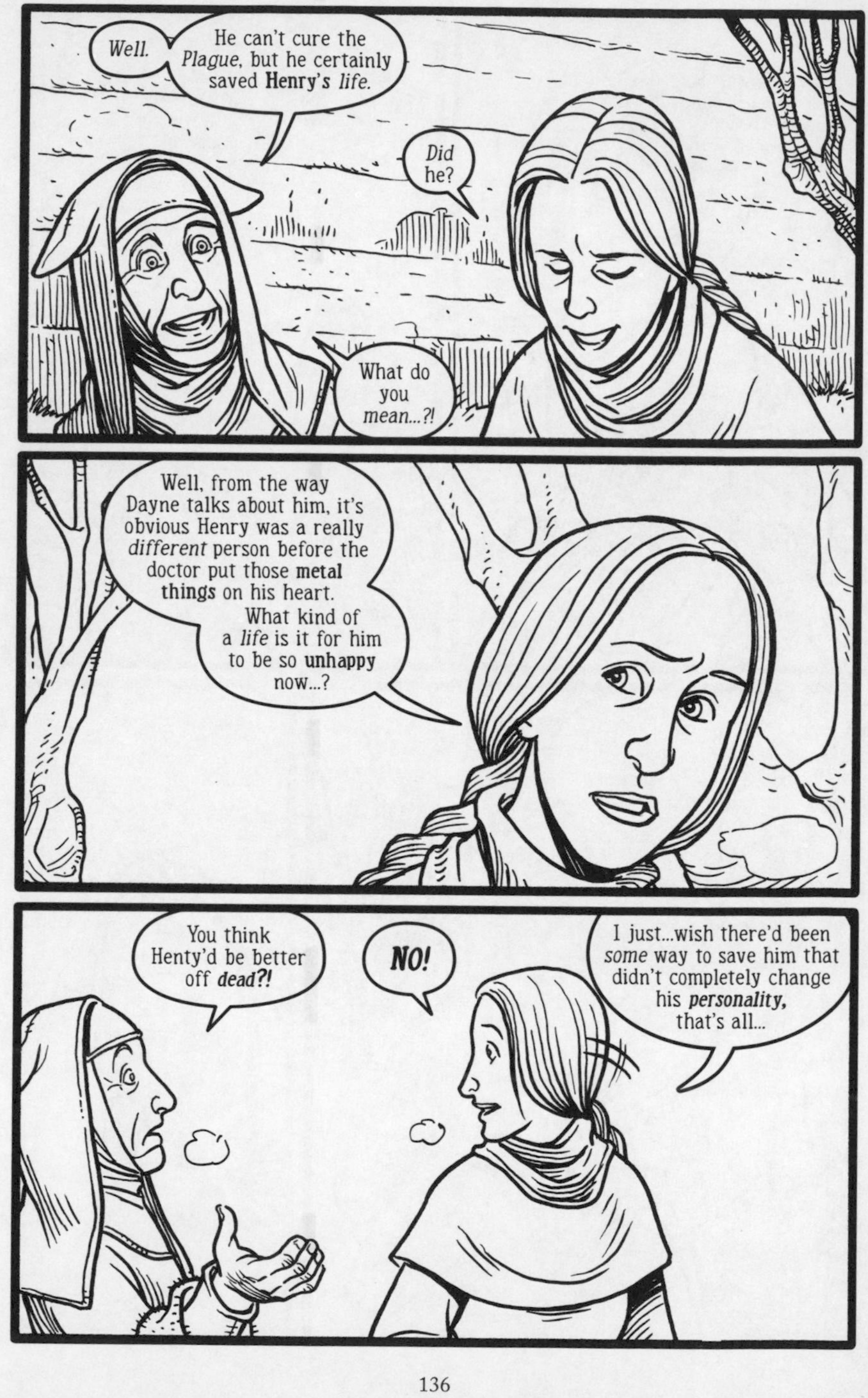
Well.
He can't cure the *Plague*, but he certainly saved **Henry's** *life.*
Did he?
What do you *mean...?!*
Well, from the way Dayne talks about him, it's obvious Henry was a really *different* person before the doctor put those **metal things** on his heart.
What kind of a *life* is it for him to be so **unhappy** now...?
You think Henty'd be better off ***dead?!***
NO!
I just...wish there'd been *some* way to save him that didn't completely change his ***personality,*** that's all...

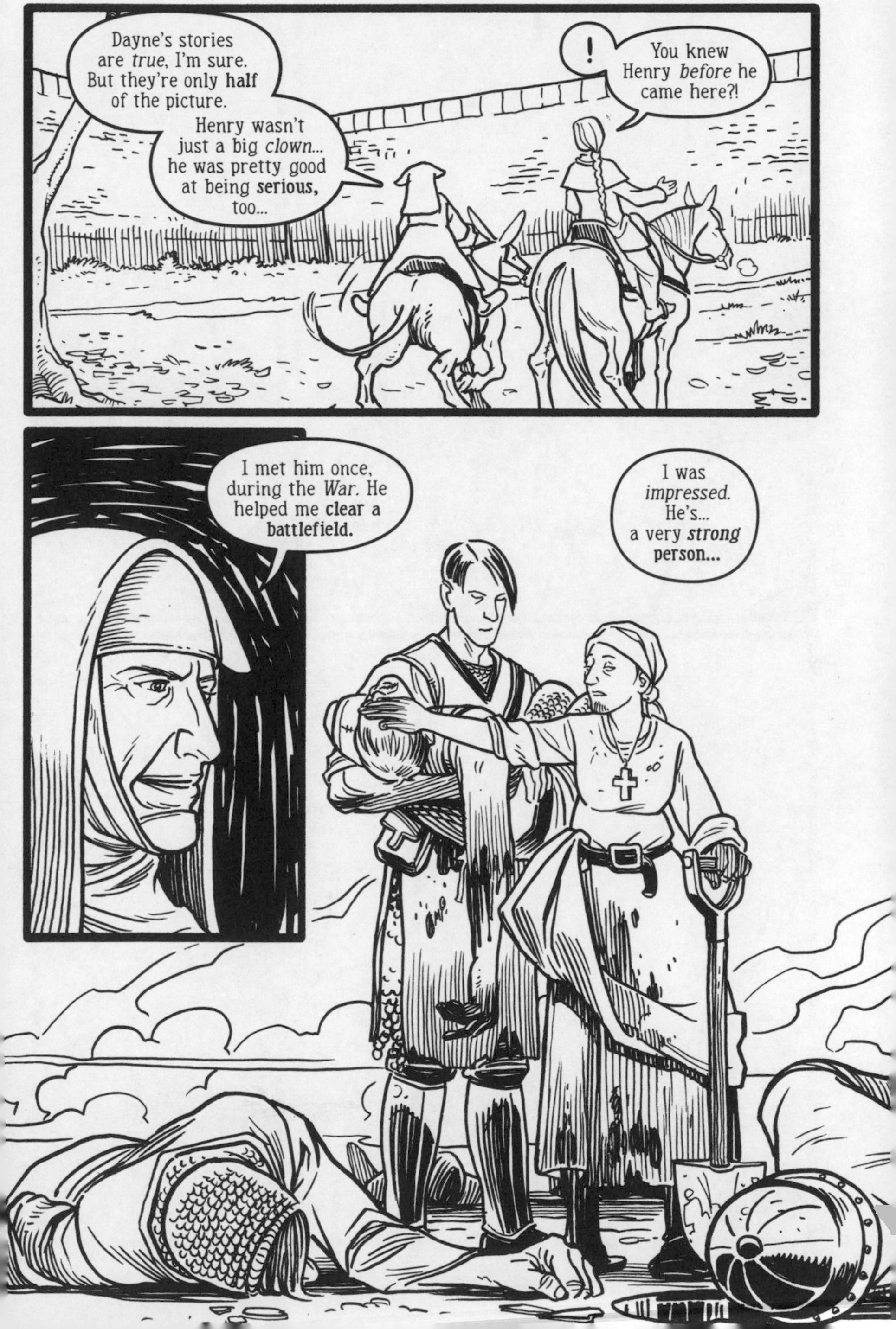
Dayne's stories are *true*, I'm sure. But they're only **half** of the picture.
Henry wasn't just a big *clown*... he was pretty good at being **serious,** too...
!
You knew Henry *before* he came here?!
I met him once, during the *War*. He helped me **clear a battlefield.**
I was *impressed*. He's... a very *strong* **person...**

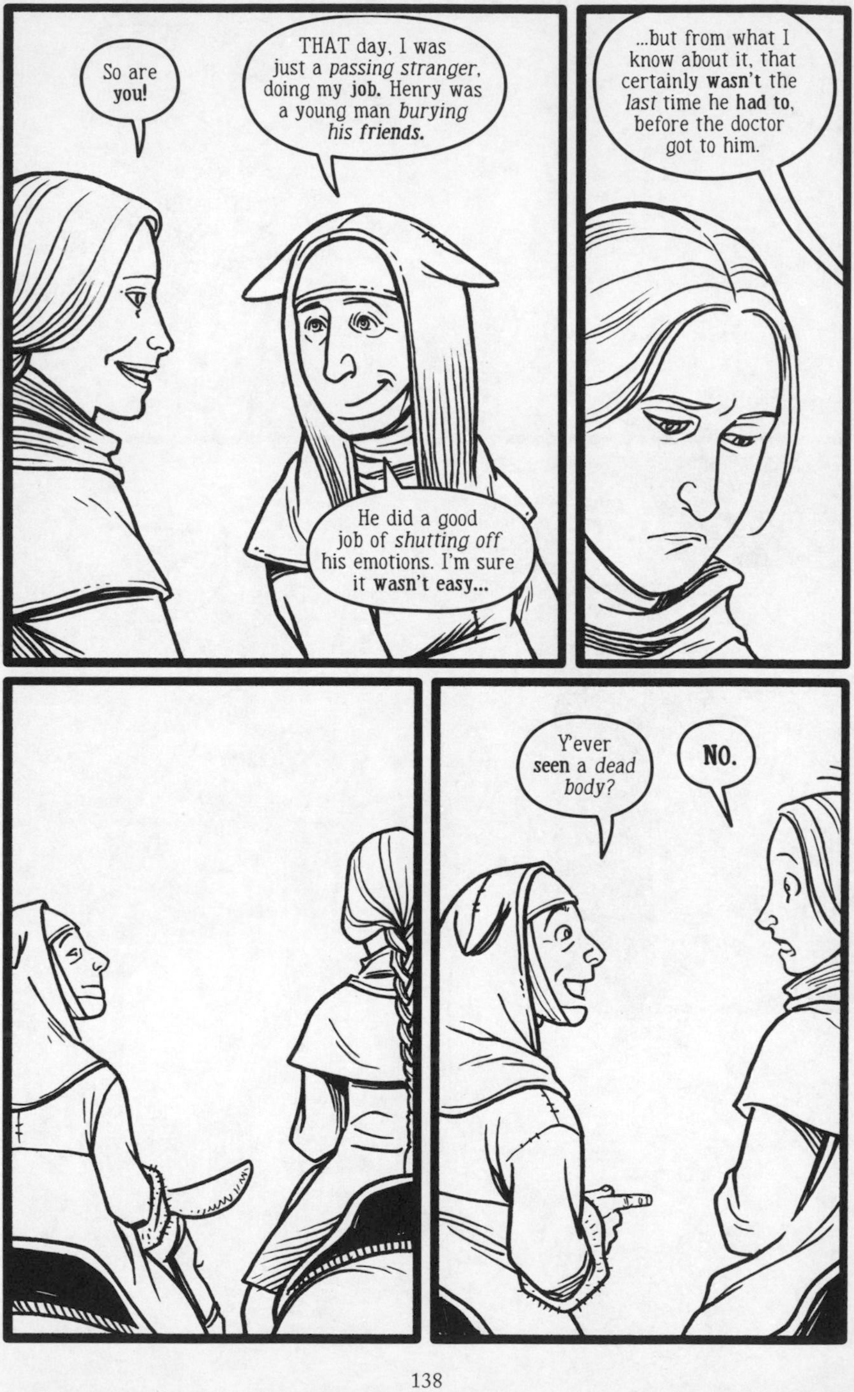
So are **you!**
THAT day, I was just a *passing stranger*, doing my **job.** Henry was a young man *burying* ***his friends.***
He did a good job of *shutting off* his emotions. I'm sure it **wasn't easy...**
...but from what I know about it, that certainly **wasn't** the *last* time he **had to**, before the doctor got to him.
Y'ever **seen** a *dead body?*
NO.

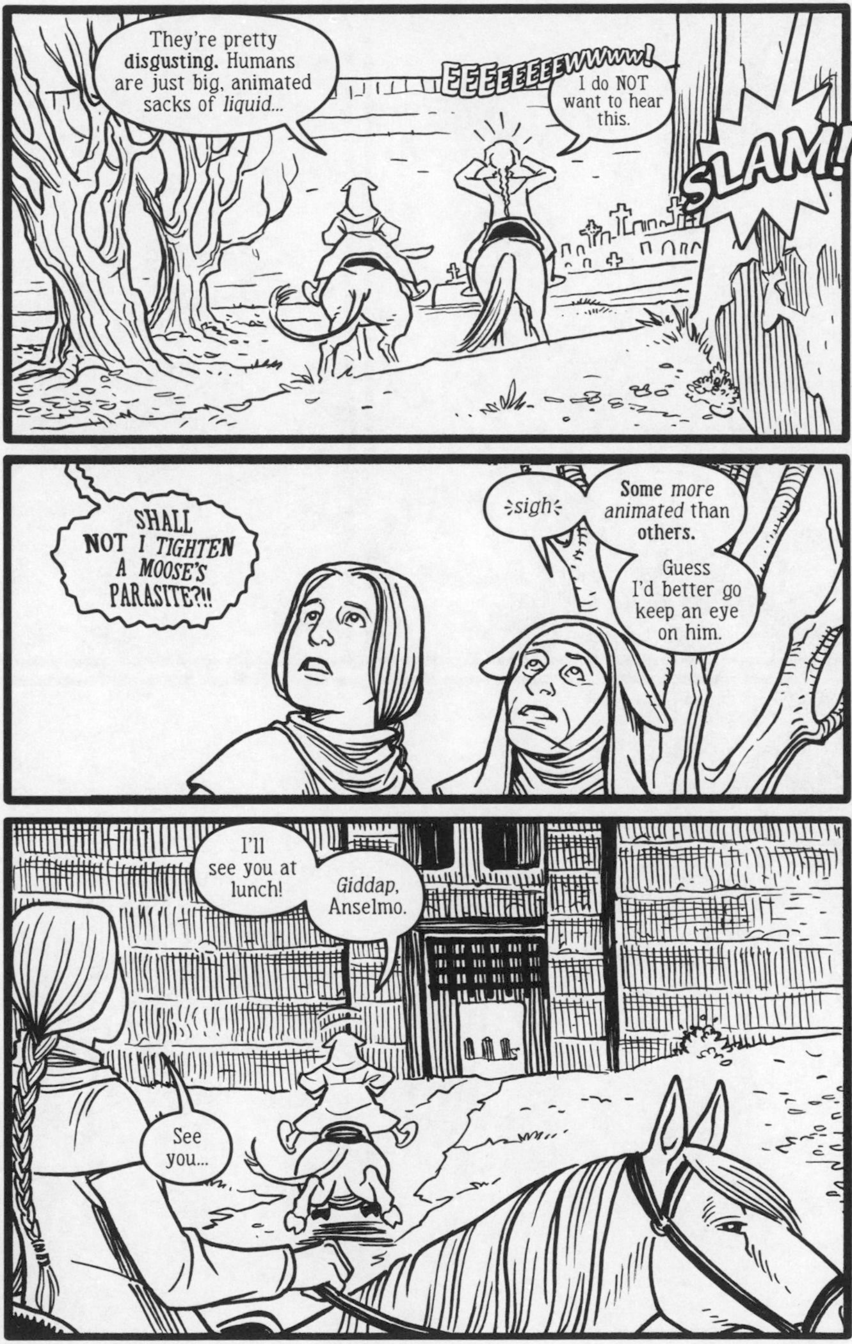

They're pretty **disgusting.** Humans are just big, animated sacks of *liquid*...
EEEEEEEEEWWWW!
I do NOT want to hear this.
SLAM!
SHALL NOT I *TIGHTEN* A *MOOSE'S* PARASITE?!!
sigh
Some *more animated* than **others.**
Guess I'd better go keep an eye on him.
I'll see you at lunch!
Giddap, Anselmo.
See you...

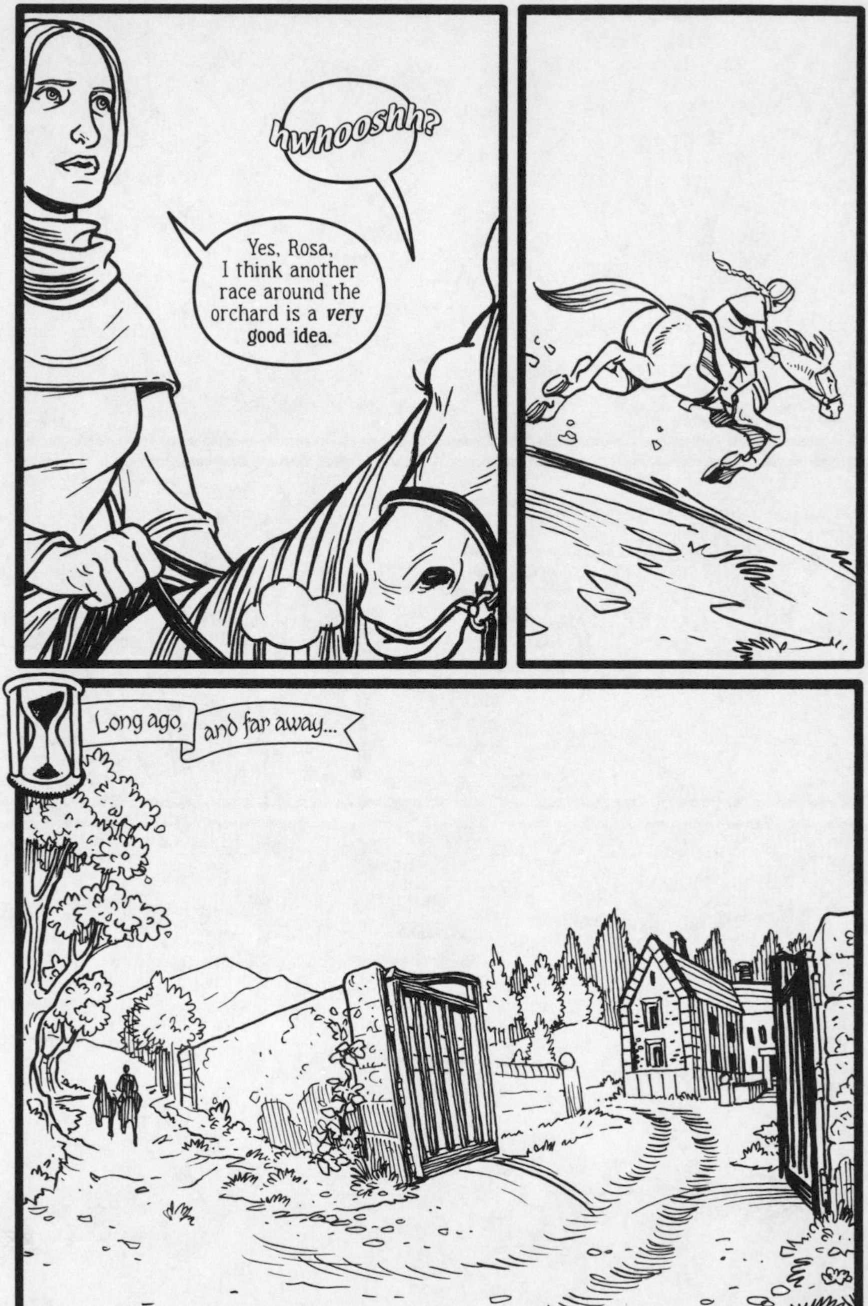
hwhooshh?
Yes, Rosa, I think another race around the orchard is a *very* **good idea.**
Long ago, and far away...

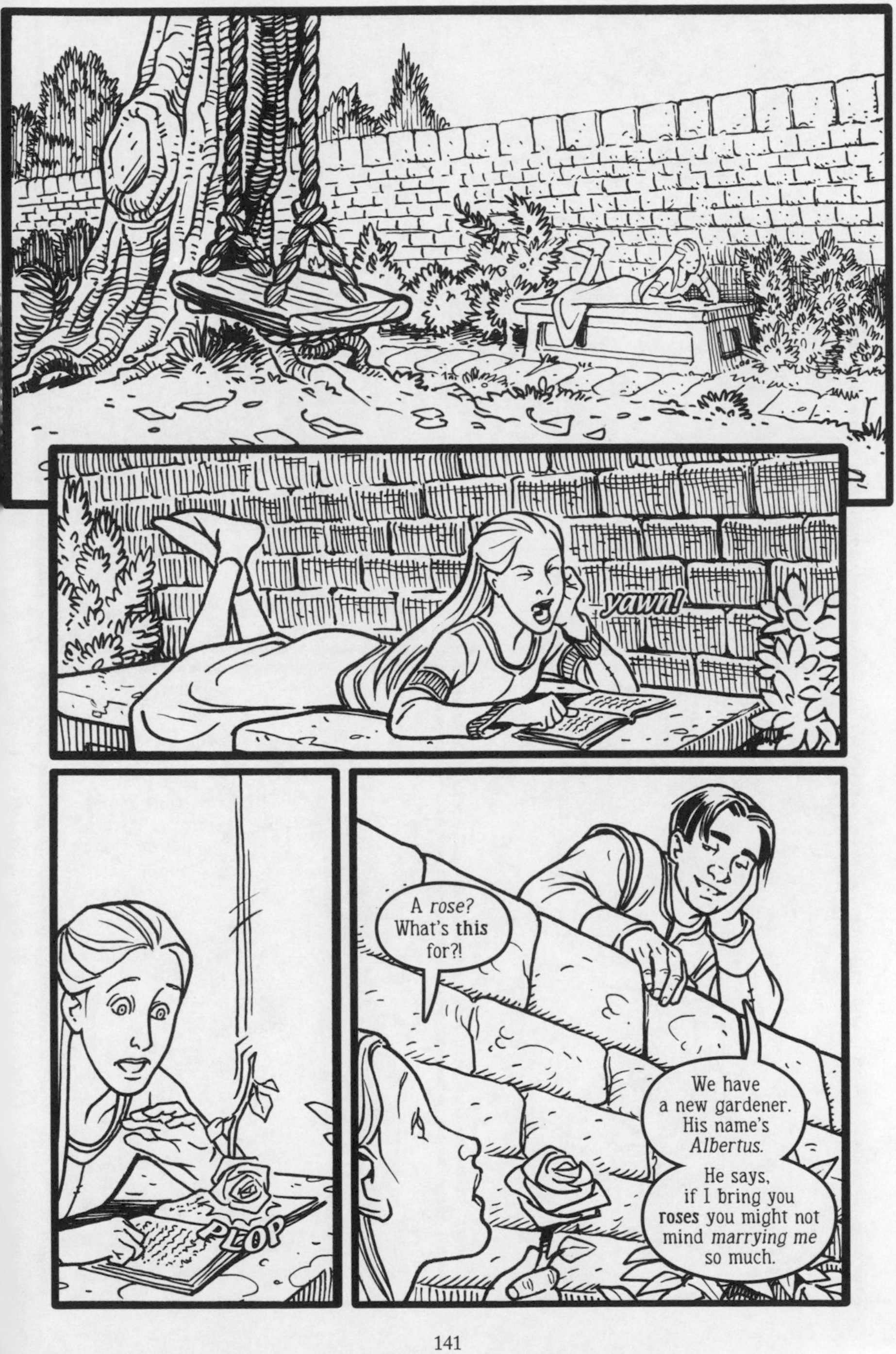
yawn!
PLOP
A *rose?* What's **this** for?!
We have a new gardener. His name's *Albertus.*
He says, if I bring you **roses** you might not mind *marrying me* so much.

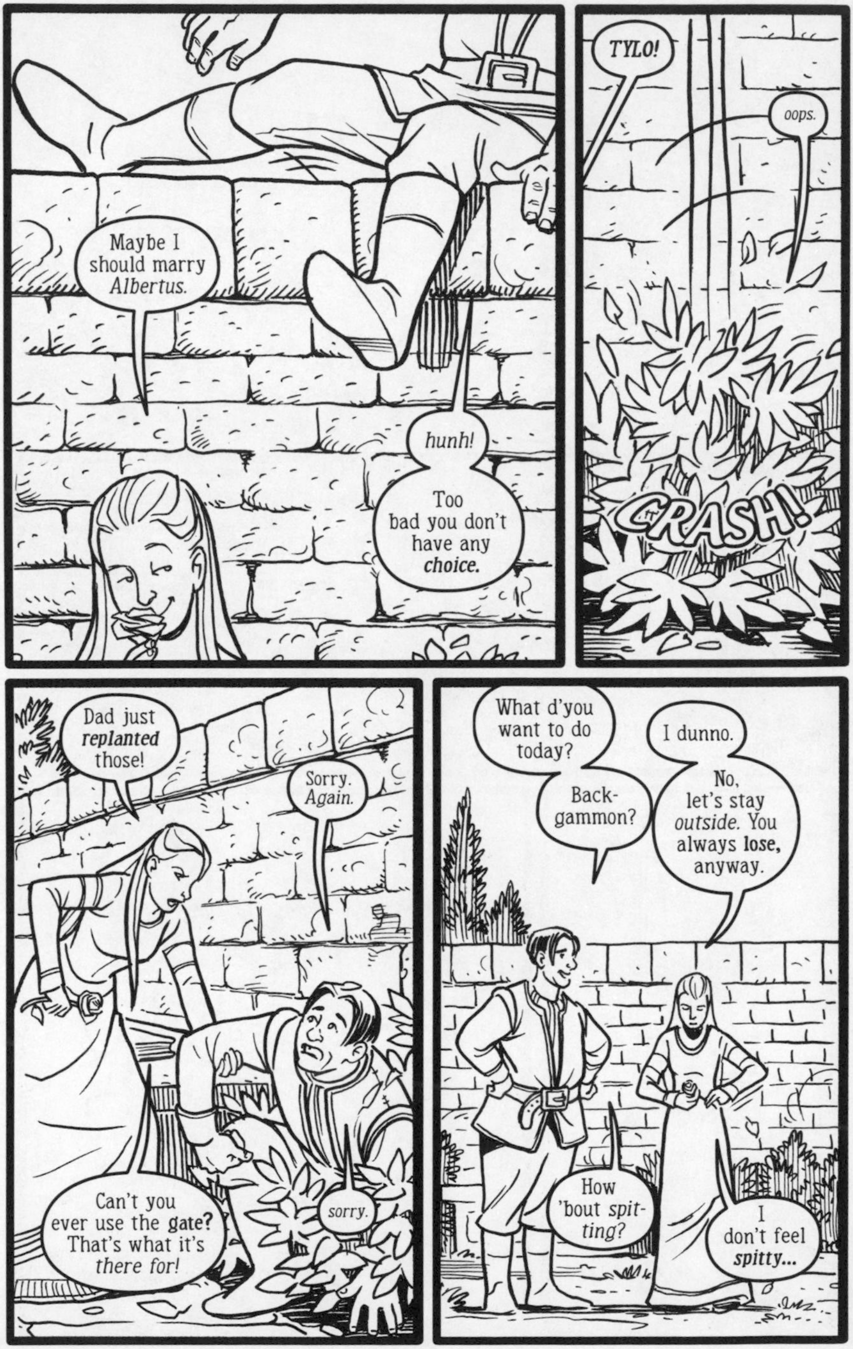
Maybe I should marry *Albertus.*
hunh!
Too bad you don't have any **choice.**
TYLO!
oops.
CRASH!
Dad just **replanted** those!
Sorry. *Again.*
Can't you ever use the **gate?** That's what it's *there for!*
sorry.
What d'you want to do today?
Back-gammon?
I dunno.
No, let's stay *outside.* You always **lose,** anyway.
How 'bout *spit-ting?*
I don't feel **spitty...**

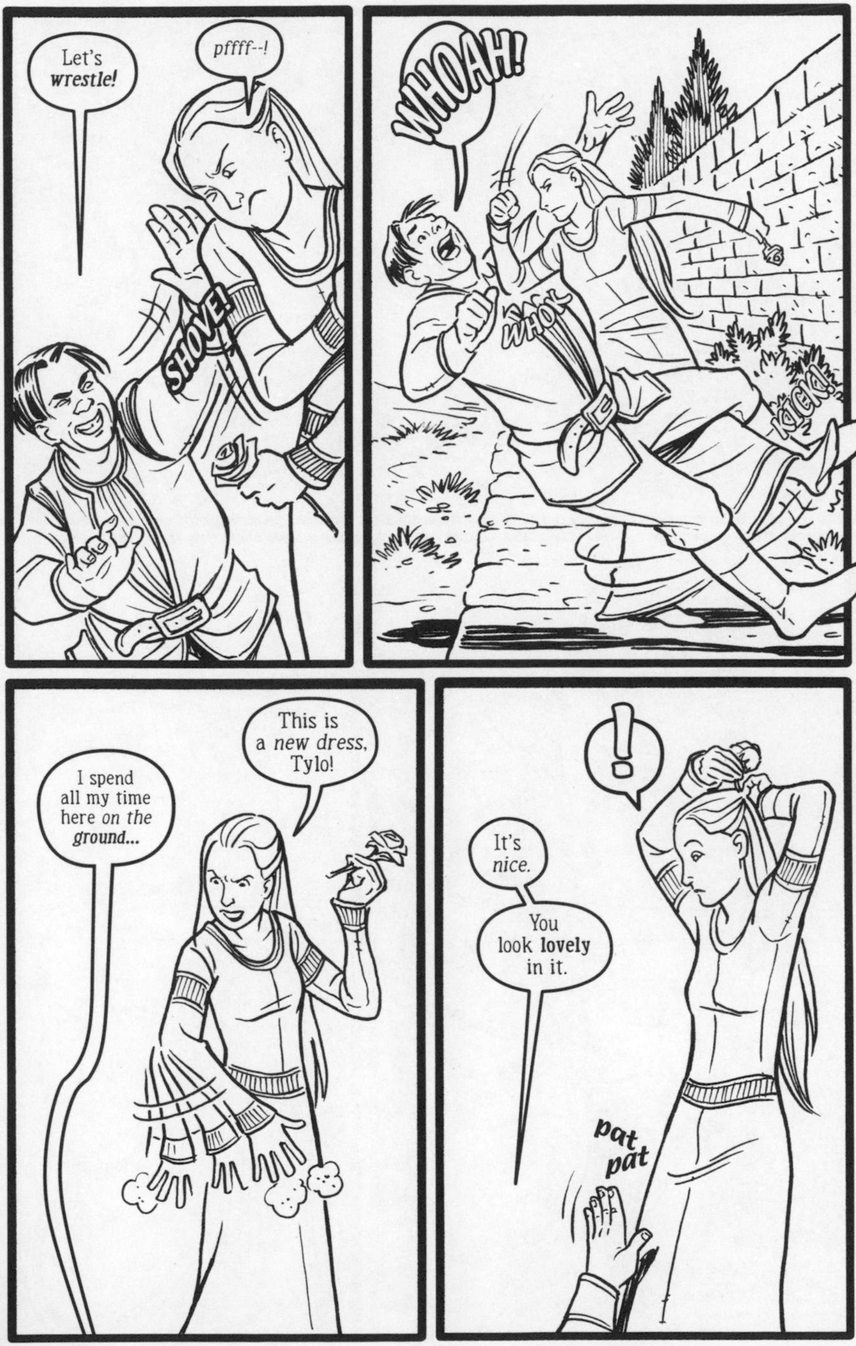
Let's *wrestle!*
pffff--!
SHOVE!
WHOAH!
WHOK
KICK!
This is a *new dress,* Tylo!
I spend all my time here *on the ground...*
!
It's *nice.*
You look **lovely** in it.
pat pat

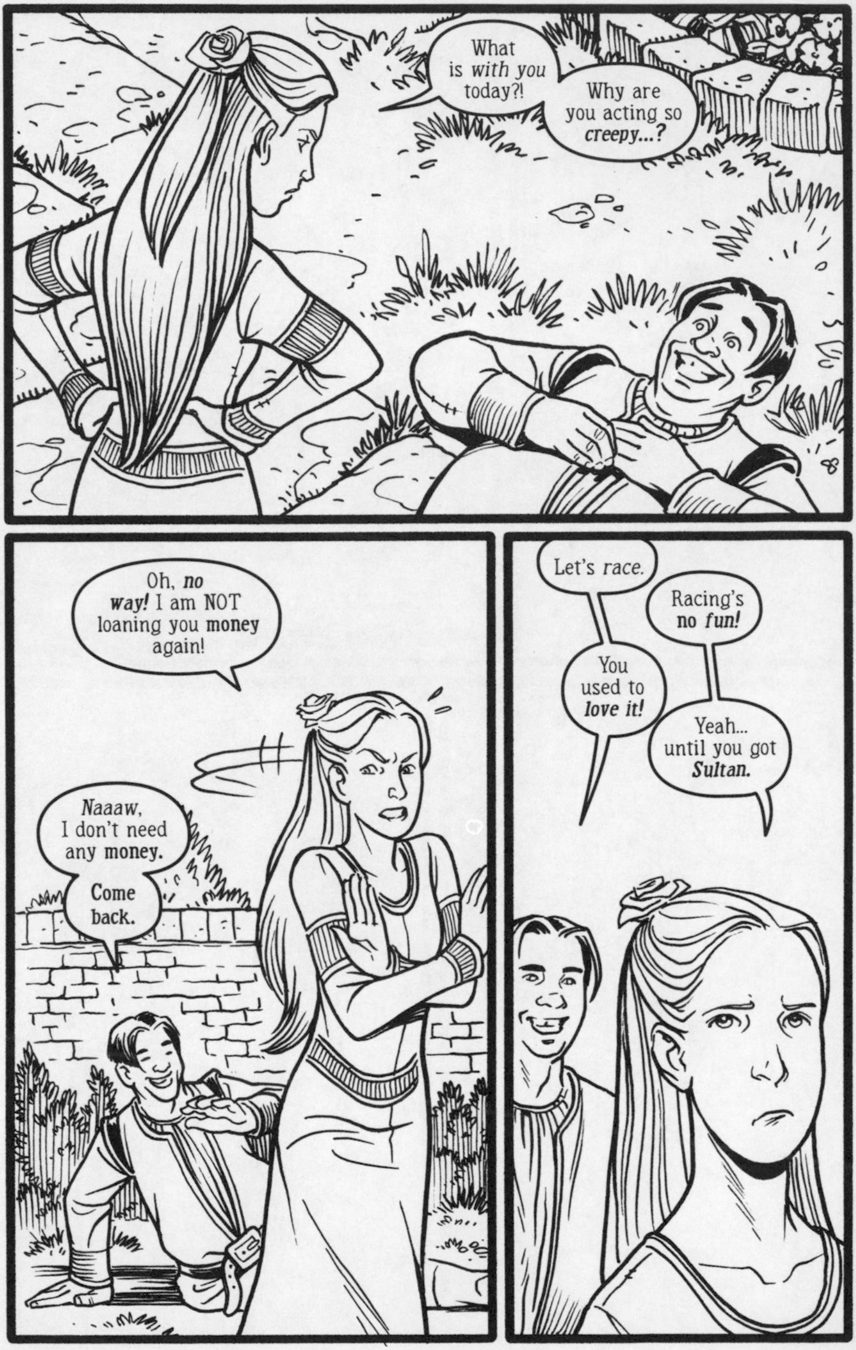
What is *with you* today?!
Why are you acting so *creepy...?*
Oh, ***no way!*** I am NOT loaning you **money** again!
Naaaw, I don't need any **money.**
Come back.
Let's *race.*
Racing's **no *fun!***
You used to ***love it!***
Yeah... until you got ***Sultan.***

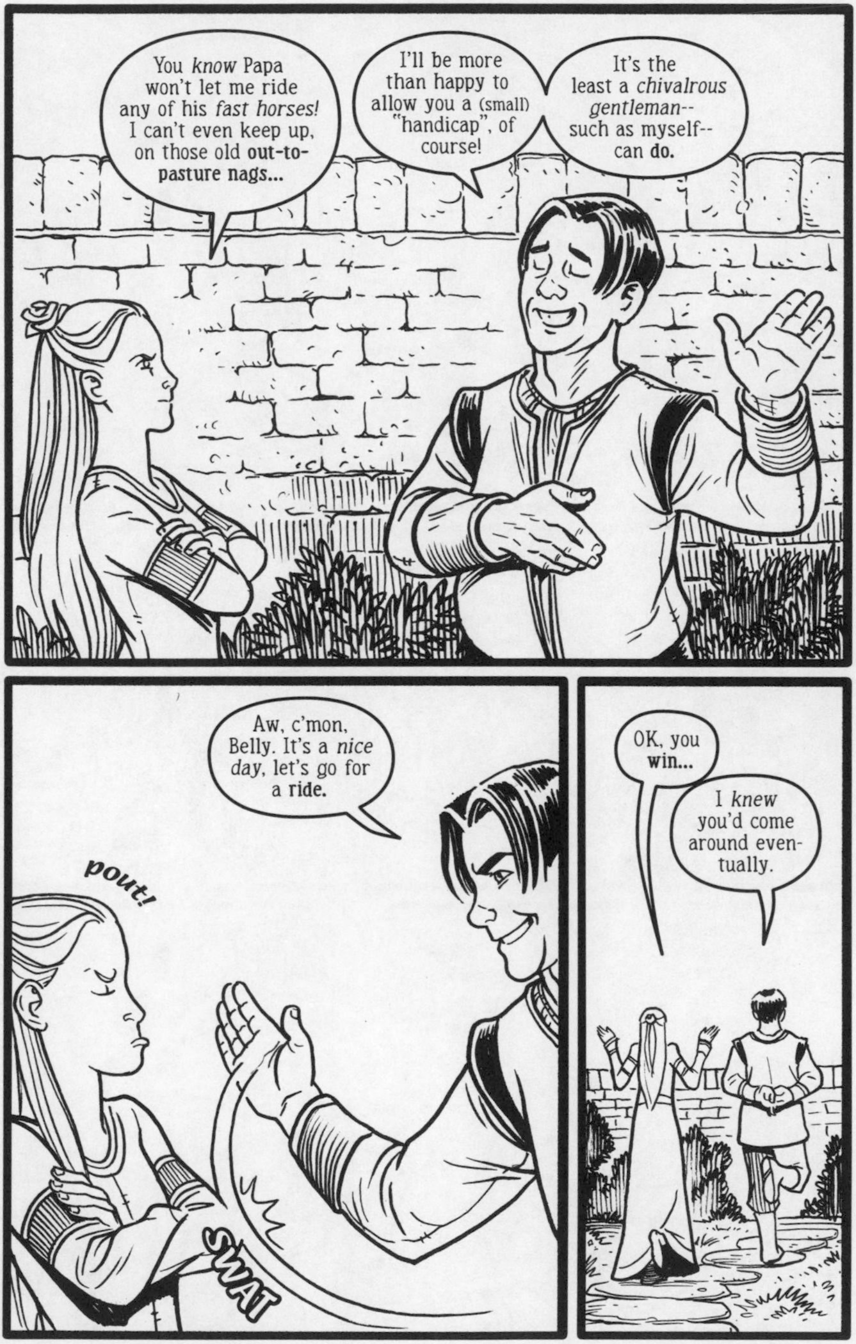

You *know* Papa won't let me ride any of his *fast horses!* I can't even keep up, on those old **out-to-pasture nags...**
I'll be more than happy to allow you a (small) "handicap", of course!
It's the least a *chivalrous gentleman*-- such as myself-- can **do.**
Aw, c'mon, Belly. It's a *nice day*, let's go for a **ride.**
pout!
SWAT
OK, you **win...**
I *knew* you'd come around eventually.

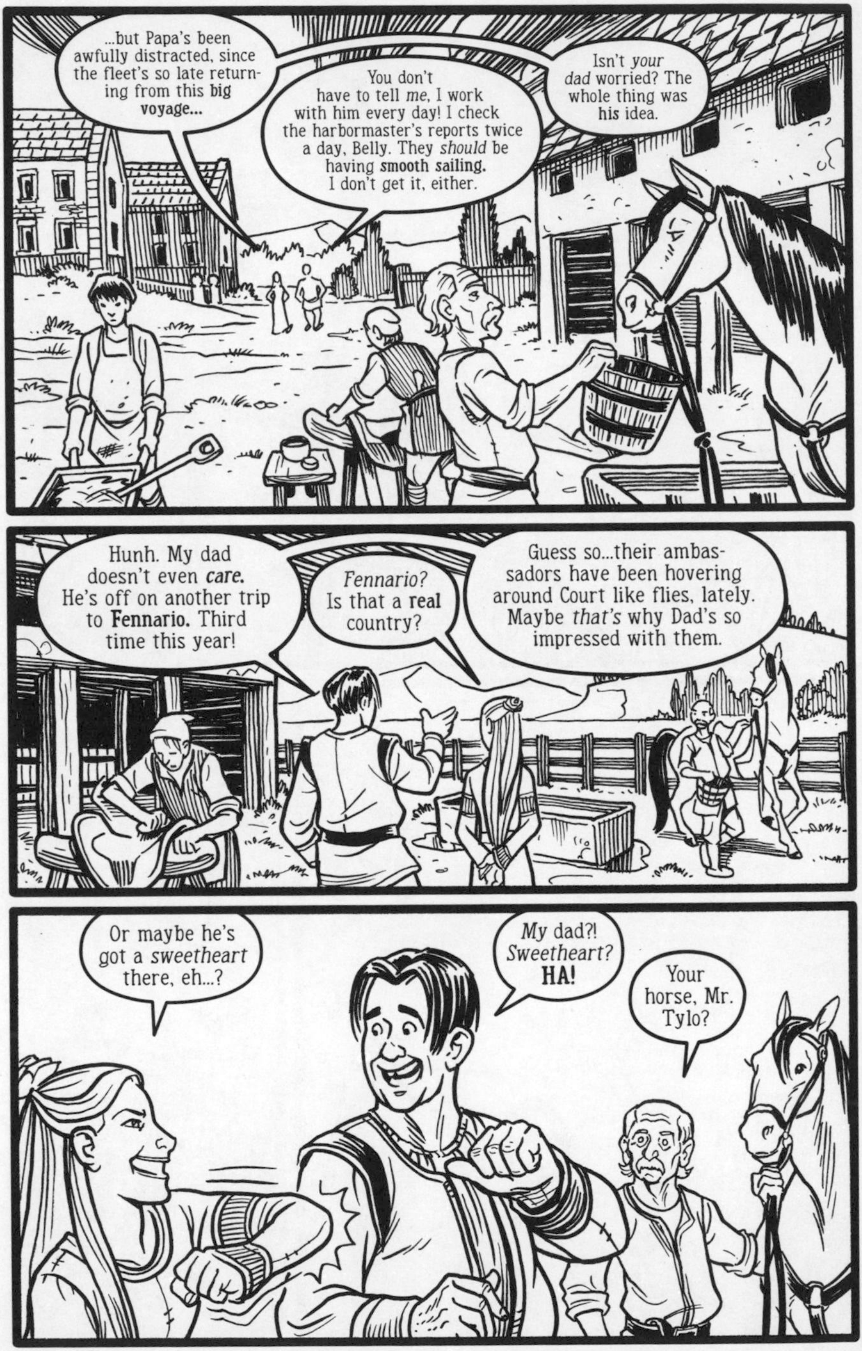
...but Papa's been awfully distracted, since the fleet's so late returning from this **big voyage...**
You don't have to tell *me*, I work with him every day! I check the harbormaster's reports twice a day, Belly. They *should* be having **smooth sailing.** I don't get it, either.
Isn't *your dad* worried? The whole thing was **his** idea.
Hunh. My dad doesn't even **care.** He's off on another trip to **Fennario.** Third time this year!
Fennario? Is that a **real** country?
Guess so...their ambassadors have been hovering around Court like flies, lately. Maybe *that's* why Dad's so impressed with them.
Or maybe he's got a *sweetheart* there, eh...?
My dad?! *Sweetheart?* **HA!**
Your horse, Mr. Tylo?

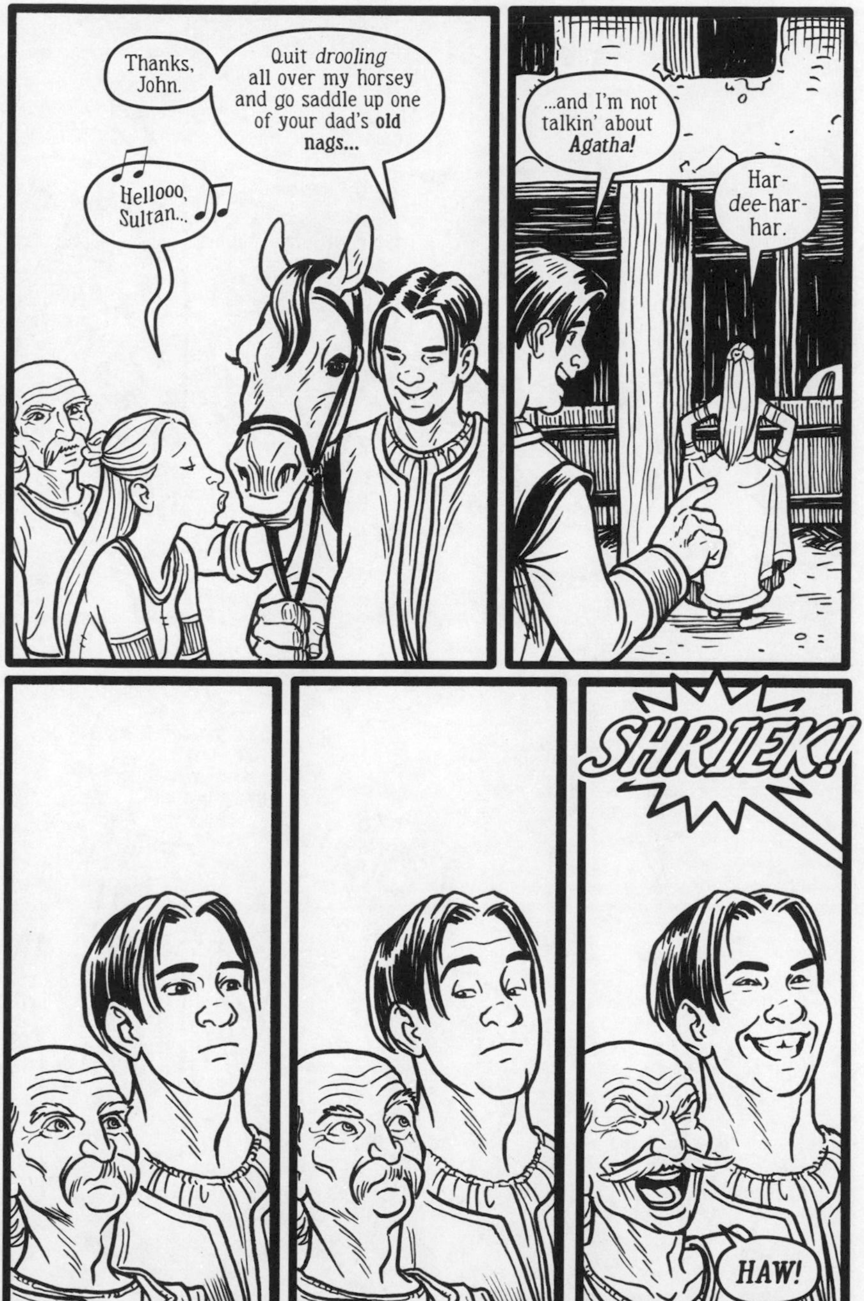
Thanks, John.
Quit *drooling* all over my horsey and go saddle up one of your dad's **old nags...**
Hellooo, Sultan...
...and I'm not talkin' about ***Agatha!***
Har-*dee*-har-har.
SHRIEK!
HAW!

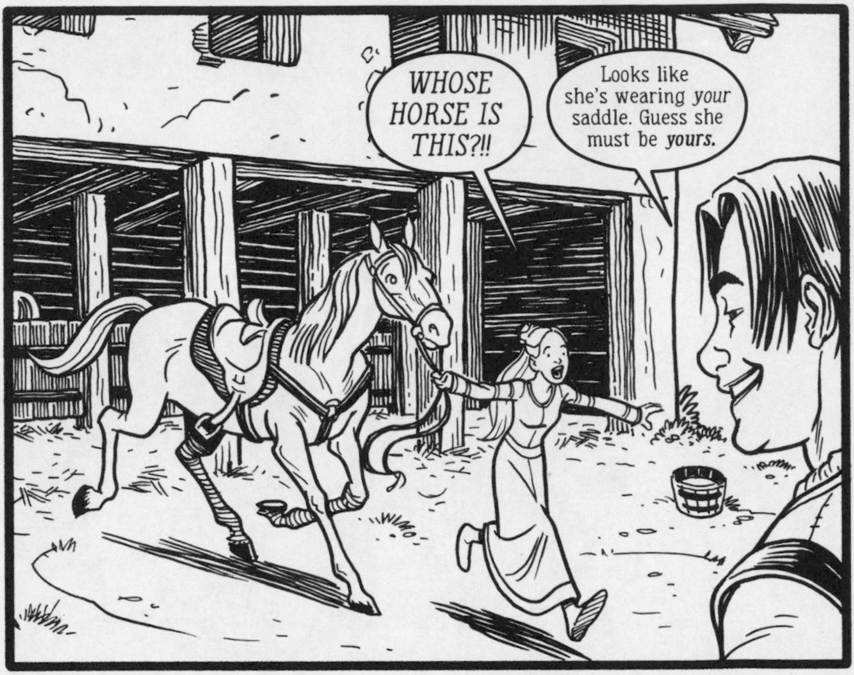
WHOSE HORSE IS THIS?!!
Looks like she's wearing *your* saddle. Guess she must be ***yours.***

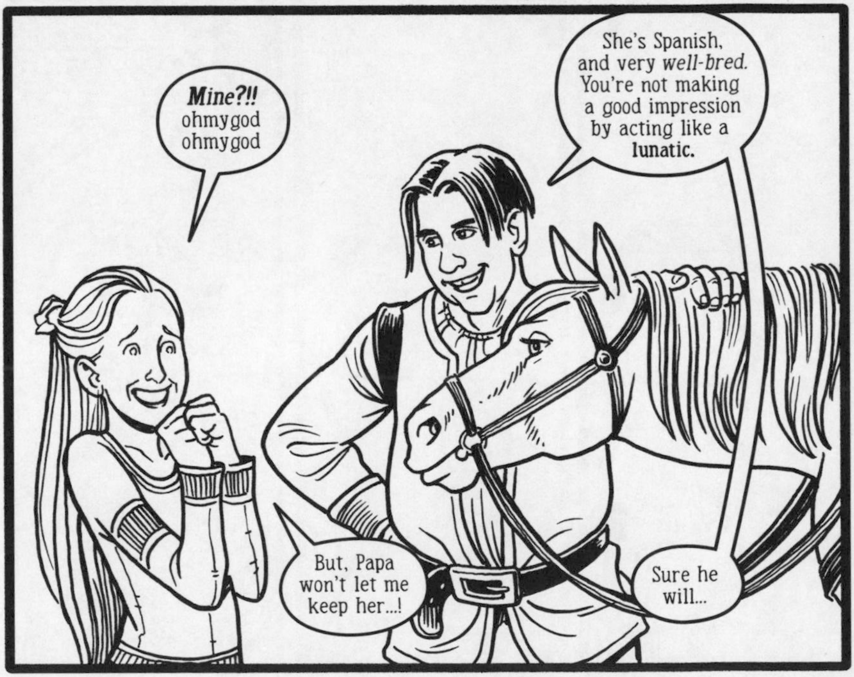
Mine?!! ohmygod ohmygod
She's Spanish, and very *well-bred.* You're not making a good impression by acting like a **lunatic.**
But, Papa won't let me keep her...!
Sure he will...

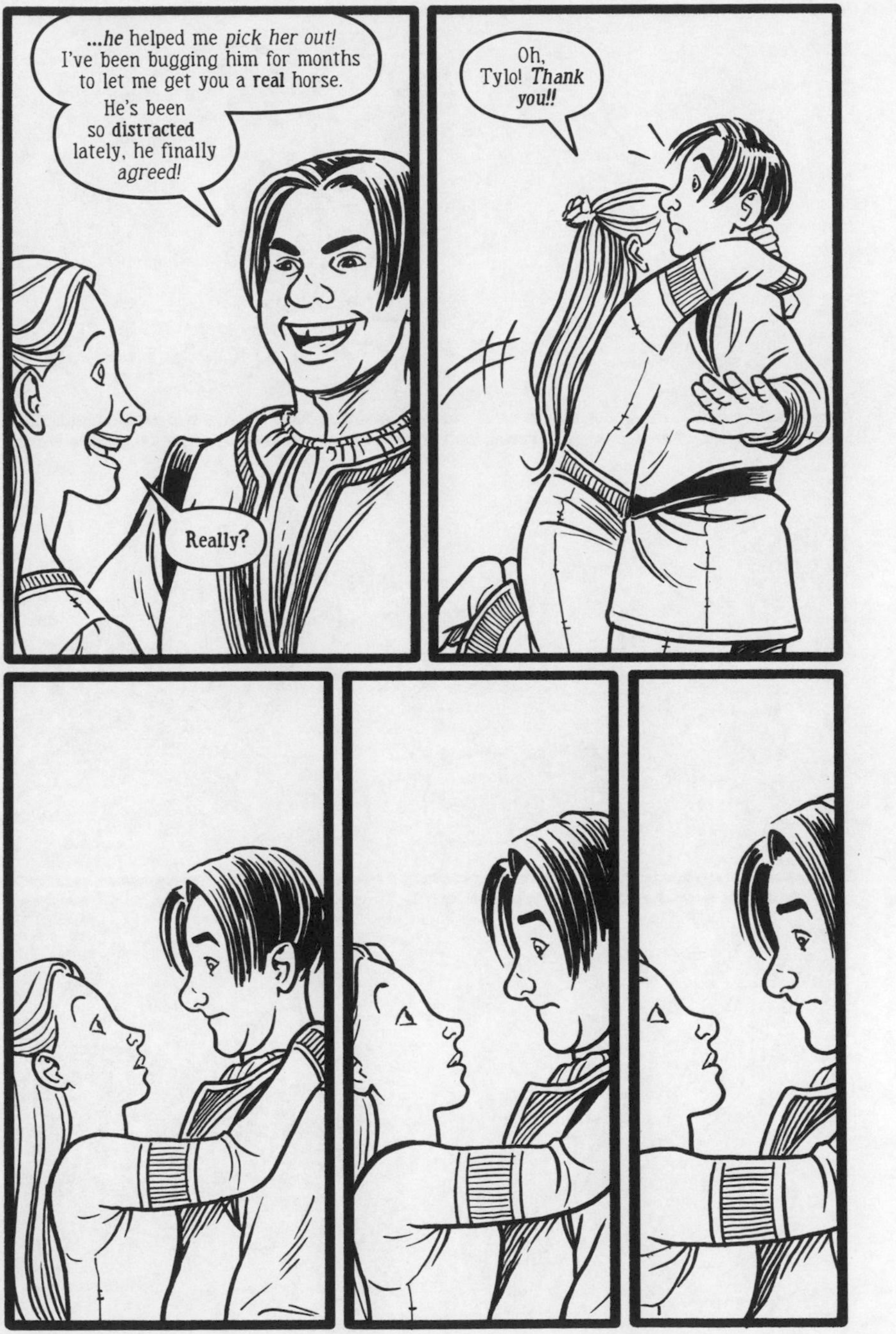
...he helped me pick her out! I've been bugging him for months to let me get you a real horse.
He's been so distracted lately, he finally agreed!
Really?
Oh, Tylo! Thank you!!

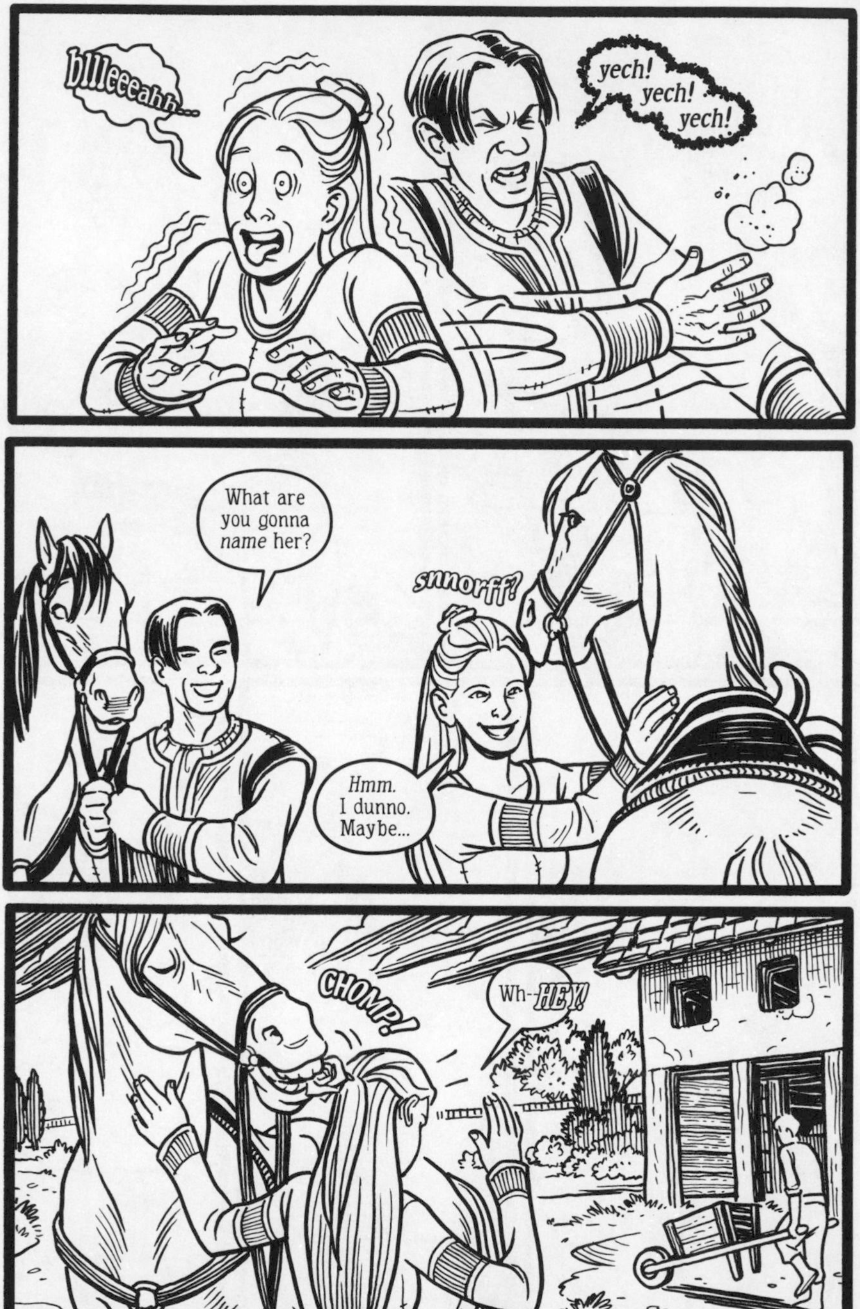
blleeeahh...
yech! yech! yech!
What are you gonna *name* her?
snnorff?
Hmm. I dunno. Maybe...
CHOMP!
Wh--HEY!

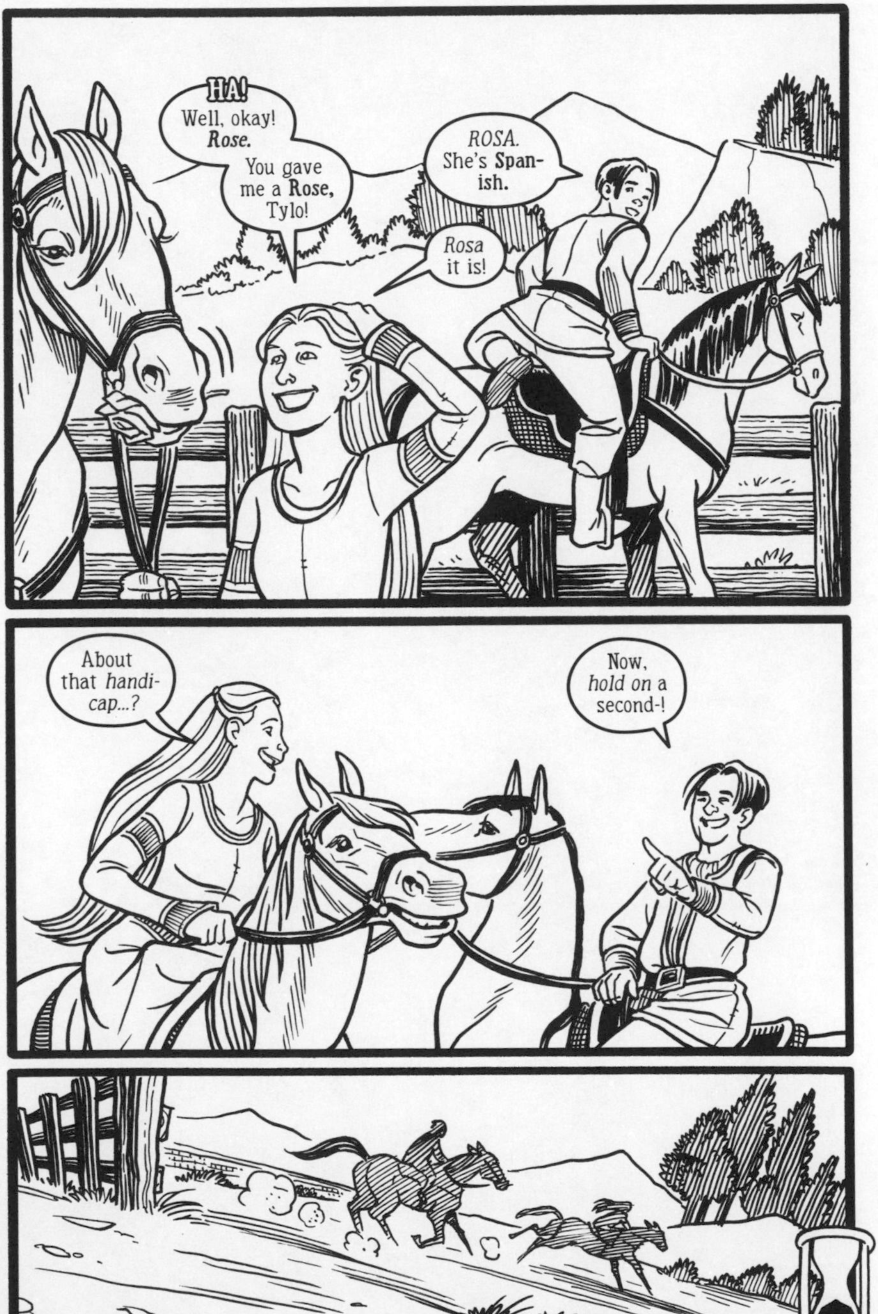
HA!
Well, okay! **Rose.**
You gave me a **Rose,** Tylo!
ROSA. She's **Span-ish.**
Rosa it is!
About that *handi-cap...?*
Now, *hold on* a second-!

Chapter 7.

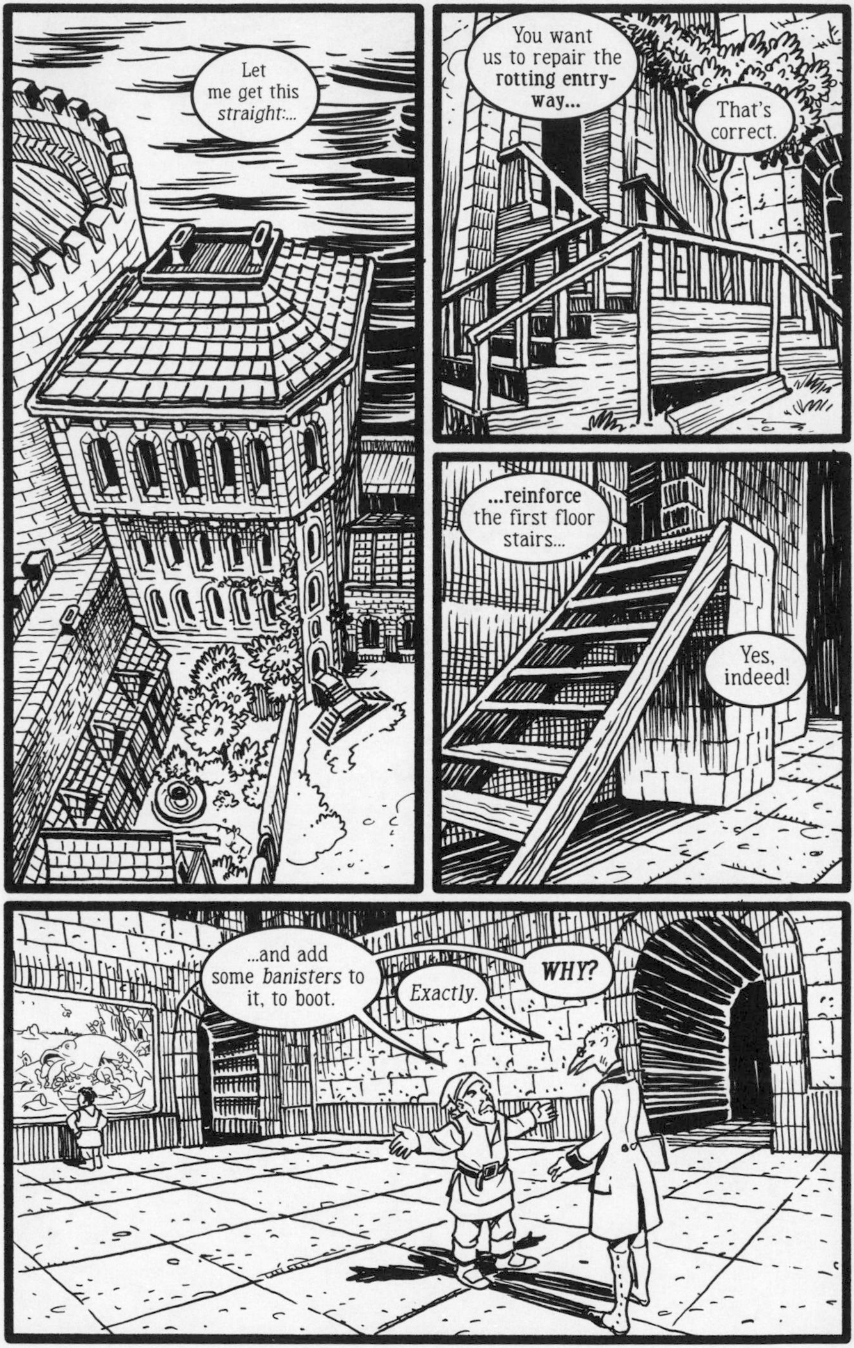
Let me get this *straight*:...
You want us to repair the **rotting entry-way...**
That's correct.
...reinforce the first floor stairs...
Yes, indeed!
...and add some *banisters* to it, to boot.
Exactly.
WHY?

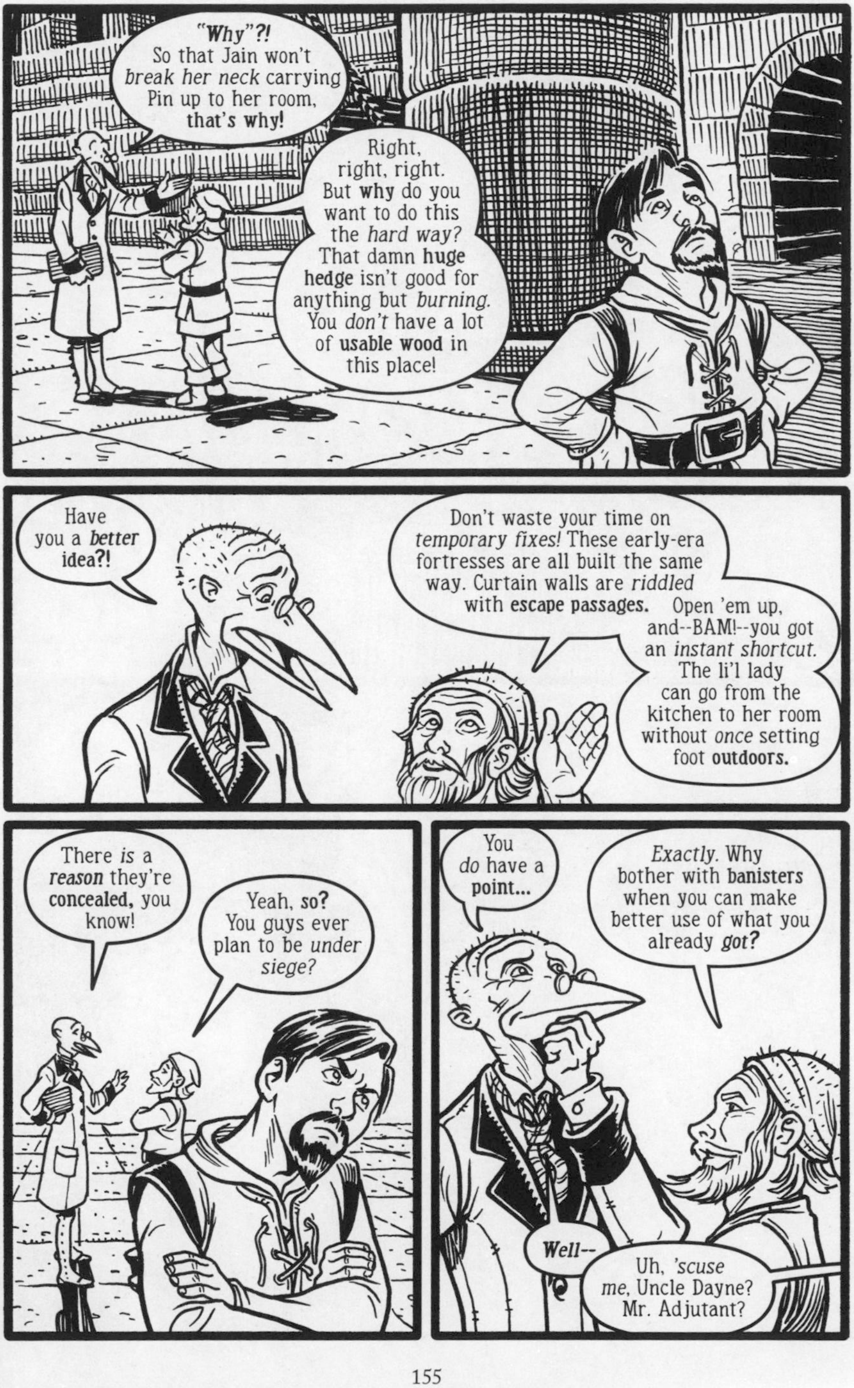
"Why"?! So that Jain won't *break her neck* carrying Pin up to her room, **that's why!**
Right, right, right. But **why** do you want to do this the *hard way?* That damn **huge hedge** isn't good for anything but *burning.* You *don't* have a lot of **usable wood** in this place!
Have you a *better* **idea?!**
Don't waste your time on *temporary fixes!* These early-era fortresses are all built the same way. Curtain walls are *riddled* with **escape passages.** Open 'em up, and--BAM!--you got an *instant shortcut.* The li'l lady can go from the kitchen to her room without *once* setting foot **outdoors.**
There *is* a *reason* they're **concealed,** you know!
Yeah, **so?** You guys ever plan to be *under siege?*
You *do* have a **point...**
Exactly. Why bother with **banisters** when you can make better use of what you already *got?*
Well--
Uh, *'scuse me,* Uncle Dayne? Mr. Adjutant?

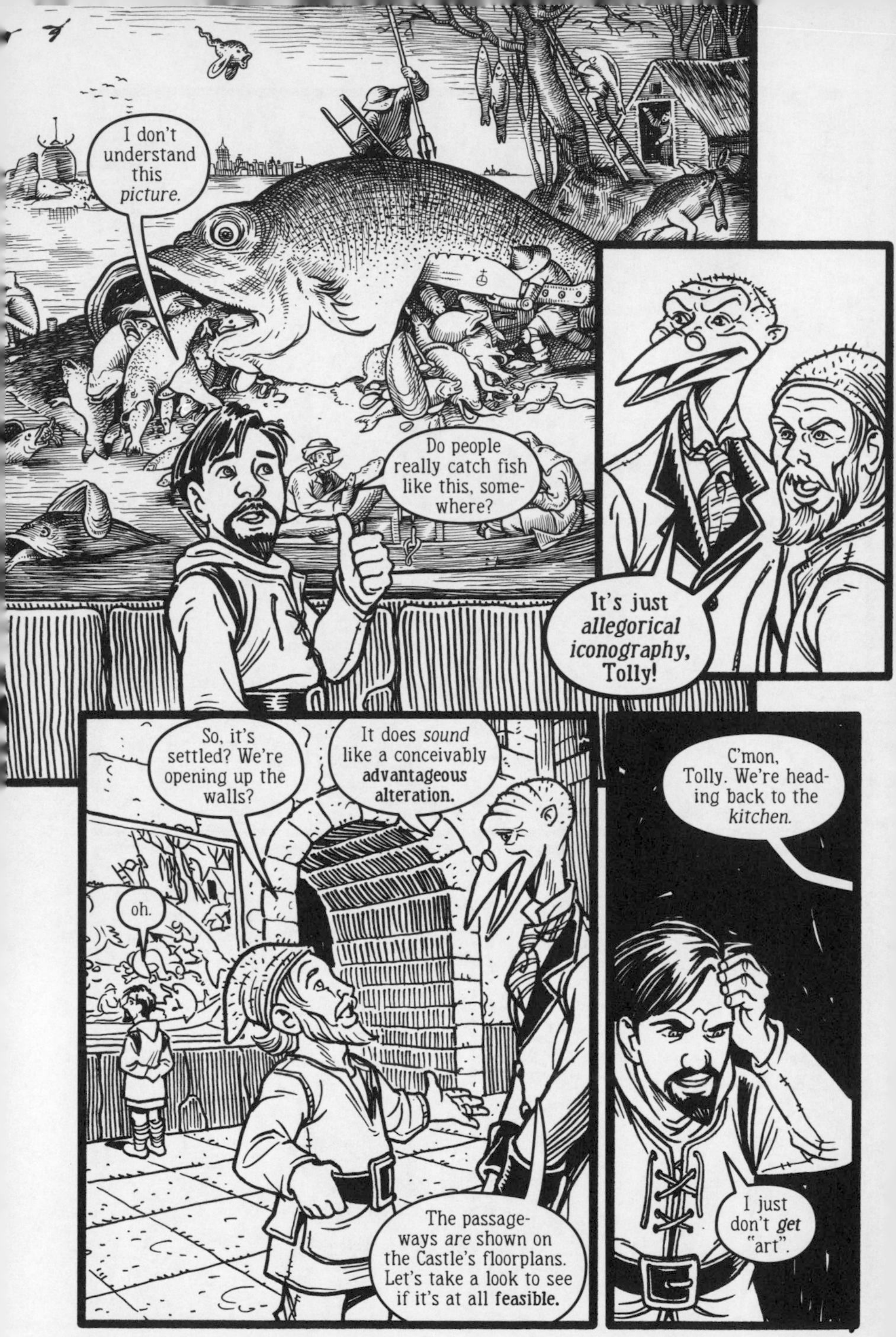
I don't understand this *picture.*
Do people really catch fish like this, some-where?
It's just *allegorical iconography,* Tolly!
So, it's settled? We're opening up the walls?
It does *sound* like a conceivably **advantageous alteration.**
oh.
The passage-ways *are* shown on the Castle's floorplans. Let's take a look to see if it's at all **feasible.**
C'mon, Tolly. We're head-ing back to the *kitchen.*
I just don't ***get*** "art".

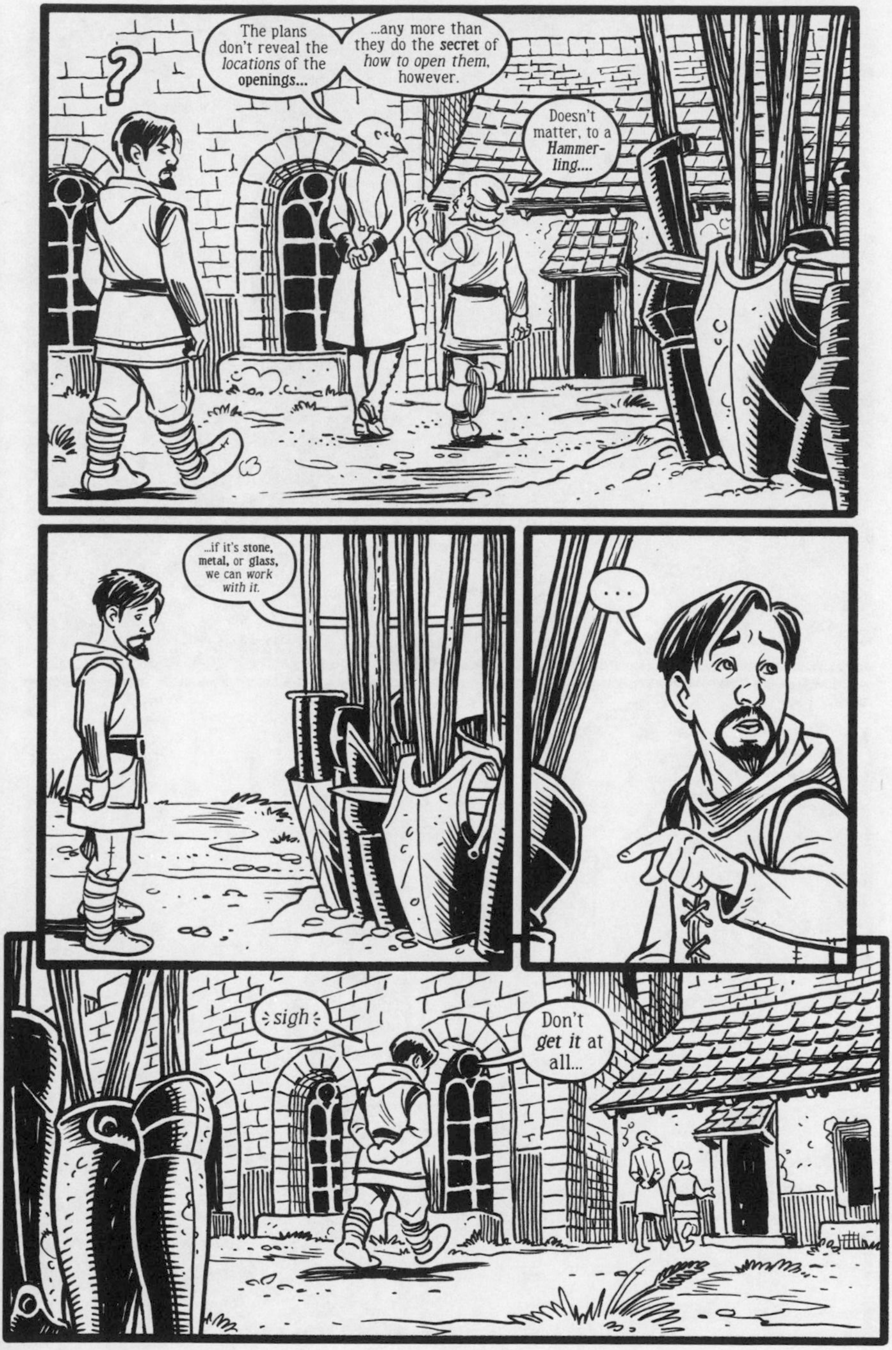
?
The plans don't reveal the *locations* of the **openings...**
...any more than they do the **secret** of *how to open them,* however.
Doesn't matter, to a **Hammer-ling....**
...if it's **stone, metal,** or **glass,** we can *work with it.*
. . .
sigh
Don't **get it** at all...

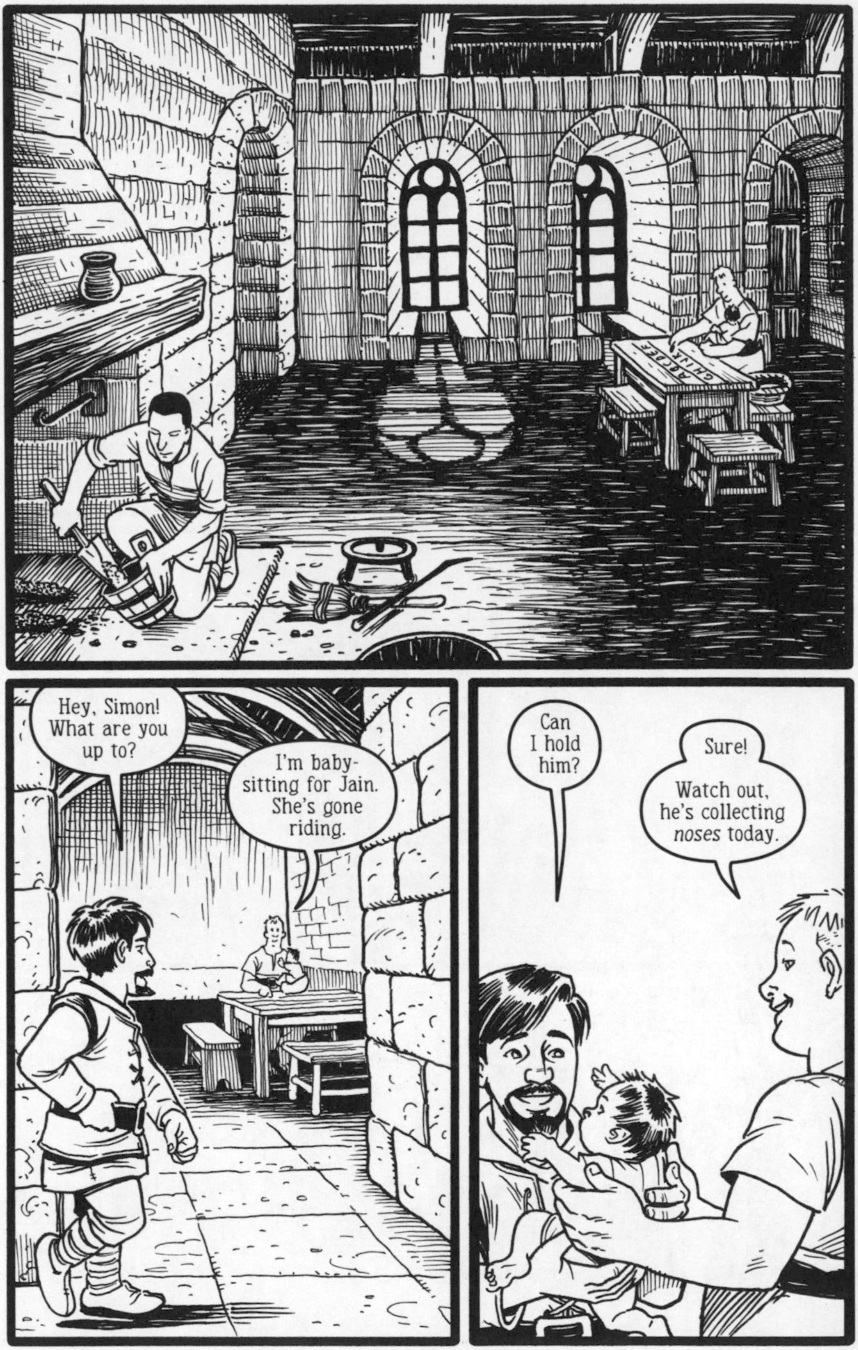
Hey, Simon! What are you up to?
I'm baby-sitting for Jain. She's gone riding.
Can I hold him?
Sure!
Watch out, he's collecting *noses* today.

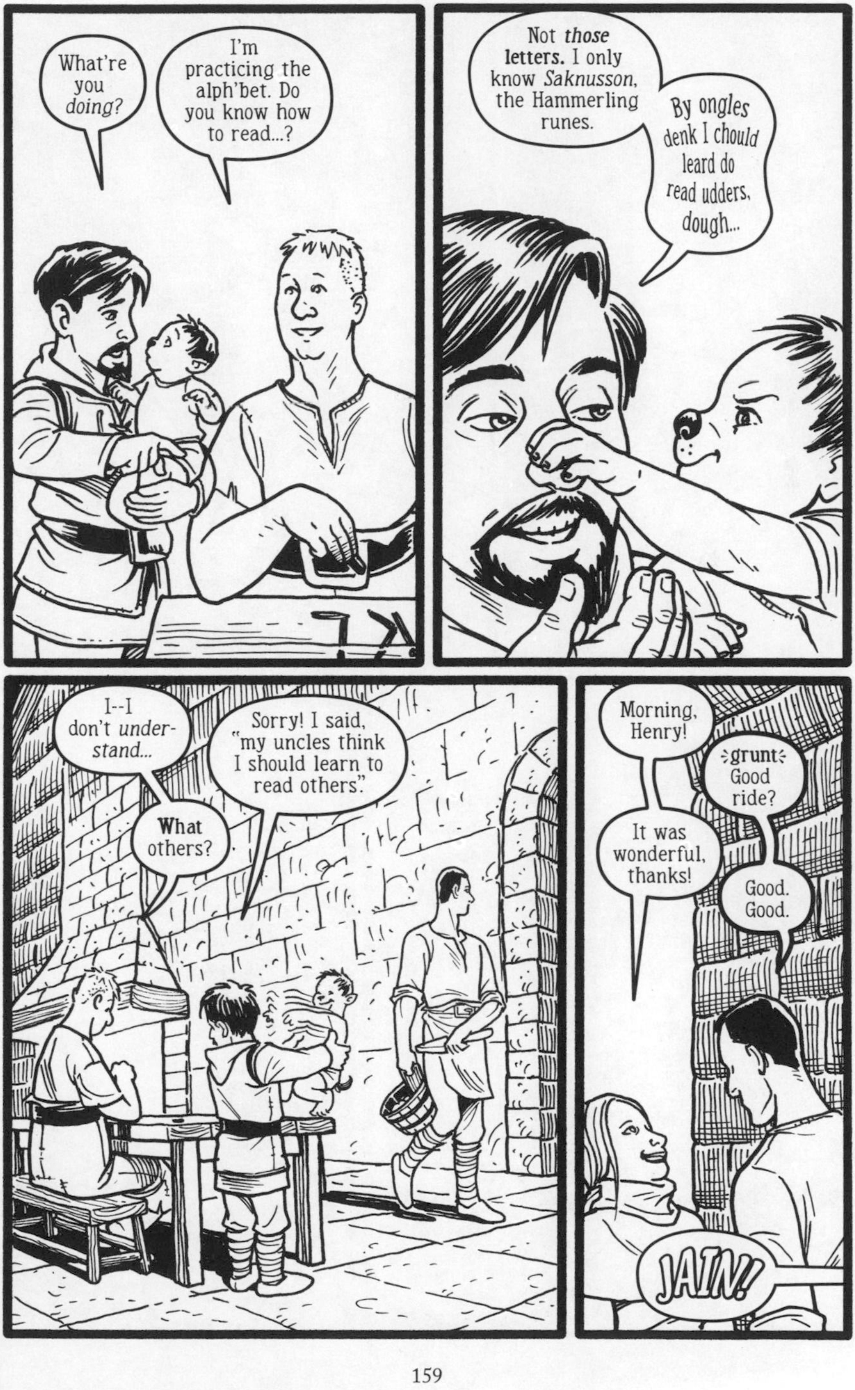
What're you *doing*?
I'm practicing the alph'bet. Do you know how to read...?
Not *those* **letters.** I only know *Saknusson*, the Hammerling runes.
By ongles denk I chould leard do read udders, dough...
I--I don't *under-stand...*
Sorry! I said, "my uncles think I should learn to read others".
What others?
Morning, Henry!
grunt Good ride?
It was wonderful, thanks!
Good. Good.
JAIN!

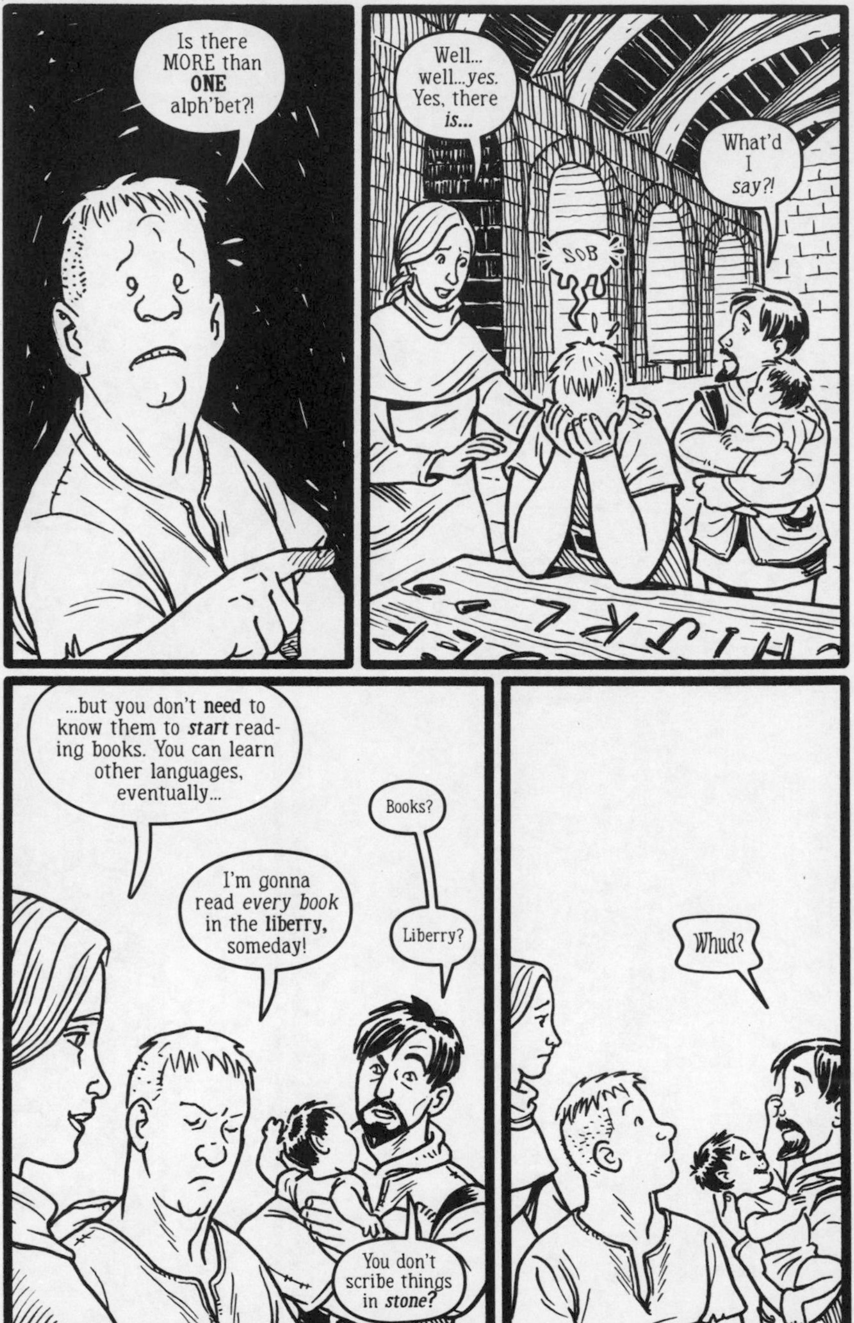
Is there MORE than **ONE** alph'bet?!
Well... well...*yes.* Yes, there *is...*
SOB
What'd I *say?!*
...but you don't **need** to know them to *start* reading books. You can learn other languages, eventually...
Books?
I'm gonna read *every book* in the **liberry,** someday!
Liberry?
You don't scribe things in *stone?*
Whud?

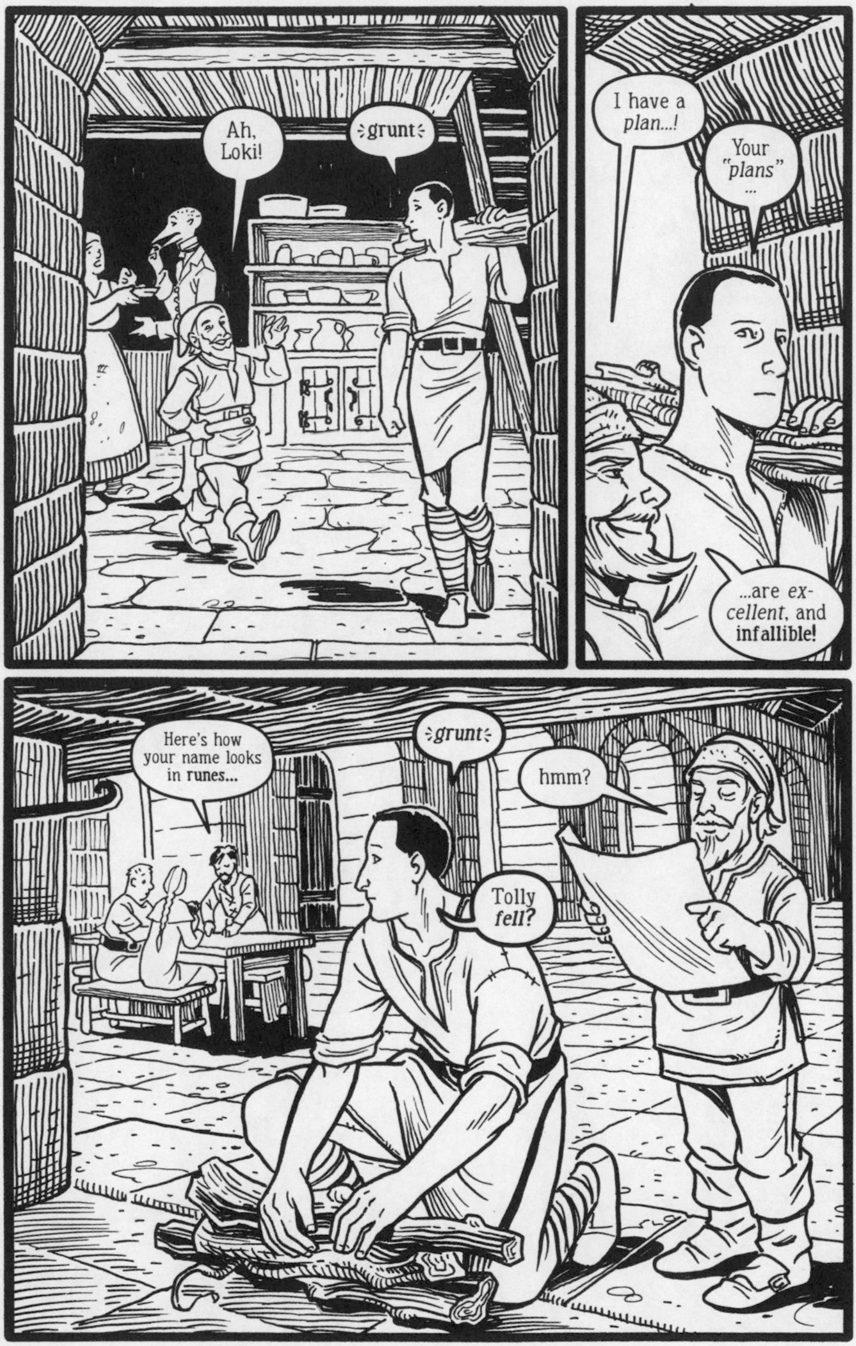
Ah, Loki!
grunt
I have a *plan*...!
Your *"plans"* ...
...are *ex-cellent*, and **infallible!**
Here's how your name looks in **runes...**
grunt
hmm?
Tolly *fell?*

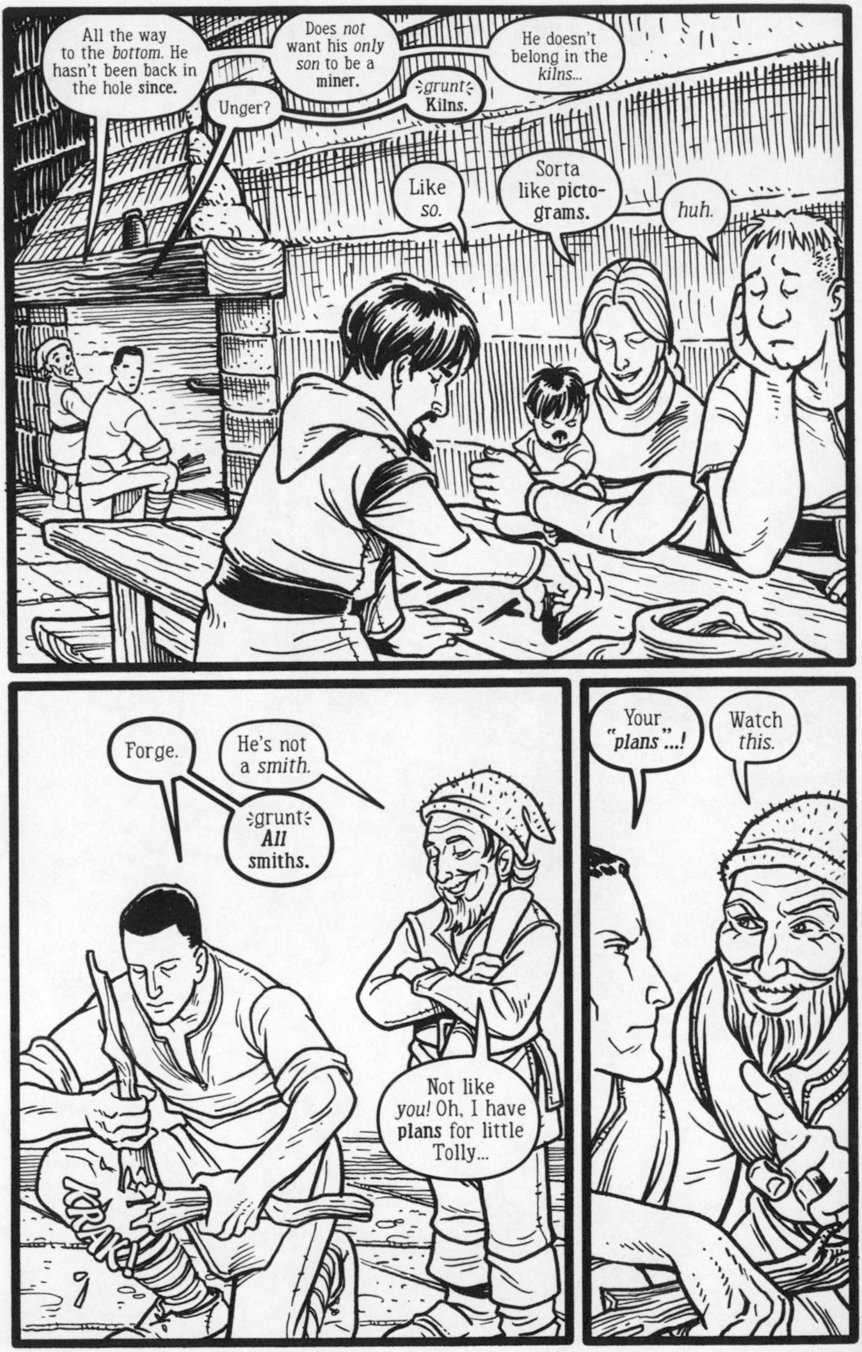
All the way to the *bottom.* He hasn't been back in the hole **since.**
Unger?
Does *not* want his *only son* to be a **miner.**
grunt **Kilns.**
He doesn't belong in the *kilns...*
Like *so.*
Sorta like **picto-grams.**
huh.
Forge.
He's not a *smith.*
grunt ***All* smiths.**
Not like *you!* Oh, I have **plans** for little Tolly...
KRAK!
Your "***plans***"...!
Watch *this.*

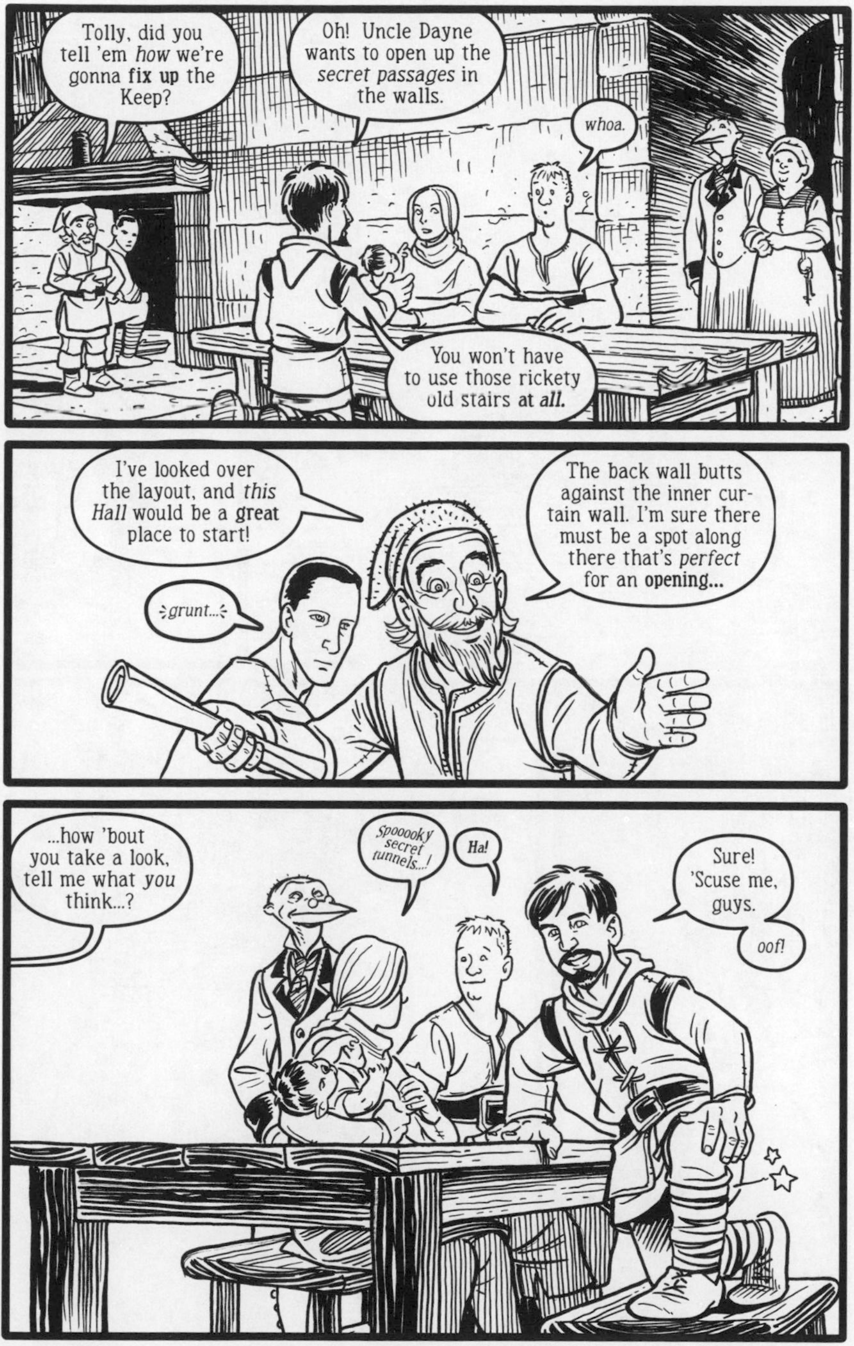
Tolly, did you tell 'em *how* we're gonna **fix up** the Keep?
Oh! Uncle Dayne wants to open up the *secret passages* in the walls.
whoa.
You won't have to use those rickety old stairs **at *all*.**
I've looked over the layout, and *this Hall* would be a **great** place to start!
grunt...
The back wall butts against the inner curtain wall. I'm sure there must be a spot along there that's *perfect* for an **opening...**
...how 'bout you take a look, tell me what *you* think...?
Spooooky secret tunnels...!
Ha!
Sure! 'Scuse me, guys.
oof!

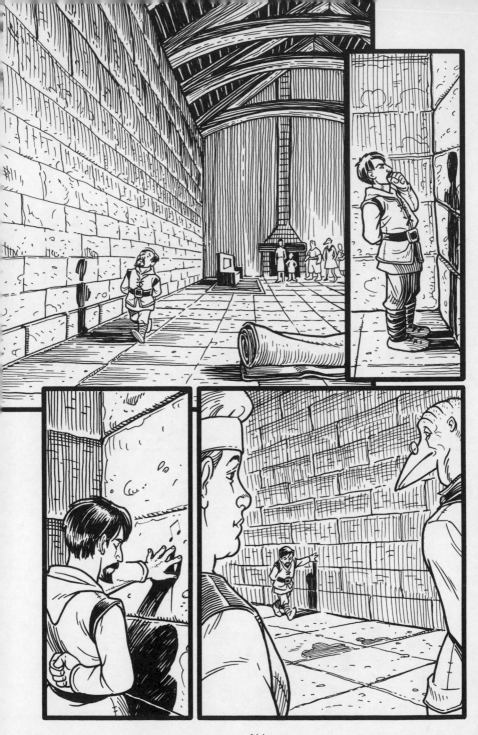

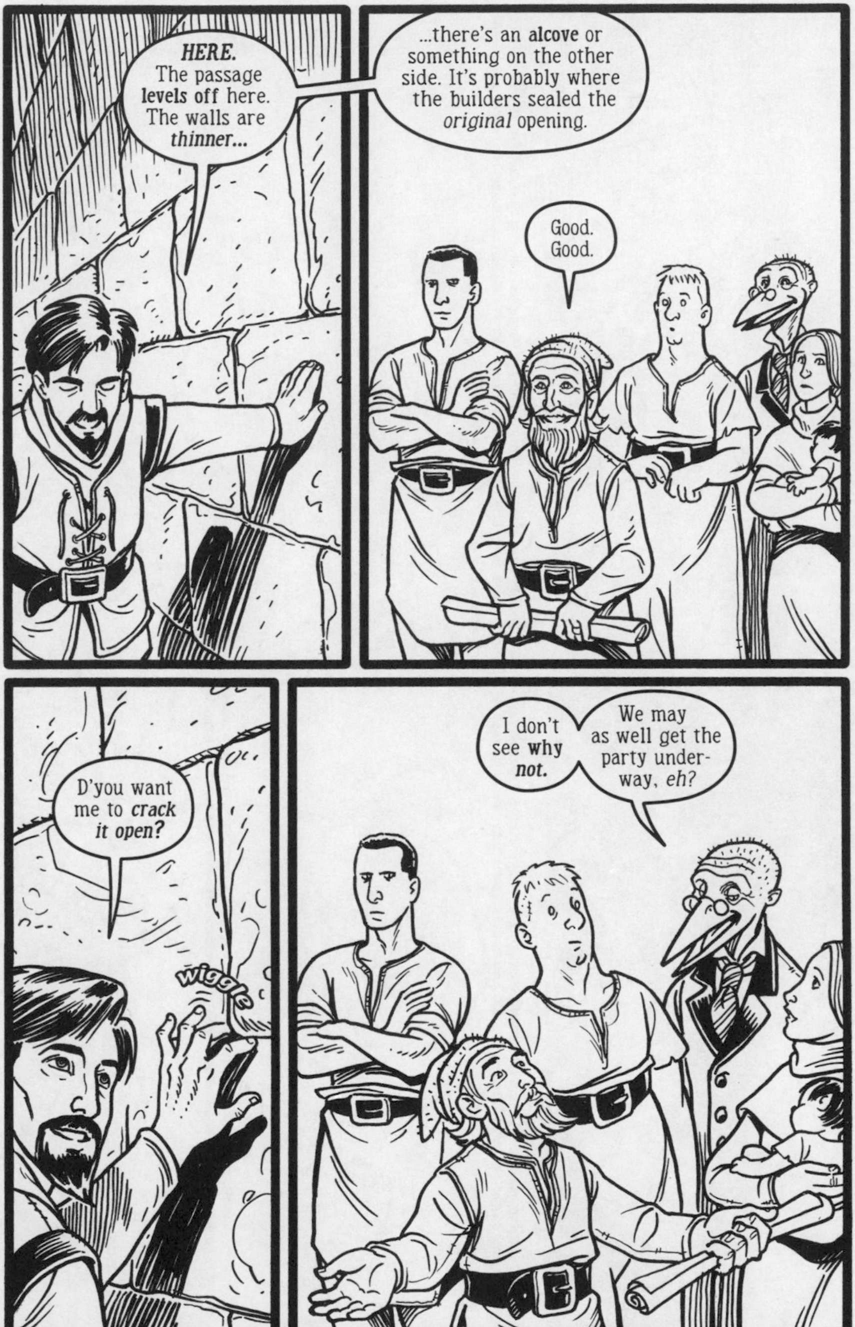
HERE.
The passage levels off here. The walls are thinner...
...there's an alcove or something on the other side. It's probably where the builders sealed the original opening.
Good. Good.
D'you want me to crack it open?
wiggle
We may as well get the party under-way, eh?
I don't see why not.

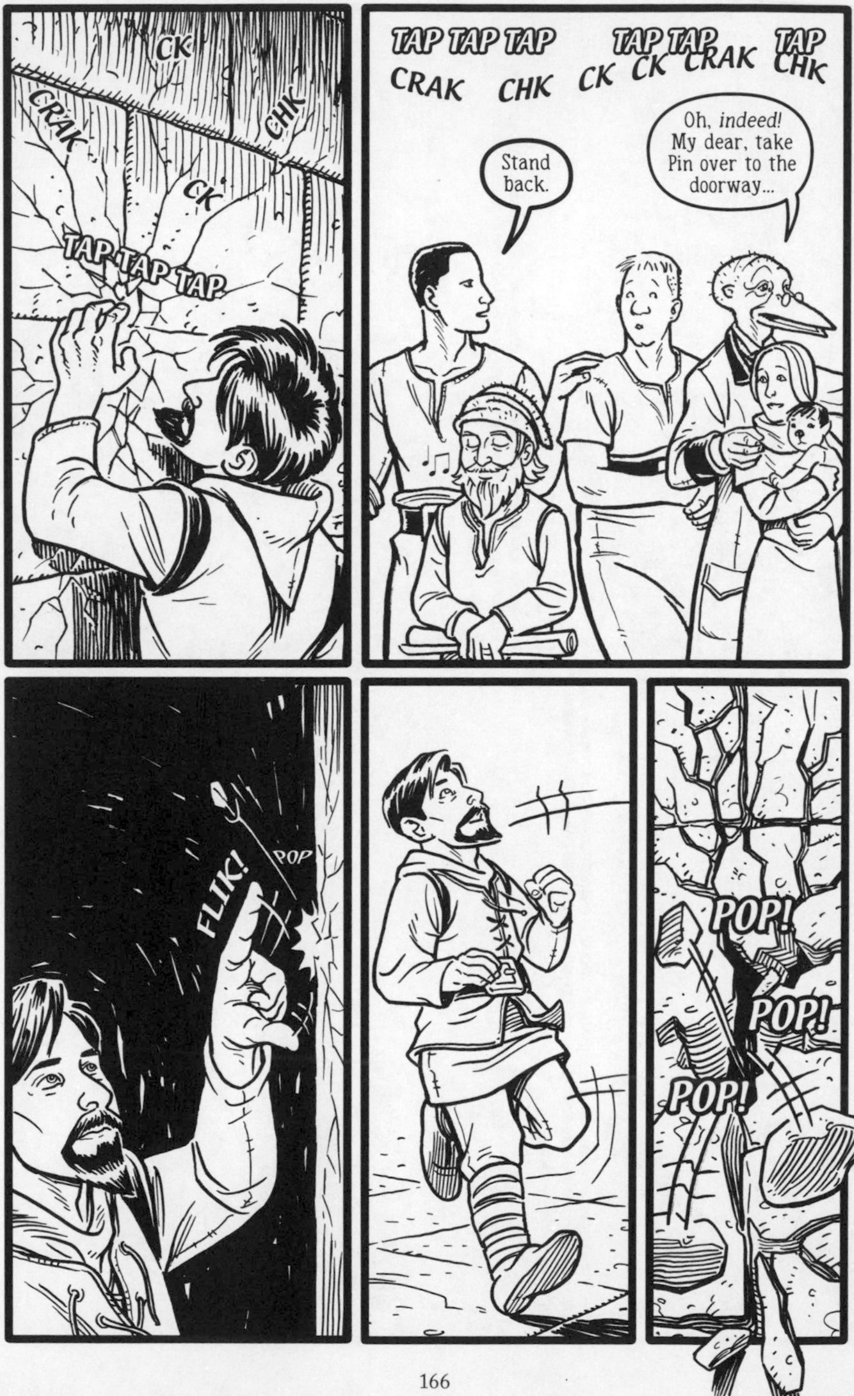
CK
CRAK
CHK
CK
TAP TAP TAP
TAP TAP TAP
CRAK
CHK
CK
TAP TAP
CK
CRAK
TAP
CHK
Stand back.
Oh, *indeed!* My dear, take Pin over to the doorway...
FLIK!
POP
POP!
POP!
POP!

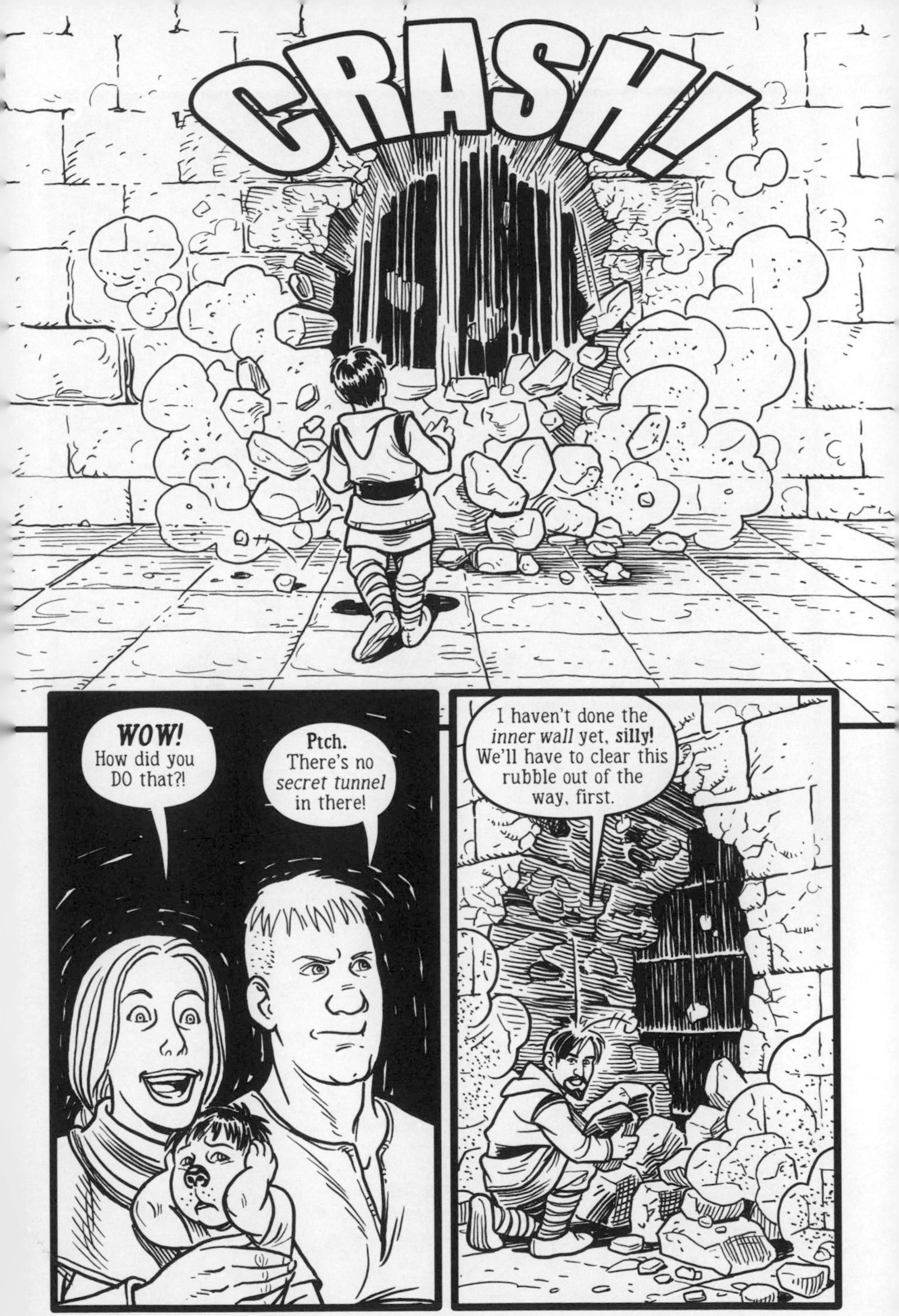
CRASH!
WOW! How did you DO that?!
Ptch. There's no *secret tunnel* in there!
I haven't done the *inner wall* yet, **silly!** We'll have to clear this rubble out of the way, first.

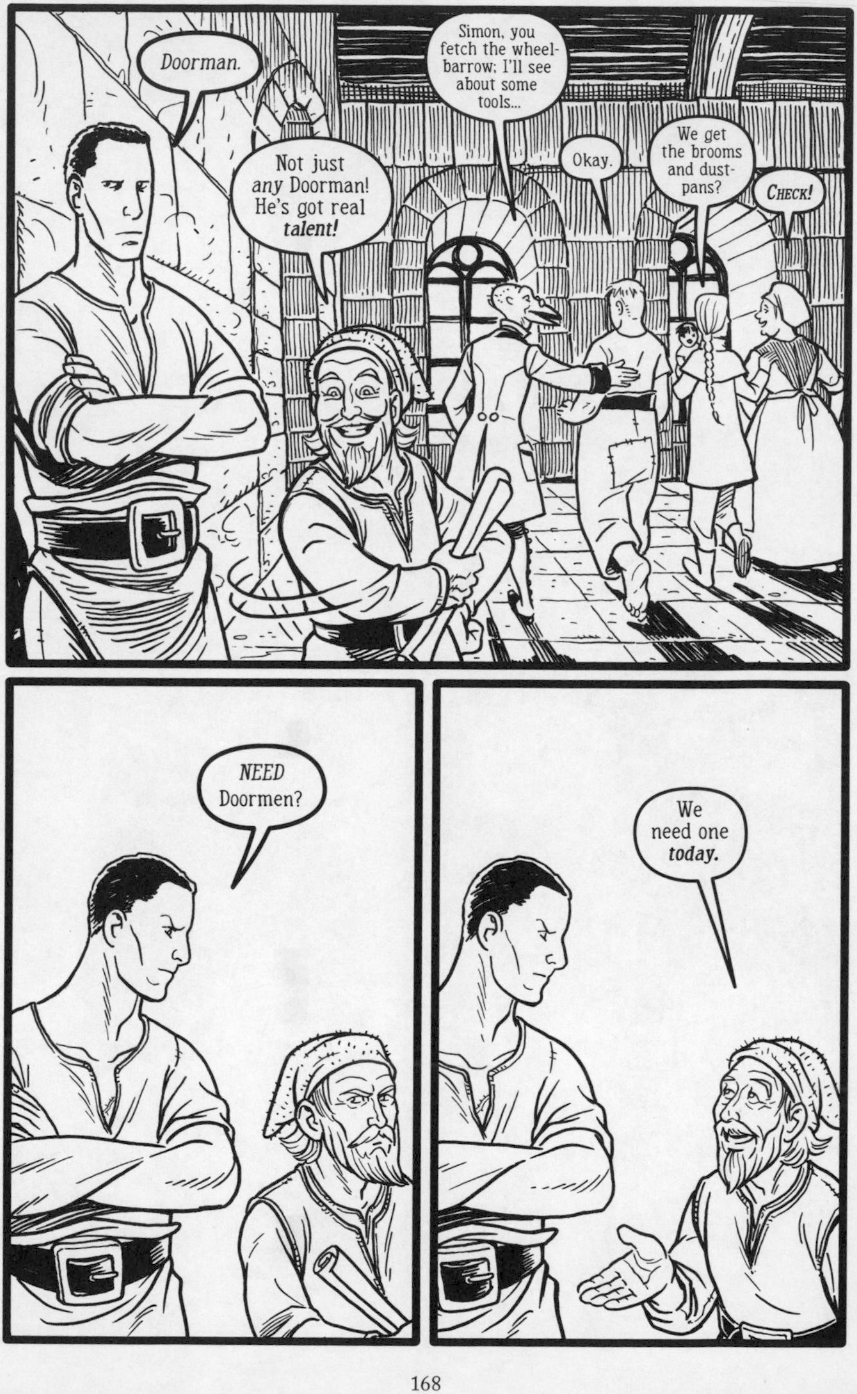
Doorman.
Not just any Doorman! He's got real *talent!*
Simon, you fetch the wheel-barrow; I'll see about some tools...
Okay.
We get the brooms and dust-pans?
CHECK!
NEED Doormen?
We need one ***today.***

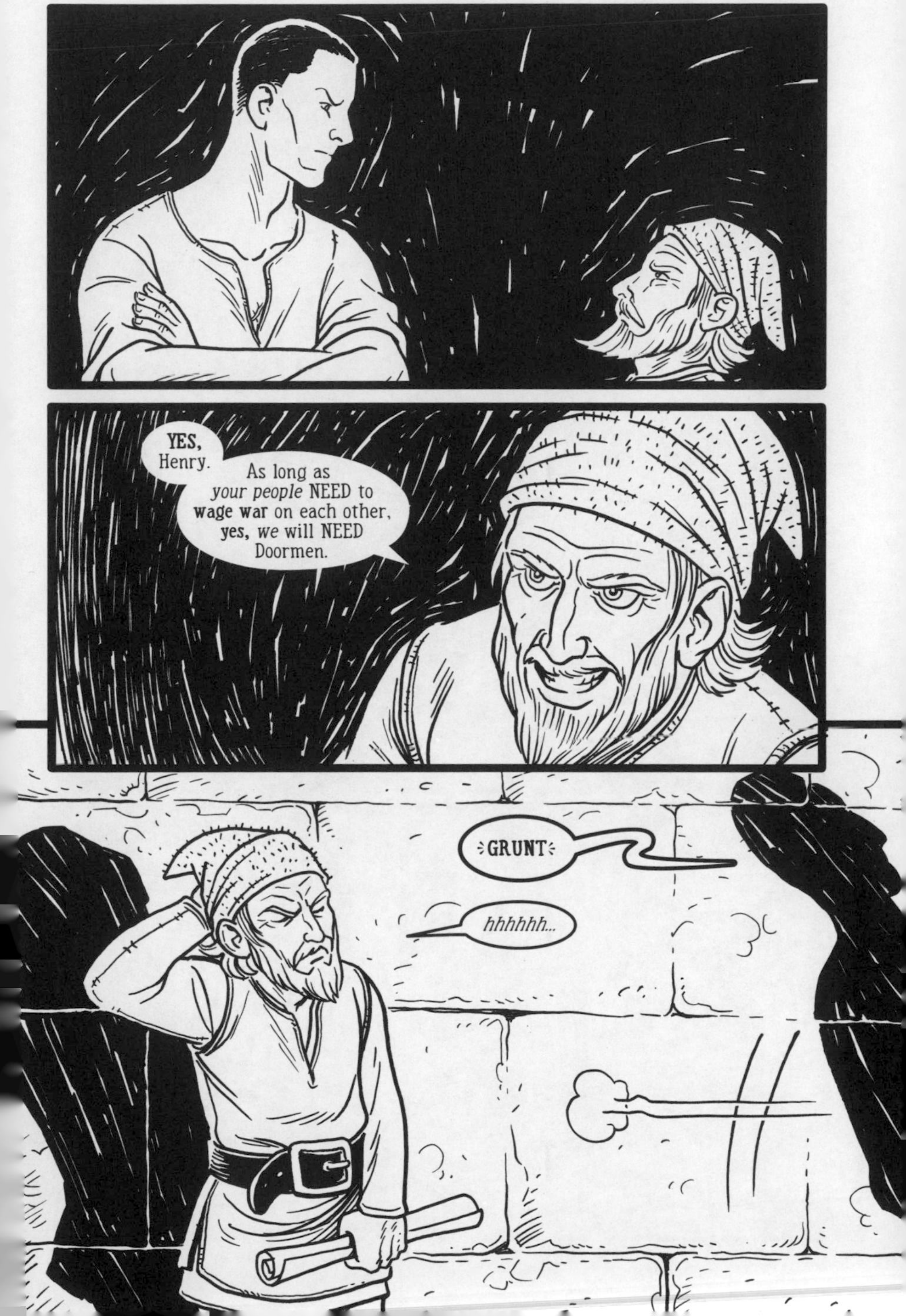
YES, Henry.
As long as *your people* NEED to **wage war** on each other, **yes,** *we* will NEED Doormen.
GRUNT
hhhhhh...

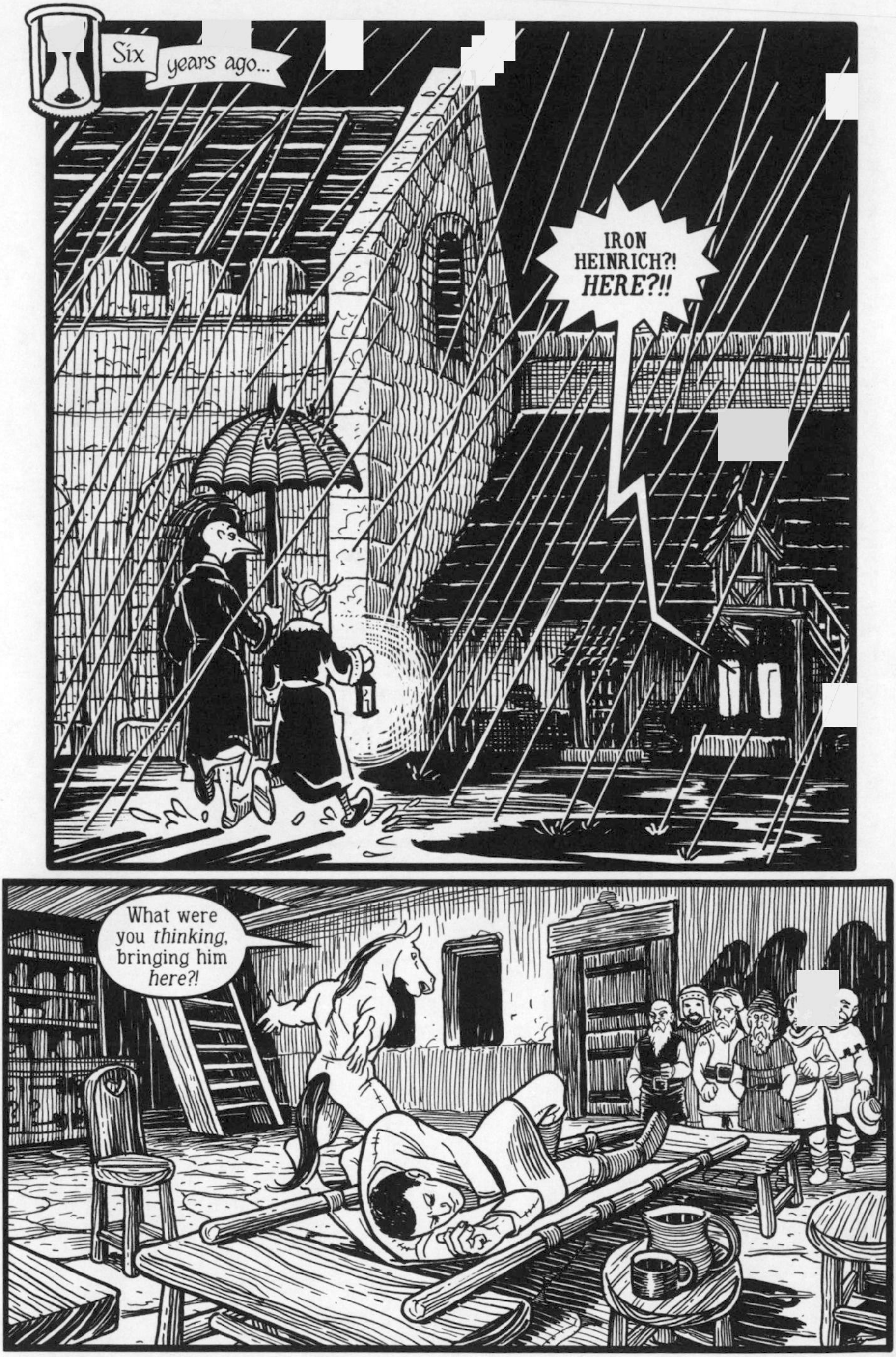
Six years ago...
IRON HEINRICH?! HERE?!!
What were you thinking, bringing him here?!

--I heard that *thousands* are dead up north! THOUSANDS! The country's a *wasteland.* How did he ESCAPE?!

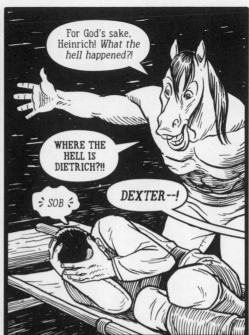

For God's sake, Heinrich! *What the hell happened?!*

WHERE THE HELL IS DIETRICH?!!

⚡ SOB ⚡

DEXTER--!

LEAVE HIM ALONE!

WHUD

OW!

We need *help*, not *harassment!*

Yeah? You--

ENOUGH!

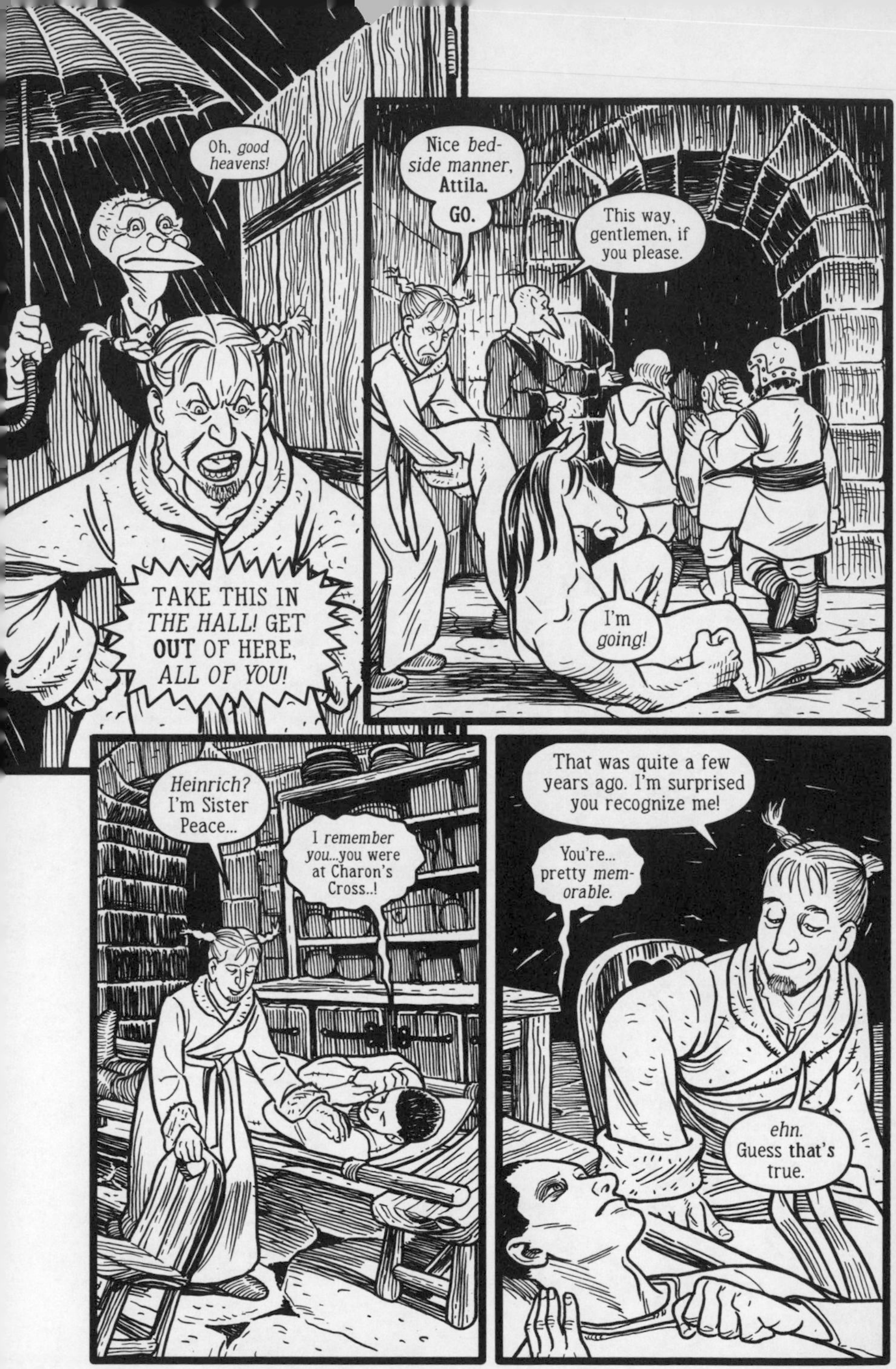
Oh, good heavens!
TAKE THIS IN THE HALL! GET OUT OF HERE, ALL OF YOU!
Nice bed-side manner, Attila.
GO.
This way, gentlemen, if you please.
I'm going!
Heinrich? I'm Sister Peace...
I remember you...you were at Charon's Cross..!
That was quite a few years ago. I'm surprised you recognize me!
You're... pretty mem-orable.
ehn. Guess that's true.

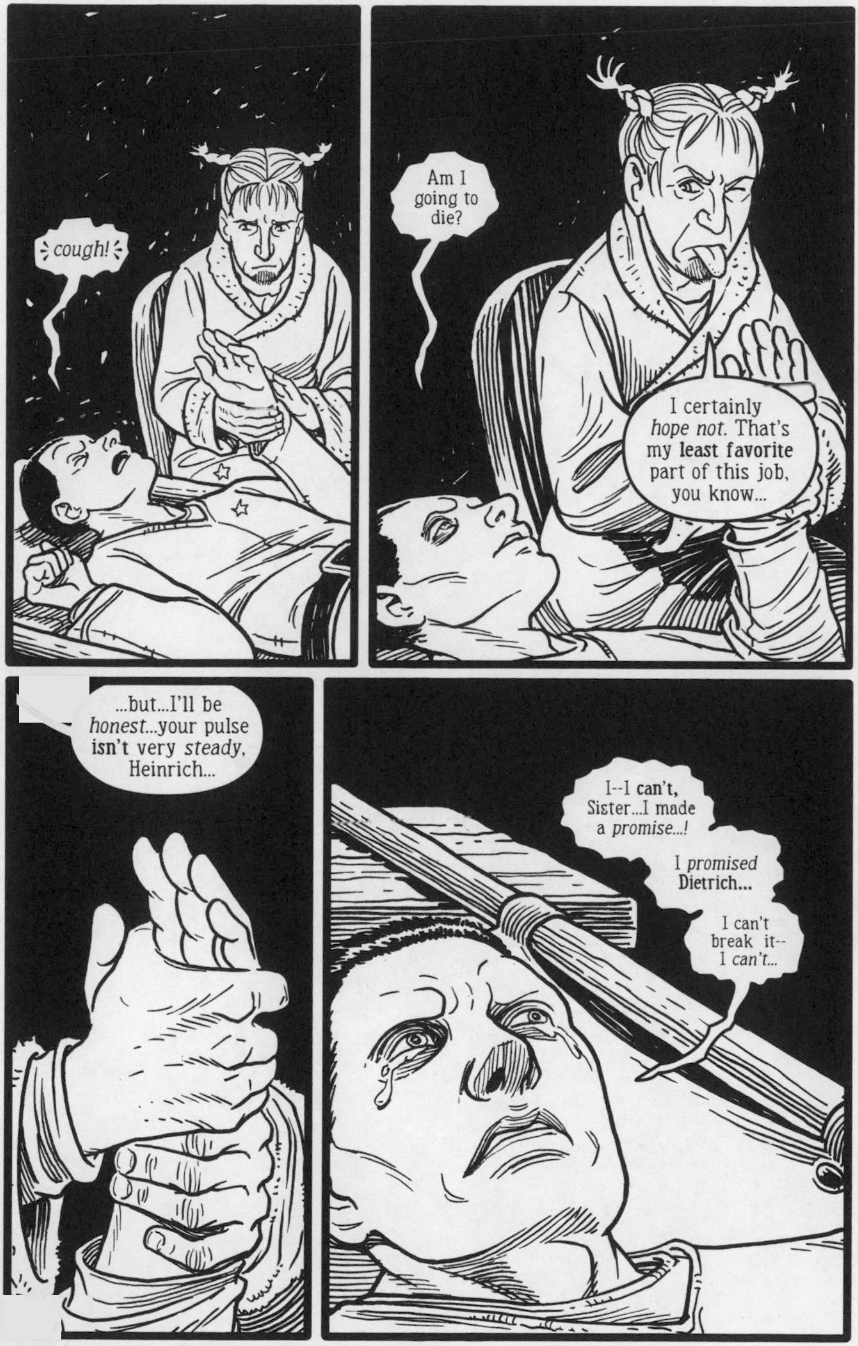
cough!
Am I going to die?
I certainly *hope not.* That's my **least favorite** part of this job, you know...
...but...I'll be *honest*...your pulse **isn't** very *steady,* Heinrich...
I--I **can't,** Sister...I made a *promise...!*
I *promised* **Dietrich...**
I can't break it-- I *can't...*

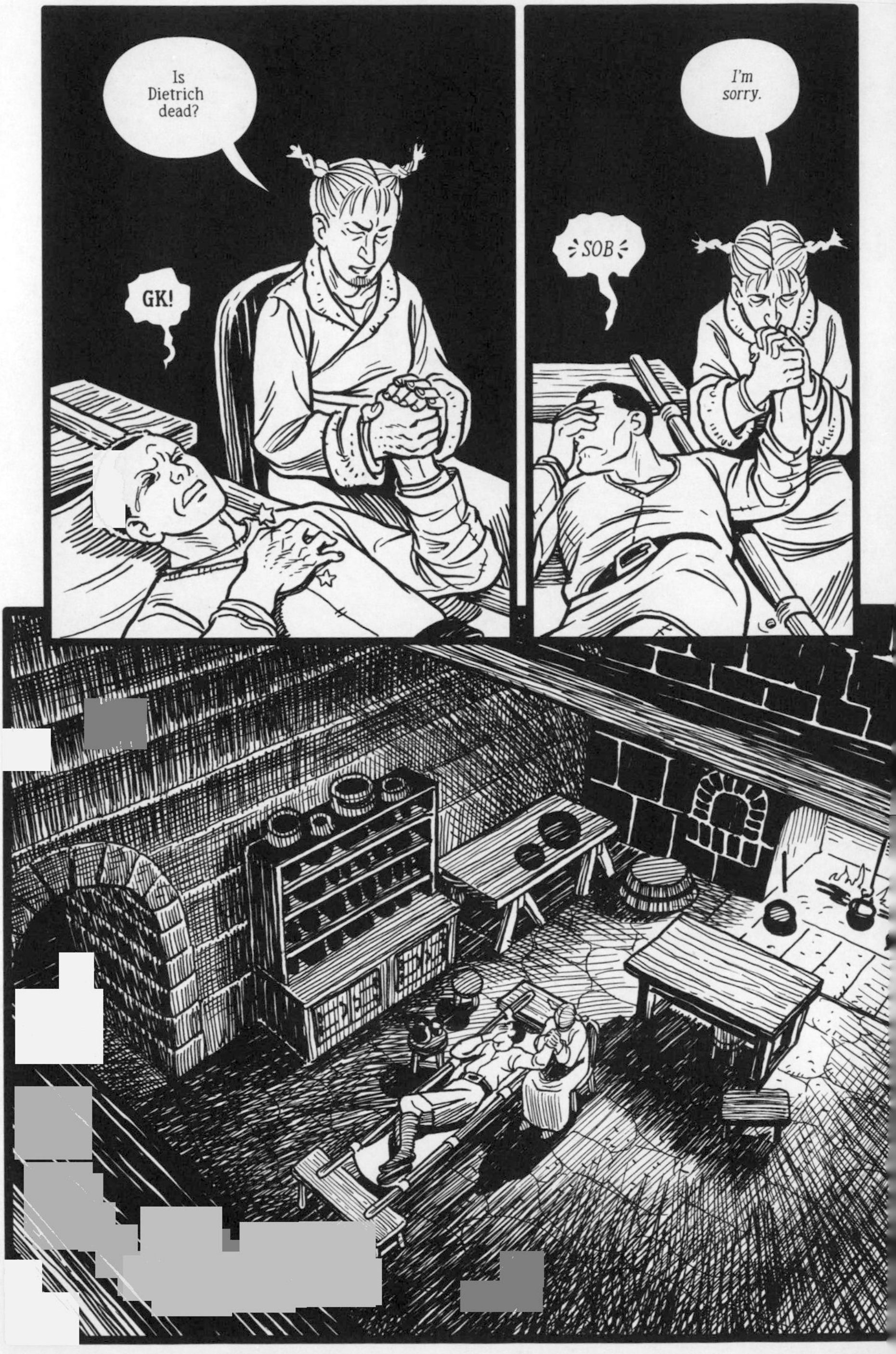
Is Dietrich dead?
GK!
I'm sorry.
SOB

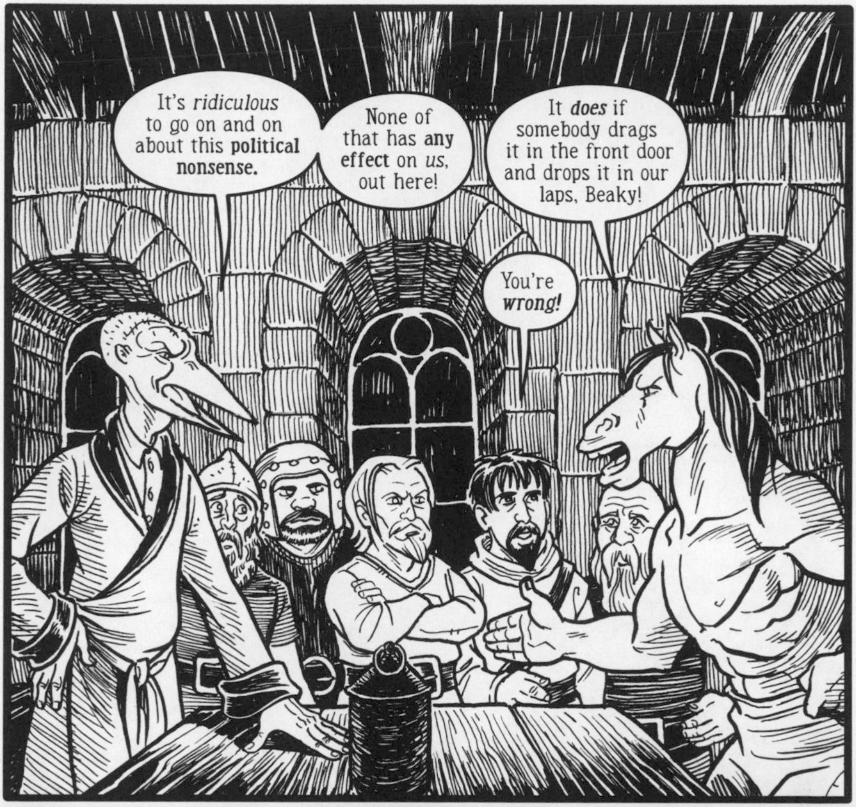
It's *ridiculous* to go on and on about this **political nonsense.**
None of that has **any effect** on *us*, out here!
It ***does*** if somebody drags it in the front door and drops it in our laps, Beaky!
You're ***wrong!***

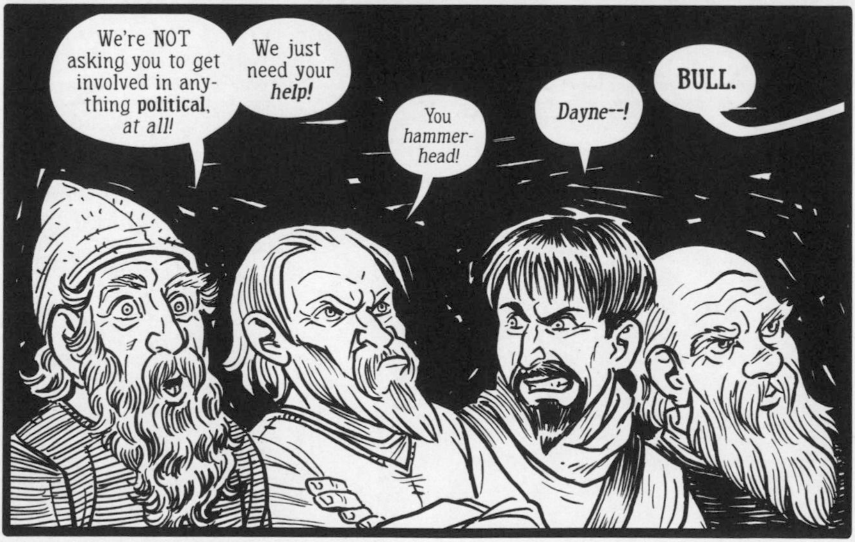
We're NOT asking you to get involved in any-thing **political**, *at all!*
We just need your ***help!***
You hammer-head!
Dayne--!
BULL.

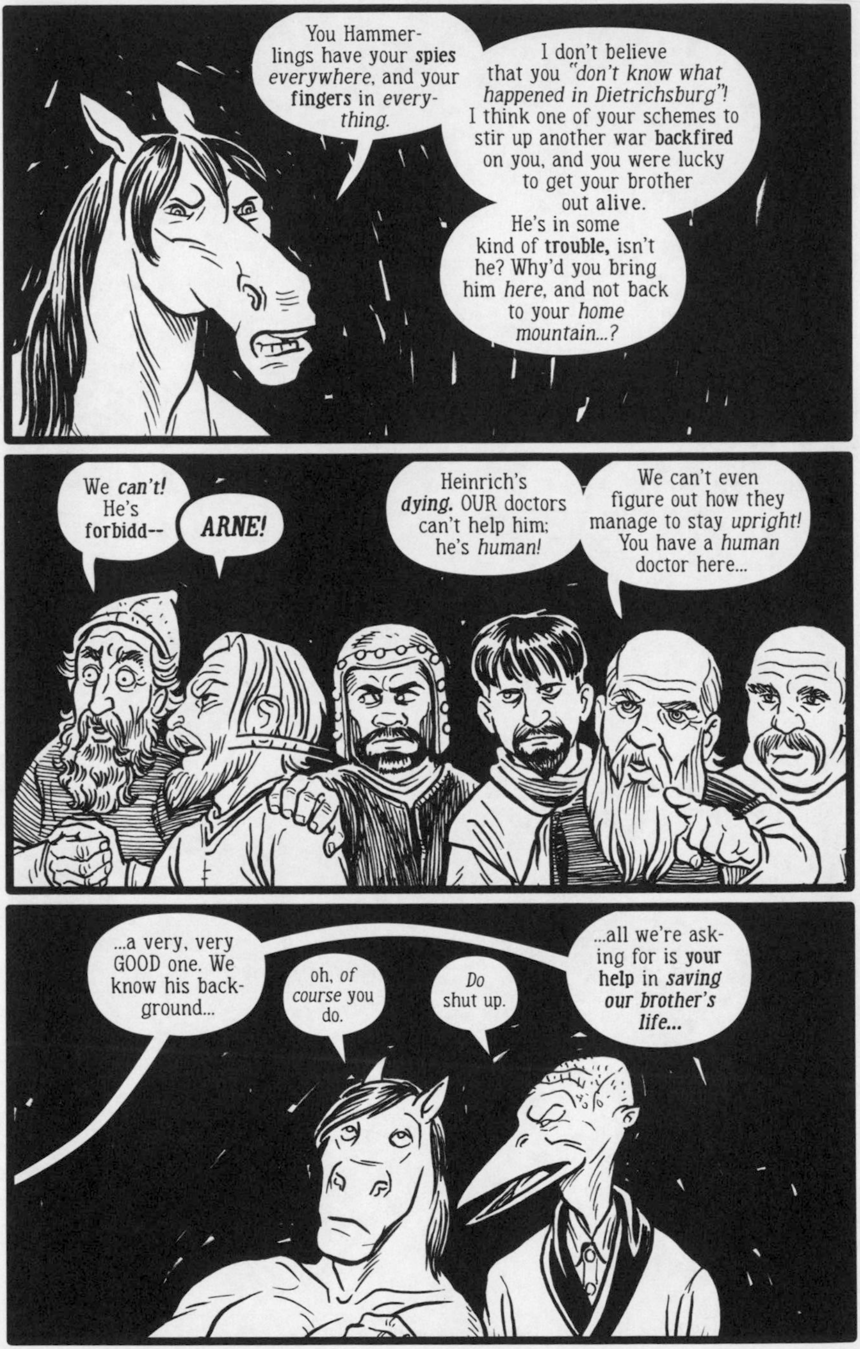
You Hammerlings have your **spies** *everywhere*, and your **fingers** in *everything.*
I don't believe that you *"don't know what happened in Dietrichsburg"*! I think one of your schemes to stir up another war **backfired** on you, and you were lucky to get your brother out alive.
He's in some kind of **trouble,** isn't he? Why'd you bring him *here*, and not back to your *home mountain...?*
We *can't!* He's **forbidd--**
ARNE!
Heinrich's ***dying.*** OUR doctors can't help him; he's *human!*
We can't even figure out how they manage to stay *upright!* You have a *human* doctor here...
...a very, very GOOD one. We know his background...
oh, *of course* you do.
Do shut up.
...all we're asking for is **your help** in ***saving our brother's life...***

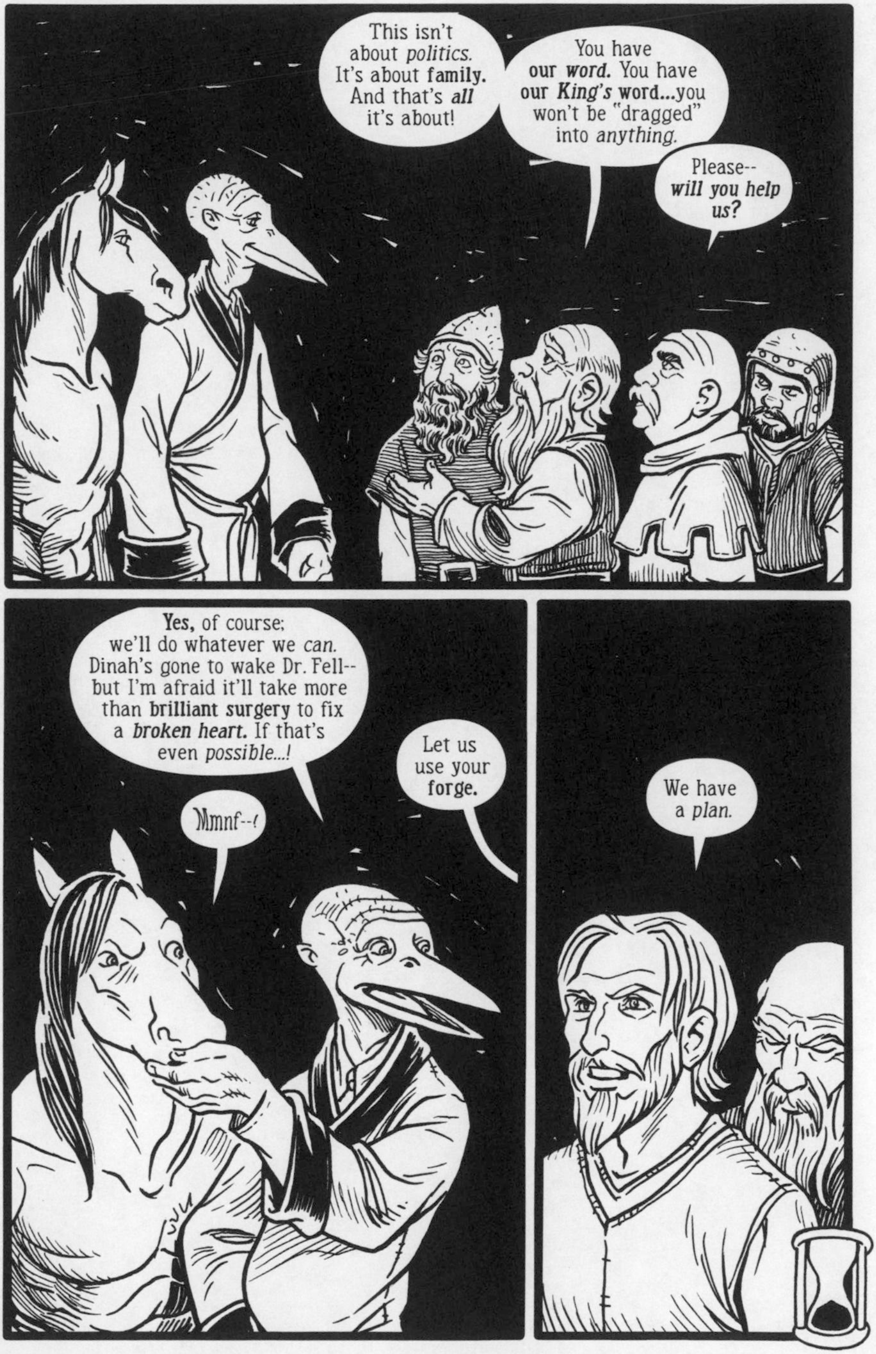
This isn't about *politics.* It's about **family.** And that's ***all*** it's about!
You have **our *word.*** You have **our *King's* word...**you won't be "dragged" into *anything.*
Please-- ***will you help us?***
Yes, of course; we'll do whatever we *can.* Dinah's gone to wake Dr. Fell-- but I'm afraid it'll take more than **brilliant surgery** to fix a ***broken heart.*** If that's even *possible...!*
Mmnf--!
Let us use your **forge.**
We have a *plan.*

Chapter 8.

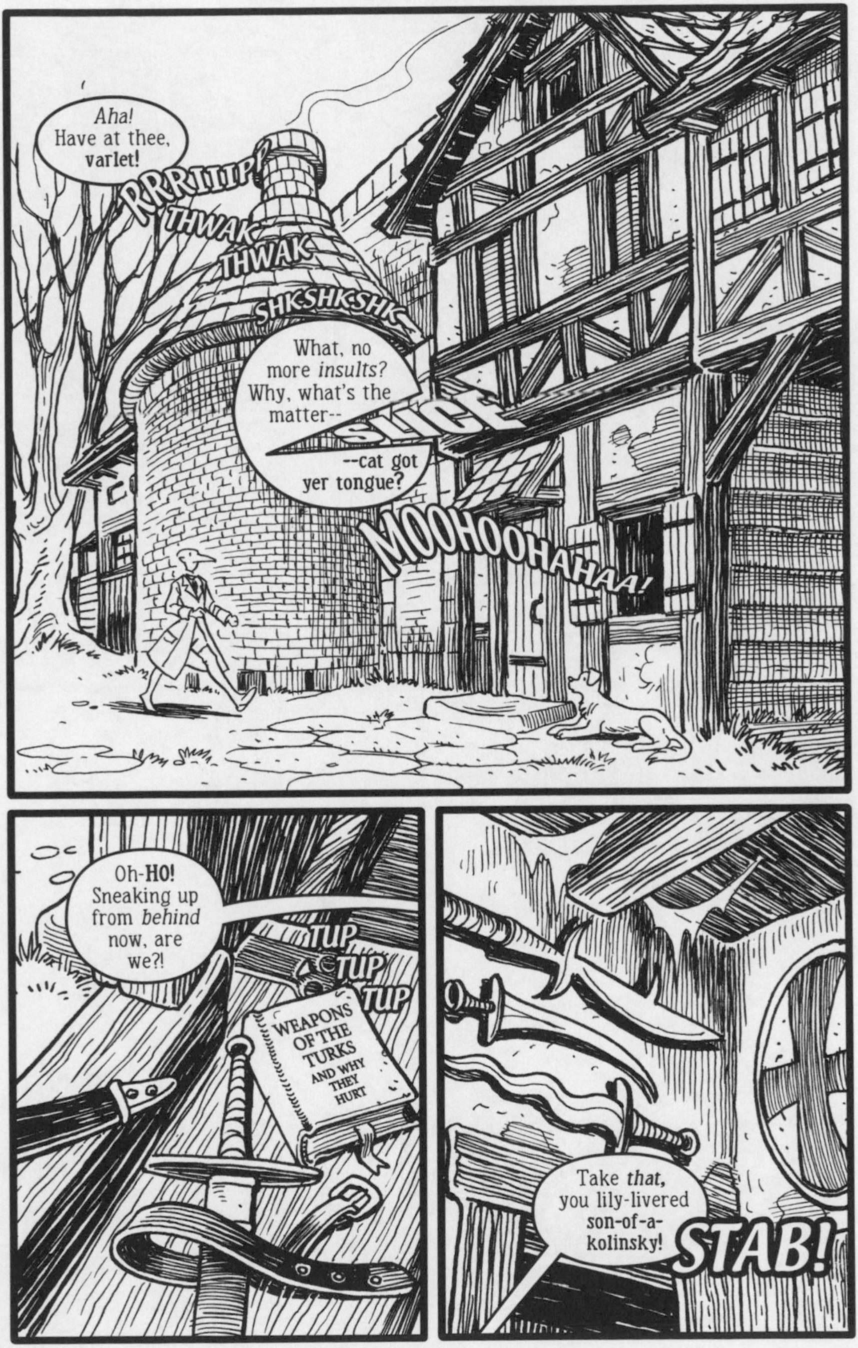
Aha! Have at thee, varlet!
RRRIIIP!
THWAK
THWAK
SHKSHKSHK
What, no more *insults*? Why, what's the matter--
SLICE
--cat got yer tongue?
MOOHOOHAHAA!
Oh-HO! Sneaking up from *behind* now, are we?!
TUP
TUP
TUP
WEAPONS OF THE TURKS AND WHY THEY HURT
Take *that*, you lily-livered son-of-a-kolinsky!
STAB!

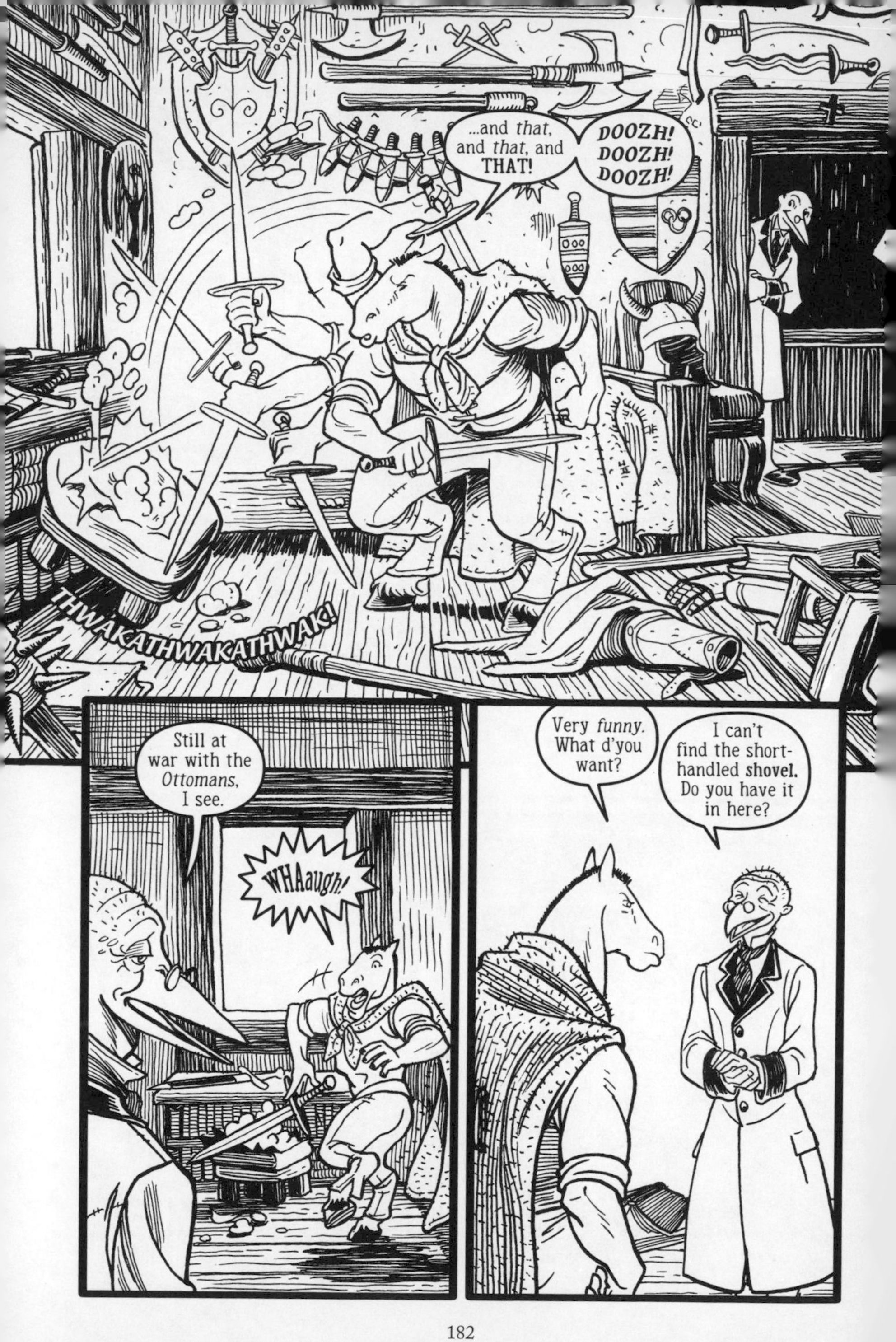
...and *that*, and *that*, and **THAT!**
DOOZH! DOOZH! DOOZH!
THWAKATHWAKATHWAK!
Still at war with the *Ottomans*, I see.
WHAaugh!
Very *funny*. What d'you want?
I can't find the short-handled **shovel.** Do you have it in here?

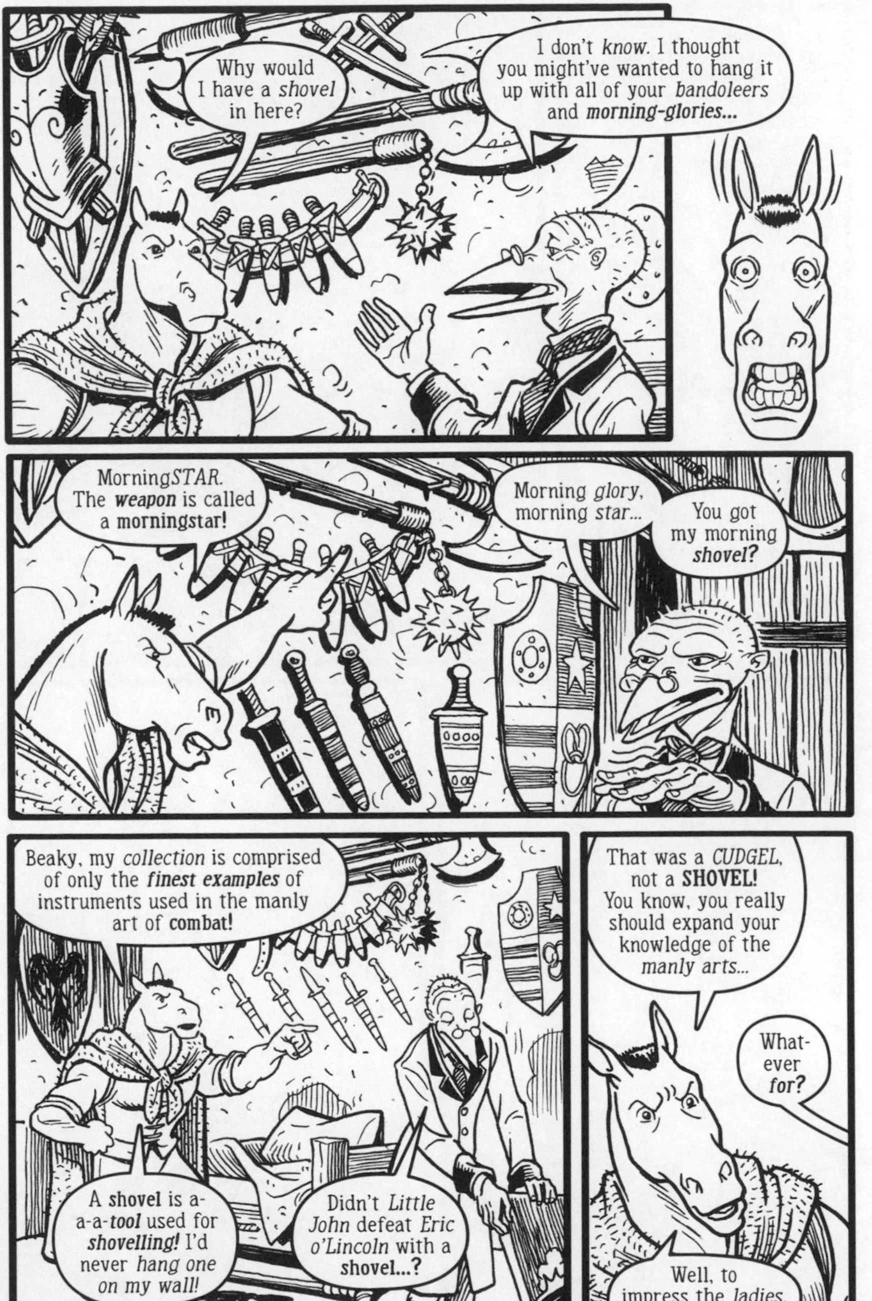
Why would I have a *shovel* in here?
I don't *know*. I thought you might've wanted to hang it up with all of your *bandoleers* and ***morning-glories...***
Morning*STAR*. The ***weapon*** is called a **morningstar!**
Morning *glory*, morning *star*...
You got my morning ***shovel?***
Beaky, my *collection* is comprised of only the ***finest examples*** of instruments used in the manly art of **combat!**
A **shovel** is a-a-a-***tool*** used for ***shovelling!*** I'd never *hang one on my wall!*
Didn't *Little John* defeat *Eric o'Lincoln* with a **shovel...?**
That was a *CUDGEL*, not a **SHOVEL!** You know, you really should expand your knowledge of the *manly arts...*
What-ever ***for?***
Well, to impress the *ladies*, for starters!

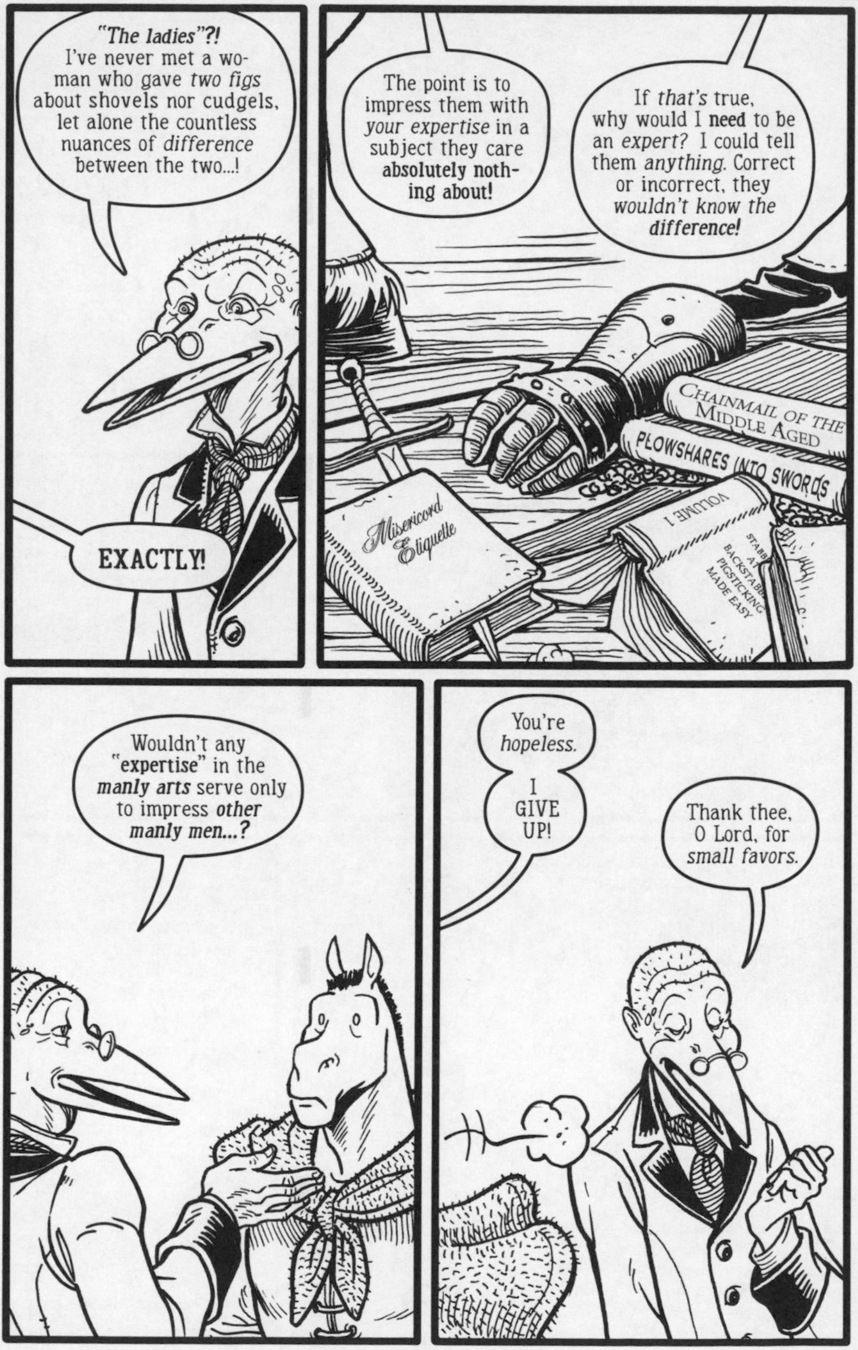
"The ladies"?! I've never met a woman who gave two figs about shovels nor cudgels, let alone the countless nuances of difference between the two...!
EXACTLY!
The point is to impress them with your expertise in a subject they care absolutely nothing about!
If that's true, why would I need to be an expert? I could tell them anything. Correct or incorrect, they wouldn't know the difference!
CHAINMAIL OF THE MIDDLE AGED
PLOWSHARES INTO SWORDS
VOLUME I
STABB AT BACKSTABB PIGSTICKING MADE EASY
Misericord Etiquette
Wouldn't any "expertise" in the manly arts serve only to impress other manly men...?
You're hopeless.
I GIVE UP!
Thank thee, O Lord, for small favors.

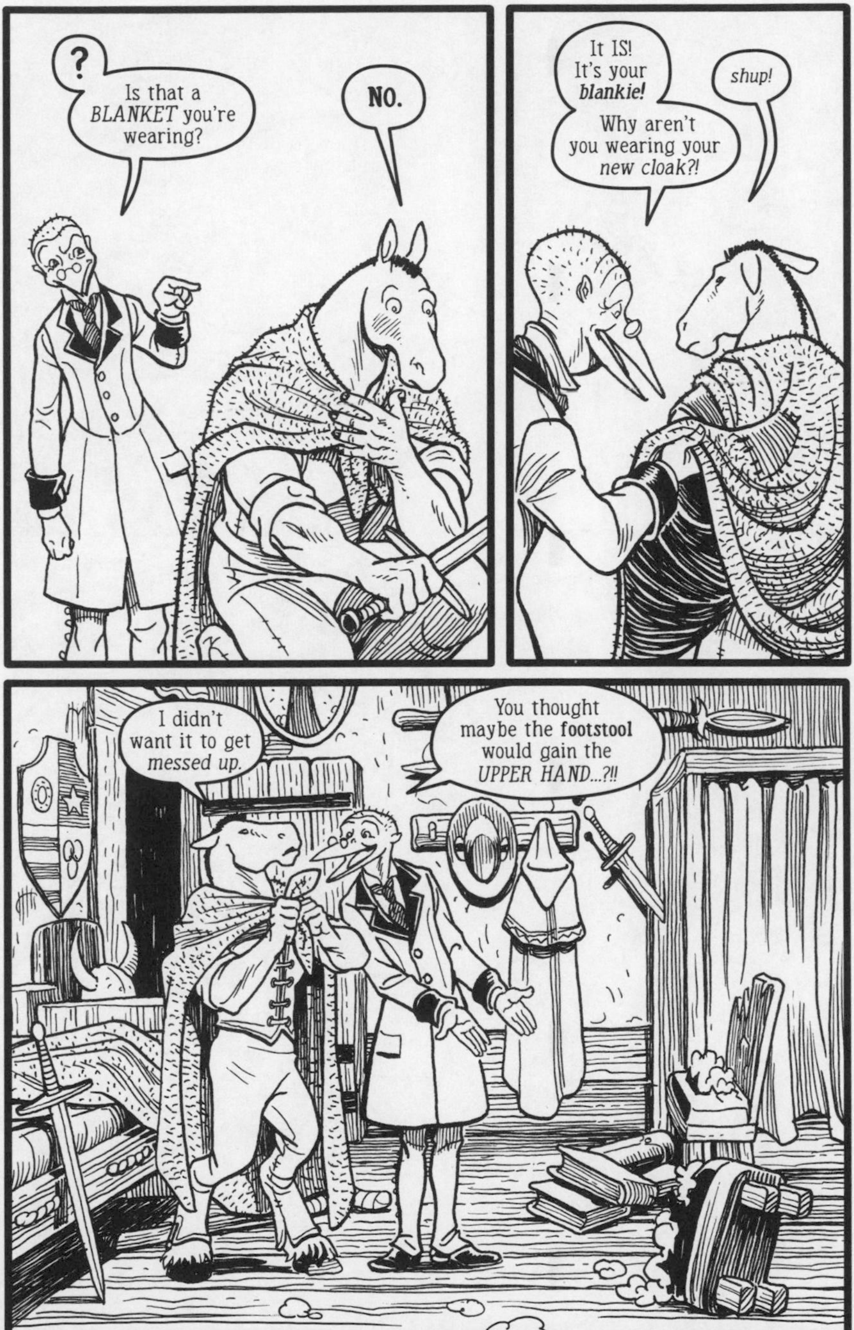
?
Is that a BLANKET you're wearing?
NO.
It IS! It's your blankie!
Why aren't you wearing your new cloak?!
shup!
I didn't want it to get messed up.
You thought maybe the footstool would gain the UPPER HAND...?!!

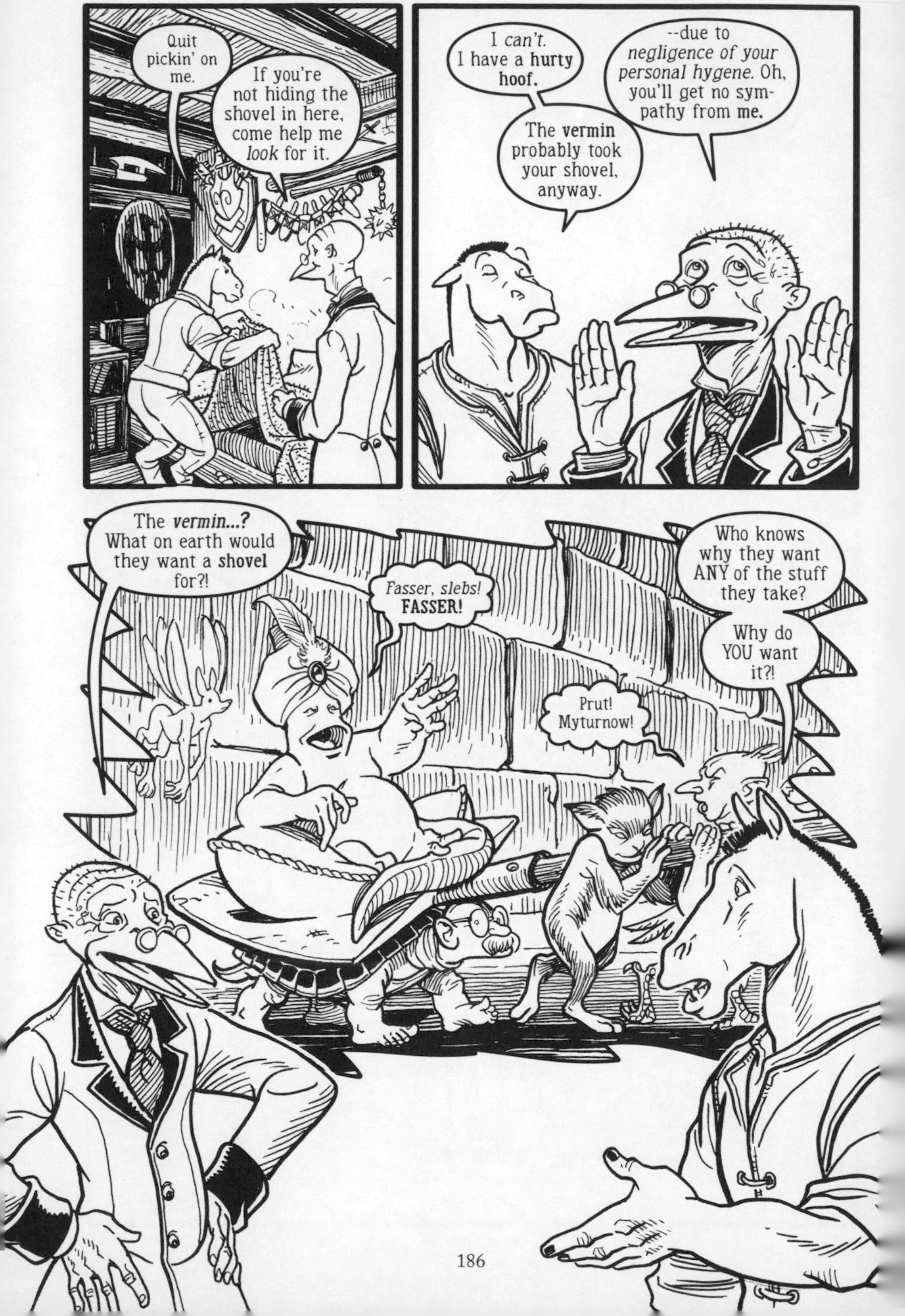
Quit pickin' on me.
If you're not hiding the shovel in here, come help me *look* for it.
I *can't*. I have a **hurty hoof.**
The **vermin** probably took your shovel, anyway.
--due to *negligence of your personal hygene.* Oh, you'll get no sympathy from **me.**
The ***vermin...?*** What on earth would they want a **shovel** for?!
Fasser, slebs! **FASSER!**
Prut! Myturnow!
Who knows why they want ANY of the stuff they take?
Why do YOU want it?!

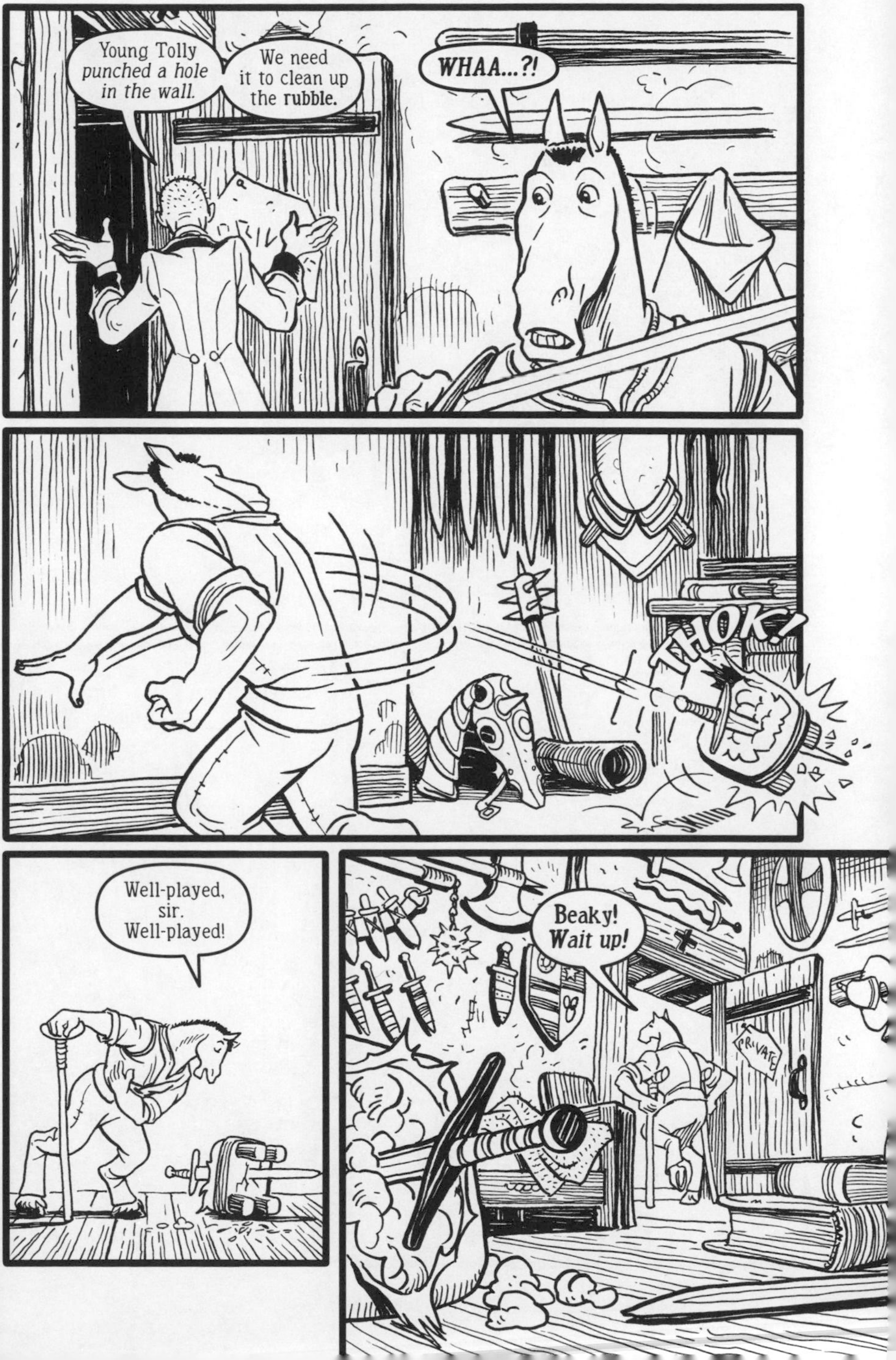

Young Tolly *punched a hole in the wall.*
We need it to clean up the **rubble.**
WHAA...?!
THOK!
Well-played, sir. Well-played!
Beaky! Wait up!
PRIVATE

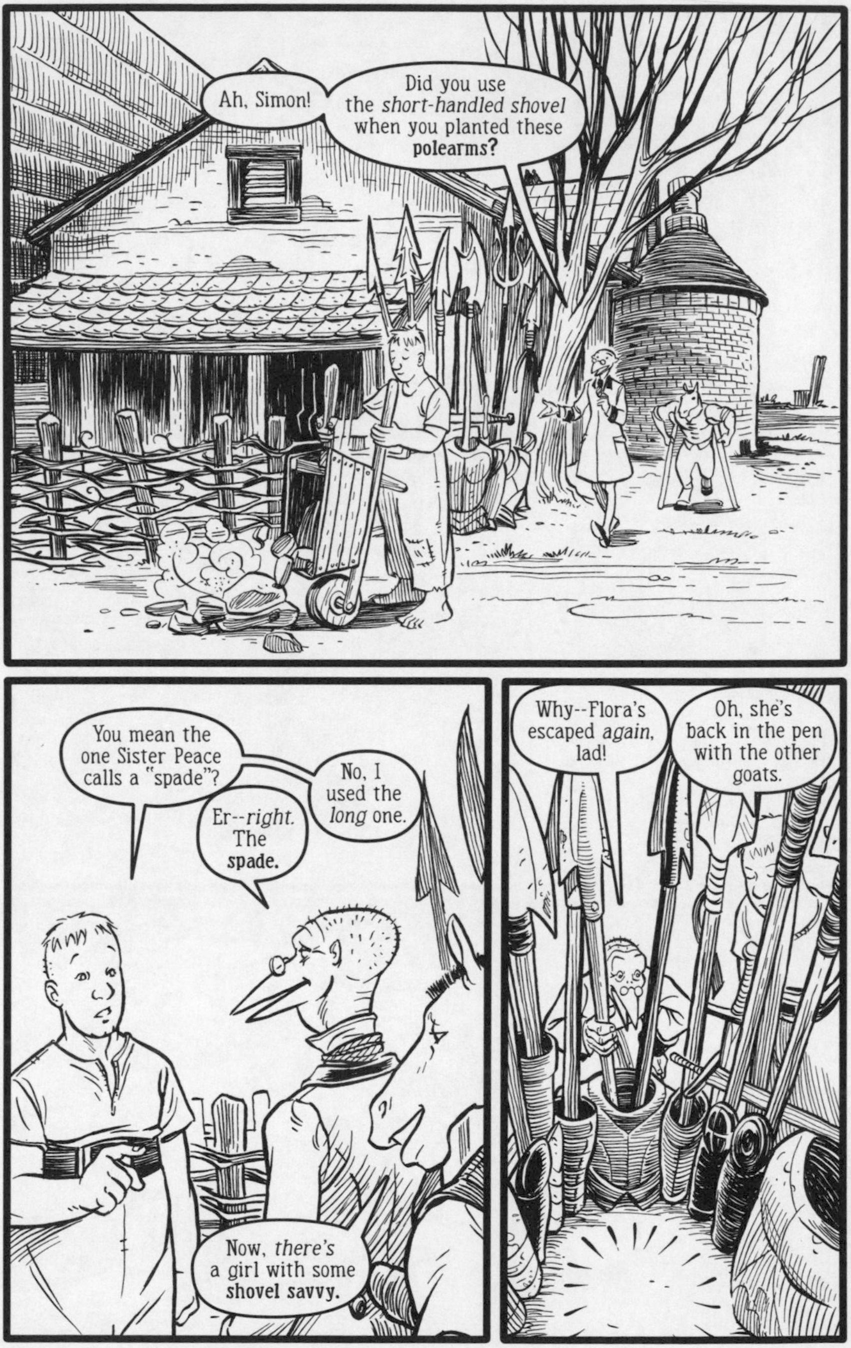
Ah, Simon!
Did you use the *short-handled shovel* when you planted these **polearms?**
You mean the one Sister Peace calls a "spade"?
No, I used the *long* one.
Er--*right.* The **spade.**
Now, *there's* a girl with some **shovel savvy.**
Why--Flora's escaped *again,* lad!
Oh, she's back in the pen with the other goats.

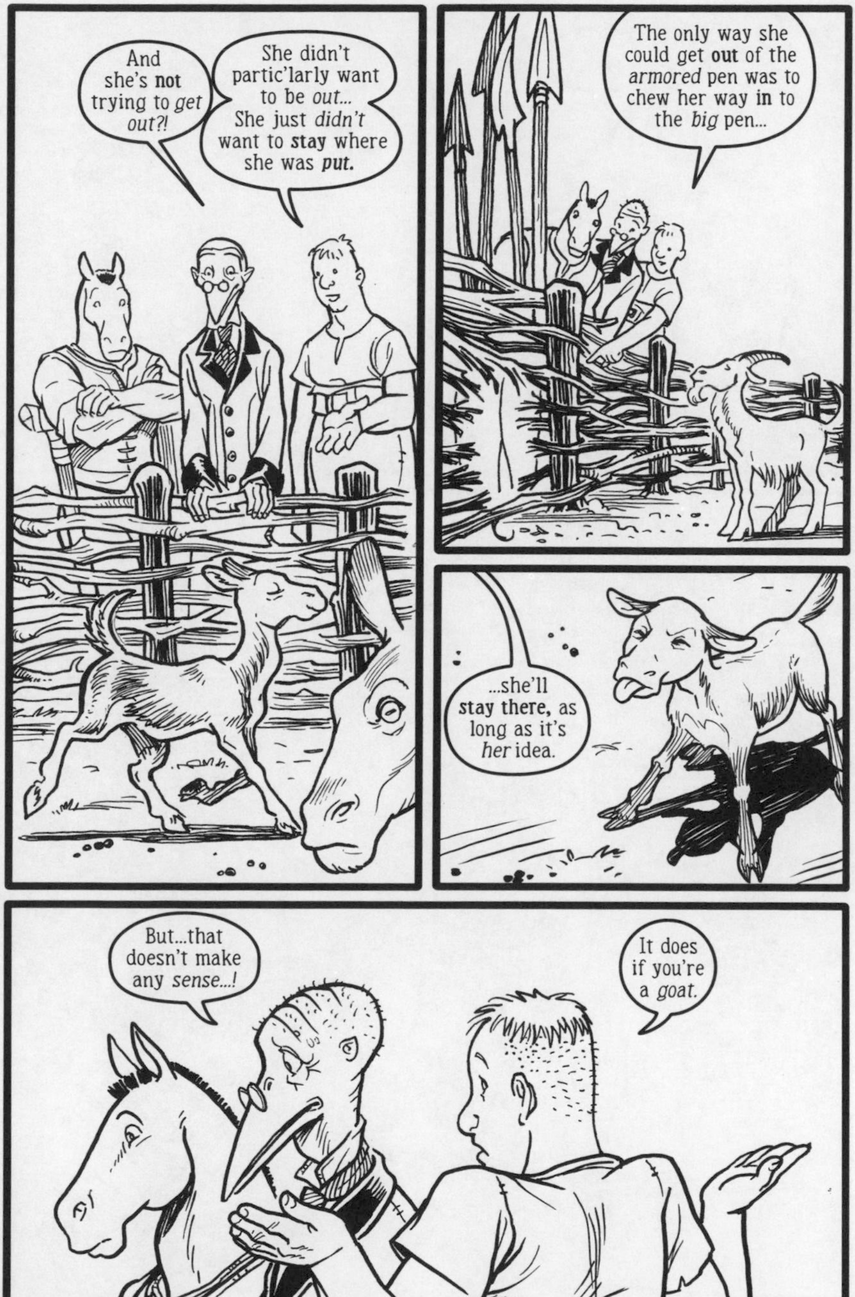
And she's **not** trying to *get out?!*
She didn't partic'larly want to be *out...* She just *didn't* want to **stay** where she was **put.**
The only way she could get **out** of the *armored* pen was to chew her way **in** to the *big* pen...
...she'll **stay there,** as long as it's *her* idea.
But...that doesn't make any *sense...!*
It does if you're a *goat.*

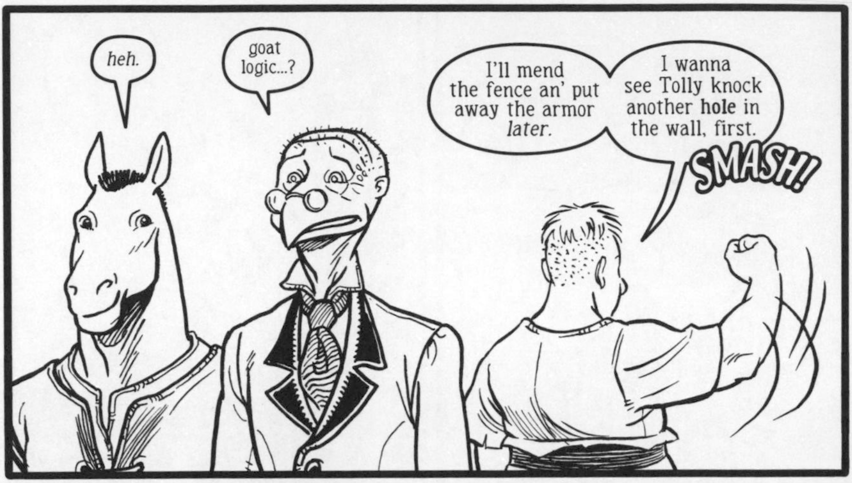
heh.
goat logic...?
I'll mend the fence an' put away the armor *later.*
I wanna see Tolly knock another **hole** in the wall, first.
SMASH!

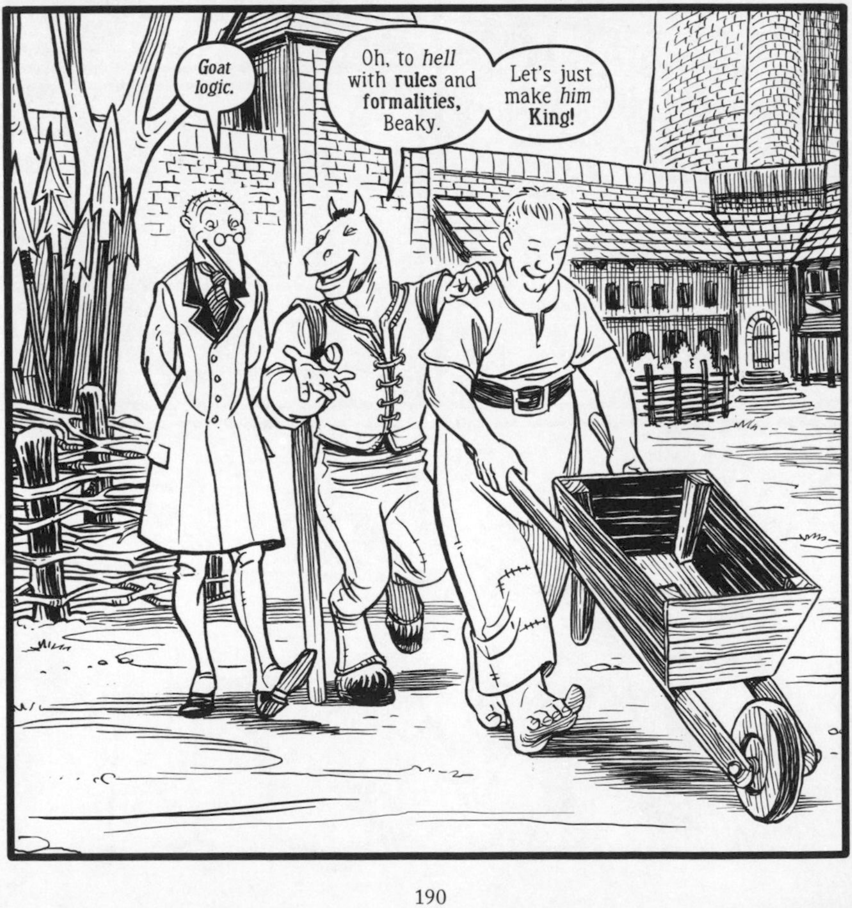
Goat logic.
Oh, to *hell* with **rules** and **formalities,** Beaky.
Let's just make *him* **King!**

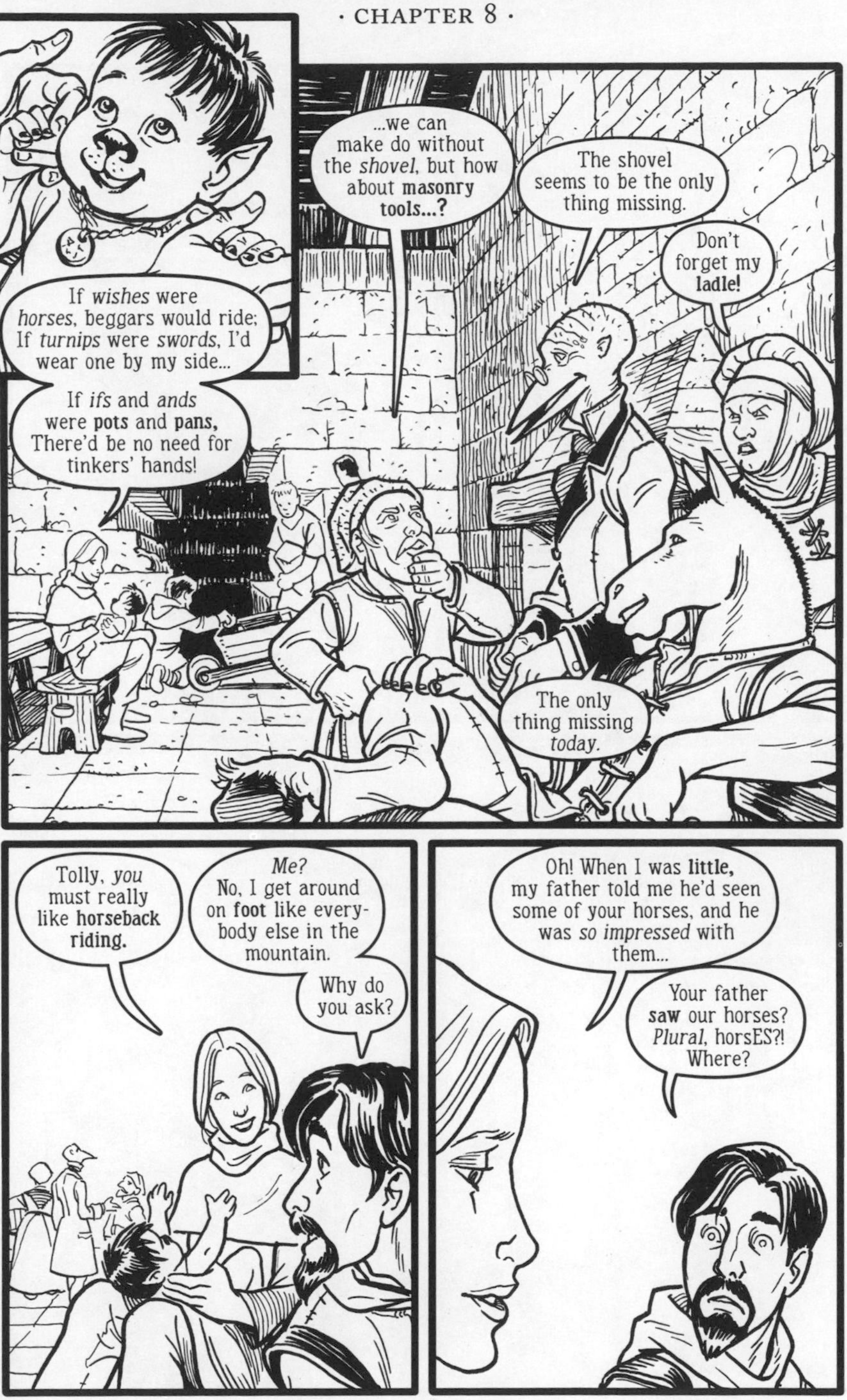
If wishes were horses, beggars would ride; If turnips were swords, I'd wear one by my side...
If ifs and ands were pots and pans, There'd be no need for tinkers' hands!
...we can make do without the shovel, but how about masonry tools...?
The shovel seems to be the only thing missing.
Don't forget my ladle!
The only thing missing today.
Tolly, you must really like horseback riding.
Me? No, I get around on foot like every-body else in the mountain.
Why do you ask?
Oh! When I was little, my father told me he'd seen some of your horses, and he was so impressed with them...
Your father saw our horses? Plural, horsES?! Where?

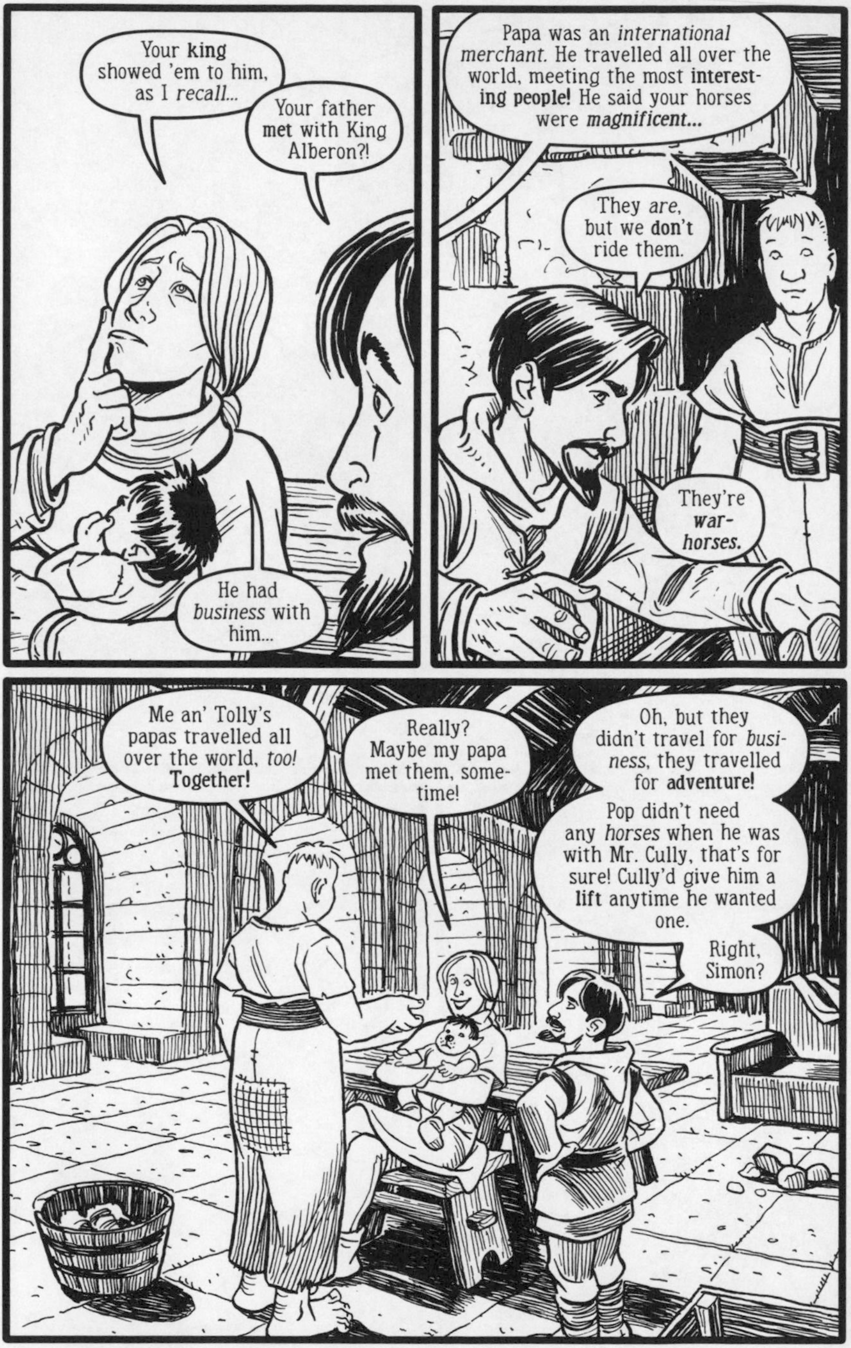
Your king showed 'em to him, as I recall...
Your father met with King Alberon?!
He had business with him...
Papa was an international merchant. He travelled all over the world, meeting the most interesting people! He said your horses were magnificent...
They are, but we don't ride them.
They're war-horses.
Me an' Tolly's papas travelled all over the world, too! Together!
Really? Maybe my papa met them, sometime!
Oh, but they didn't travel for business, they travelled for adventure!
Pop didn't need any horses when he was with Mr. Cully, that's for sure! Cully'd give him a lift anytime he wanted one.
Right, Simon?

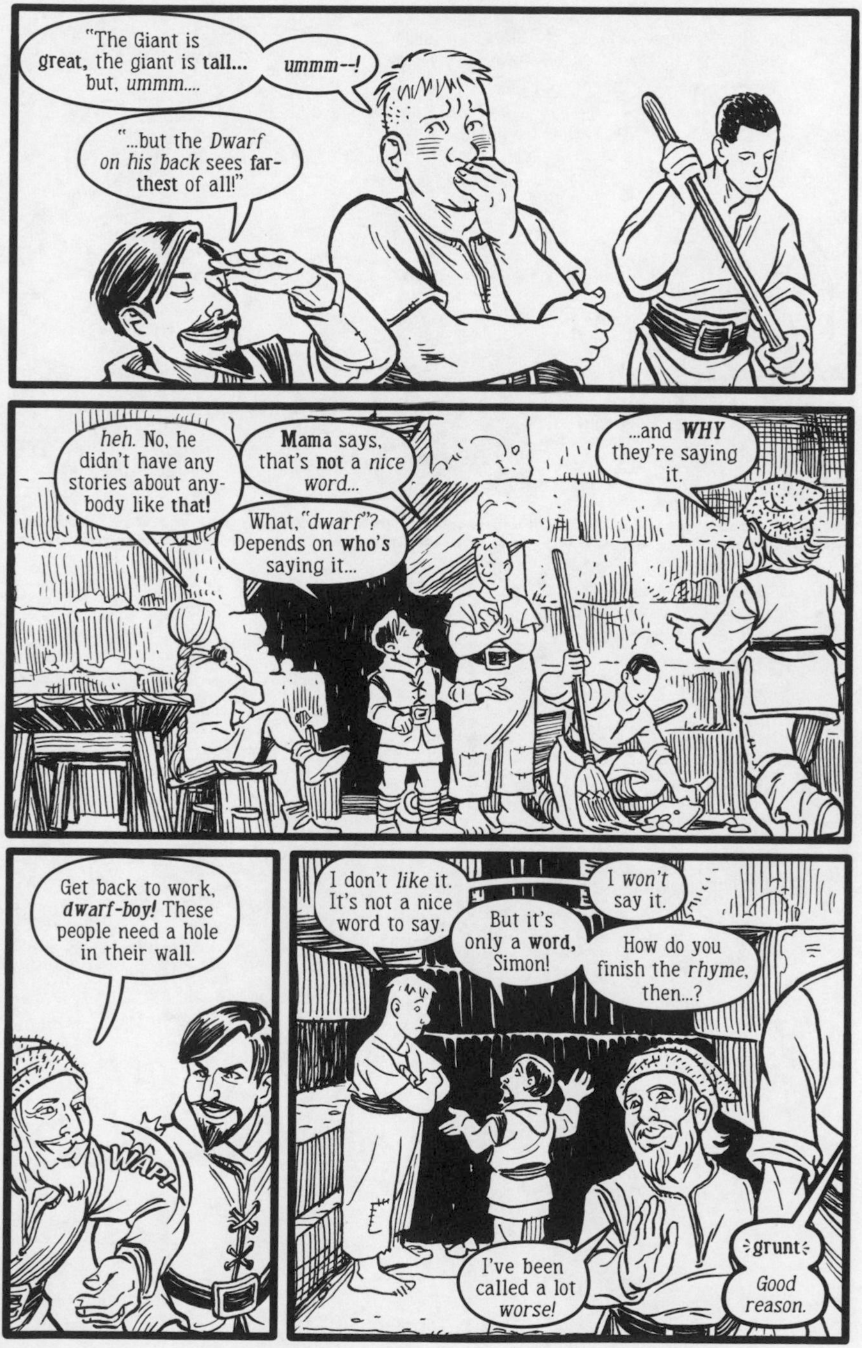
"The Giant is **great,** the giant is **tall...** but, *ummm....*
ummm--!
"...but the *Dwarf on his back* sees **far-thest** of all!"
heh. No, he didn't have any stories about any-body like **that!**
Mama says, that's **not** a *nice word...*
What, "*dwarf*"? Depends on **who's** saying it...
...and **WHY** they're saying it.
Get back to work, ***dwarf-boy!*** These people need a hole in their wall.
WAP!
I don't *like* it. It's not a nice word to say.
I *won't* say it.
But it's only a **word,** Simon!
How do you finish the *rhyme,* then...?
I've been called a lot *worse!*
grunt
Good reason.

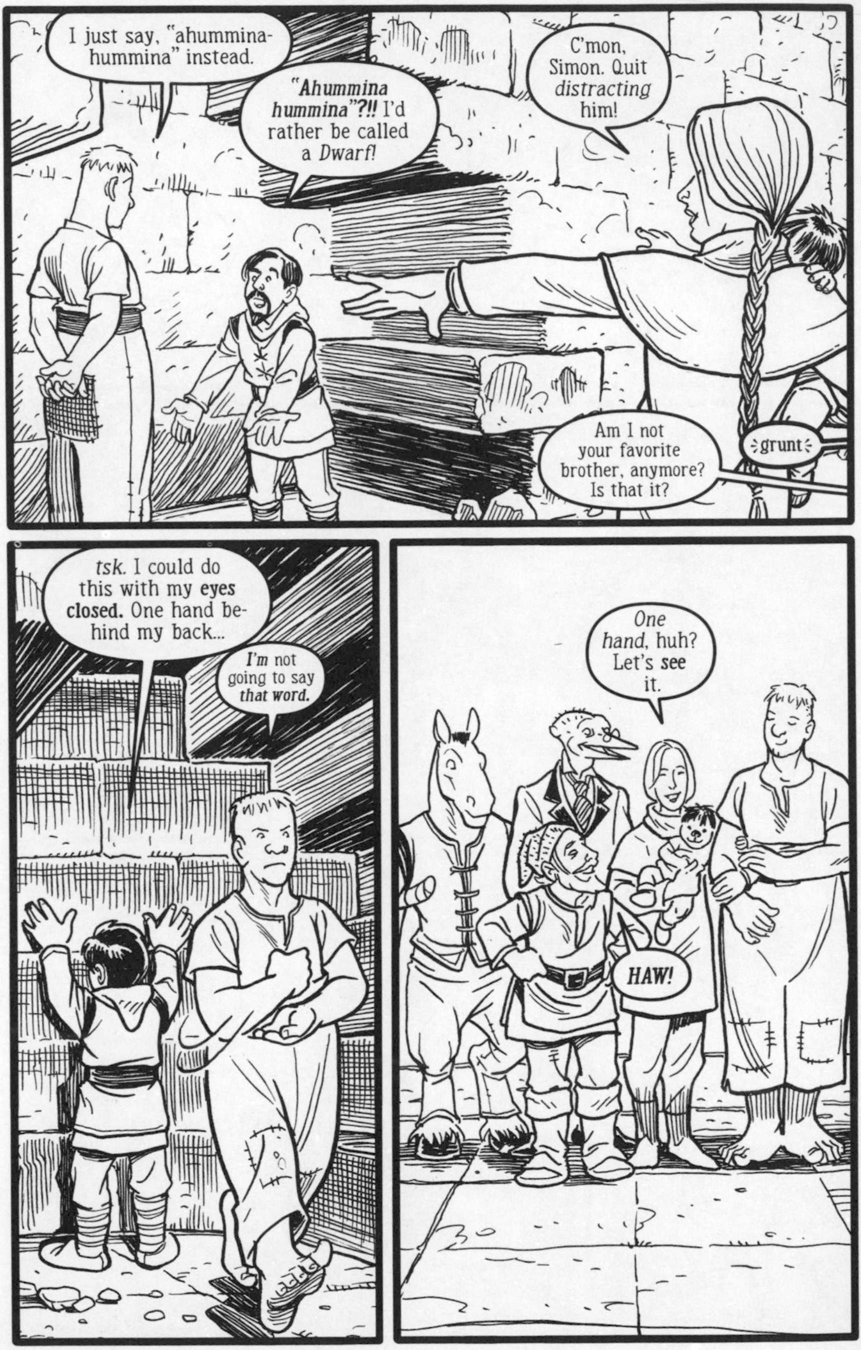
I just say, "ahummina-hummina" instead.
"Ahummina hummina"?!! I'd rather be called a Dwarf!
C'mon, Simon. Quit distracting him!
Am I not your favorite brother, anymore? Is that it?
grunt
tsk. I could do this with my eyes closed. One hand be-hind my back...
I'm not going to say that word.
One hand, huh? Let's see it.
HAW!

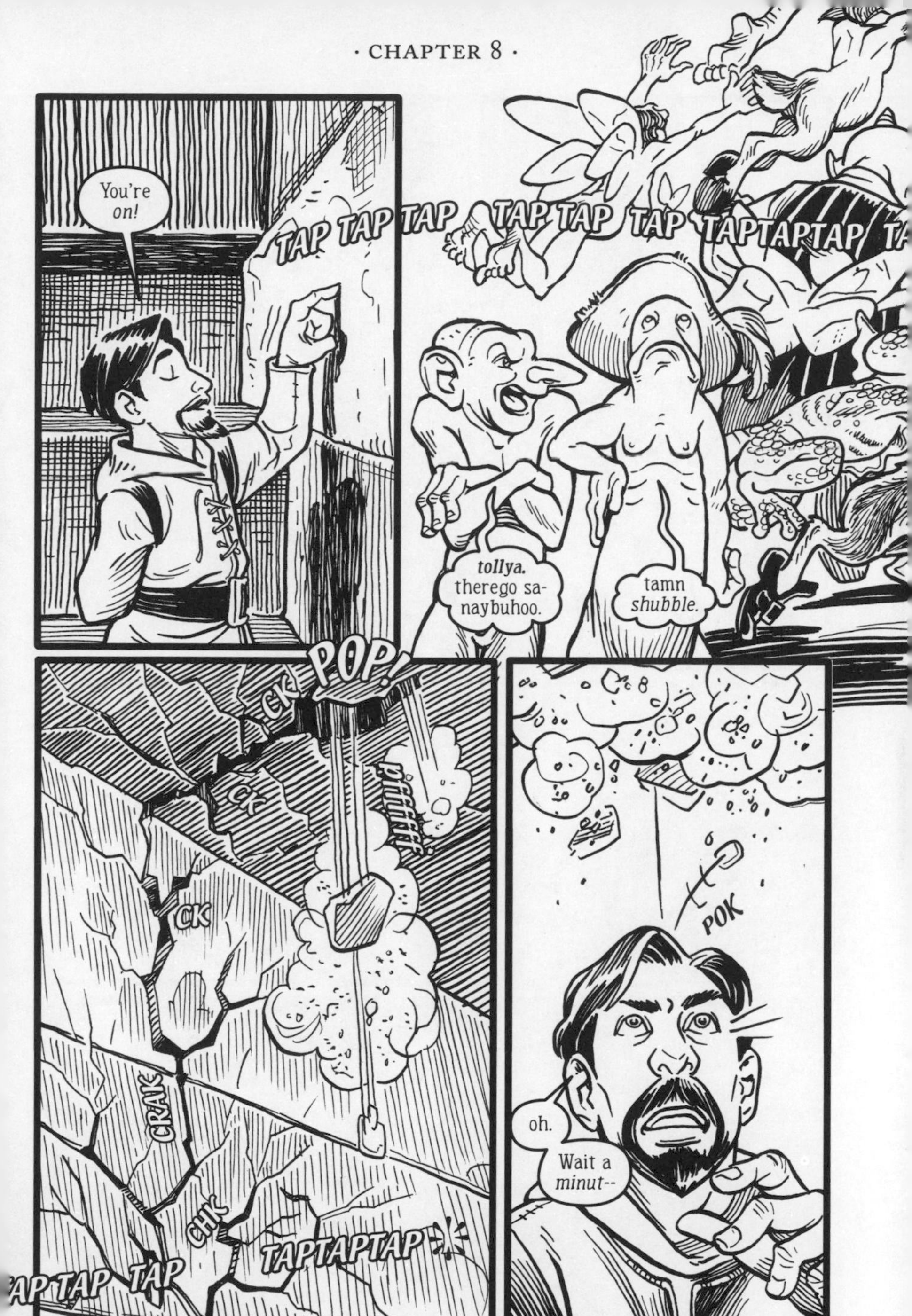
You're on!
TAP TAP TAP TAP TAP TAP TAPTAPTAP
tollya. therego sa-naybuhoo.
tamn shubble.
CK POP!
CK
pffffff
CK
CRAK
CHK
TAP TAP TAP
TAPTAPTAP
POK
oh.
Wait a minut--

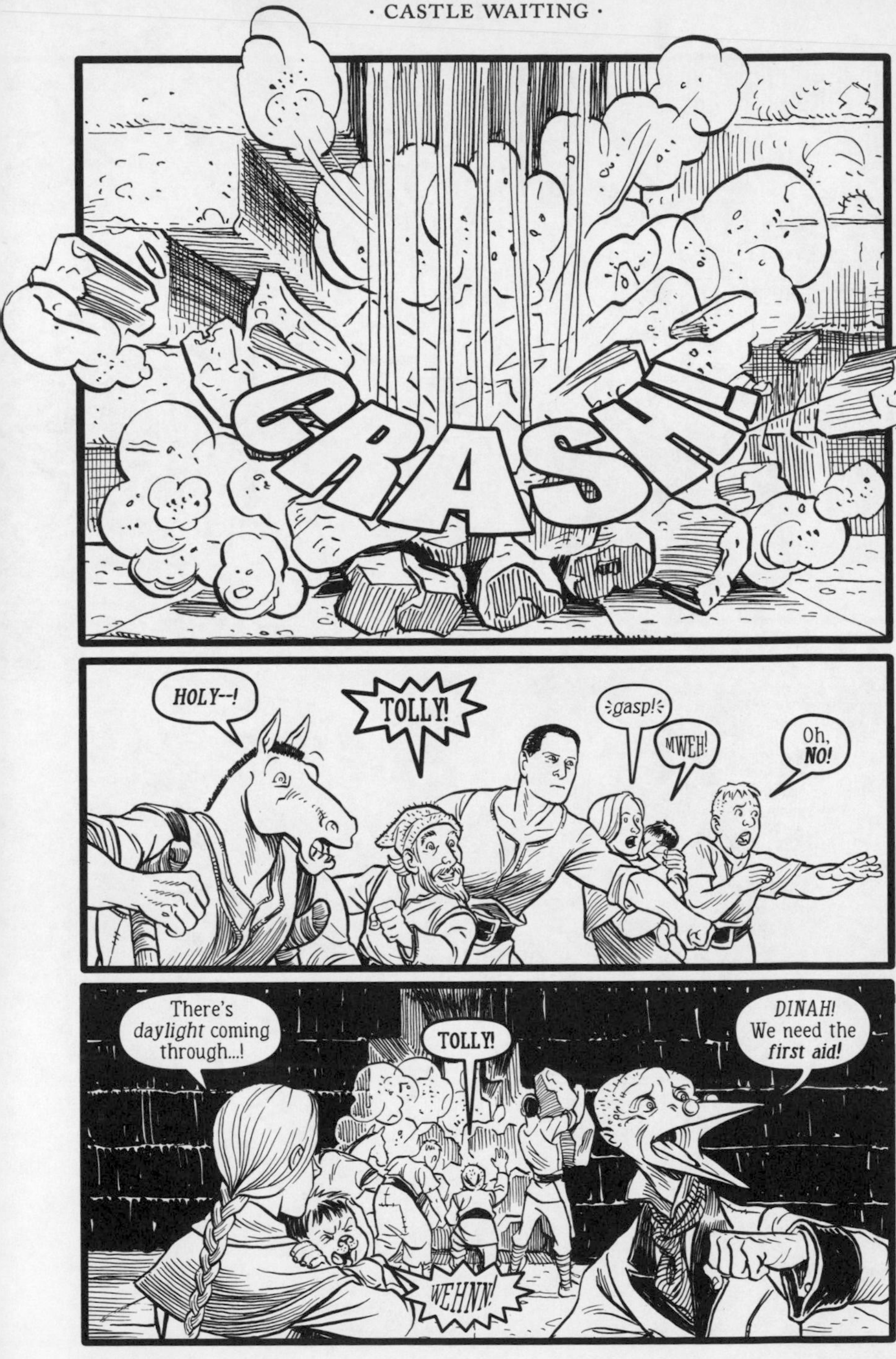
CRASH!
HOLY--!
TOLLY!
gasp!
MWEH!
Oh, NO!
There's daylight coming through...!
TOLLY!
DINAH! We need the first aid!
WEHNN!

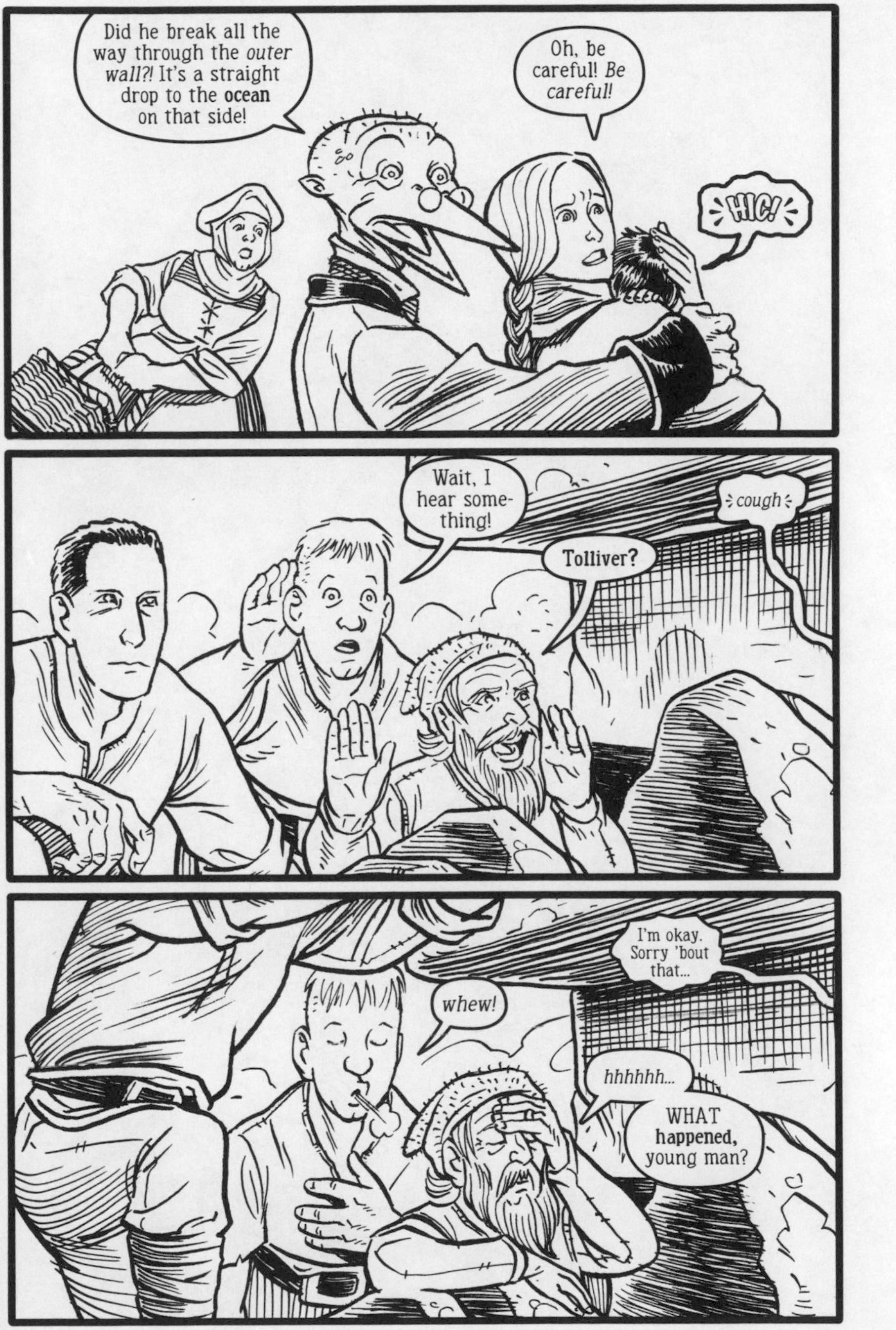
Did he break all the way through the *outer wall?!* It's a straight drop to the **ocean** on that side!
Oh, be careful! *Be careful!*
HIC!
Wait, I hear some-thing!
cough
Tolliver?
I'm okay. Sorry 'bout that...
whew!
hhhhhh...
WHAT **happened,** young man?

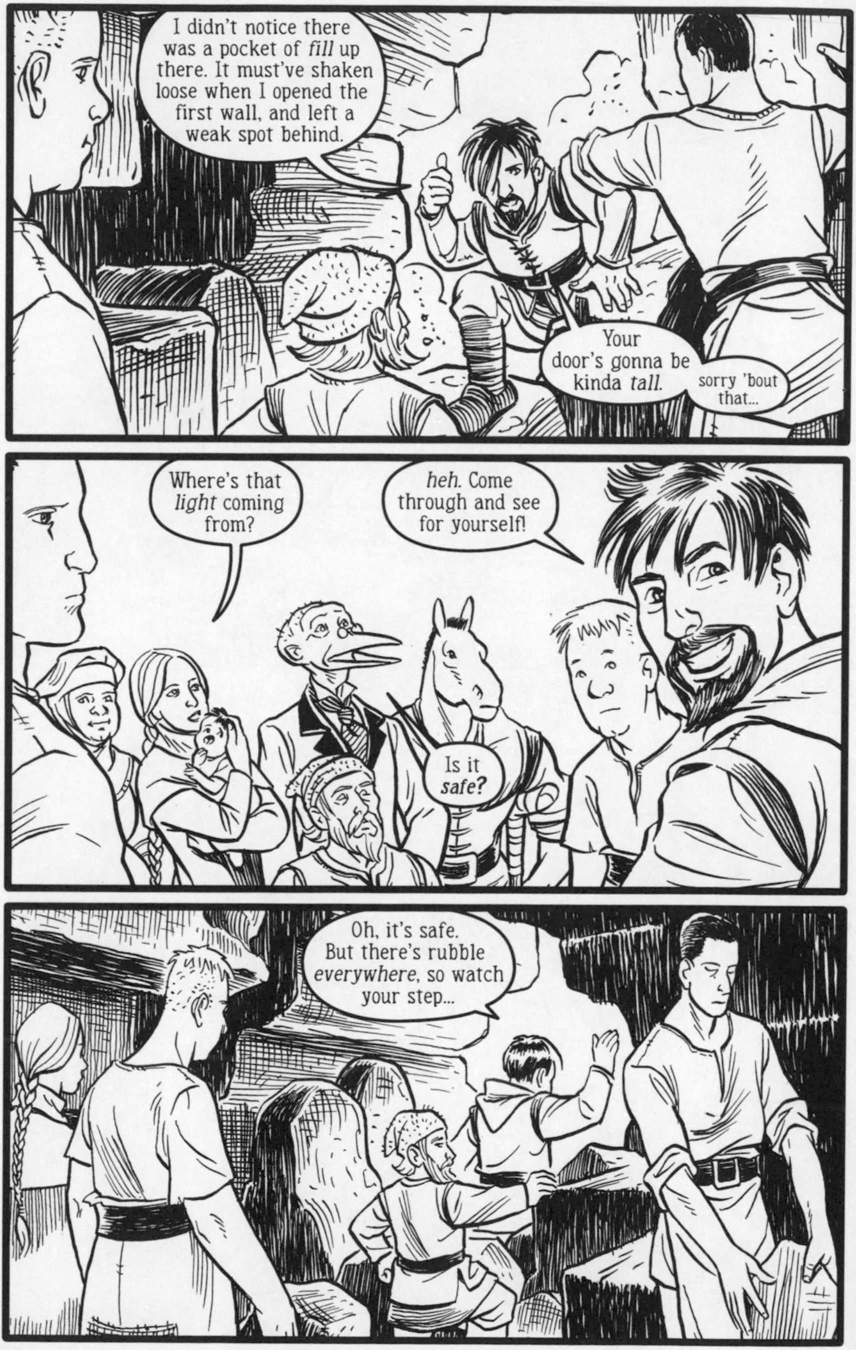
I didn't notice there was a pocket of *fill* up there. It must've shaken loose when I opened the first wall, and left a weak spot behind.
Your door's gonna be kinda *tall.*
sorry 'bout that...
Where's that *light* coming from?
heh. Come through and see for yourself!
Is it *safe?*
Oh, it's safe. But there's rubble *everywhere*, so watch your step...

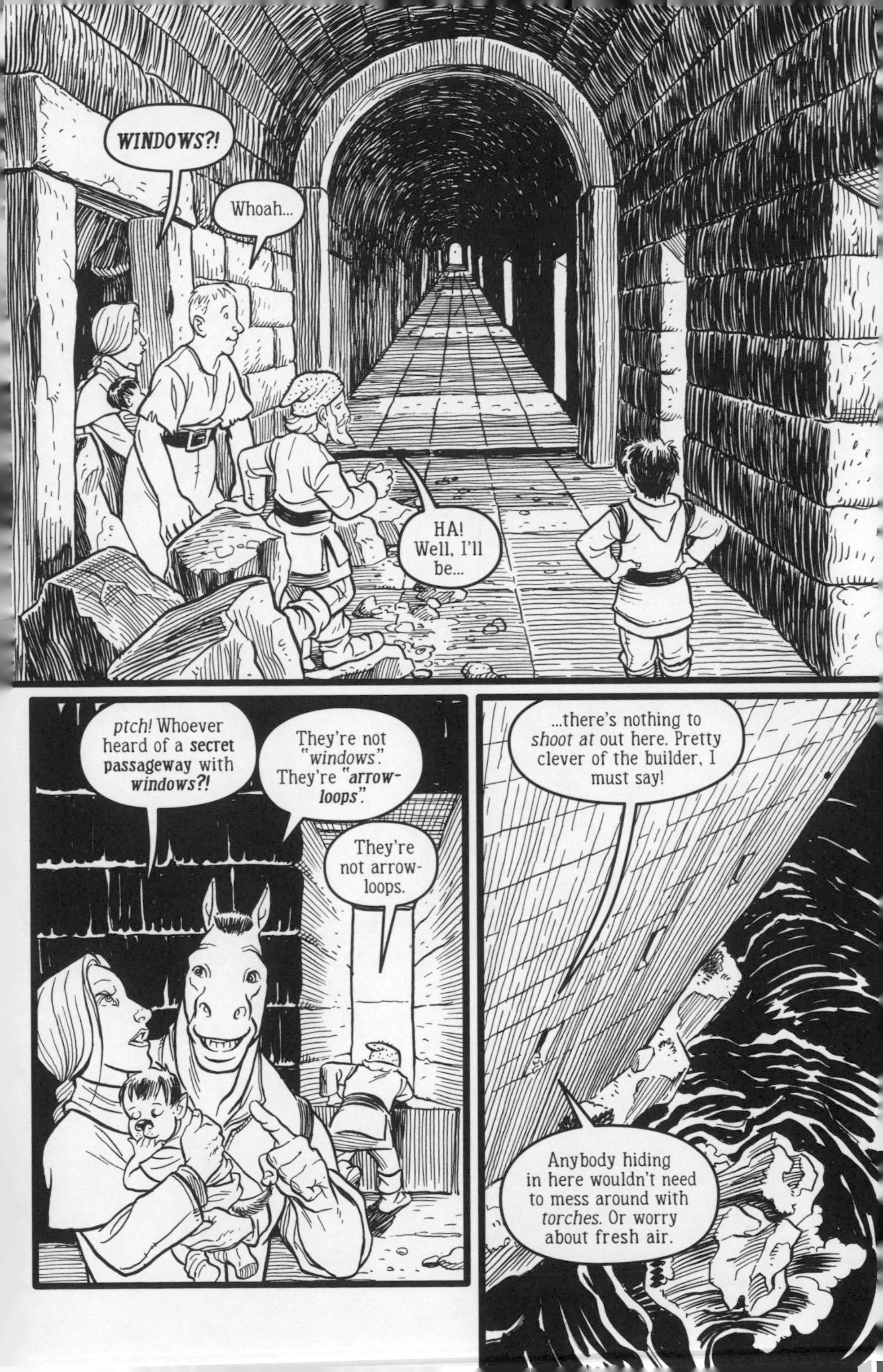

WINDOWS?!
Whoah...
HA! Well, I'll be...
ptch! Whoever heard of a secret passageway with windows?!
They're not "windows." They're "arrow-loops".
They're not arrow-loops.
...there's nothing to shoot at out here. Pretty clever of the builder, I must say!
Anybody hiding in here wouldn't need to mess around with torches. Or worry about fresh air.

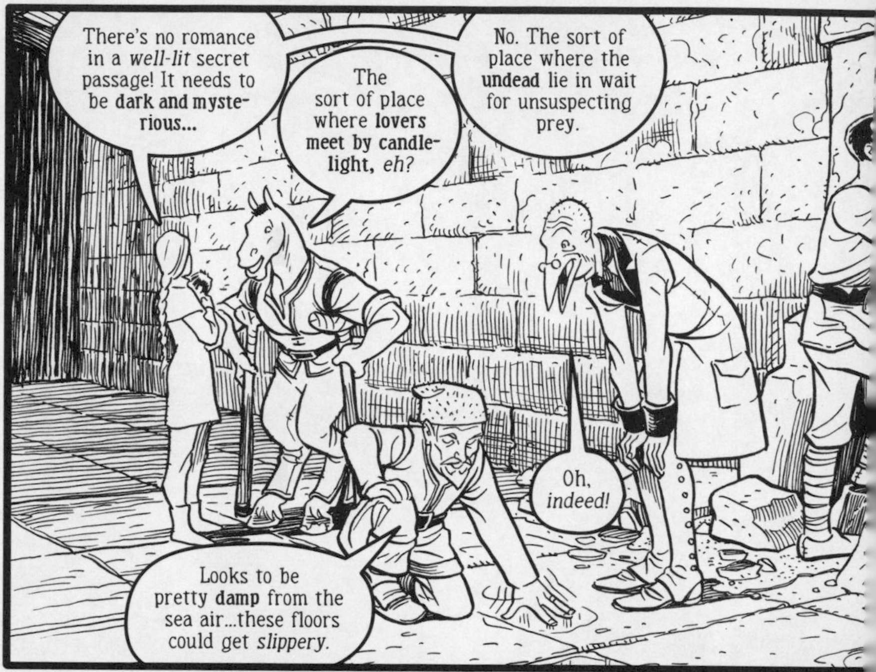
There's no romance in a *well-lit* secret passage! It needs to be **dark and mysterious...**
The sort of place where **lovers meet by candlelight,** *eh?*
No. The sort of place where the **undead** lie in wait for unsuspecting prey.
Oh, *indeed!*
Looks to be pretty **damp** from the sea air...these floors could get *slippery.*

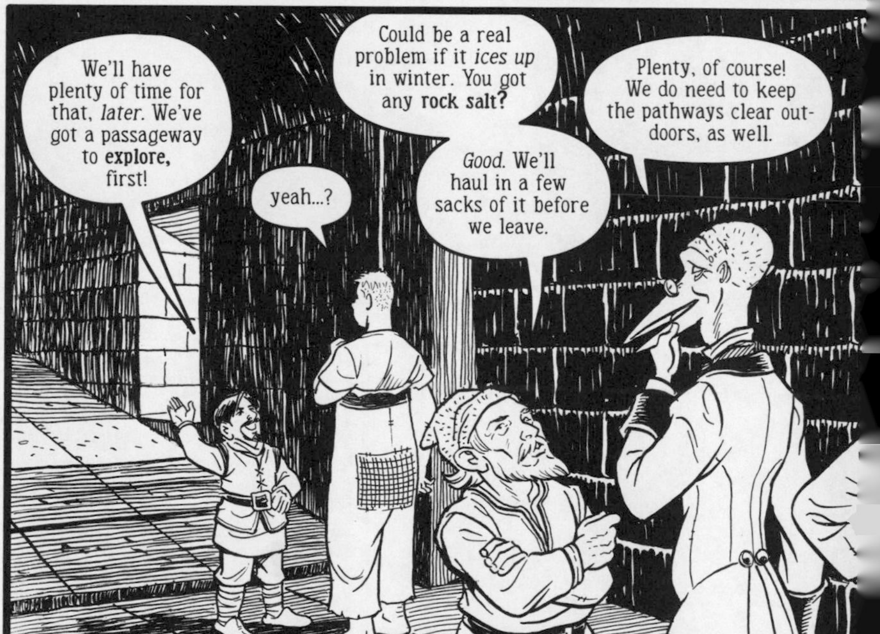
We'll have plenty of time for that, *later.* We've got a passageway to **explore,** first!
yeah...?
Could be a real problem if it *ices up* in winter. You got any **rock salt?**
Plenty, of course! We do need to keep the pathways clear outdoors, as well.
Good. We'll haul in a few sacks of it before we leave.

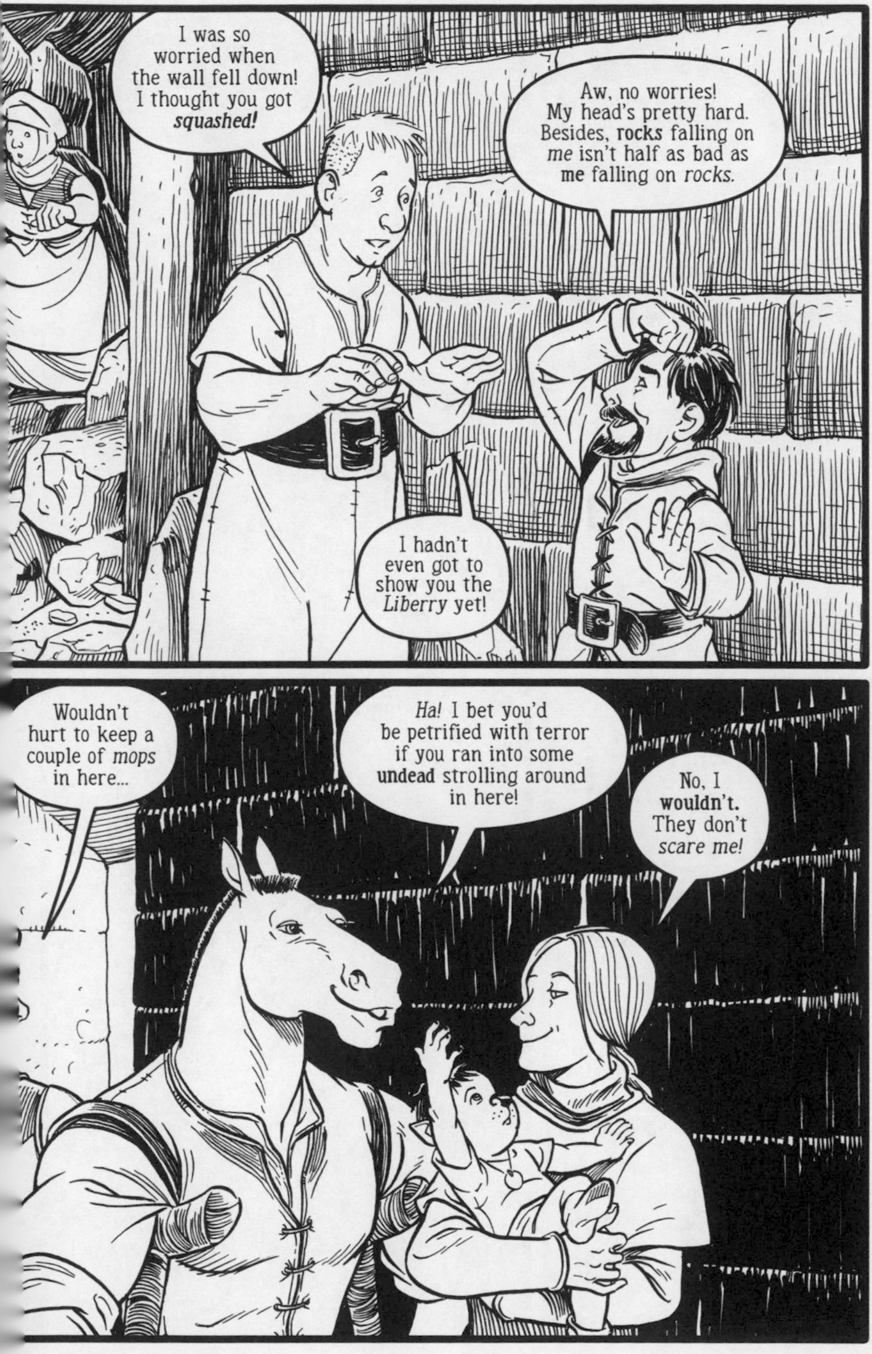
I was so worried when the wall fell down! I thought you got *squashed!*
Aw, no worries! My head's pretty hard. Besides, **rocks** falling on *me* isn't half as bad as **me** falling on *rocks.*
I hadn't even got to show you the *Liberry* yet!
Wouldn't hurt to keep a couple of *mops* in here...
Ha! I bet you'd be petrified with terror if you ran into some **undead** strolling around in here!
No, I **wouldn't.** They don't *scare me!*

C'mon, Jain! Come explore the passage with us!
C'mon!
Oh, I *can't...*
Now, now, don't be *scared!* I'll come along to **protect** you.
You ***caaaan't,*** you have a ***hurty hoooooof.***
BEAKY.
C'mon, it'll be **fun!** Don't you want to explore the *great unknown,* like your **dad** did?
heh. Papa didn't have a *squirmy infant* in tow, like **I** do...

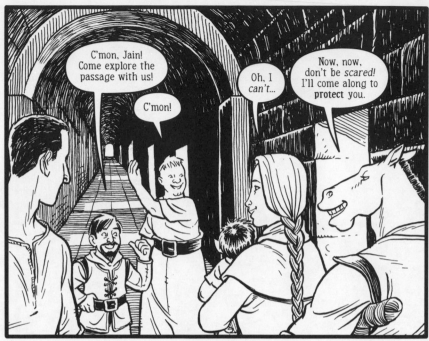

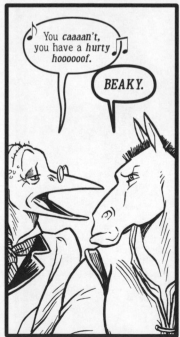

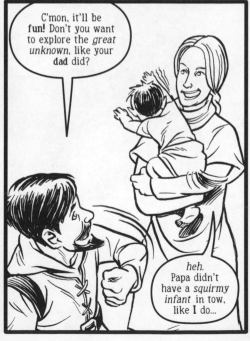

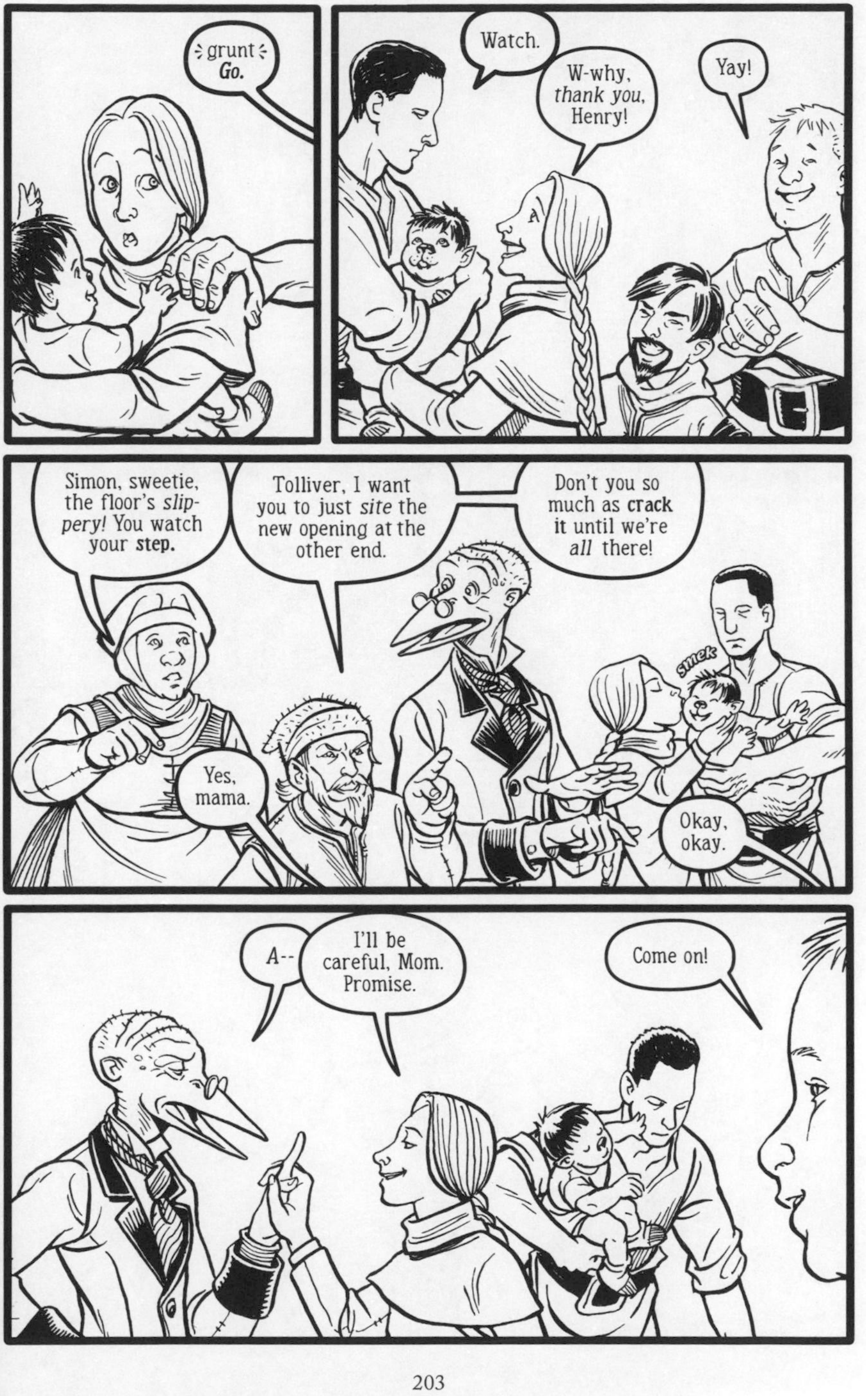
grunt
Go.
Watch.
W-why, thank you, Henry!
Yay!
Simon, sweetie, the floor's slippery! You watch your step.
Yes, mama.
Tolliver, I want you to just site the new opening at the other end.
Don't you so much as crack it until we're all there!
Okay, okay.
smek
A--
I'll be careful, Mom. Promise.
Come on!

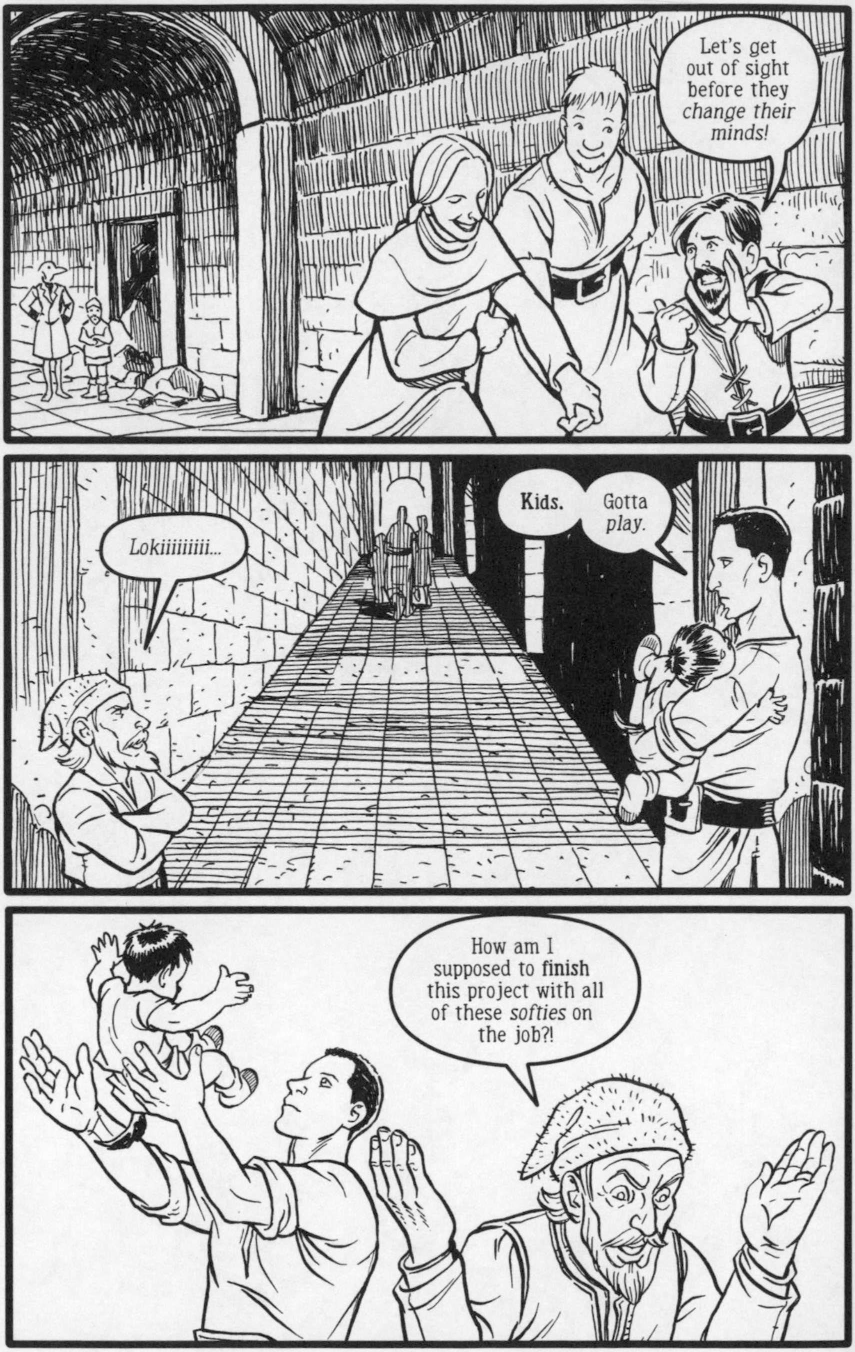
Let's get out of sight before they *change their minds!*
Lokiiiiiiii...
Kids.
Gotta *play.*
How am I supposed to **finish** this project with all of these *softies* on the job?!

Chapter 9.

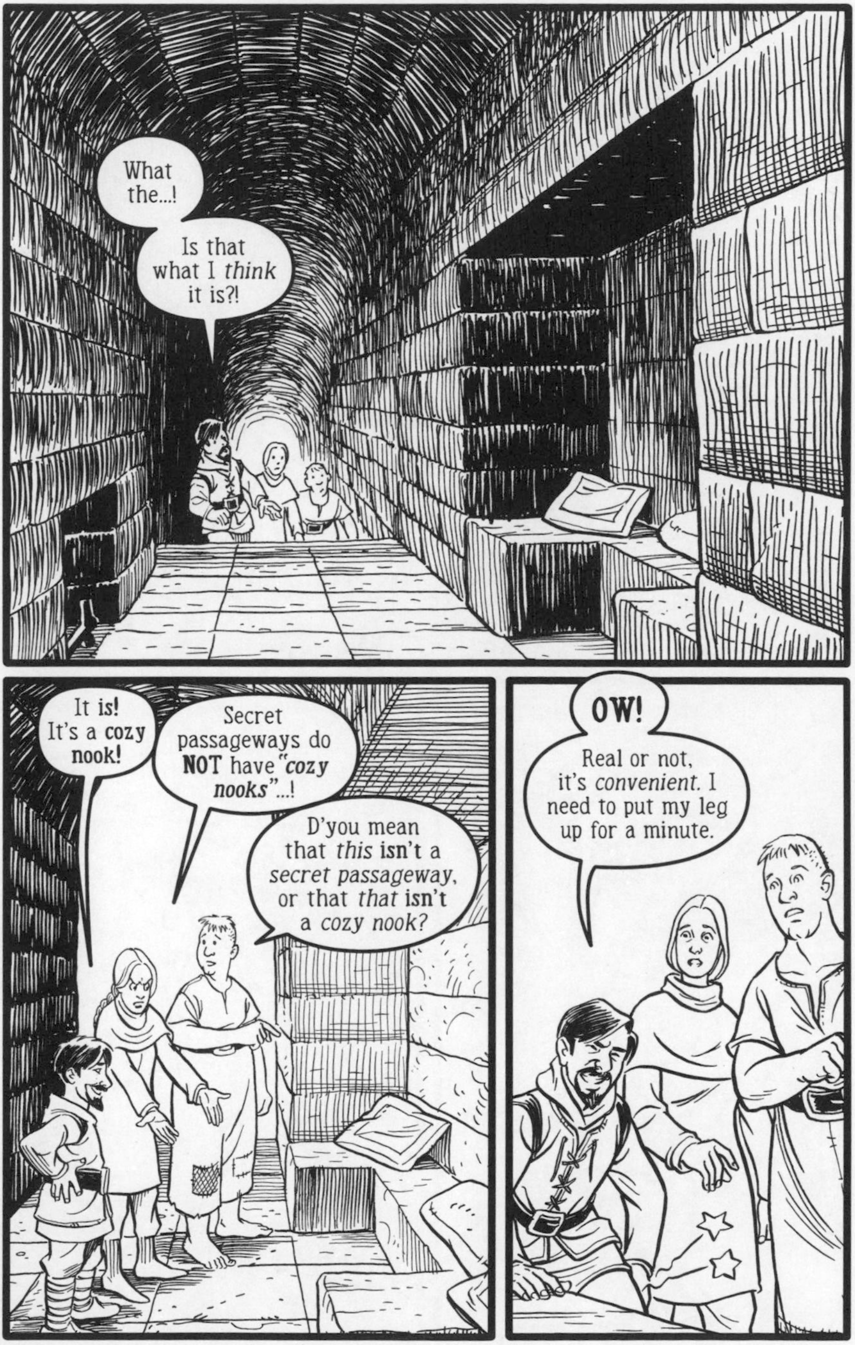
What the...!
Is that what I *think* it is?!
It is! It's a **cozy nook!**
Secret passageways do **NOT** have "*cozy nooks*"...!
D'you mean that *this* **isn't** a *secret passageway*, or that *that* **isn't** a *cozy nook*?
OW!
Real or not, it's *convenient*. I need to put my leg up for a minute.

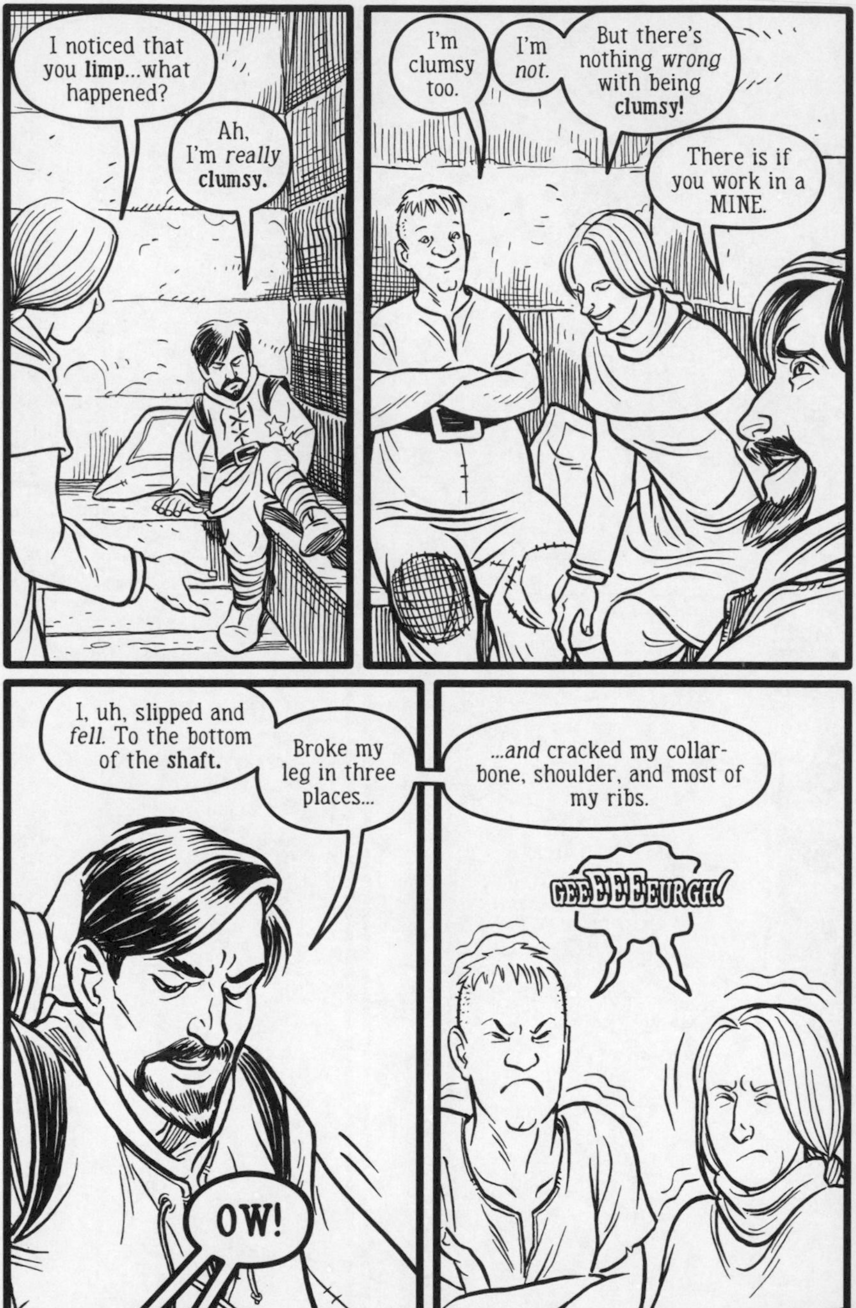
I noticed that you limp...what happened?
Ah, I'm really clumsy.
I'm clumsy too.
I'm not.
But there's nothing wrong with being clumsy!
There is if you work in a MINE.
I, uh, slipped and fell. To the bottom of the shaft.
Broke my leg in three places...
...and cracked my collar-bone, shoulder, and most of my ribs.
GEEEEEEURGH!
OW!

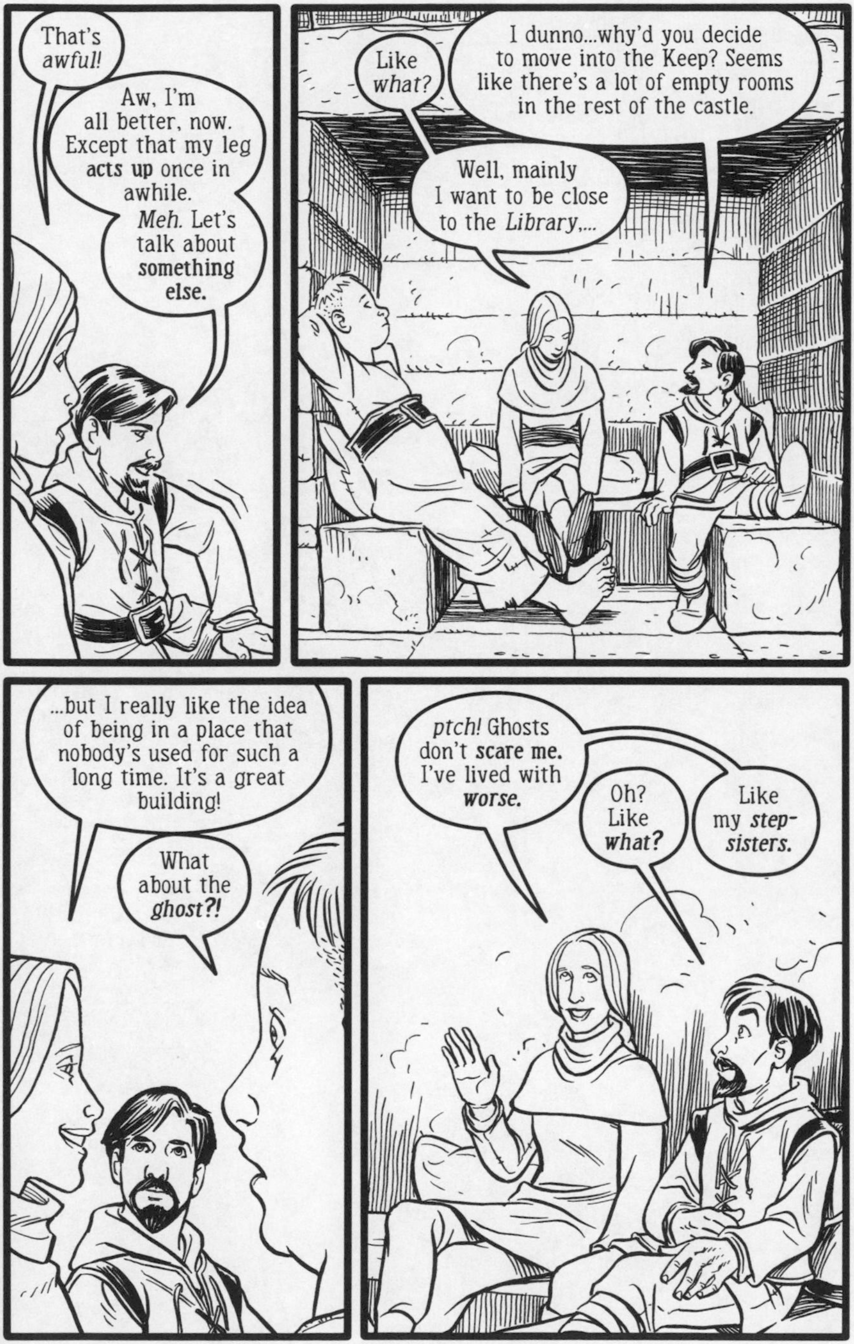
That's *awful!*
Aw, I'm all better, now. Except that my leg **acts up** once in awhile.
Meh. Let's talk about **something else.**
Like *what?*
I dunno...why'd you decide to move into the Keep? Seems like there's a lot of empty rooms in the rest of the castle.
Well, mainly I want to be close to the *Library*,...
...but I really like the idea of being in a place that nobody's used for such a long time. It's a great building!
What about the ***ghost?!***
ptch! Ghosts don't **scare me.** I've lived with ***worse.***
Oh? Like ***what?***
Like my ***step-sisters.***

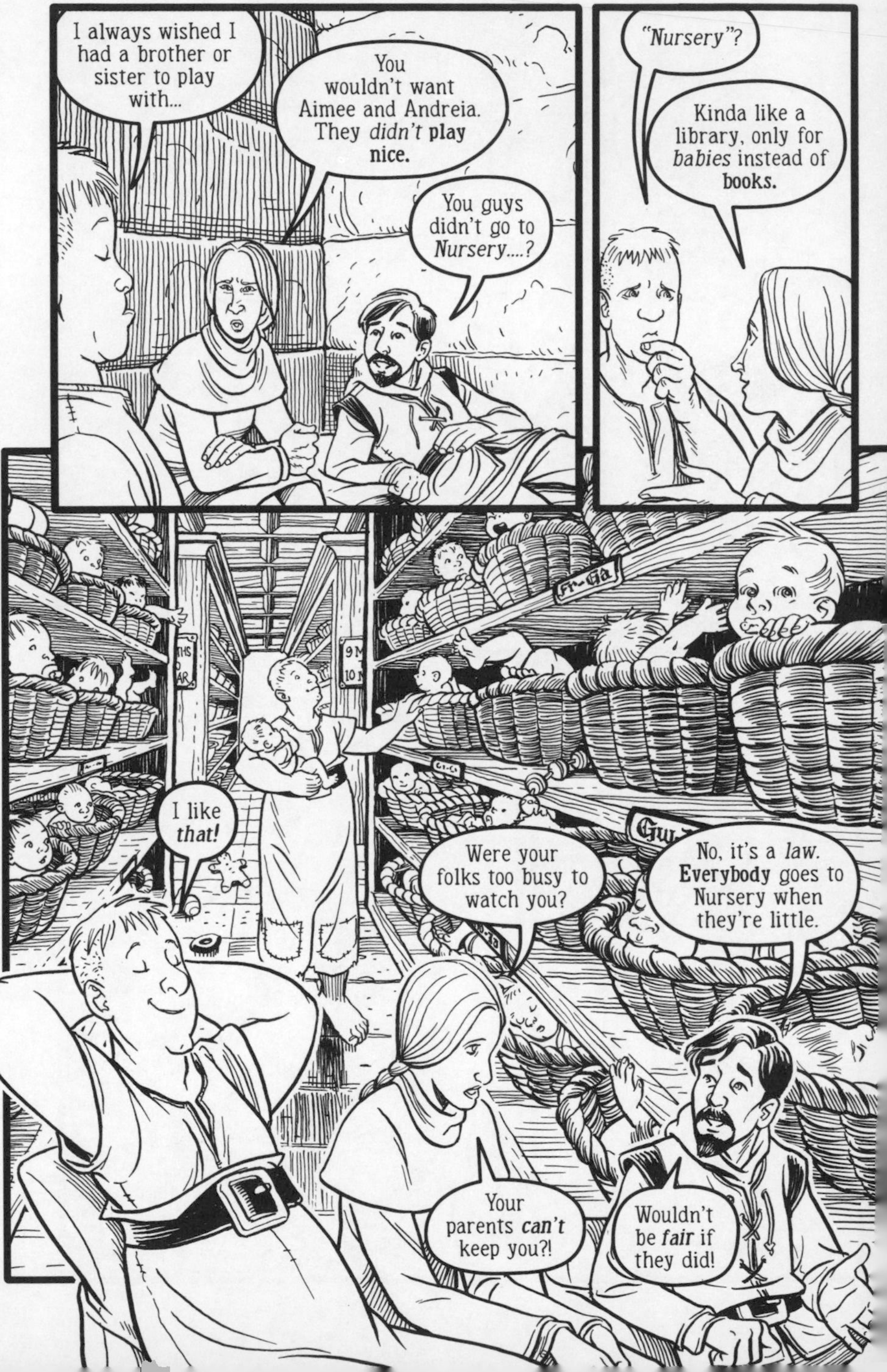
I always wished I had a brother or sister to play with...
You wouldn't want Aimee and Andreia. They *didn't* **play nice.**
You guys didn't go to *Nursery*....?
"Nursery"?
Kinda like a library, only for *babies* instead of **books.**
Fr-Ga
I like *that!*
Were your folks too busy to watch you?
No, it's a *law.* **Everybody** goes to Nursery when they're little.
Your parents ***can't*** keep you?!
Wouldn't be ***fair*** if they did!

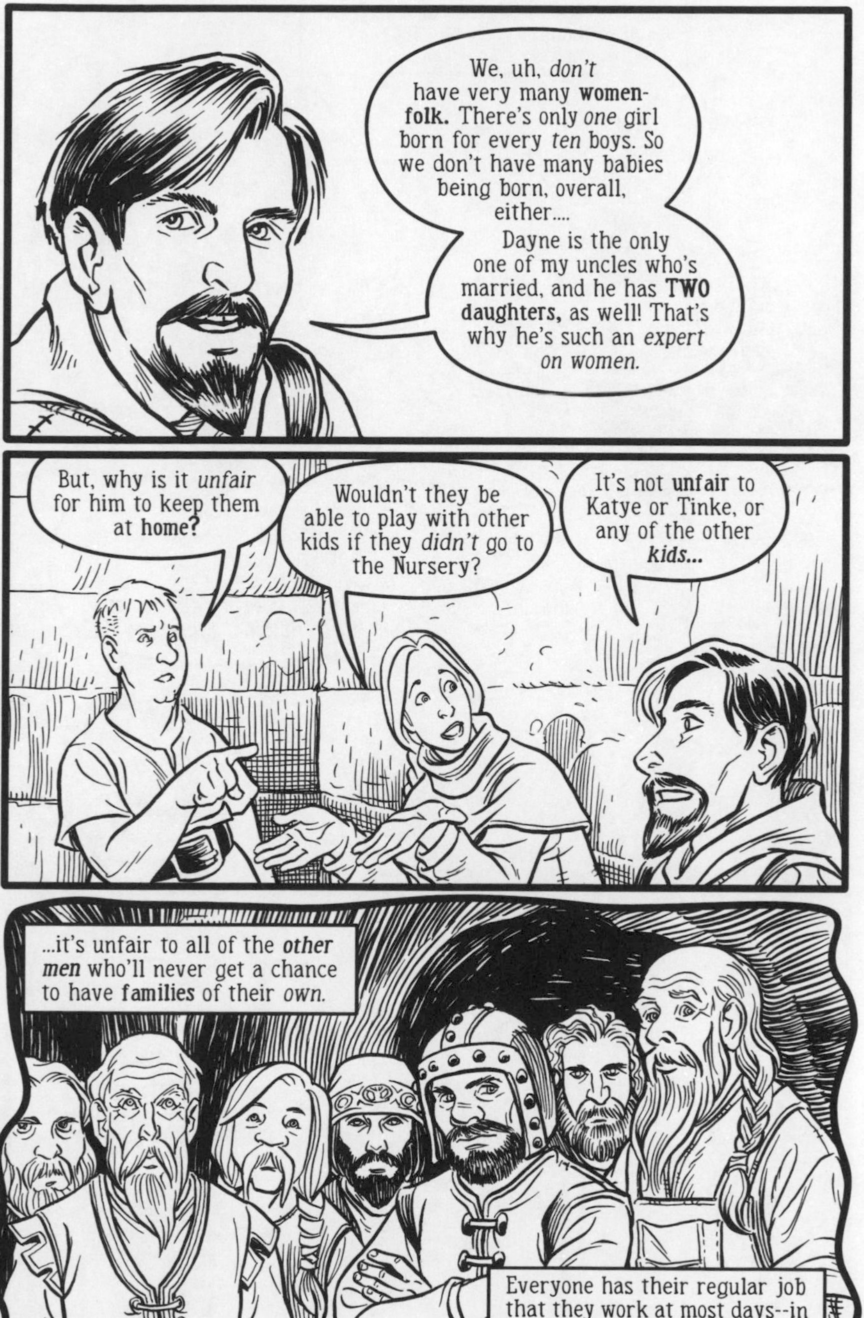
We, uh, *don't* have very many **women-folk.** There's only *one* girl born for every *ten* boys. So we don't have many babies being born, overall, either....
Dayne is the only one of my uncles who's married, and he has **TWO daughters,** as well! That's why he's such an *expert on women.*
But, why is it *unfair* for him to keep them at **home?**
Wouldn't they be able to play with other kids if they *didn't* go to the Nursery?
It's not **unfair** to Katye or Tinke, or any of the other ***kids...***
...it's unfair to all of the ***other men*** who'll never get a chance to have **families** of their *own.*
Everyone has their regular job that they work at most days--in the mines, for instance...

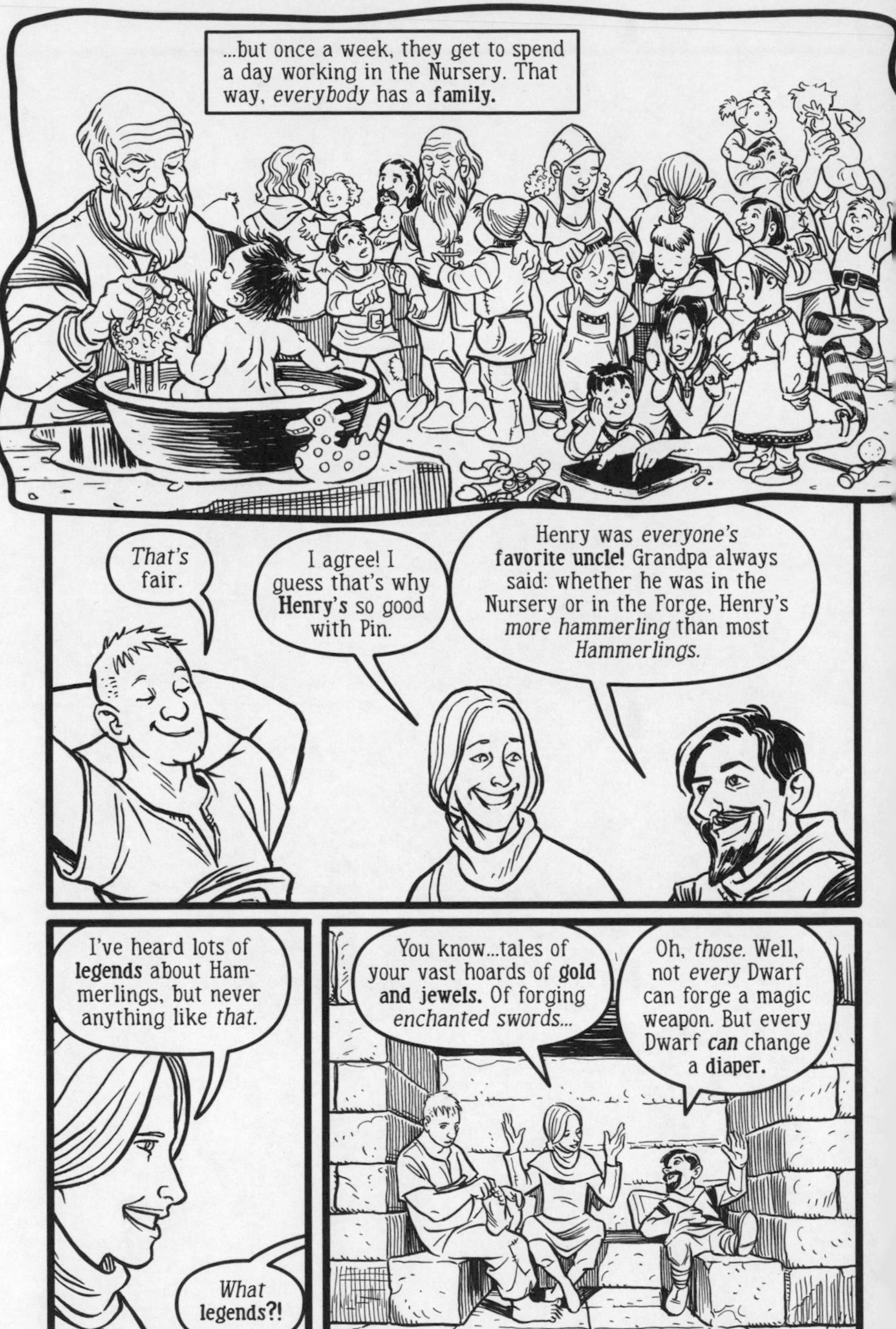
...but once a week, they get to spend a day working in the Nursery. That way, *everybody* has a **family.**
That's fair.
I agree! I guess that's why **Henry's** so good with Pin.
Henry was *everyone's* **favorite uncle!** Grandpa always said: whether he was in the Nursery or in the Forge, Henry's *more hammerling* than most *Hammerlings.*
I've heard lots of **legends** about Hammerlings, but never anything like *that.*
What **legends?!**
You know...tales of your vast hoards of **gold and jewels.** Of forging *enchanted swords...*
Oh, *those.* Well, not *every* Dwarf can forge a magic weapon. But every Dwarf ***can*** change a **diaper.**

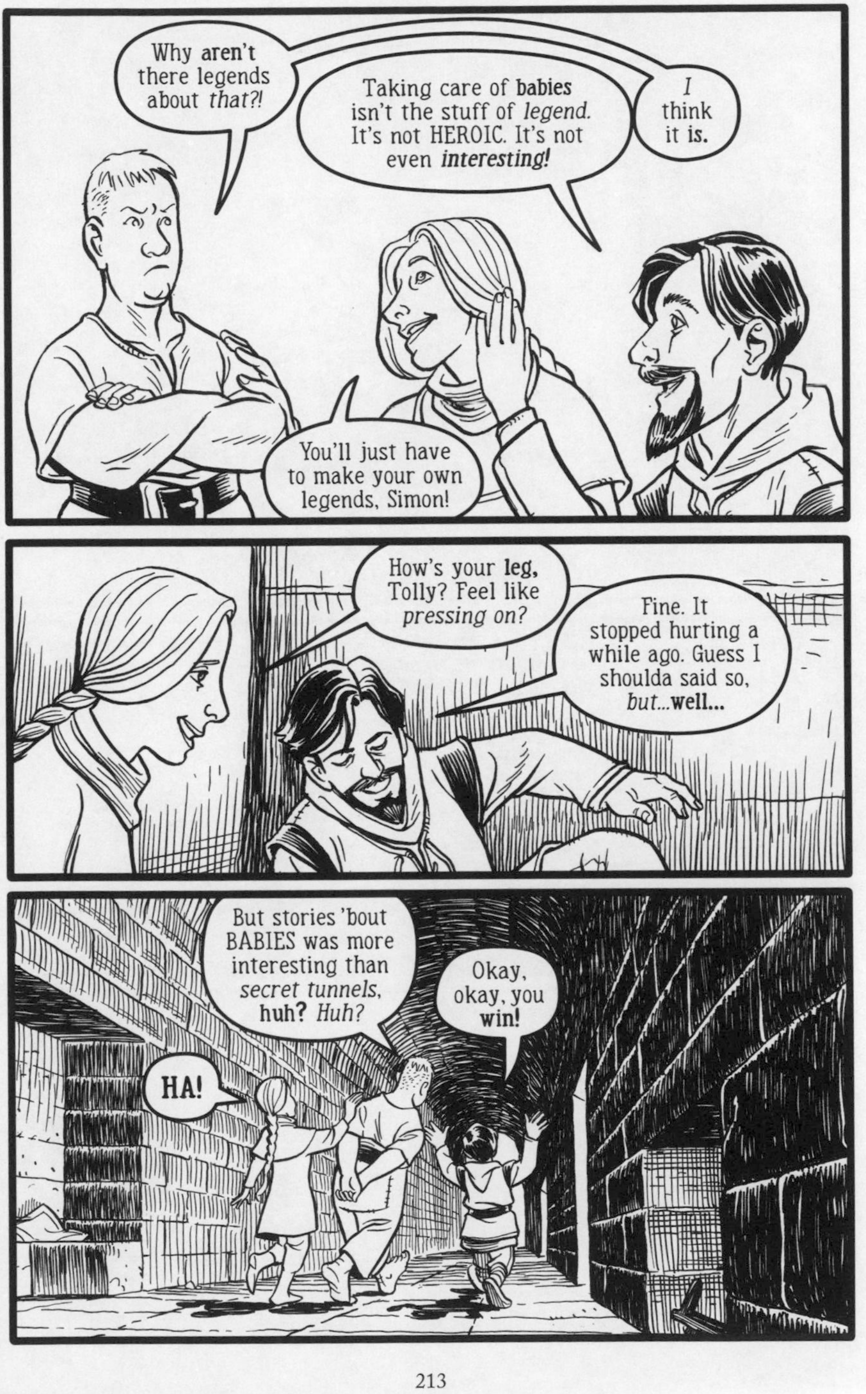
Why **aren't** there legends about *that?!*
Taking care of **babies** isn't the stuff of *legend.* It's not HEROIC. It's not even ***interesting!***
I think it **is.**
You'll just have to make your own legends, Simon!
How's your **leg,** Tolly? Feel like *pressing on?*
Fine. It stopped hurting a while ago. Guess I shoulda said so, *but...***well...**
But stories 'bout BABIES was more interesting than *secret tunnels,* **huh?** *Huh?*
Okay, okay, you **win!**
HA!

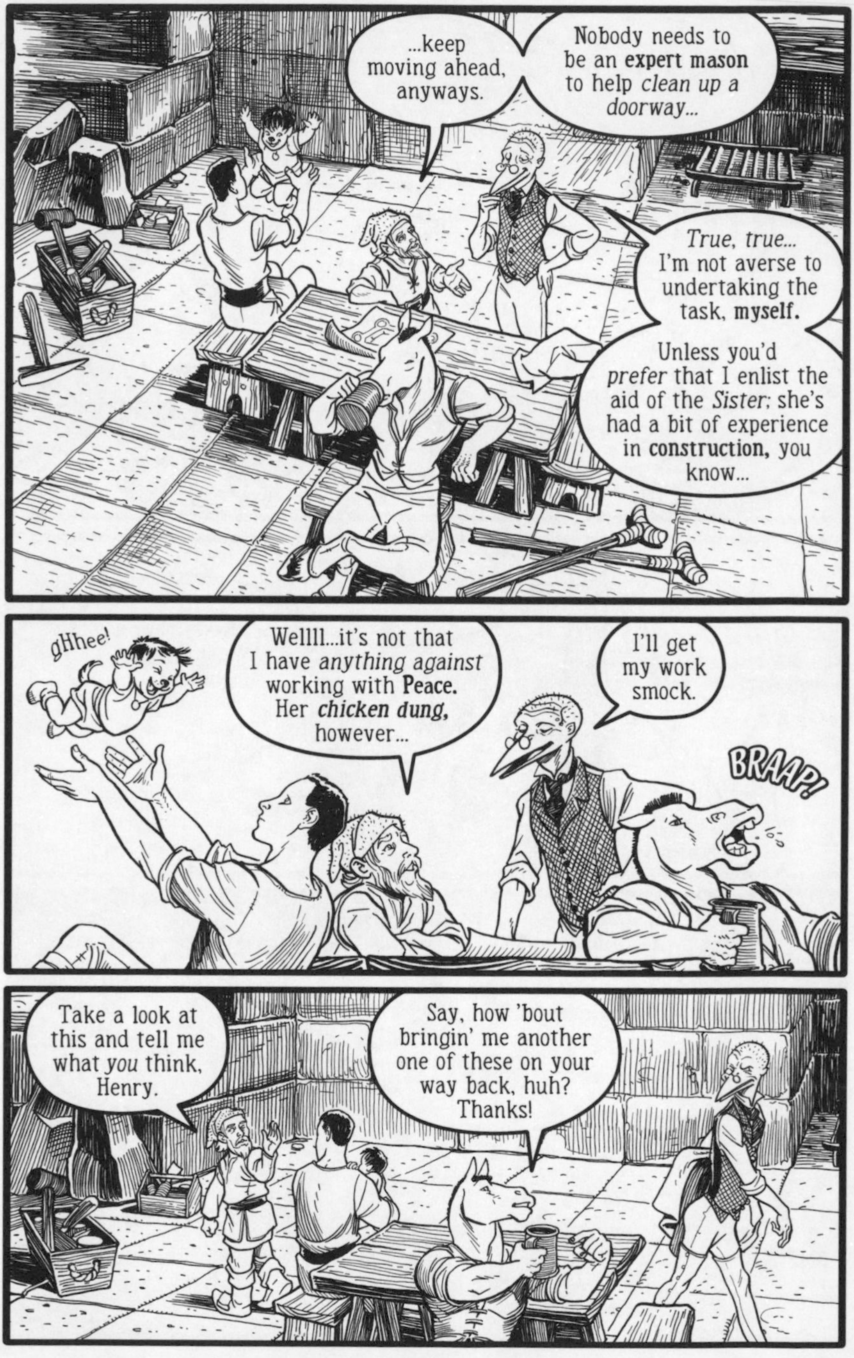
...keep moving ahead, anyways.
Nobody needs to be an **expert mason** to help *clean up a doorway...*
True, true... I'm not averse to undertaking the task, **myself.**
Unless you'd *prefer* that I enlist the aid of the *Sister;* she's had a bit of experience in **construction,** you know...
gHhee!
Wellll...it's not that I have *anything against* working with **Peace.** Her ***chicken dung,*** however...
I'll get my work smock.
BRAAP!
Take a look at this and tell me what *you* think, Henry.
Say, how 'bout bringin' me another one of these on your way back, huh? Thanks!

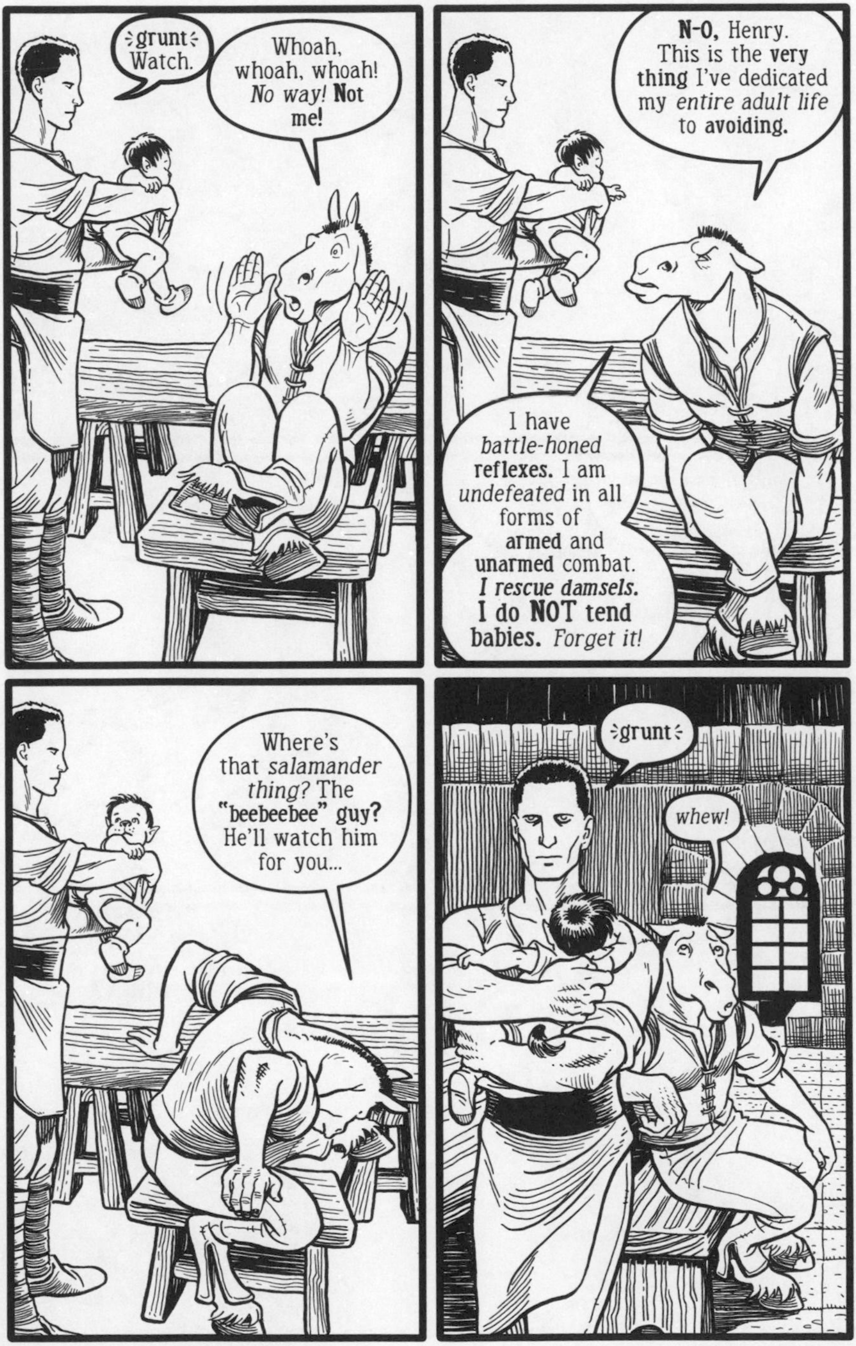
grunt
Watch.
Whoah, whoah, whoah! *No way!* **Not me!**
N-O, Henry. This is the **very thing** I've dedicated my *entire adult life* to **avoiding.**
I have *battle-honed* **reflexes.** I am *undefeated* in all forms of **armed** and **unarmed** combat. *I rescue damsels.* **I do NOT tend babies.** *Forget it!*
Where's that *salamander thing?* The **"beebeebee" guy?** He'll watch him for you...
grunt
whew!

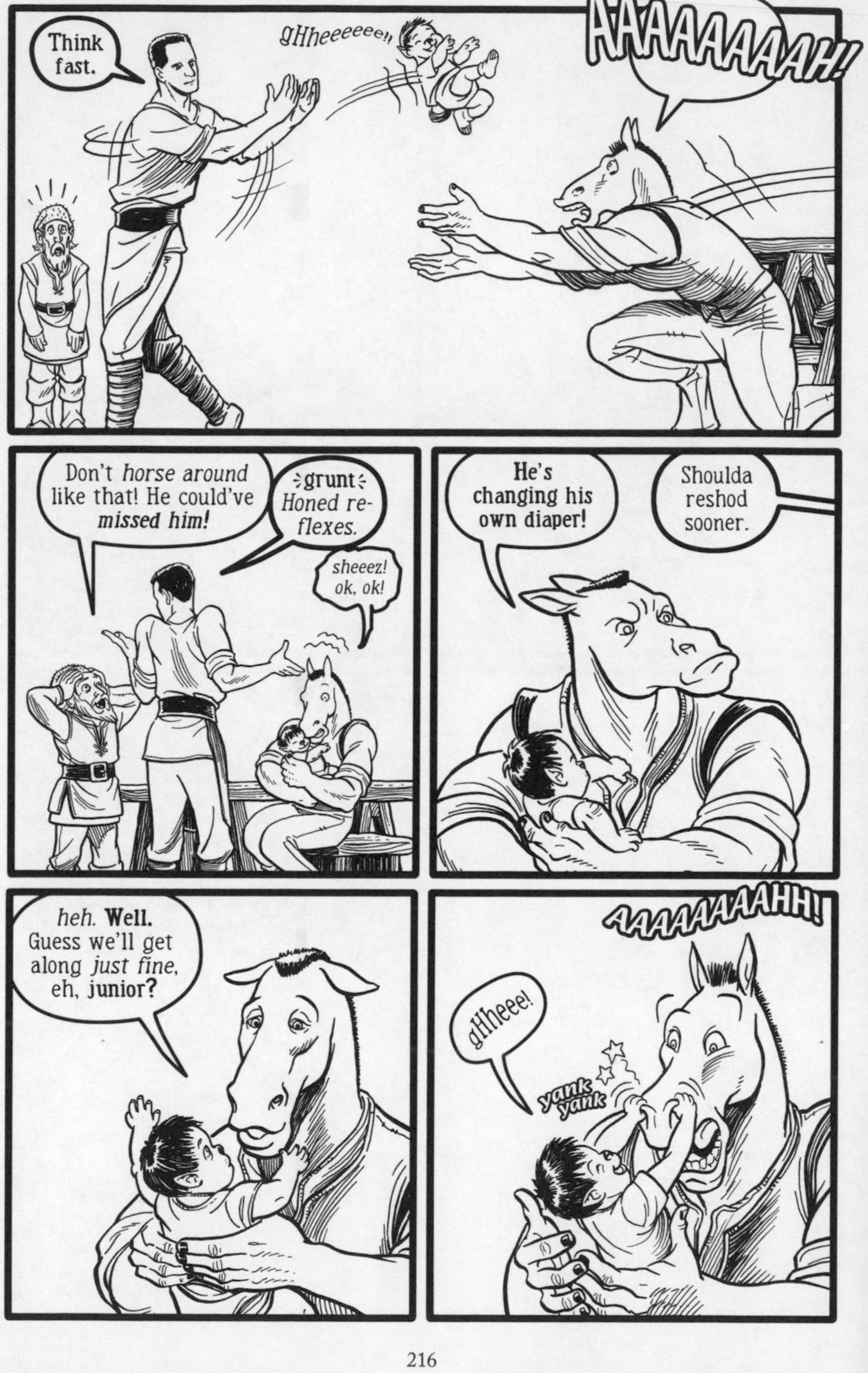
Think fast.
gHheeeeee!!
AAAAAAAAAH!
Don't *horse around* like that! He could've ***missed him!***
grunt Honed re-flexes.
sheeez! ok, ok!
He's changing his own diaper!
Shoulda reshod sooner.
heh. **Well.** Guess we'll get along *just fine*, eh, **junior?**
AAAAAAAAHH!
gHheee!
yank yank

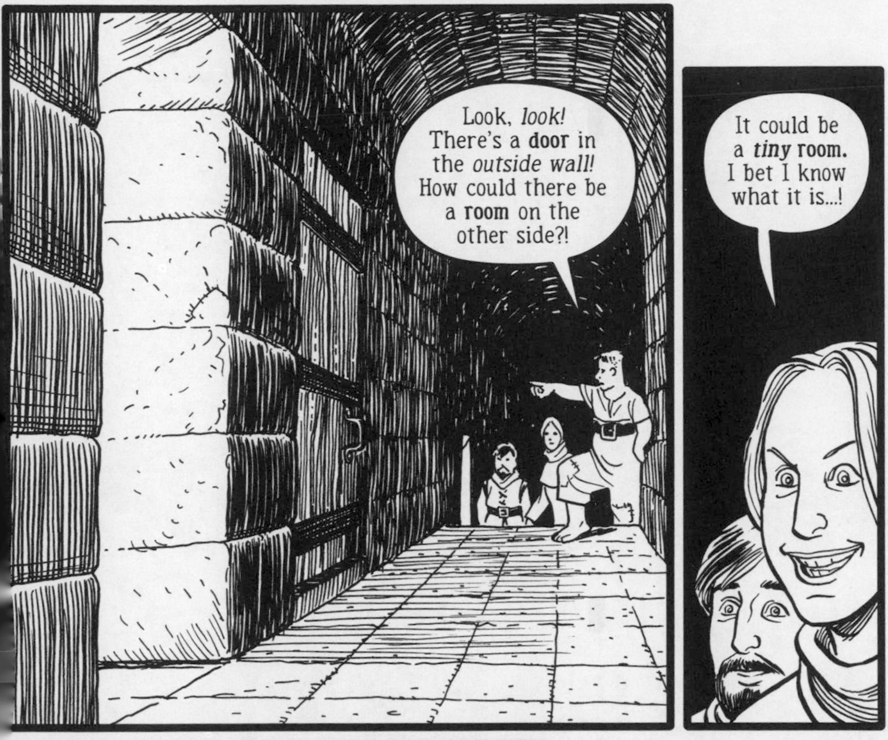
Look, *look!* There's a **door** in the *outside wall!* How could there be a **room** on the other side?!
It could be a ***tiny* room.** I bet I know what it is...!

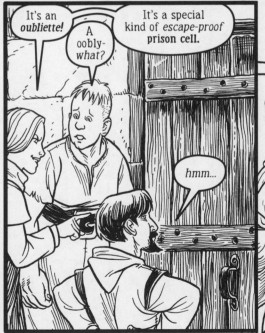

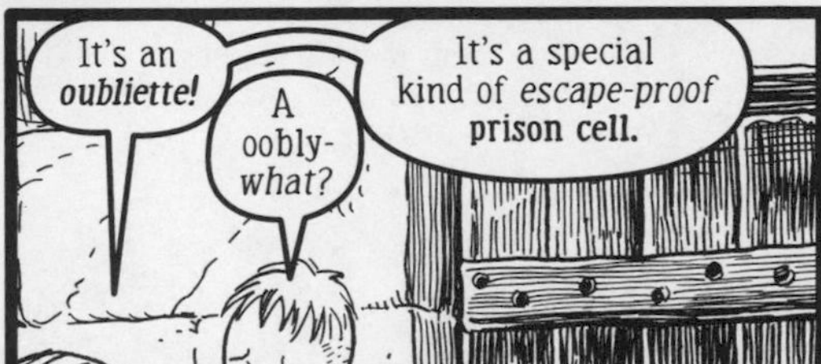
It's an ***oubliette!***
A oobly-*what?*
It's a special kind of *escape-proof* **prison cell.**
hmm...

Gaolers force their prisoners into 'em, then *forget all about them!* The prisoner's left to **starve to death!**

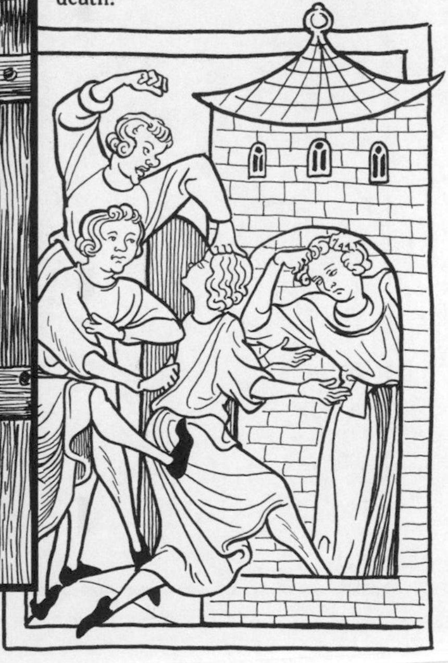

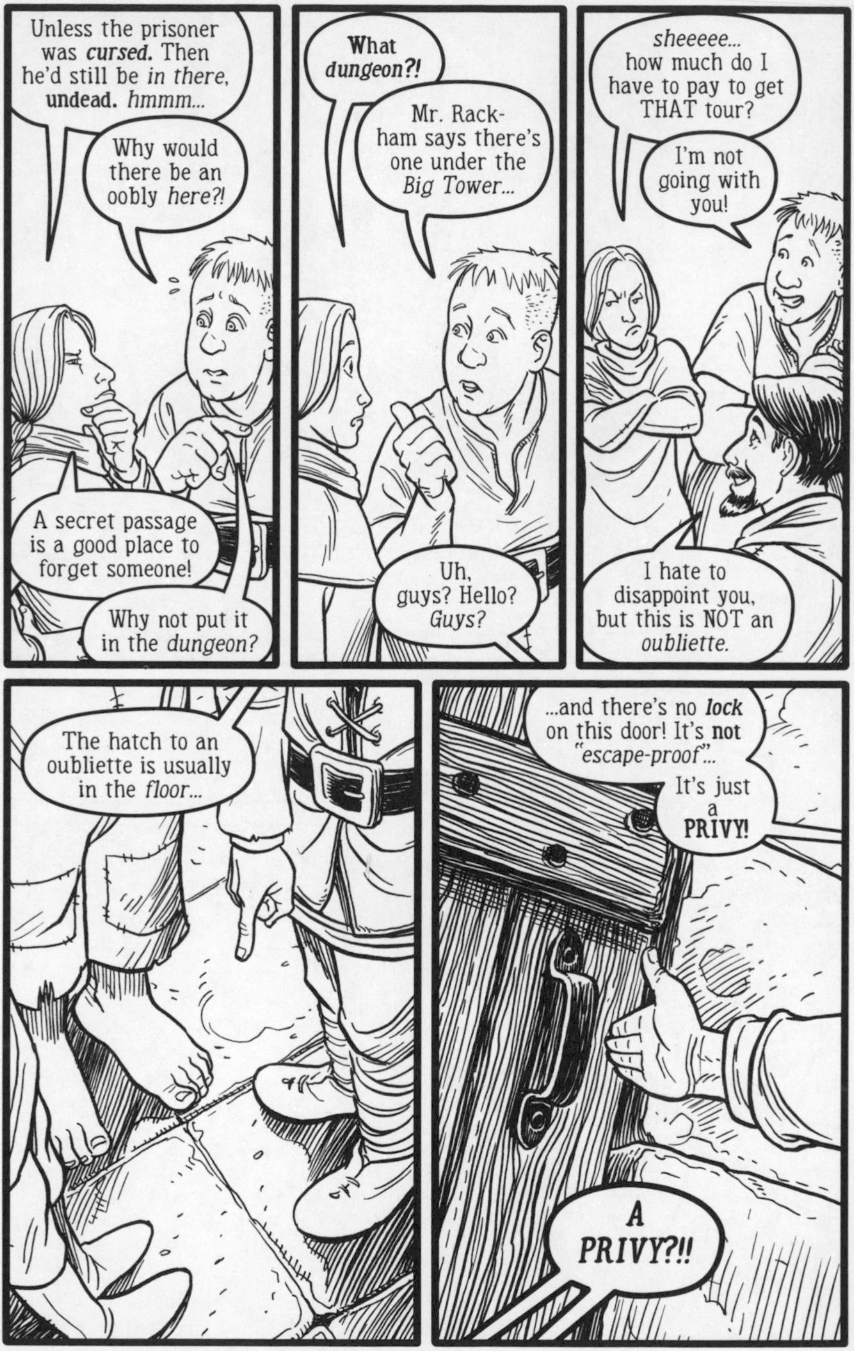
Unless the prisoner was *cursed.* Then he'd still be *in there,* **undead.** *hmmm...*
Why would there be an oobly *here?!*
A secret passage is a good place to forget someone!
Why not put it in the *dungeon?*
What *dungeon?!*
Mr. Rack-ham says there's one under the *Big Tower...*
Uh, guys? Hello? *Guys?*
sheeeee... how much do I have to pay to get THAT tour?
I'm not going with you!
I hate to disappoint you, but this is NOT an *oubliette.*
The hatch to an oubliette is usually in the *floor...*
...and there's no ***lock*** on this door! It's **not** *"escape-proof"...*
It's just a **PRIVY!**
A PRIVY?!!

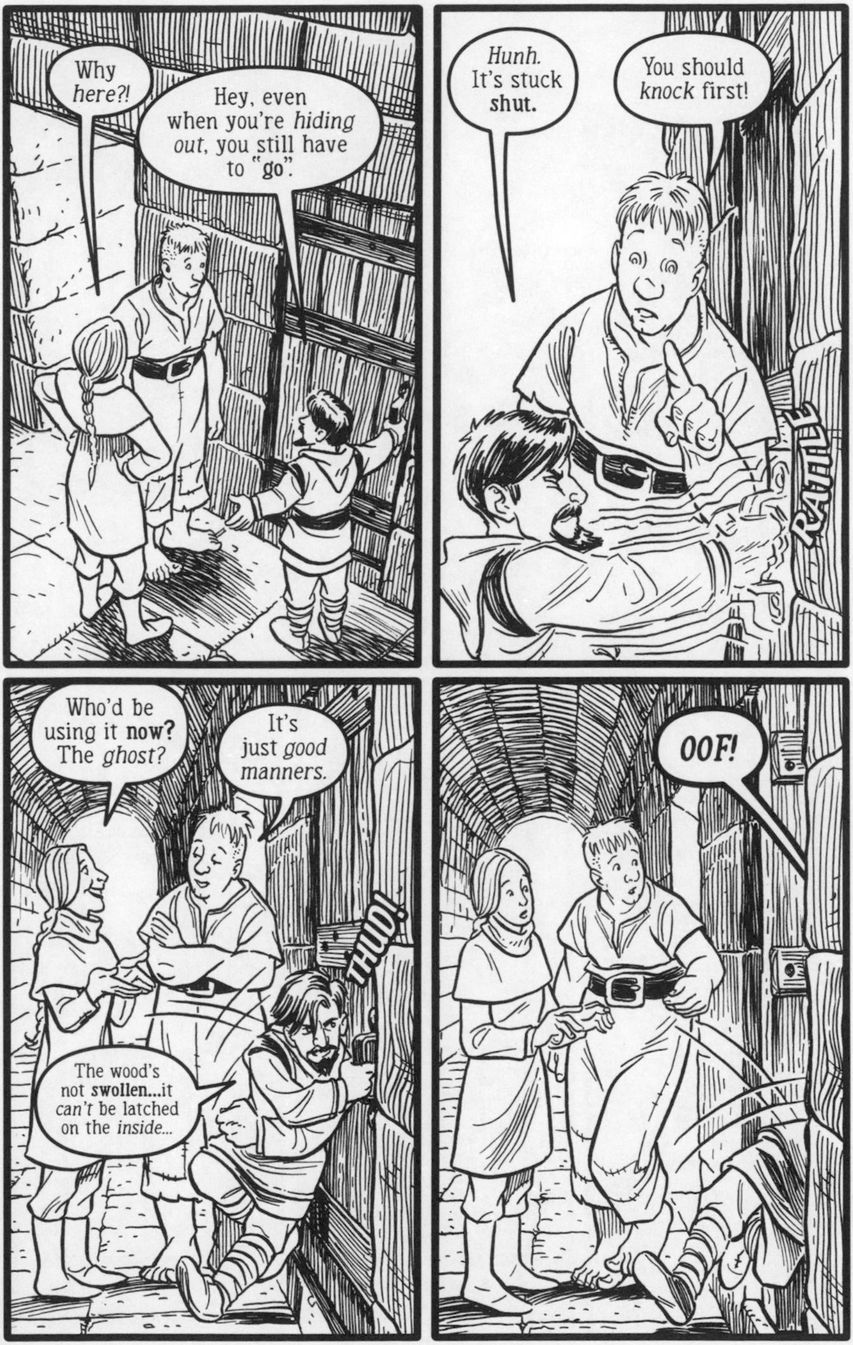
Why *here?!*
Hey, even when you're *hiding out*, you still have to "**go**".
Hunh. It's stuck **shut.**
You should *knock* first!
RATTLE
Who'd be using it **now?** The *ghost?*
It's just *good manners.*
THUD!
The wood's not **swollen...**it *can't* be latched on the *inside...*
OOF!

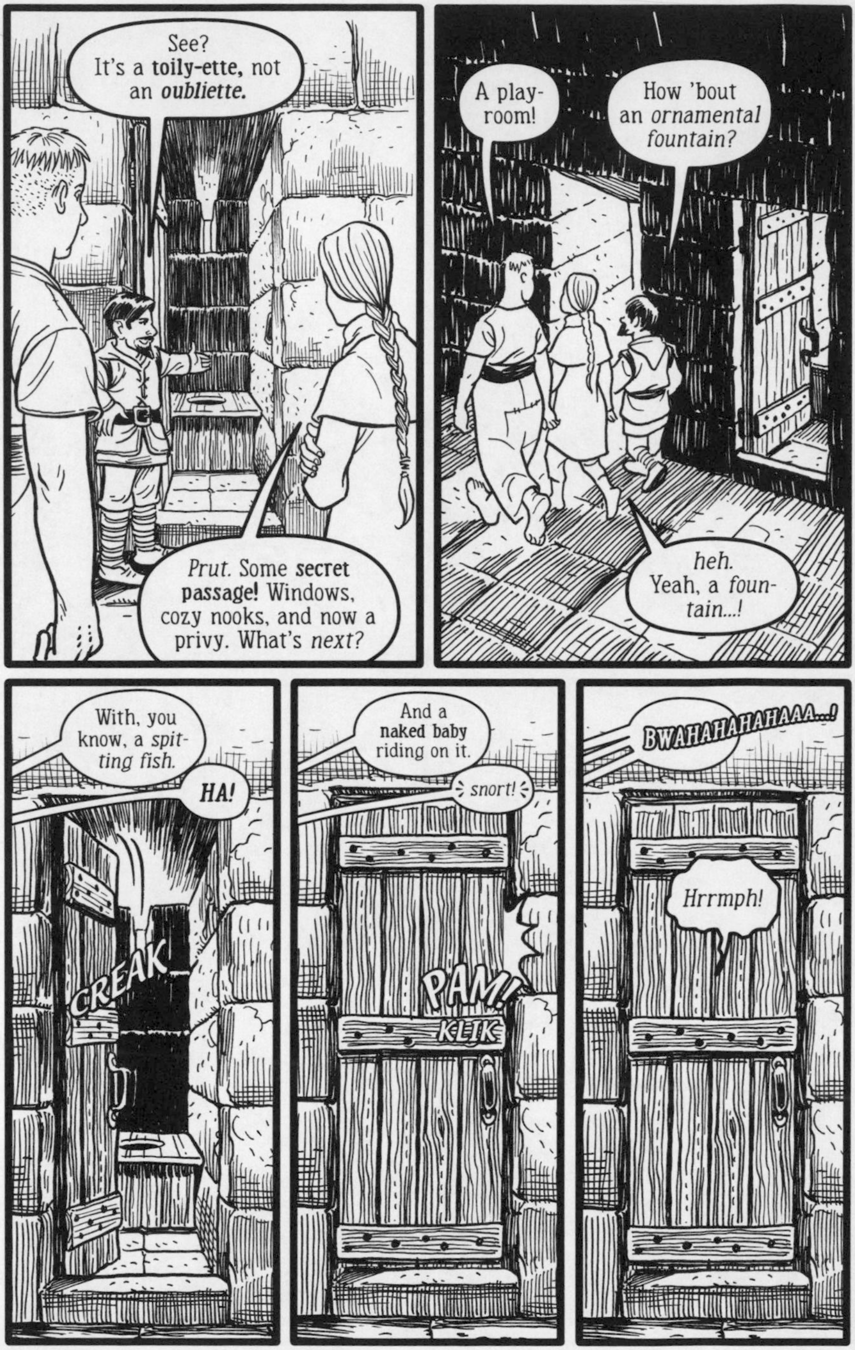
See?
It's a **toily-ette,** not an ***oubliette.***
Prut. Some **secret passage!** Windows, cozy nooks, and now a privy. What's *next?*
A play-room!
How 'bout an *ornamental fountain?*
heh.
Yeah, a *foun-tain...!*
With, you know, a *spit-ting fish.*
HA!
CREAK
And a **naked baby** riding on it.
snort!
PAM!
KLIK
BWAHAHAHAHAAA...!
Hrrmph!

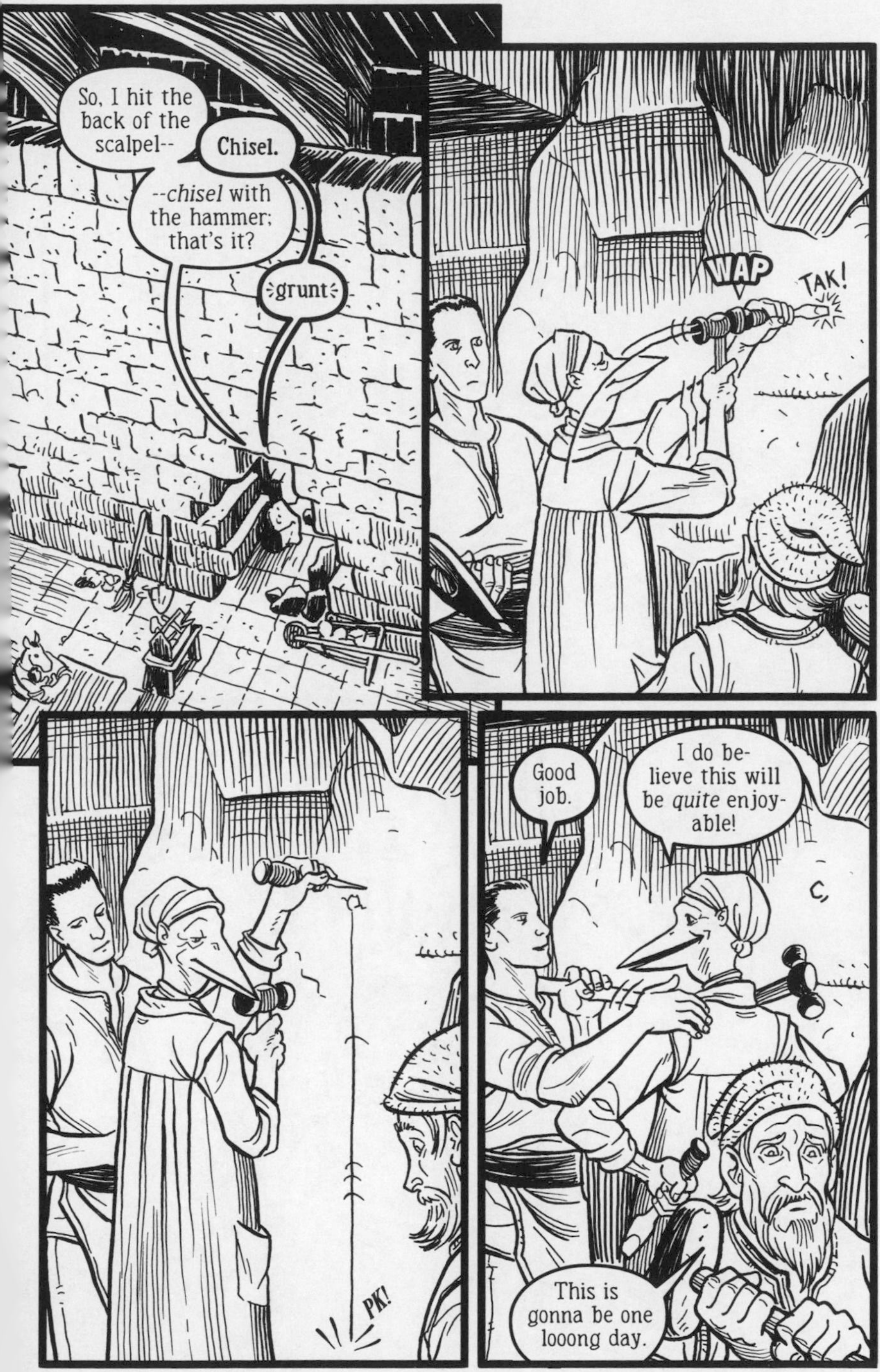
So, I hit the back of the scalpel--
Chisel.
--*chisel* with the hammer; that's it?
grunt
WAP
TAK!
PK!
Good job.
I do be-lieve this will be *quite* enjoy-able!
This is gonna be one looong day.

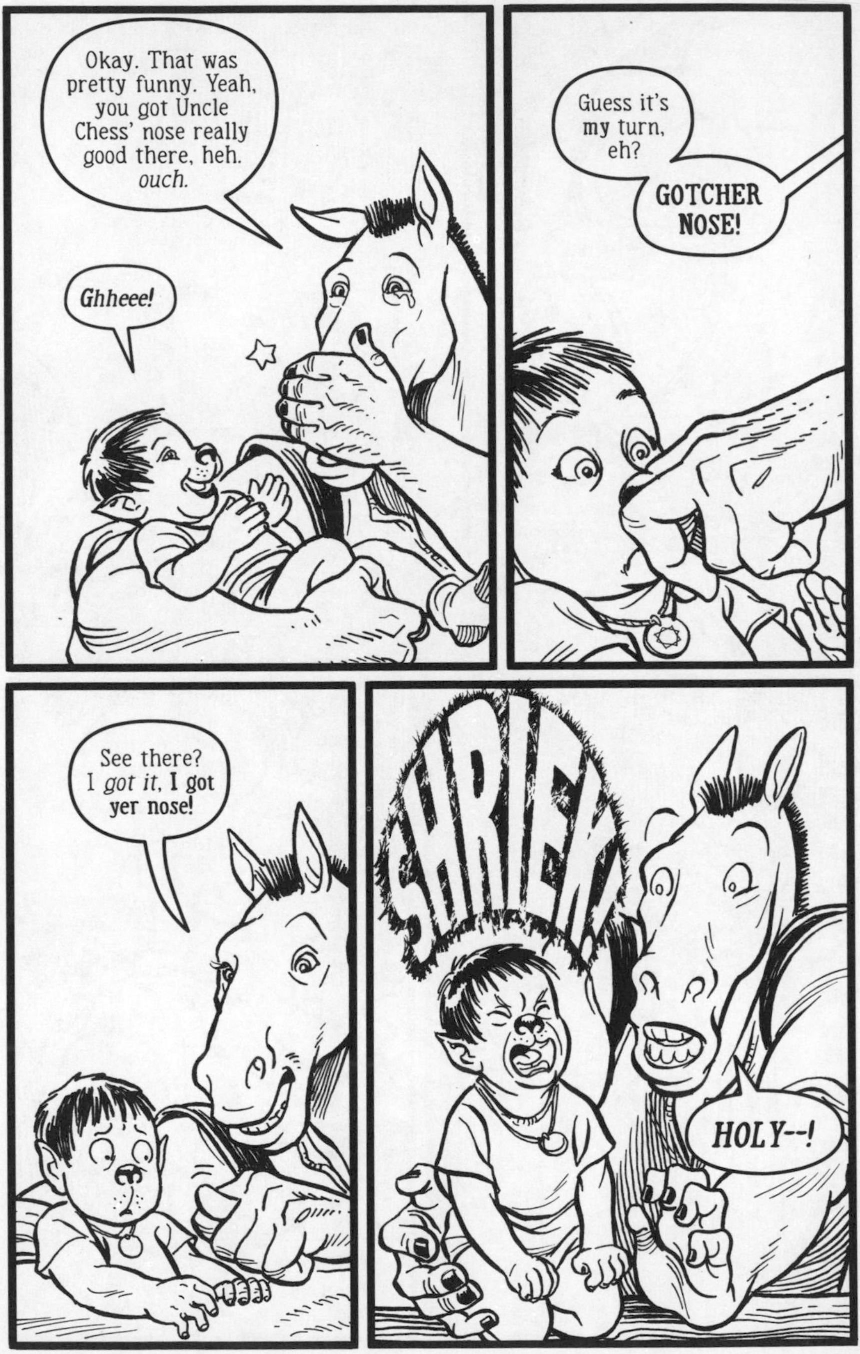
Okay. That was pretty funny. Yeah, you got Uncle Chess' nose really good there, heh. *ouch.*
Ghheee!
Guess it's my turn, eh?
GOTCHER NOSE!
See there? I *got it*, I got yer nose!
SHRIEK
HOLY--!

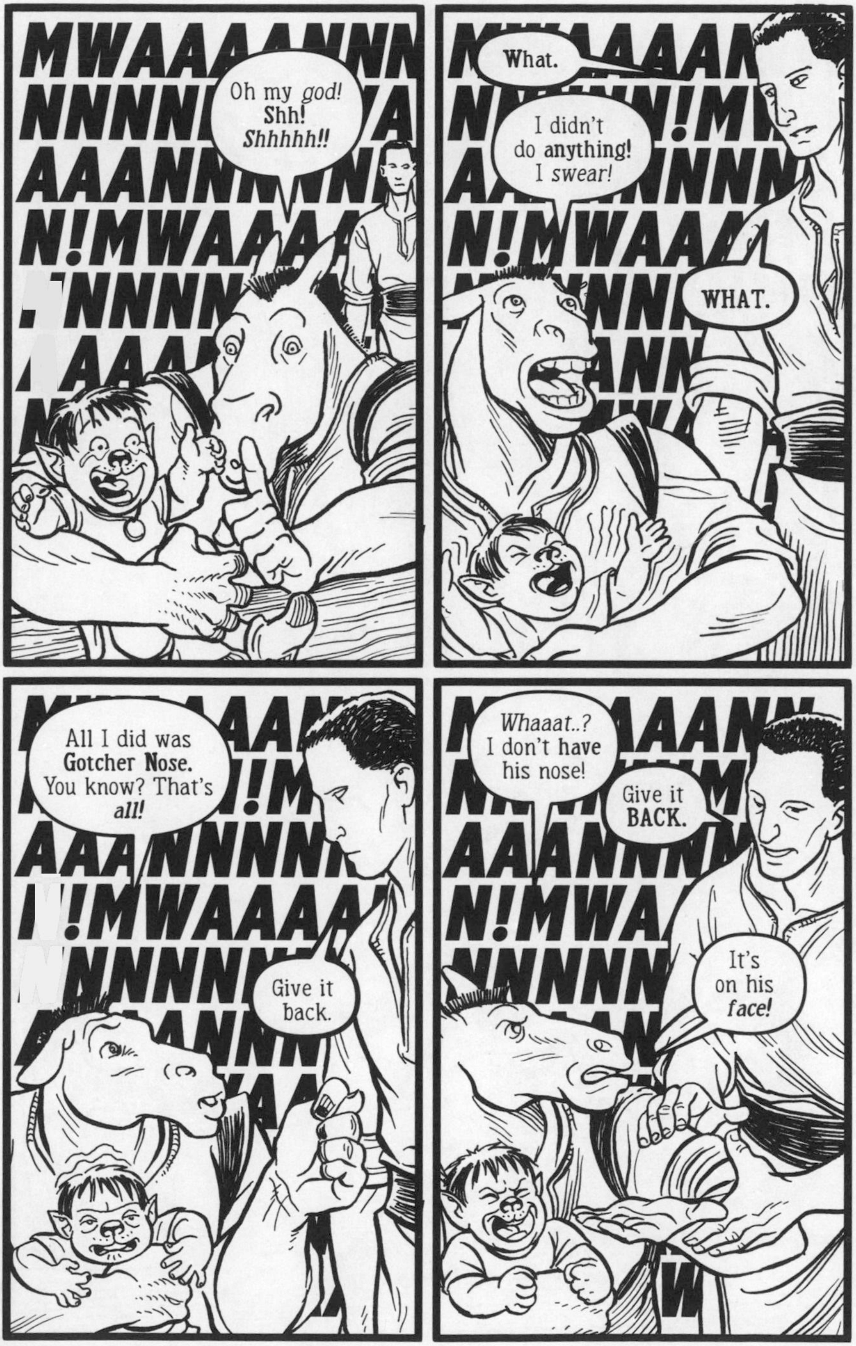

MWAAAANNN
Oh my god! Shh! Shhhhh!!
What.
I didn't do anything! I swear!
WHAT.
All I did was Gotcher Nose. You know? That's all!
Give it back.
Whaaat..? I don't have his nose!
Give it BACK.
It's on his face!

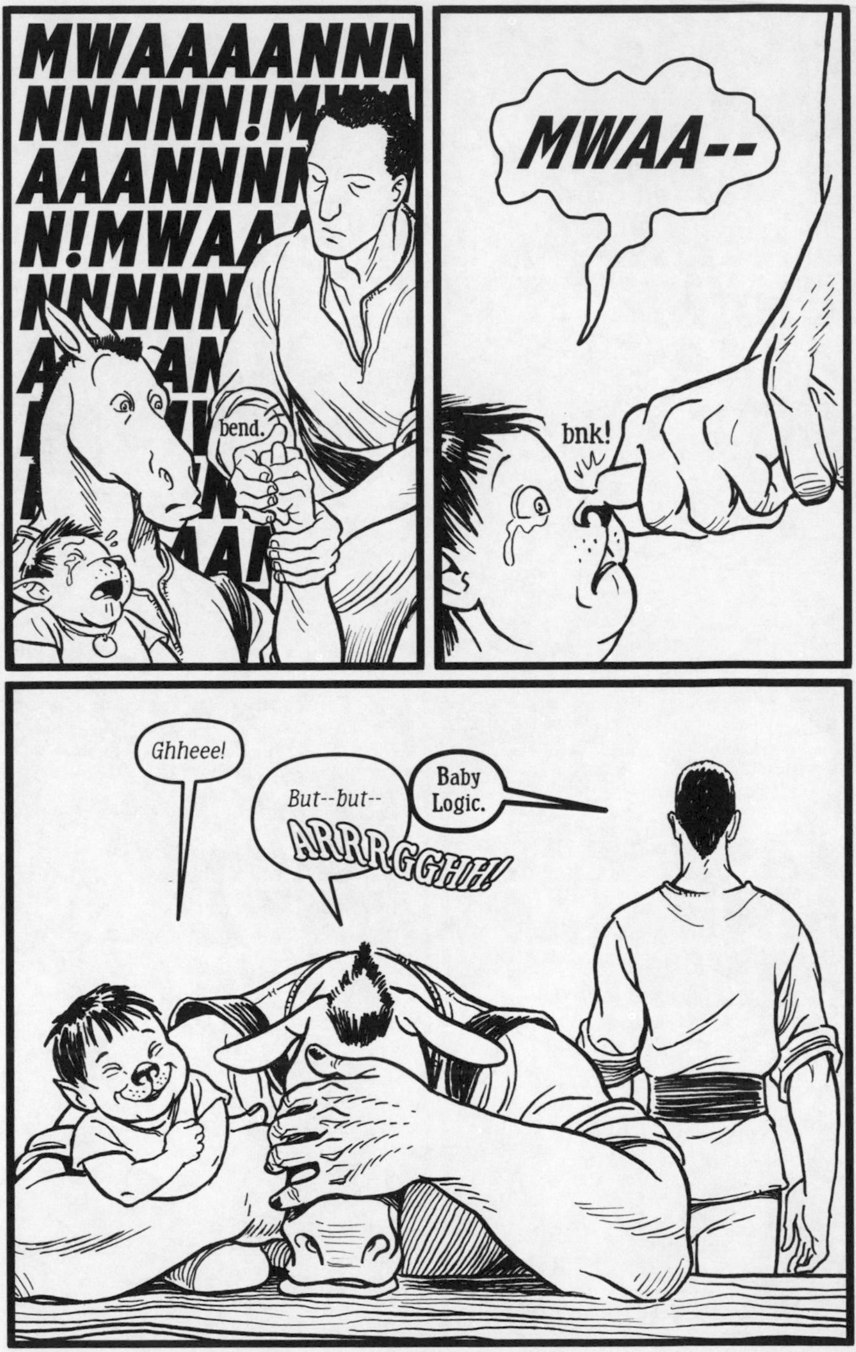
MWAAAANNN
NNNNN!MWA
AAANNNN
N!MWAA
NNNNN
bend.
MWAA--
bnk!
Ghheee!
But--but--
ARRRGGHH!
Baby Logic.

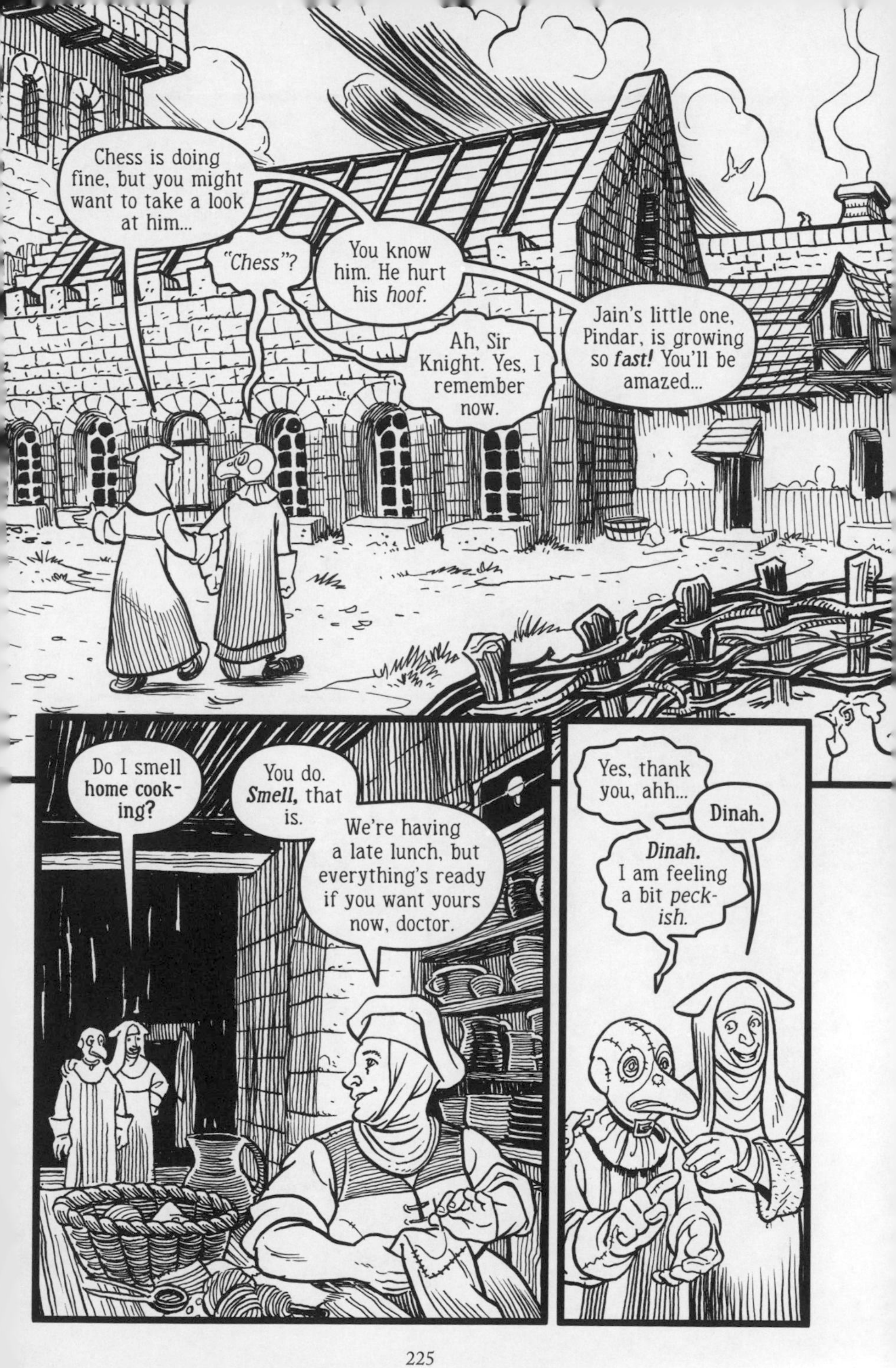
Chess is doing fine, but you might want to take a look at him...
"Chess"?
You know him. He hurt his *hoof.*
Ah, Sir Knight. Yes, I remember now.
Jain's little one, Pindar, is growing so *fast!* You'll be amazed...
Do I smell **home cook-ing?**
You do. ***Smell,*** that is.
We're having a late lunch, but everything's ready if you want yours now, doctor.
Yes, thank you, ahh...
Dinah.
Dinah. I am feeling a bit *peck-ish.*

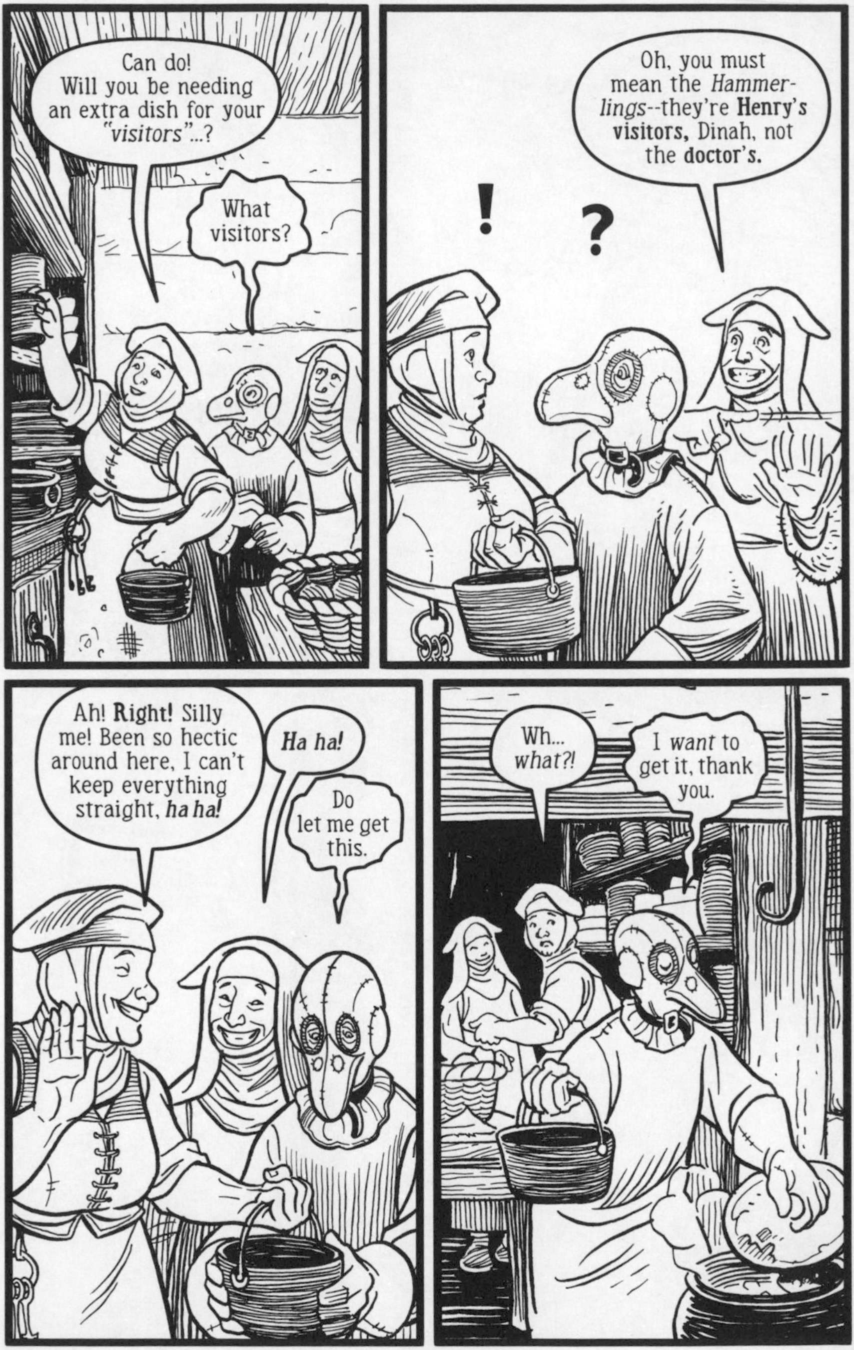
Can do!
Will you be needing an extra dish for your *"visitors"*...?
What visitors?
Oh, you must mean the *Hammerlings*--they're **Henry's visitors,** Dinah, not the **doctor's.**
!
?
Ah! **Right!** Silly me! Been so hectic around here, I can't keep everything straight, ***ha ha!***
Ha ha!
Do let me get this.
Wh... *what?!*
I *want* to get it, thank you.

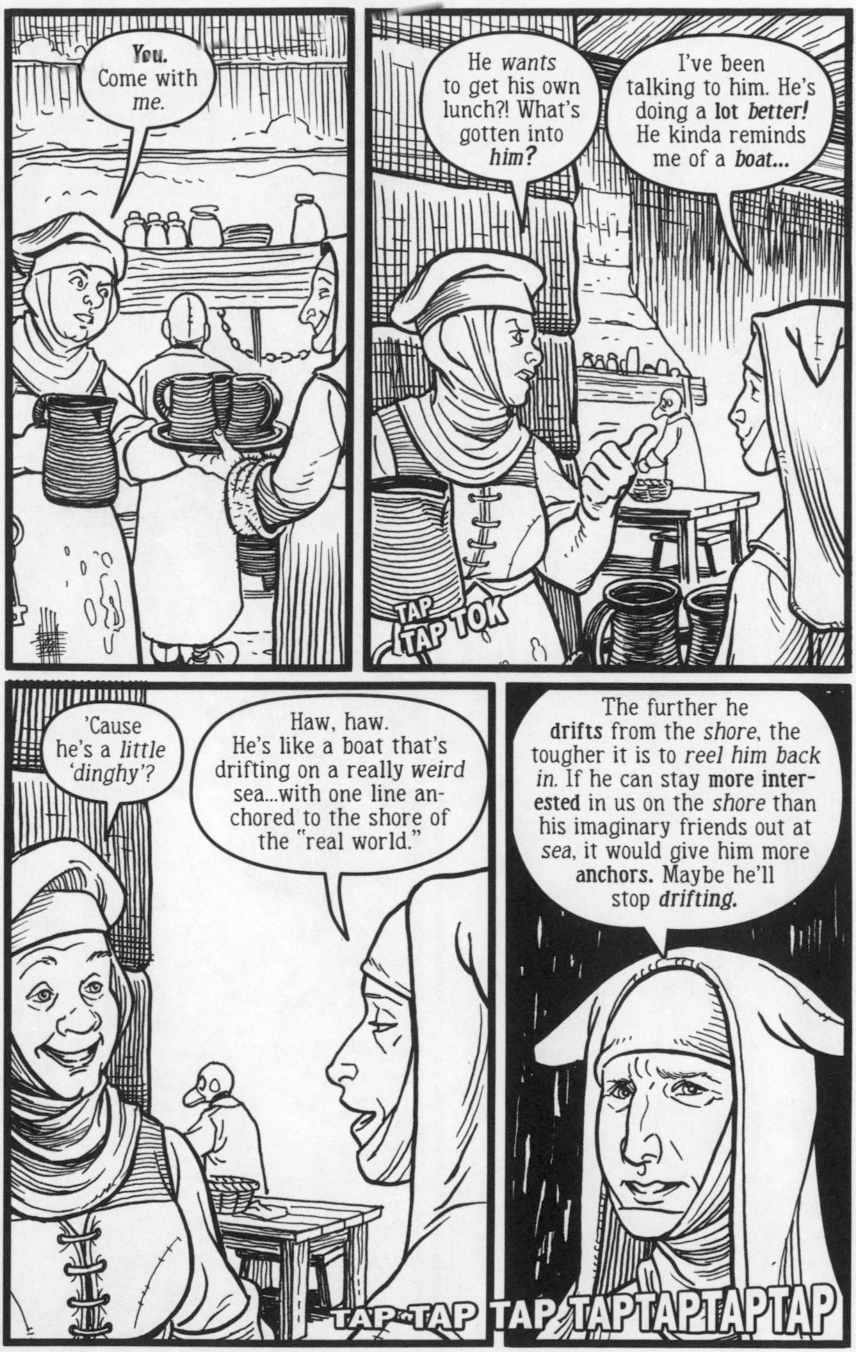
You. Come with me.
He wants to get his own lunch?! What's gotten into him?
I've been talking to him. He's doing a lot better! He kinda reminds me of a boat...
TAP TAP TOK
'Cause he's a little 'dinghy'?
Haw, haw. He's like a boat that's drifting on a really weird sea...with one line anchored to the shore of the "real world."
The further he drifts from the shore, the tougher it is to reel him back in. If he can stay more interested in us on the shore than his imaginary friends out at sea, it would give him more anchors. Maybe he'll stop drifting.
TAP TAP TAP TAPTAPTAPTAP

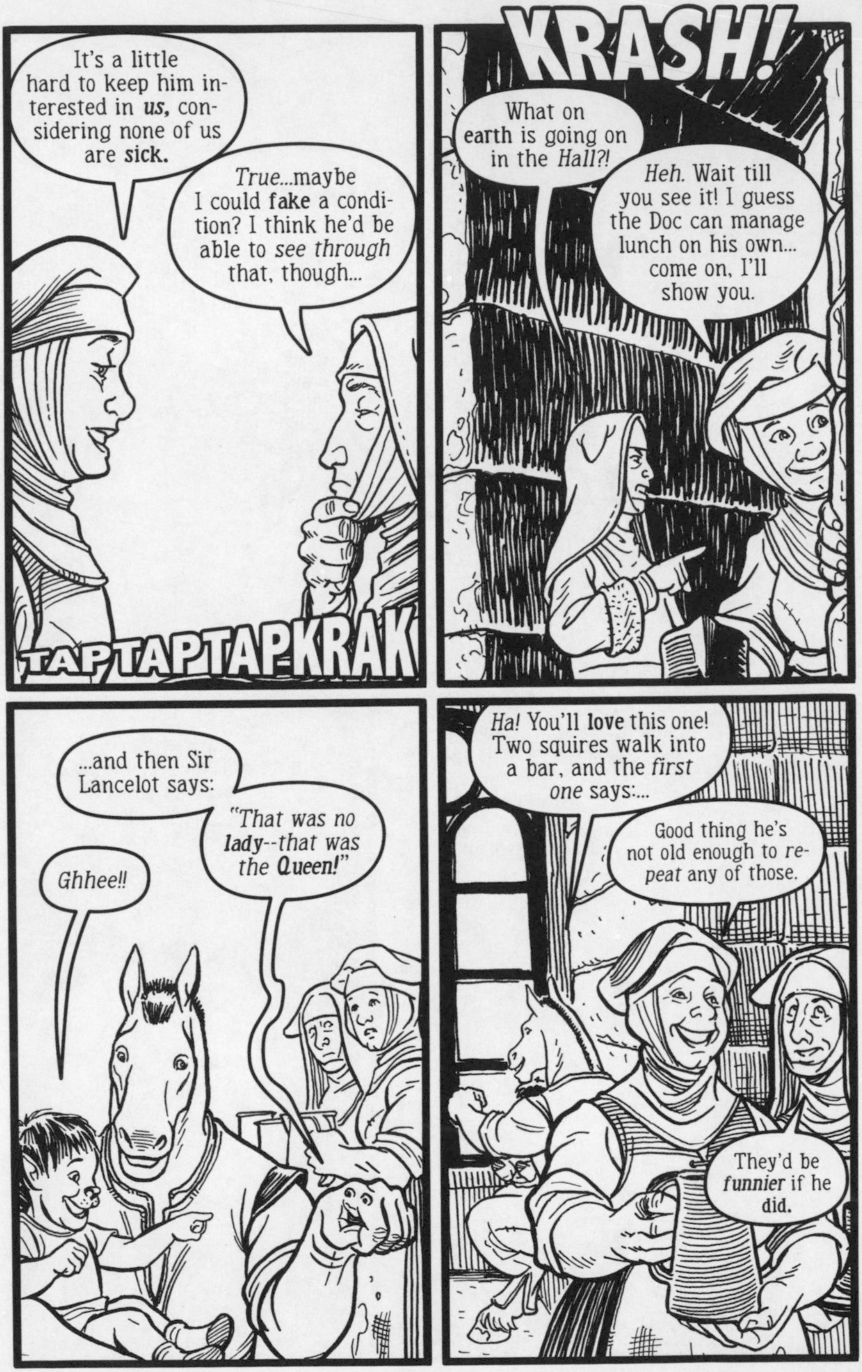
It's a little hard to keep him interested in *us,* considering none of us are **sick.**
True...maybe I could **fake** a condition? I think he'd be able to *see through* that, though...
TAPTAPTAPKRAK
KRASH!
What on **earth** is going on in the *Hall?!*
Heh. Wait till you see it! I guess the Doc can manage lunch on his own... come on, I'll show you.
...and then Sir Lancelot says:
*"That was no **lady**--that was the **Queen!**"*
Ghhee!!
Ha! You'll **love** this one! Two squires walk into a bar, and the *first one* says:...
Good thing he's not old enough to *repeat* any of those.
They'd be *funnier* if he **did.**

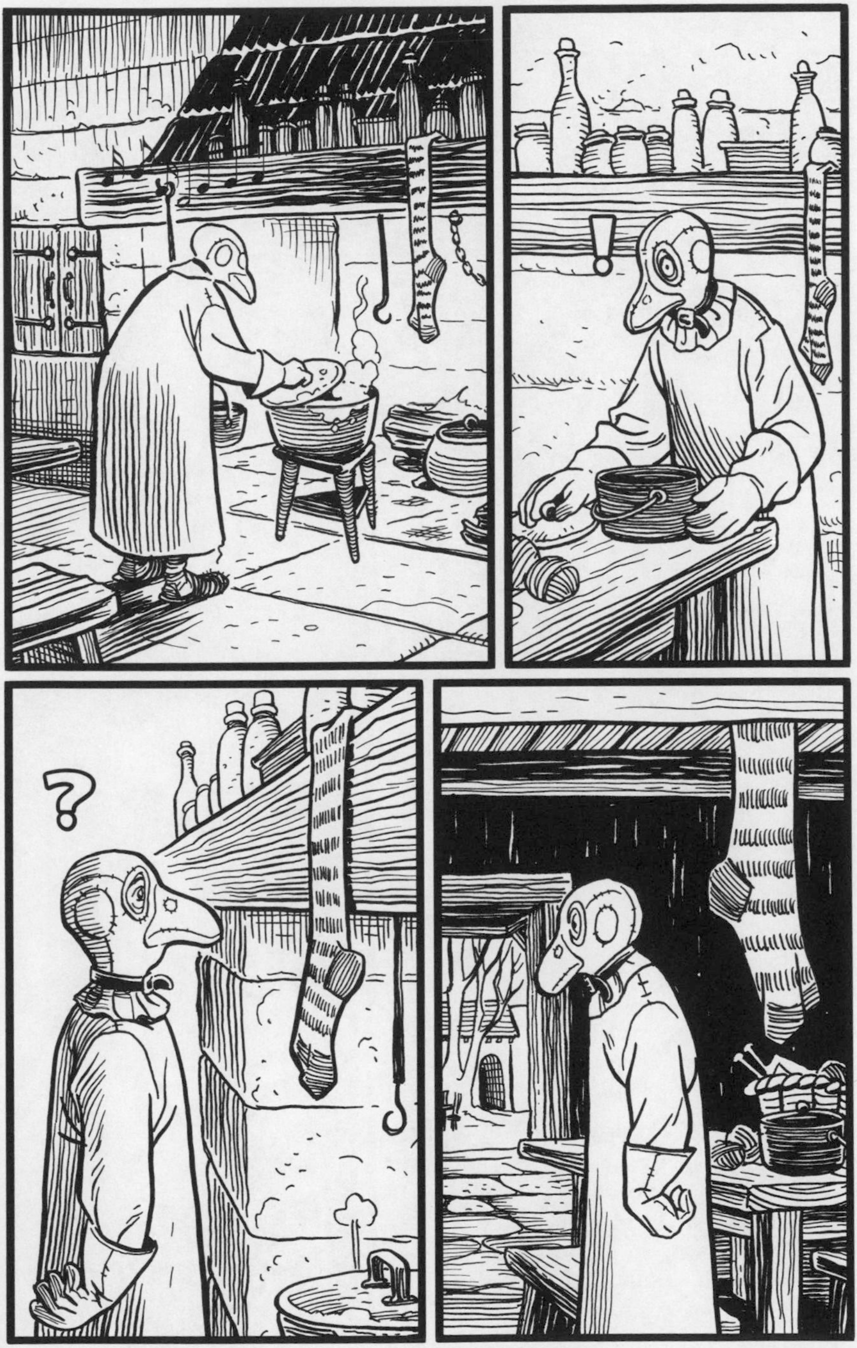
!
?

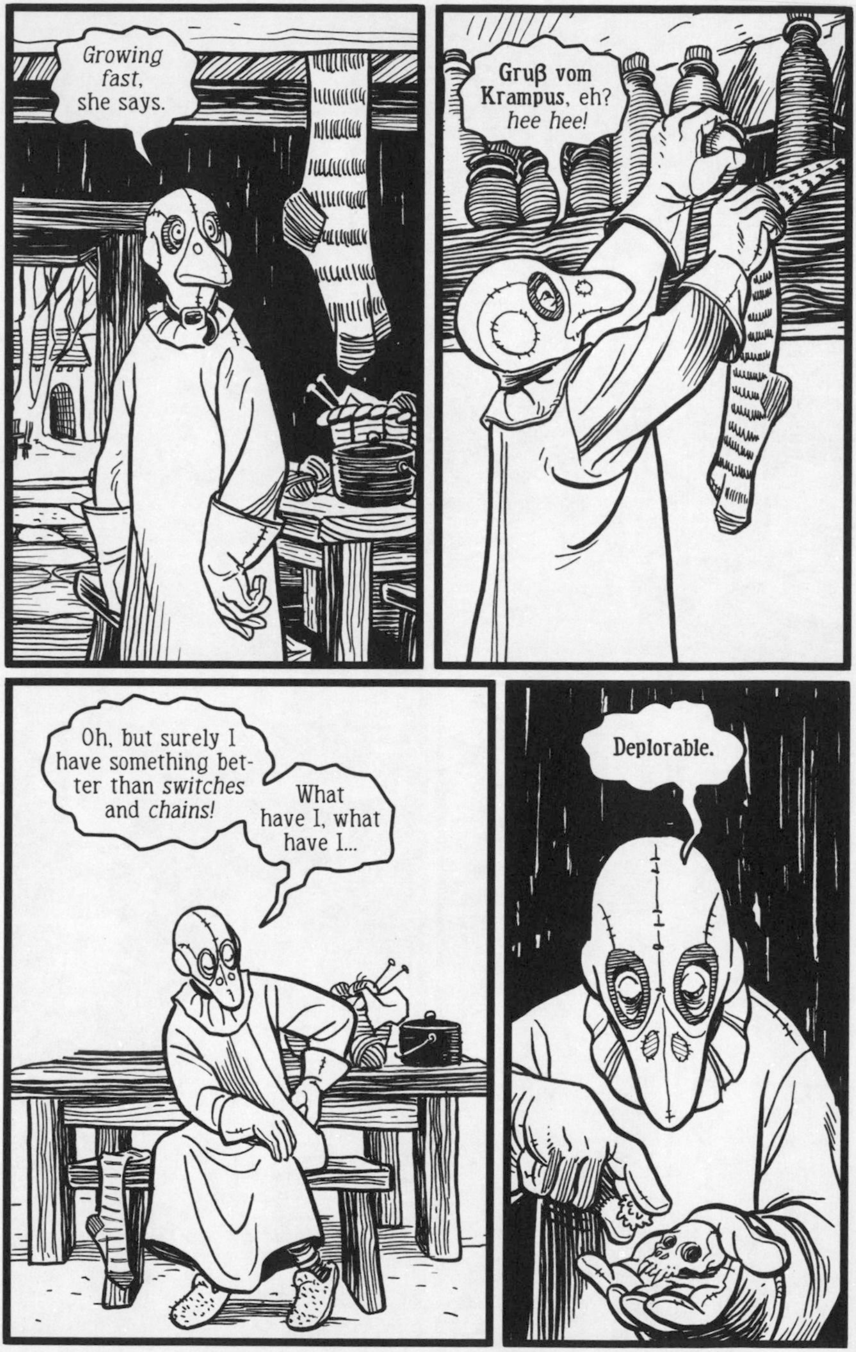

Growing *fast*, she says.
Gruß vom Krampus, eh? *hee hee!*
Oh, but surely I have something better than *switches* and *chains!*
What have I, what have I...
Deplorable.

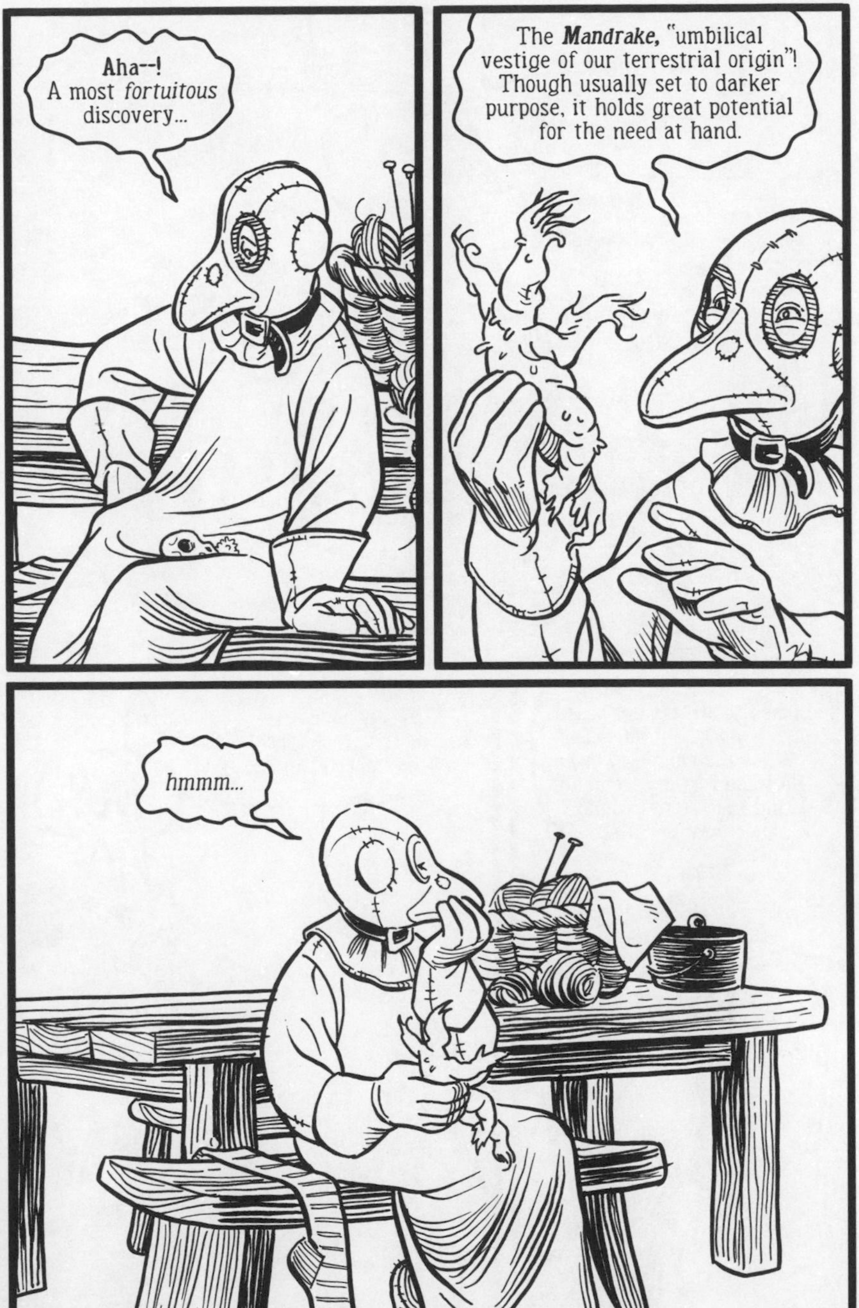
Aha--!
A most *fortuitous* discovery...
The **Mandrake,** "umbilical vestige of our terrestrial origin"! Though usually set to darker purpose, it holds great potential for the need at hand.
hmmm...

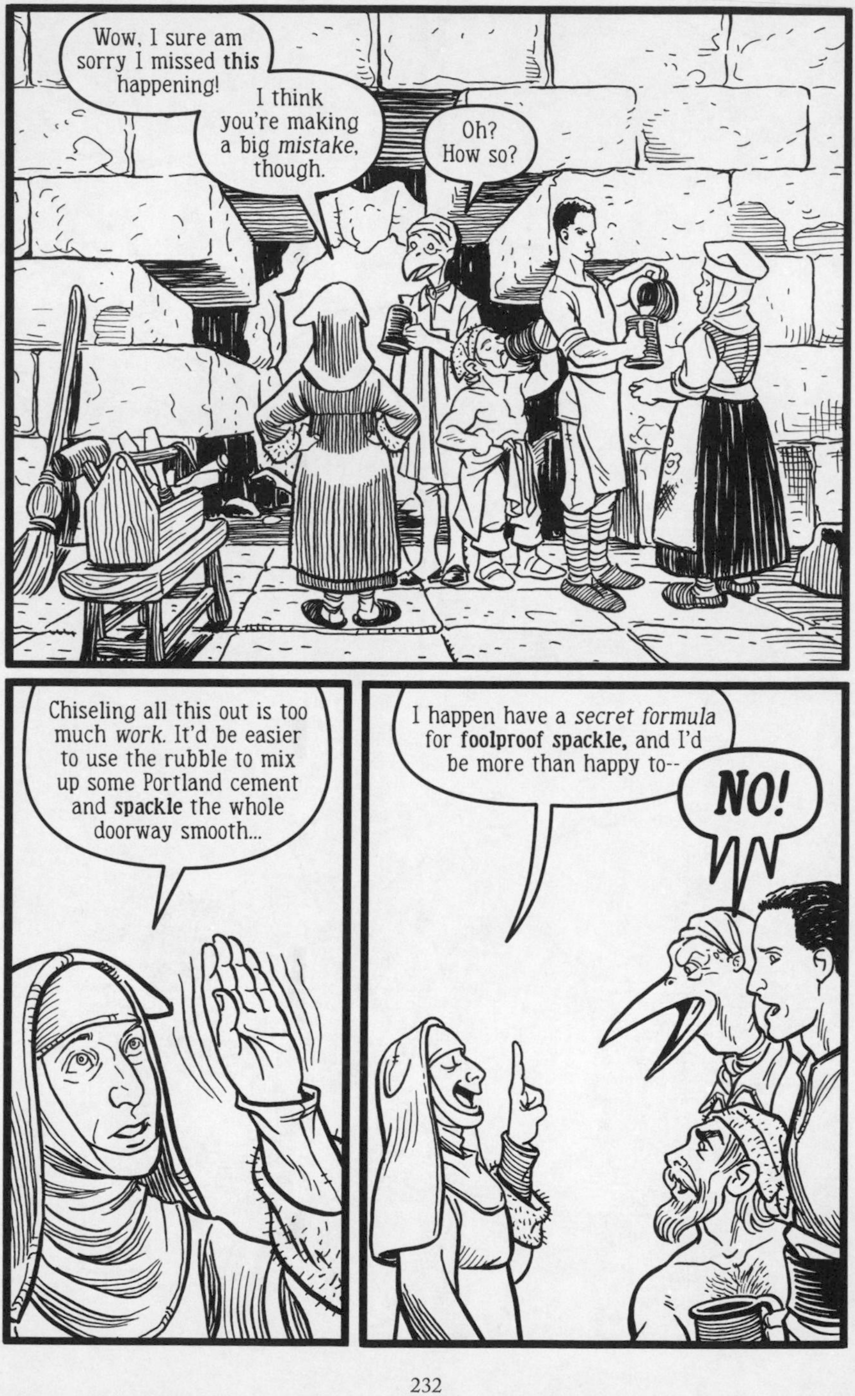
Wow, I sure am sorry I missed **this** happening!
I think you're making a big *mistake*, though.
Oh? How so?
Chiseling all this out is too much *work*. It'd be easier to use the rubble to mix up some Portland cement and **spackle** the whole doorway smooth...
I happen have a *secret formula* for **foolproof spackle,** and I'd be more than happy to--
NO!

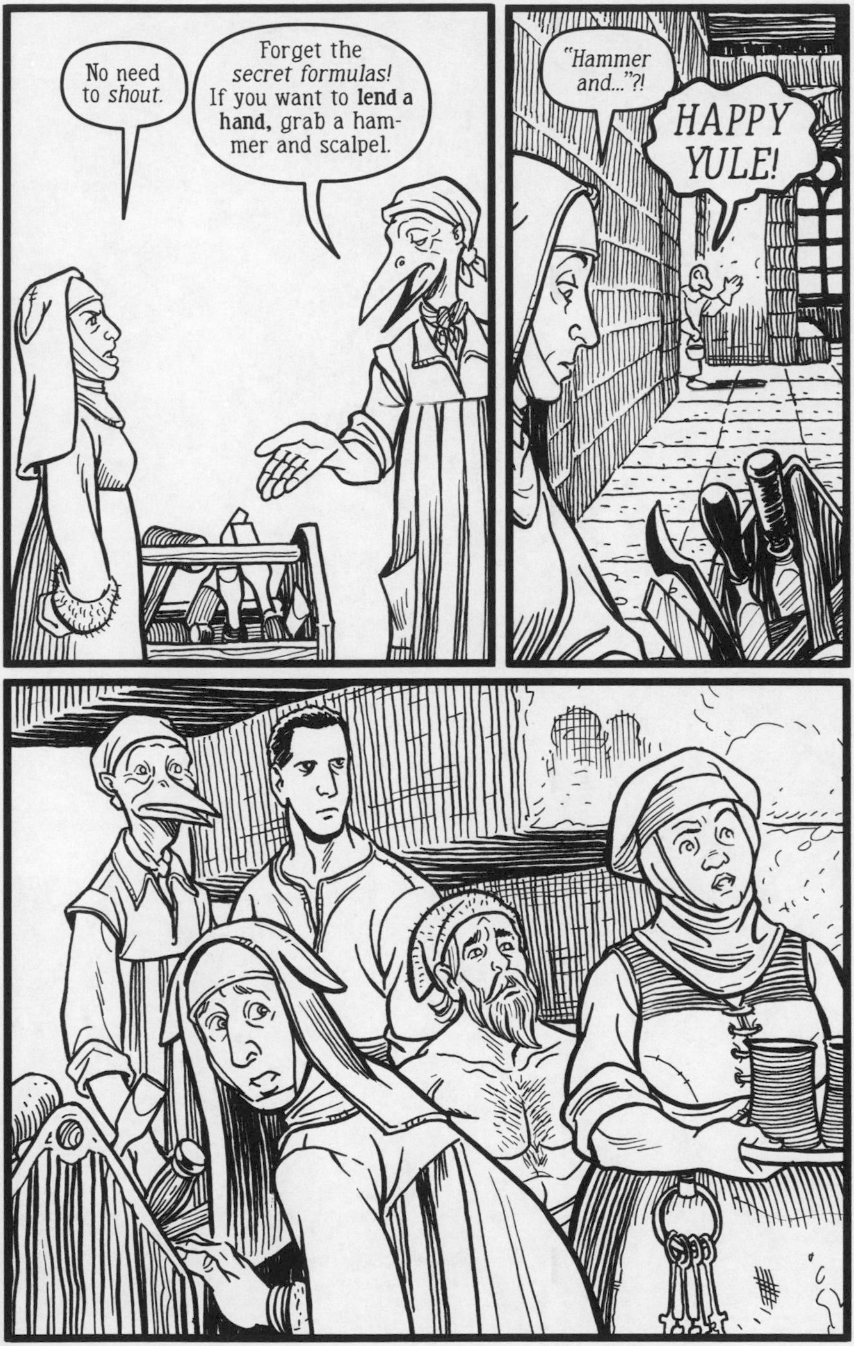
No need to *shout.*
Forget the *secret formulas!* If you want to **lend a hand,** grab a hammer and scalpel.
"Hammer and..."?!
HAPPY YULE!

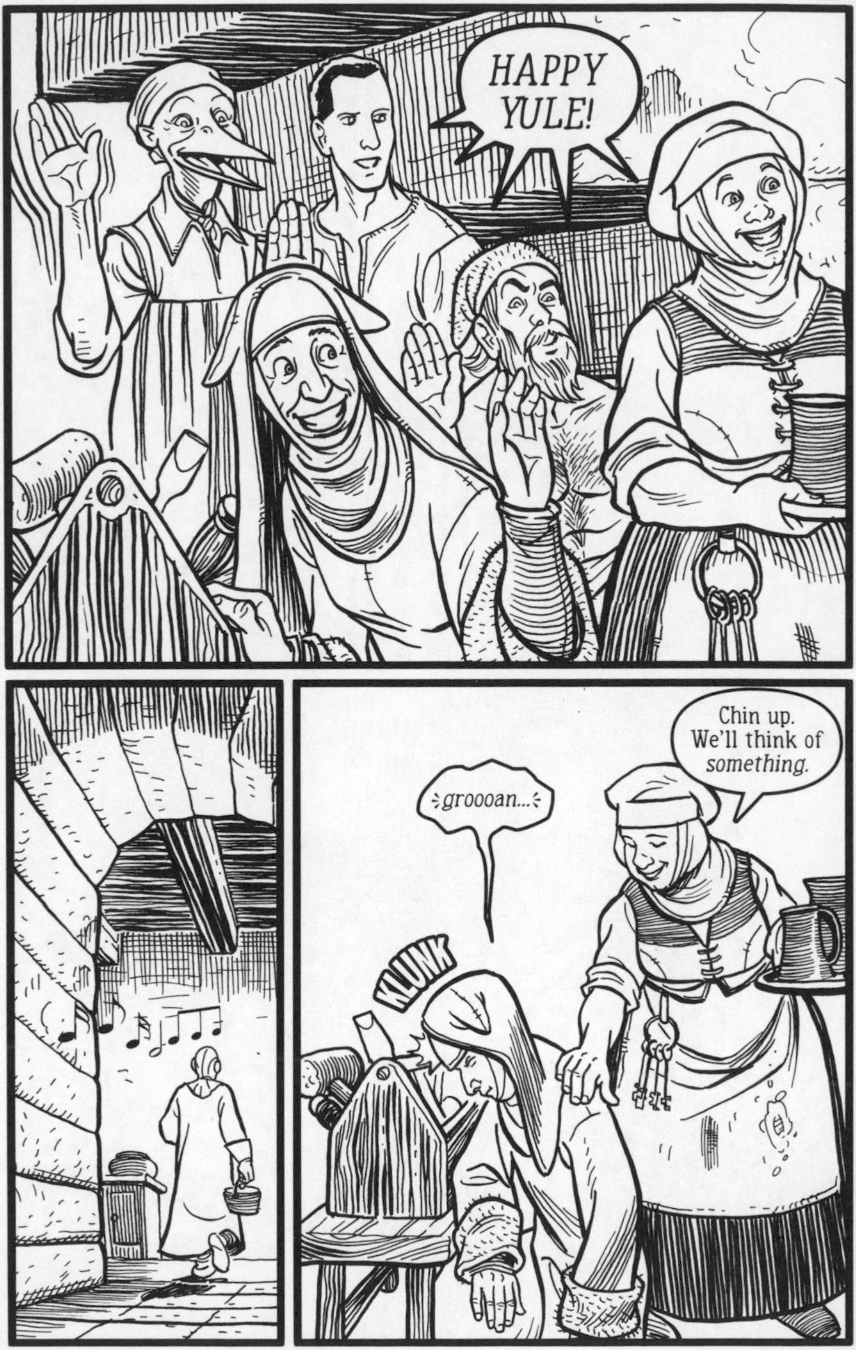
HAPPY YULE!
KLUNK
grooooan...
Chin up. We'll think of *something.*

Chapter 10.

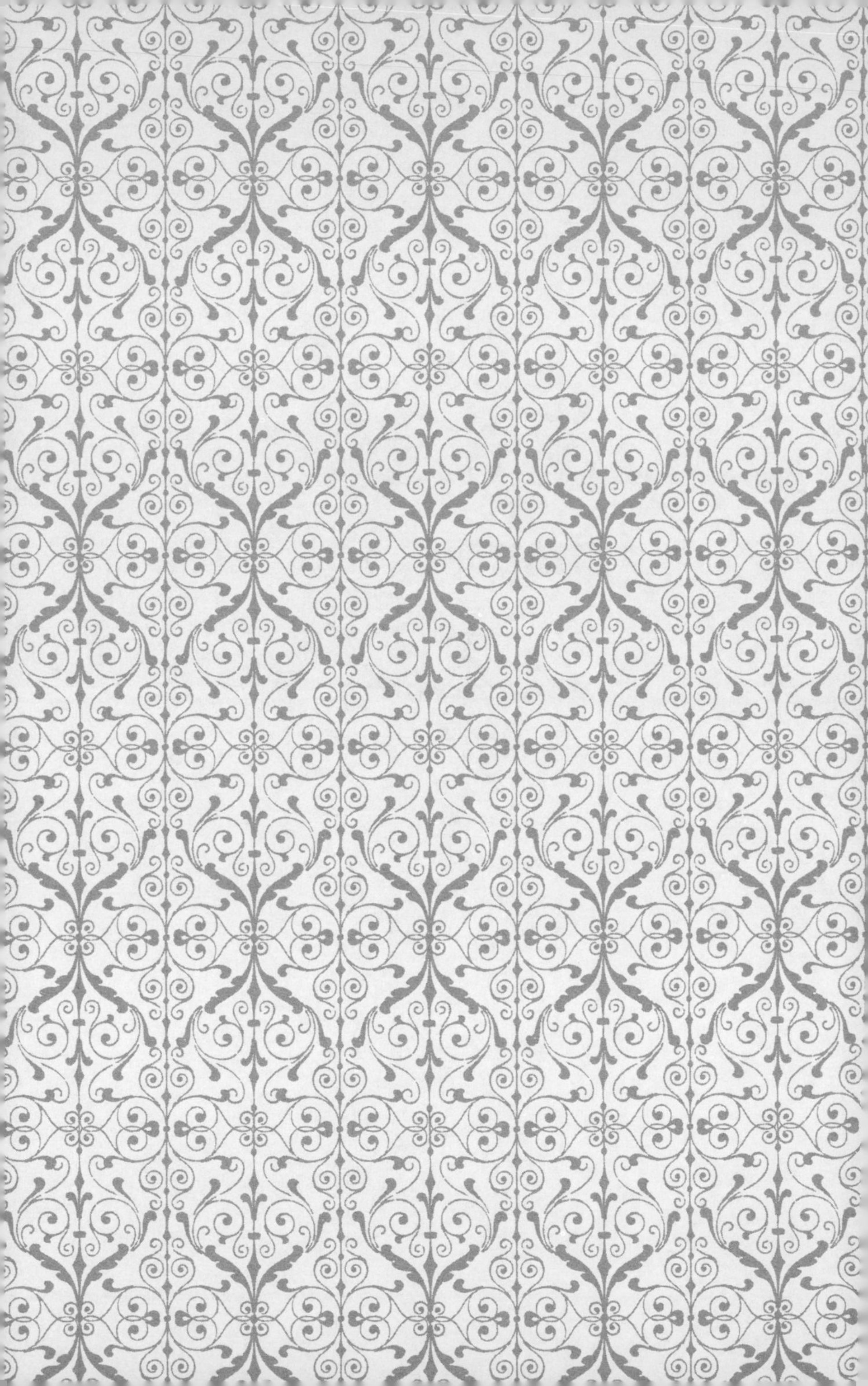

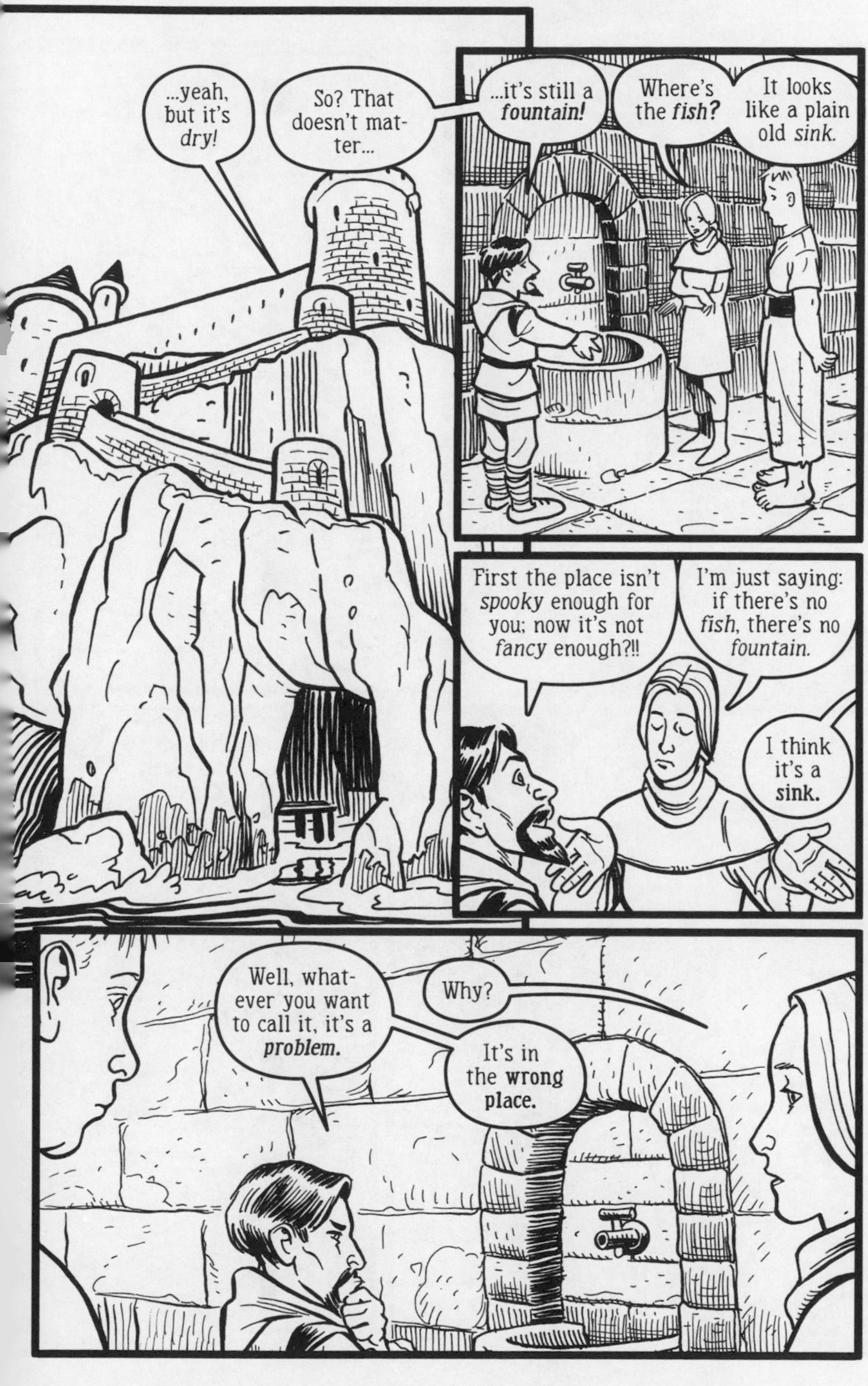

...yeah, but it's *dry!*
So? That doesn't matter...
...it's still a ***fountain!***
Where's the ***fish?***
It looks like a plain old *sink.*
First the place isn't *spooky* enough for you; now it's not *fancy* enough?!!
I'm just saying: if there's no *fish*, there's no *fountain.*
I think it's a **sink.**
Well, whatever you want to call it, it's a ***problem.***
Why?
It's in the **wrong place.**

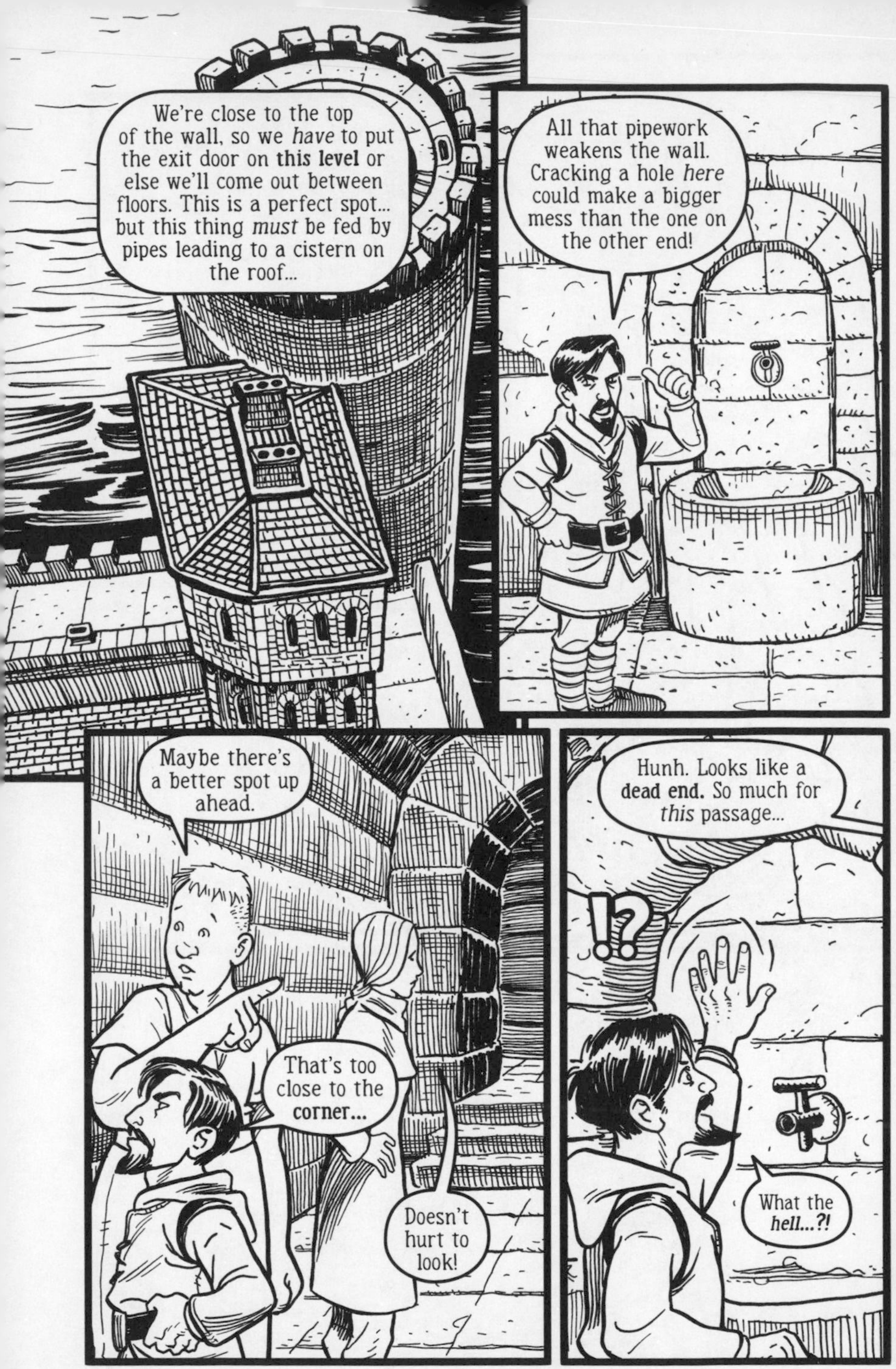
We're close to the top of the wall, so we *have* to put the exit door on **this level** or else we'll come out between floors. This is a perfect spot... but this thing *must* be fed by pipes leading to a cistern on the roof...
All that pipework weakens the wall. Cracking a hole *here* could make a bigger mess than the one on the other end!
Maybe there's a better spot up ahead.
That's too close to the **corner...**
Doesn't hurt to look!
Hunh. Looks like a **dead end.** So much for *this* passage...
!?
What the ***hell...?!***

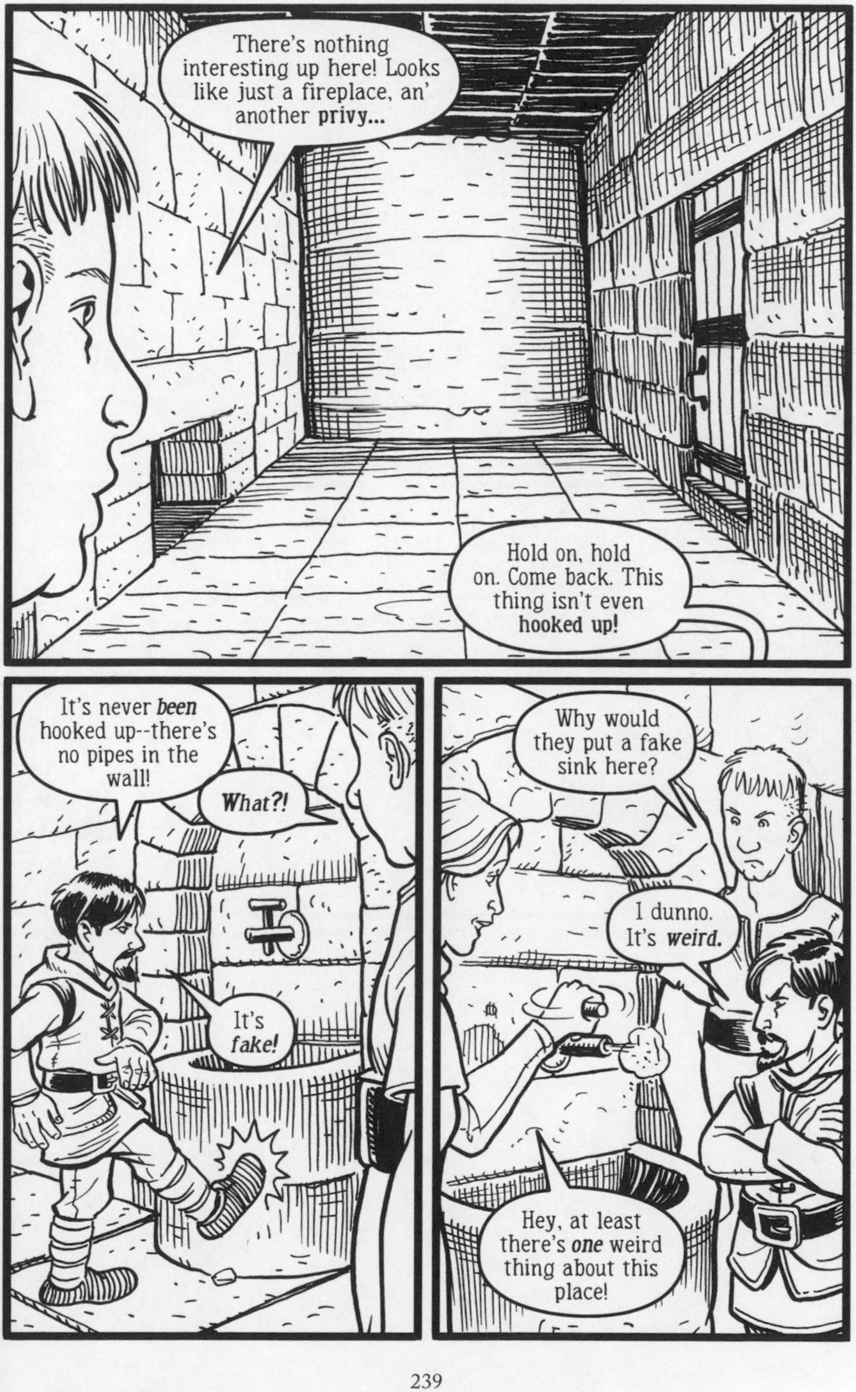
There's nothing interesting up here! Looks like just a fireplace, an' another **privy...**
Hold on, hold on. Come back. This thing isn't even **hooked up!**
It's never *been* hooked up--there's no pipes in the wall!
What?!
It's *fake!*
Why would they put a fake sink here?
I dunno. It's **weird.**
Hey, at least there's *one* weird thing about this place!

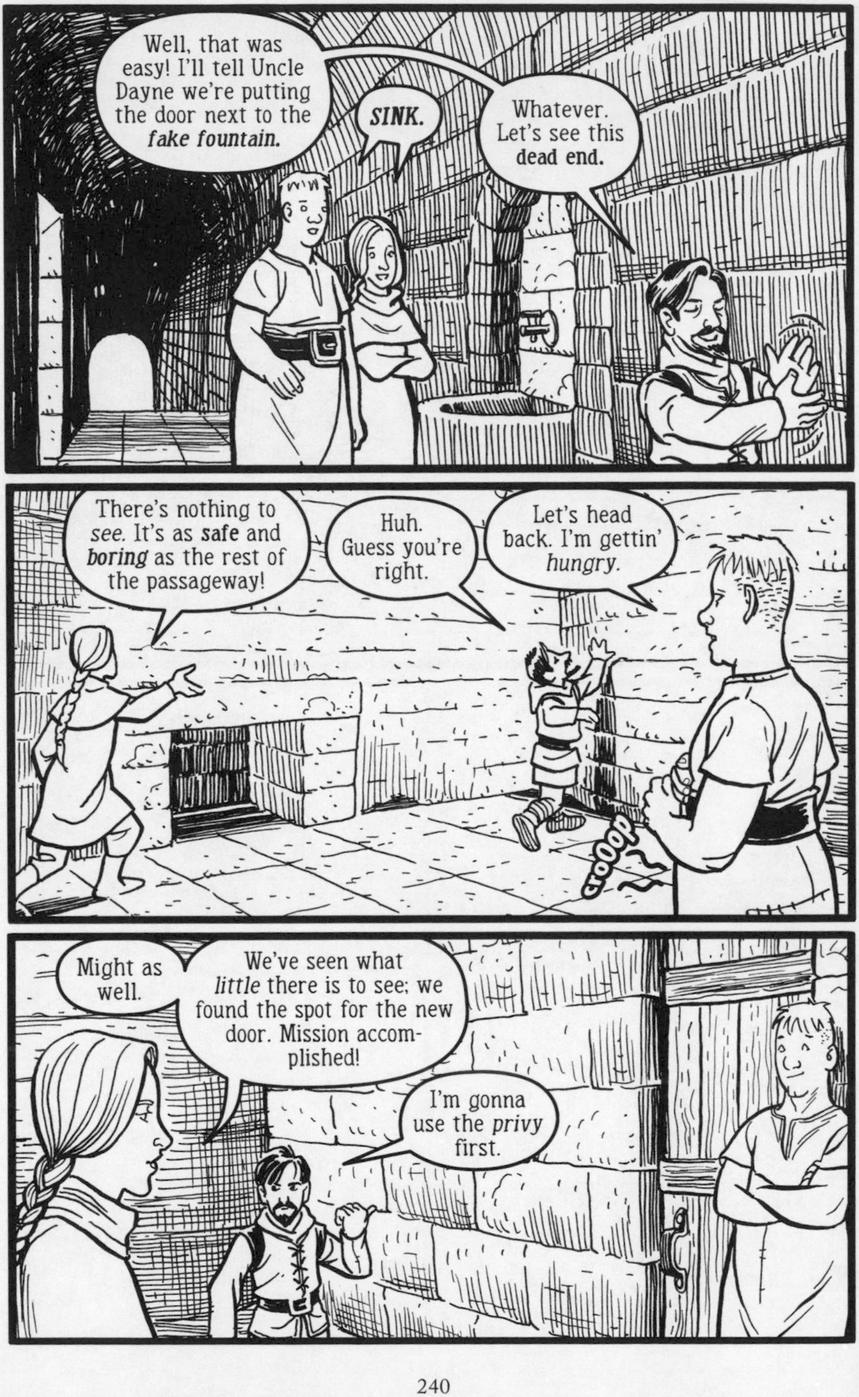
Well, that was easy! I'll tell Uncle Dayne we're putting the door next to the *fake fountain.*
SINK.
Whatever. Let's see this **dead end.**
There's nothing to *see.* It's as **safe** and *boring* as the rest of the passageway!
Huh. Guess you're right.
Let's head back. I'm gettin' *hungry.*
Might as well.
We've seen what *little* there is to see; we found the spot for the new door. Mission accom-plished!
I'm gonna use the *privy* first.

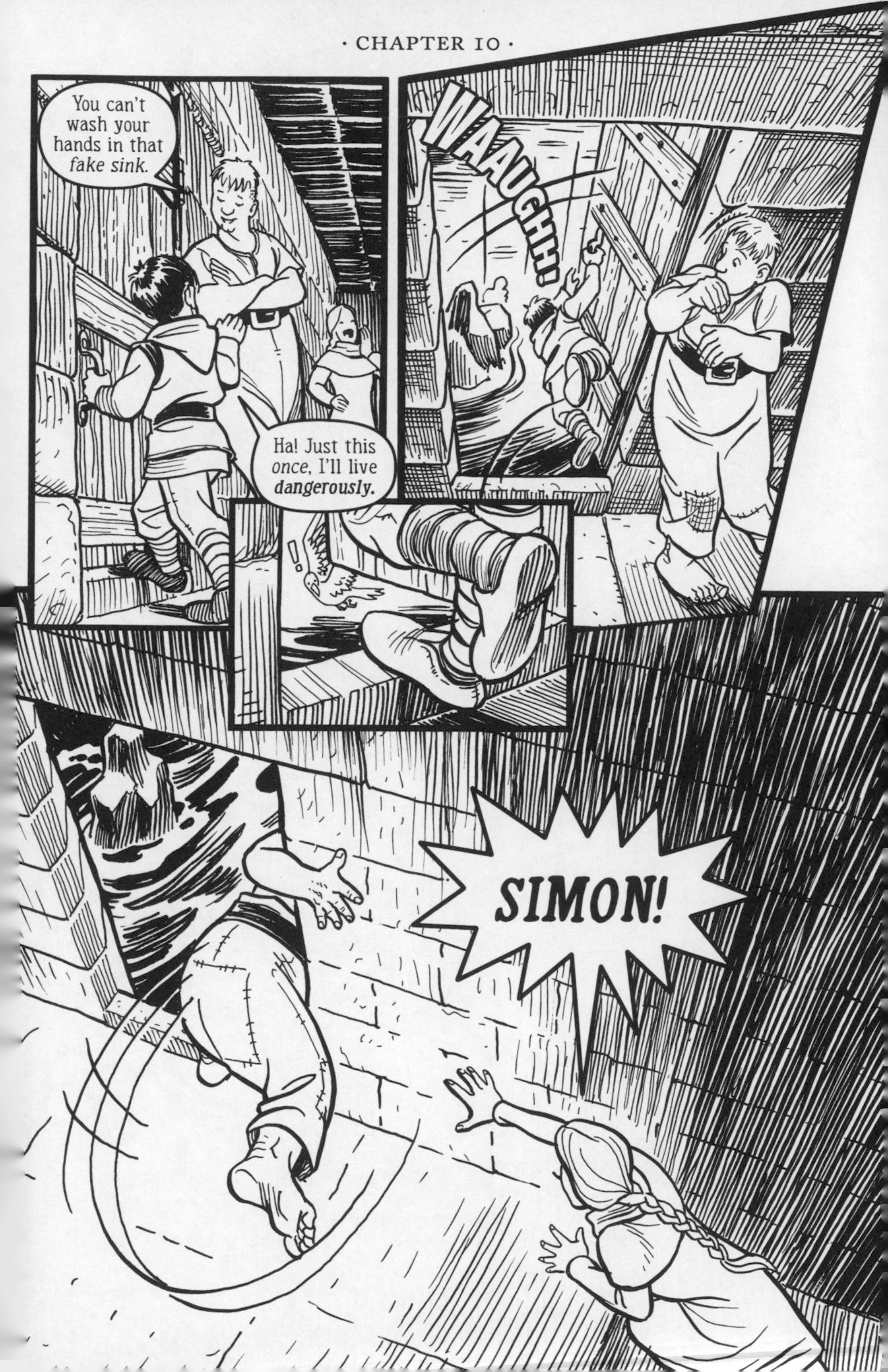
You can't wash your hands in that *fake sink.*
Ha! Just this *once*, I'll live ***dangerously.***
WAAUGHH!
!
SIMON!

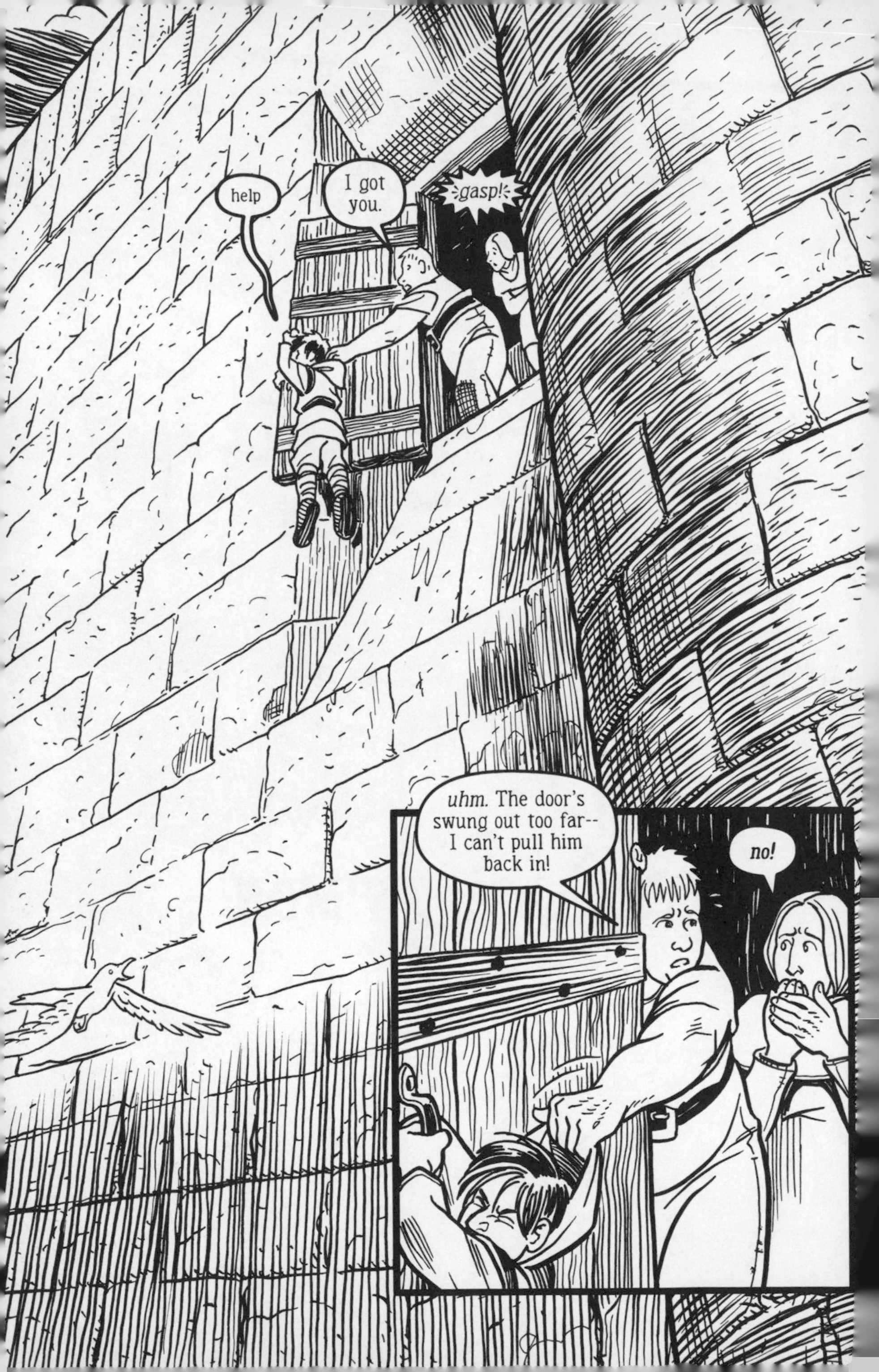
help
I got you.
gasp!
uhm. The door's swung out too far-- I can't pull him back in!
no!

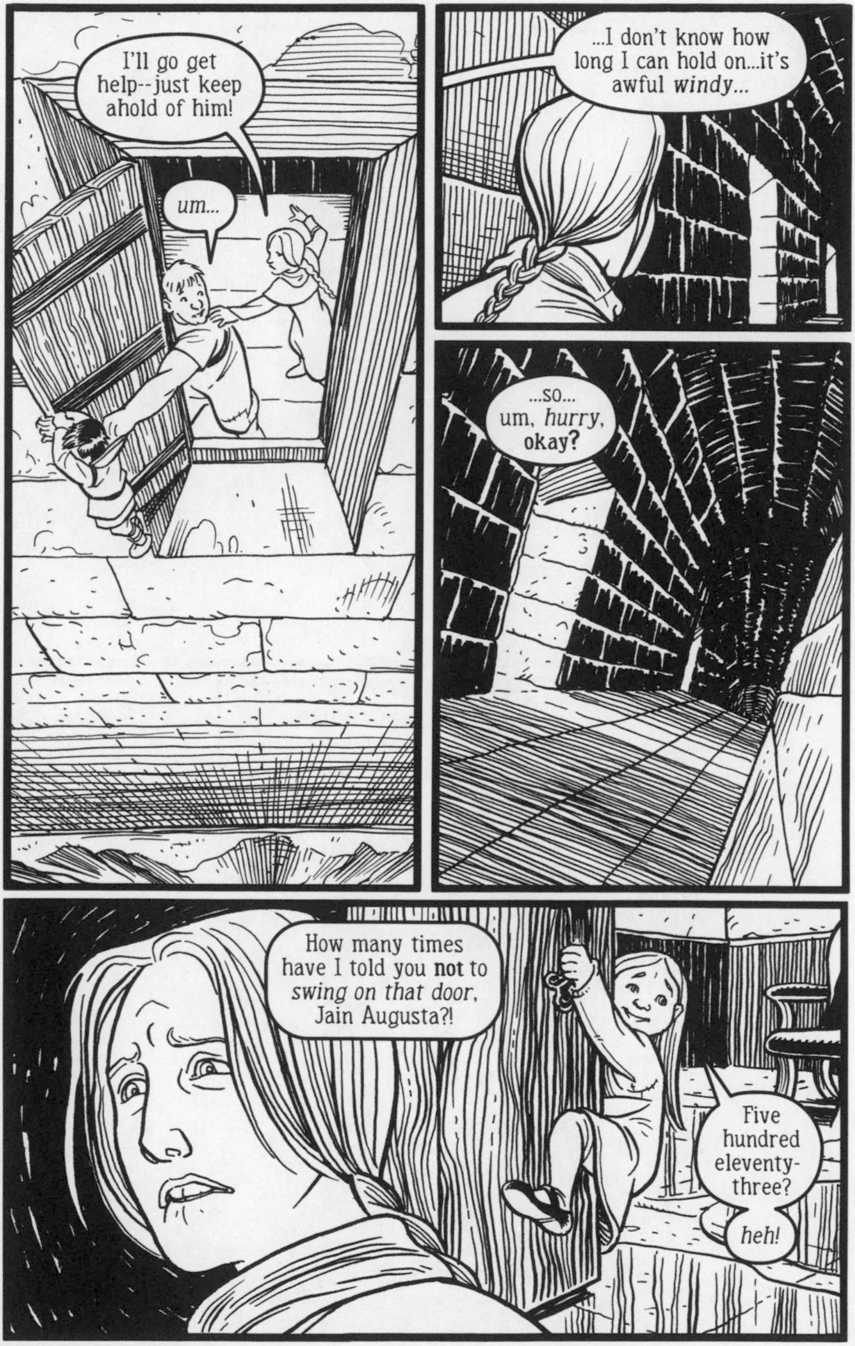
I'll go get help--just keep ahold of him!
um...
...I don't know how long I can hold on...it's awful *windy*...
...so... um, *hurry*, **okay?**
How many times have I told you **not** to *swing on that door*, Jain Augusta?!
Five hundred eleventy-three?
heh!

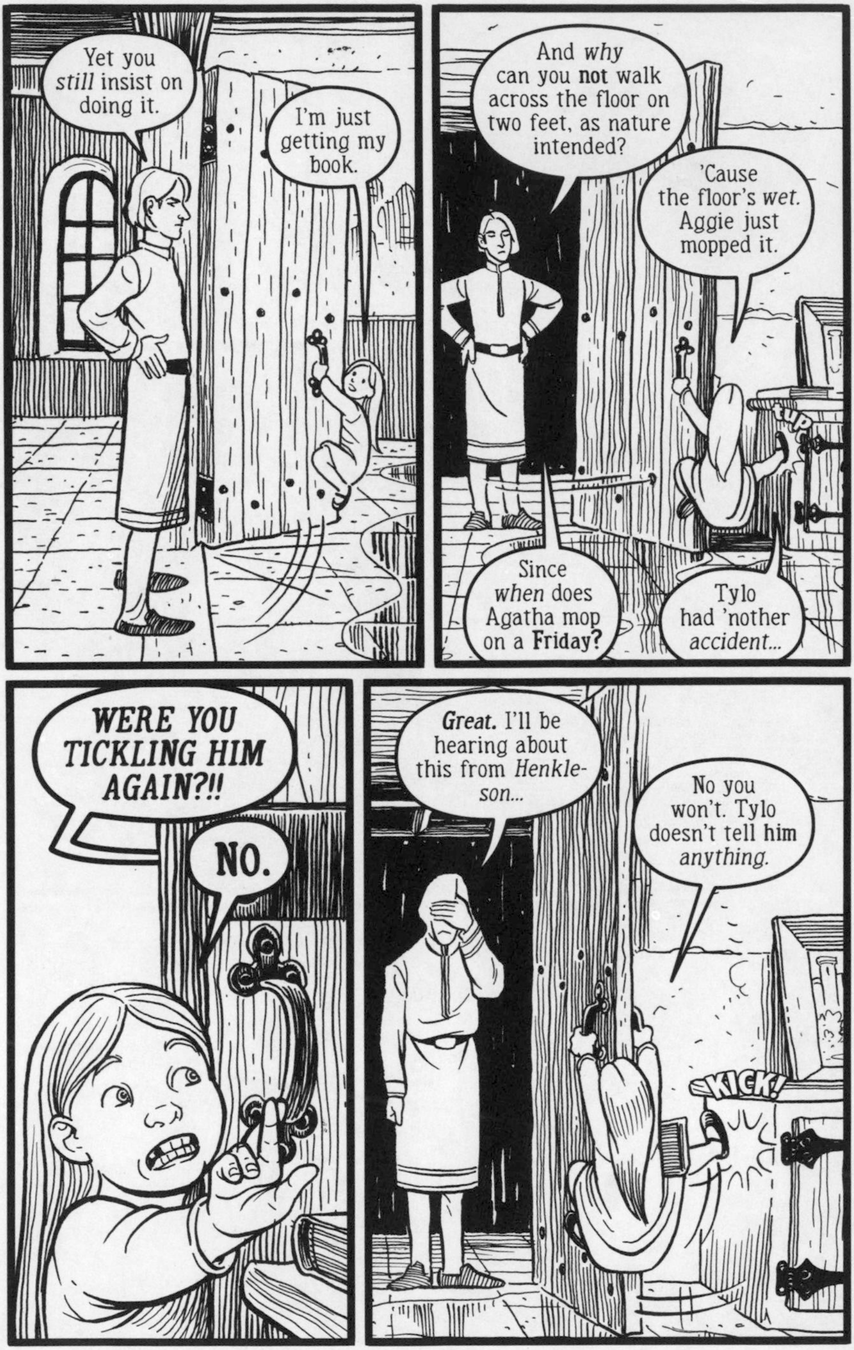

Yet you *still* insist on doing it.
I'm just getting my book.
And *why* can you **not** walk across the floor on two feet, as nature intended?
'Cause the floor's *wet.* Aggie just mopped it.
TUP
Since *when* does Agatha mop on a **Friday?**
Tylo had 'nother *accident...*
WERE YOU TICKLING HIM AGAIN?!!
NO.
Great. I'll be hearing about this from *Henkle-son...*
No you won't. Tylo doesn't tell **him** *anything.*
KICK!

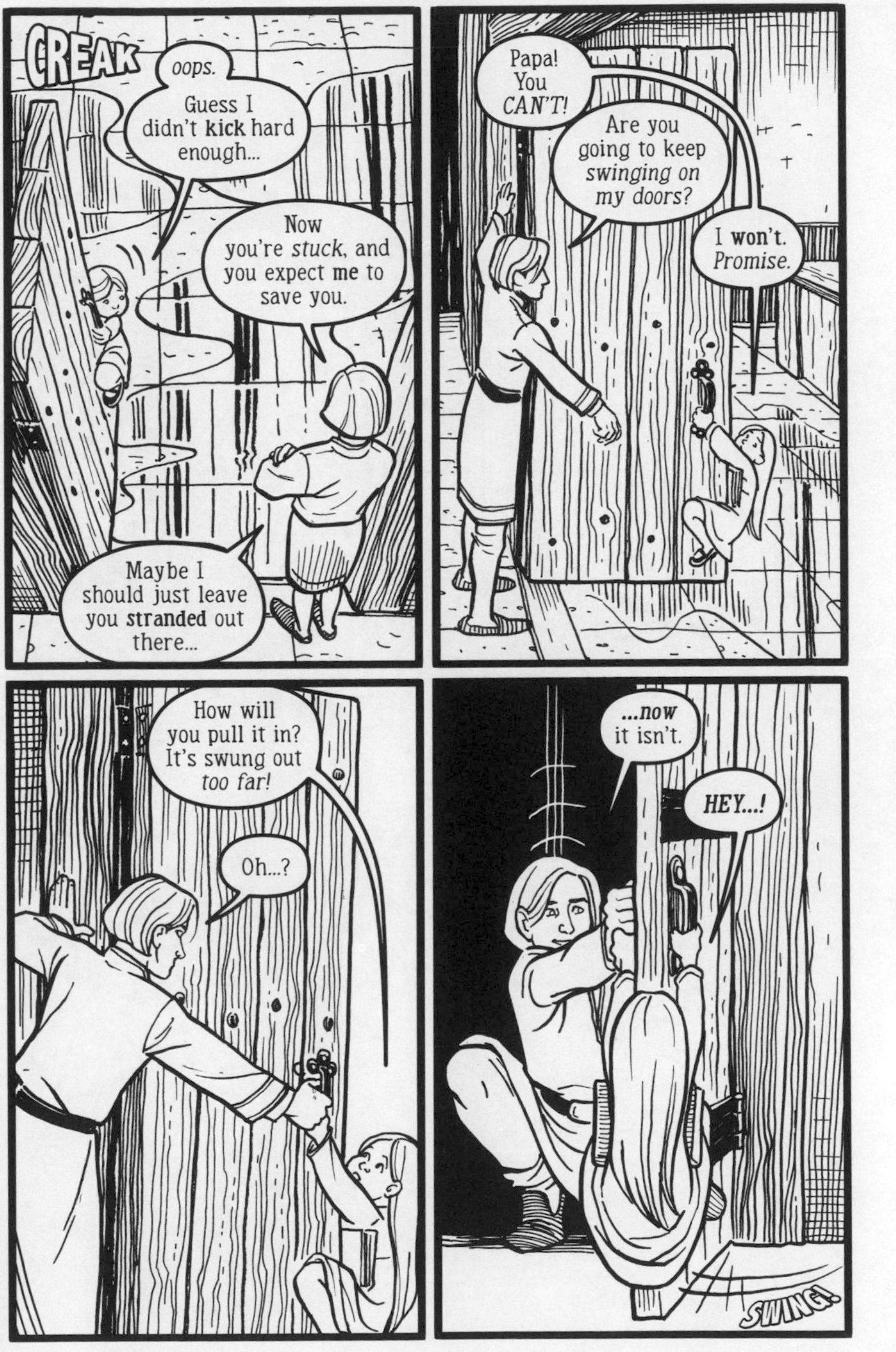
CREAK
oops.
Guess I didn't kick hard enough...
Now you're stuck, and you expect me to save you.
Maybe I should just leave you stranded out there...
Papa! You CAN'T!
Are you going to keep swinging on my doors?
I won't. Promise.
How will you pull it in? It's swung out too far!
Oh...?
...now it isn't.
HEY...!
SWING!

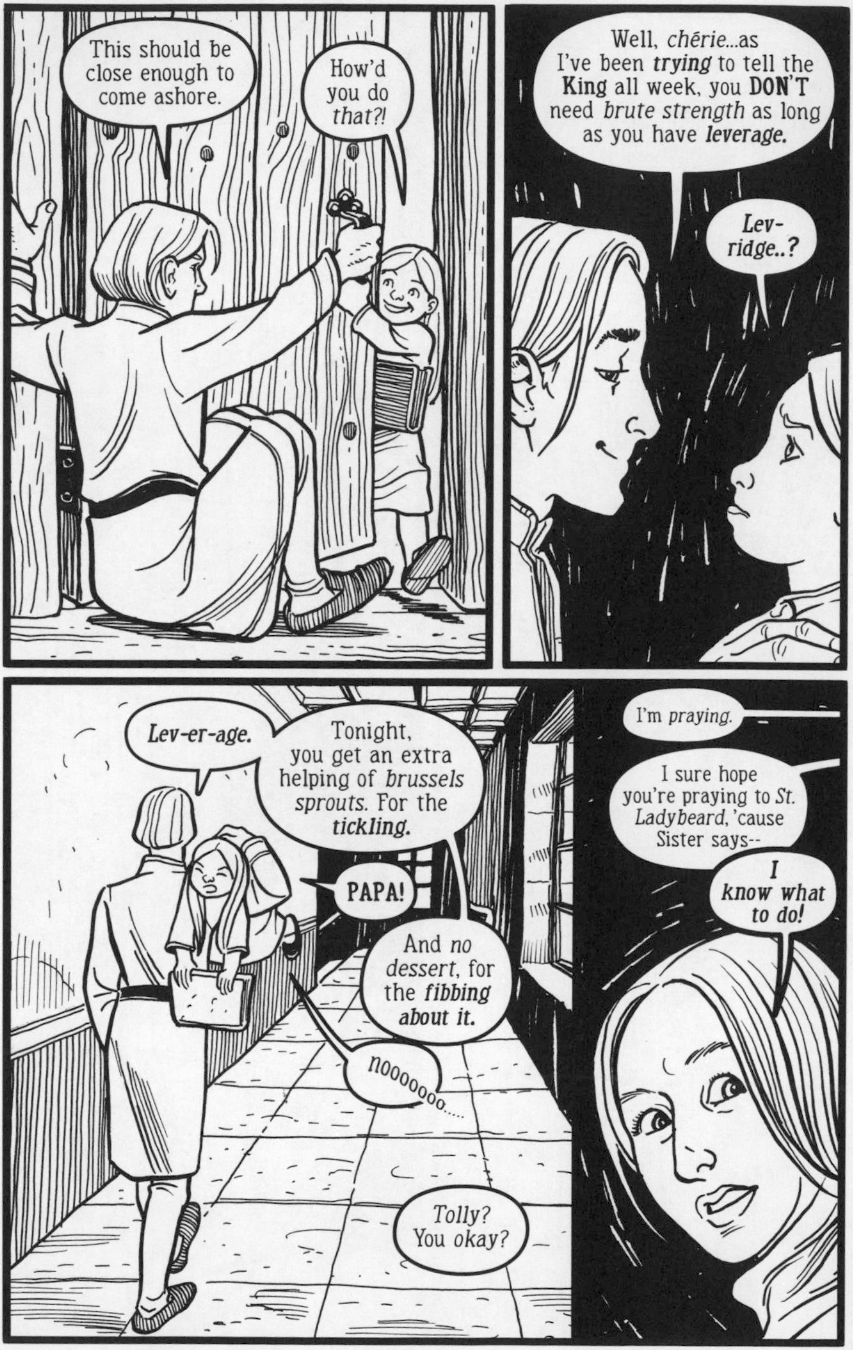
This should be close enough to come ashore.
How'd you do *that?!*
Well, *chérie*...as I've been ***trying*** to tell the **King** all week, you **DON'T** need *brute strength* as long as you have ***leverage.***
Lev-ridge..?
Lev-er-age.
Tonight, you get an extra helping of *brussels sprouts.* For the ***tickling.***
PAPA!
And *no dessert*, for the ***fibbing about it.***
nooooooo.....
Tolly? You *okay?*
I'm *praying.*
I sure hope you're praying to *St. Ladybeard,* 'cause Sister says--
I know what to do!

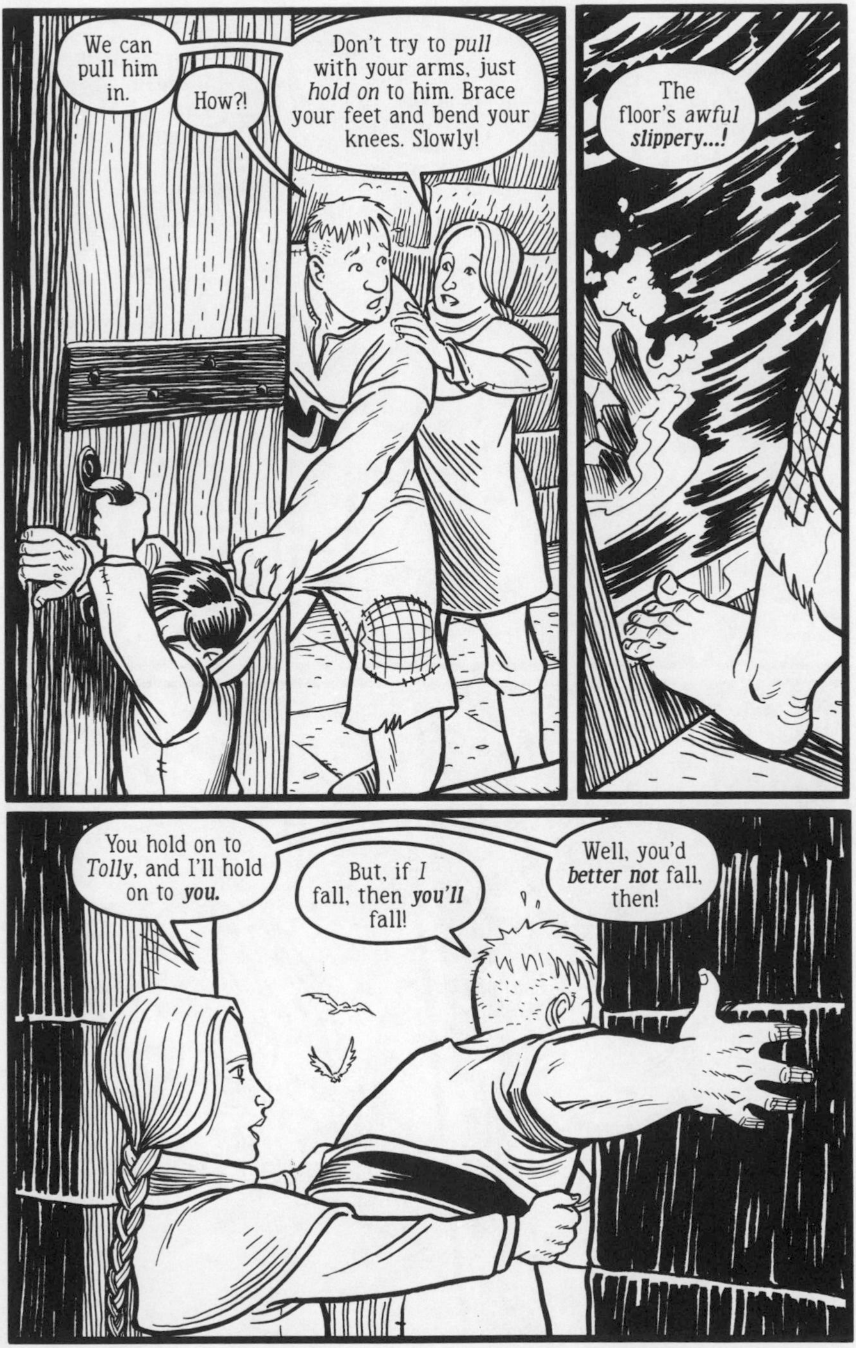
We can pull him in.
How?!
Don't try to *pull* with your arms, just *hold on* to him. Brace your feet and bend your knees. Slowly!
The floor's *awful* ***slippery...!***
You hold on to *Tolly*, and I'll hold on to ***you.***
But, if *I* fall, then ***you'll*** fall!
Well, you'd ***better not*** fall, then!

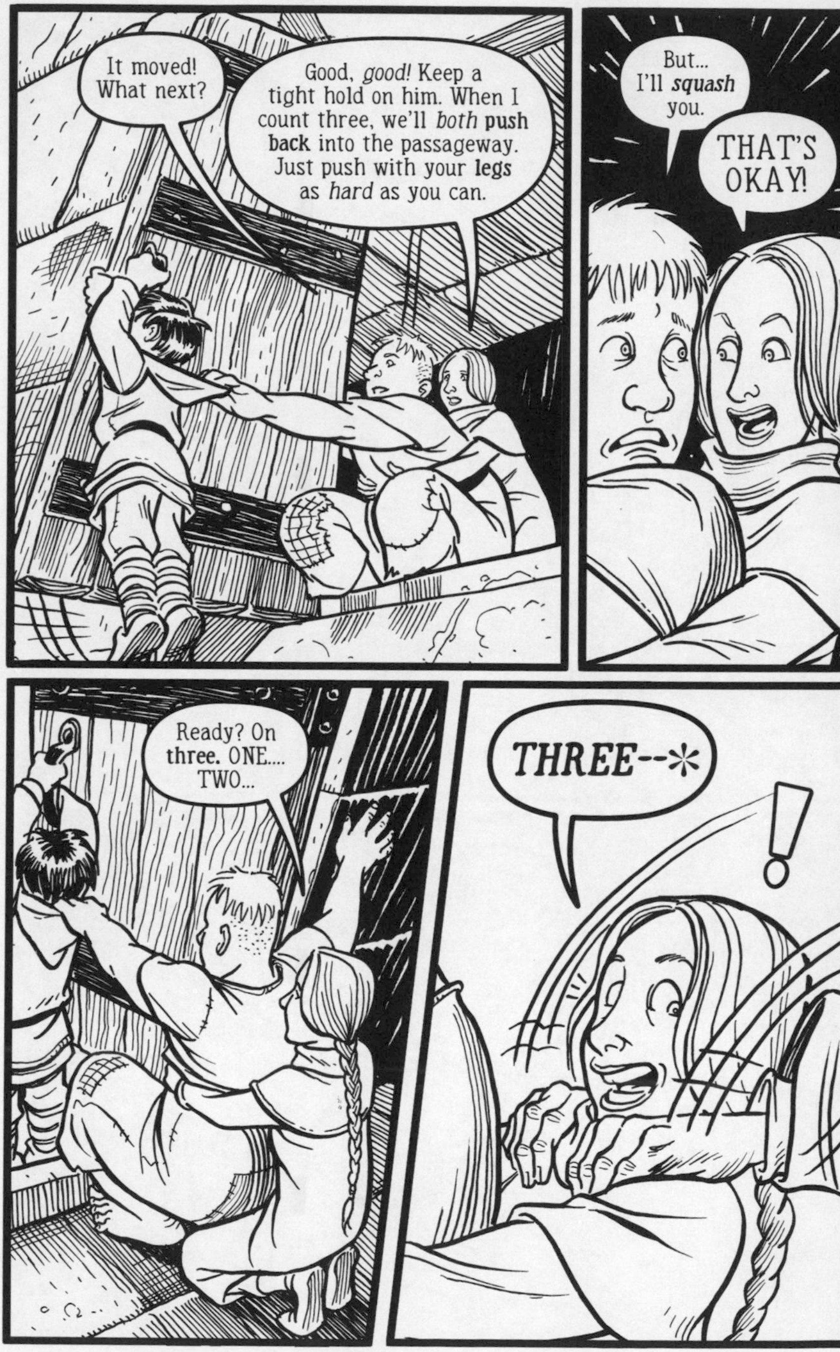
It moved! What next?
Good, *good!* Keep a tight hold on him. When I count three, we'll *both* **push back** into the passageway. Just push with your **legs** as *hard* as you can.
But... I'll *squash* you.
THAT'S OKAY!
Ready? On **three.** ONE.... TWO...
THREE--*
!

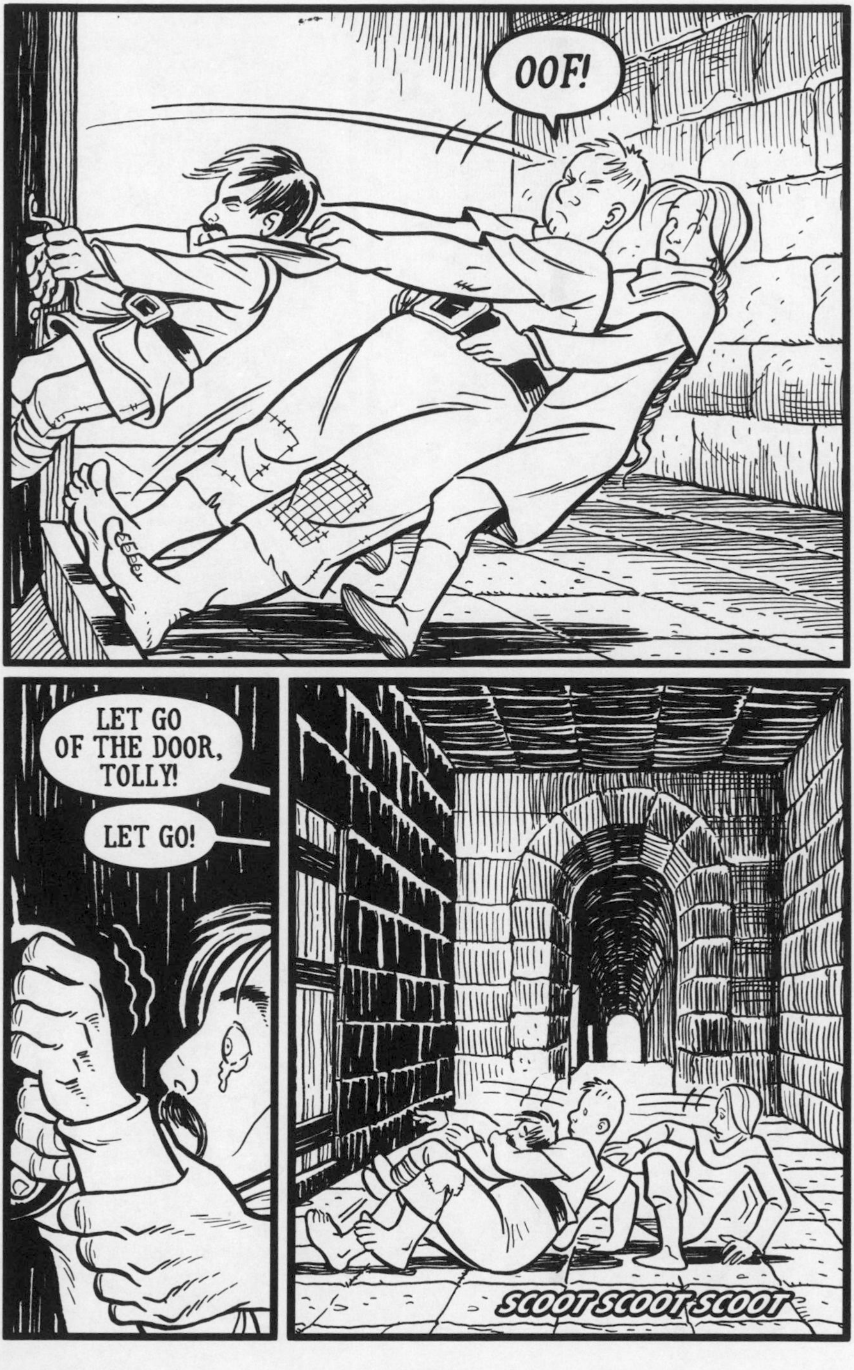
OOF!
LET GO OF THE DOOR, TOLLY!
LET GO!
SCOOT SCOOT SCOOT

Are you okay, Tolly?

can't breathe

You can *let go* now, Simon!

oops!

⸓*cough cough*⸓ Thanks for saving me...I'm really, **really** sorry about that...!

Hey, don't **apologize**--it wasn't **your fault!** Any one of us could've opened that door...

Yeah, but *I* should've **noticed** something was wrong *before* I opened it. I could've gotten both of you killed! I screwed up, just like I did in the mine... Please, don't tell my **Uncles** about this, okay?

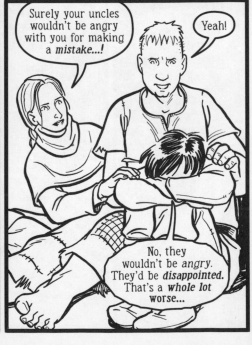

Surely your uncles wouldn't be angry with you for making a *mistake...!*

Yeah!

No, they wouldn't be *angry*. They'd be *disappointed*. That's a *whole lot* worse...

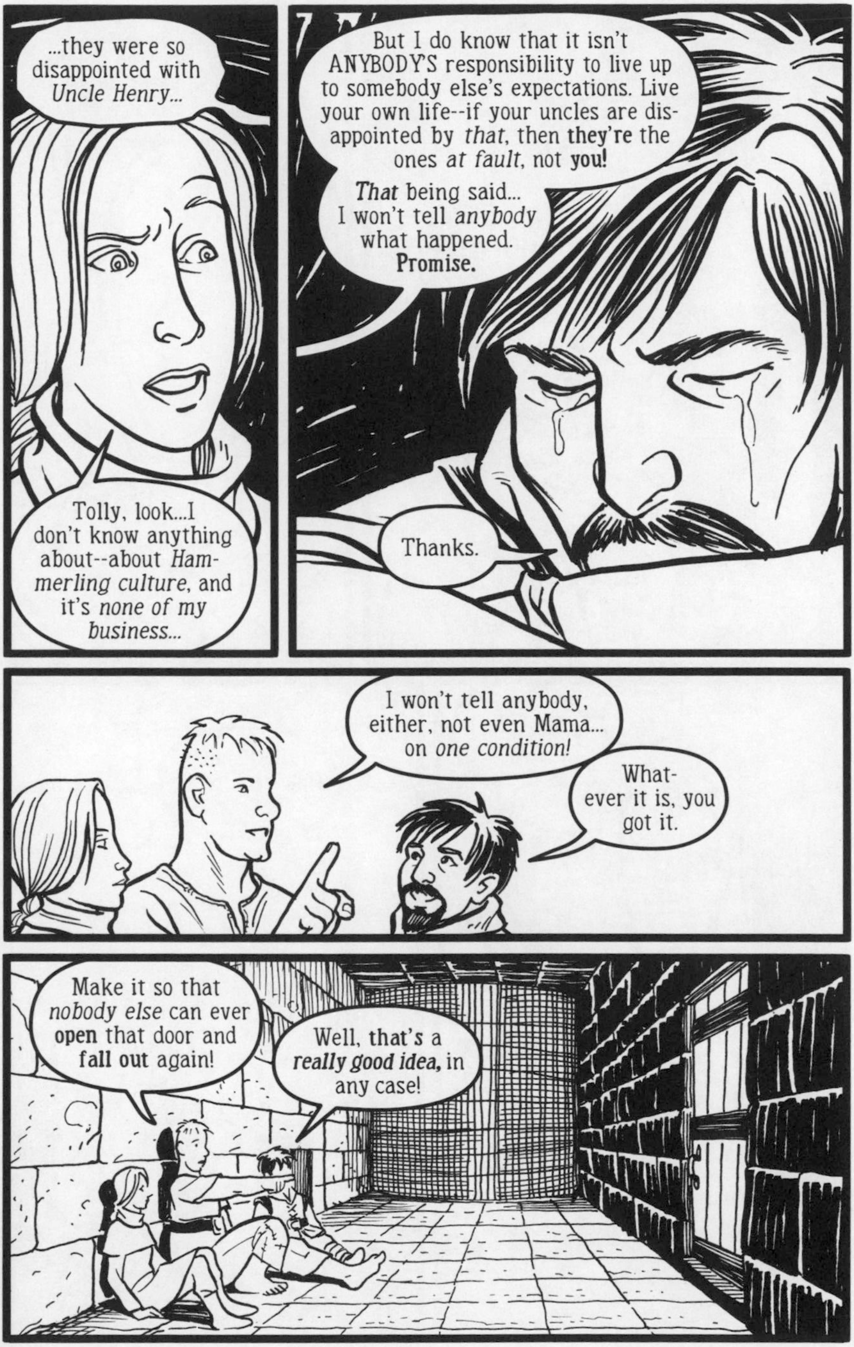
...they were so disappointed with *Uncle Henry*...
Tolly, look...I don't know anything about--about *Hammerling culture*, and it's *none of my business*...
But I do know that it isn't ANYBODY'S responsibility to live up to somebody else's expectations. Live your own life--if your uncles are disappointed by *that*, then **they're** the ones *at fault*, not **you!**
That being said... I won't tell *anybody* what happened. **Promise.**
Thanks.
I won't tell anybody, either, not even Mama... on *one condition!*
Whatever it is, you got it.
Make it so that *nobody else* can ever **open** that door and **fall out** again!
Well, **that's** a ***really good idea,*** in any case!

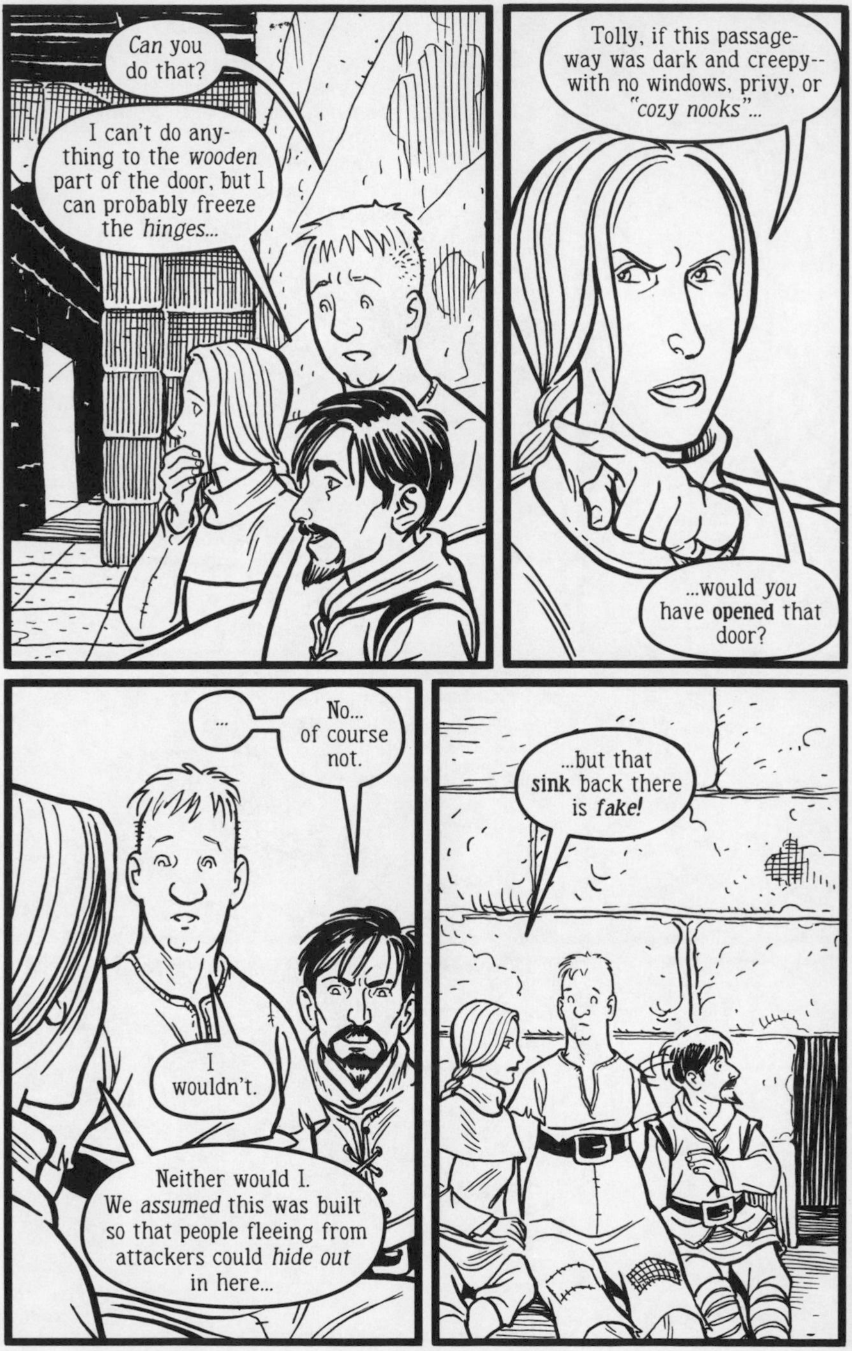
Can you do that?
I can't do anything to the wooden part of the door, but I can probably freeze the hinges...
Tolly, if this passageway was dark and creepy-- with no windows, privy, or "cozy nooks"...
...would you have opened that door?
...
No... of course not.
I wouldn't.
Neither would I. We assumed this was built so that people fleeing from attackers could hide out in here...
...but that sink back there is fake!

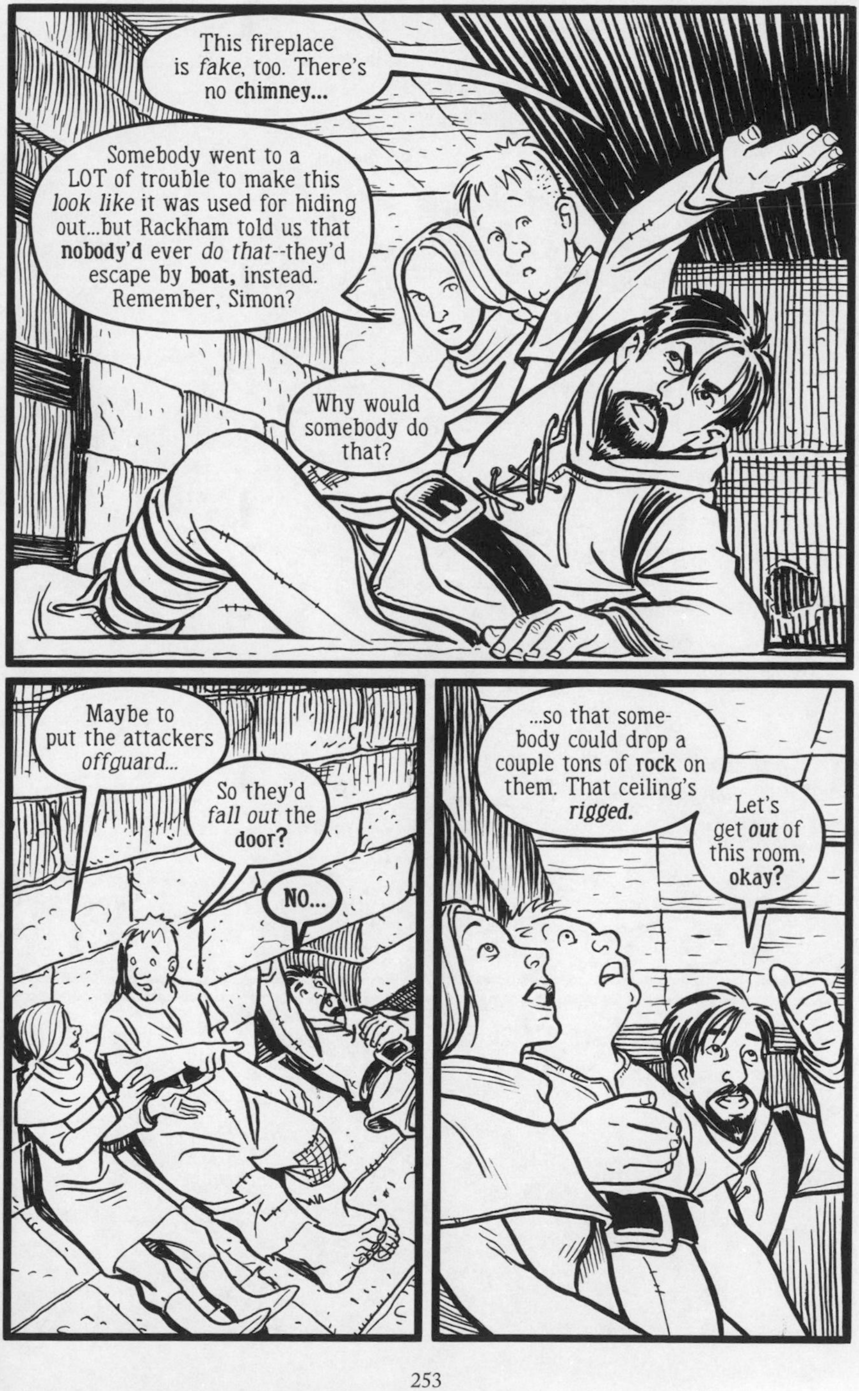
This fireplace is *fake*, too. There's no **chimney...**
Somebody went to a LOT of trouble to make this *look like* it was used for hiding out...but Rackham told us that **nobody'd** ever *do that*--they'd escape by **boat,** instead. Remember, Simon?
Why would somebody do that?
Maybe to put the attackers *offguard...*
So they'd *fall out* the **door?**
NO...
...so that somebody could drop a couple tons of **rock** on them. That ceiling's ***rigged.***
Let's get ***out*** of this room, **okay?**

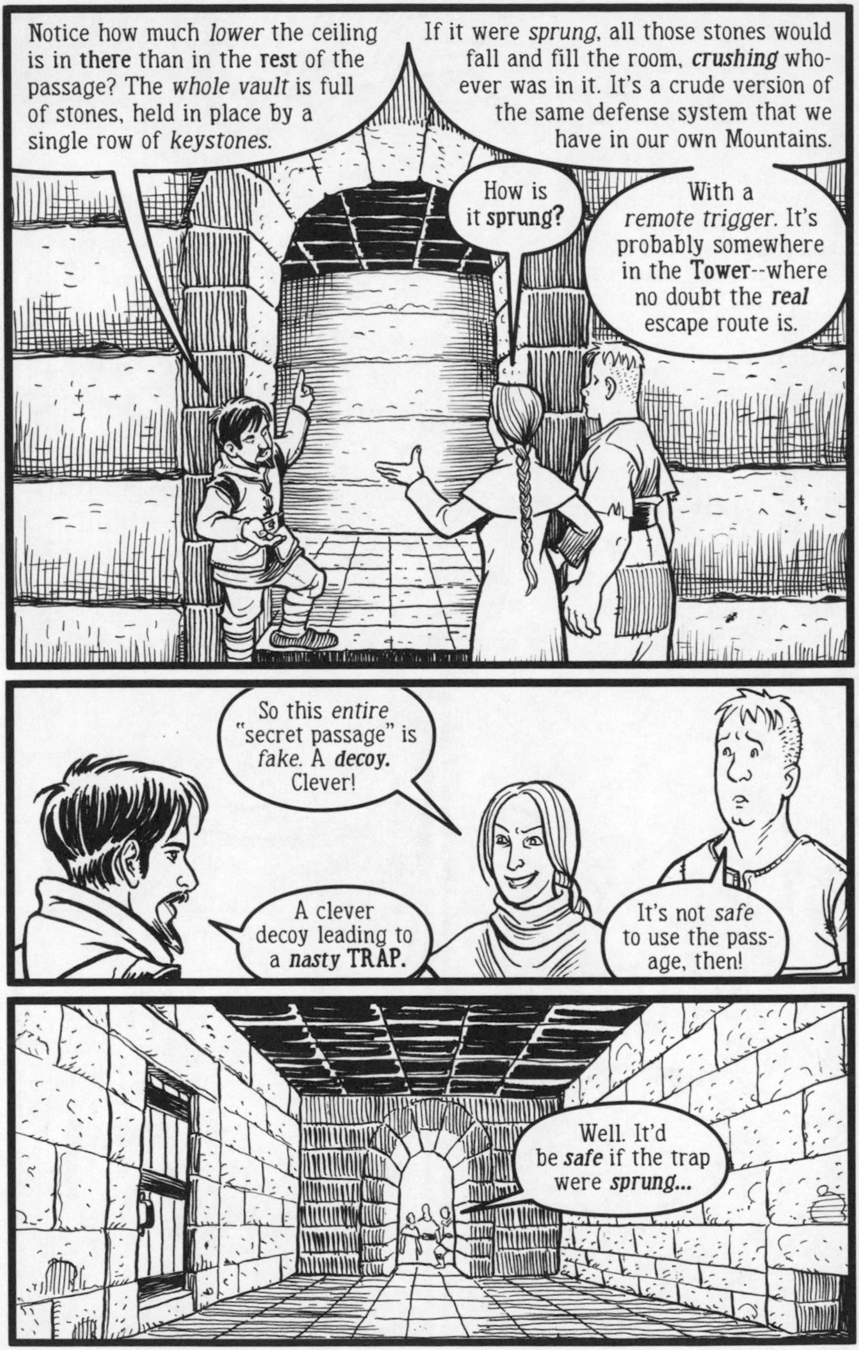
Notice how much *lower* the ceiling is in **there** than in the **rest** of the passage? The *whole vault* is full of stones, held in place by a single row of *keystones.*
If it were *sprung*, all those stones would fall and fill the room, ***crushing*** whoever was in it. It's a crude version of the same defense system that we have in our own Mountains.
How is it **sprung?**
With a *remote trigger.* It's probably somewhere in the **Tower**--where no doubt the ***real*** escape route is.
So this *entire* "secret passage" is *fake.* A ***decoy.*** Clever!
A clever decoy leading to a ***nasty*** **TRAP.**
It's not *safe* to use the passage, then!
Well. It'd be ***safe*** if the trap were ***sprung...***

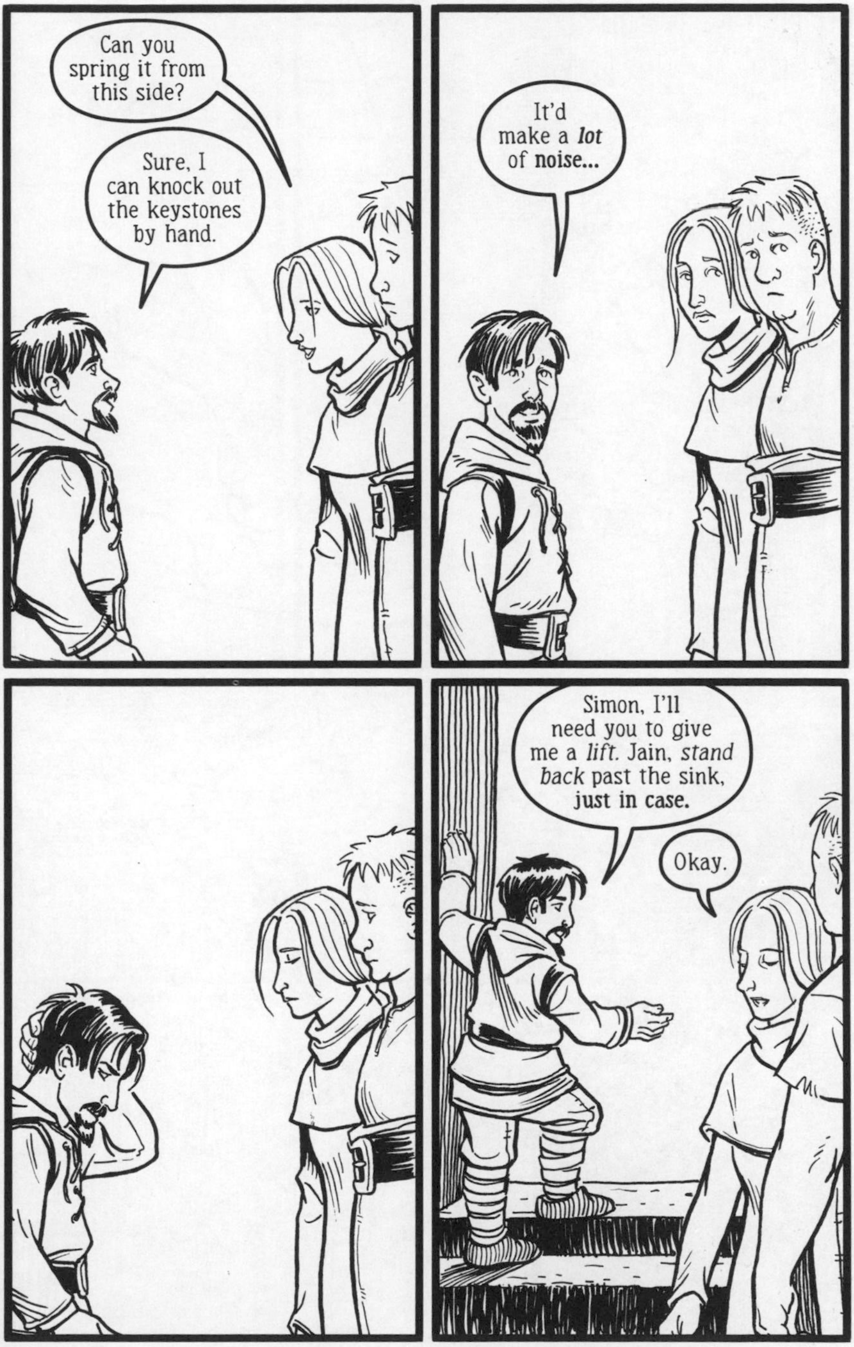
Can you spring it from this side?
Sure, I can knock out the keystones by hand.
It'd make a *lot* of **noise...**
Simon, I'll need you to give me a *lift*. Jain, *stand back* past the sink, **just in case.**
Okay.

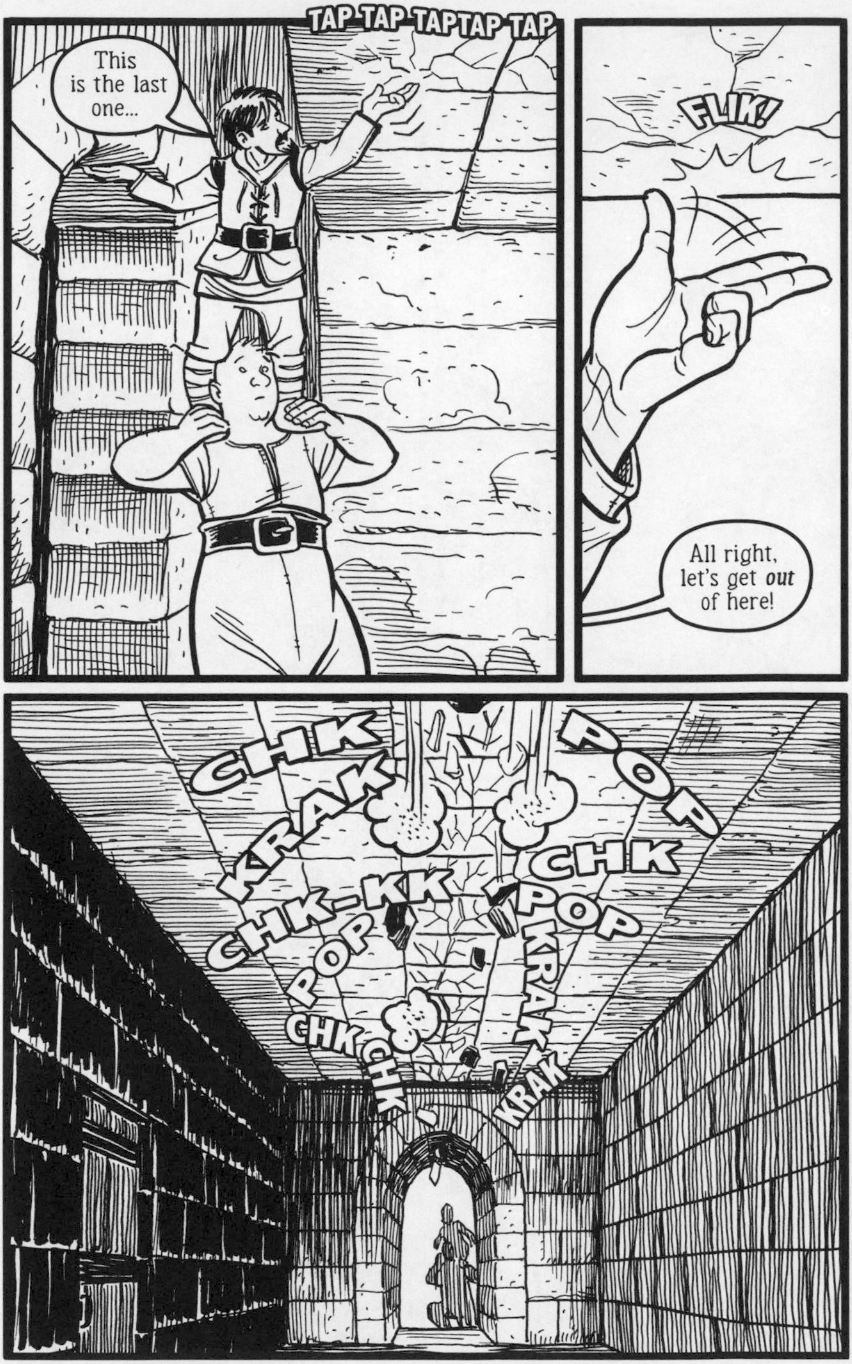
TAP TAP TAPTAP TAP
This is the last one...
FLIK!
All right, let's get *out* of here!
CHK
KRAK
POP
CHK
CHK-KK
POP
POP
KRAK
CHK
CHK
KRAK

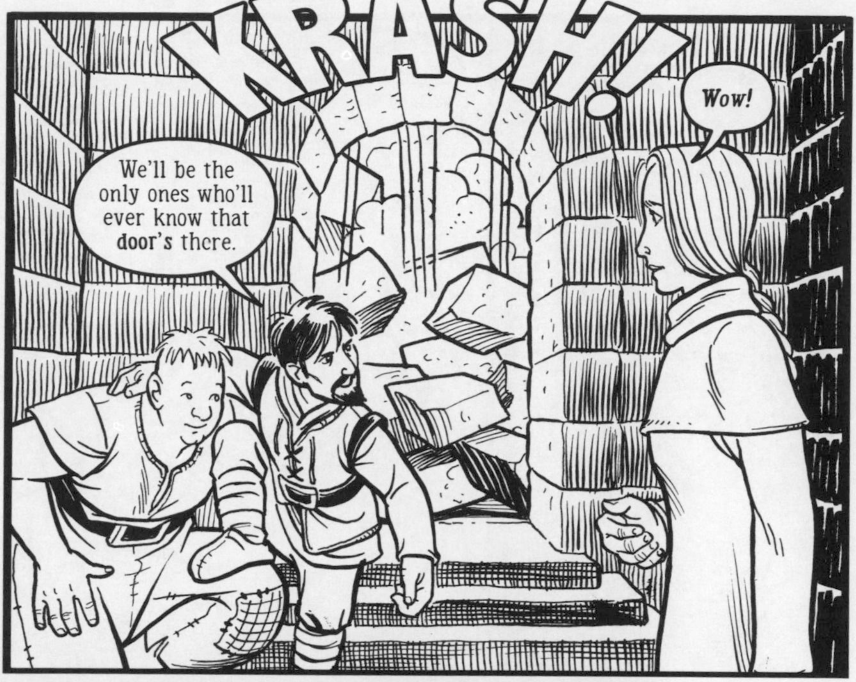
KRASH!
We'll be the only ones who'll ever know that door's there.
Wow!

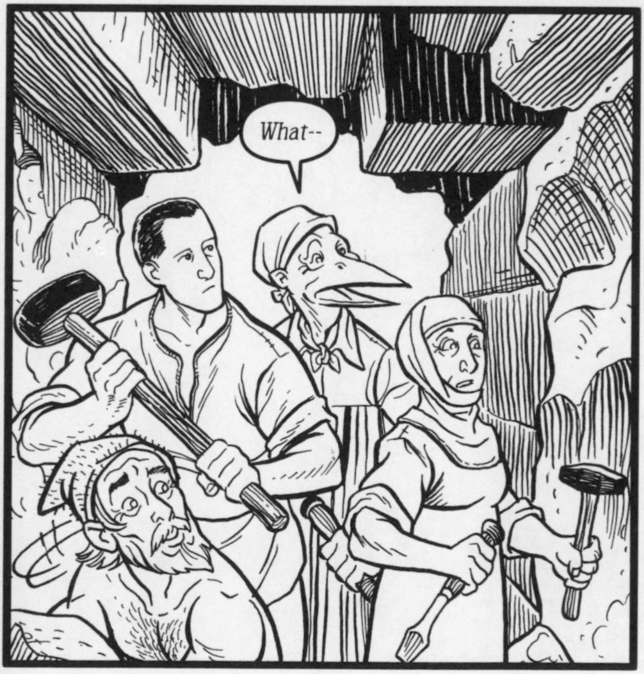
What--

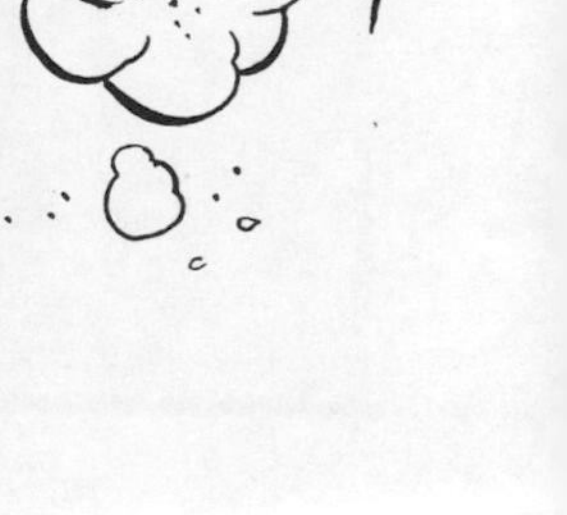

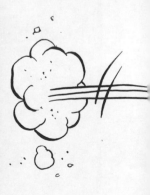

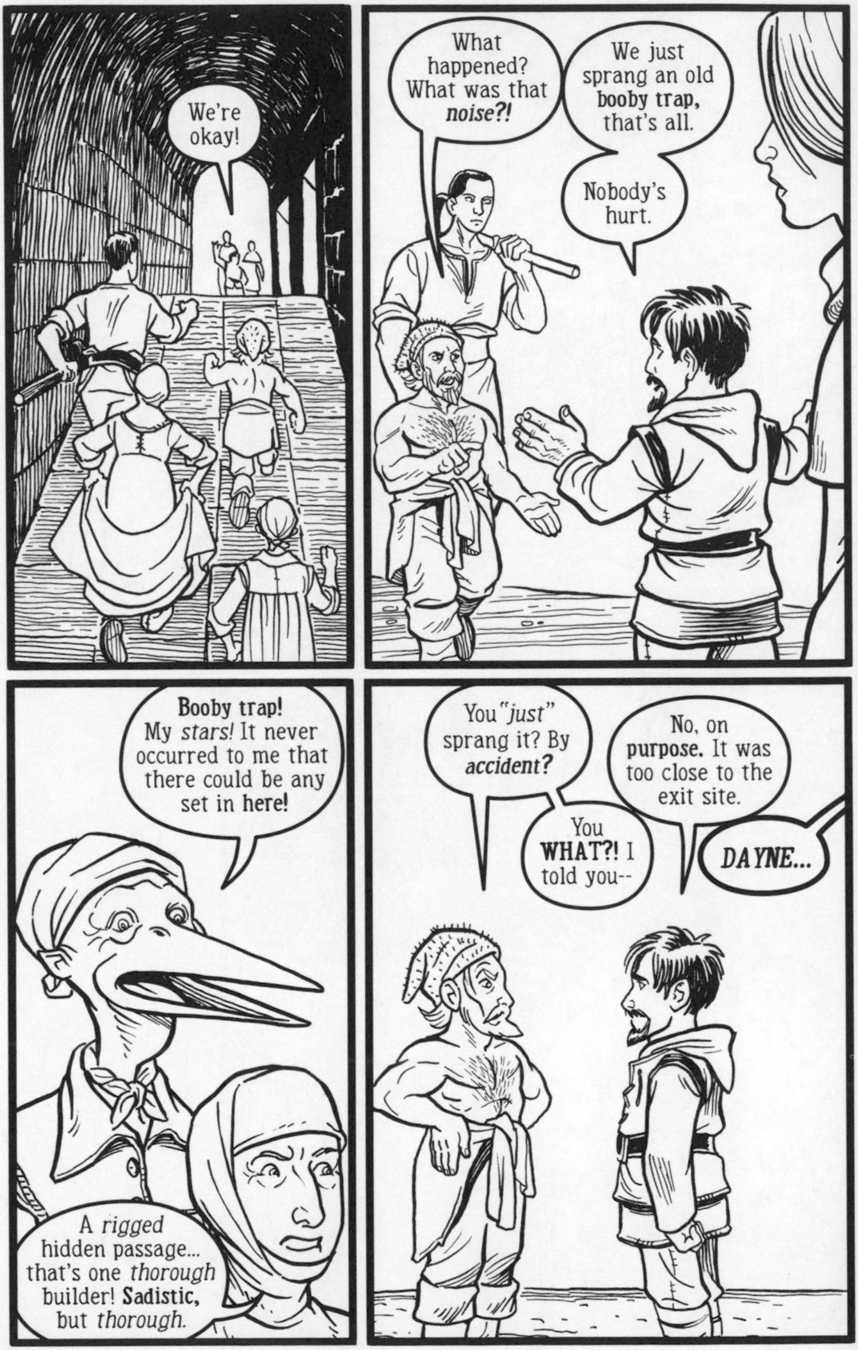
We're okay!
What happened? What was that *noise?!*
We just sprang an old **booby trap,** that's all.
Nobody's hurt.
Booby trap! My *stars!* It never occurred to me that there could be any set in **here!**
A *rigged* hidden passage... that's one *thorough* builder! **Sadistic,** but *thorough.*
You *"just"* sprang it? By ***accident?***
You **WHAT?!** I told you--
No, on **purpose.** It was too close to the exit site.
DAYNE...

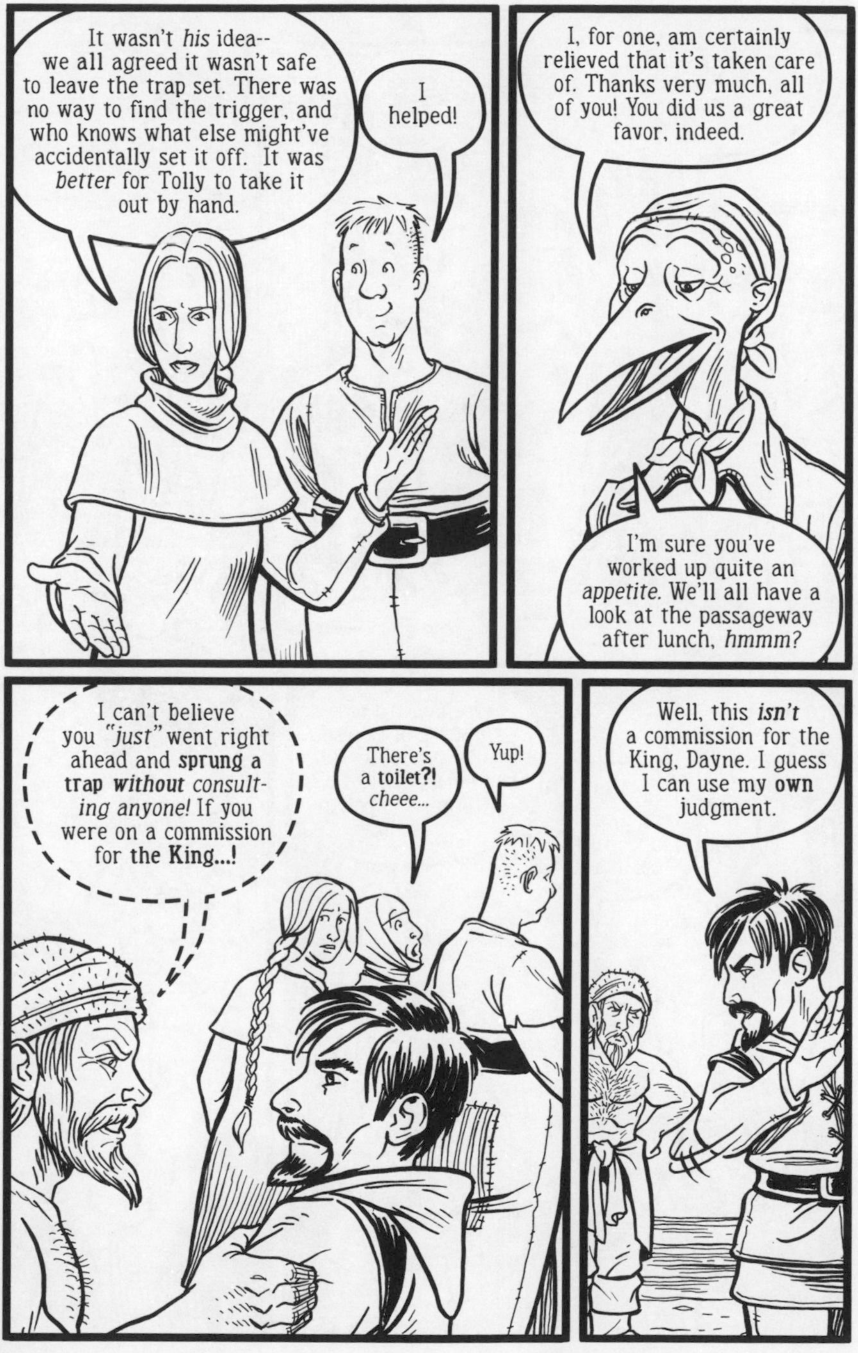
It wasn't *his* idea-- we all agreed it wasn't safe to leave the trap set. There was no way to find the trigger, and who knows what else might've accidentally set it off. It was *better* for Tolly to take it out by hand.
I helped!
I, for one, am certainly relieved that it's taken care of. Thanks very much, all of you! You did us a great favor, indeed.
I'm sure you've worked up quite an *appetite*. We'll all have a look at the passageway after lunch, *hmmm?*
I can't believe you *"just"* went right ahead and **sprung** a **trap *without*** *consult-ing anyone!* If you were on a commission for **the King...!**
There's a **toilet?!** *cheee...*
Yup!
Well, this ***isn't*** a commission for the King, Dayne. I guess I can use my **own** judgment.

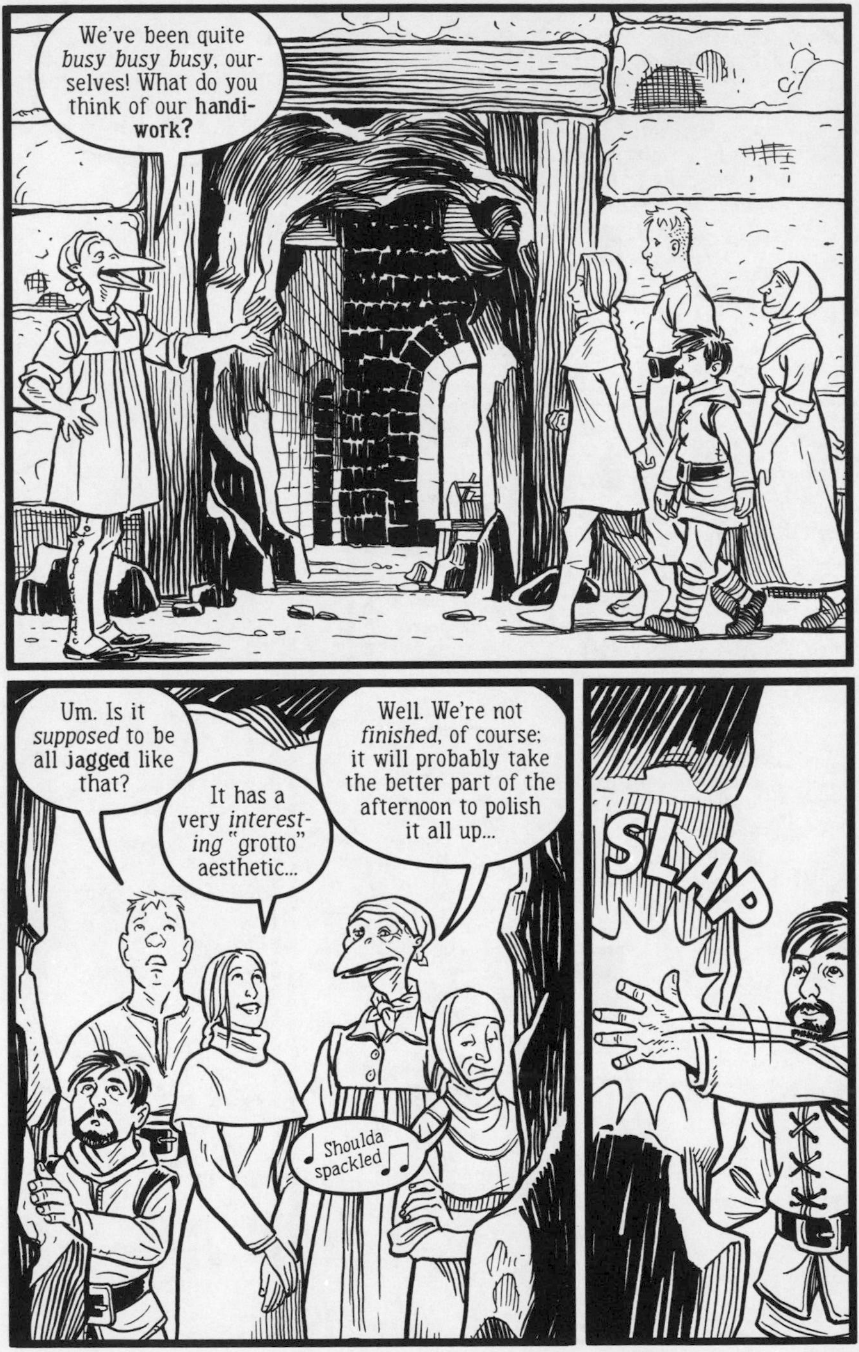
We've been quite *busy busy busy*, ourselves! What do you think of our **handiwork?**
Um. Is it *supposed* to be all **jagged** like that?
It has a very *interesting* "grotto" aesthetic...
Well. We're not *finished*, of course; it will probably take the better part of the afternoon to polish it all up...
♩ Shoulda spackled ♫
SLAP

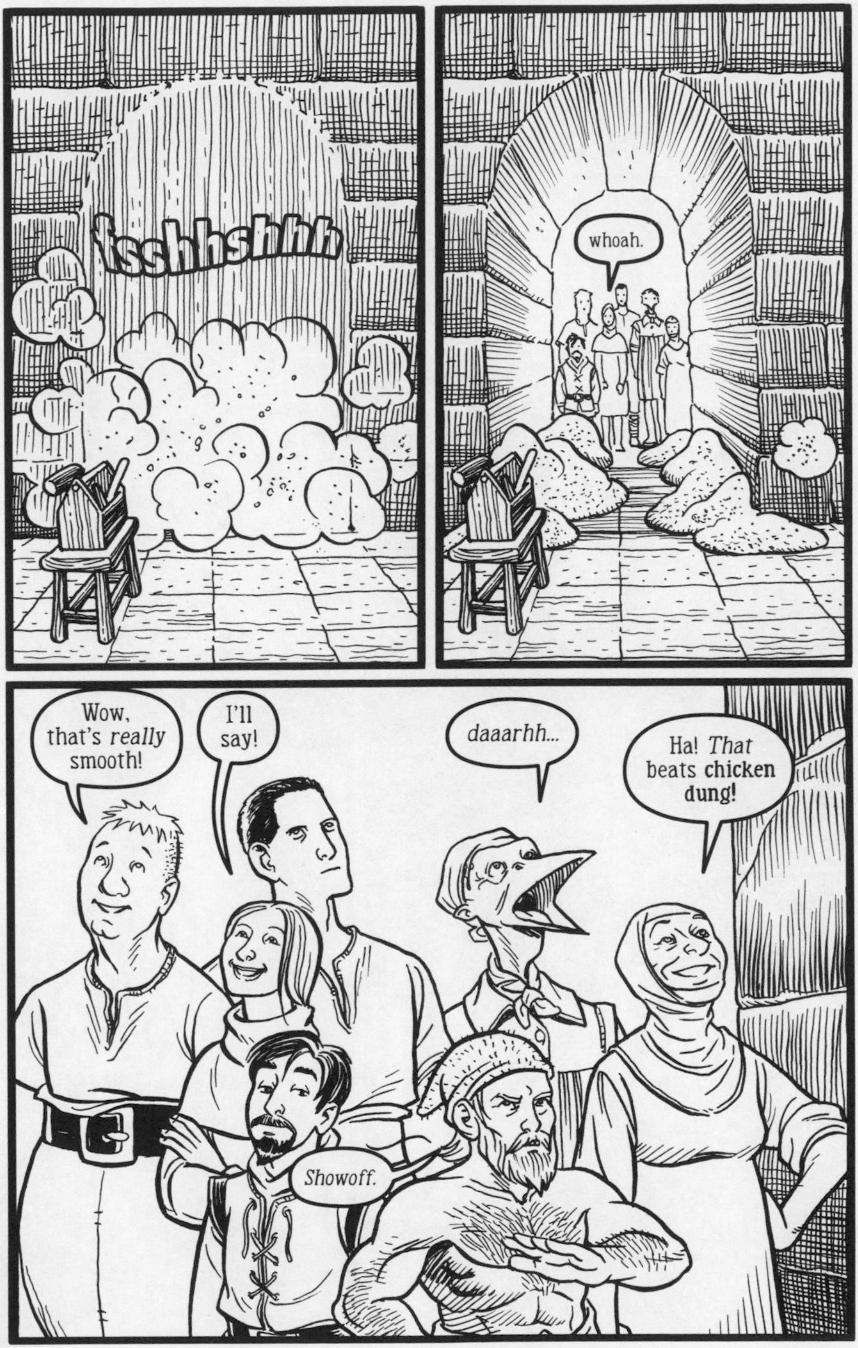
fsshhshhh
whoah.
Wow, that's *really* smooth!
I'll say!
daaarhh...
Ha! *That* beats **chicken dung!**
Showoff.

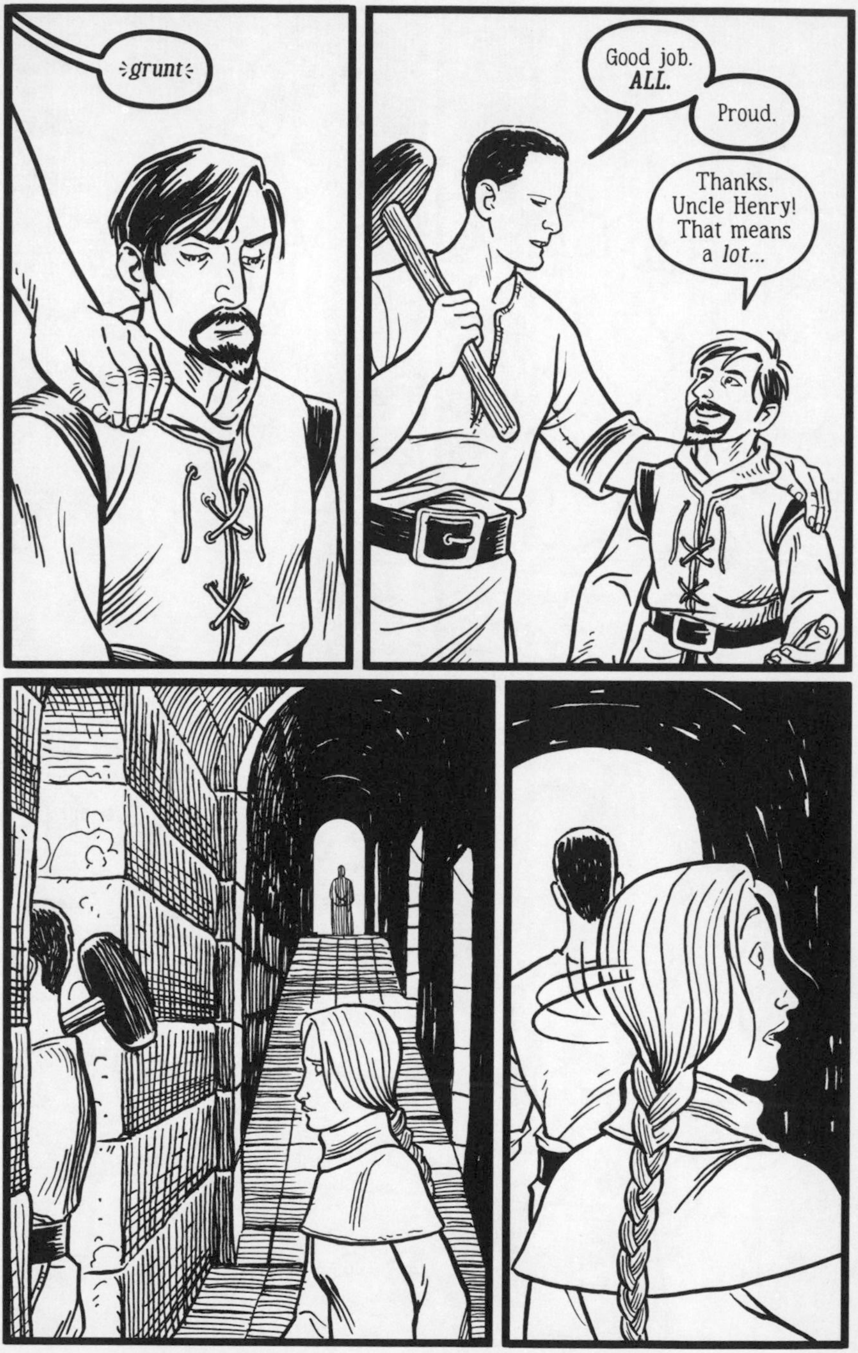
grunt
Good job. **ALL.**
Proud.
Thanks, Uncle Henry! That means a *lot*...

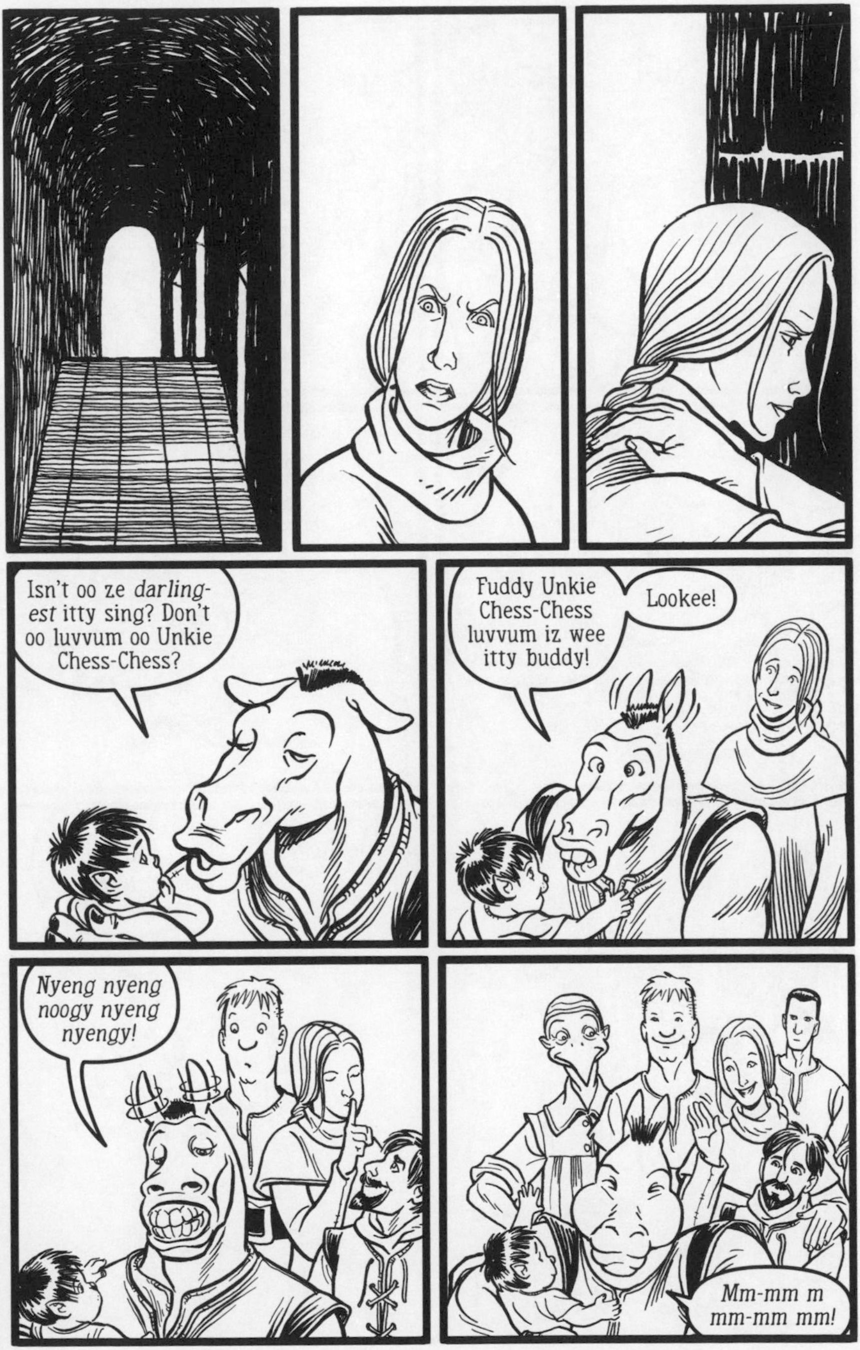
Isn't oo ze *darling-est* itty sing? Don't oo luvvum oo Unkie Chess-Chess?
Fuddy Unkie Chess-Chess luvvum iz wee itty buddy!
Lookee!
Nyeng nyeng noogy nyeng nyengy!
Mm-mm m mm-mm mm!

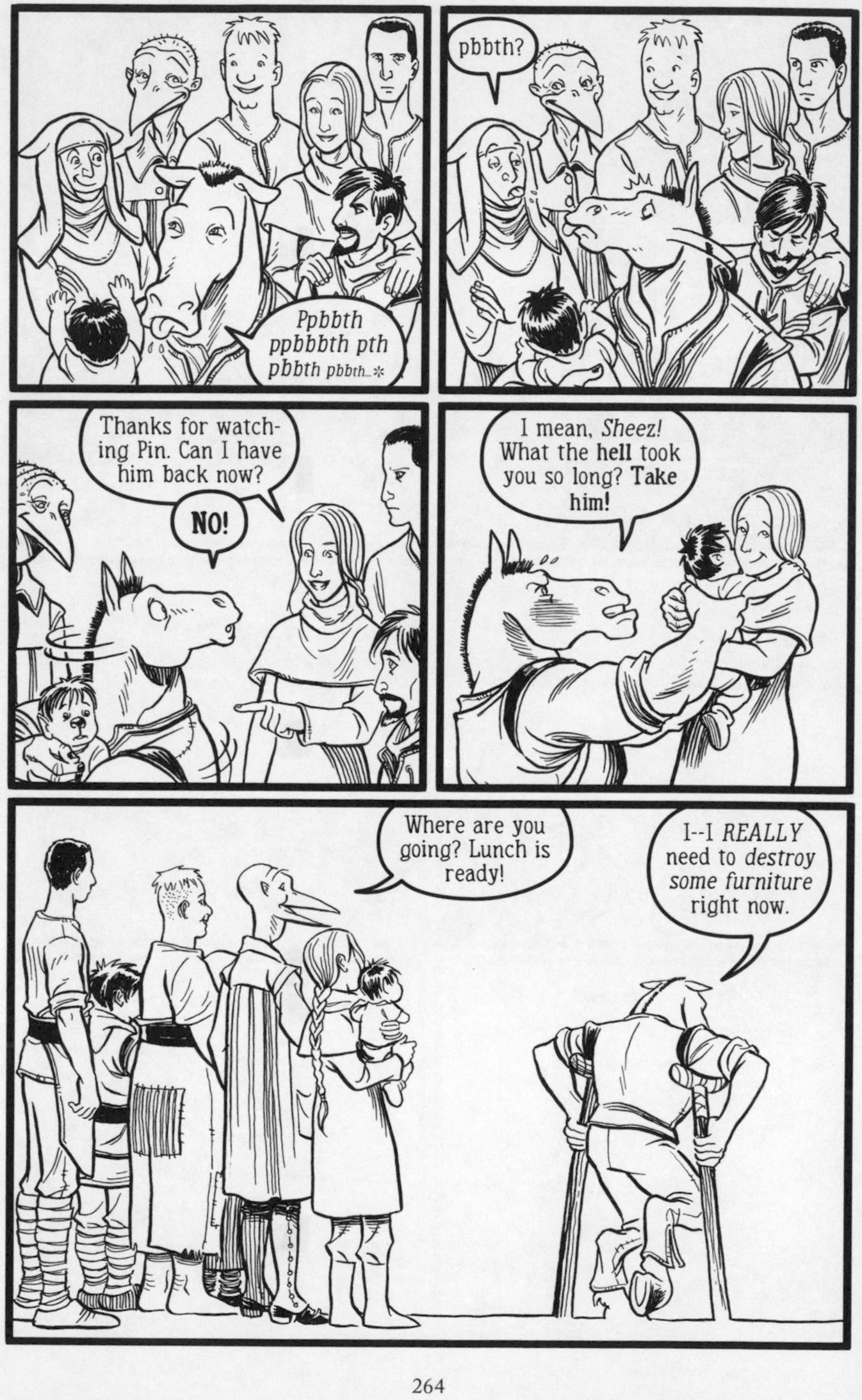
Ppbbth ppbbbth pth pbbth pbbth...*
pbbth?
Thanks for watching Pin. Can I have him back now?
NO!
I mean, *Sheez!* What the **hell** took you so long? **Take** him!
Where are you going? Lunch is ready!
I--I *REALLY* need to *destroy some furniture* right now.

Chapter 11.

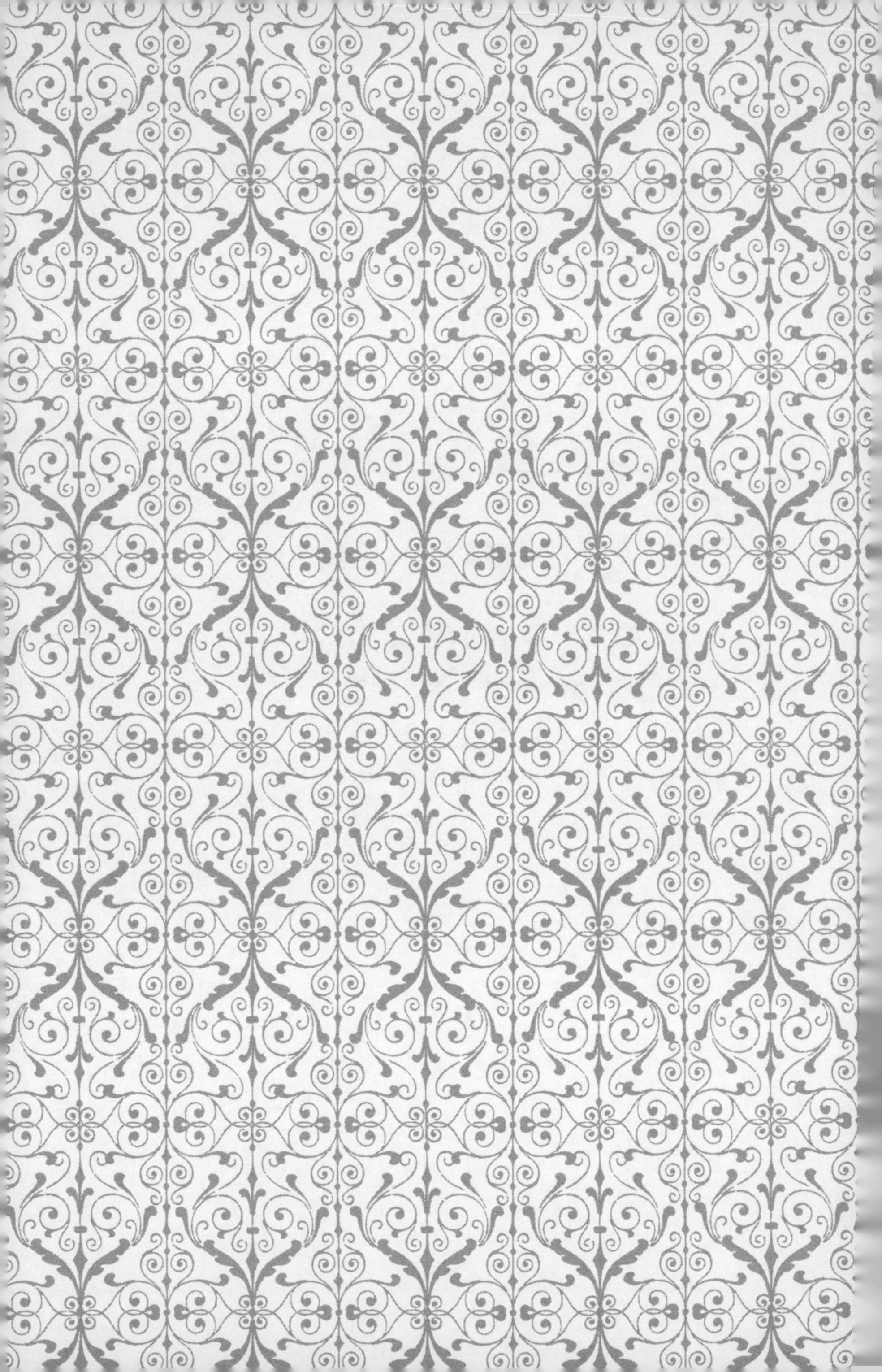

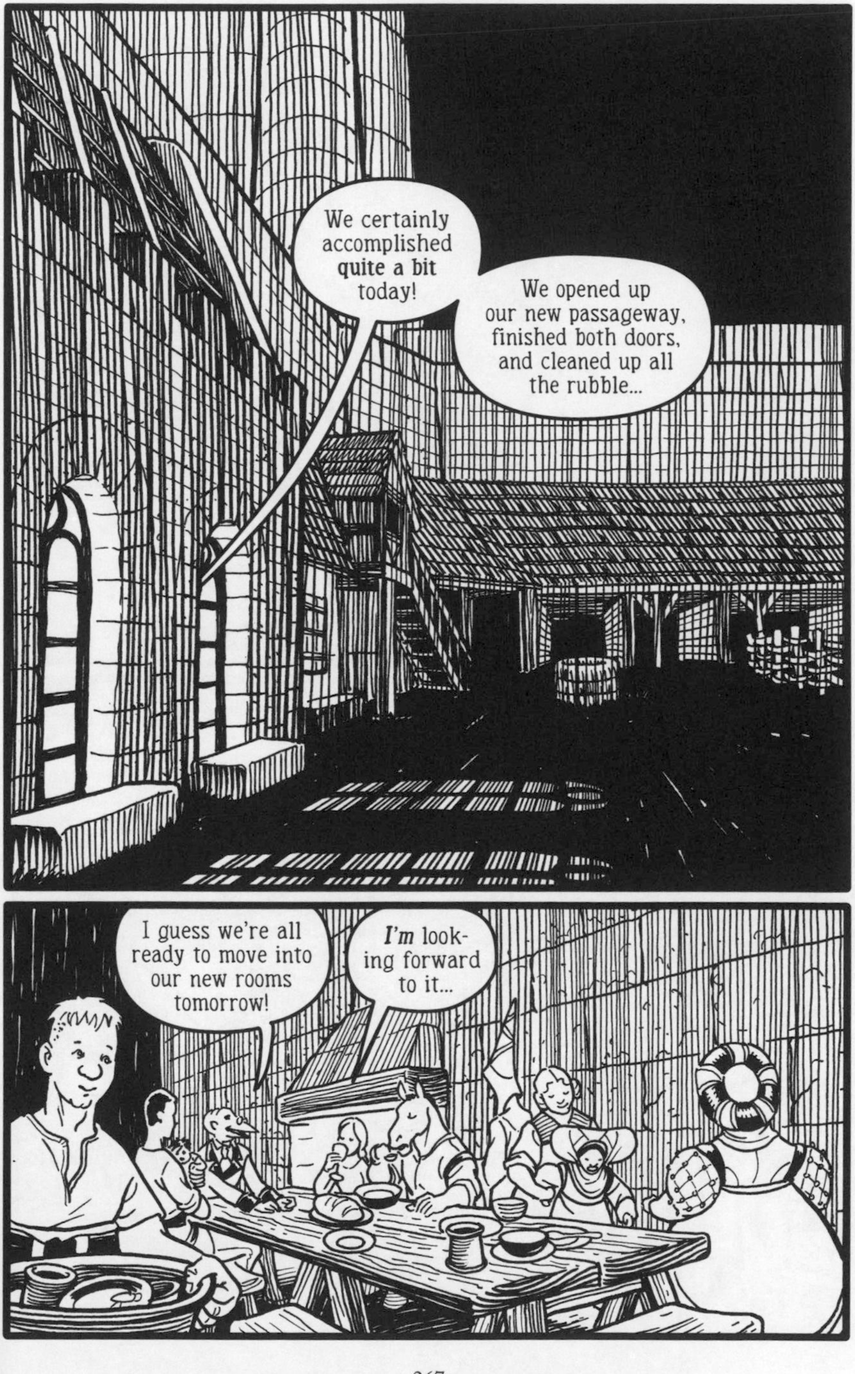
We certainly accomplished **quite a bit** today!
We opened up our new passageway, finished both doors, and cleaned up all the rubble...
I guess we're all ready to move into our new rooms tomorrow!
I'm looking forward to it...

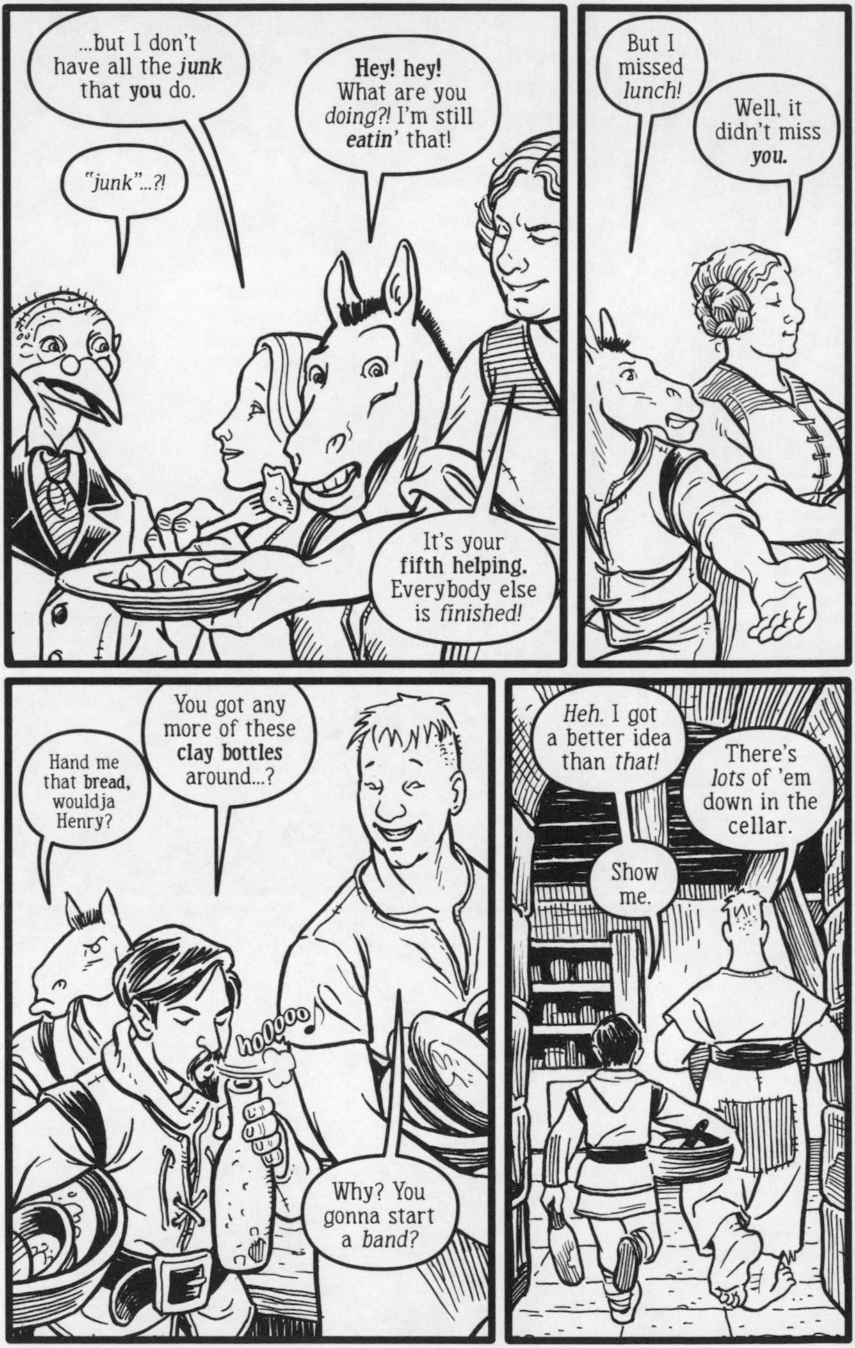
...but I don't have all the *junk* that **you** do.
"*junk*"...?!
Hey! hey! What are you *doing?!* I'm still ***eatin'*** that!
It's your **fifth helping.** Everybody else is *finished!*
But I missed *lunch!*
Well, it didn't miss ***you.***
Hand me that **bread,** wouldja Henry?
You got any more of these **clay bottles** around...?
hoOooo
Why? You gonna start a *band?*
Heh. I got a better idea than *that!*
There's *lots* of 'em down in the cellar.
Show me.

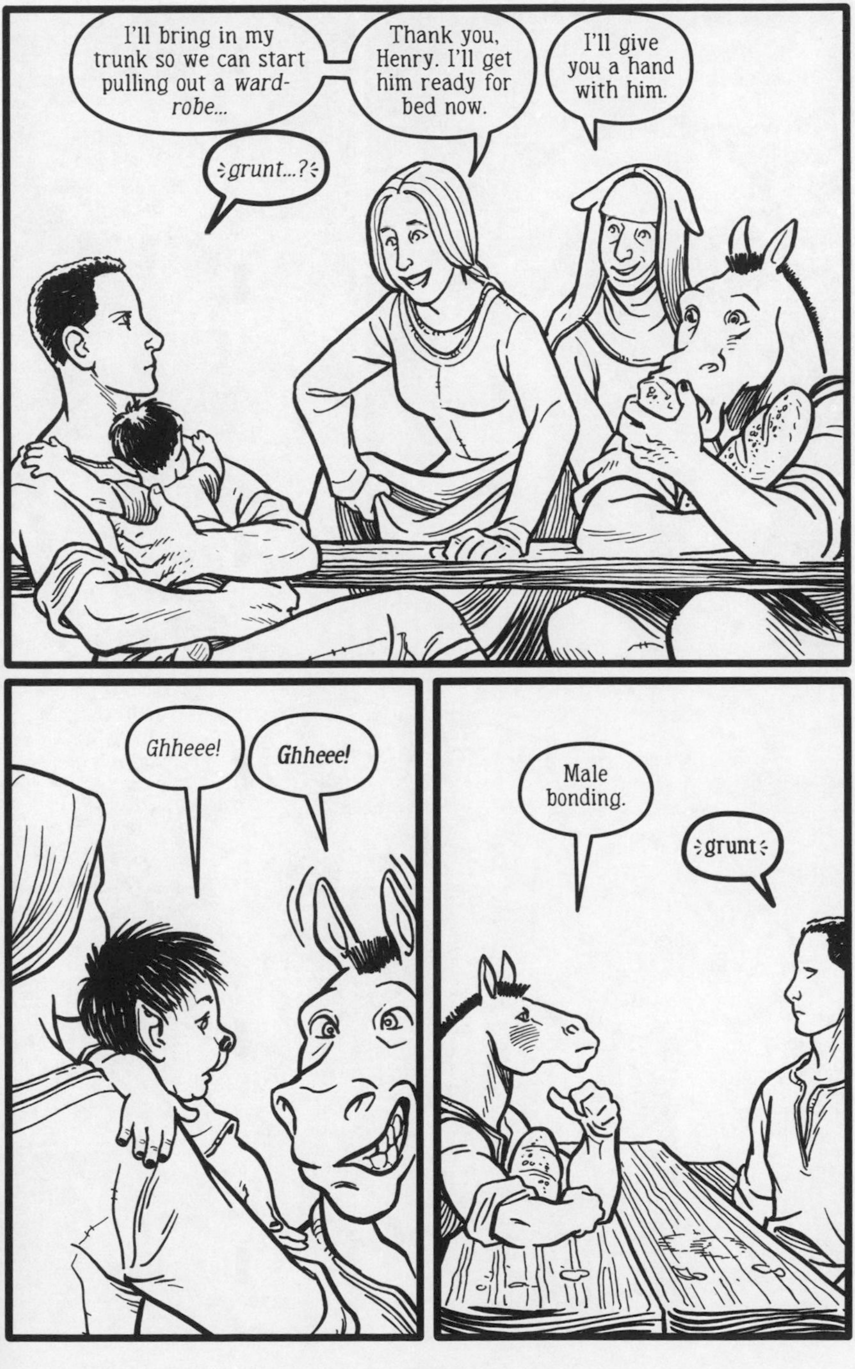
I'll bring in my trunk so we can start pulling out a *ward-robe*...
Thank you, Henry. I'll get him ready for bed now.
I'll give you a hand with him.
grunt...?
Ghheee!
Ghheee!
Male bonding.
grunt

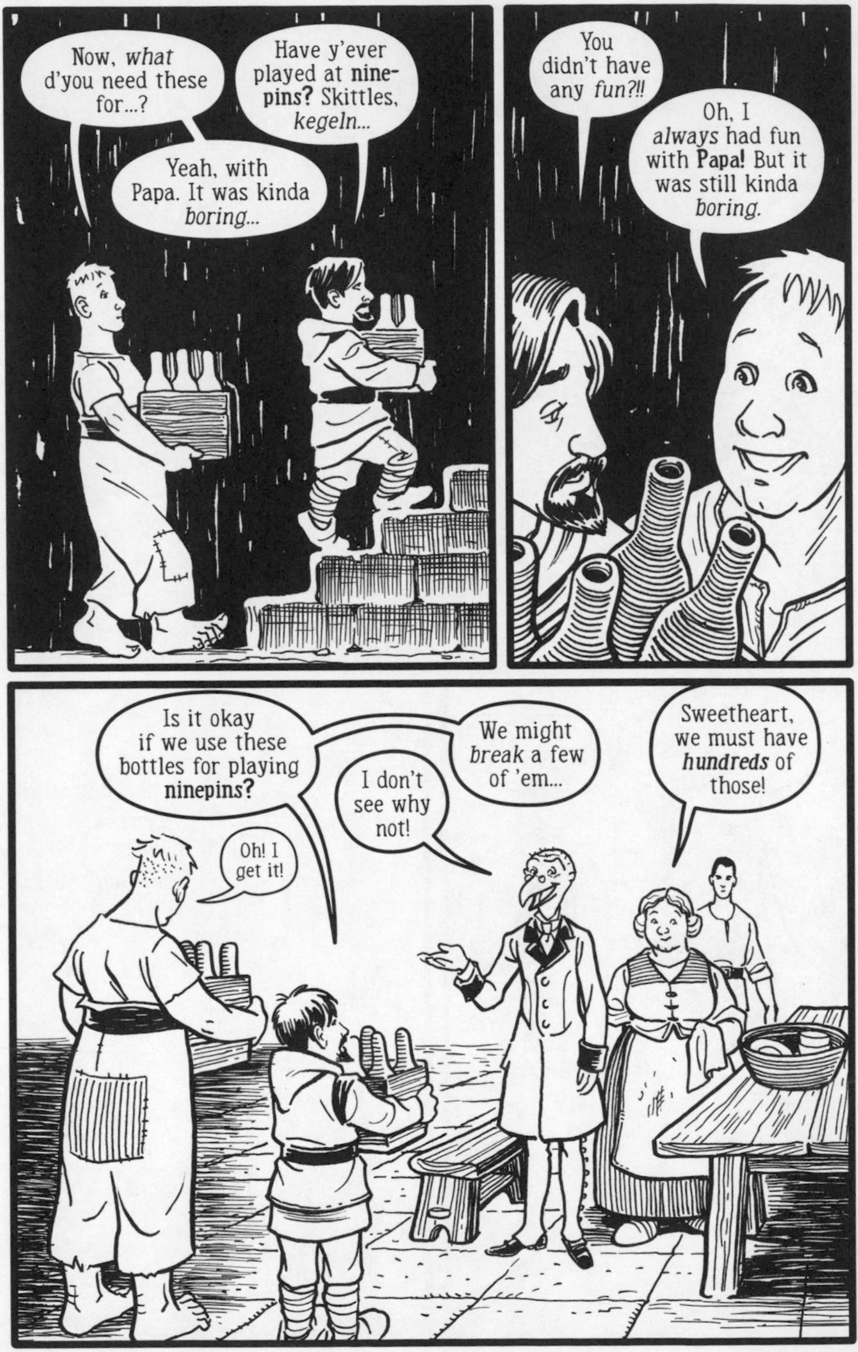
Now, *what* d'you need these for...?
Have y'ever played at **nine-pins?** Skittles, *kegeln...*
Yeah, with Papa. It was kinda *boring...*
You didn't have any *fun?!!*
Oh, I *always* had fun with **Papa!** But it was still kinda *boring.*
Is it okay if we use these bottles for playing **ninepins?**
Oh! I get it!
I don't see why not!
We might *break* a few of 'em...
Sweetheart, we must have ***hundreds*** of those!

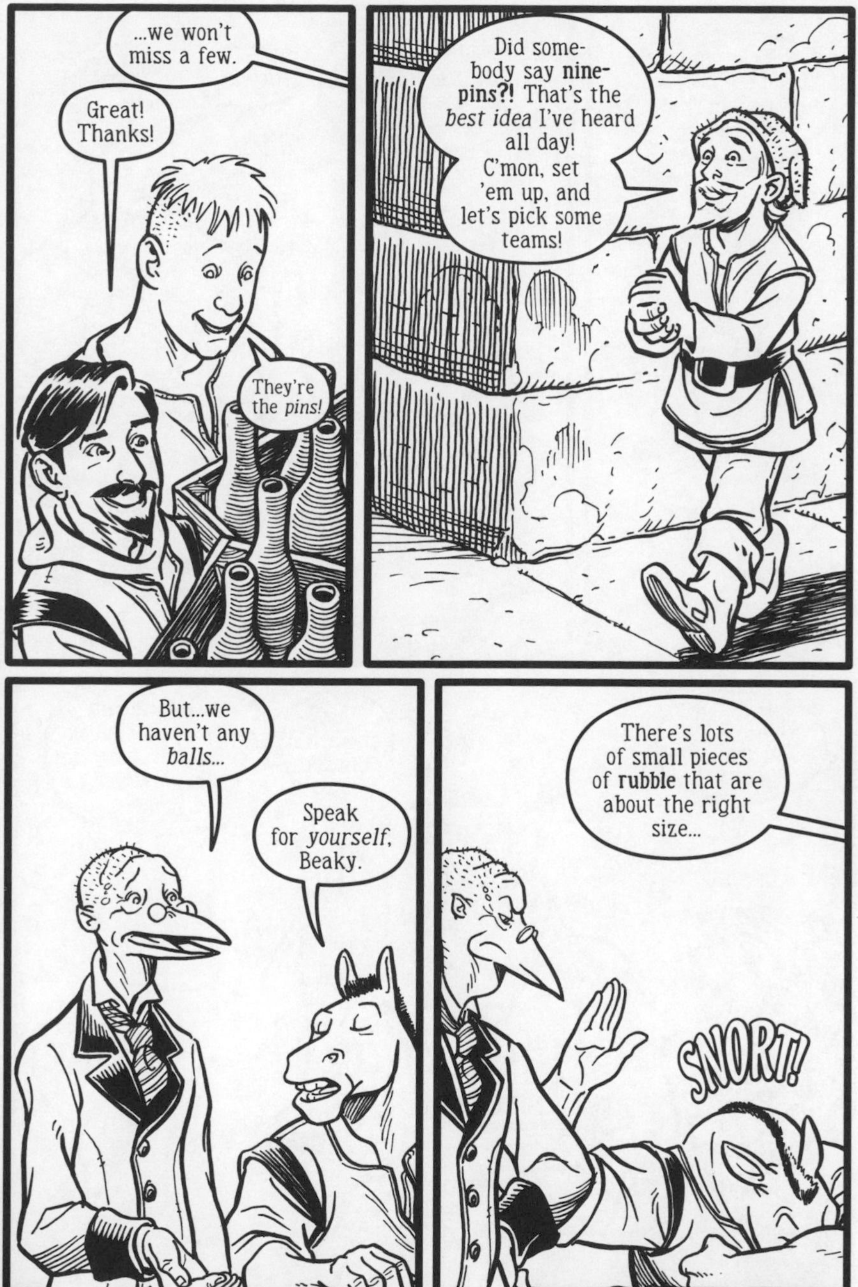
...we won't miss a few.
Great! Thanks!
They're the *pins!*
Did somebody say **nine-pins?!** That's the *best idea* I've heard all day! C'mon, set 'em up, and let's pick some teams!
But...we haven't any *balls...*
Speak for *yourself,* Beaky.
There's lots of small pieces of **rubble** that are about the right size...
SNORT!

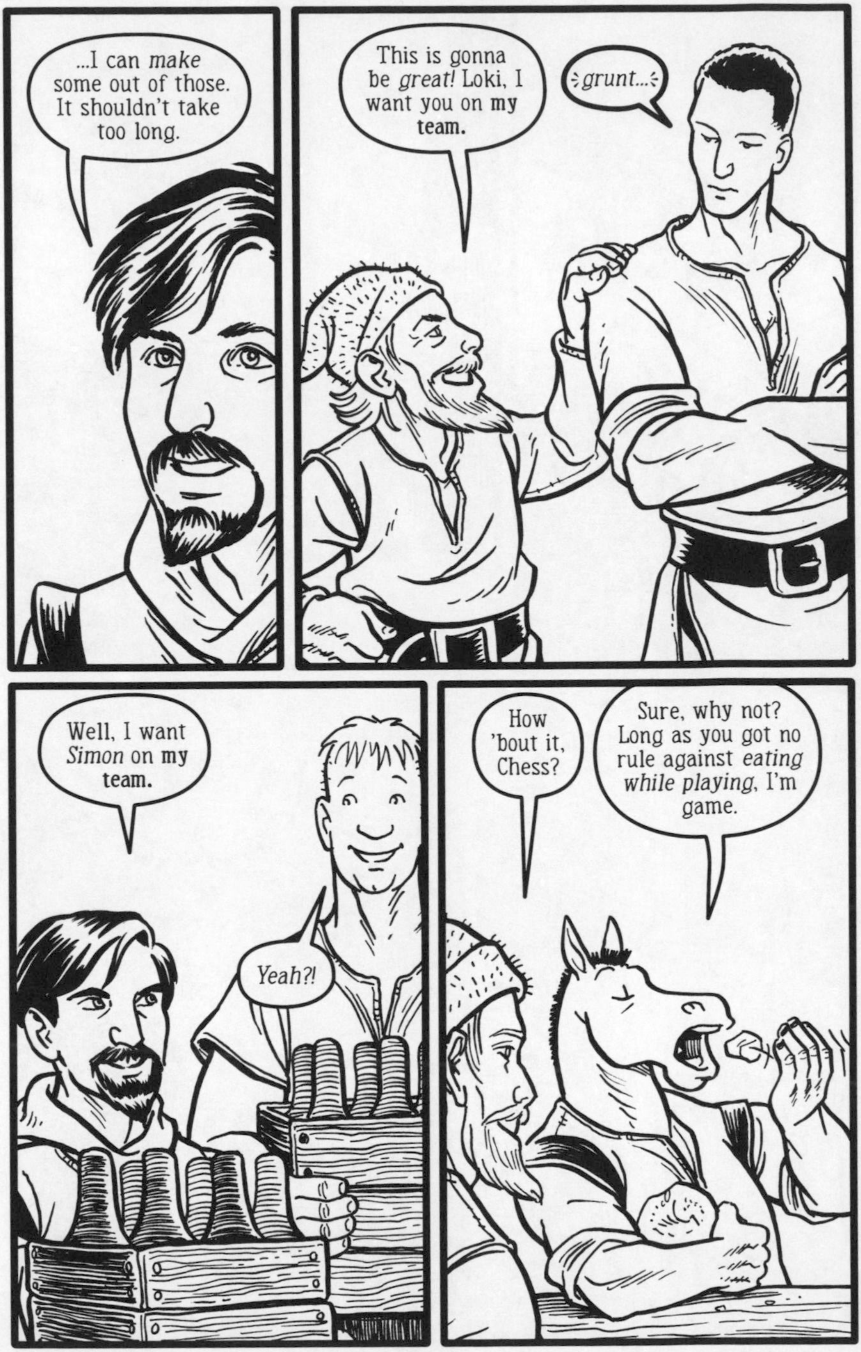
...I can *make* some out of those. It shouldn't take too long.
This is gonna be *great!* Loki, I want you on **my team.**
grunt...
Well, I want *Simon* on **my team.**
Yeah?!
How 'bout it, Chess?
Sure, why not? Long as you got no rule against *eating while playing*, I'm game.

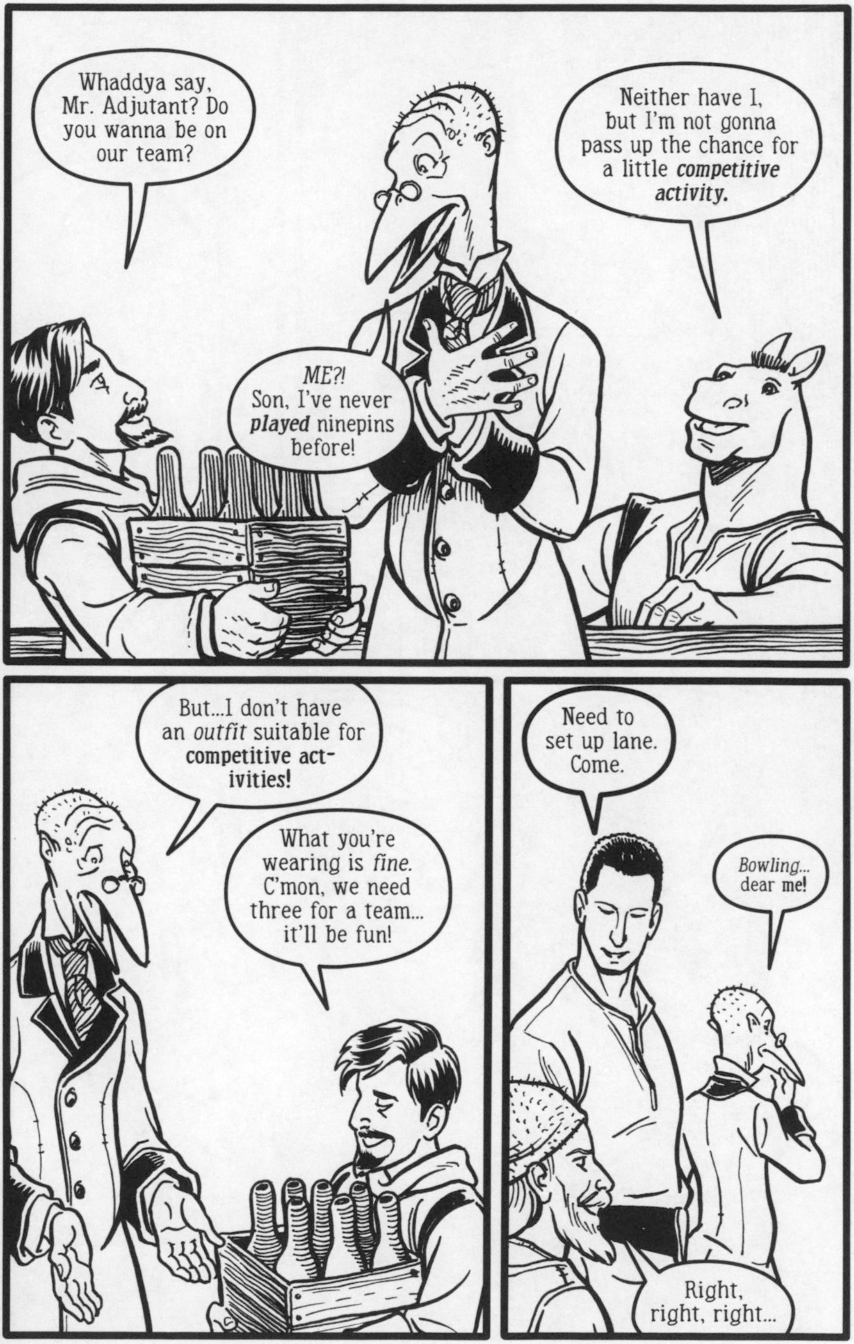
Whaddya say, Mr. Adjutant? Do you wanna be on our team?
ME?! Son, I've never *played* ninepins before!
Neither have I, but I'm not gonna pass up the chance for a little **competitive activity.**
But...I don't have an *outfit* suitable for **competitive act-ivities!**
What you're wearing is *fine.* C'mon, we need three for a team... it'll be fun!
Need to set up lane. Come.
Bowling... dear **me!**
Right, right, right...

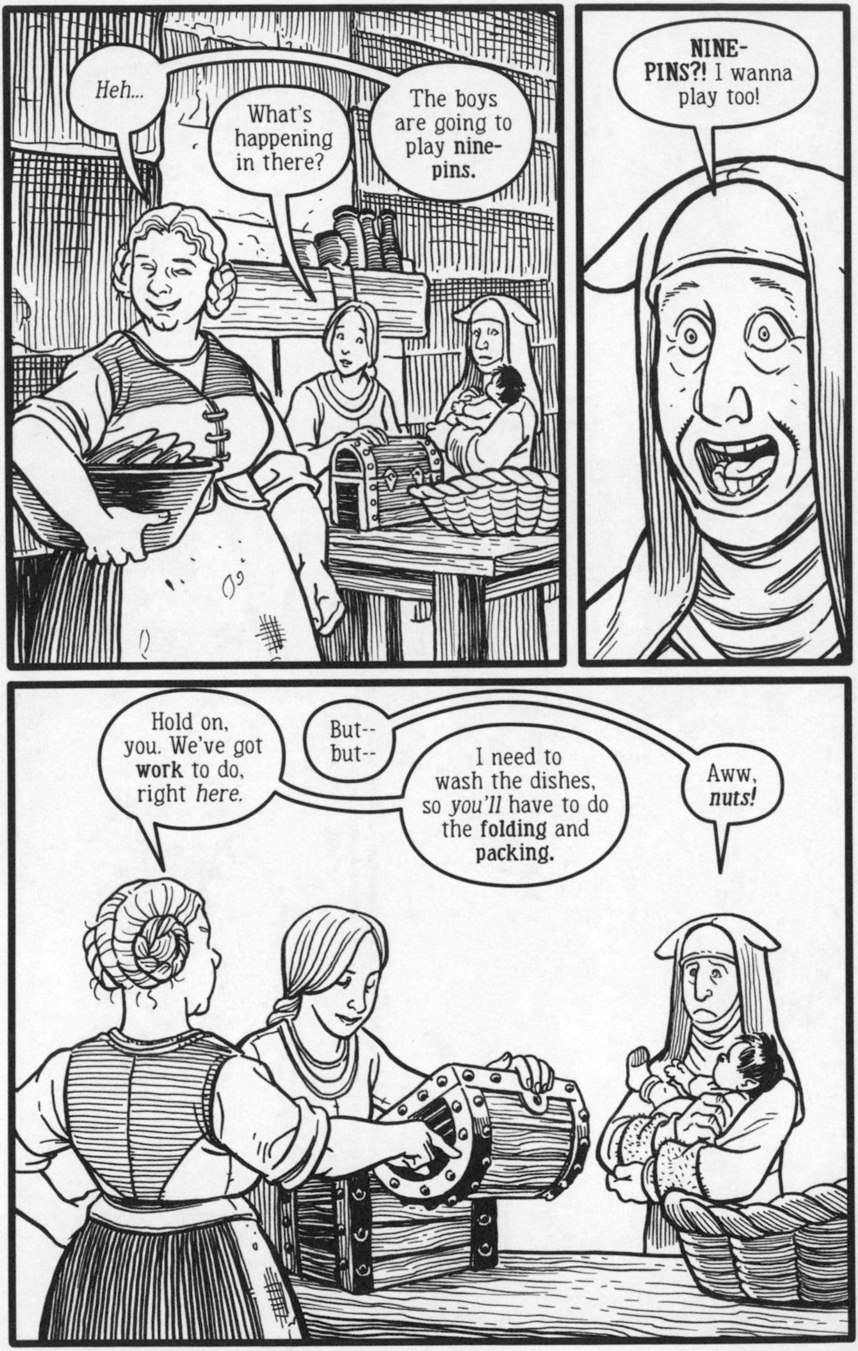
Heh...
What's happening in there?
The boys are going to play **nine-pins.**
NINE-PINS?! I wanna play too!
Hold on, you. We've got **work** to do, right *here.*
But-- but--
I need to wash the dishes, so *you'll* have to do the **folding** and **packing.**
Aww, *nuts!*

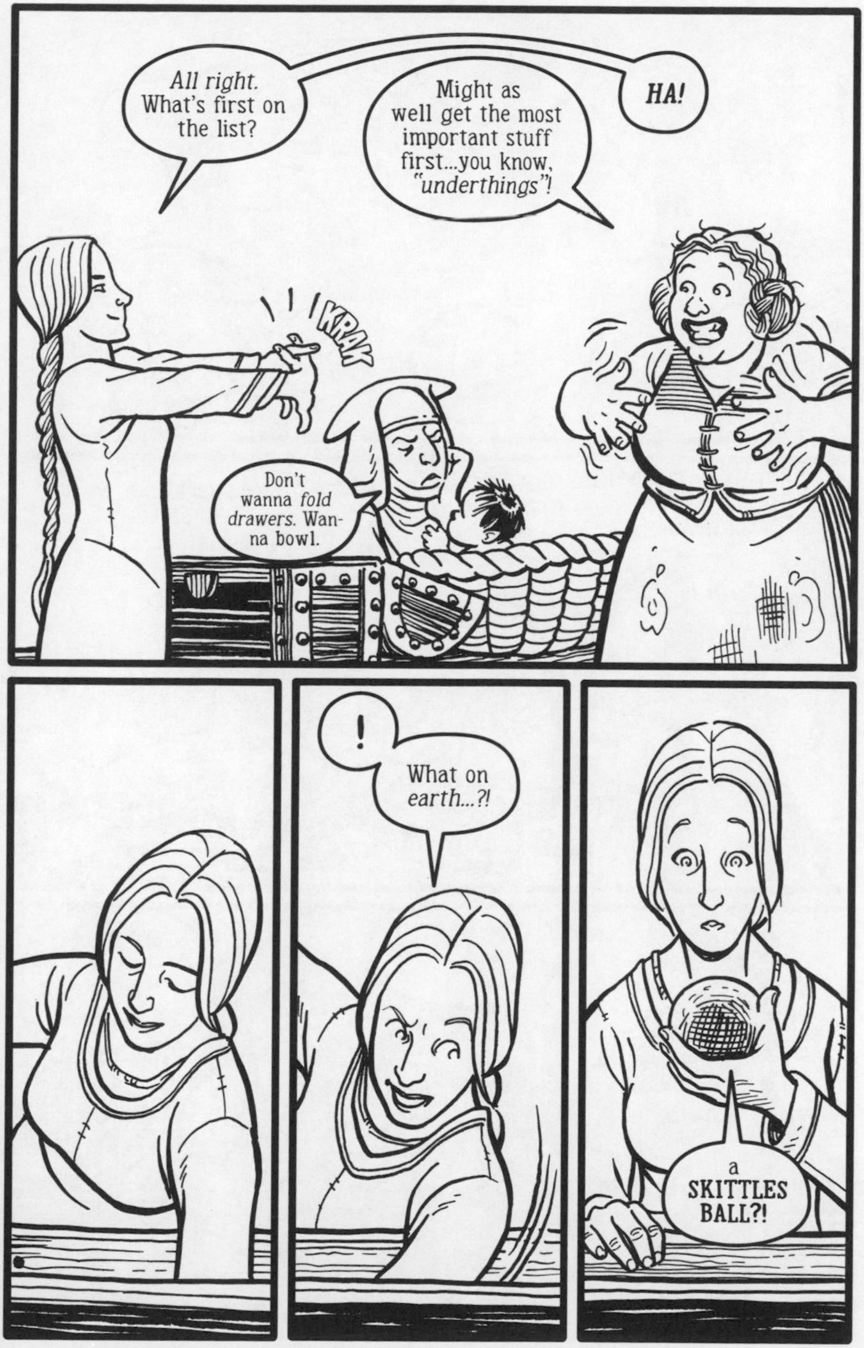
All right. What's first on the list?
Might as well get the most important stuff first...you know, "underthings"!
HA!
KRAK
Don't wanna fold drawers. Wanna bowl.
!
What on earth...?!
a SKITTLES BALL?!

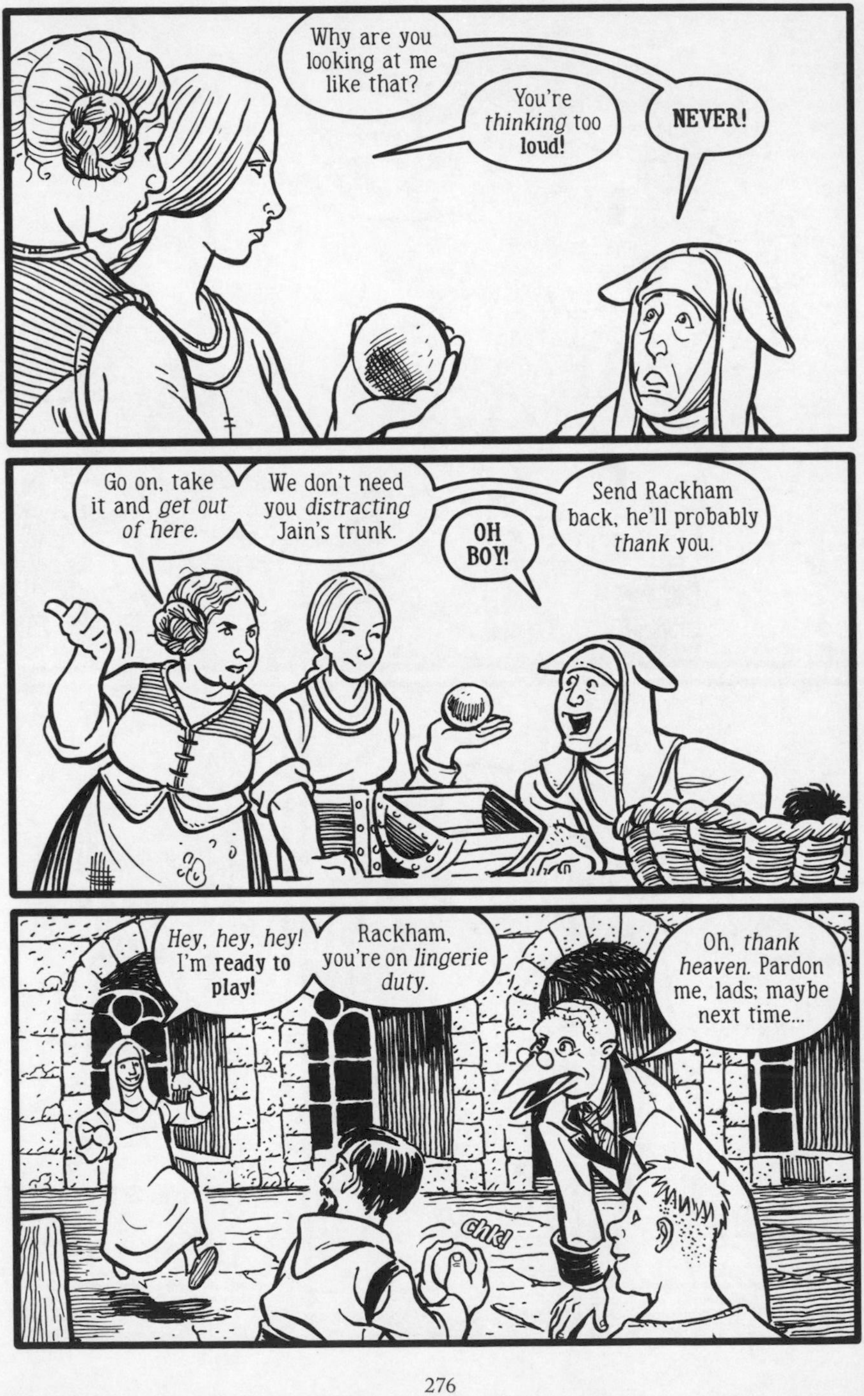
Why are you looking at me like that?
You're *thinking* too **loud!**
NEVER!
Go on, take it and *get out of here.*
We don't need you *distracting* Jain's trunk.
Send Rackham back, he'll probably *thank* you.
OH BOY!
Hey, hey, hey! I'm **ready to play!**
Rackham, you're on *lingerie duty.*
Oh, *thank heaven.* Pardon me, lads; maybe next time...
chk!

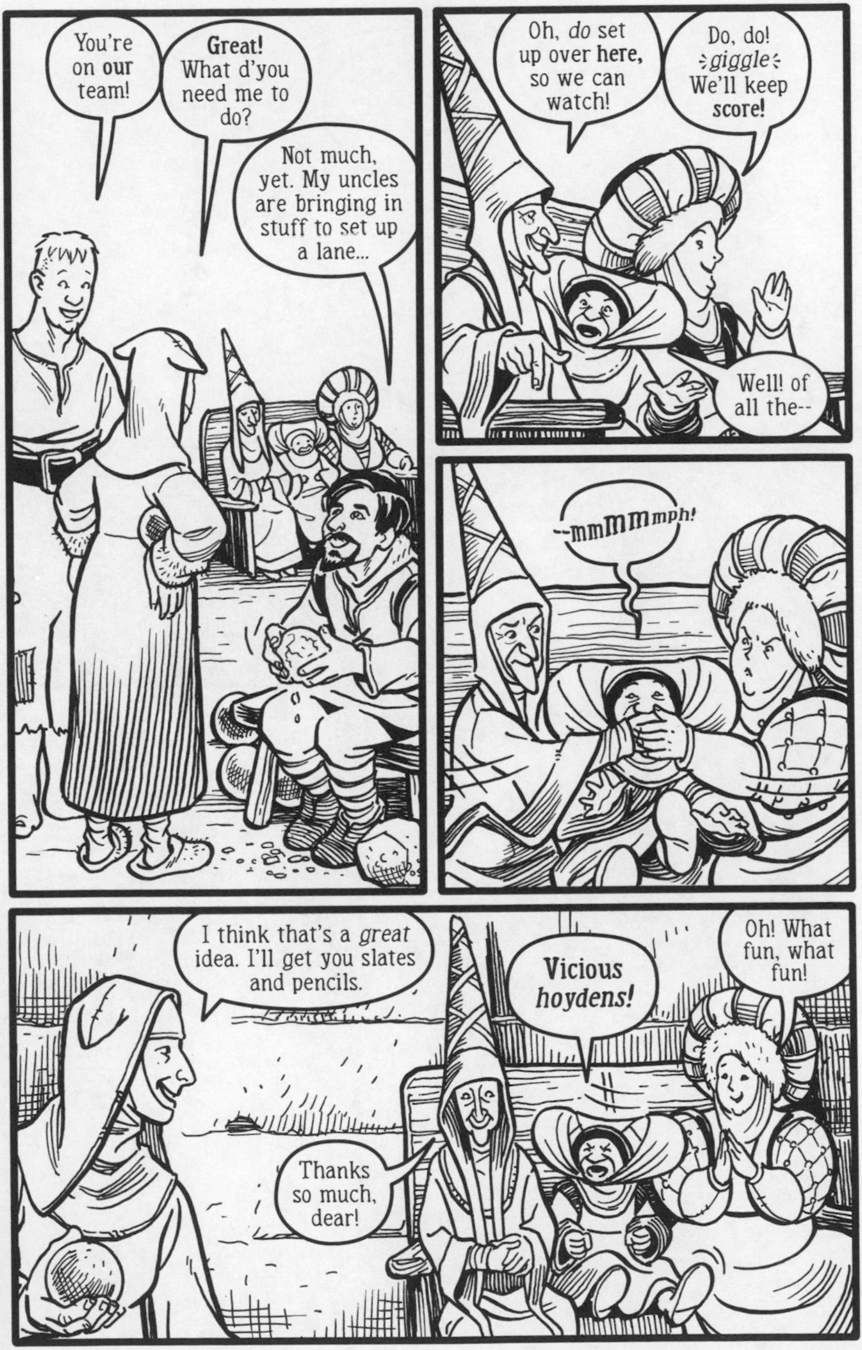
You're on **our** team!
Great! What d'you need me to do?
Not much, yet. My uncles are bringing in stuff to set up a lane...
Oh, *do* set up over **here,** so we can watch!
Do, do! *giggle* We'll keep **score!**
Well! of all the--
--mmMMmph!
I think that's a *great* idea. I'll get you slates and pencils.
Thanks so much, dear!
Vicious *hoydens!*
Oh! What fun, what fun!

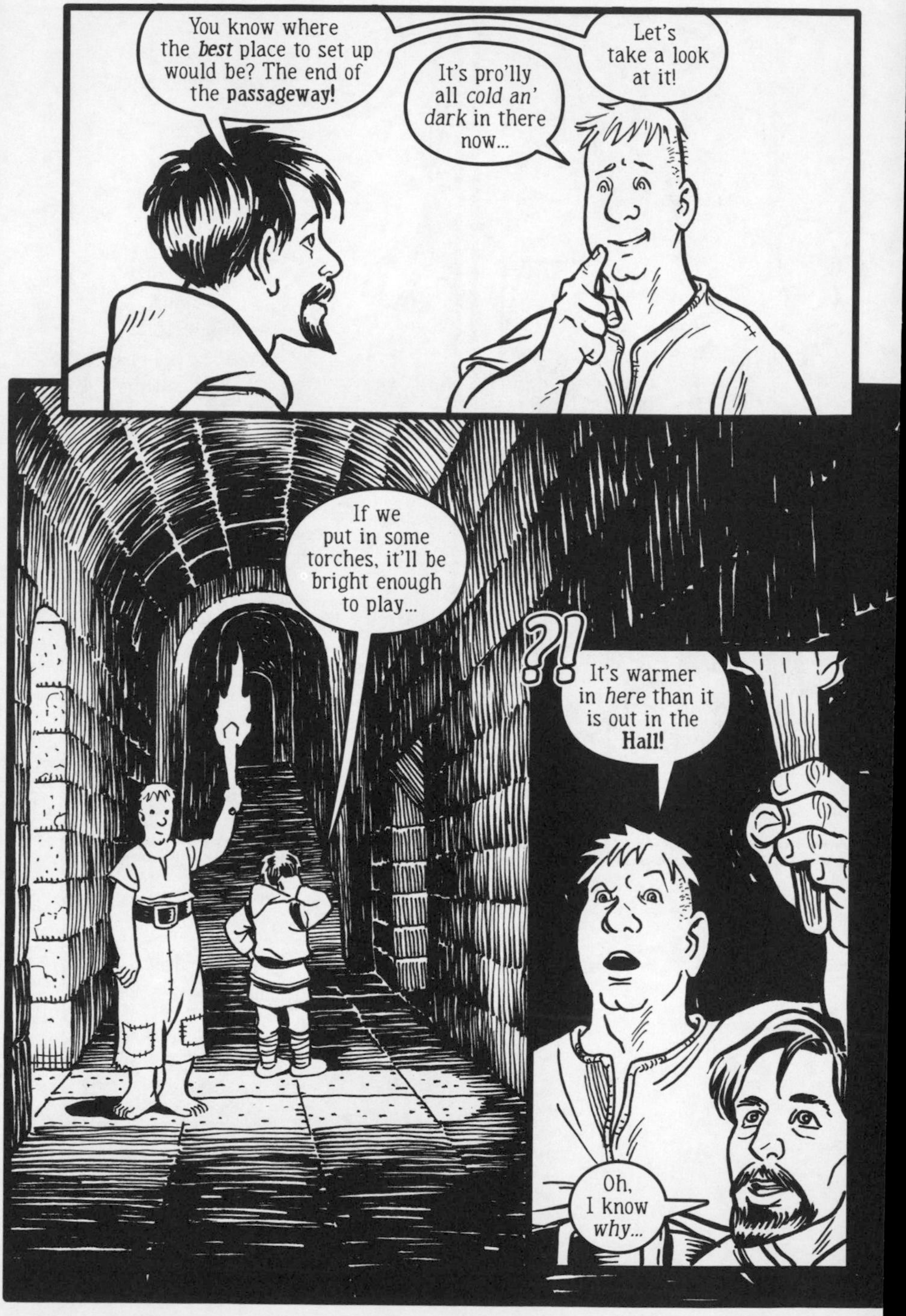
You know where the *best* place to set up would be? The end of the **passageway!**
It's pro'lly all *cold an' dark* in there now...
Let's take a look at it!
If we put in some torches, it'll be bright enough to play...
?!
It's warmer in *here* than it is out in the **Hall!**
Oh, I know *why*...

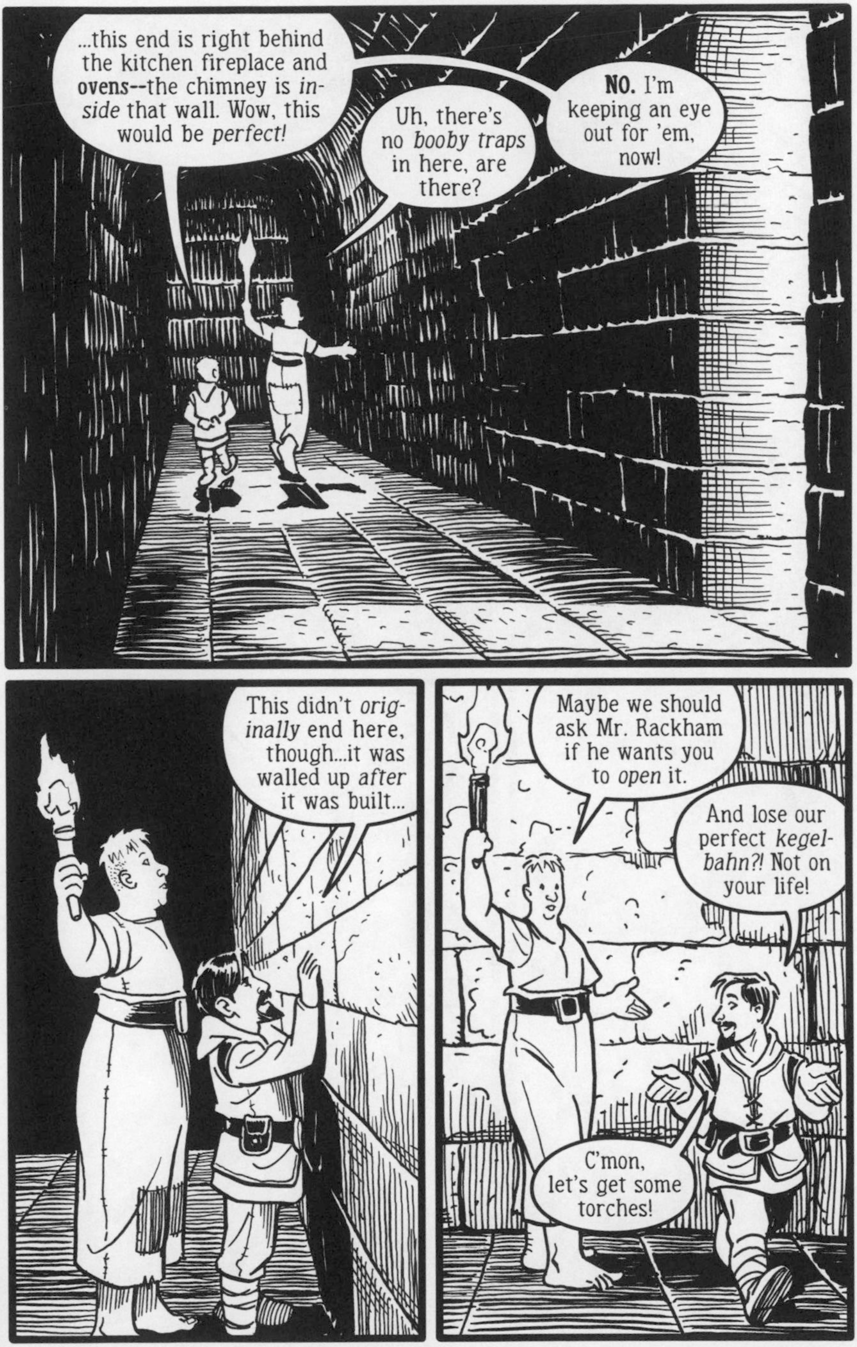
...this end is right behind the kitchen fireplace and **ovens**--the chimney is *in-side* that wall. Wow, this would be *perfect!*
Uh, there's no *booby traps* in here, are there?
NO. I'm keeping an eye out for 'em, now!
This didn't *orig-inally* end here, though...it was walled up *after* it was built...
Maybe we should ask Mr. Rackham if he wants you to *open* it.
And lose our perfect *kegel-bahn?!* Not on your life!
C'mon, let's get some torches!

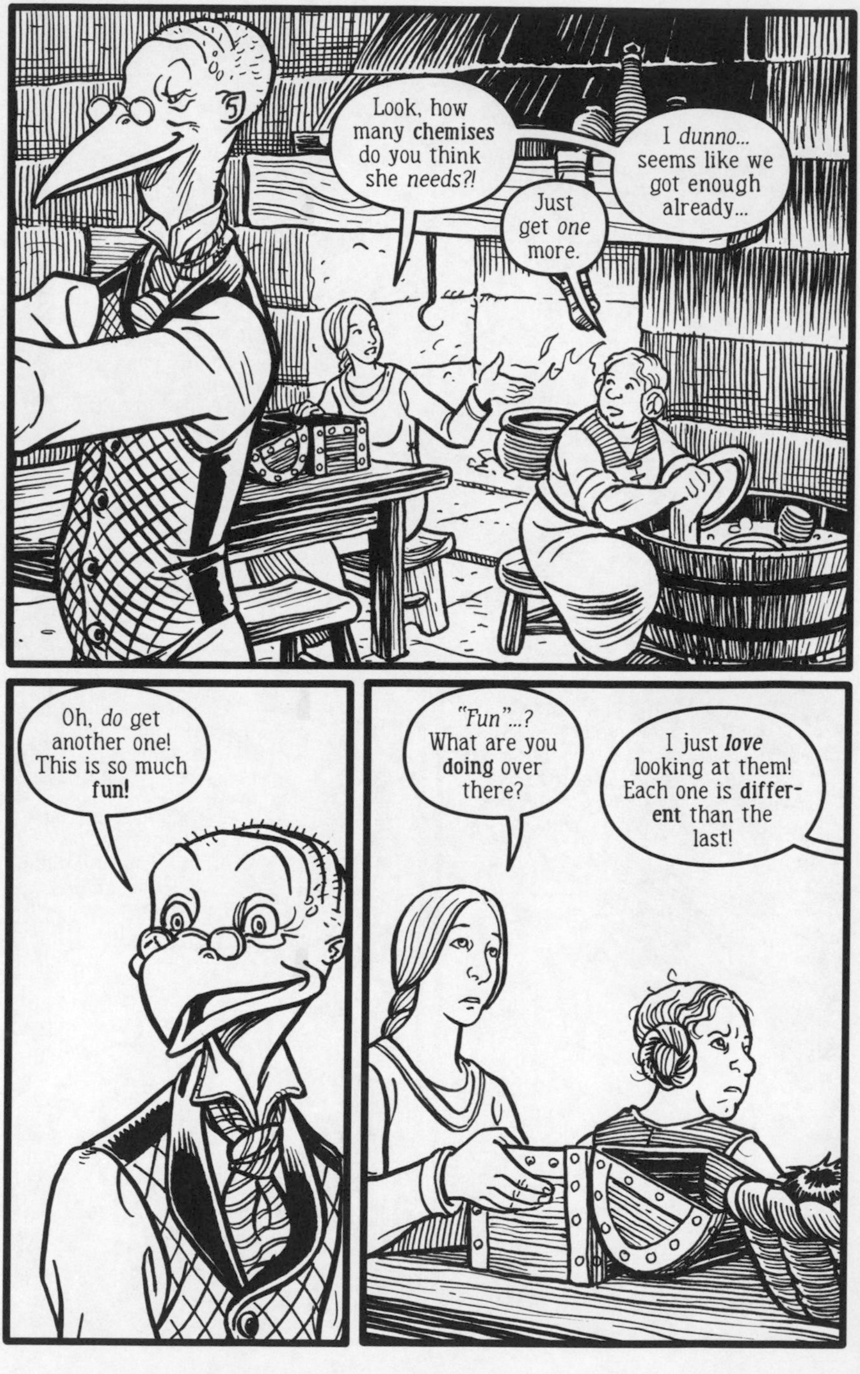
Look, how many **chemises** do you think she *needs?!*
I *dunno...* seems like we got enough already...
Just get *one* more.
Oh, *do* get another one! This is so much **fun!**
"Fun"...? What are you **doing** over there?
I just ***love*** looking at them! Each one is **differ-ent** than the last!

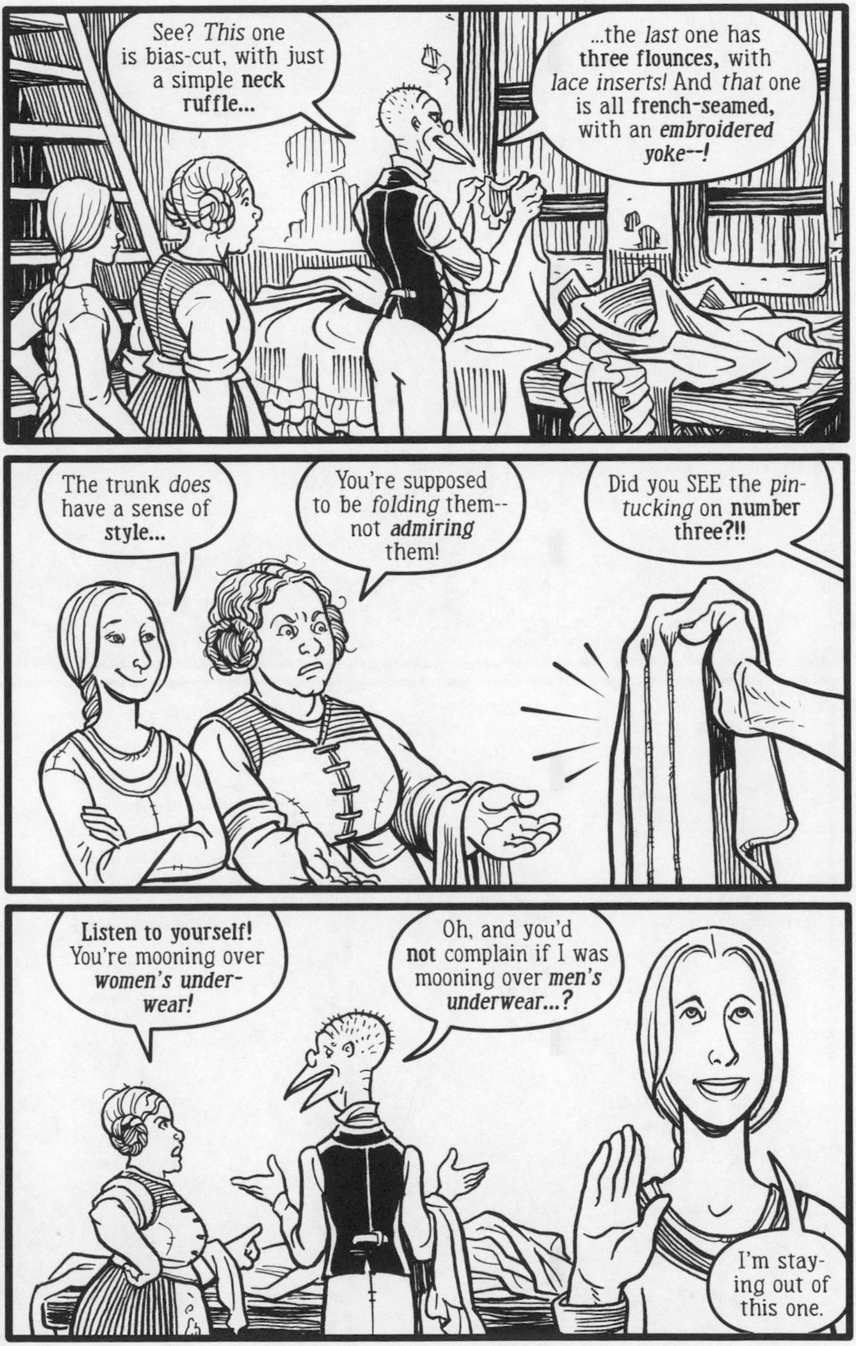
See? *This* one is bias-cut, with just a simple **neck ruffle...**
...the *last* one has **three flounces,** with *lace inserts!* And *that* one is all **french-seamed,** with an ***embroidered yoke--!***
The trunk *does* have a sense of **style...**
You're supposed to be *folding* them-- not ***admiring*** them!
Did you SEE the *pin-tucking* on **number three?!!**
Listen to yourself! You're mooning over ***women's underwear!***
Oh, and you'd **not** complain if I was mooning over ***men's underwear...?***
I'm staying out of this one.

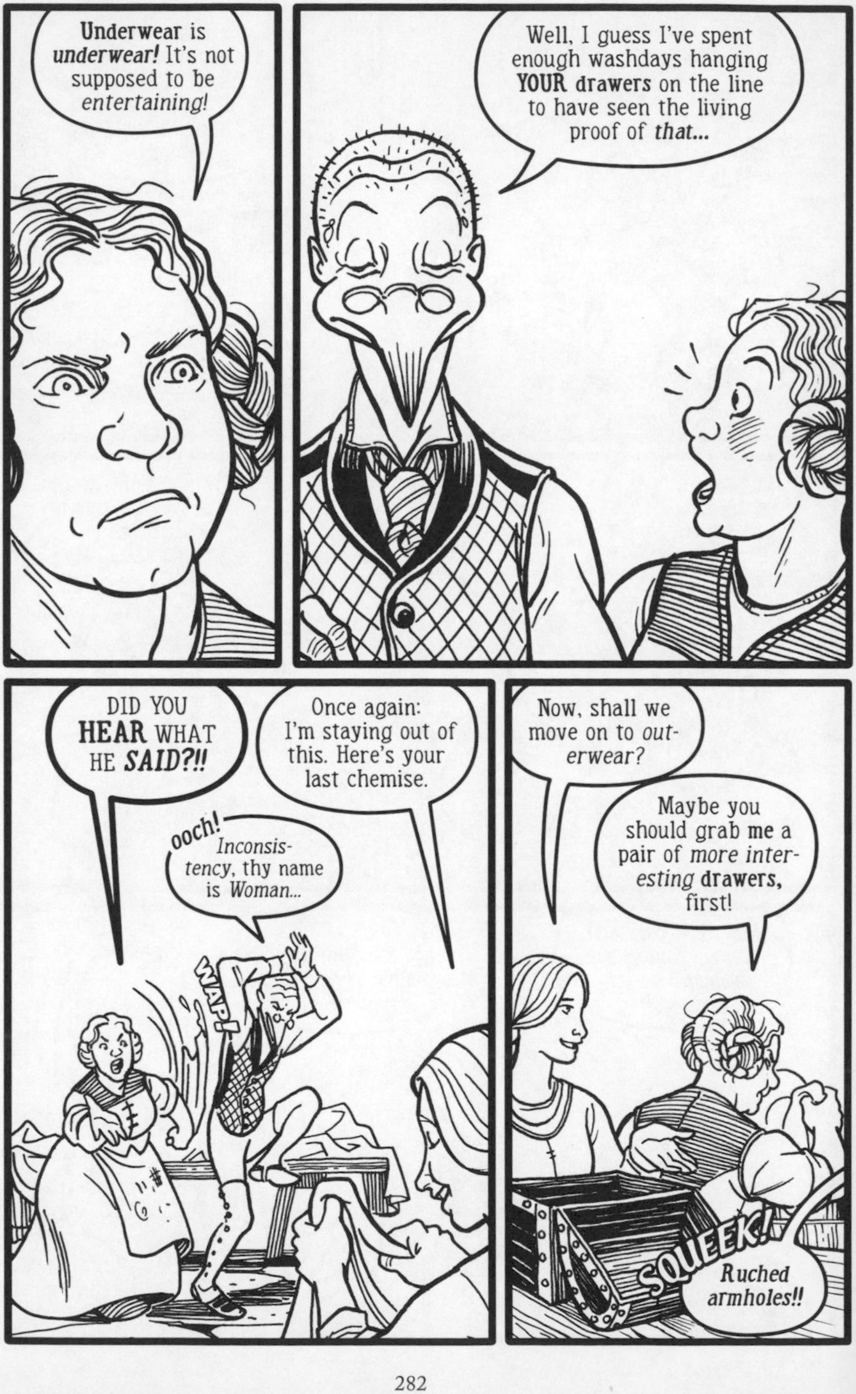
Underwear is underwear! It's not supposed to be entertaining!
Well, I guess I've spent enough washdays hanging YOUR drawers on the line to have seen the living proof of that...
DID YOU HEAR WHAT HE SAID?!!
Once again: I'm staying out of this. Here's your last chemise.
ooch!
Inconsistency, thy name is Woman...
WAP!
Now, shall we move on to outerwear?
Maybe you should grab me a pair of more interesting drawers, first!
SQUEEK!
Ruched armholes!!

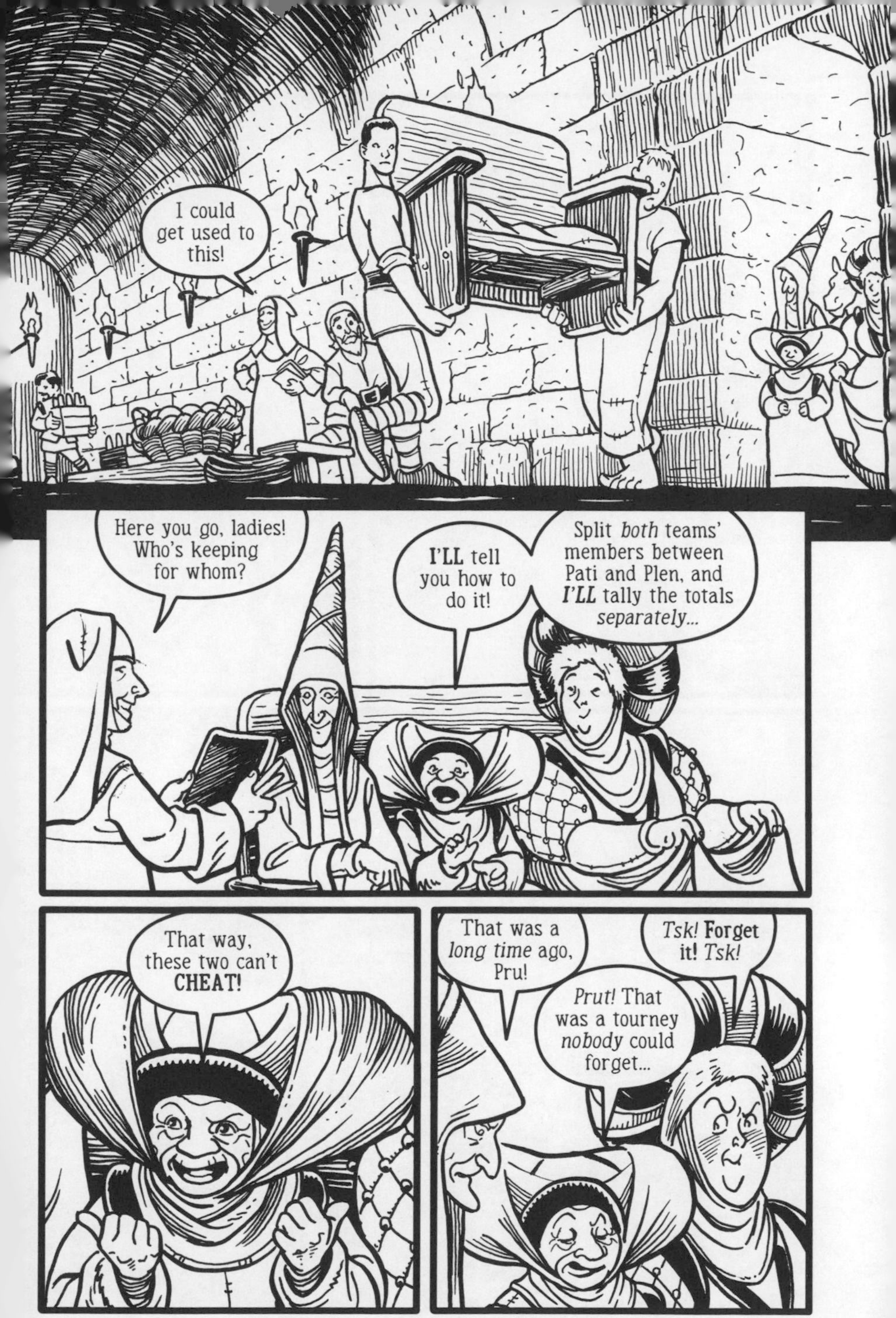
I could get used to this!
Here you go, ladies! Who's keeping for whom?
I'LL tell you how to do it!
Split *both* teams' members between Pati and Plen, and ***I'LL*** tally the totals *separately*...
That way, these two can't **CHEAT!**
That was a *long time* ago, Pru!
Tsk! **Forget it!** *Tsk!*
Prut! That was a tourney *nobody* could forget...

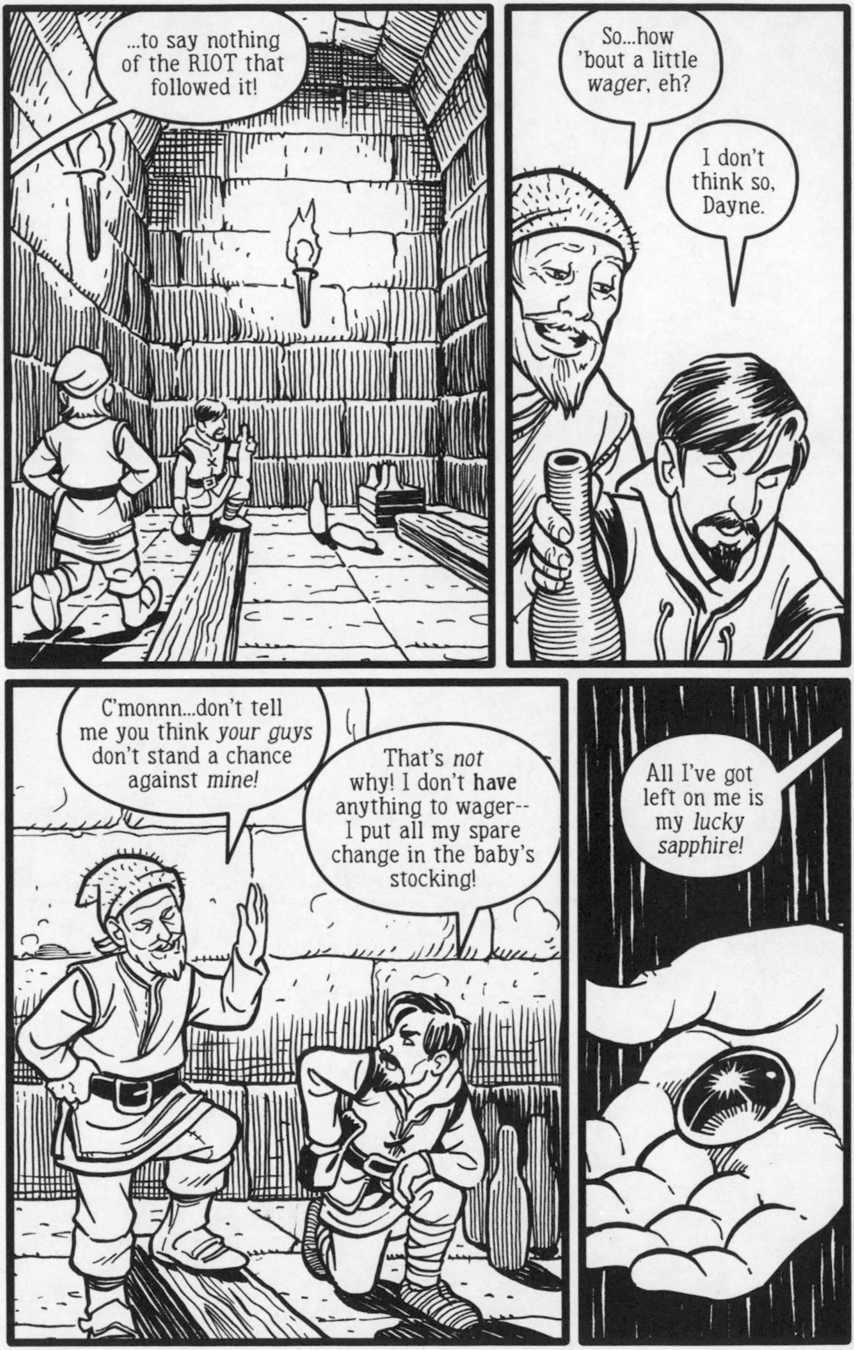
...to say nothing of the RIOT that followed it!
So...how 'bout a little *wager*, eh?
I don't think so, Dayne.
C'monnn...don't tell me you think *your guys* don't stand a chance against *mine!*
That's *not* why! I don't **have** anything to wager-- I put all my spare change in the baby's stocking!
All I've got left on me is my *lucky sapphire!*

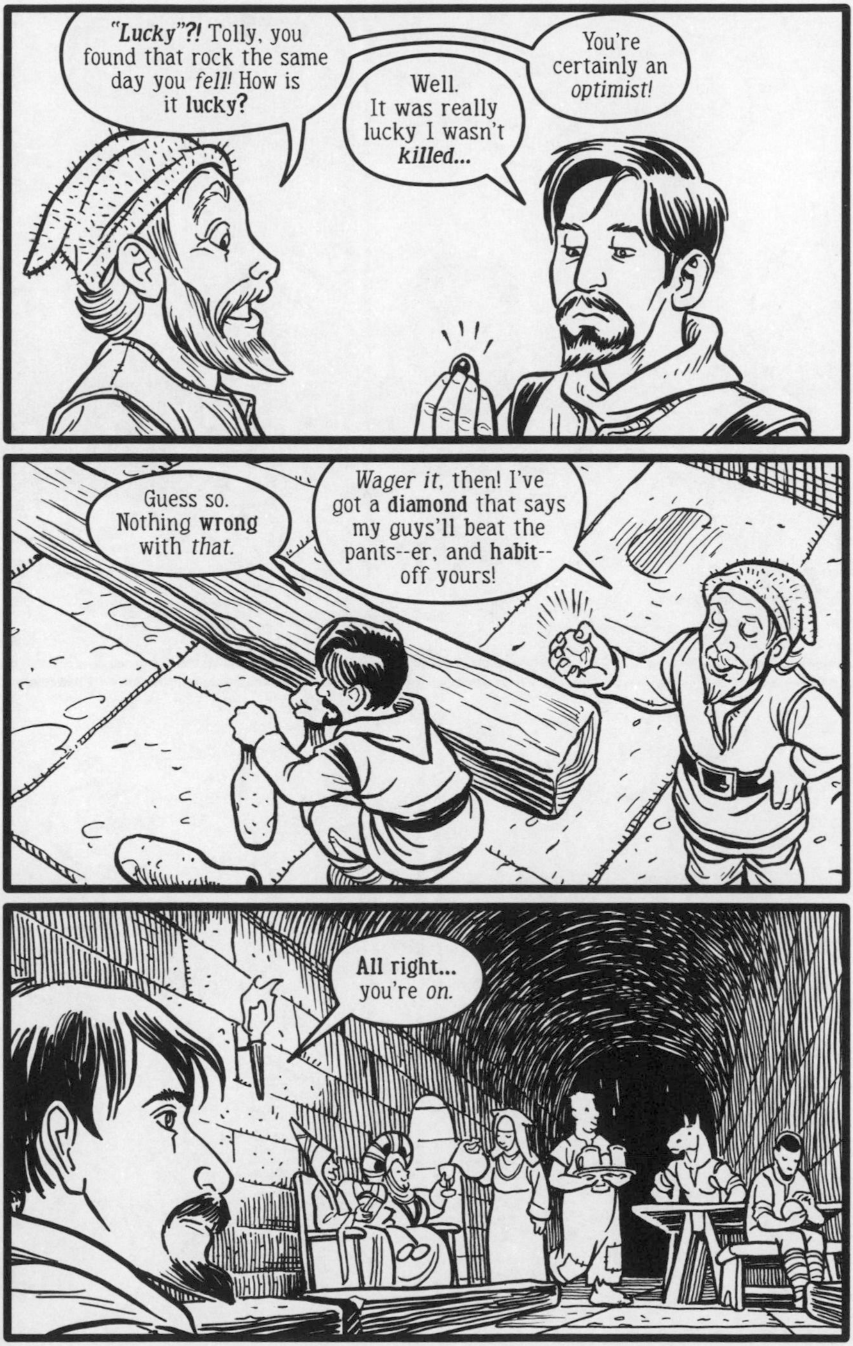
"Lucky"?! Tolly, you found that rock the same day you fell! How is it lucky?
Well. It was really lucky I wasn't killed...
You're certainly an optimist!
Guess so. Nothing wrong with that.
Wager it, then! I've got a diamond that says my guys'll beat the pants--er, and habit--off yours!
All right... you're on.

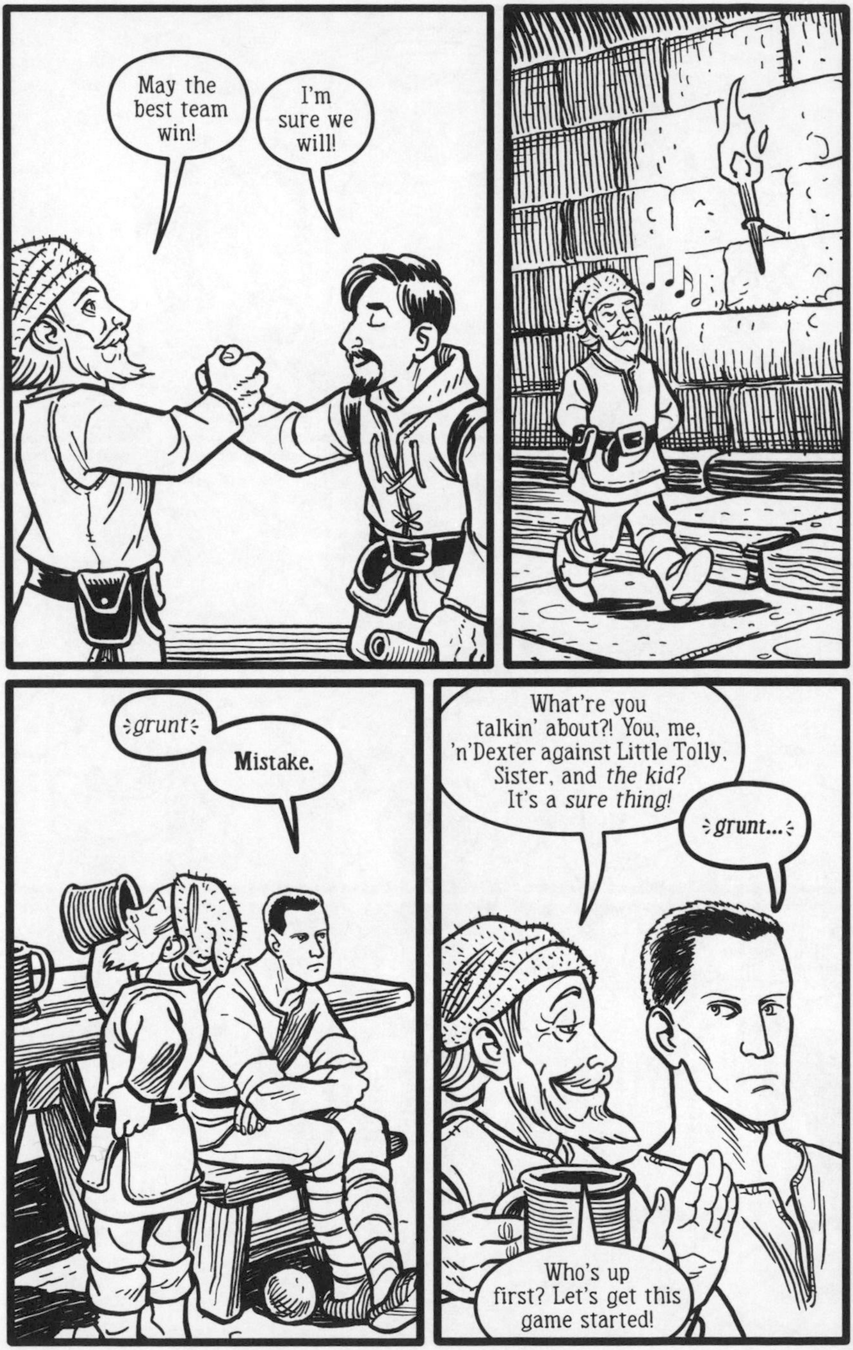
May the best team win!
I'm sure we will!
grunt
Mistake.
What're you talkin' about?! You, me, 'n'Dexter against Little Tolly, Sister, and *the kid*? It's a *sure thing*!
grunt...
Who's up first? Let's get this game started!

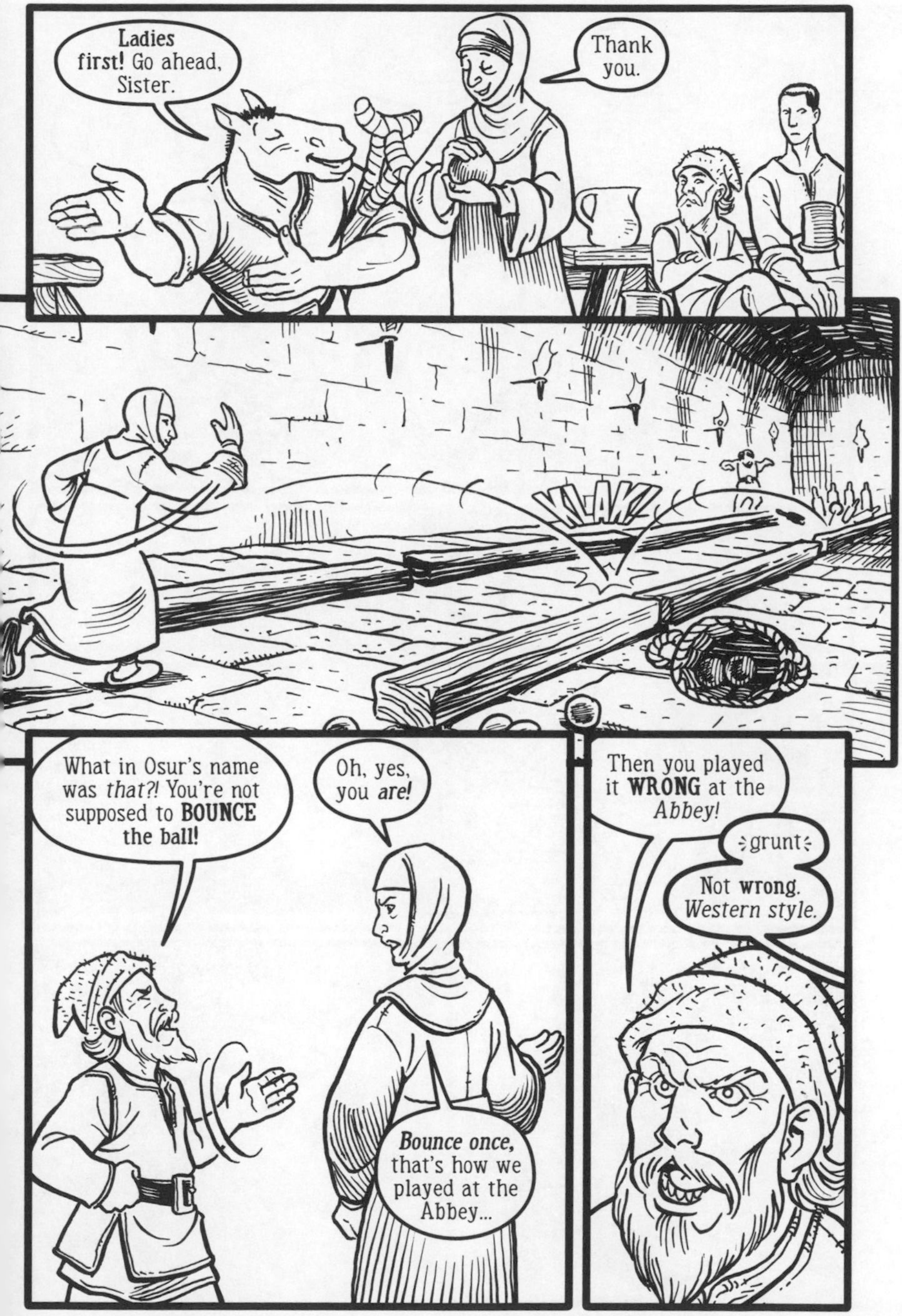
Ladies first! Go ahead, Sister.
Thank you.
VLAK!
What in Osur's name was *that?!* You're not supposed to **BOUNCE** the ball!
Oh, yes, you *are!*
Bounce once, that's how we played at the Abbey...
Then you played it **WRONG** at the *Abbey!*
grunt
Not **wrong**. *Western style.*

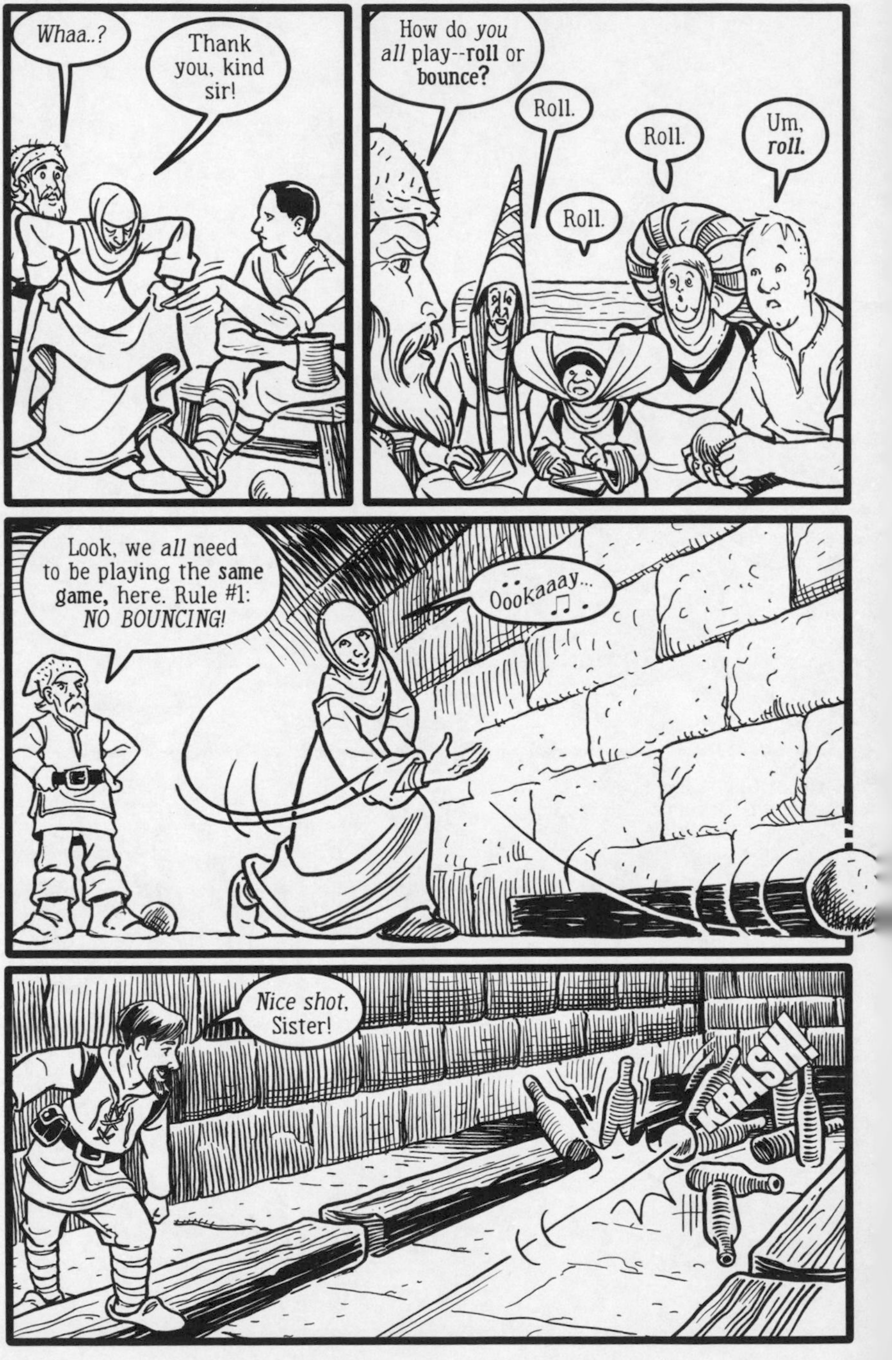
Whaa..?
Thank you, kind sir!
How do *you all* play--**roll** or **bounce?**
Roll.
Roll.
Roll.
Um, *roll.*
Look, we *all* need to be playing the **same game,** here. Rule #1: *NO BOUNCING!*
Oookaaay...
Nice shot, Sister!
KRASH!

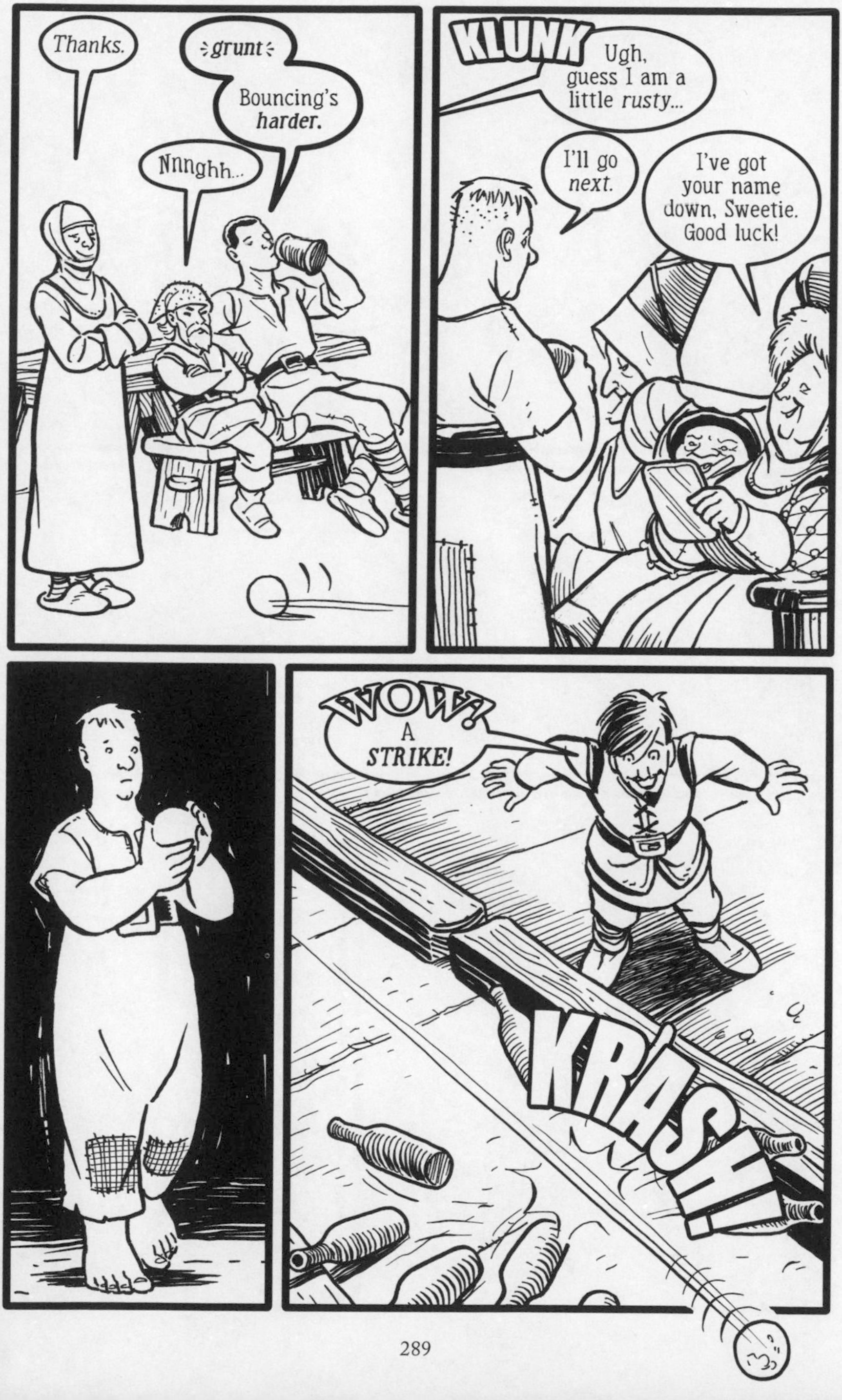
Thanks.
grunt
Bouncing's *harder.*
Nnnghh...
KLUNK
Ugh, guess I am a little *rusty*...
I'll go *next.*
I've got your name down, Sweetie. Good luck!
WOW! A *STRIKE!*
KRASH

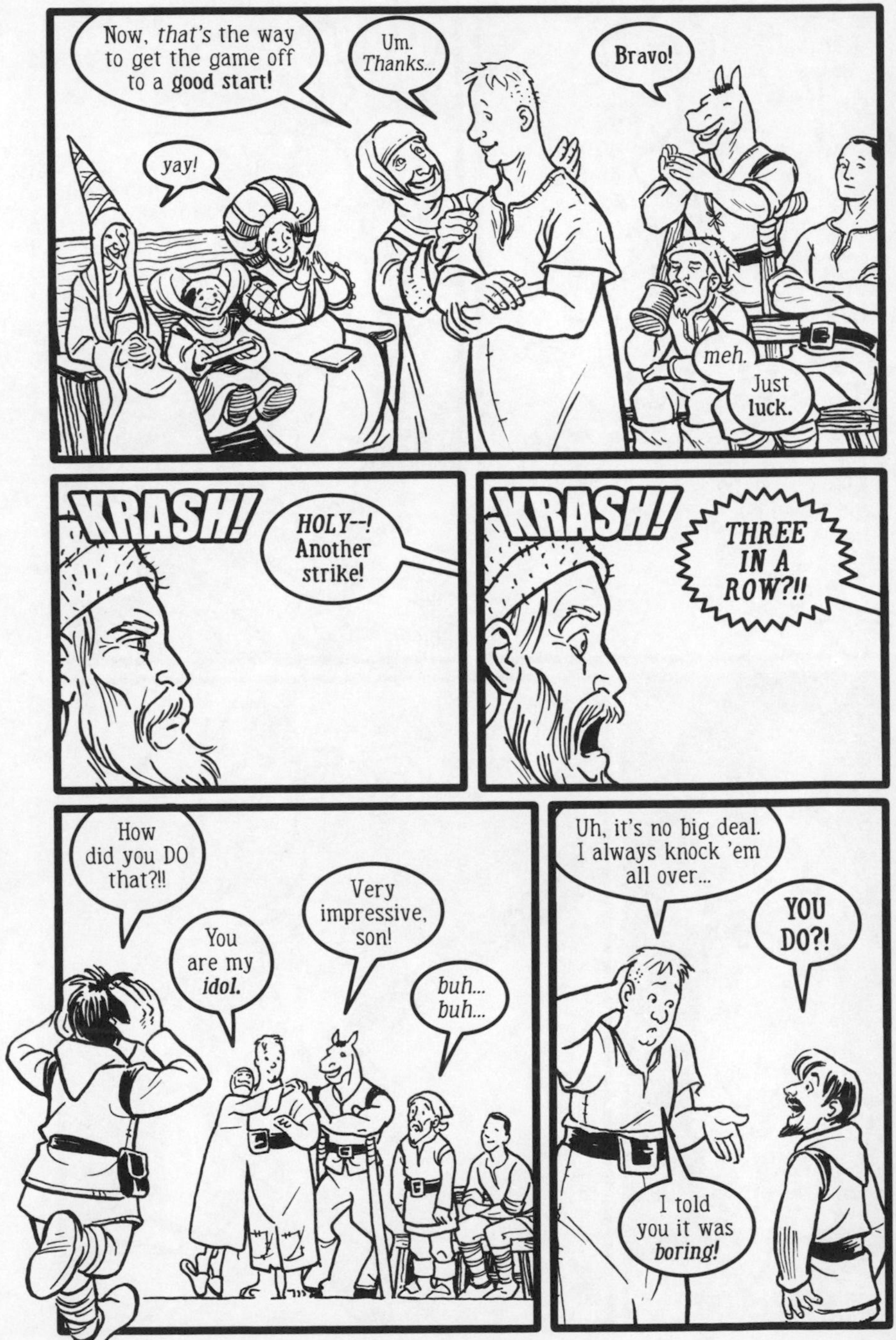
Now, *that's* the way to get the game off to a **good start!**
Um. Thanks...
Bravo!
yay!
meh.
Just **luck.**
KRASH!
HOLY--! Another strike!
KRASH!
THREE IN A ROW?!!
How did you DO that?!!
You are my ***idol.***
Very impressive, son!
buh... buh...
Uh, it's no big deal. I always knock 'em all over...
YOU DO?!
I told you it was ***boring!***

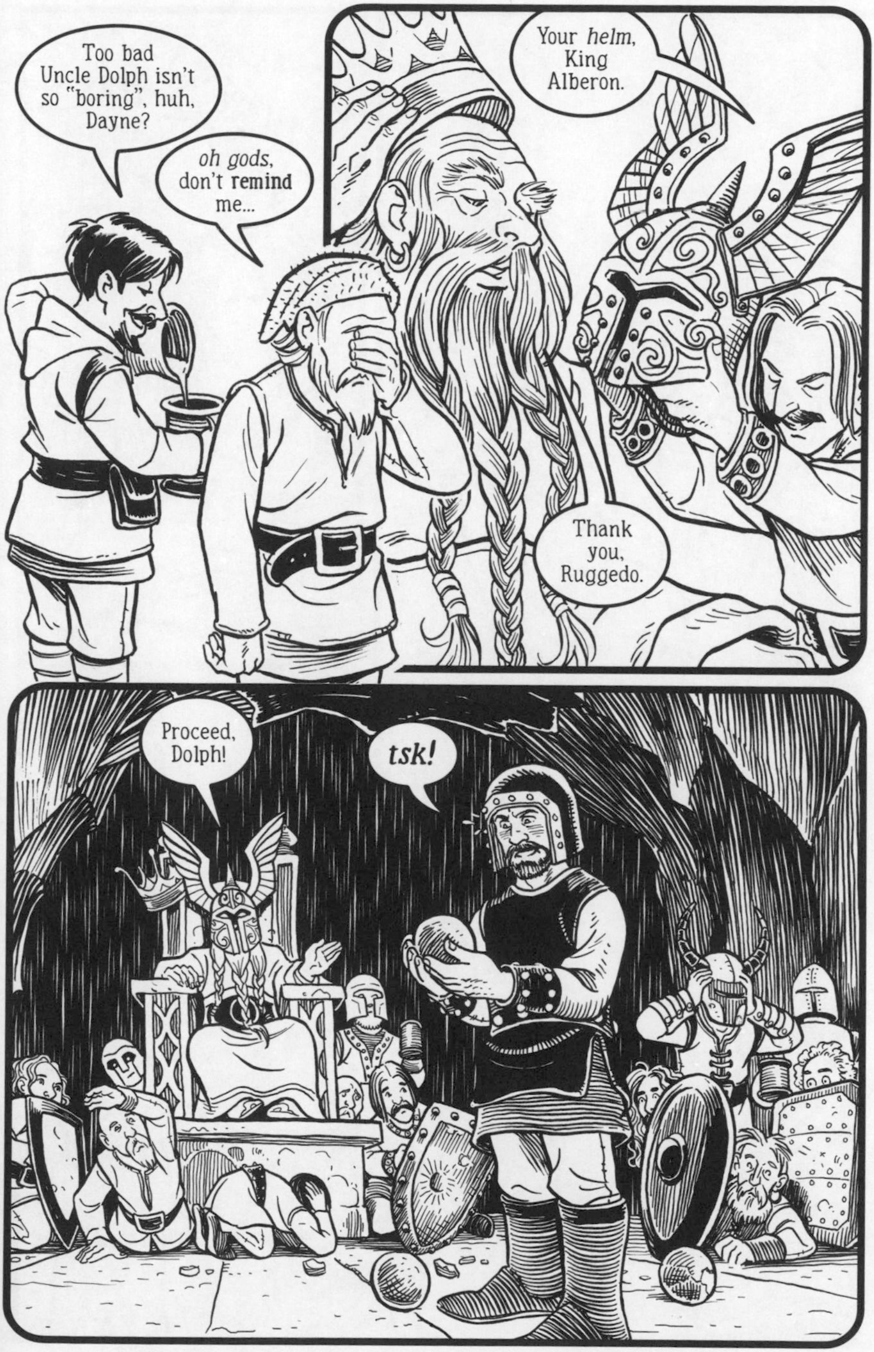
Too bad Uncle Dolph isn't so "boring", huh, Dayne?
oh gods, don't **remind** me...
Your *helm*, King Alberon.
Thank you, Ruggedo.
Proceed, Dolph!
tsk!

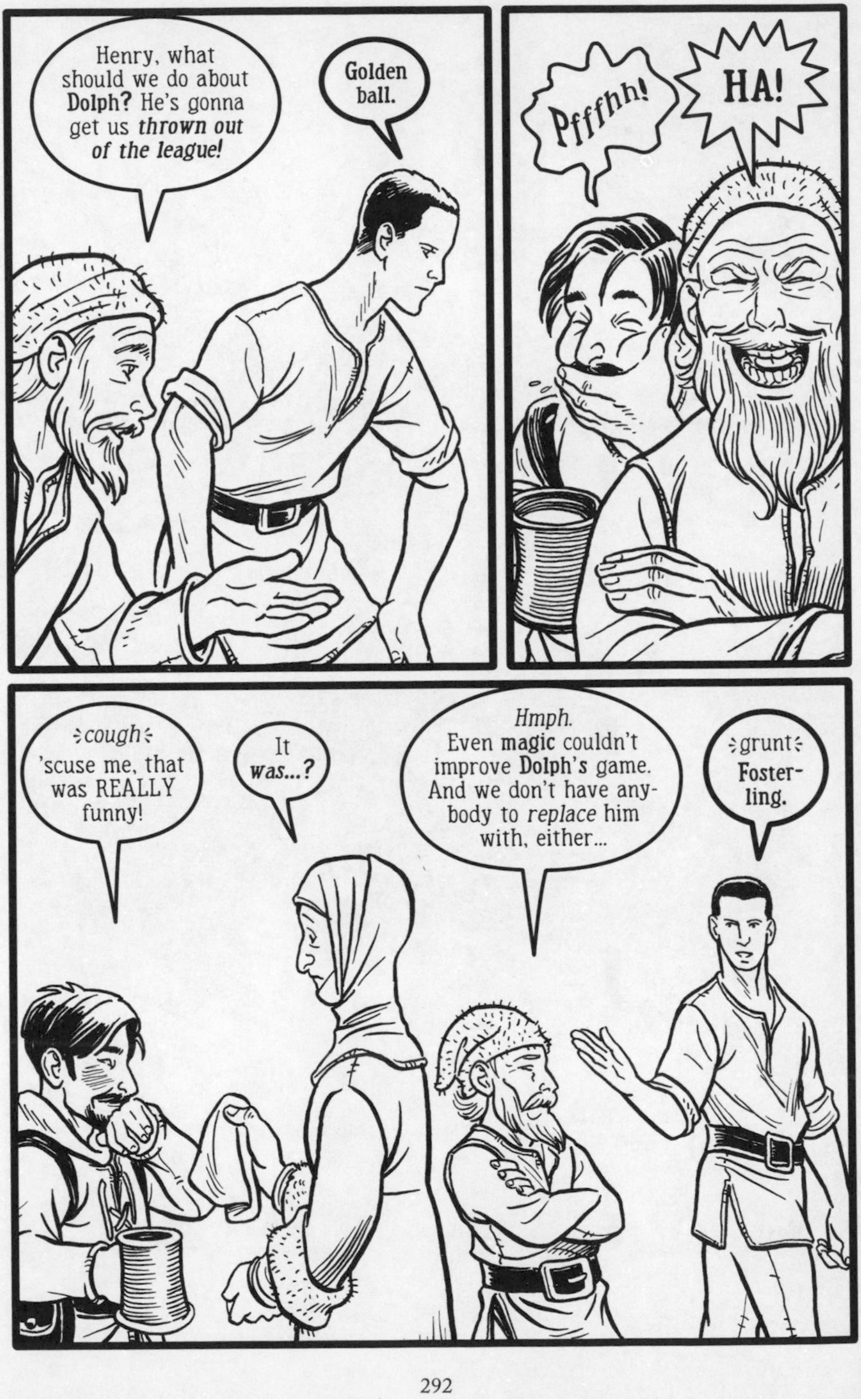
Henry, what should we do about Dolph? He's gonna get us thrown out of the league!
Golden ball.
Pfffhh!
HA!
cough 'scuse me, that was REALLY funny!
It was...?
Hmph. Even magic couldn't improve Dolph's game. And we don't have anybody to replace him with, either...
grunt Fosterling.

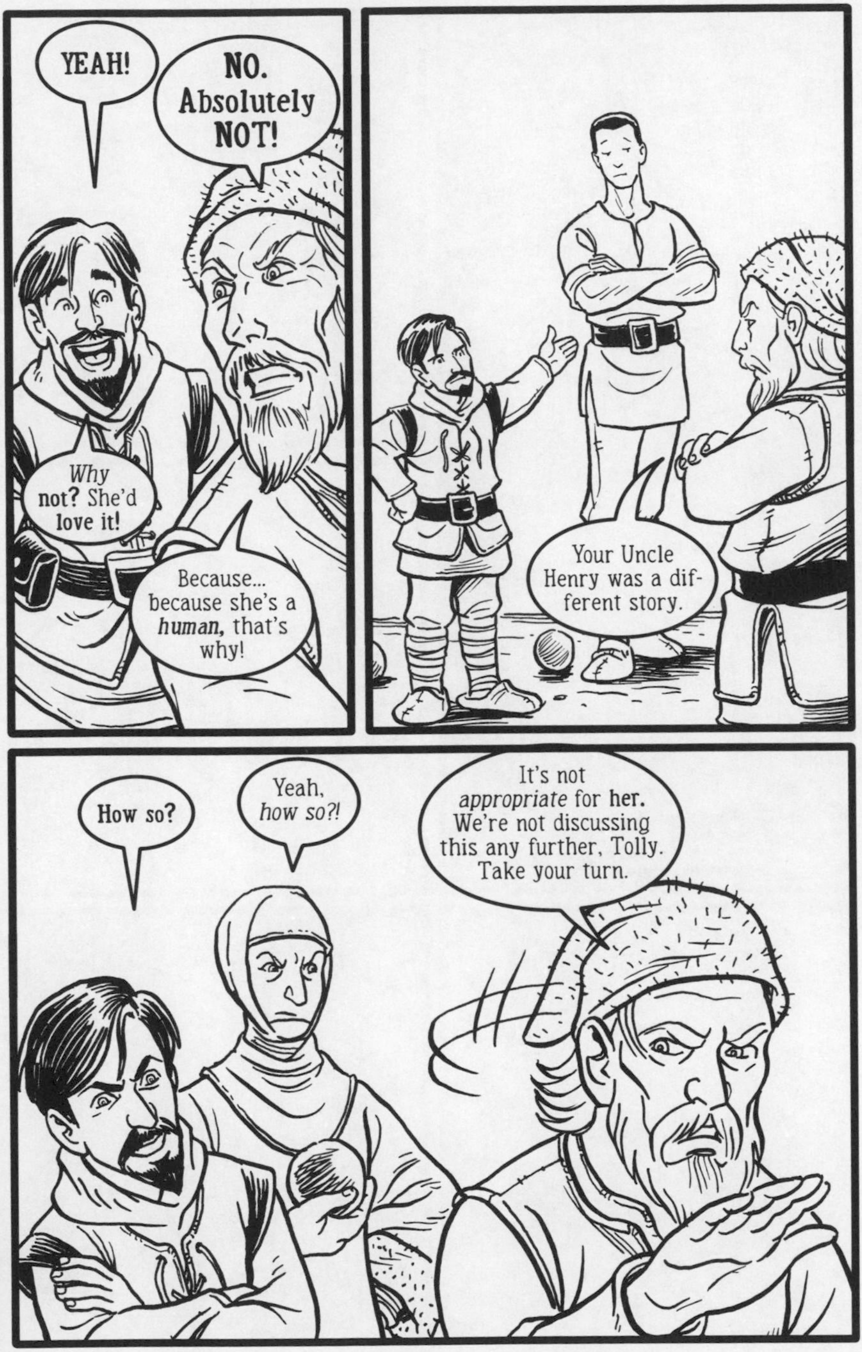
YEAH!
NO. Absolutely NOT!
Why not? She'd love it!
Because... because she's a human, that's why!
Your Uncle Henry was a different story.
How so?
Yeah, how so?!
It's not appropriate for her. We're not discussing this any further, Tolly. Take your turn.

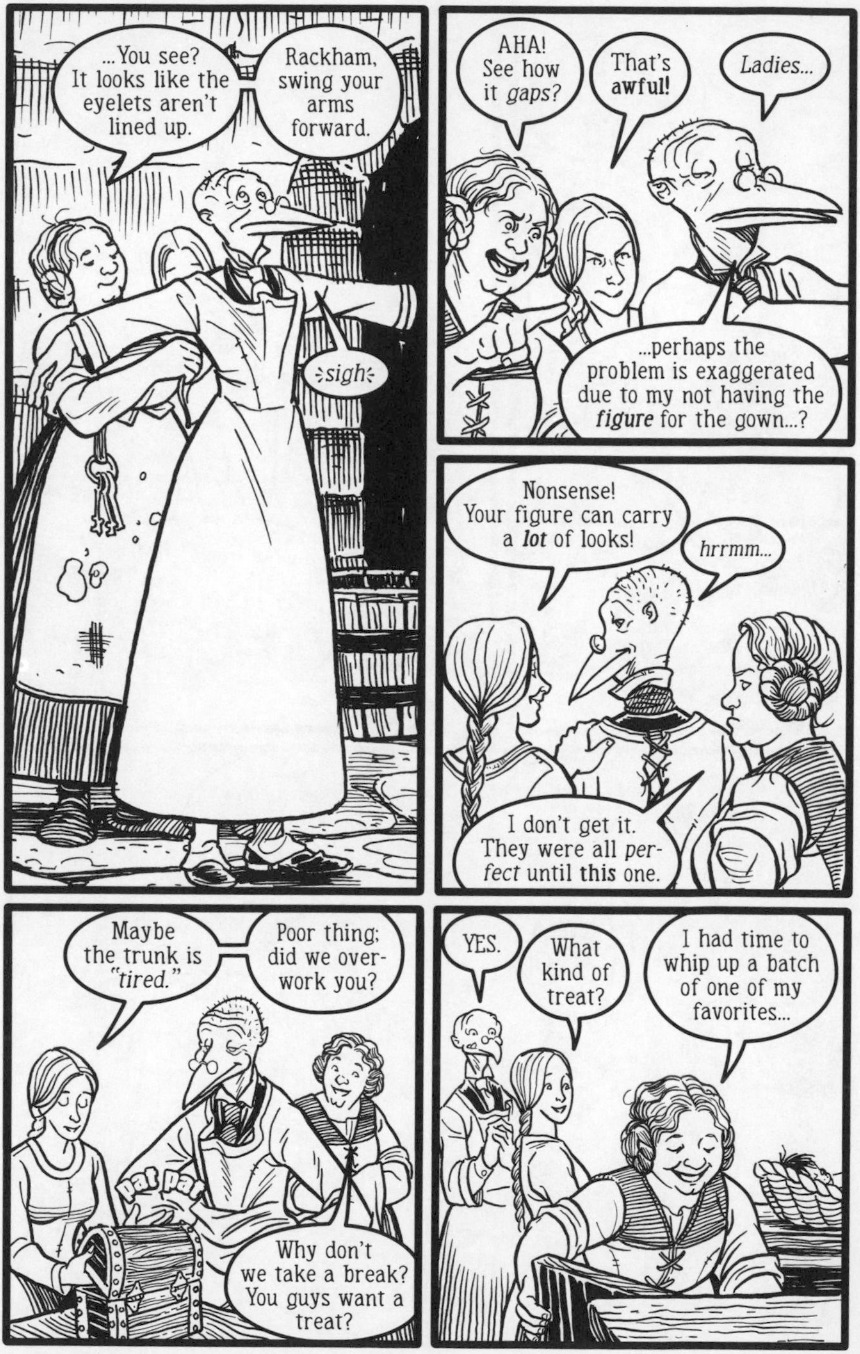
...You see? It looks like the eyelets aren't lined up.
Rackham, swing your arms forward.
sigh
AHA! See how it *gaps*?
That's **awful!**
Ladies...
...perhaps the problem is exaggerated due to my not having the ***figure*** for the gown...?
Nonsense! Your figure can carry a ***lot*** of looks!
hrrmm...
I don't get it. They were all *perfect* until **this** one.
Maybe the trunk is *"tired."*
Poor thing; did we overwork you?
pat pat
Why don't we take a break? You guys want a treat?
YES.
What kind of treat?
I had time to whip up a batch of one of my favorites...

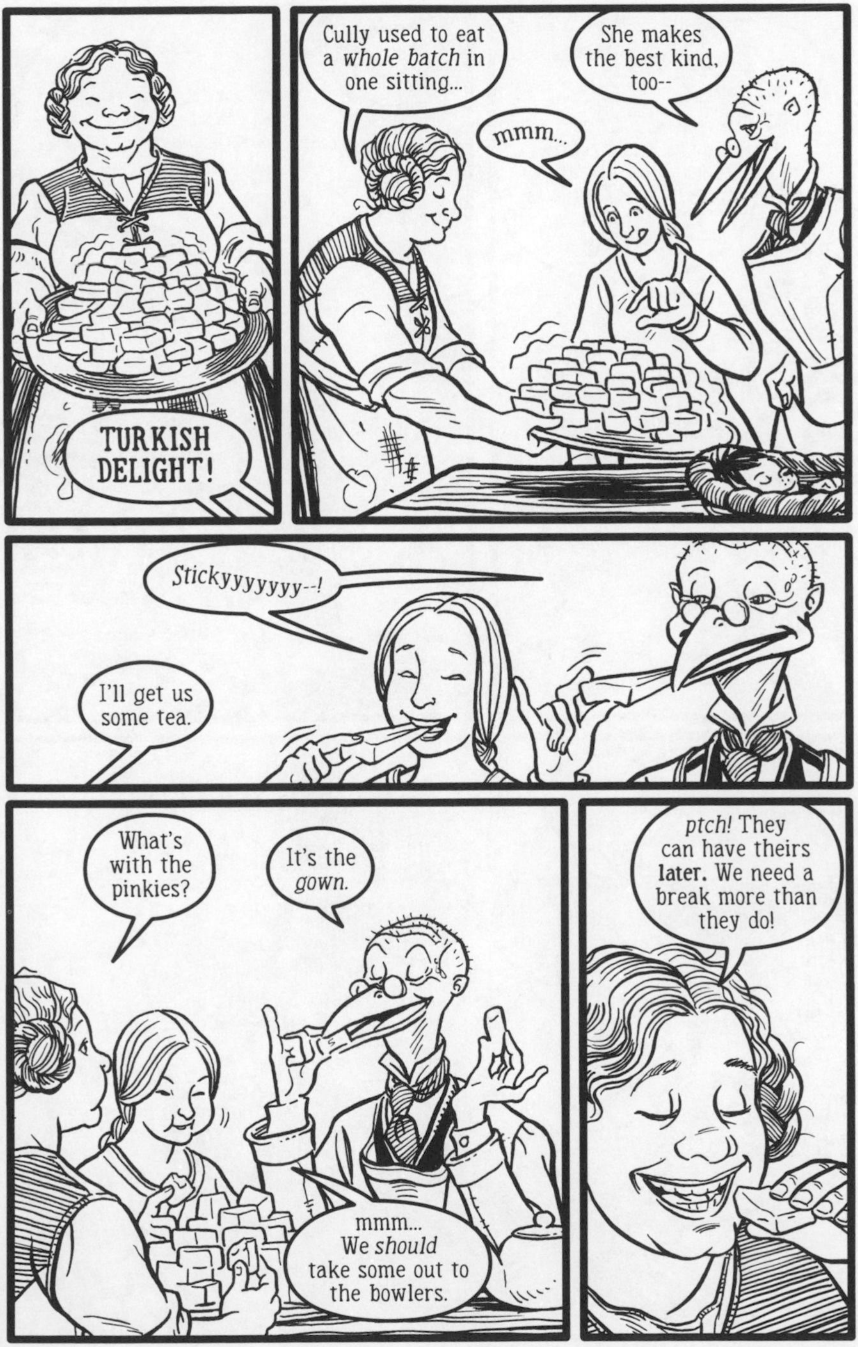
TURKISH DELIGHT!
Cully used to eat a *whole batch* in one sitting...
She makes the best kind, too--
mmm...
Stickyyyyyyy--!
I'll get us some tea.
What's with the pinkies?
It's the *gown.*
mmm... We *should* take some out to the bowlers.
ptch! They can have theirs **later.** We need a break more than they do!

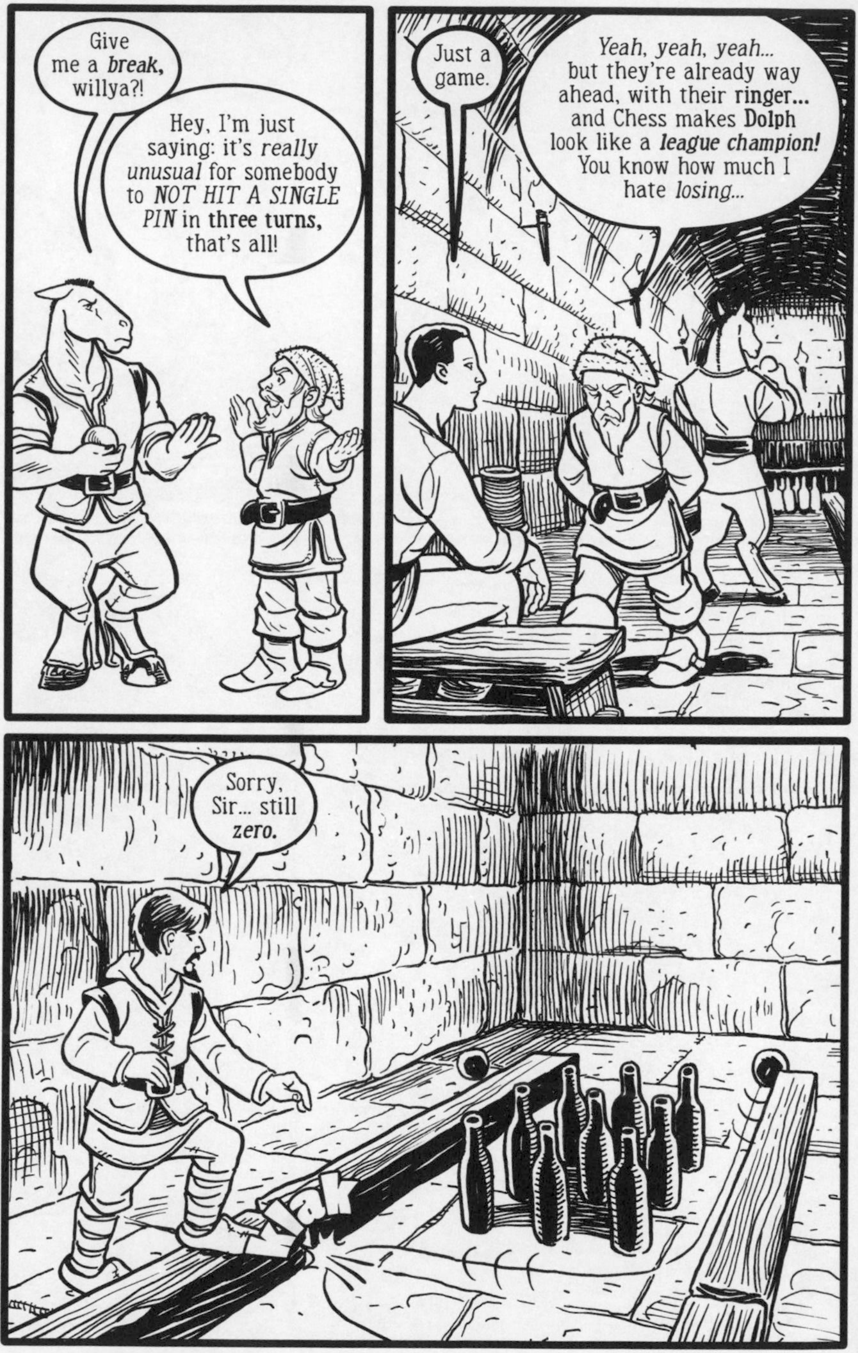
Give me a *break,* willya?!
Hey, I'm just saying: it's *really unusual* for somebody to *NOT HIT A SINGLE PIN* in **three turns,** that's all!
Just a game.
Yeah, yeah, yeah... but they're already way ahead, with their **ringer...** and Chess makes **Dolph** look like a ***league champion!*** You know how much I hate *losing...*
Sorry, Sir... still **zero.**

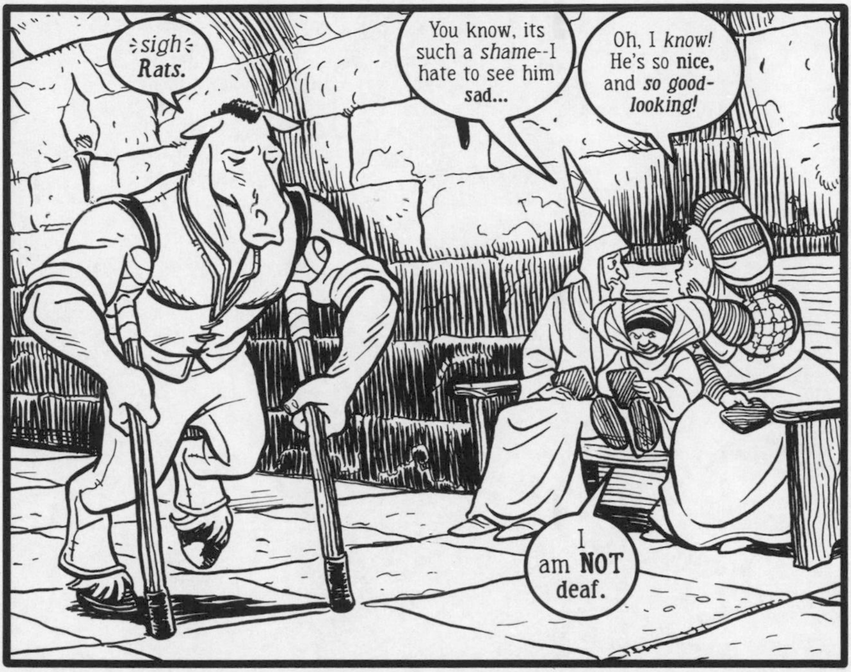
sigh
Rats.
You know, its such a shame--I hate to see him sad...
Oh, I know! He's so nice, and so good-looking!
I am NOT deaf.

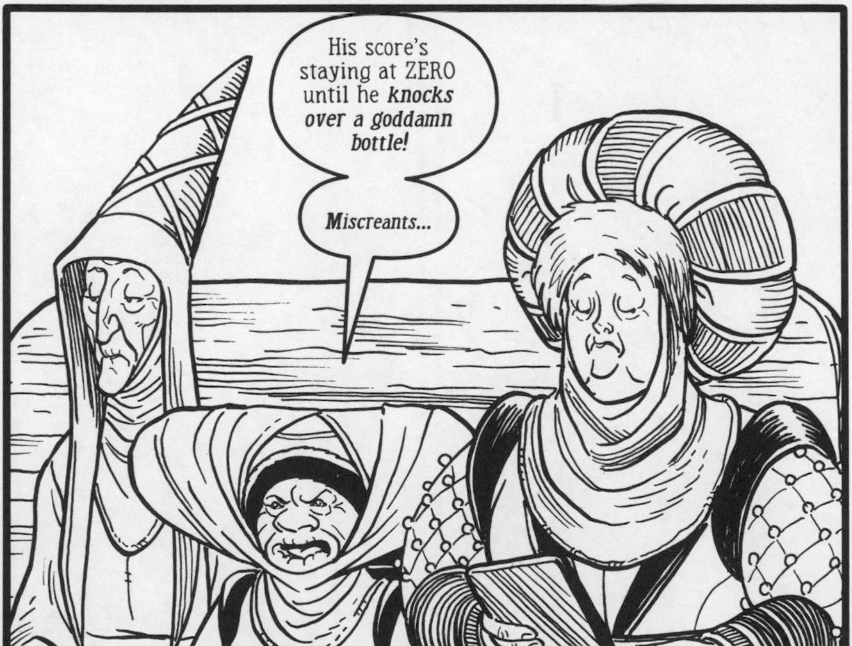
His score's staying at ZERO until he knocks over a goddamn bottle!
Miscreants...

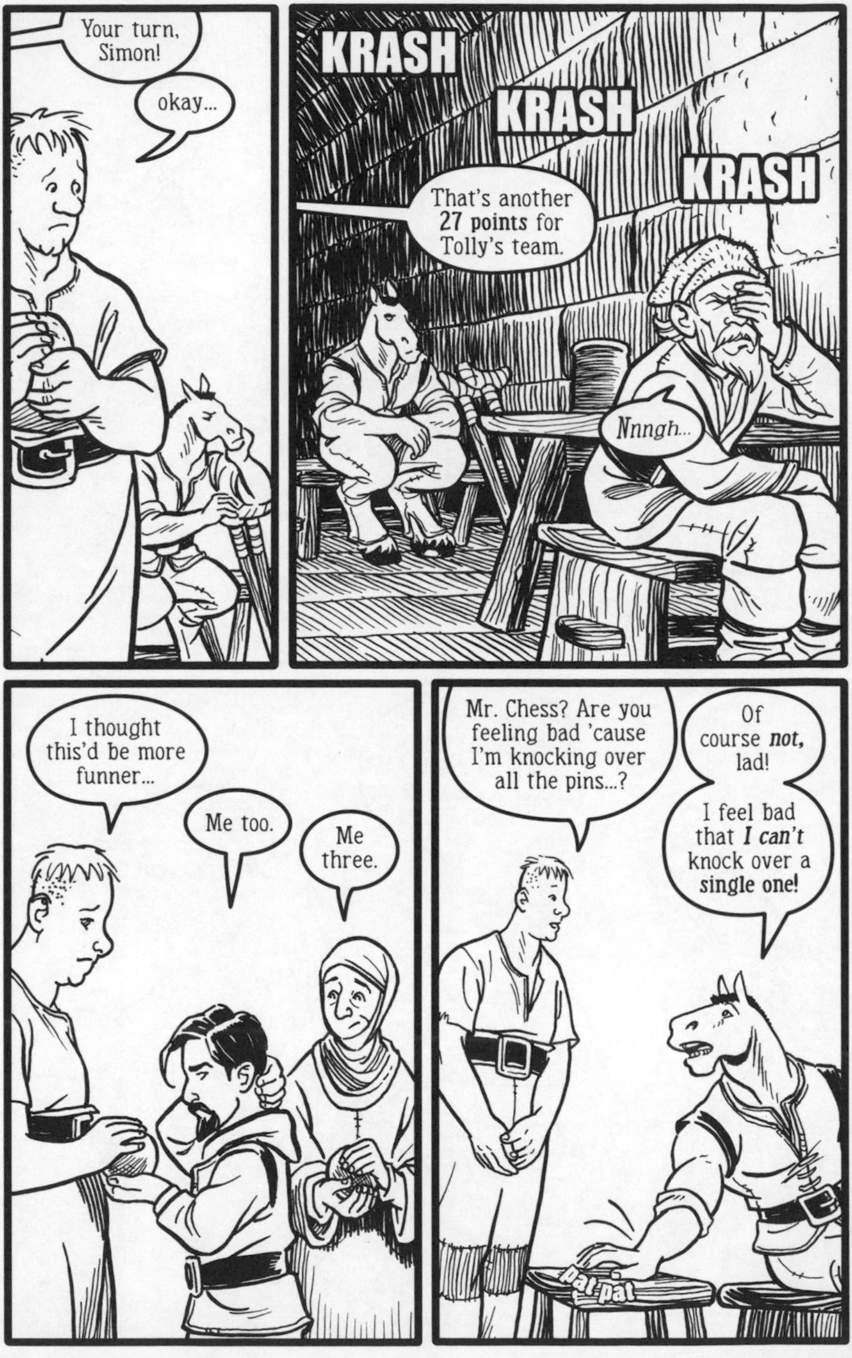
Your turn, Simon!
okay...
KRASH
KRASH
KRASH
That's another **27 points** for Tolly's team.
Nnngh...
I thought this'd be more funner...
Me too.
Me three.
Mr. Chess? Are you feeling bad 'cause I'm knocking over all the pins...?
Of course ***not,*** lad!
I feel bad that ***I can't*** knock over a **single one!**
pat pat

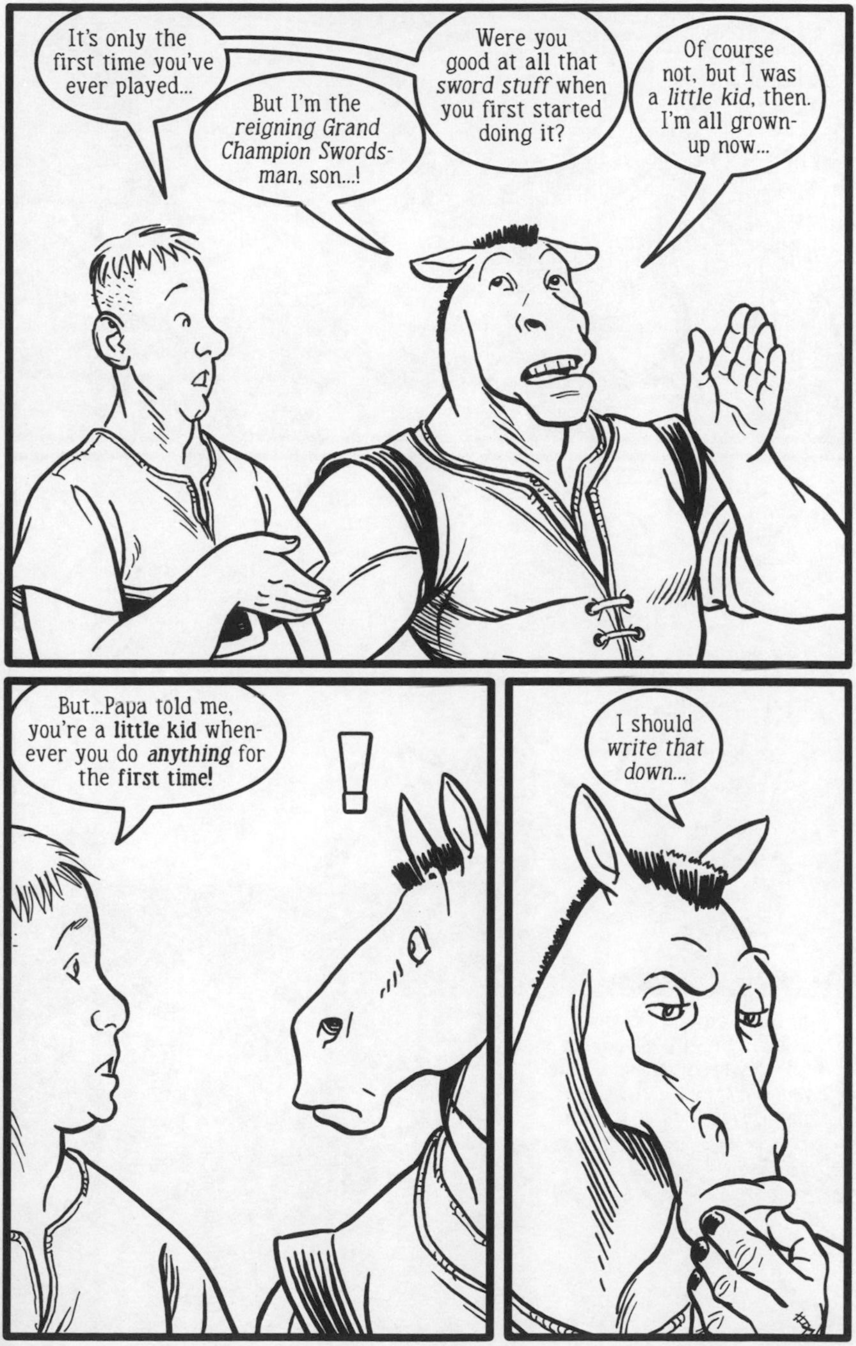
It's only the first time you've ever played...
But I'm the *reigning Grand Champion Swordsman*, son...!
Were you good at all that *sword stuff* when you first started doing it?
Of course not, but I was a *little kid*, then. I'm all grown-up now...
But...Papa told me, you're a **little kid** whenever you do *anything* for the **first time**!
!
I should *write that down*...

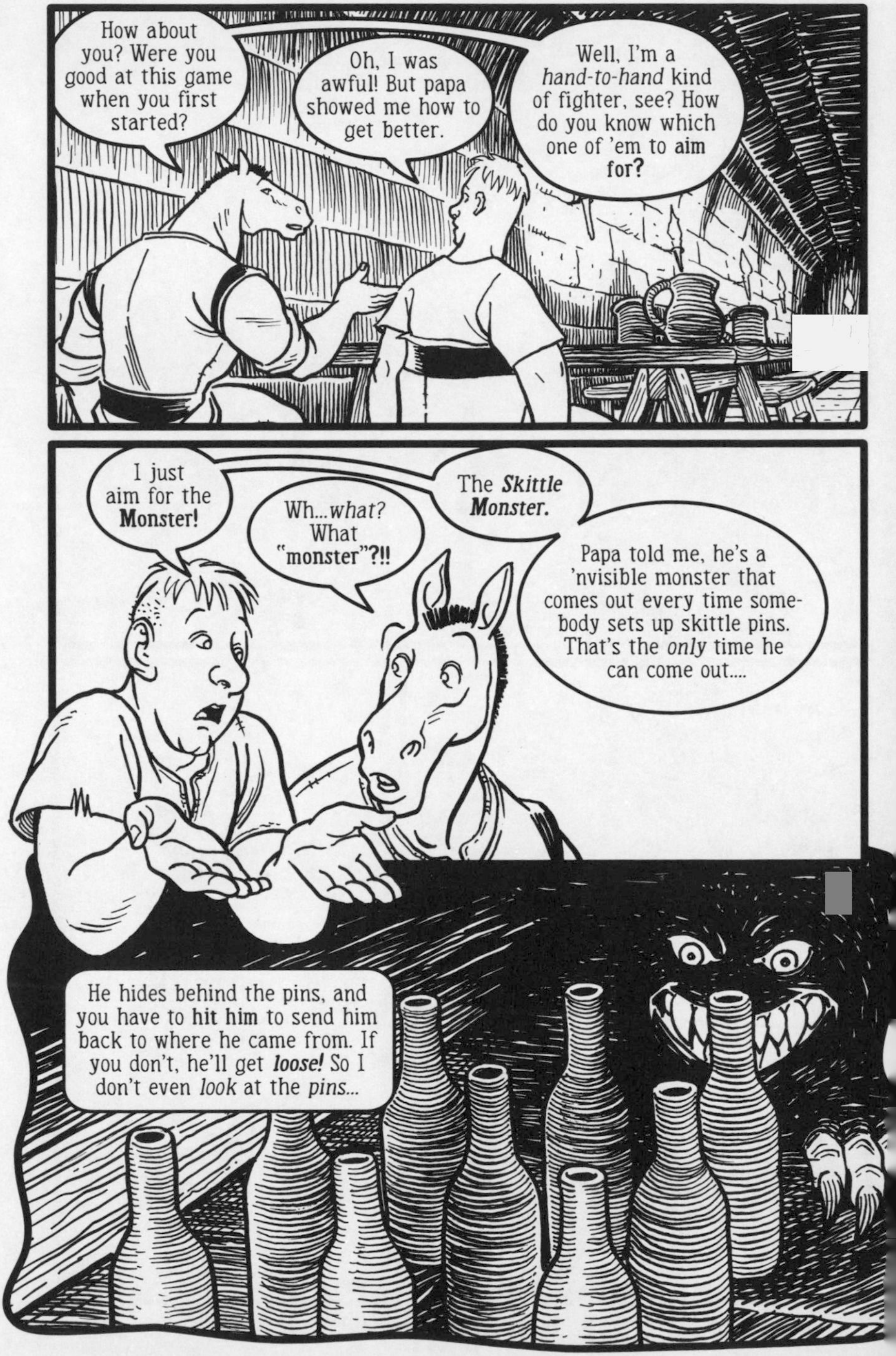
How about you? Were you good at this game when you first started?
Oh, I was awful! But papa showed me how to get better.
Well, I'm a *hand-to-hand* kind of fighter, see? How do you know which one of 'em to **aim for?**
I just aim for the **Monster!**
Wh...*what?* What "**monster**"?!!
The ***Skittle Monster.***
Papa told me, he's a 'nvisible monster that comes out every time somebody sets up skittle pins. That's the *only* time he can come out....
He hides behind the pins, and you have to **hit him** to send him back to where he came from. If you don't, he'll get ***loose!*** So I don't even *look* at the *pins*...

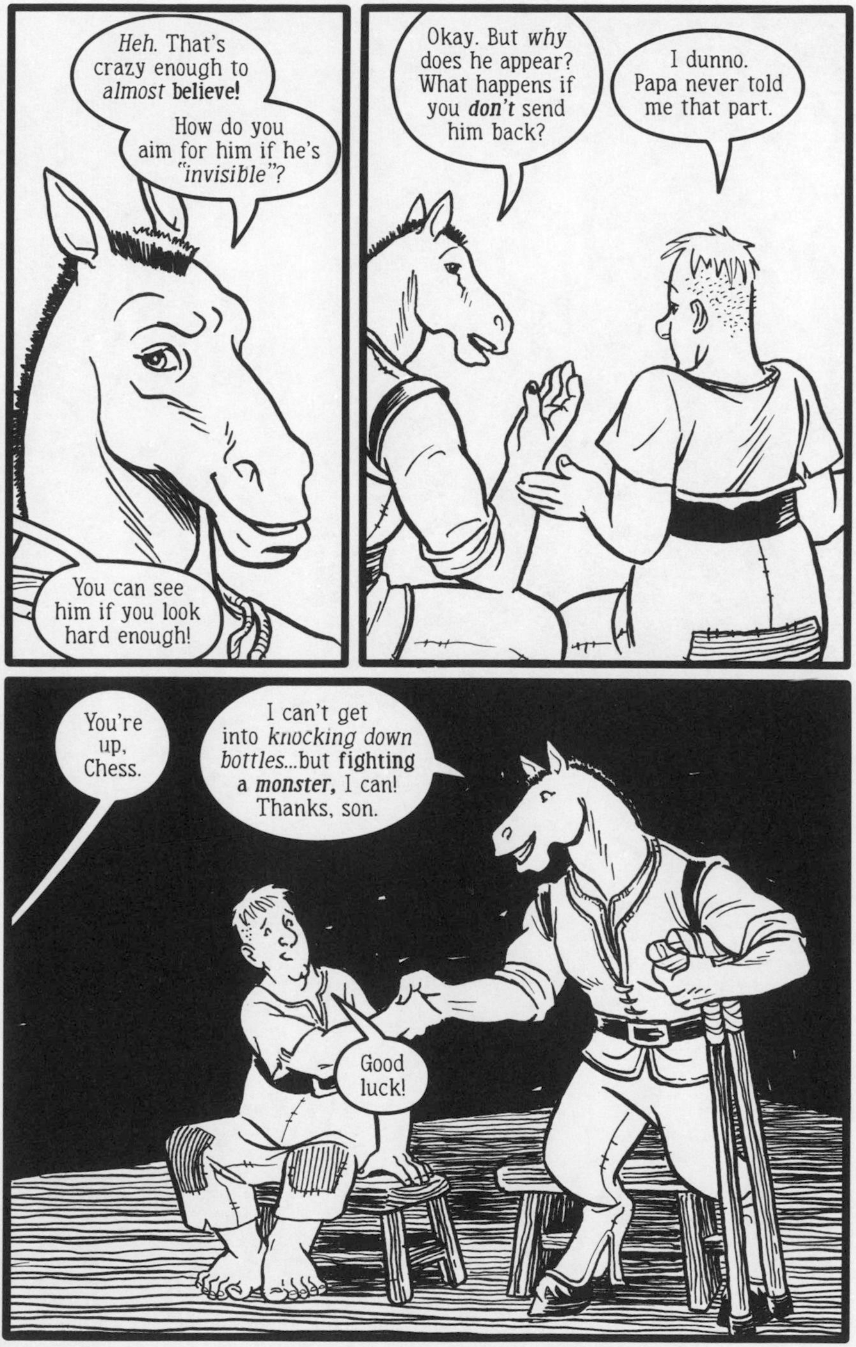
Heh. That's crazy enough to *almost* **believe!**
How do you aim for him if he's "*invisible*"?
You can see him if you look hard enough!
Okay. But *why* does he appear? What happens if you ***don't*** send him back?
I dunno. Papa never told me that part.
You're up, Chess.
I can't get into *knocking down bottles*...but **fighting a *monster*,** I can! Thanks, son.
Good luck!

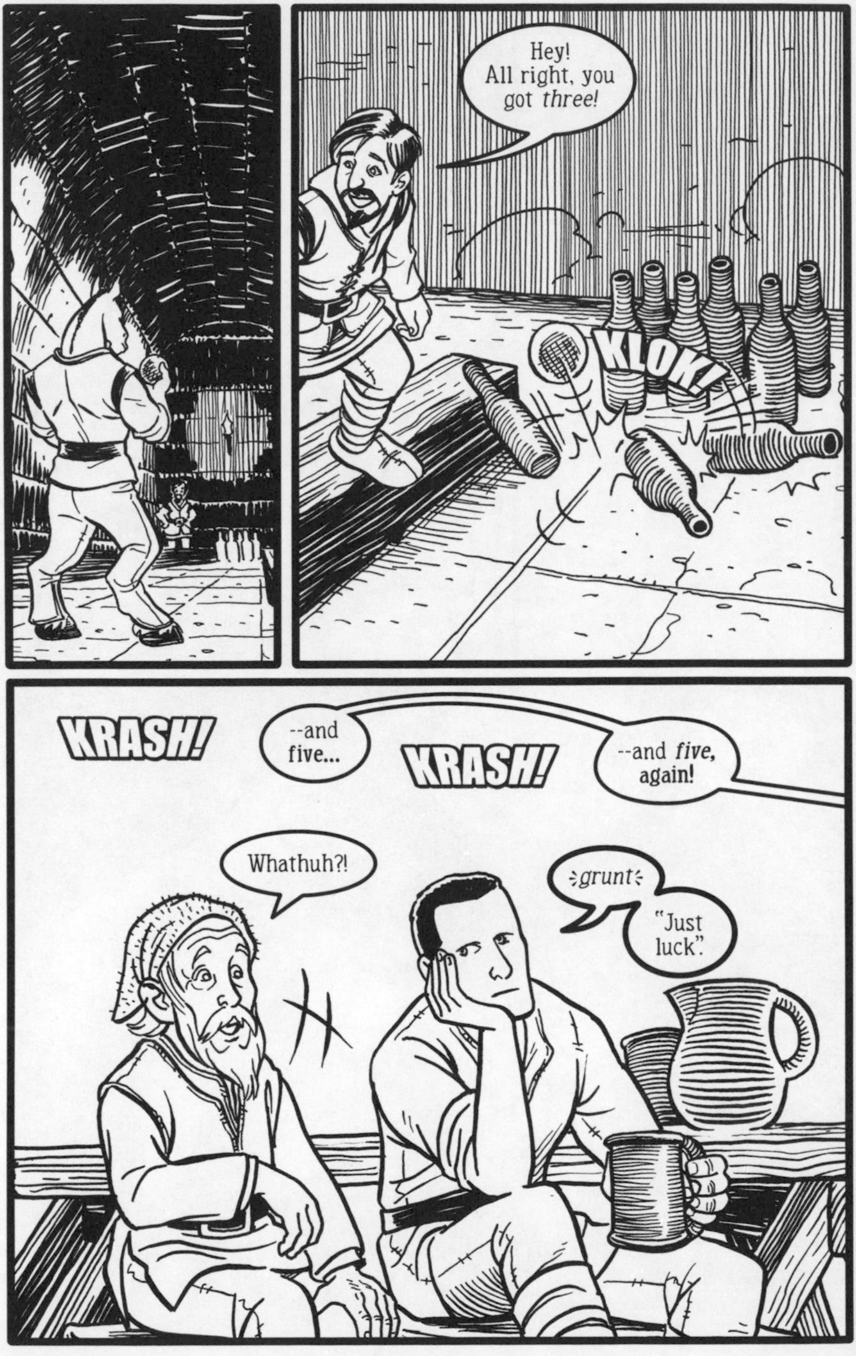
Hey!
All right, you got *three!*
KLOK!
KRASH!
--and five...
KRASH!
--and *five,* again!
Whathuh?!
grunt
"Just luck".

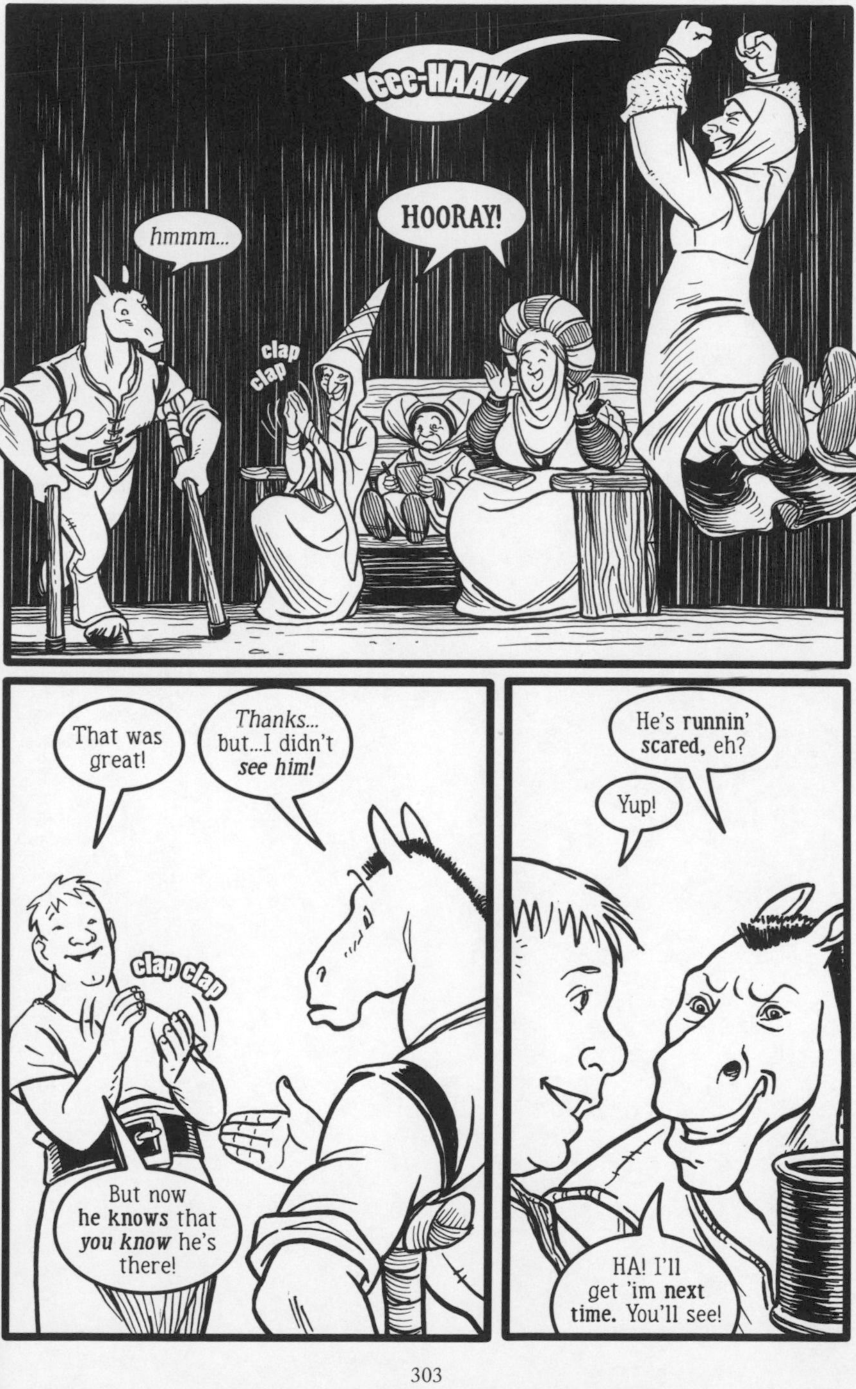
Yeee-HAAW!
hmmm...
HOORAY!
clap clap
That was great!
Thanks... but...I didn't *see him!*
clap clap
But now **he knows** that *you know* he's there!
He's **runnin' scared,** eh?
Yup!
HA! I'll get 'im **next time.** You'll see!

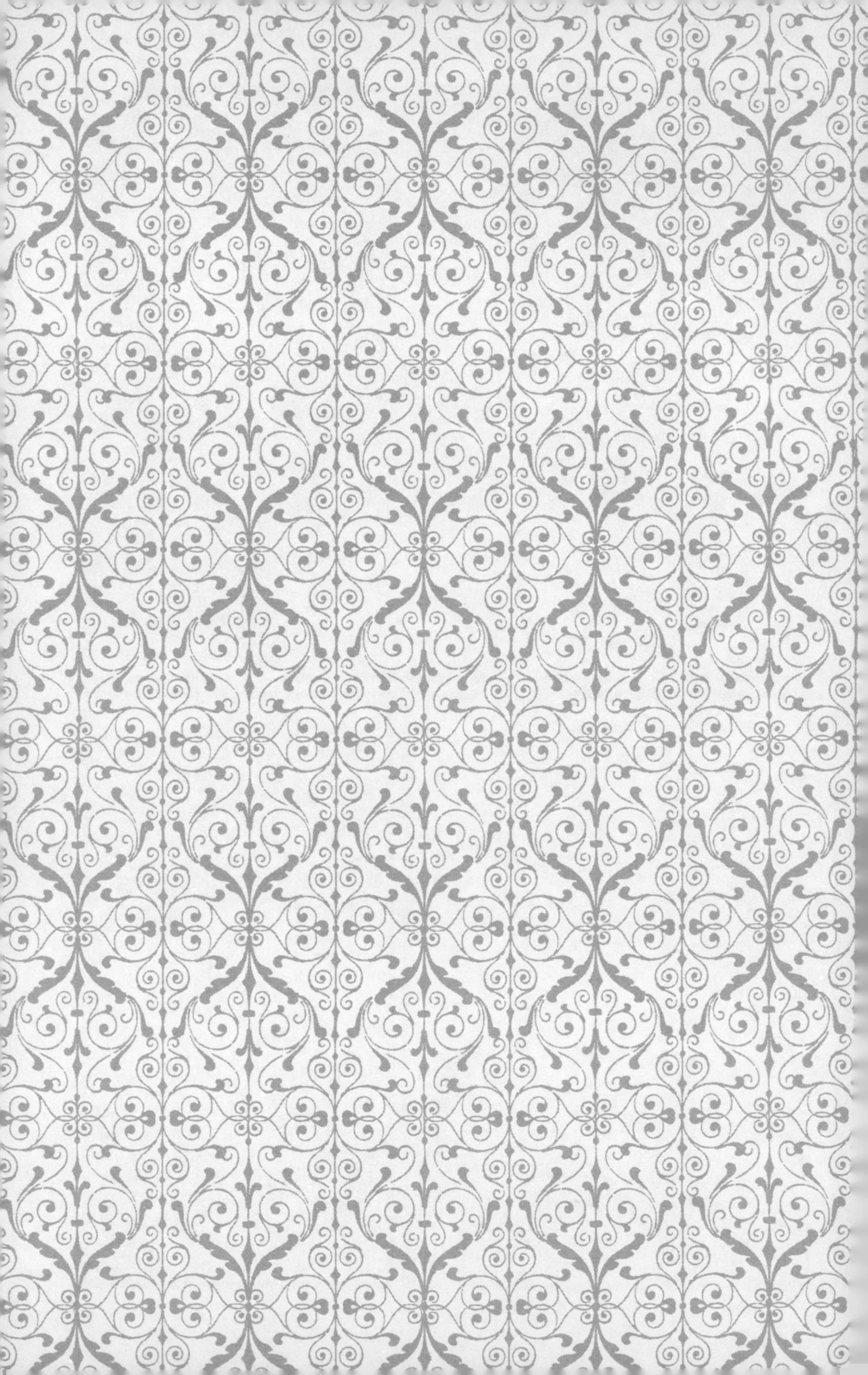

Chapter 12.

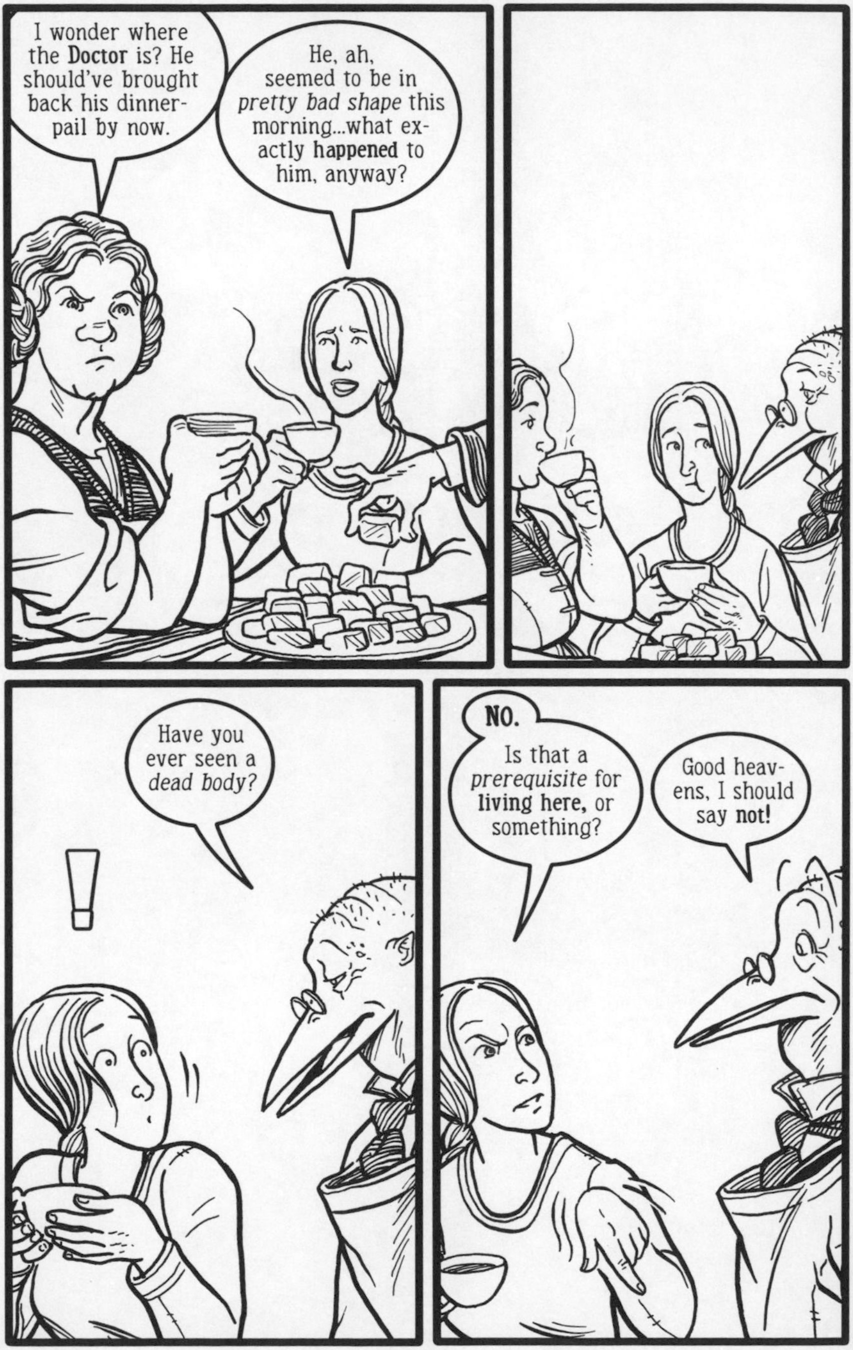
I wonder where the **Doctor** is? He should've brought back his dinner-pail by now.
He, ah, seemed to be in *pretty bad shape* this morning...what exactly **happened** to him, anyway?
Have you ever seen a *dead body*?
!
NO.
Is that a *prerequisite* for **living here,** or something?
Good heavens, I should say **not!**

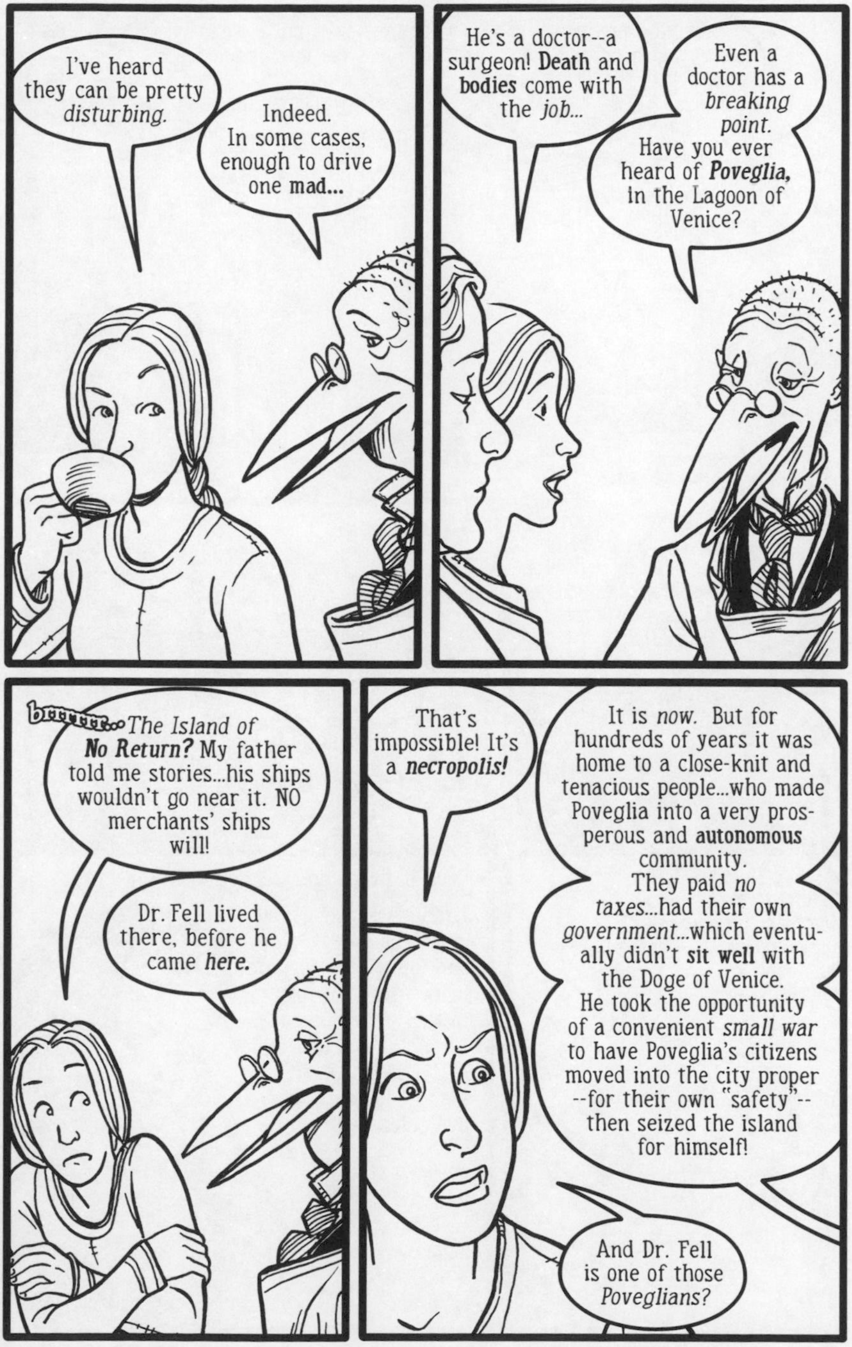
I've heard they can be pretty *disturbing.*
Indeed. In some cases, enough to drive one **mad...**
He's a doctor--a surgeon! **Death** and **bodies** come with the *job...*
Even a doctor has a *breaking point.* Have you ever heard of ***Poveglia,*** in the Lagoon of Venice?
brrrrrr...*The Island of* ***No Return?*** My father told me stories...his ships wouldn't go near it. NO merchants' ships will!
Dr. Fell lived there, before he came ***here.***
That's impossible! It's a ***necropolis!***
It is *now.* But for hundreds of years it was home to a close-knit and tenacious people...who made Poveglia into a very prosperous and **autonomous** community. They paid *no taxes*...had their own *government*...which eventually didn't **sit well** with the Doge of Venice. He took the opportunity of a convenient *small war* to have Poveglia's citizens moved into the city proper --for their own "safety"-- then seized the island for himself!
And Dr. Fell is one of those *Poveglians?*

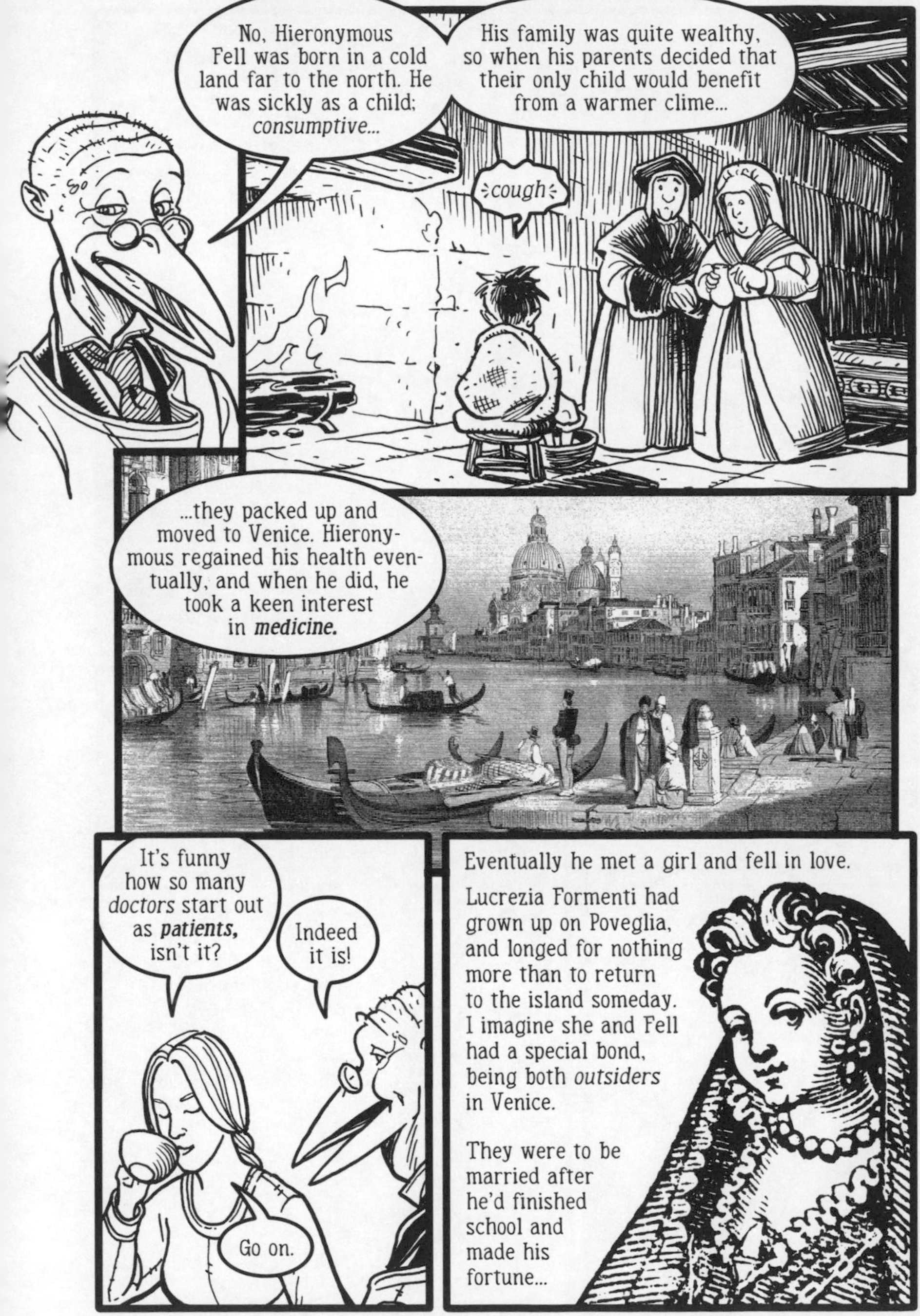
No, Hieronymous Fell was born in a cold land far to the north. He was sickly as a child; *consumptive...*
His family was quite wealthy, so when his parents decided that their only child would benefit from a warmer clime...
cough
...they packed up and moved to Venice. Hieronymous regained his health eventually, and when he did, he took a keen interest in ***medicine.***
It's funny how so many *doctors* start out as ***patients,*** isn't it?
Indeed it is!
Go on.
Eventually he met a girl and fell in love.
Lucrezia Formenti had grown up on Poveglia, and longed for nothing more than to return to the island someday. I imagine she and Fell had a special bond, being both *outsiders* in Venice.
They were to be married after he'd finished school and made his fortune...

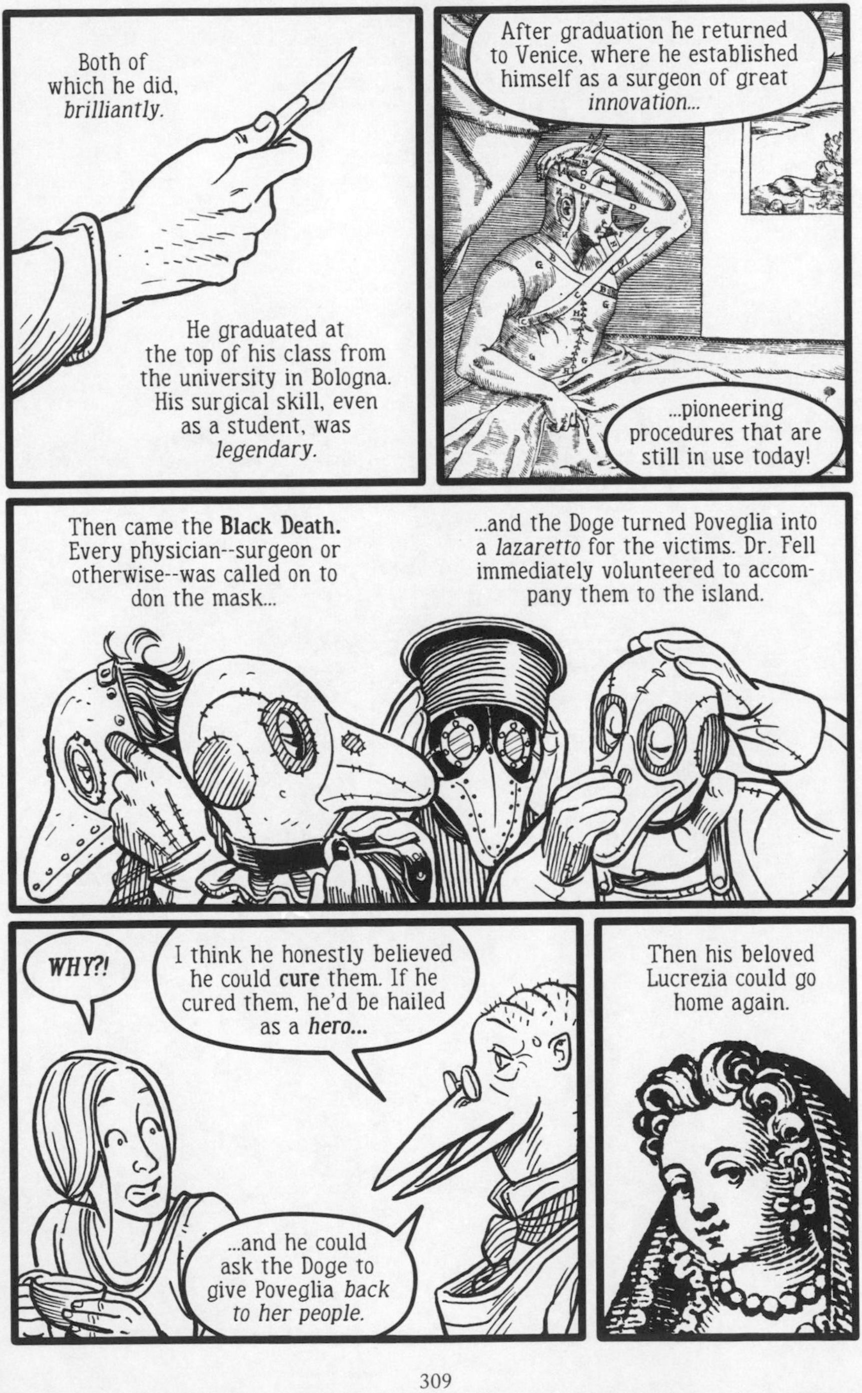
Both of which he did, *brilliantly.*
He graduated at the top of his class from the university in Bologna. His surgical skill, even as a student, was *legendary.*
After graduation he returned to Venice, where he established himself as a surgeon of great *innovation...*
...pioneering procedures that are still in use today!
Then came the **Black Death.** Every physician--surgeon or otherwise--was called on to don the mask...
...and the Doge turned Poveglia into a *lazaretto* for the victims. Dr. Fell immediately volunteered to accompany them to the island.
WHY?!
I think he honestly believed he could **cure** them. If he cured them, he'd be hailed as a ***hero...***
...and he could ask the Doge to give Poveglia *back to her people.*
Then his beloved Lucrezia could go home again.

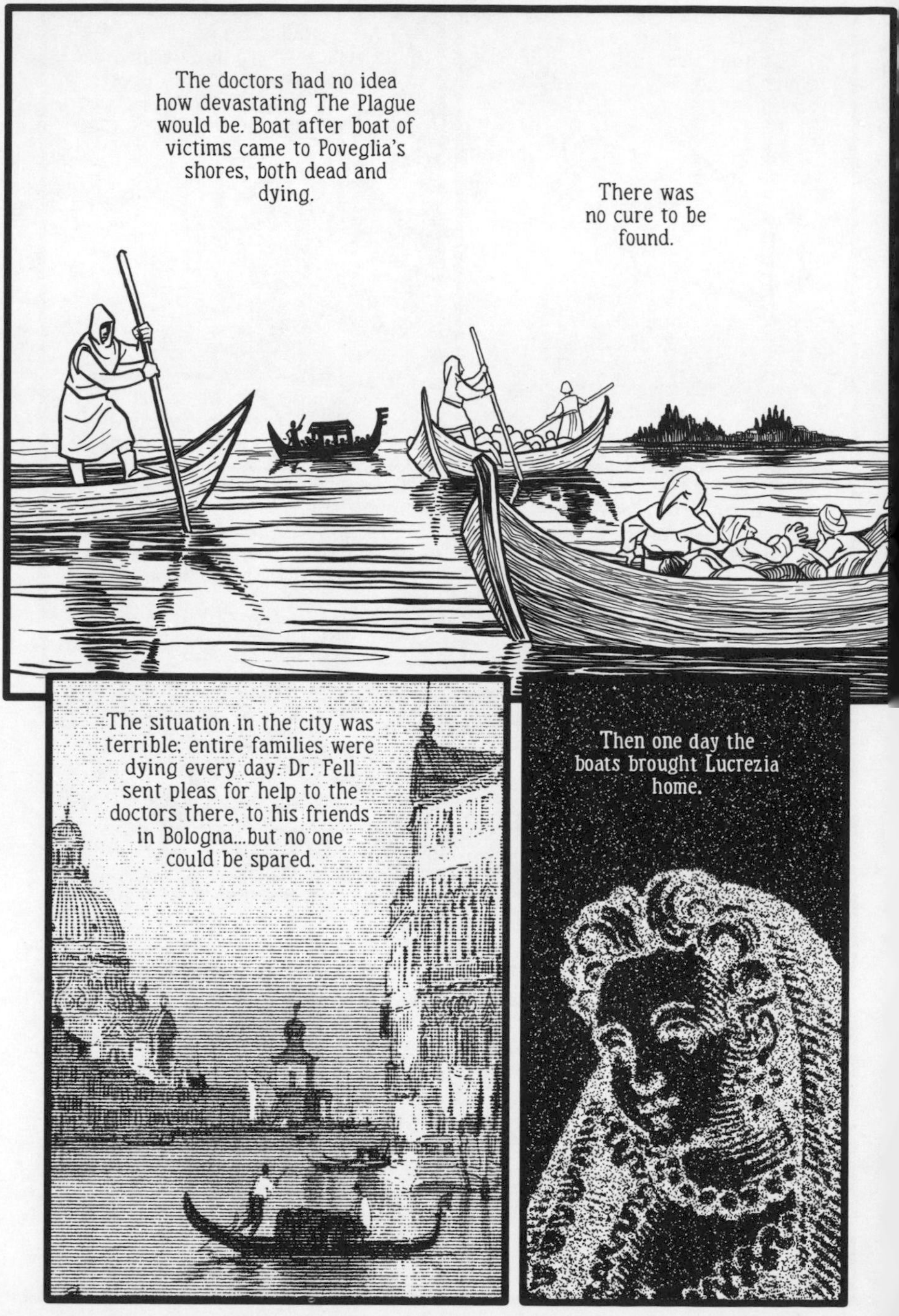
The doctors had no idea how devastating The Plague would be. Boat after boat of victims came to Poveglia's shores, both dead and dying.
There was no cure to be found.
The situation in the city was terrible; entire families were dying every day. Dr. Fell sent pleas for help to the doctors there, to his friends in Bologna...but no one could be spared.
Then one day the boats brought Lucrezia home.

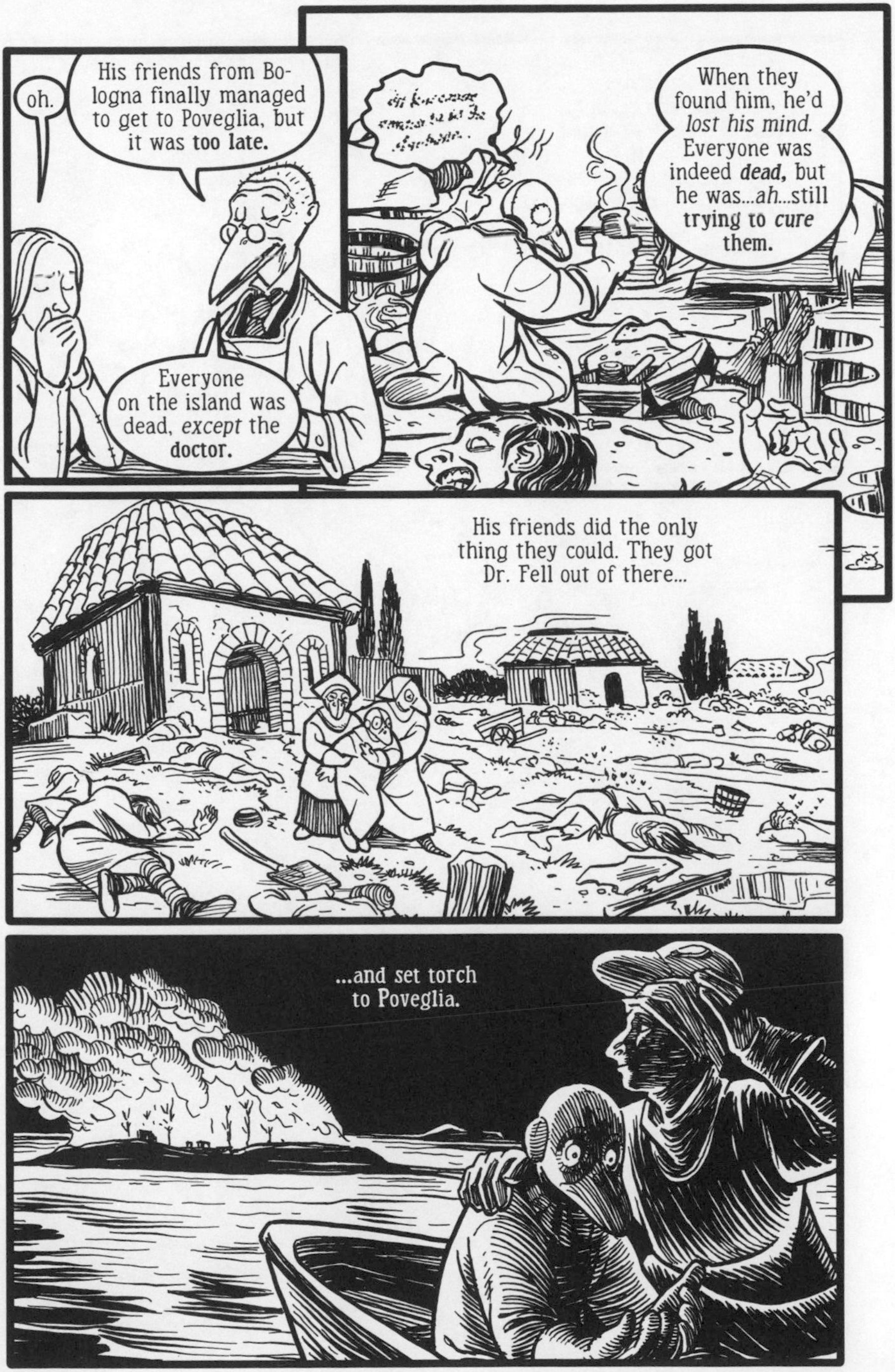
oh.
His friends from Bologna finally managed to get to Poveglia, but it was **too late.**
Everyone on the island was dead, *except* the **doctor.**
When they found him, he'd *lost his mind.* Everyone was indeed ***dead,*** but he was...*ah*...still **trying to *cure* them.**
His friends did the only thing they could. They got Dr. Fell out of there...
...and set torch to Poveglia.

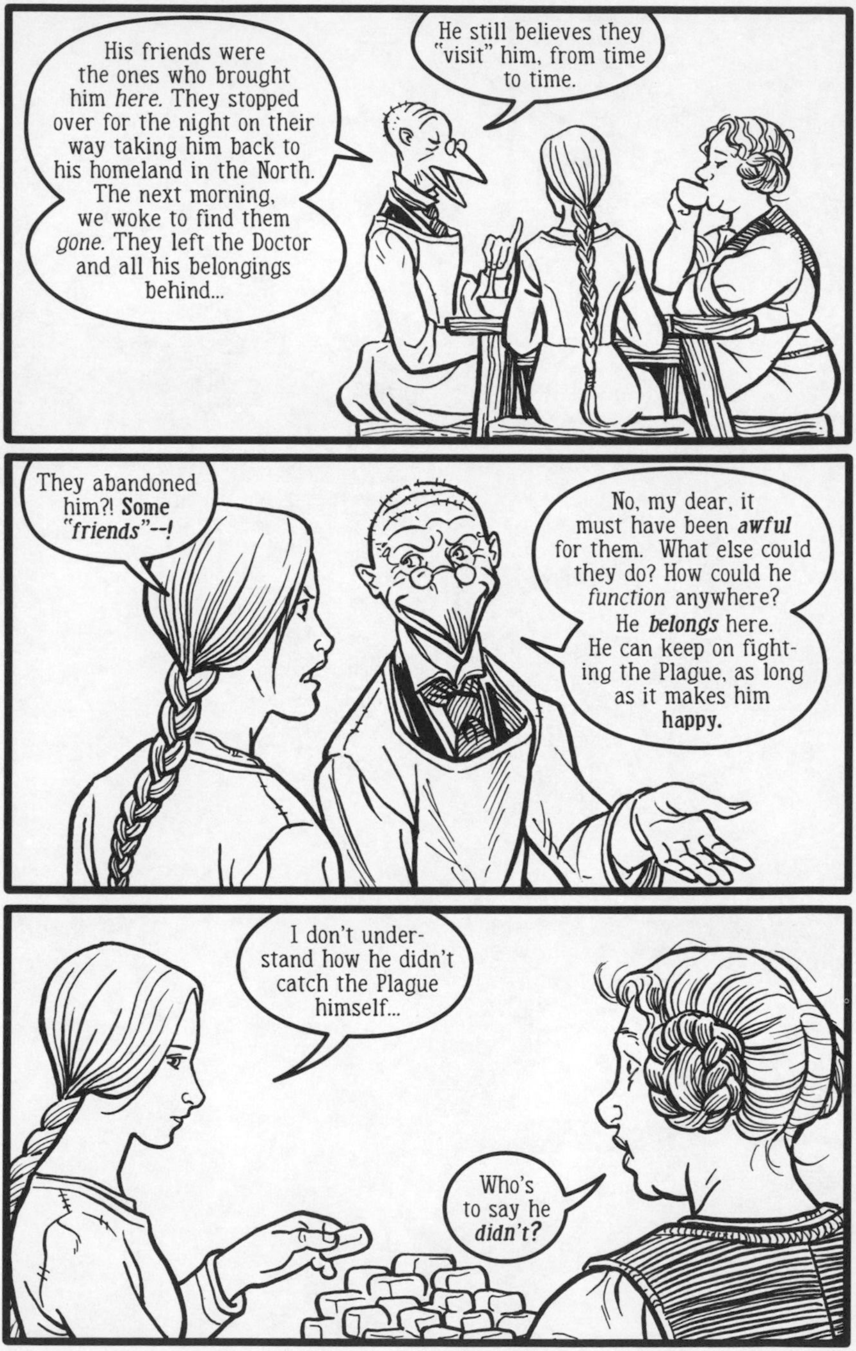
His friends were the ones who brought him *here.* They stopped over for the night on their way taking him back to his homeland in the North. The next morning, we woke to find them *gone.* They left the Doctor and all his belongings behind...
He still believes they "visit" him, from time to time.
They abandoned him?! **Some *"friends"*--!**
No, my dear, it must have been ***awful*** for them. What else could they do? How could he *function* anywhere? He ***belongs*** here. He can keep on fighting the Plague, as long as it makes him **happy.**
I don't understand how he didn't catch the Plague himself...
Who's to say he ***didn't?***

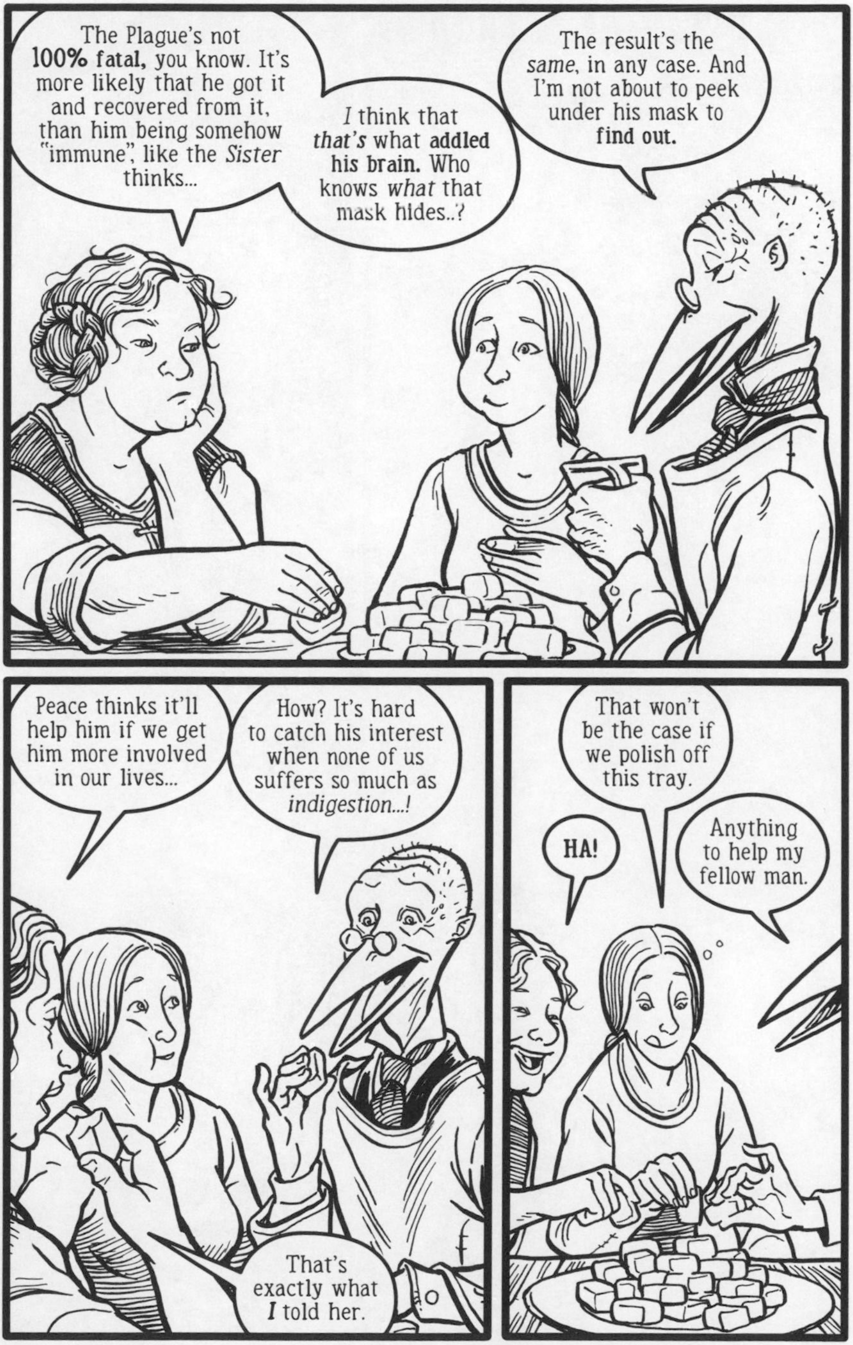
The Plague's not **100% fatal,** you know. It's more likely that he got it and recovered from it, than him being somehow "immune", like the *Sister* thinks...
I think that *that's* what **addled his brain.** Who knows *what* that mask hides..?
The result's the *same*, in any case. And I'm not about to peek under his mask to **find out.**
Peace thinks it'll help him if we get him more involved in our lives...
How? It's hard to catch his interest when none of us suffers so much as *indigestion...!*
That's exactly what ***I*** told her.
That won't be the case if we polish off this tray.
HA!
Anything to help my fellow man.

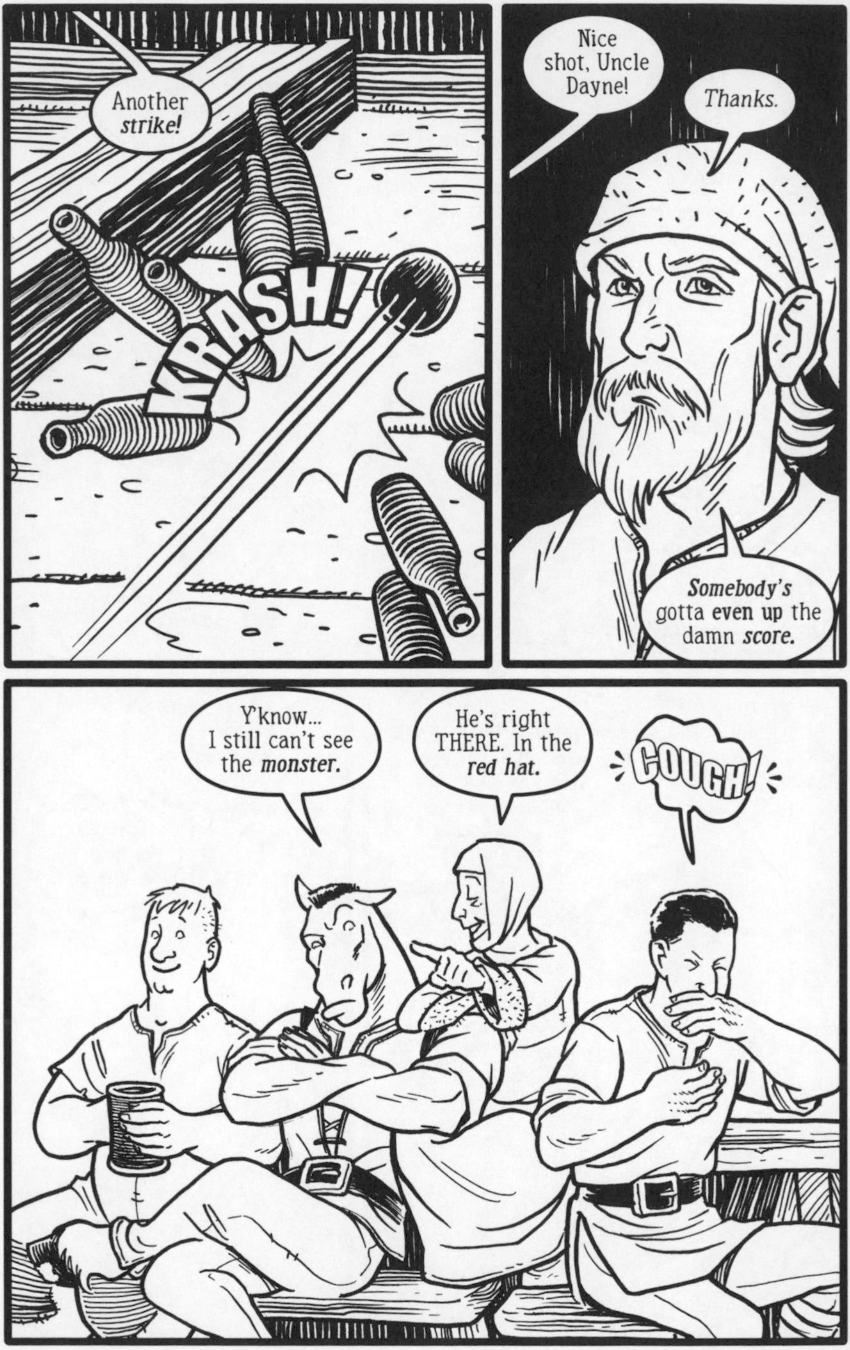
Another strike!
KRASH!
Nice shot, Uncle Dayne!
Thanks.
Somebody's gotta even up the damn score.
Y'know... I still can't see the monster.
He's right THERE. In the red hat.
COUGH!

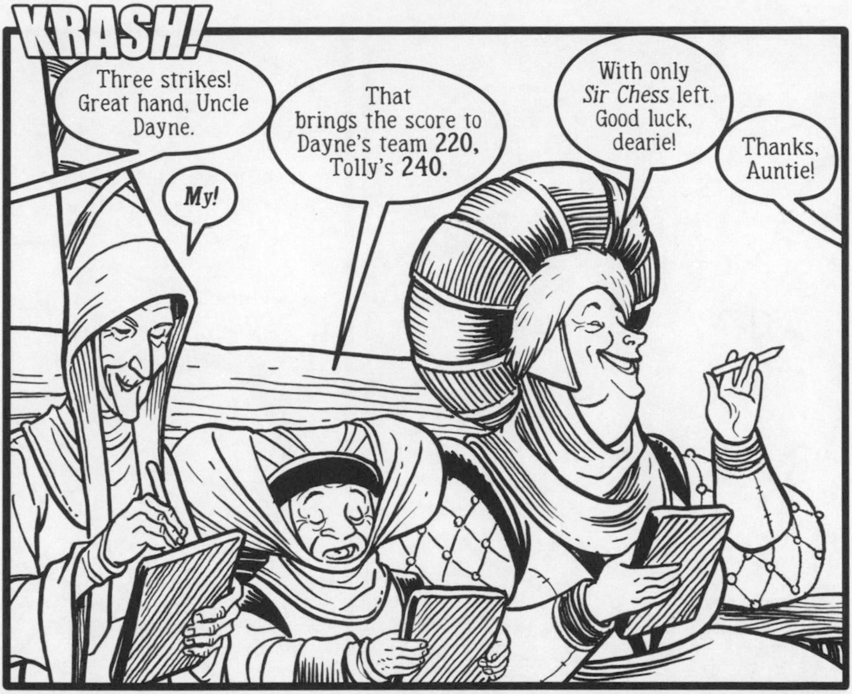
KRASH!
Three strikes! Great hand, Uncle Dayne.
My!
That brings the score to Dayne's team **220,** Tolly's **240.**
With only *Sir Chess* left. Good luck, dearie!
Thanks, Auntie!

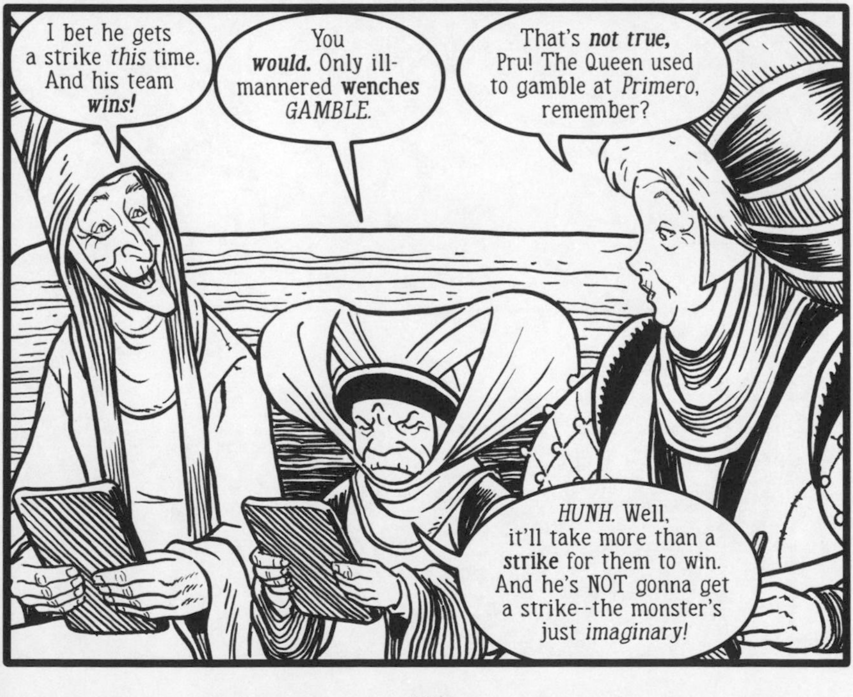
I bet he gets a strike *this* time. And his team ***wins!***
You ***would.*** Only ill-mannered **wenches** *GAMBLE.*
That's ***not true,*** Pru! The Queen used to gamble at *Primero,* remember?
HUNH. Well, it'll take more than a **strike** for them to win. And he's NOT gonna get a strike--the monster's just *imaginary!*

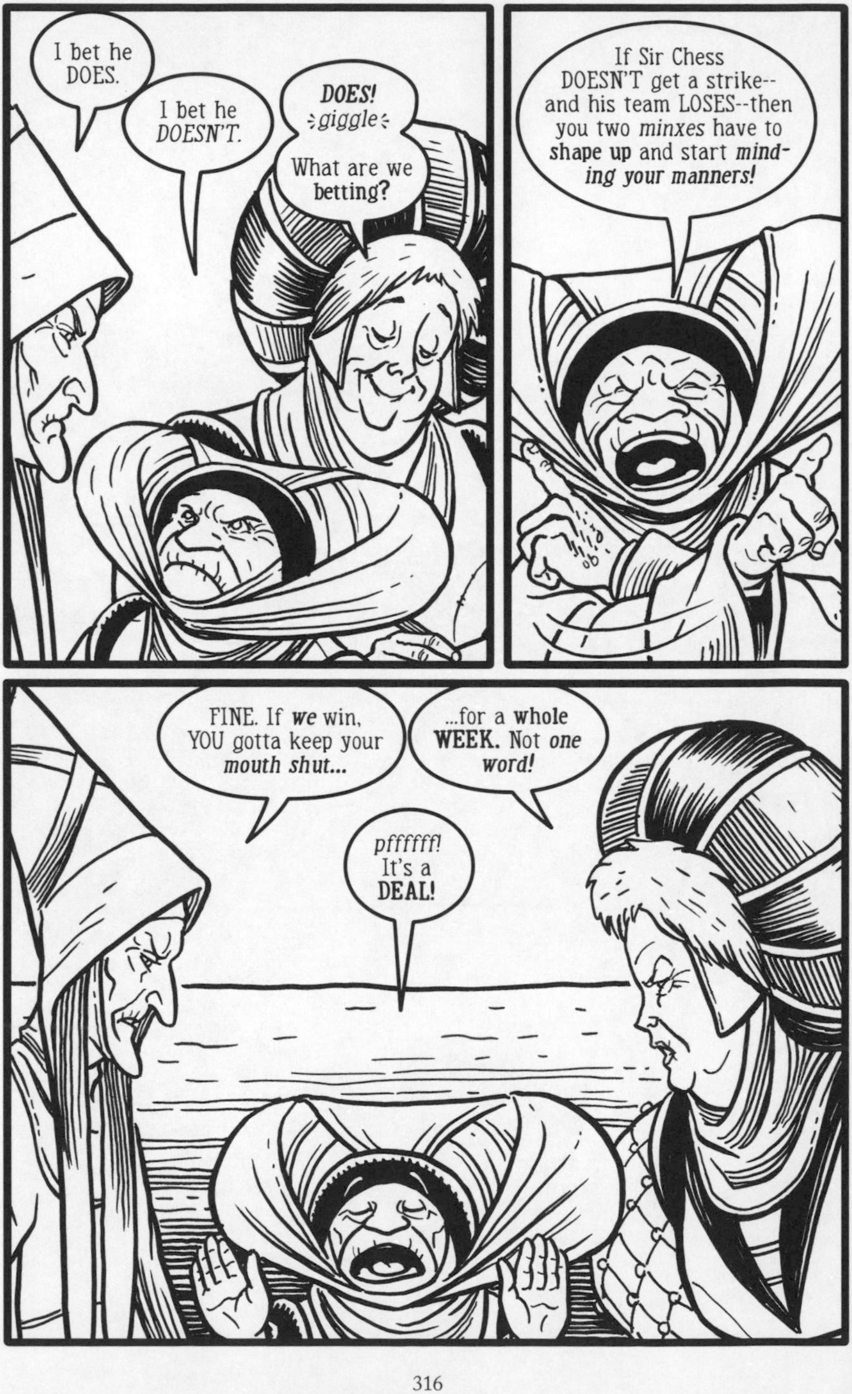
I bet he DOES.
I bet he *DOESN'T.*
DOES! *giggle*
What are we **betting?**
If Sir Chess DOESN'T get a strike--and his team LOSES--then you two *minxes* have to **shape up** and start ***minding your manners!***
FINE. If ***we*** win, YOU gotta keep your ***mouth shut...***
...for a **whole WEEK.** Not ***one word!***
pffffff! It's a **DEAL!**

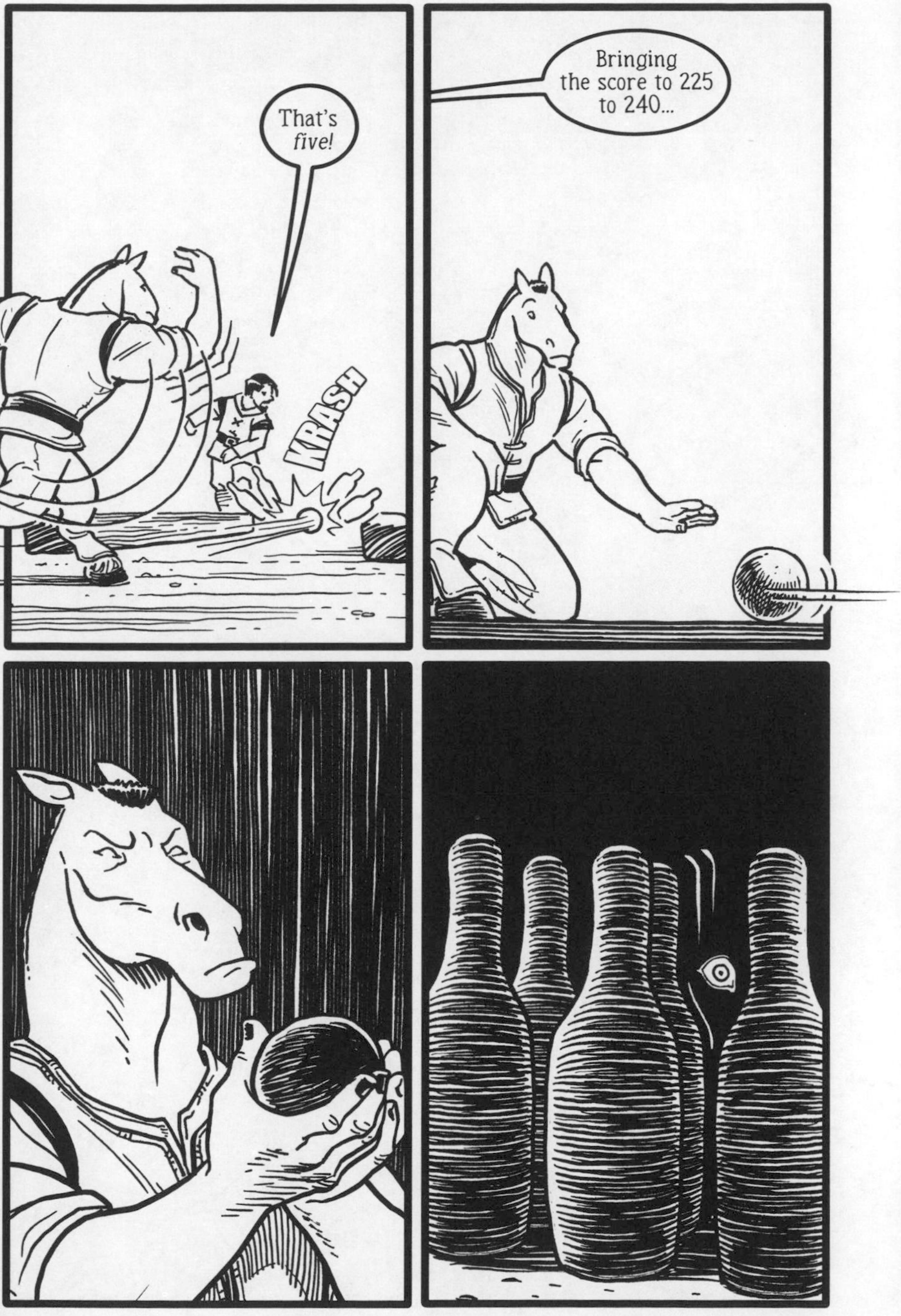
That's *five!*
KRASH
Bringing the score to 225 to 240...

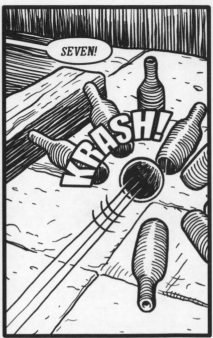

SEVEN!

KRASH!

Something *moved!* I saw it!

rub rub

I am NOT *blind.*

WHAT?!! My sleeve was caught!

232 to 240! If Chess gets a *strike,* his team *wins.*

And so do *we!* *giggle*

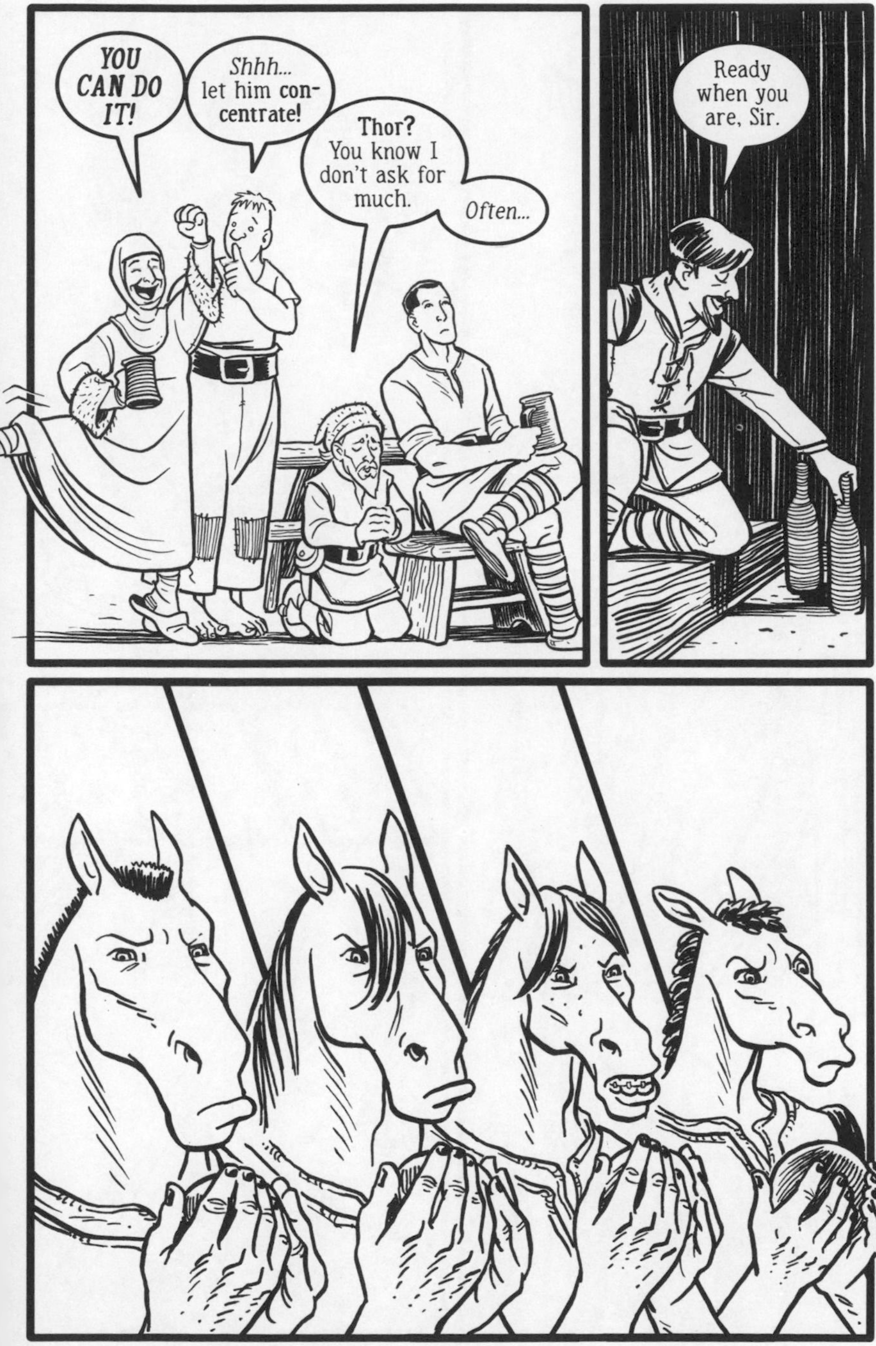
YOU CAN DO IT!
Shhh... let him concentrate!
Thor? You know I don't ask for much.
Often...
Ready when you are, Sir.

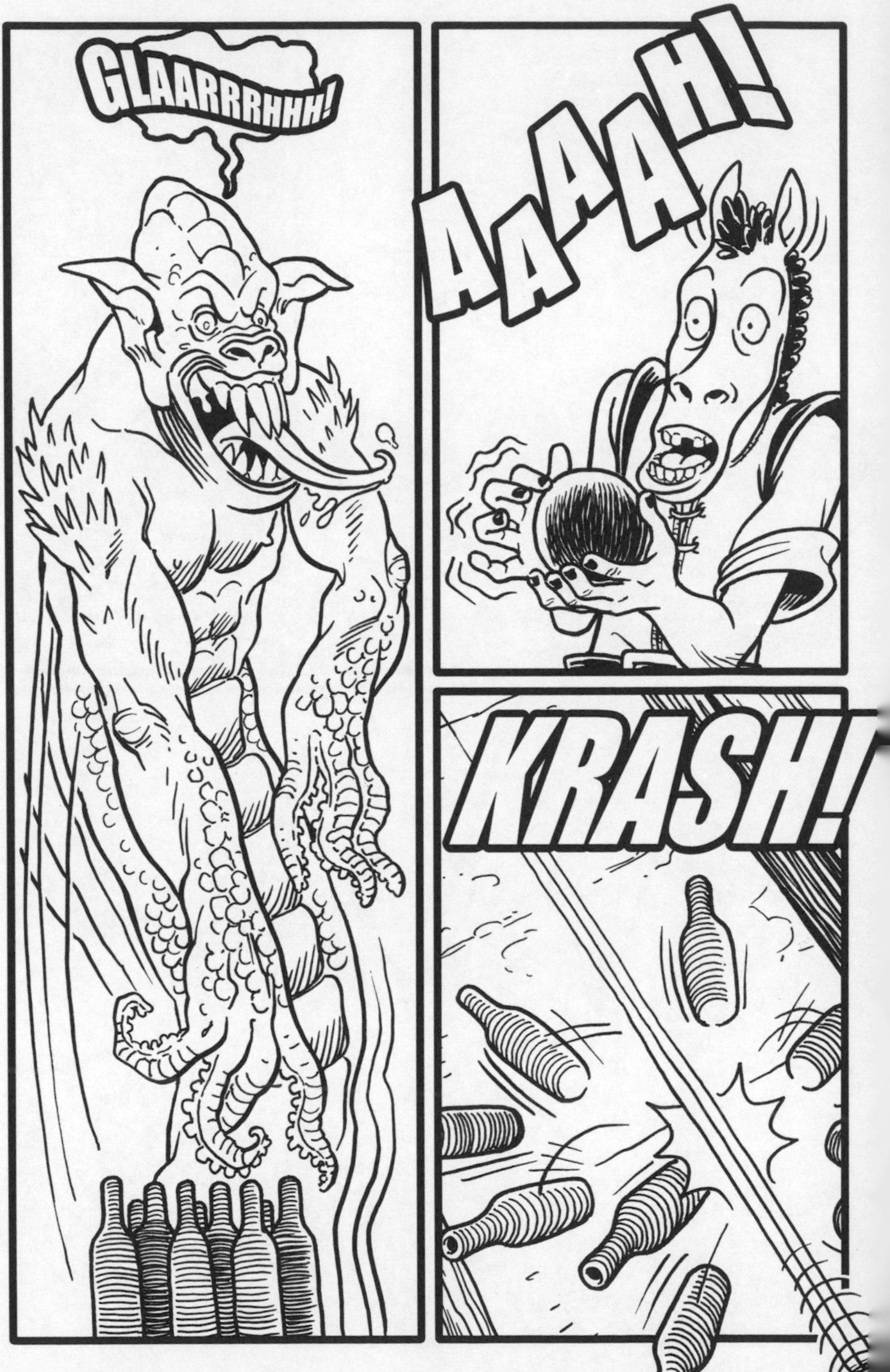
GLAARRRHHH!
AAAAH!
KRASH!

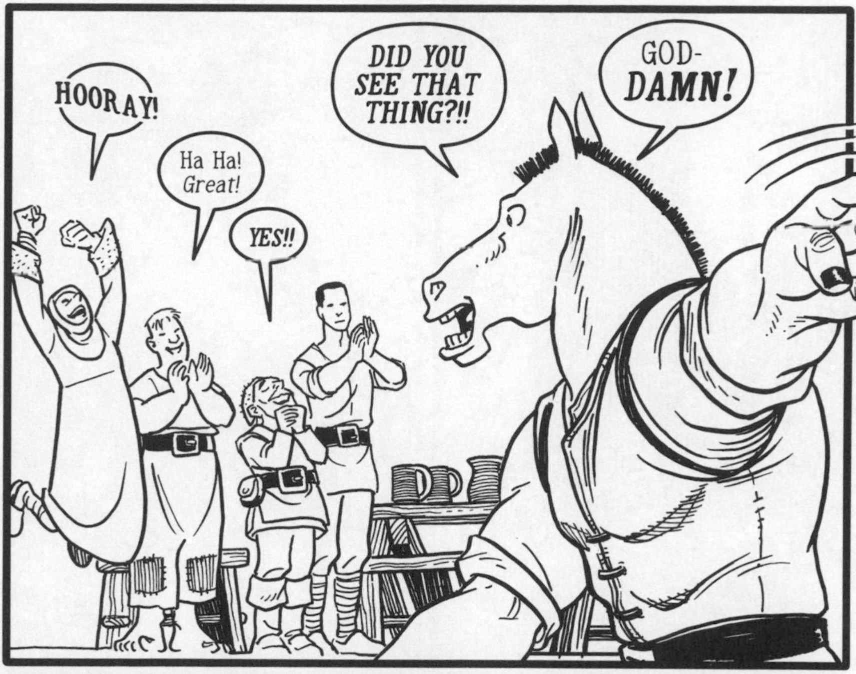
HOORAY!
Ha Ha! *Great!*
YES!!
DID YOU SEE THAT THING?!!
GOD-**DAMN!**

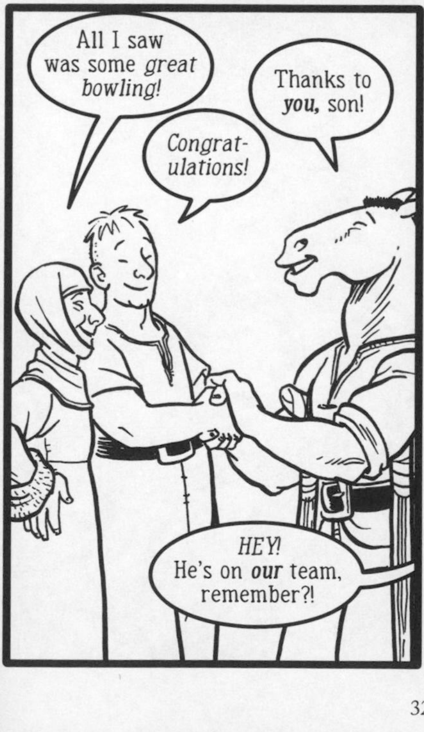
All I saw was some *great bowling!*
Congrat-ulations!
Thanks to ***you,*** son!
HEY! He's on ***our*** team, remember?!

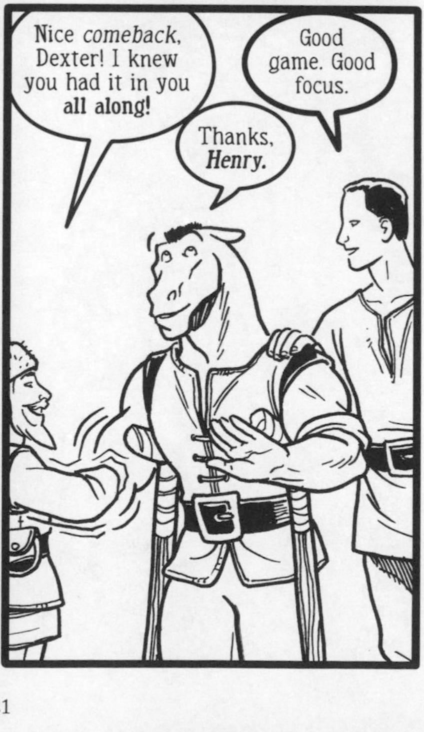
Nice *comeback,* Dexter! I knew you had it in you **all along!**
Good game. Good focus.
Thanks, ***Henry.***

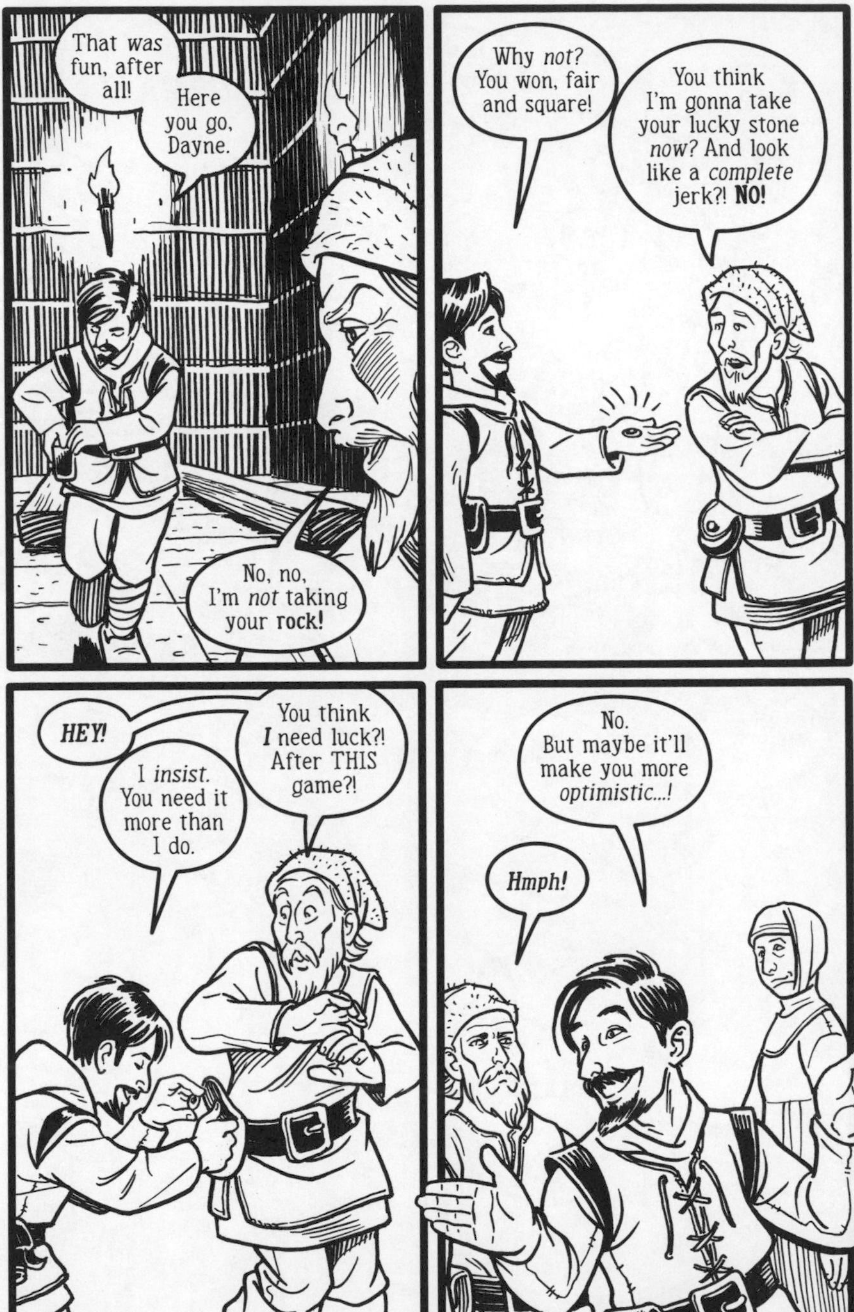
That *was* fun, after all!
Here you go, Dayne.
No, no, I'm *not* taking your **rock**!
Why *not*? You won, fair and square!
You think I'm gonna take your lucky stone *now?* And look like a *complete* jerk?! **NO!**
HEY!
You think *I* need luck?! After THIS game?!
I *insist*. You need it more than I do.
No. But maybe it'll make you more *optimistic...!*
Hmph!

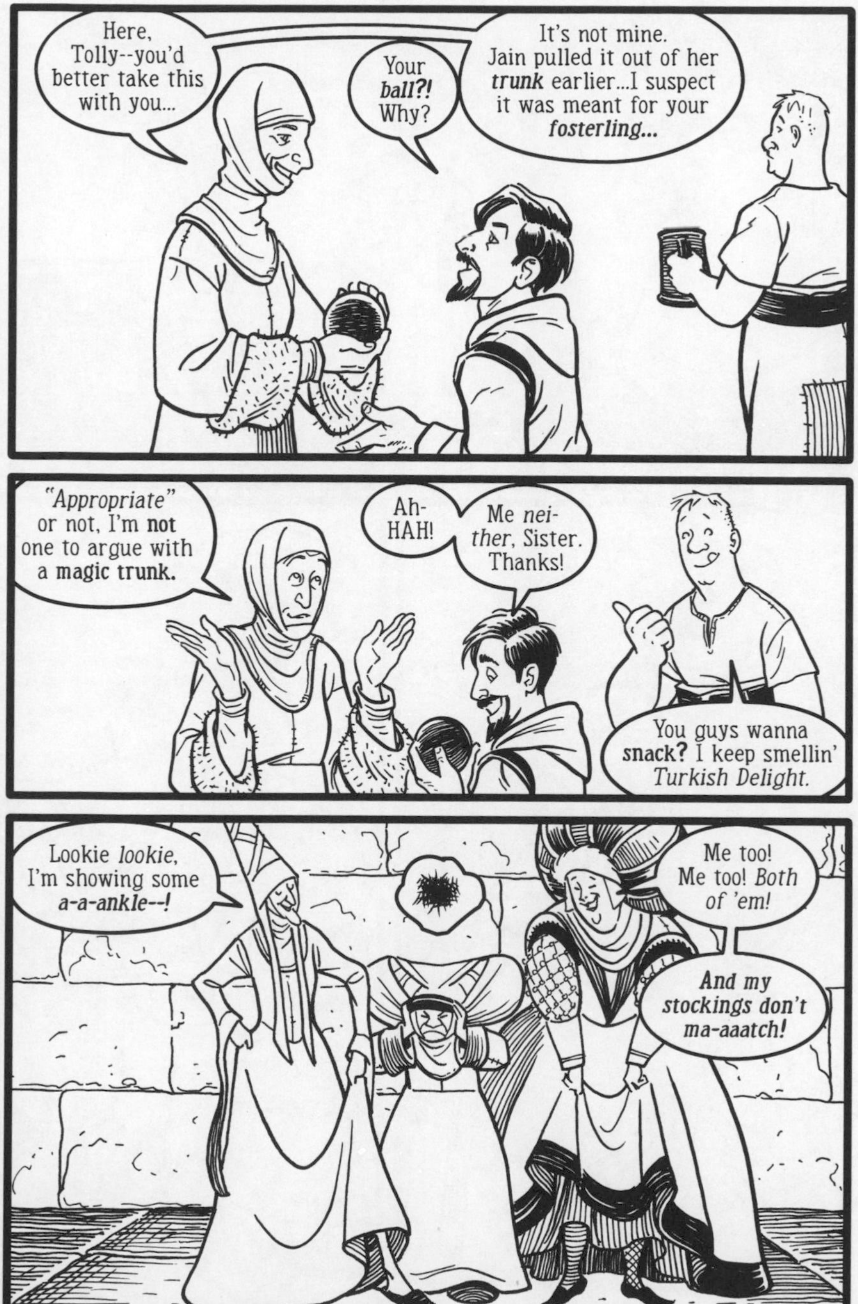
Here, Tolly--you'd better take this with you...
Your *ball?!* Why?
It's not mine. Jain pulled it out of her *trunk* earlier...I suspect it was meant for your *fosterling...*
"Appropriate" or not, I'm **not** one to argue with a **magic trunk.**
Ah-HAH!
Me *nei-ther*, Sister. Thanks!
You guys wanna **snack?** I keep smellin' *Turkish Delight.*
Lookie *lookie*, I'm showing some *a-a-ankle--!*
Me too! Me too! *Both of 'em!*
And my stockings don't ma-aaatch!

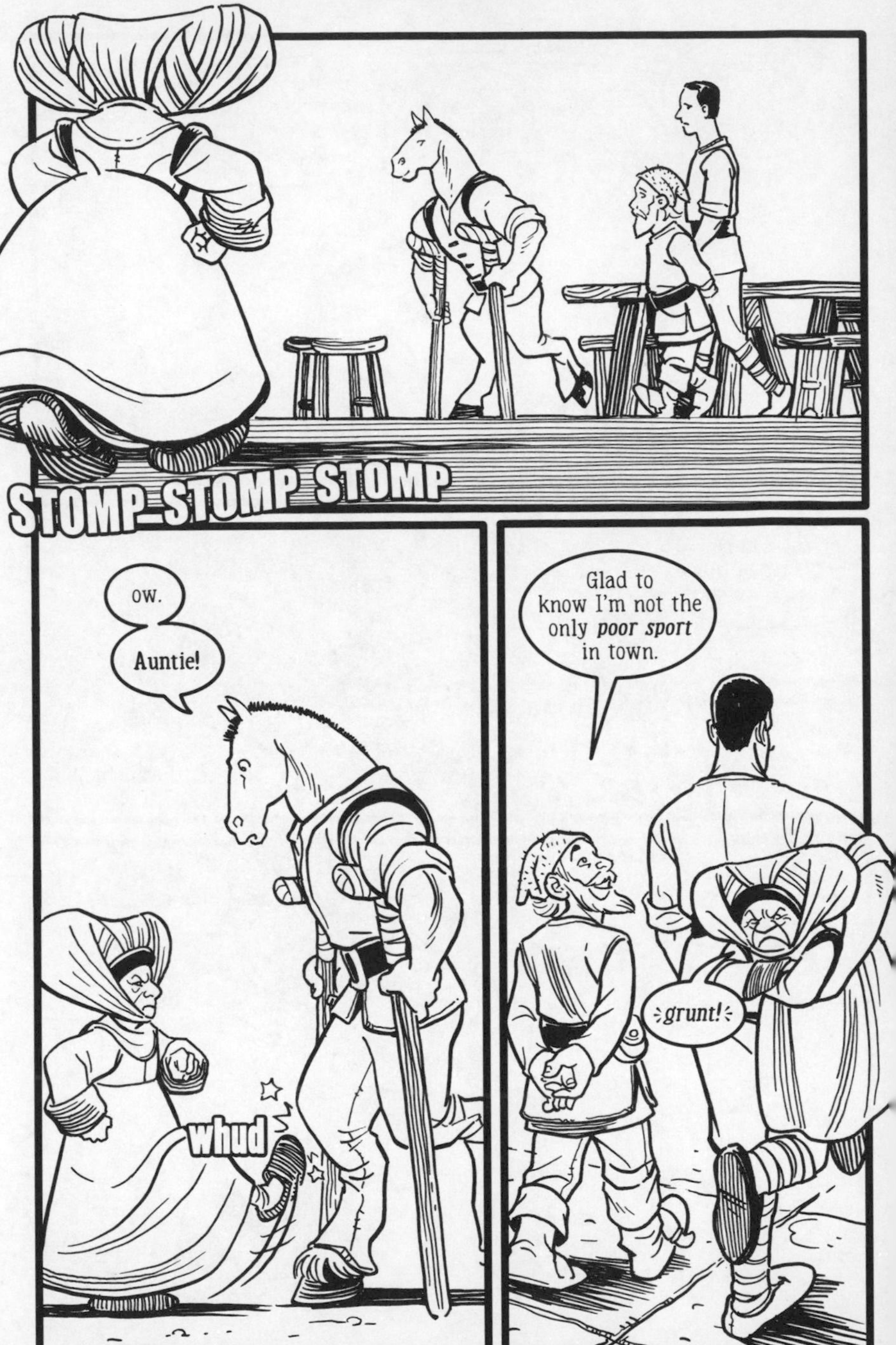
STOMP STOMP STOMP
OW.
Auntie!
whud
Glad to know I'm not the only *poor sport* in town.
grunt!

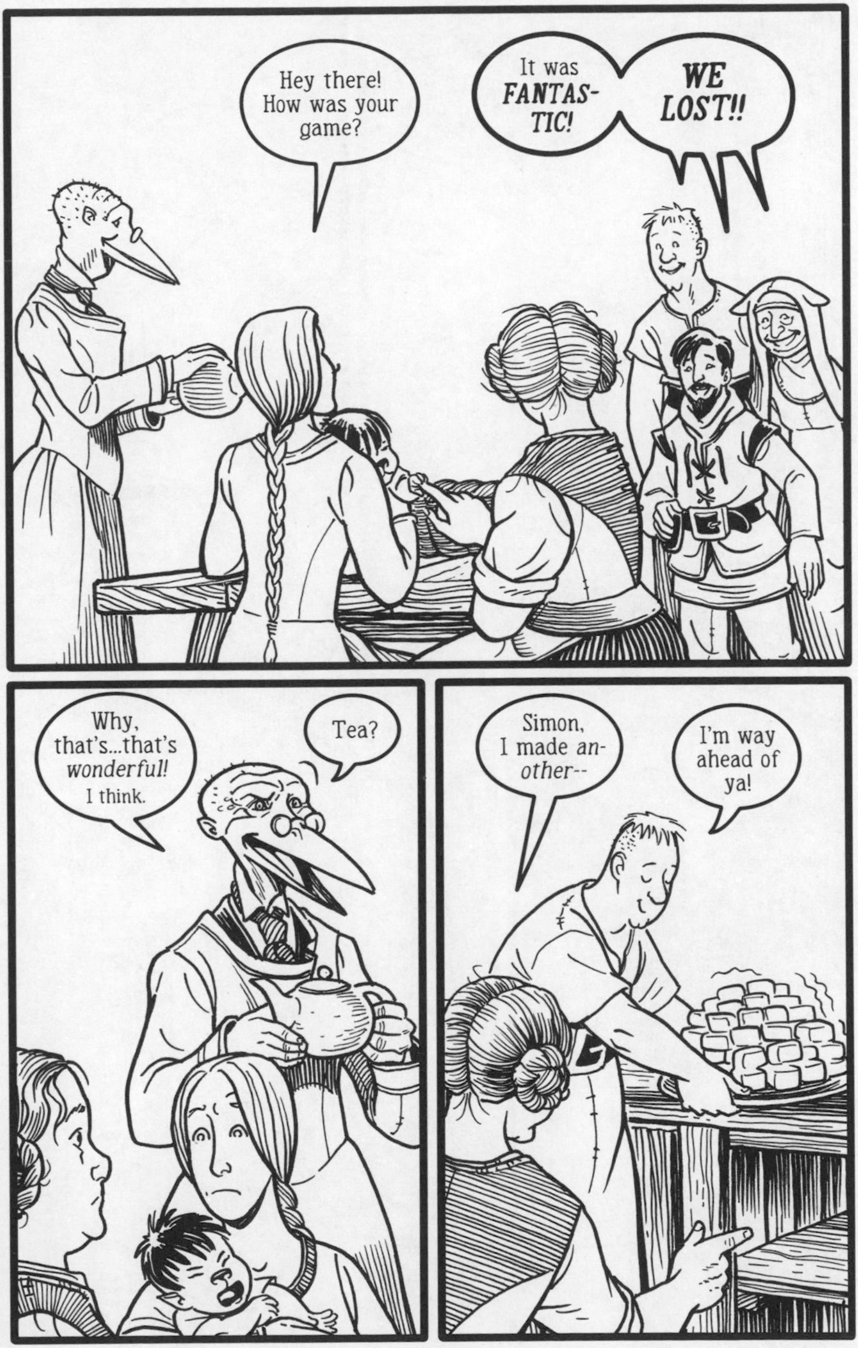
Hey there! How was your game?
It was *FANTAS-TIC!*
WE LOST!!
Why, that's...that's *wonderful!* I think.
Tea?
Simon, I made *an-other--*
I'm way ahead of ya!

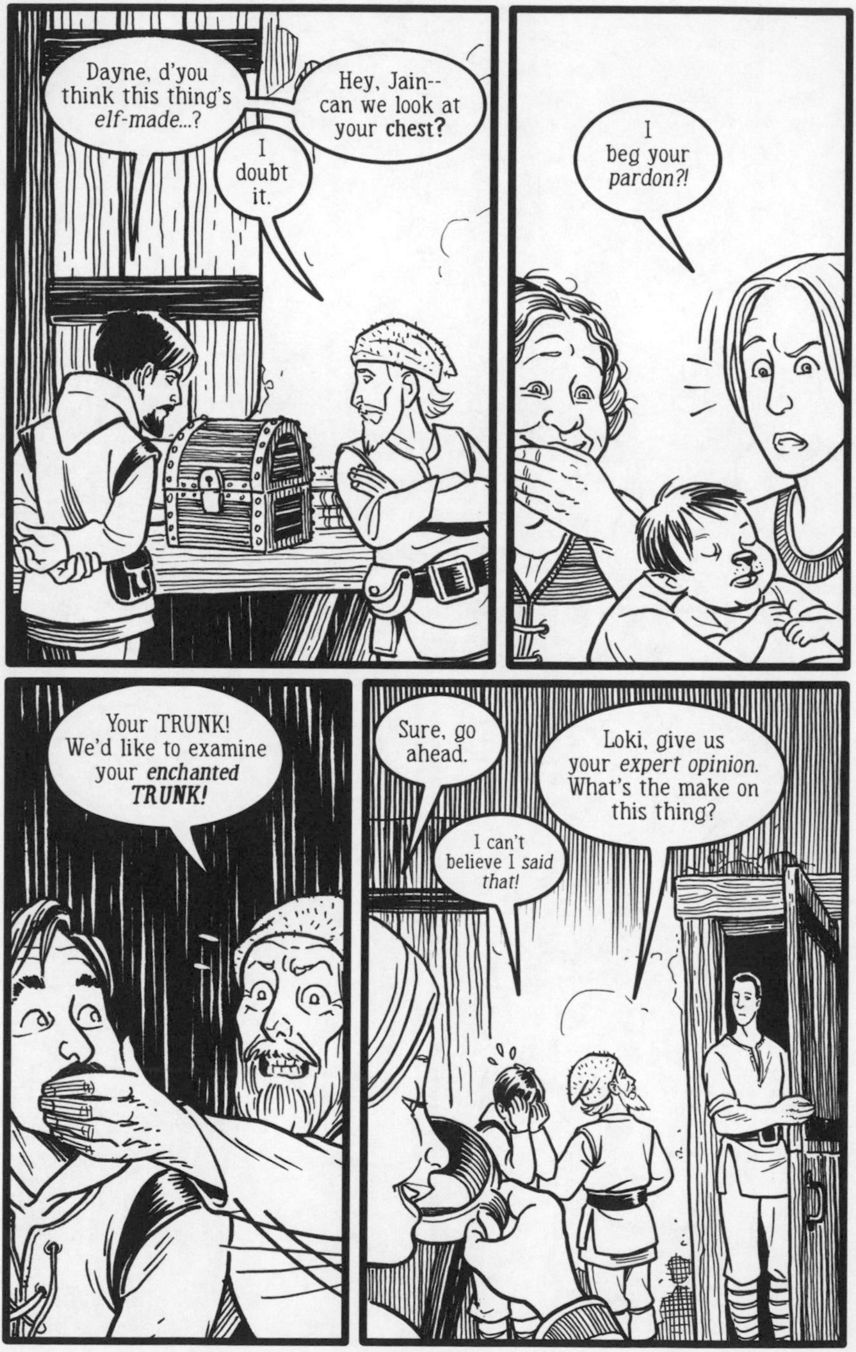
Dayne, d'you think this thing's *elf-made...?*
Hey, Jain-- can we look at your **chest?**
I doubt it.
I beg your *pardon?!*
Your TRUNK! We'd like to examine your *enchanted* ***TRUNK!***
Sure, go ahead.
Loki, give us your *expert opinion.* What's the make on this thing?
I can't believe I *said that!*

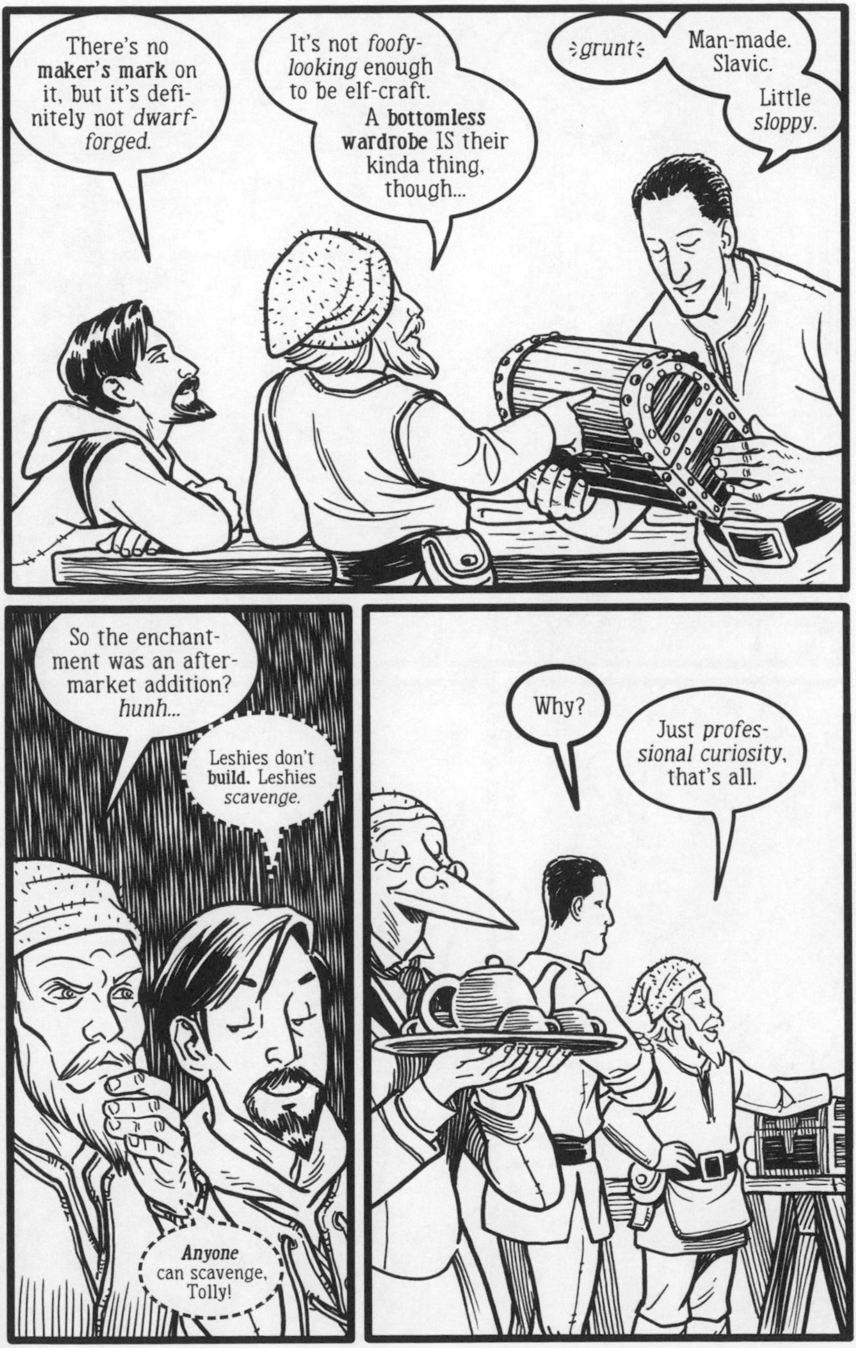
There's no **maker's mark** on it, but it's definitely not *dwarf-forged.*
It's not *foofy-looking* enough to be elf-craft.
A **bottomless wardrobe** IS their kinda thing, though...
grunt
Man-made. Slavic.
Little *sloppy.*
So the enchantment was an after-market addition? *hunh...*
Leshies don't **build.** Leshies *scavenge.*
Anyone can scavenge, Tolly!
Why?
Just *professional curiosity,* that's all.

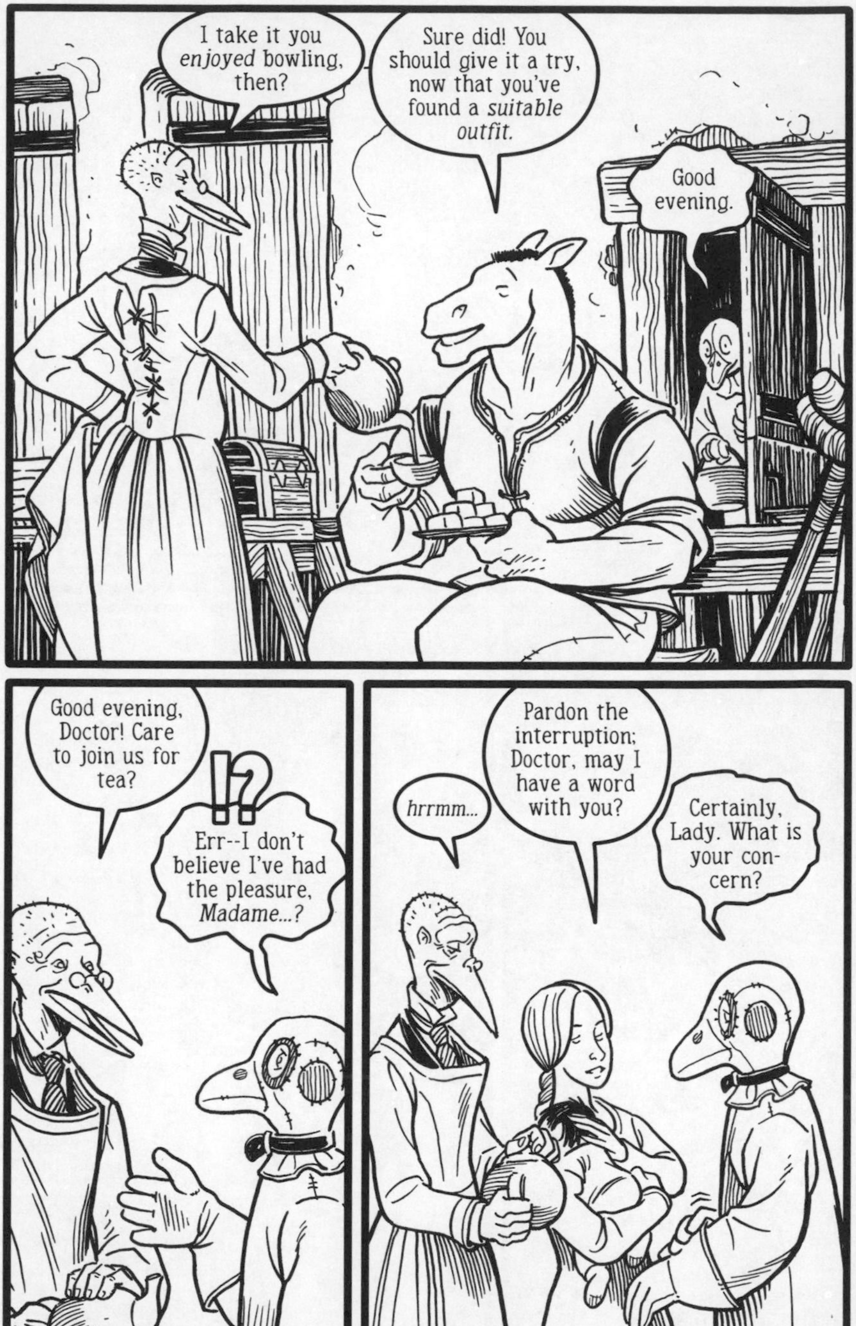
I take it you *enjoyed* bowling, then?
Sure did! You should give it a try, now that you've found a *suitable outfit.*
Good evening.
Good evening, Doctor! Care to join us for tea?
!?
Err--I don't believe I've had the pleasure, *Madame...?*
hrrmm...
Pardon the interruption; Doctor, may I have a word with you?
Certainly, Lady. What is your concern?

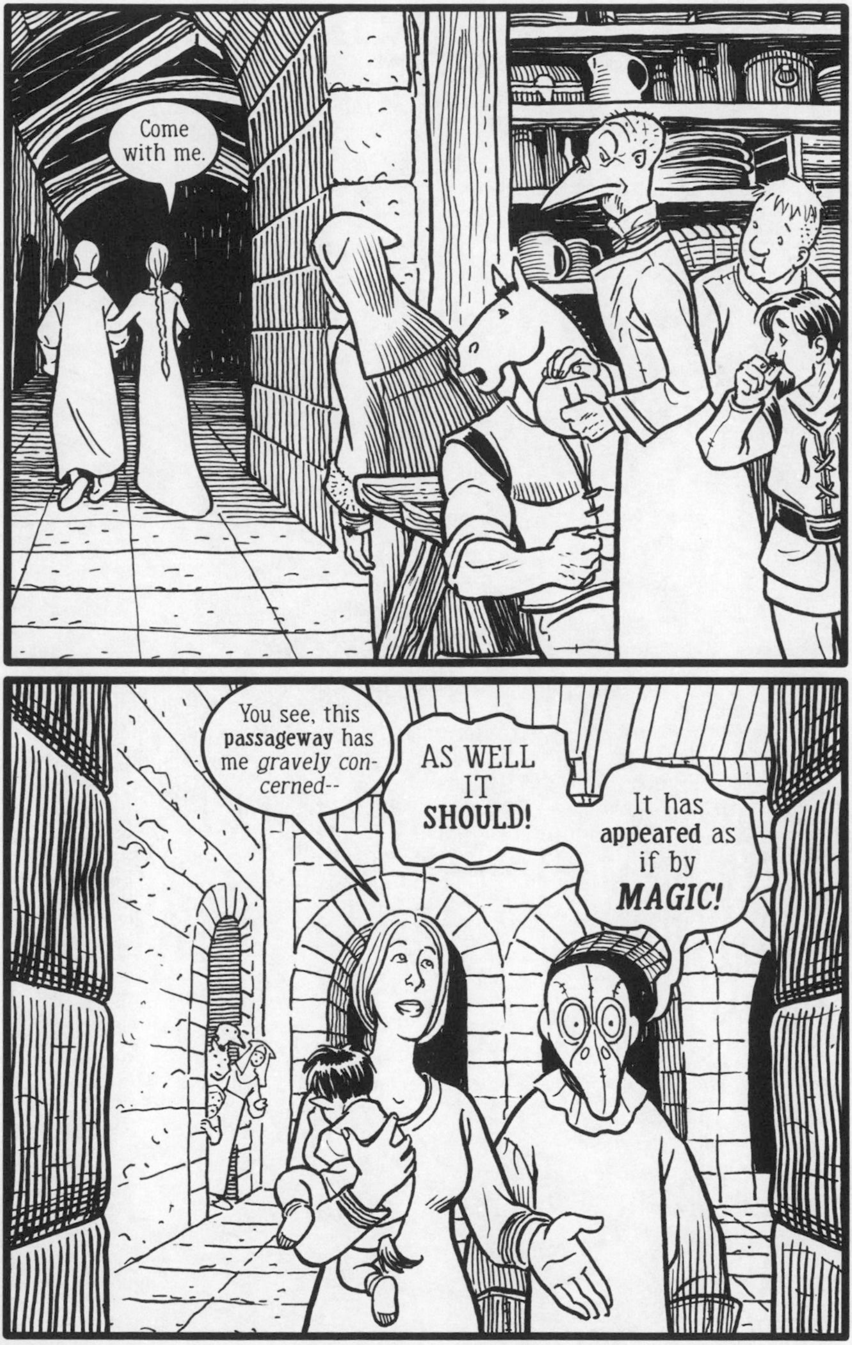
Come with me.
You see, this passageway has me gravely concerned--
AS WELL IT SHOULD!
It has appeared as if by MAGIC!

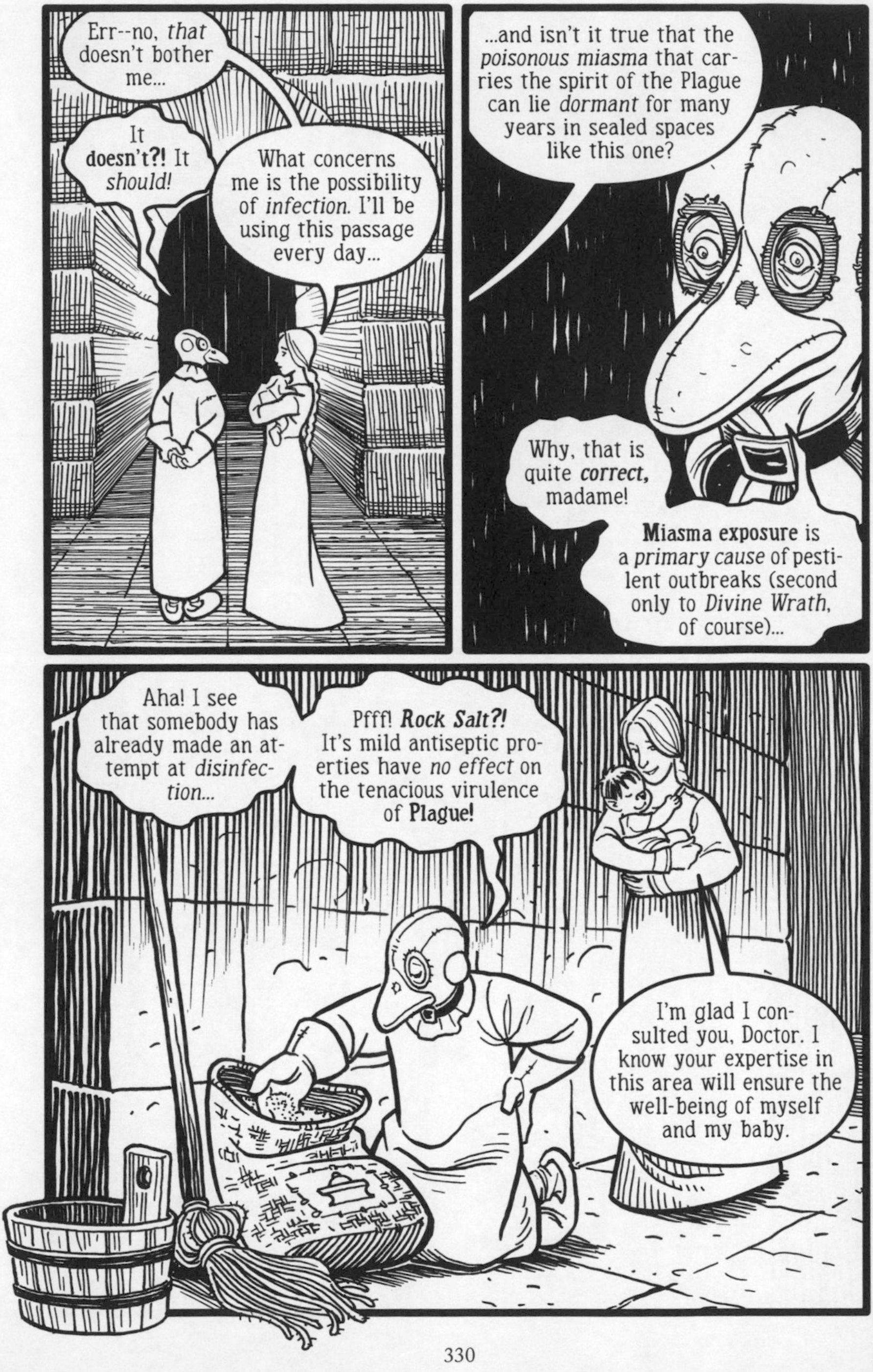
Err--no, *that* doesn't bother me...
It **doesn't?!** It *should!*
What concerns me is the possibility of *infection.* I'll be using this passage every day...
...and isn't it true that the *poisonous miasma* that carries the spirit of the Plague can lie *dormant* for many years in sealed spaces like this one?
Why, that is quite ***correct,*** madame!
Miasma exposure is a *primary cause* of pestilent outbreaks (second only to *Divine Wrath,* of course)...
Aha! I see that somebody has already made an attempt at *disinfection...*
Pfff! ***Rock Salt?!*** It's mild antiseptic properties have *no effect* on the tenacious virulence of **Plague!**
I'm glad I consulted you, Doctor. I know your expertise in this area will ensure the well-being of myself and my baby.

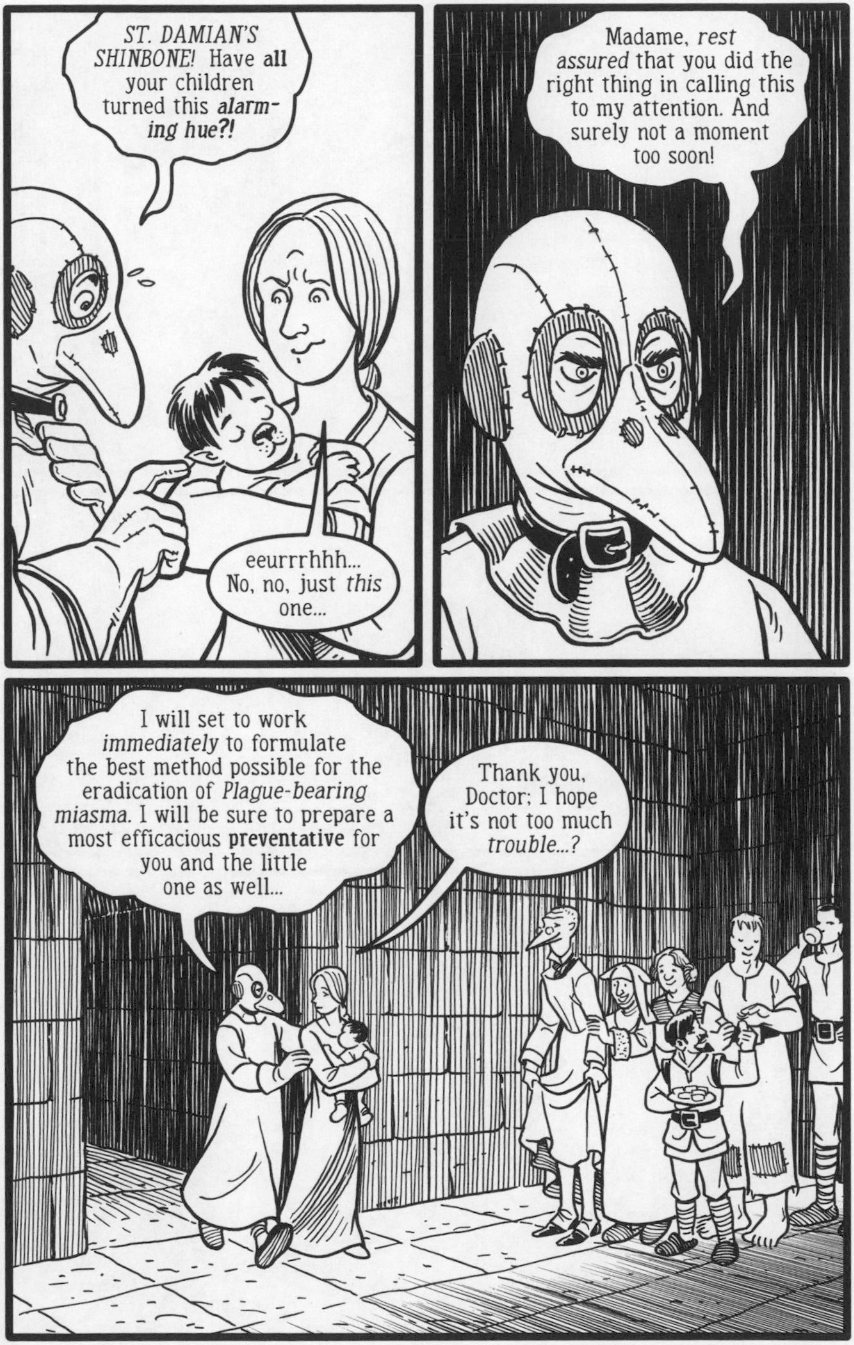
ST. DAMIAN'S SHINBONE! Have **all** your children turned this ***alarming hue?!***
eeurrrhhh... No, no, just *this* one...
Madame, *rest assured* that you did the right thing in calling this to my attention. And surely not a moment too soon!
I will set to work *immediately* to formulate the best method possible for the eradication of *Plague-bearing miasma.* I will be sure to prepare a most efficacious **preventative** for you and the little one as well...
Thank you, Doctor; I hope it's not too much *trouble...?*

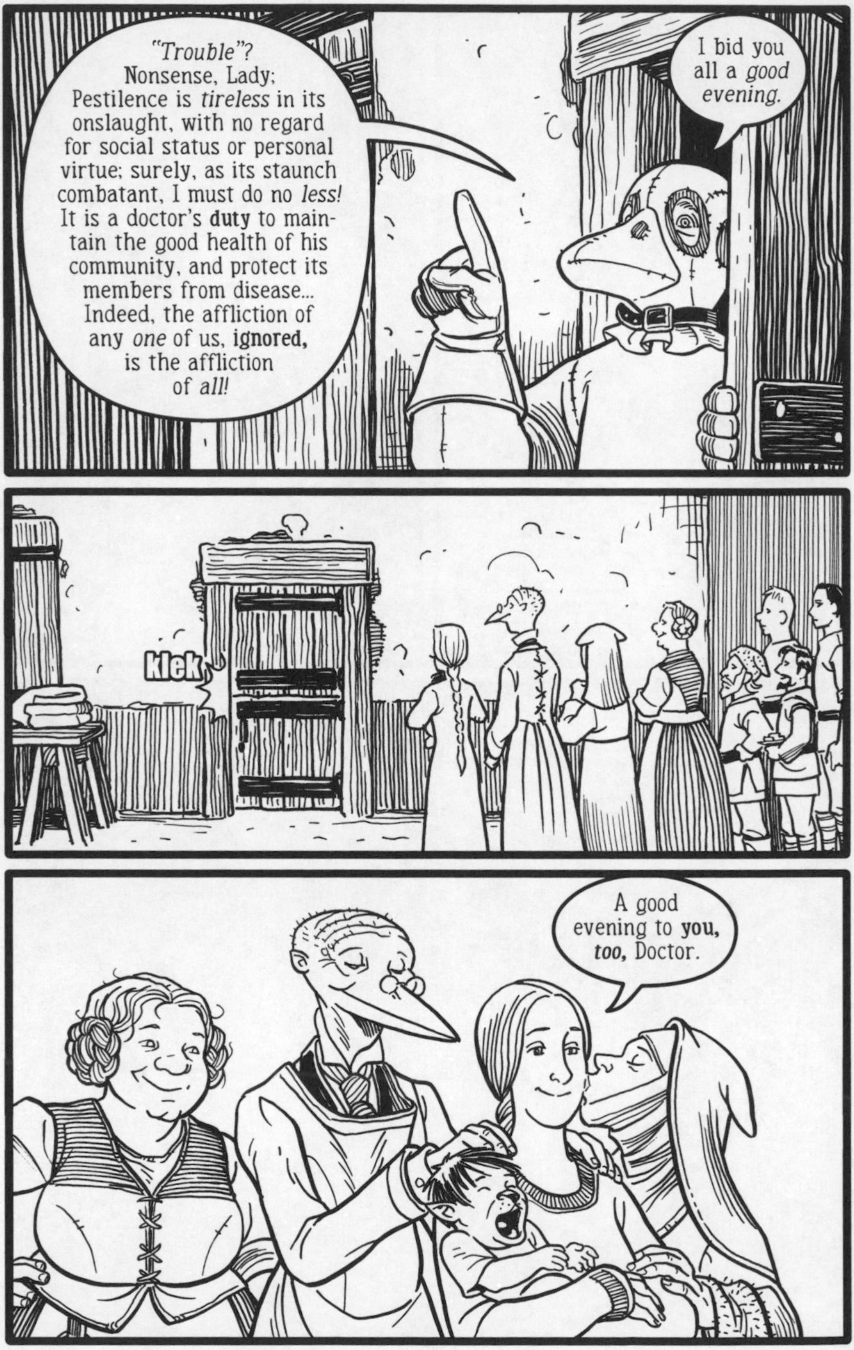
"*Trouble*"? Nonsense, Lady; Pestilence is *tireless* in its onslaught, with no regard for social status or personal virtue; surely, as its staunch combatant, I must do no *less!* It is a doctor's **duty** to maintain the good health of his community, and protect its members from disease... Indeed, the affliction of any *one* of us, **ignored,** is the affliction of *all!*
I bid you all a *good evening.*
klek
A good evening to **you,** ***too,*** Doctor.

Chapter 13.

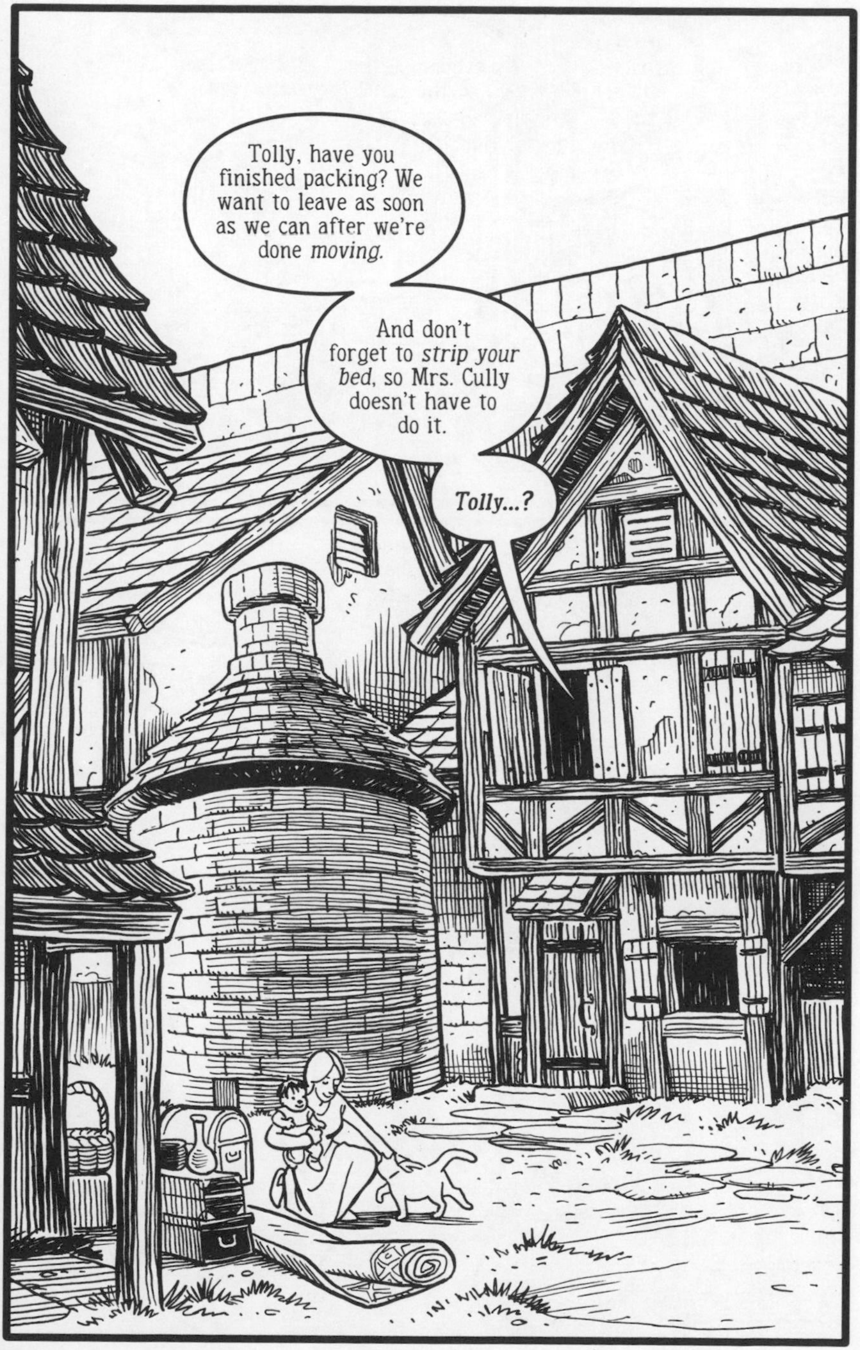
Tolly, have you finished packing? We want to leave as soon as we can after we're done *moving.*
And don't forget to *strip your bed*, so Mrs. Cully doesn't have to do it.
Tolly...?

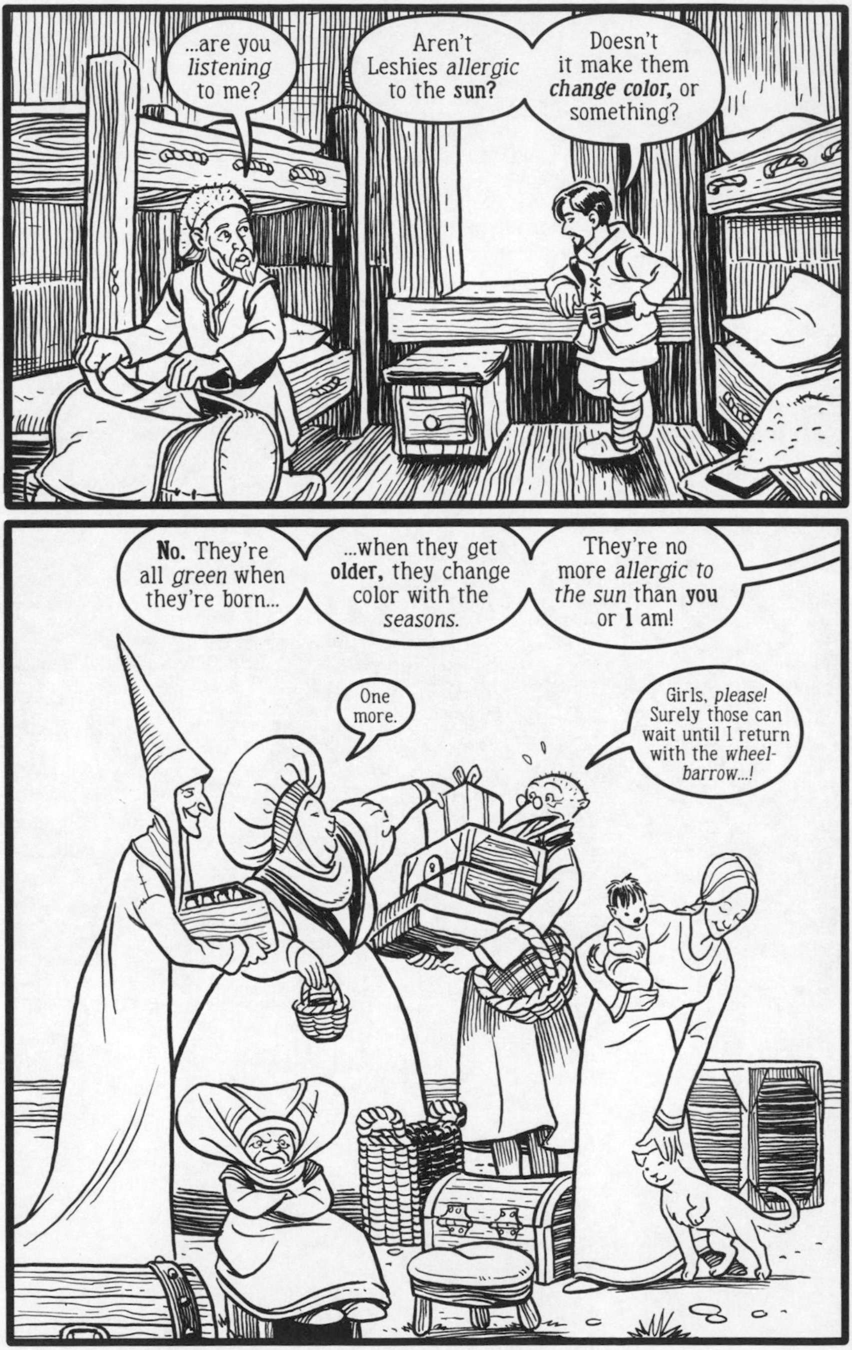
...are you *listening* to me?
Aren't Leshies *allergic* to the **sun?**
Doesn't it make them ***change color,*** or something?
No. They're all *green* when they're born...
...when they get **older,** they change color with the *seasons.*
They're no more *allergic to the sun* than **you** or **I** am!
One more.
Girls, *please!* Surely those can wait until I return with the *wheel-barrow*...!

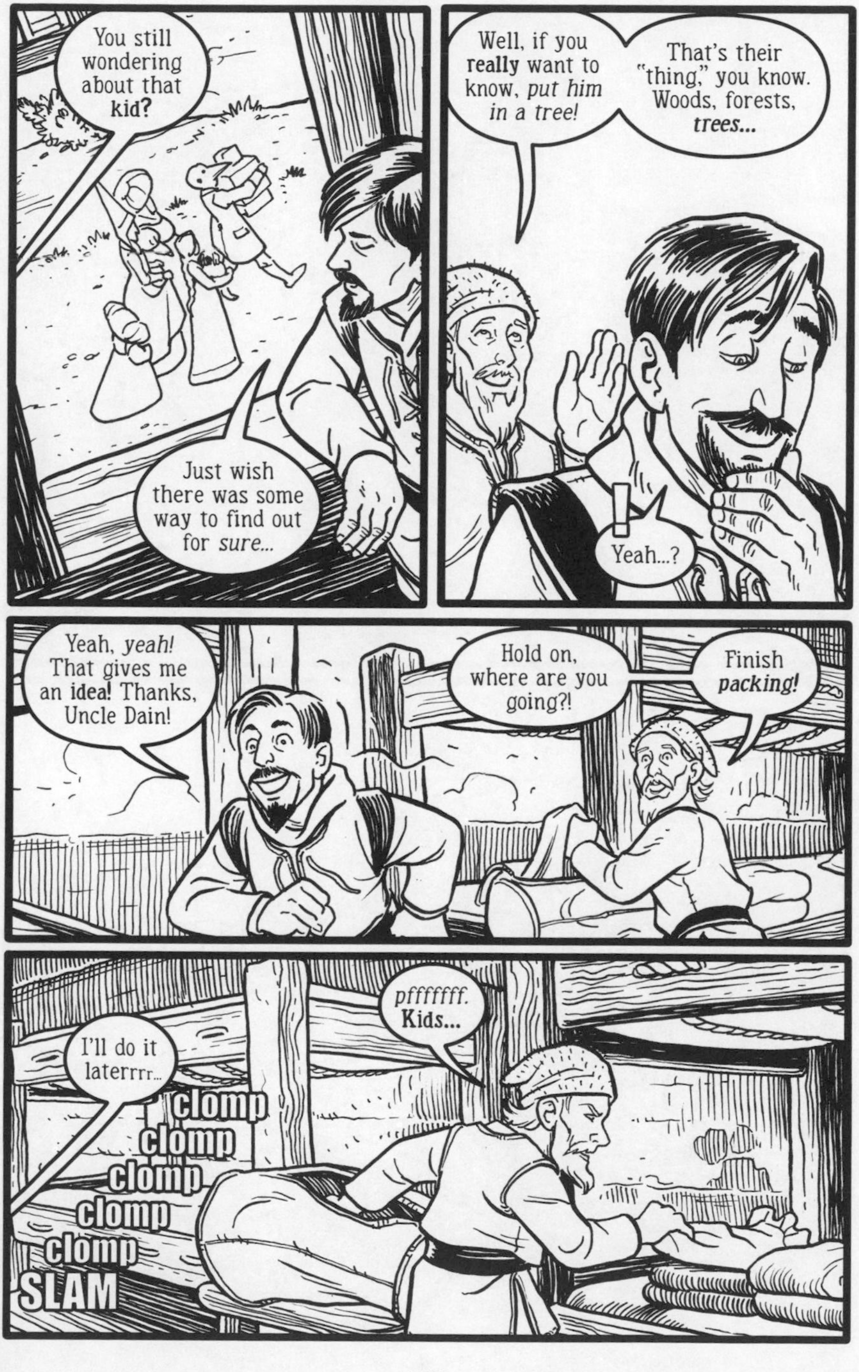
You still wondering about that **kid?**
Just wish there was some way to find out for *sure...*
Well, if you **really** want to know, *put him in a tree!*
That's their "thing," you know. Woods, forests, ***trees...***
!
Yeah...?
Yeah, *yeah!* That gives me an **idea!** Thanks, Uncle Dain!
Hold on, where are you going?!
Finish ***packing!***
I'll do it laterrrr...
clomp
clomp
clomp
clomp
clomp
SLAM
pfffffff. **Kids...**

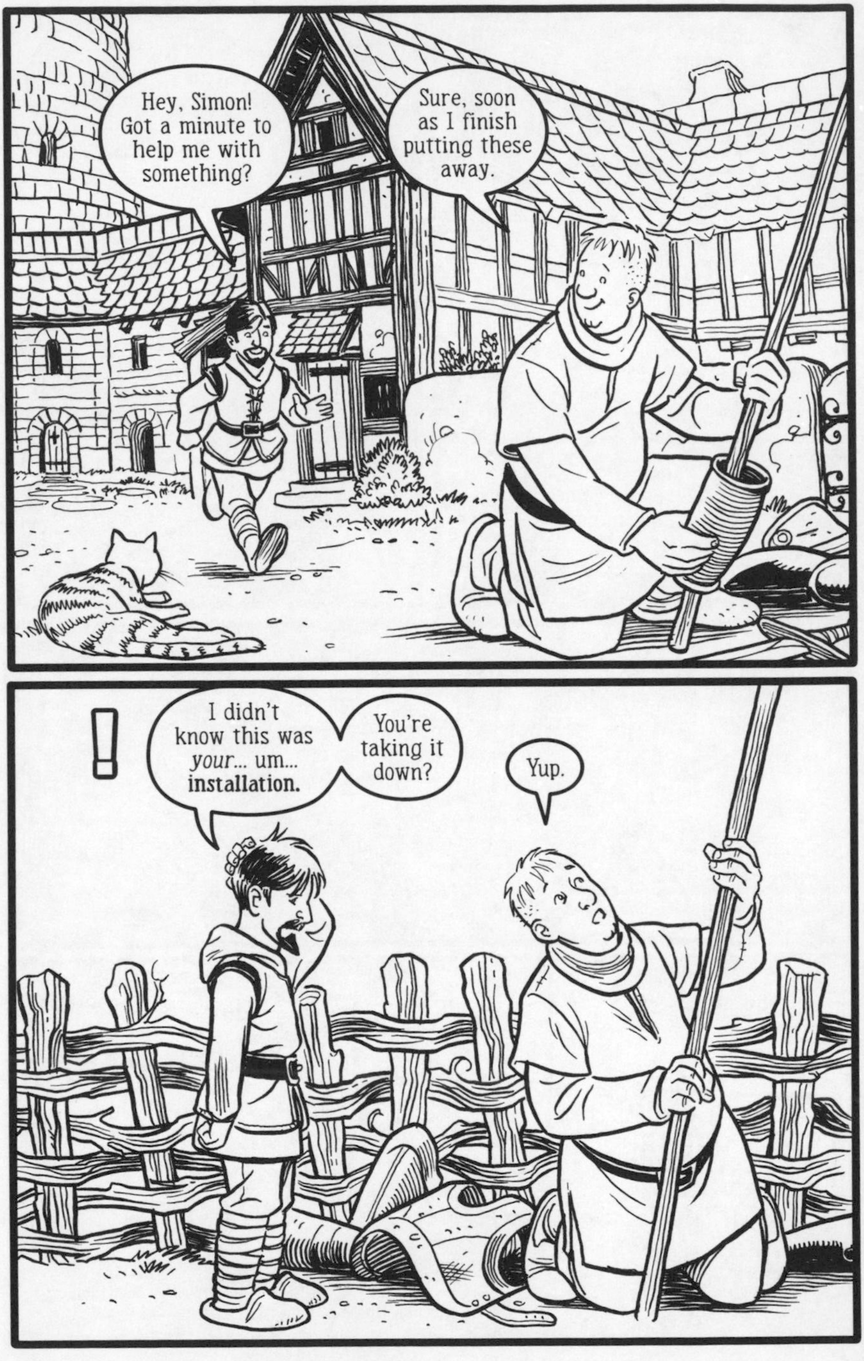
Hey, Simon! Got a minute to help me with something?
Sure, soon as I finish putting these away.
!
I didn't know this was *your*... um... **installation.**
You're taking it down?
Yup.

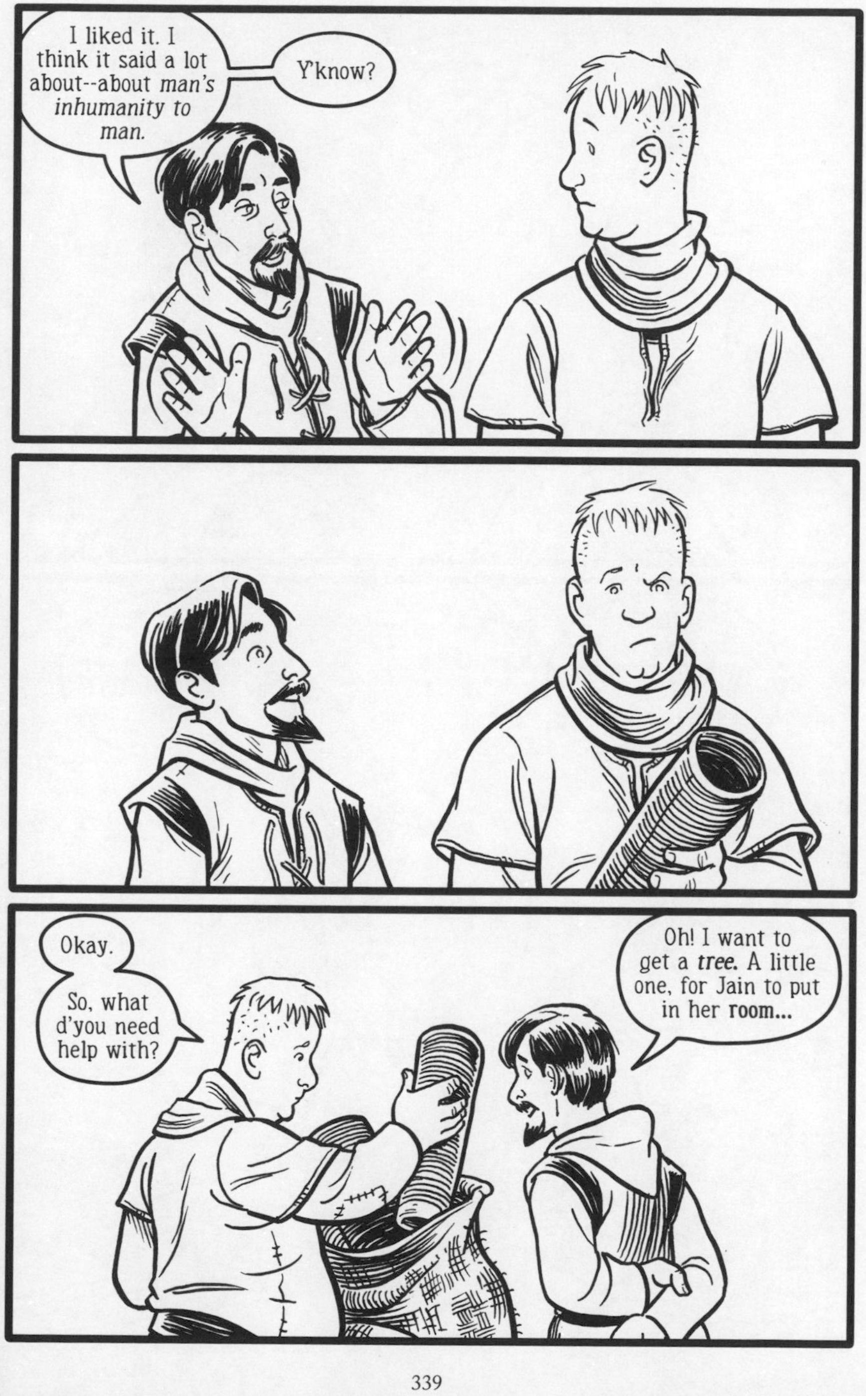
I liked it. I think it said a lot about--about *man's inhumanity to man.*
Y'know?
Okay.
So, what d'you need help with?
Oh! I want to get a ***tree.*** A little one, for Jain to put in her **room...**

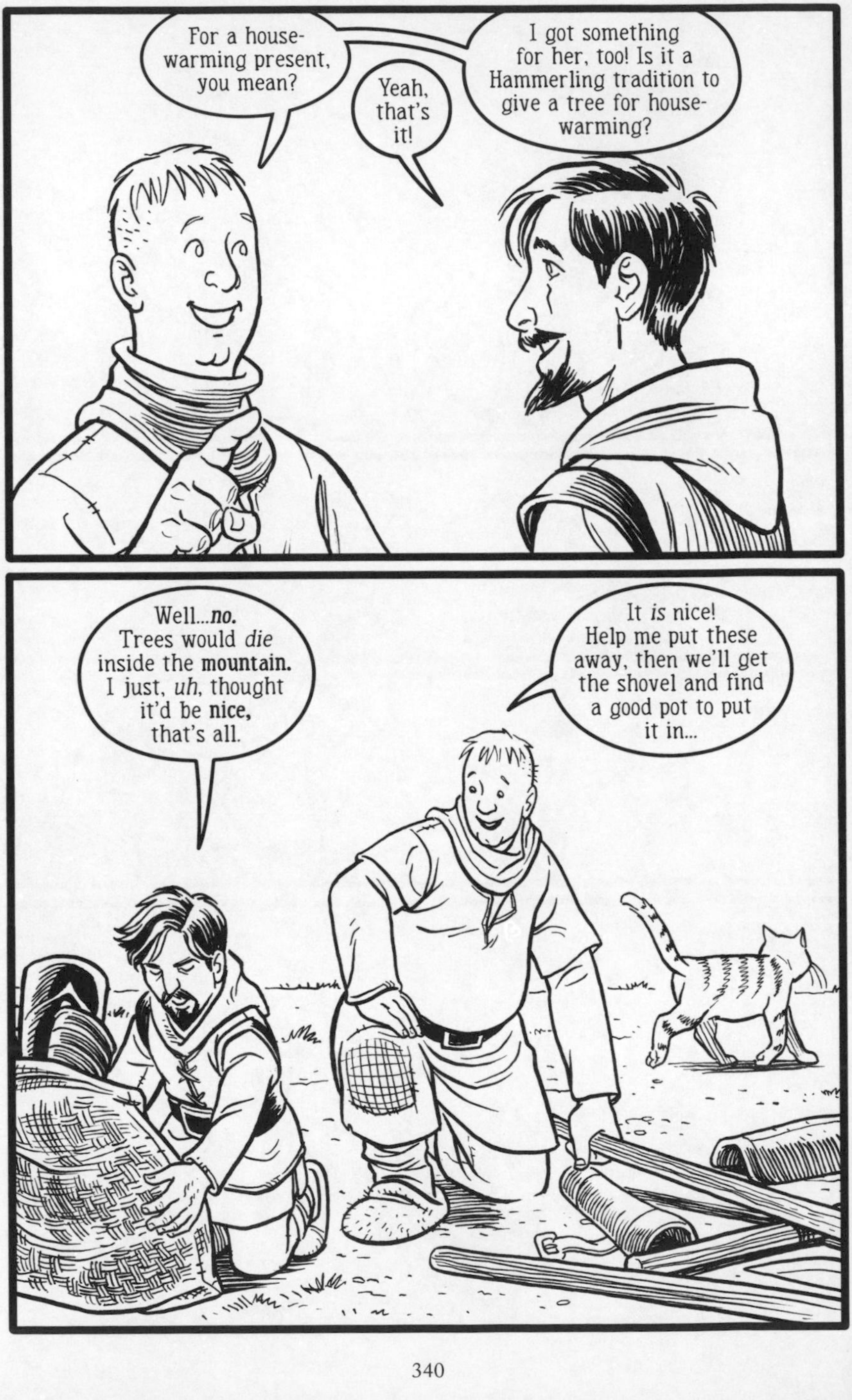
For a house-warming present, you mean?
Yeah, that's it!
I got something for her, too! Is it a Hammerling tradition to give a tree for house-warming?
Well...**no.** Trees would *die* inside the **mountain.** I just, *uh,* thought it'd be **nice,** that's all.
It *is* nice! Help me put these away, then we'll get the shovel and find a good pot to put it in...

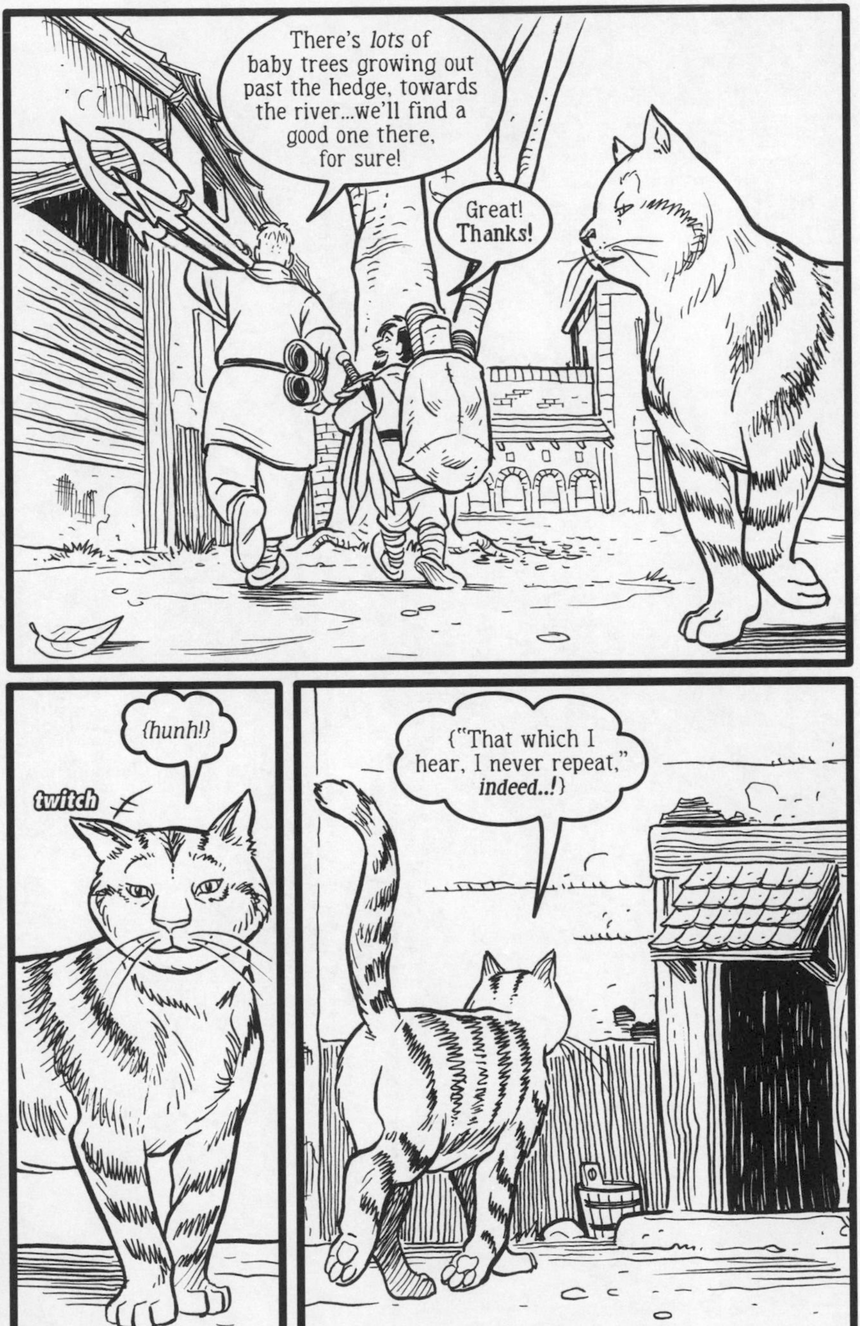
There's *lots* of baby trees growing out past the hedge, towards the river...we'll find a good one there, for sure!
Great! **Thanks!**
{hunh!}
twitch
{"That which I hear, I never repeat," *indeed...!*}

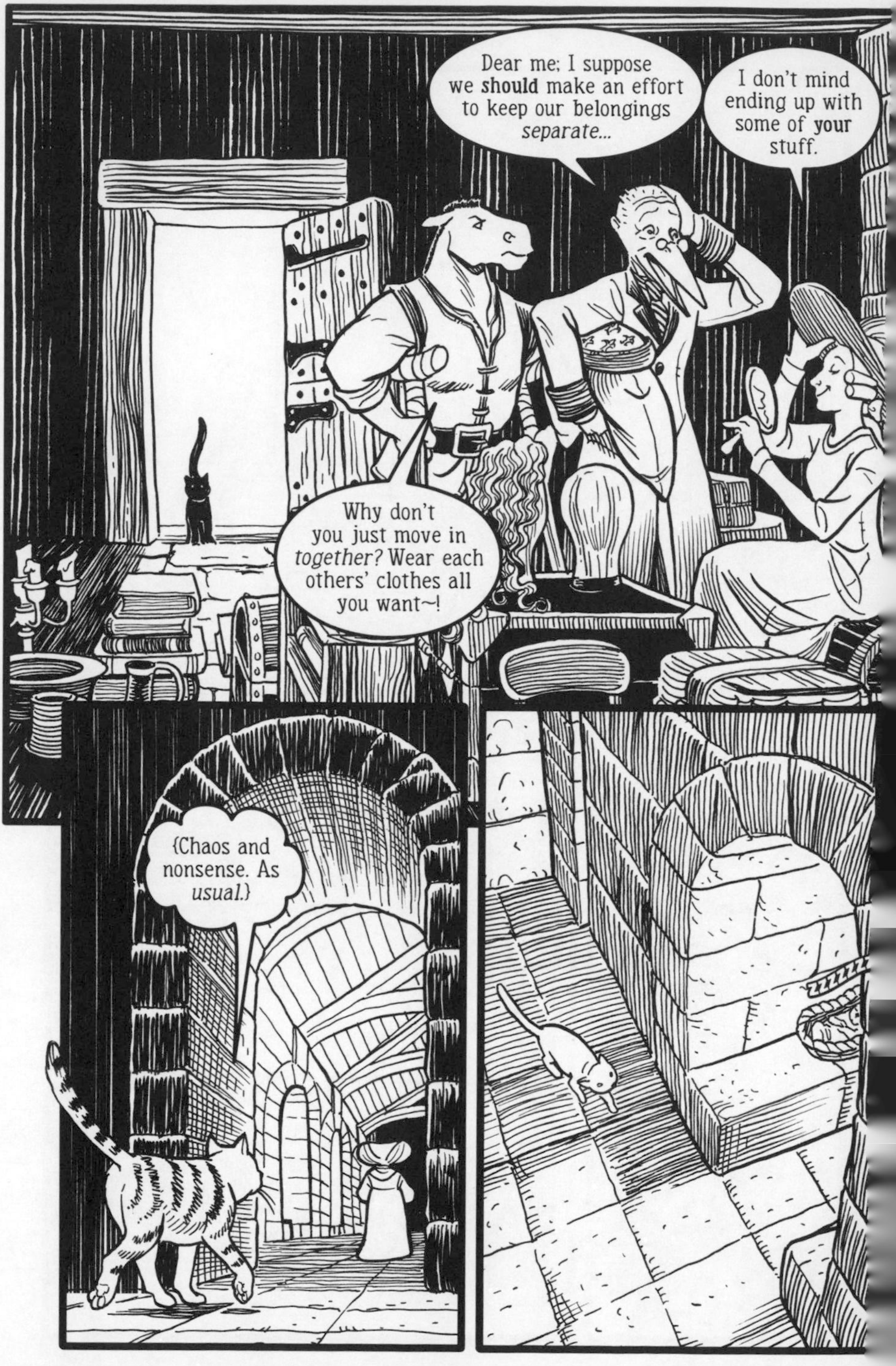
Dear me; I suppose we **should** make an effort to keep our belongings *separate*...
I don't mind ending up with some of **your** stuff.
Why don't you just move in *together*? Wear each others' clothes all you want~!
{Chaos and nonsense. As *usual*.}
ZZZZZZ

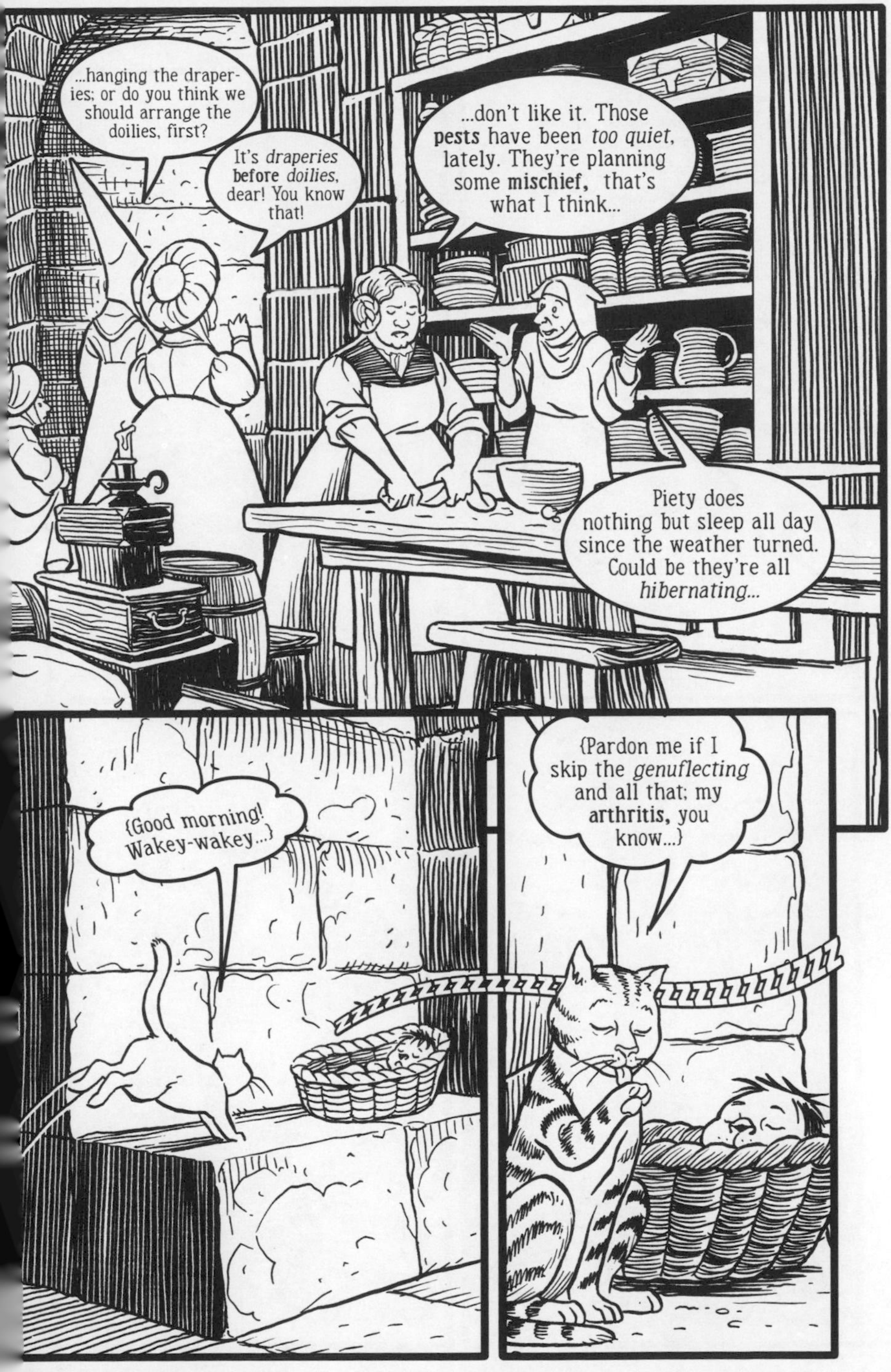
...hanging the draperies; or do you think we should arrange the doilies, first?
It's *draperies* **before** *doilies*, dear! You know that!
...don't like it. Those **pests** have been *too quiet*, lately. They're planning some **mischief**, that's what I think...
Piety does nothing but sleep all day since the weather turned. Could be they're all *hibernating*...
{Good morning! Wakey-wakey...}
{Pardon me if I skip the *genuflecting* and all that; my **arthritis**, you know...}
ZZZZZZZZZZZZZZZZZZZZZZZZZZZZZZZ

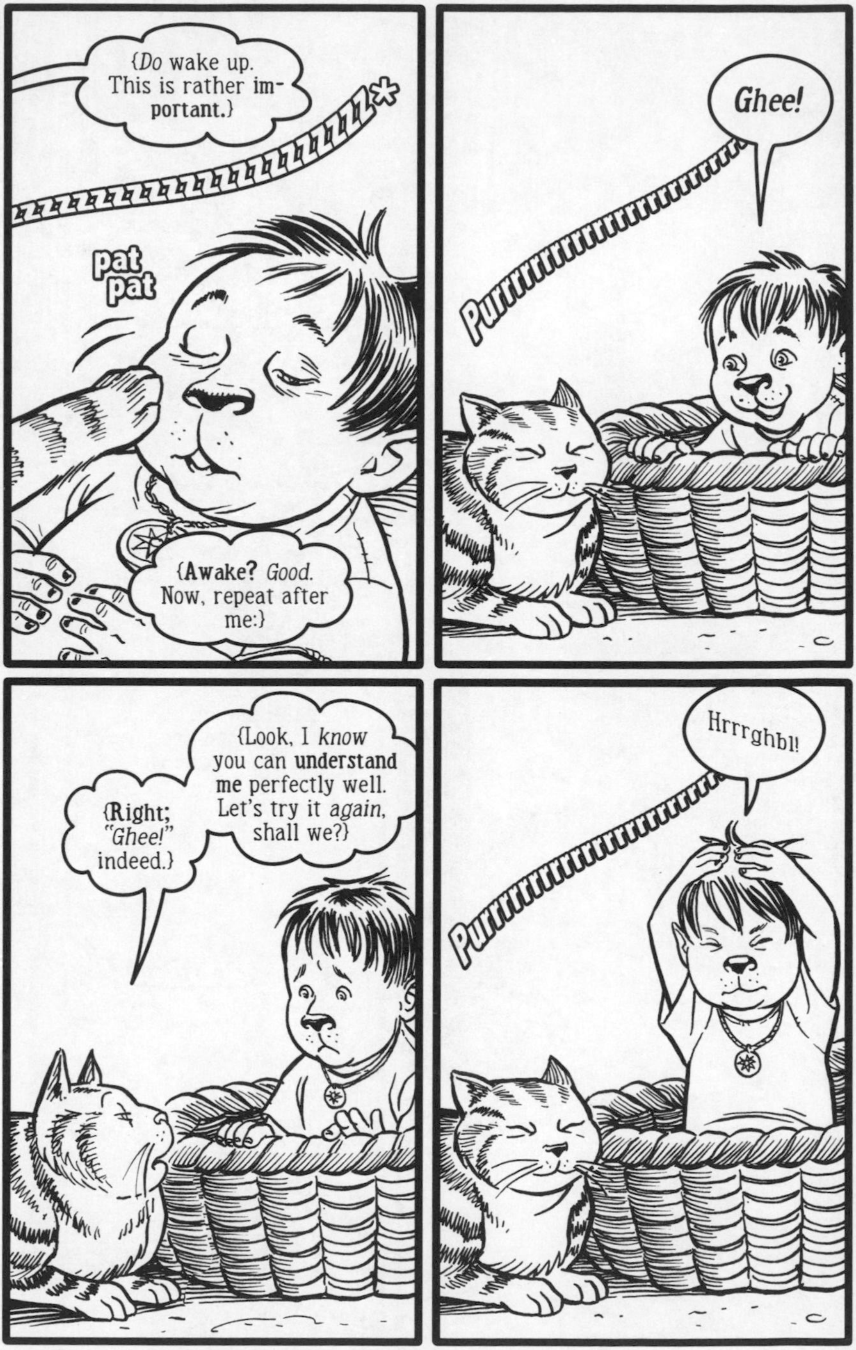
{*Do* wake up. This is rather important.}
zzzzzzzzzzzzzzzzzzzzzzzzzzzzz*
pat pat
{**Awake?** *Good.* Now, repeat after me:}
Ghee!
Purrrrrrrrrrrrrrrrrrrrrrrr
{**Right;** *"Ghee!"* indeed.}
{Look, I *know* you can **understand** me perfectly well. Let's try it *again*, shall we?}
Hrrrghbl!
Purrrrrrrrrrrrrrrrrrrrrrr

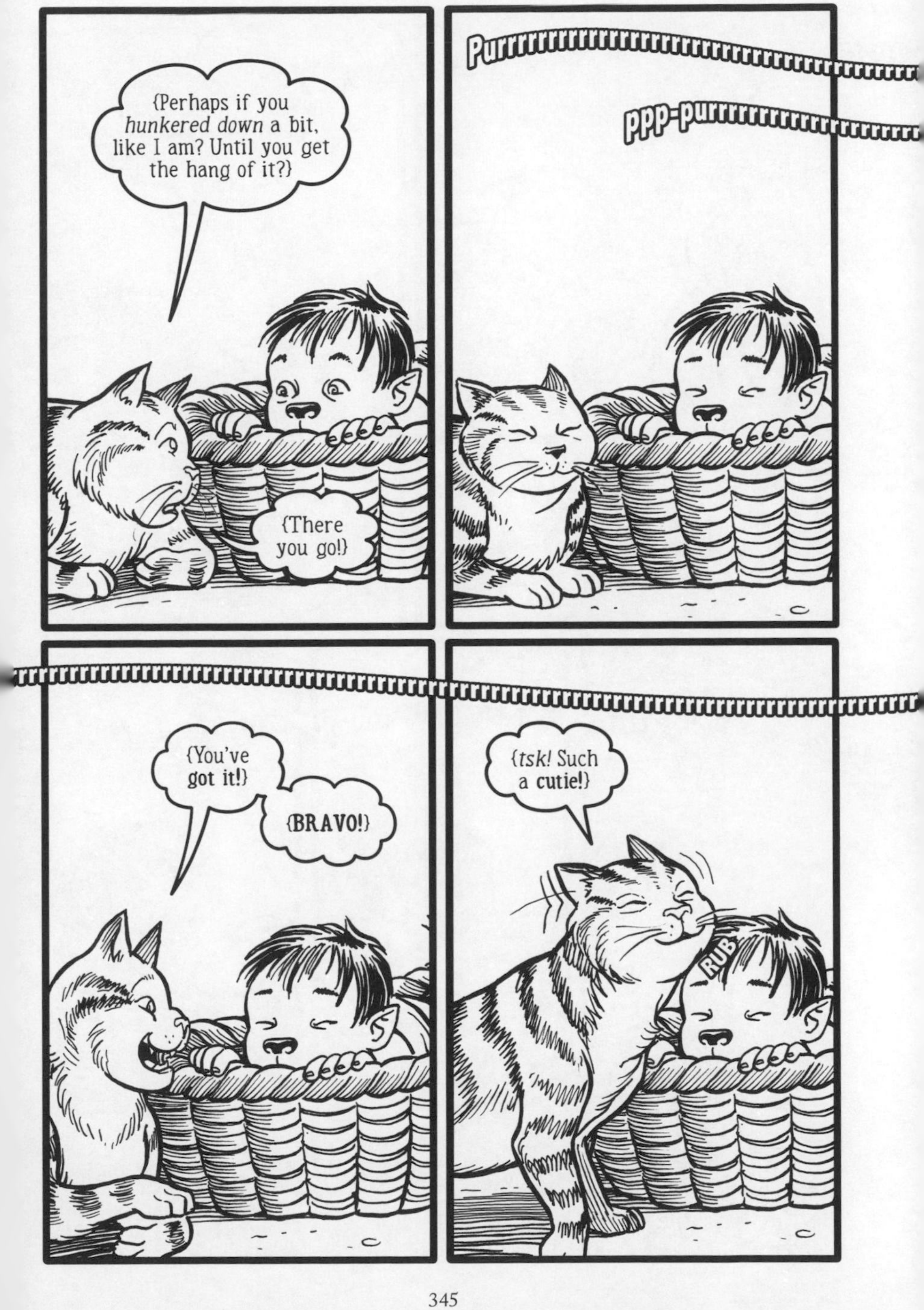
{Perhaps if you *hunkered down* a bit, like I am? Until you get the hang of it?}
{There you go!}
Purrrrrrrrrrrrrrrrrrrrrrrrrrrrrrrrrrrrrrrr
ppp-purrrrrrrrrrrrrrrrrrr
rrrrrrrrrrrrrrrrrrrrrrrrrrrrrrrrrrrrrrrrrrrrrrrrrrrrrrrrrrrrrrrr
{You've **got it!**}
{**BRAVO!**}
{*tsk!* Such a **cutie!**}
RUB

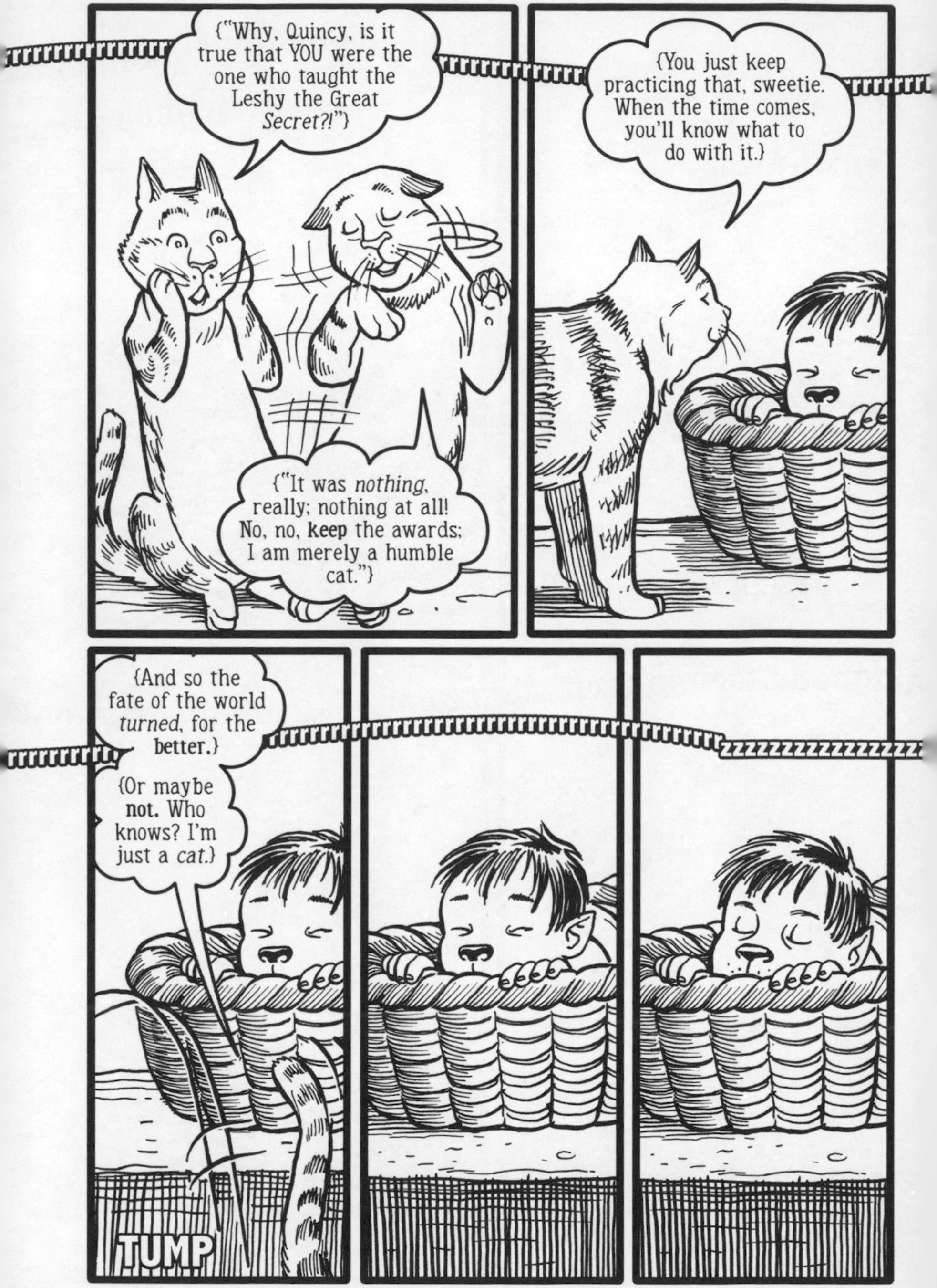
rrrrrrrrrrrrrr
{"Why, Quincy, is it true that YOU were the one who taught the Leshy the Great *Secret?!*"}
rrrrrrrrrrrrrrr
{"It was *nothing*, really; nothing at all! No, no, **keep** the awards; I am merely a humble cat."}
{You just keep practicing that, sweetie. When the time comes, you'll know what to do with it.}
rrrrrrrr
rrrrrrrrrr
{And so the fate of the world *turned*, for the **better.**}
{Or maybe **not.** Who knows? I'm just a *cat.*}
TUMP
rrrrrrrrrrrrrrrrrrrrrrrrrrrrrrrrrrrrrrrrrrrrrrr
zzzzzzzzzzzzzzzzz

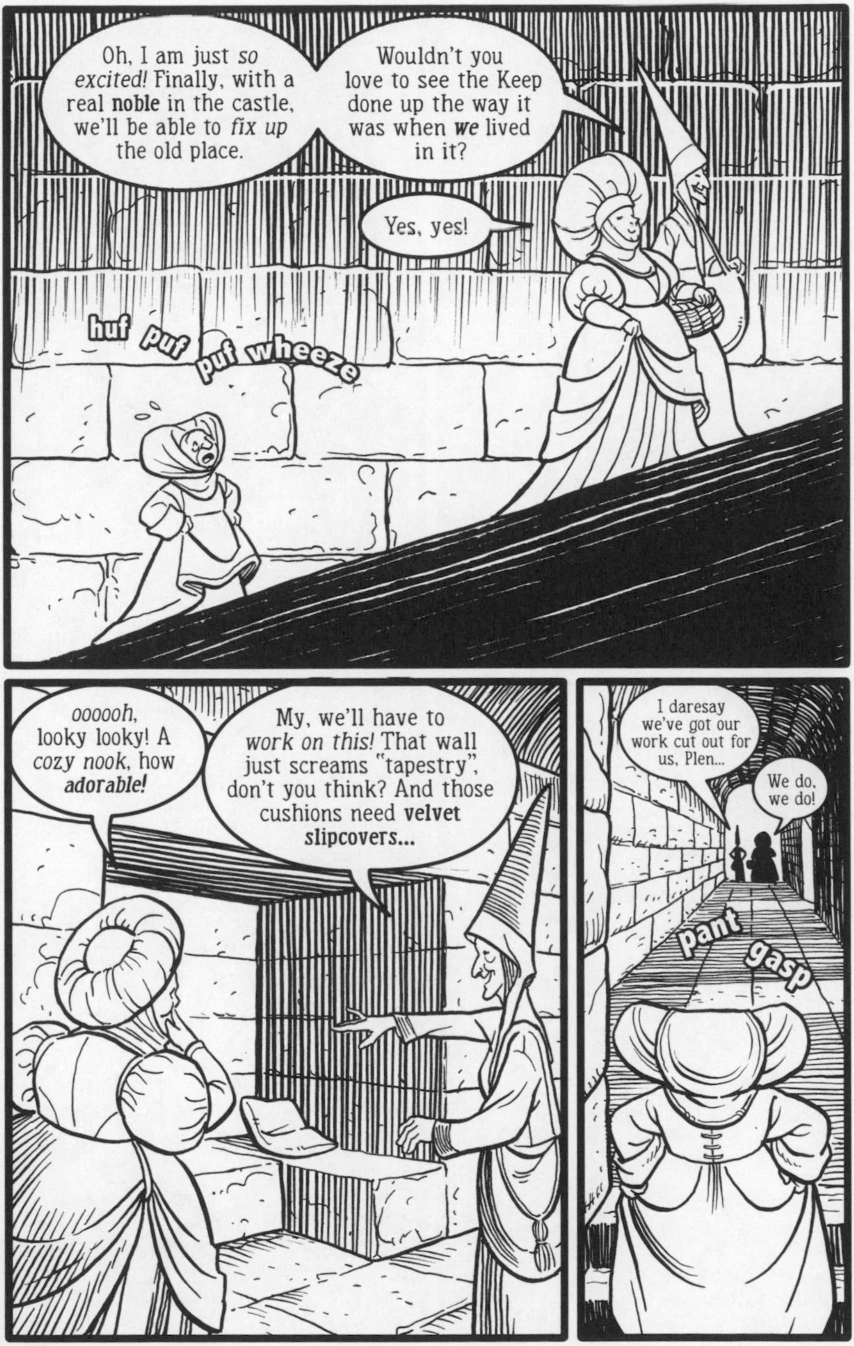
Oh, I am just *so excited!* Finally, with a real **noble** in the castle, we'll be able to *fix up* the old place.
Wouldn't you love to see the Keep done up the way it was when ***we*** lived in it?
Yes, yes!
huf puf puf wheeze
oooooh, looky looky! A *cozy nook*, how ***adorable!***
My, we'll have to *work on this!* That wall just screams "tapestry", don't you think? And those cushions need **velvet slipcovers...**
I daresay we've got our work cut out for us, Plen...
We do, we do!
pant gasp

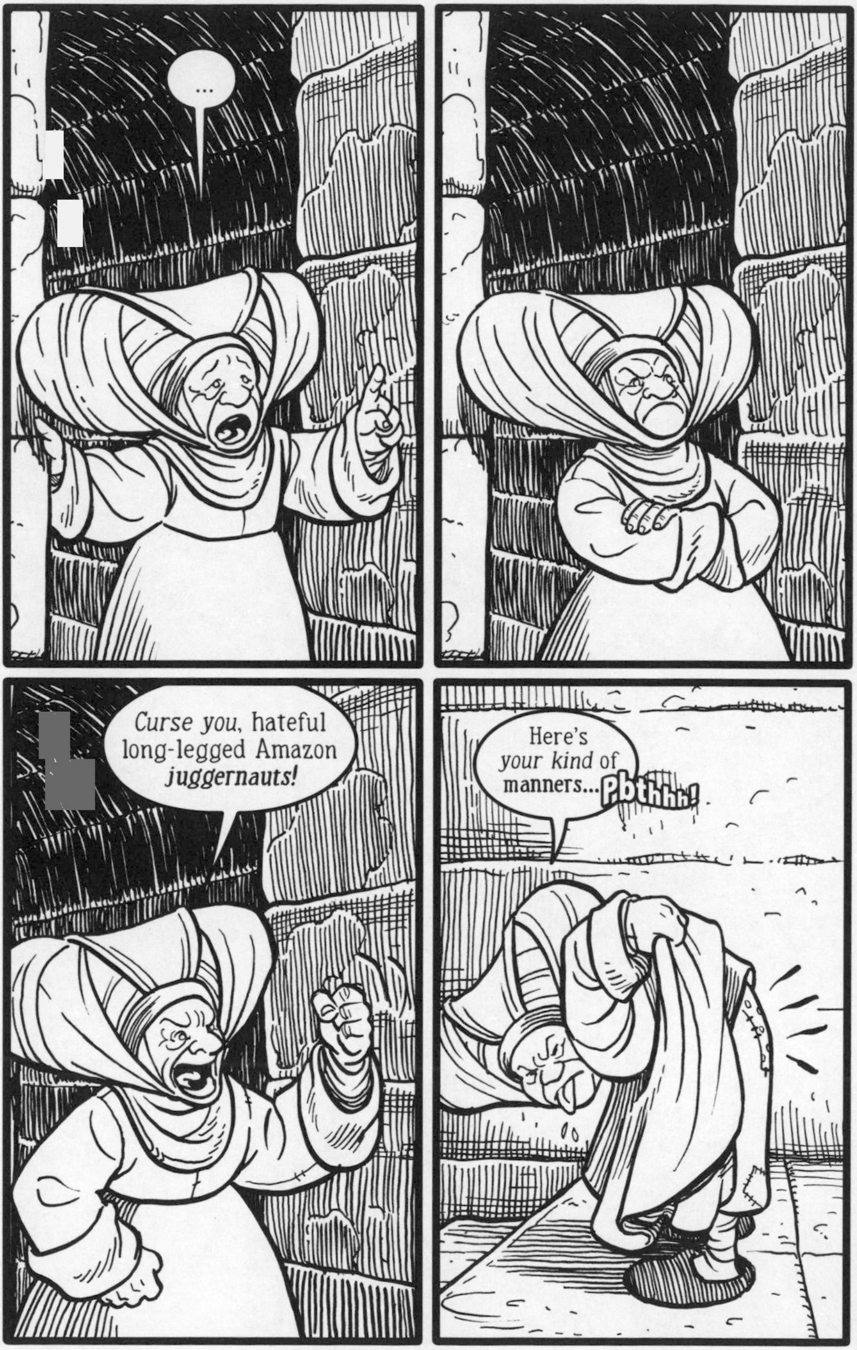
...
Curse you, hateful long-legged Amazon juggernauts!
Here's your kind of manners...
Pbthhh!

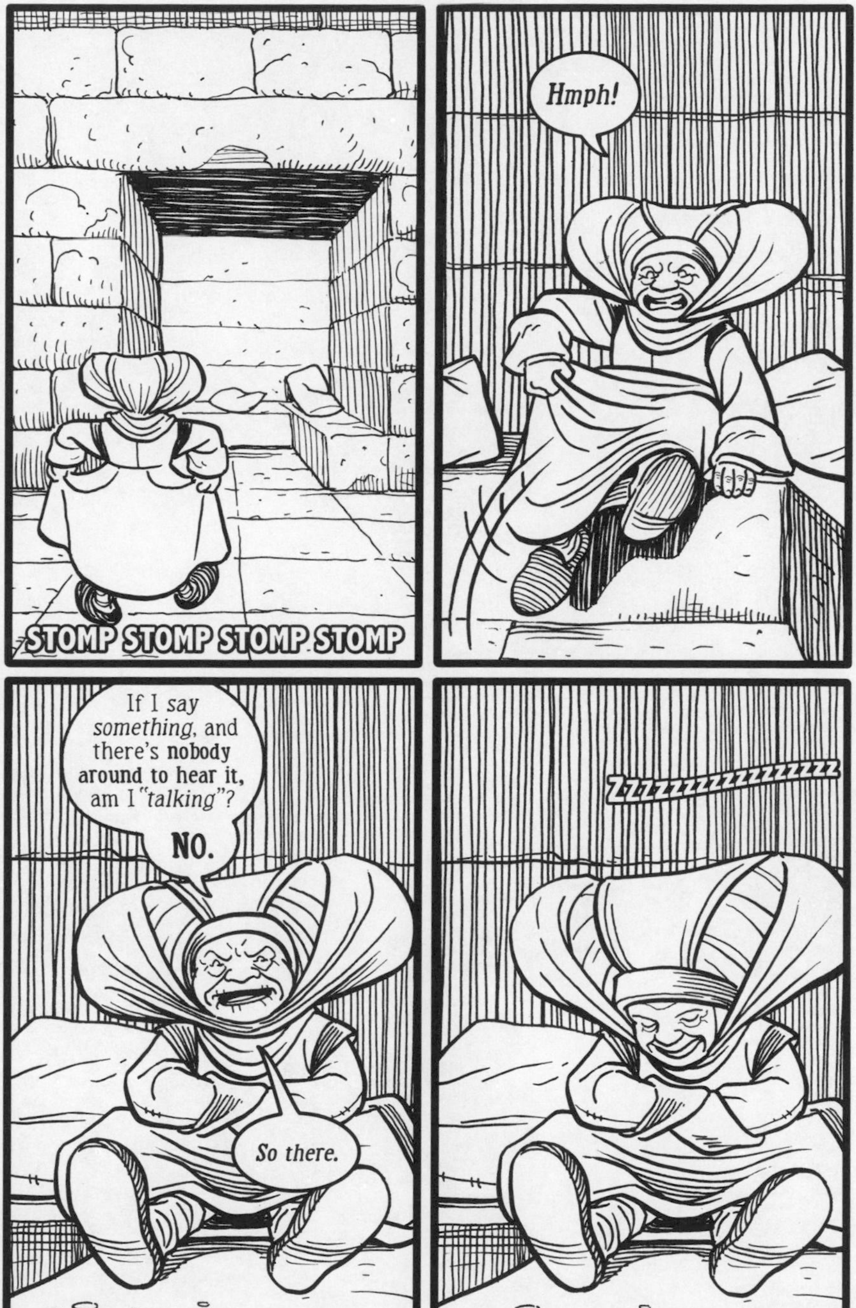
STOMP STOMP STOMP STOMP
Hmph!
If I *say* *something*, and there's **nobody** around to hear it, am I "*talking*"?
NO.
So there.
Zzzzzzzzzzzzzzzzz

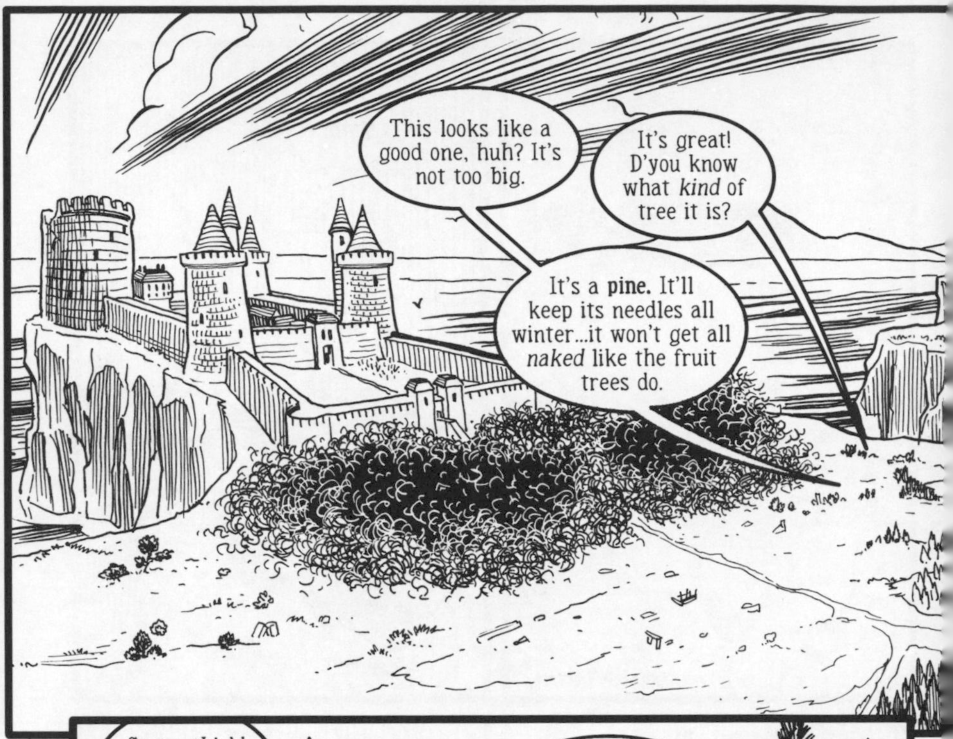
This looks like a good one, huh? It's not too big.
It's great! D'you know what *kind* of tree it is?
It's a **pine.** It'll keep its needles all winter...it won't get all *naked* like the fruit trees do.

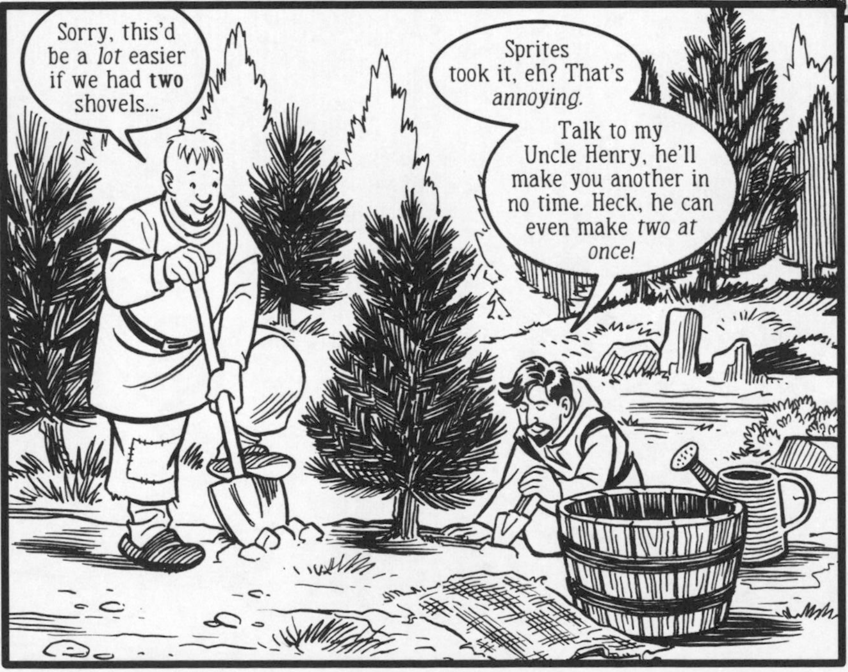
Sorry, this'd be a *lot* easier if we had **two** shovels...
Sprites took it, eh? That's *annoying.*
Talk to my Uncle Henry, he'll make you another in no time. Heck, he can even make *two at once!*

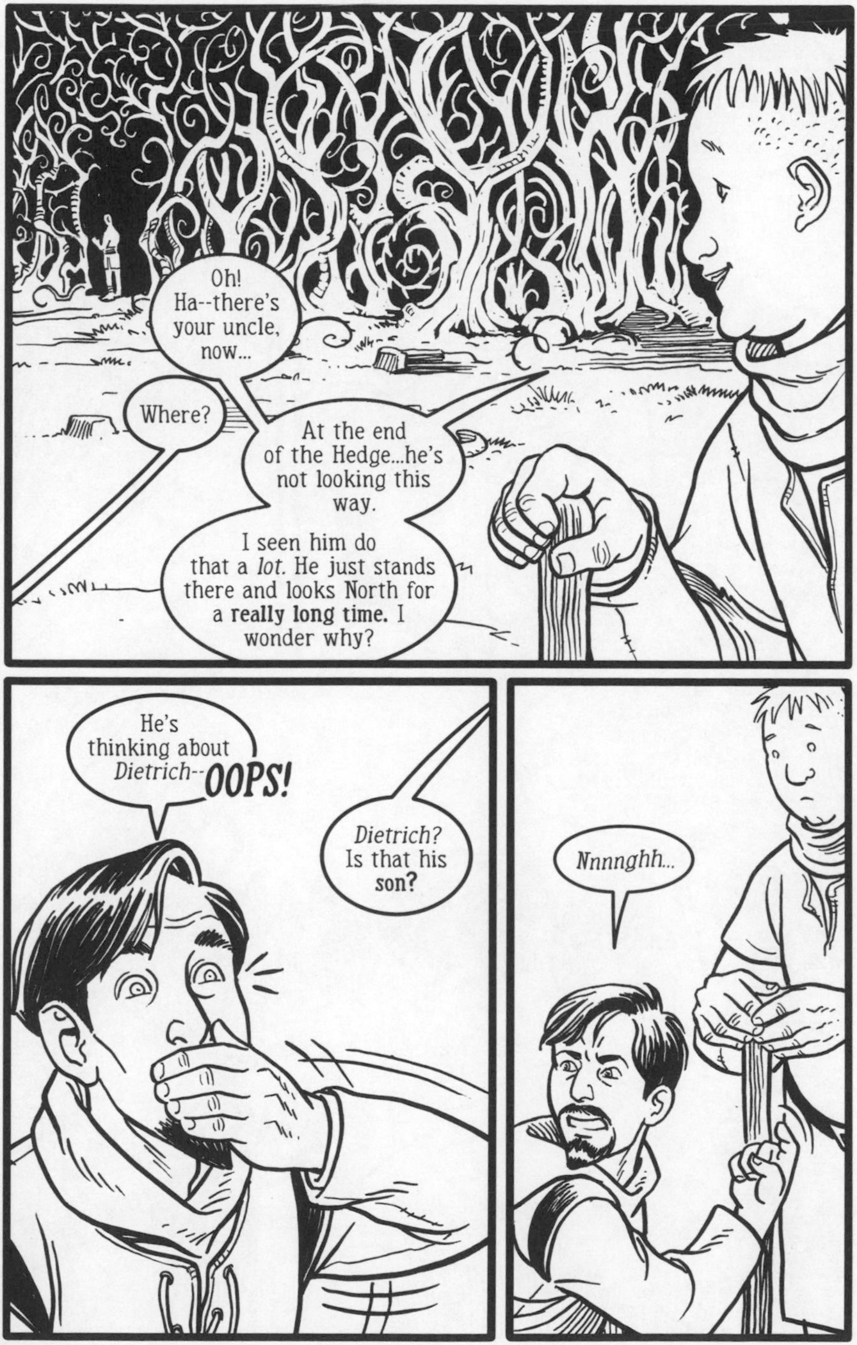
Oh! Ha--there's your uncle, now...
Where?
At the end of the Hedge...he's not looking this way.
I seen him do that a *lot*. He just stands there and looks North for a **really long time.** I wonder why?
He's thinking about *Dietrich*--**OOPS!**
Dietrich? Is that his **son?**
Nnnnghh...

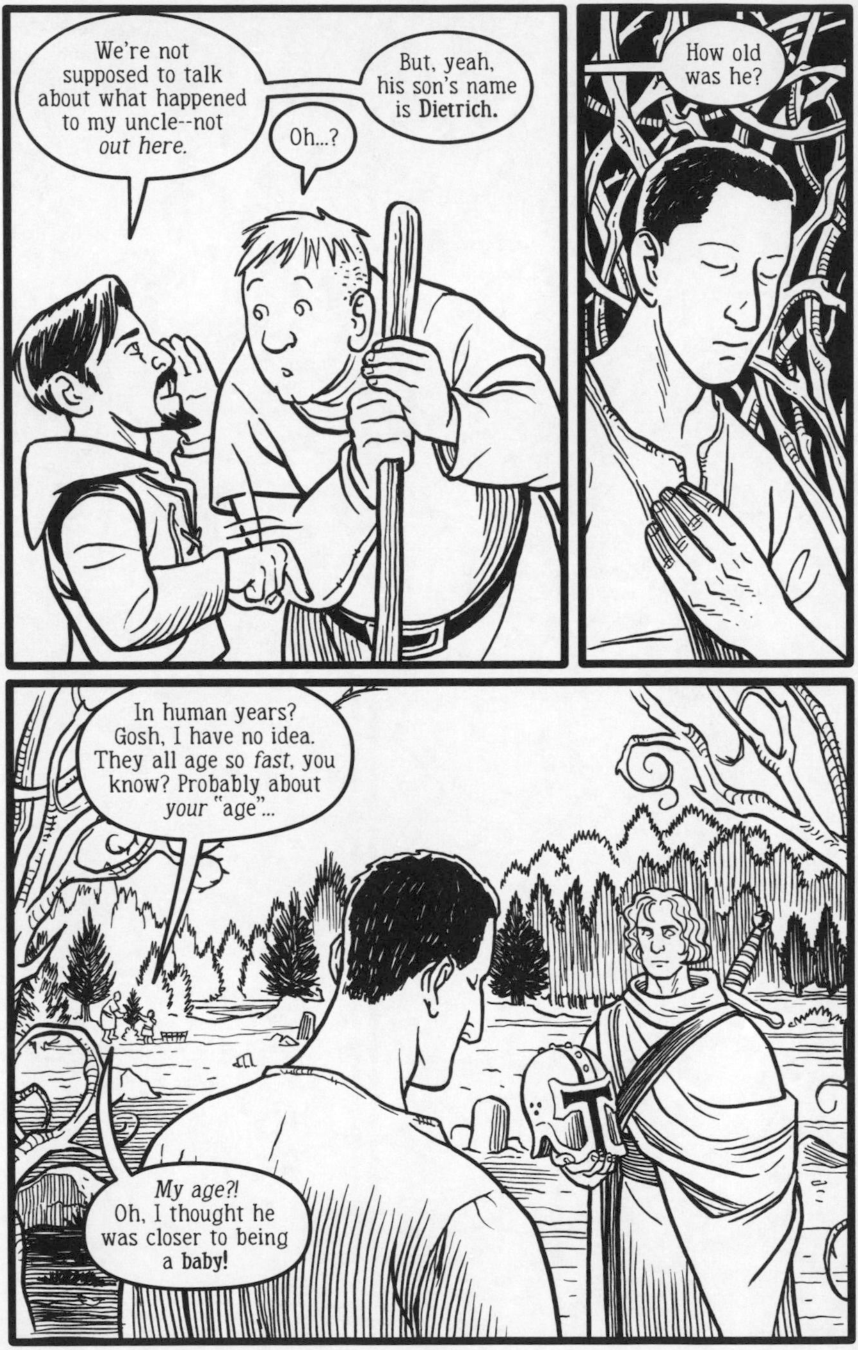
We're not supposed to talk about what happened to my uncle--not *out here.*
Oh...?
But, yeah, his son's name is **Dietrich.**
How old was he?
In human years? Gosh, I have no idea. They all age so *fast*, you know? Probably about *your* "age"...
My age?! Oh, I thought he was closer to being a **baby!**

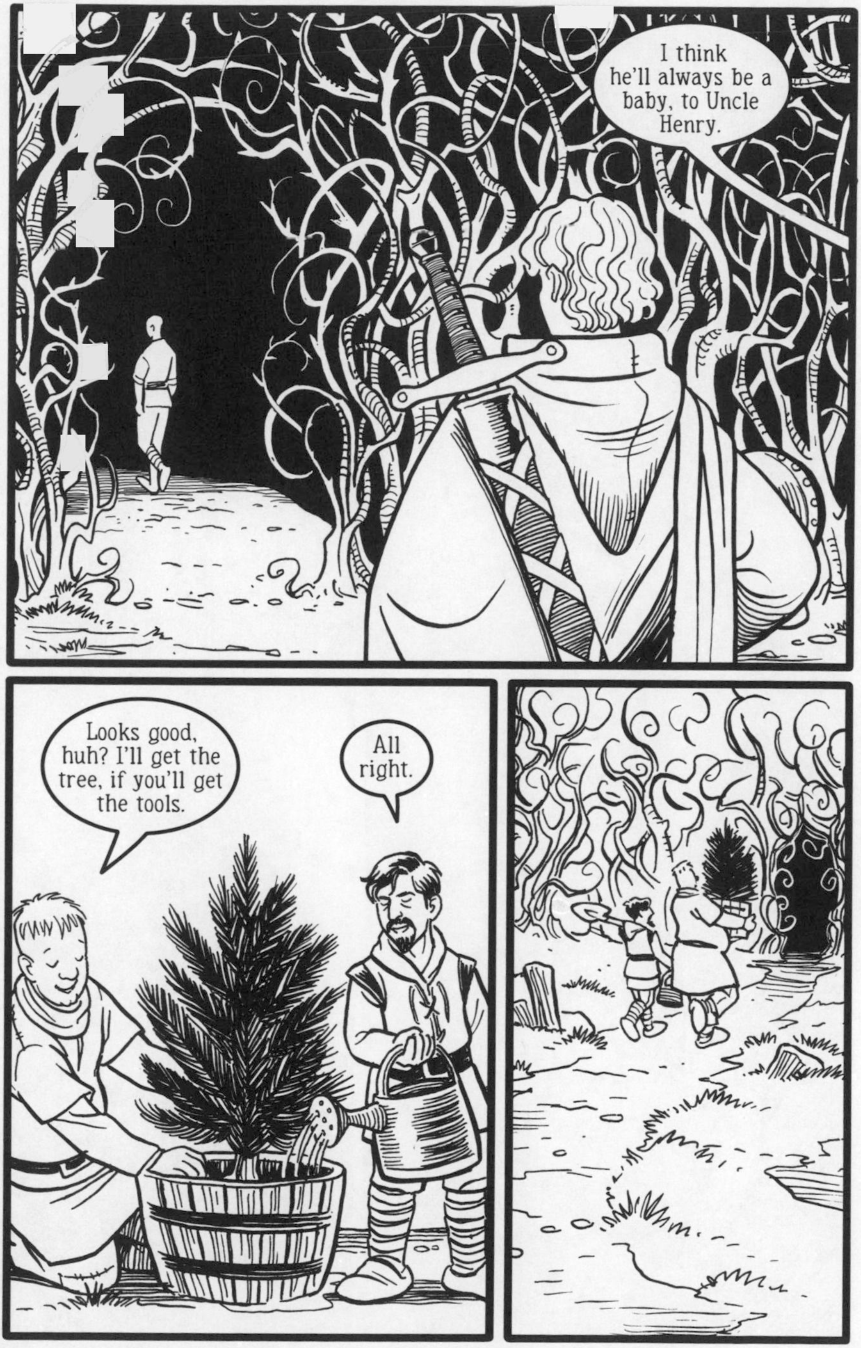
I think he'll always be a baby, to Uncle Henry.
Looks good, huh? I'll get the tree, if you'll get the tools.
All right.

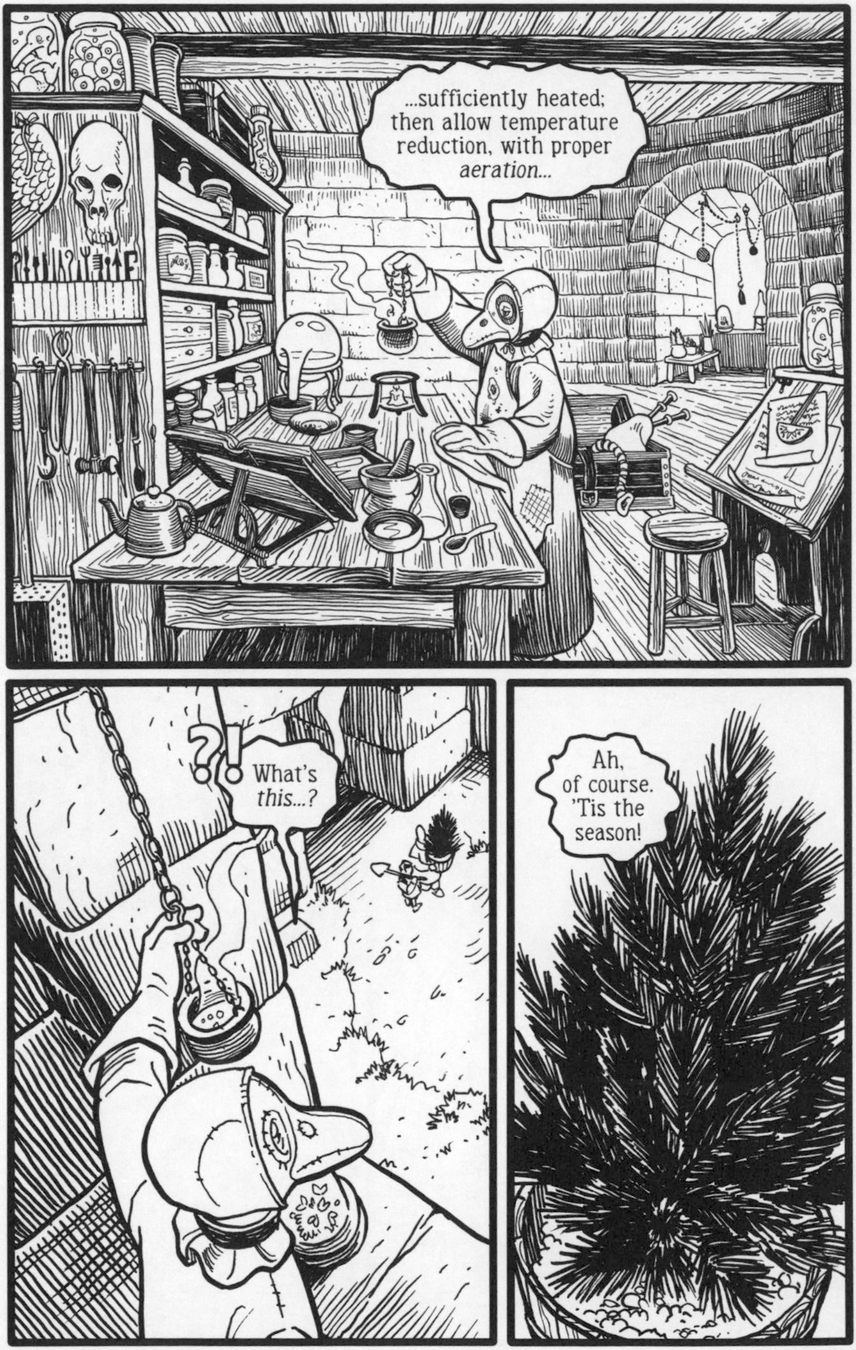
...sufficiently heated; then allow temperature reduction, with proper *aeration*...
?!
What's *this*...?
Ah, of course. 'Tis the season!

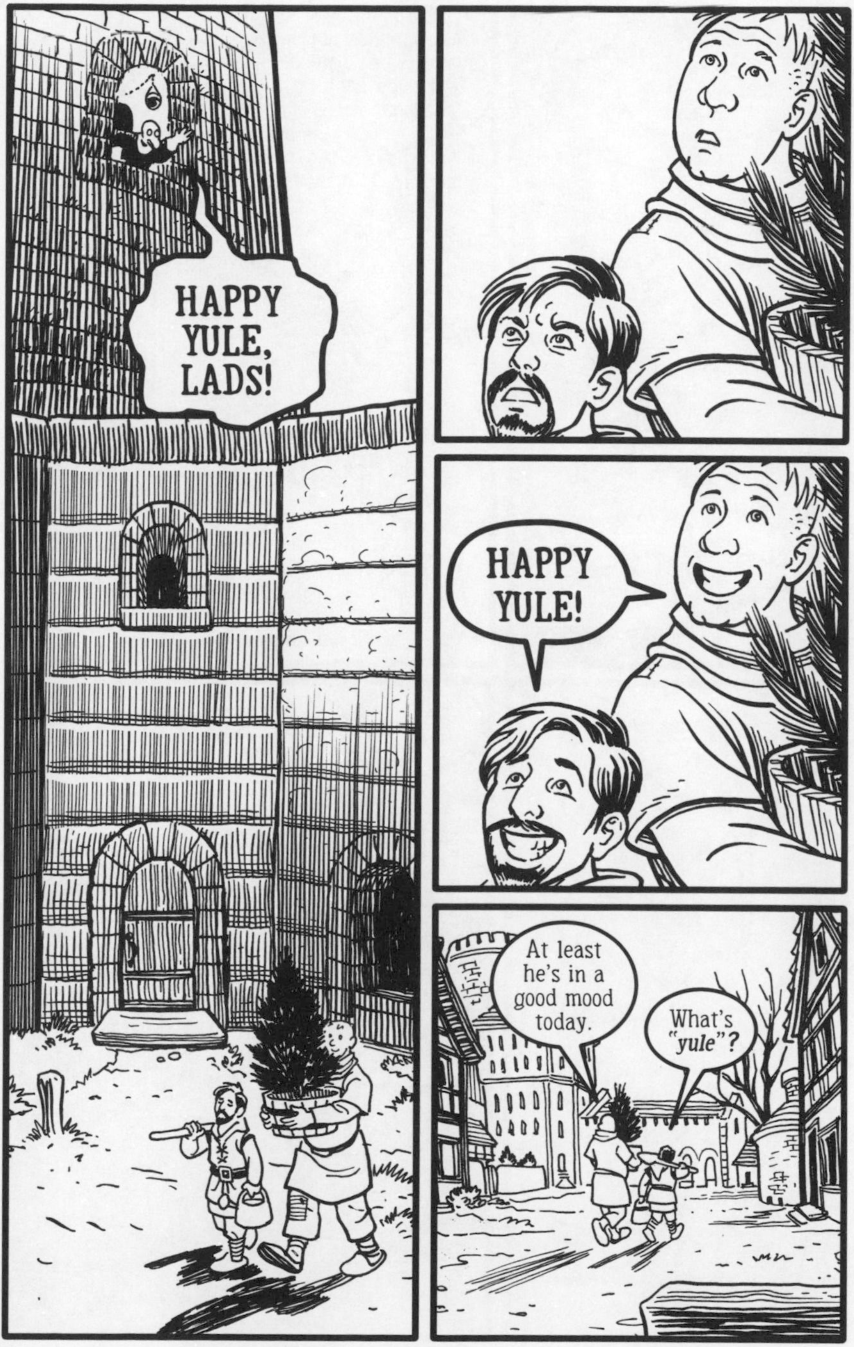
HAPPY YULE, LADS!
HAPPY YULE!
At least he's in a good mood today.
What's "*yule*"?

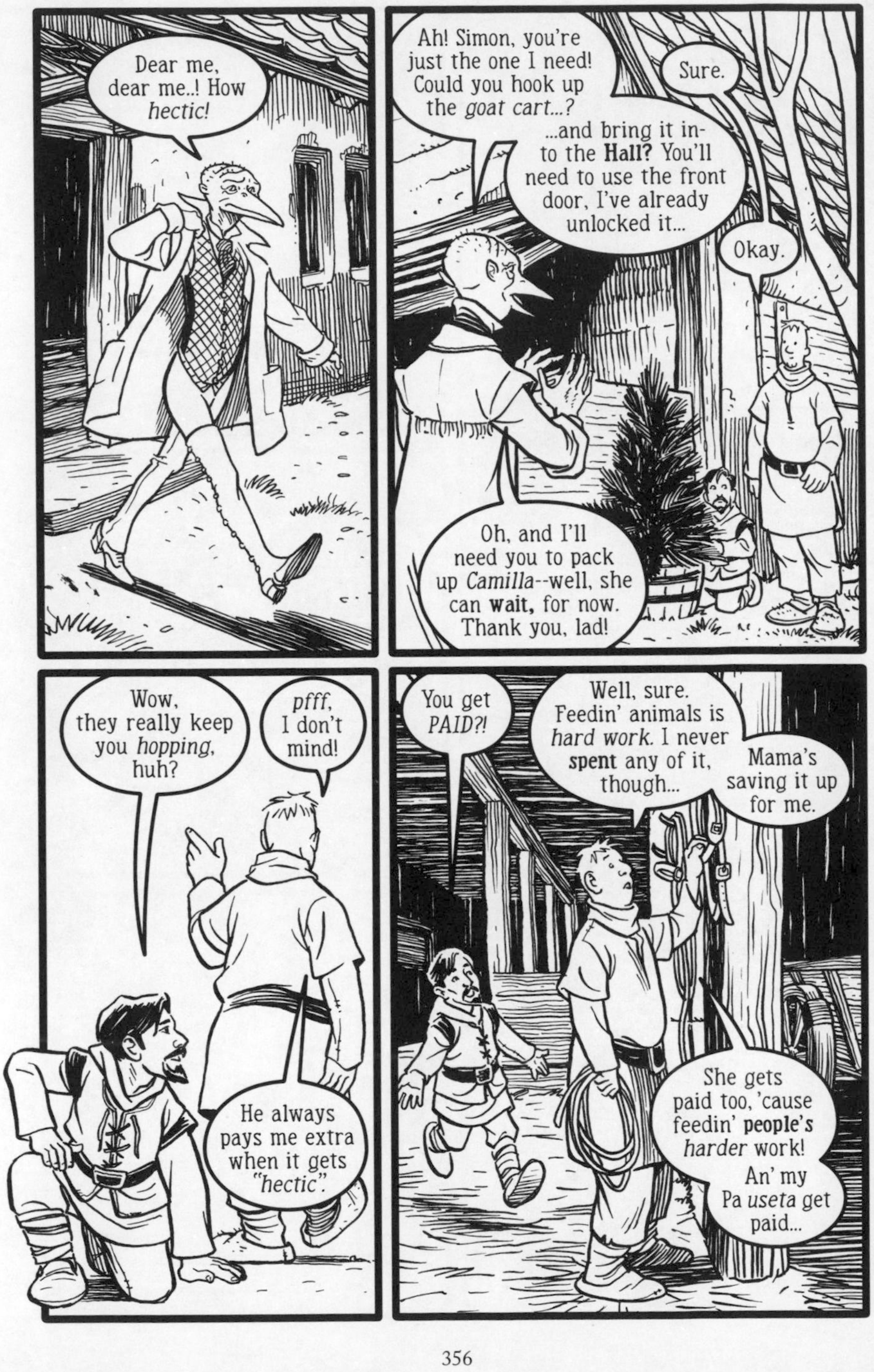
Dear me, dear me..! How *hectic!*
Ah! Simon, you're just the one I need! Could you hook up the *goat cart*...?
Sure.
...and bring it in-to the **Hall?** You'll need to use the front door, I've already unlocked it...
Okay.
Oh, and I'll need you to pack up *Camilla*--well, she can **wait,** for now. Thank you, lad!
Wow, they really keep you *hopping,* huh?
pfff, I don't mind!
He always pays me extra when it gets *"hectic".*
You get *PAID?!*
Well, sure. Feedin' animals is *hard work.* I never **spent** any of it, though...
Mama's saving it up for me.
She gets paid too, 'cause feedin' **people's** *harder* work!
An' my Pa *useta* get paid...

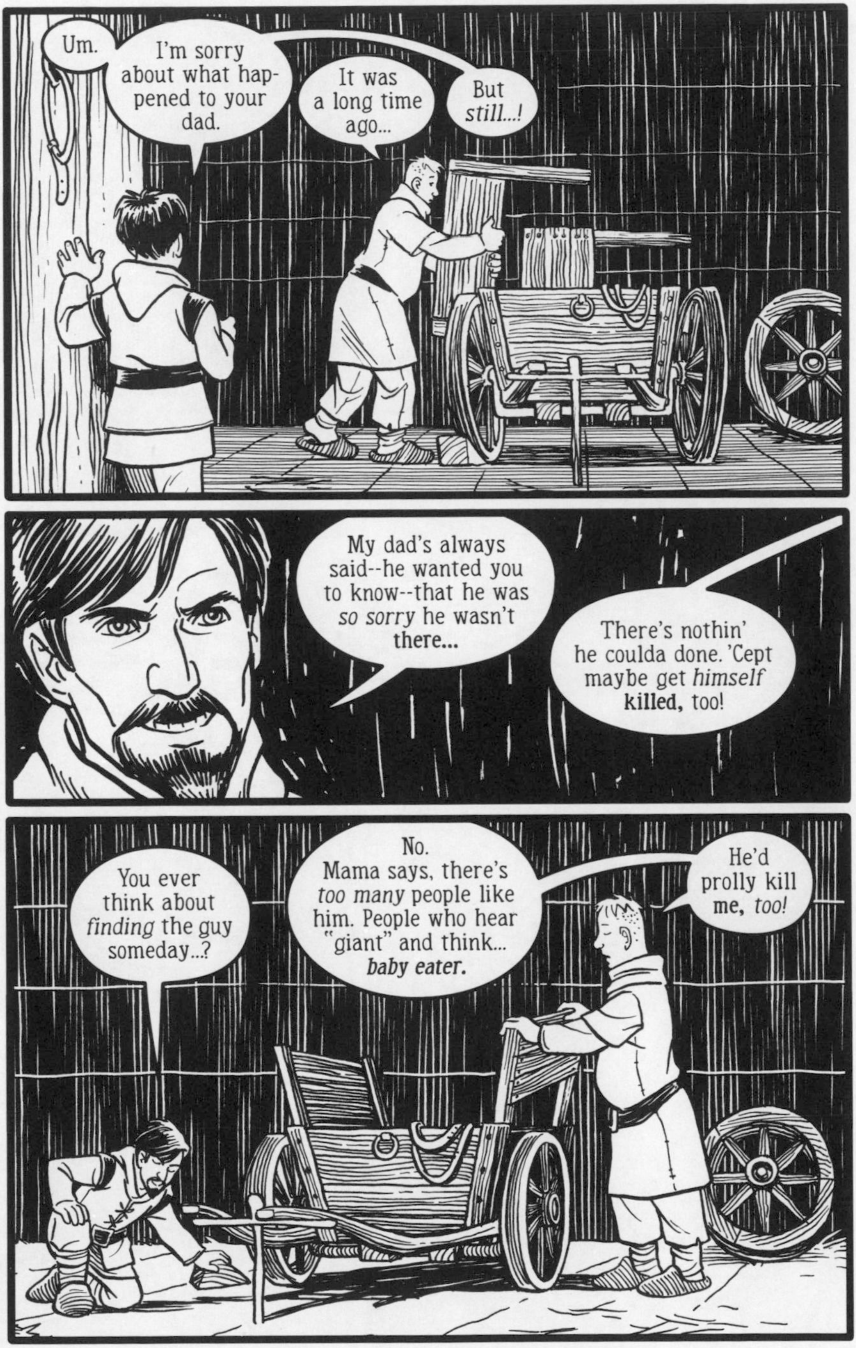
Um.
I'm sorry about what happened to your dad.
It was a long time ago...
But *still...!*
My dad's always said--he wanted you to know--that he was *so sorry* he wasn't **there...**
There's nothin' he coulda done. 'Cept maybe get *himself* **killed,** too!
You ever think about *finding* the guy someday...?
No.
Mama says, there's *too many* people like him. People who hear "giant" and think... ***baby eater.***
He'd prolly kill **me,** *too!*

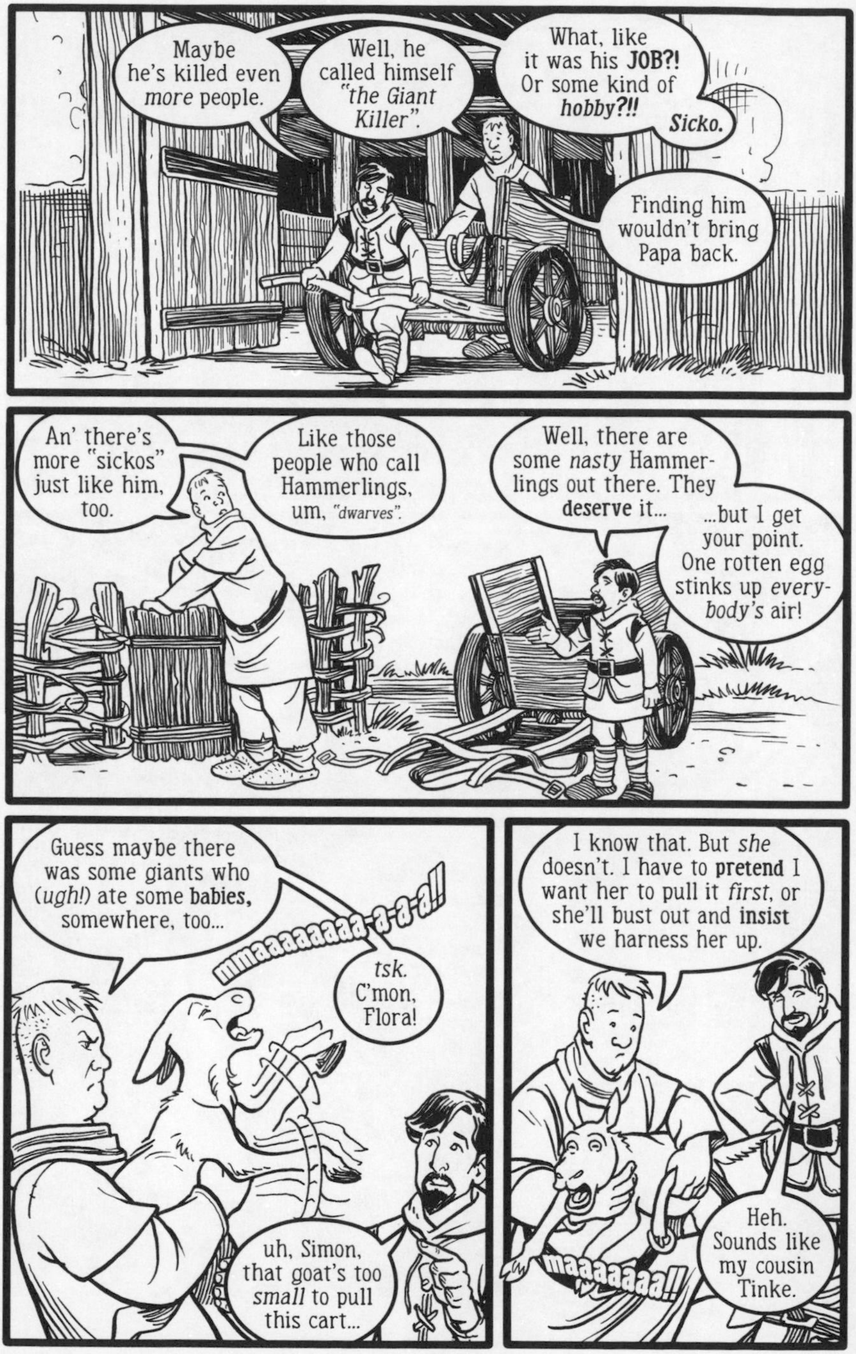
Maybe he's killed even *more* people.
Well, he called himself *"the Giant Killer"*.
What, like it was his **JOB?!** Or some kind of ***hobby?!!***
Sicko.
Finding him wouldn't bring Papa back.
An' there's more "sickos" just like him, too.
Like those people who call Hammerlings, um, *"dwarves"*.
Well, there are some *nasty* Hammerlings out there. They **deserve** it...
...but I get your point. One rotten egg stinks up *every-body's* air!
Guess maybe there was some giants who (*ugh!*) ate some **babies,** somewhere, too...
mmaaaaaaaaa-a-a-a!!
tsk. C'mon, Flora!
uh, Simon, that goat's too *small* to pull this cart...
I know that. But *she* doesn't. I have to **pretend** I want her to pull it *first*, or she'll bust out and **insist** we harness her up.
maaaaaaa!!
Heh. Sounds like my cousin Tinke.

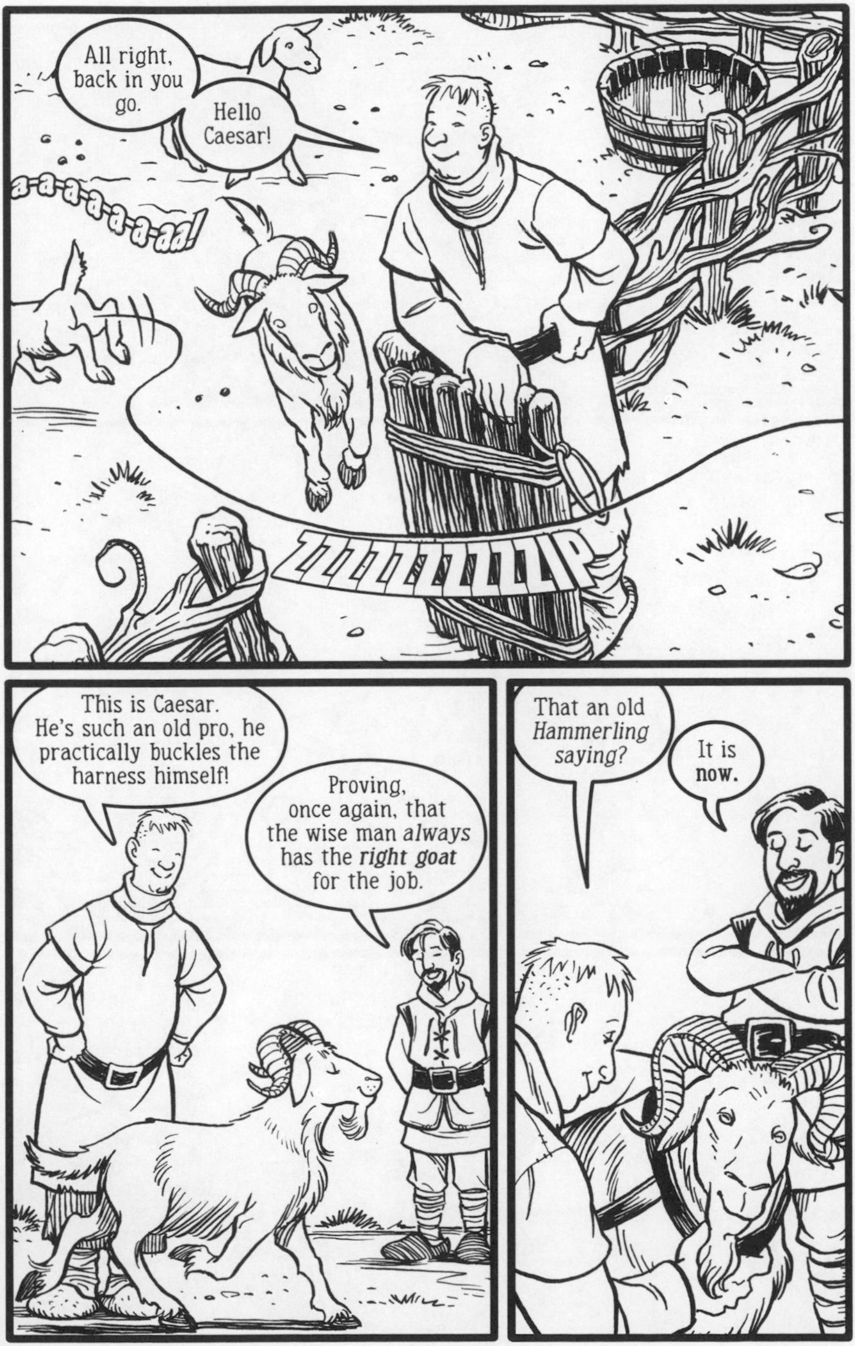
All right, back in you go.
Hello Caesar!
a-a-a-a-a-a-a-aa!
ZZZZZZZZZZZIP
This is Caesar. He's such an old pro, he practically buckles the harness himself!
Proving, once again, that the wise man *always* has the ***right goat*** for the job.
That an old *Hammerling saying?*
It is **now.**

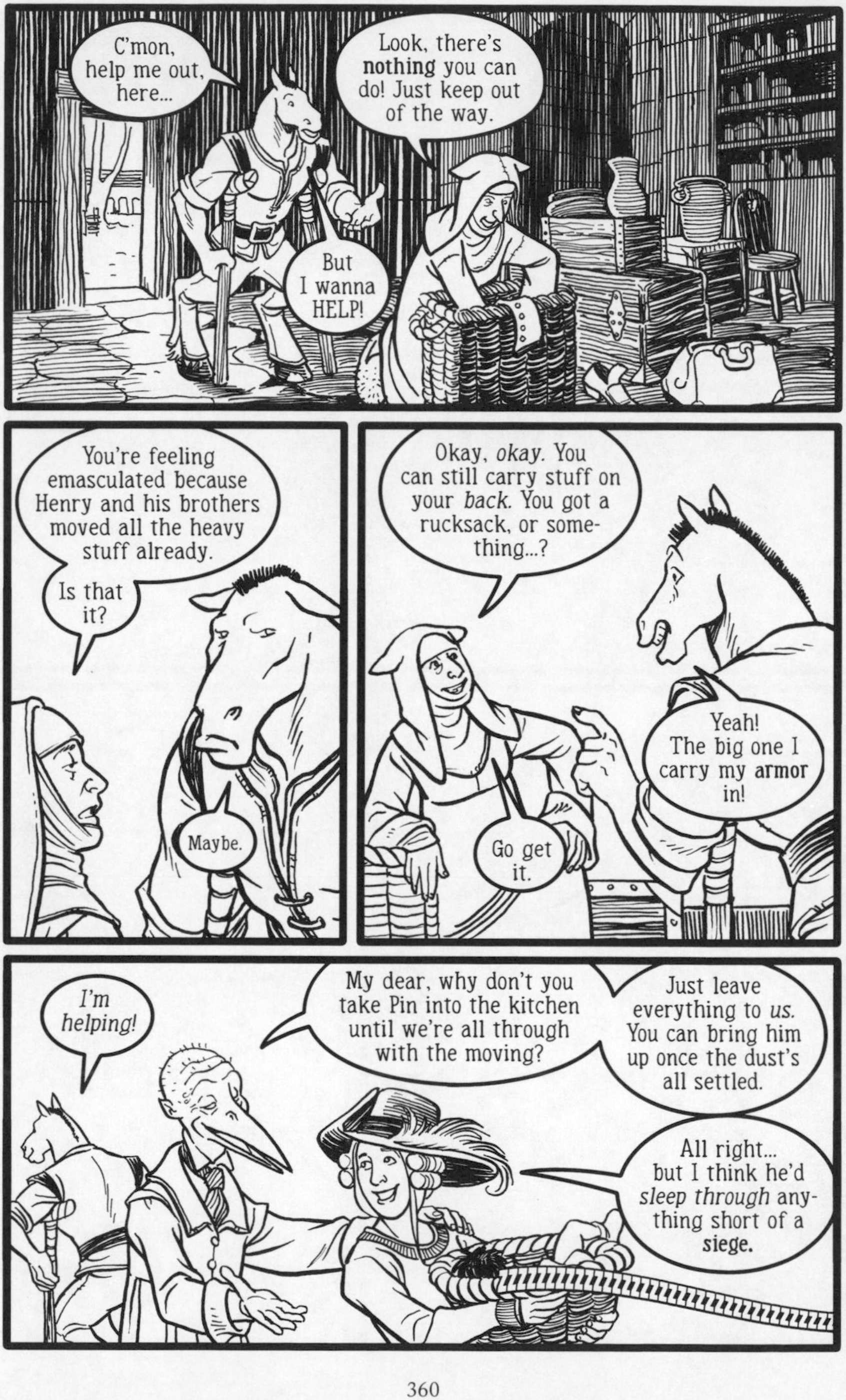
C'mon, help me out, here...
Look, there's **nothing** you can do! Just keep out of the way.
But I wanna HELP!
You're feeling emasculated because Henry and his brothers moved all the heavy stuff already.
Is that it?
Maybe.
Okay, *okay.* You can still carry stuff on your *back.* You got a rucksack, or something...?
Yeah! The big one I carry my **armor** in!
Go get it.
I'm helping!
My dear, why don't you take Pin into the kitchen until we're all through with the moving?
Just leave everything to *us.* You can bring him up once the dust's all settled.
All right... but I think he'd *sleep through* anything short of a **siege.**

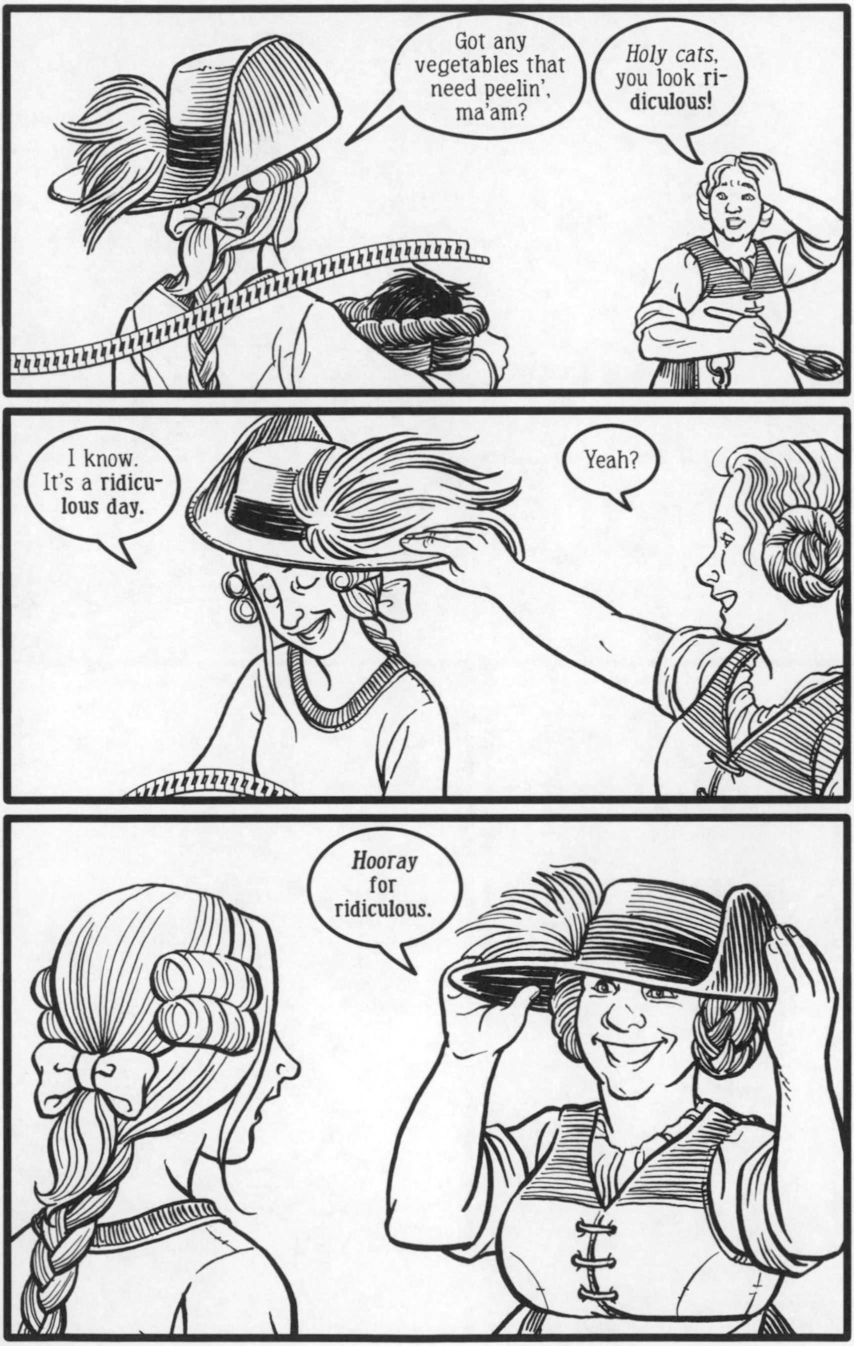
Got any vegetables that need peelin', ma'am?
Holy cats, you look **ri-diculous!**
I know. It's a **ridicu-lous day.**
Yeah?
Hooray **for ridiculous.**

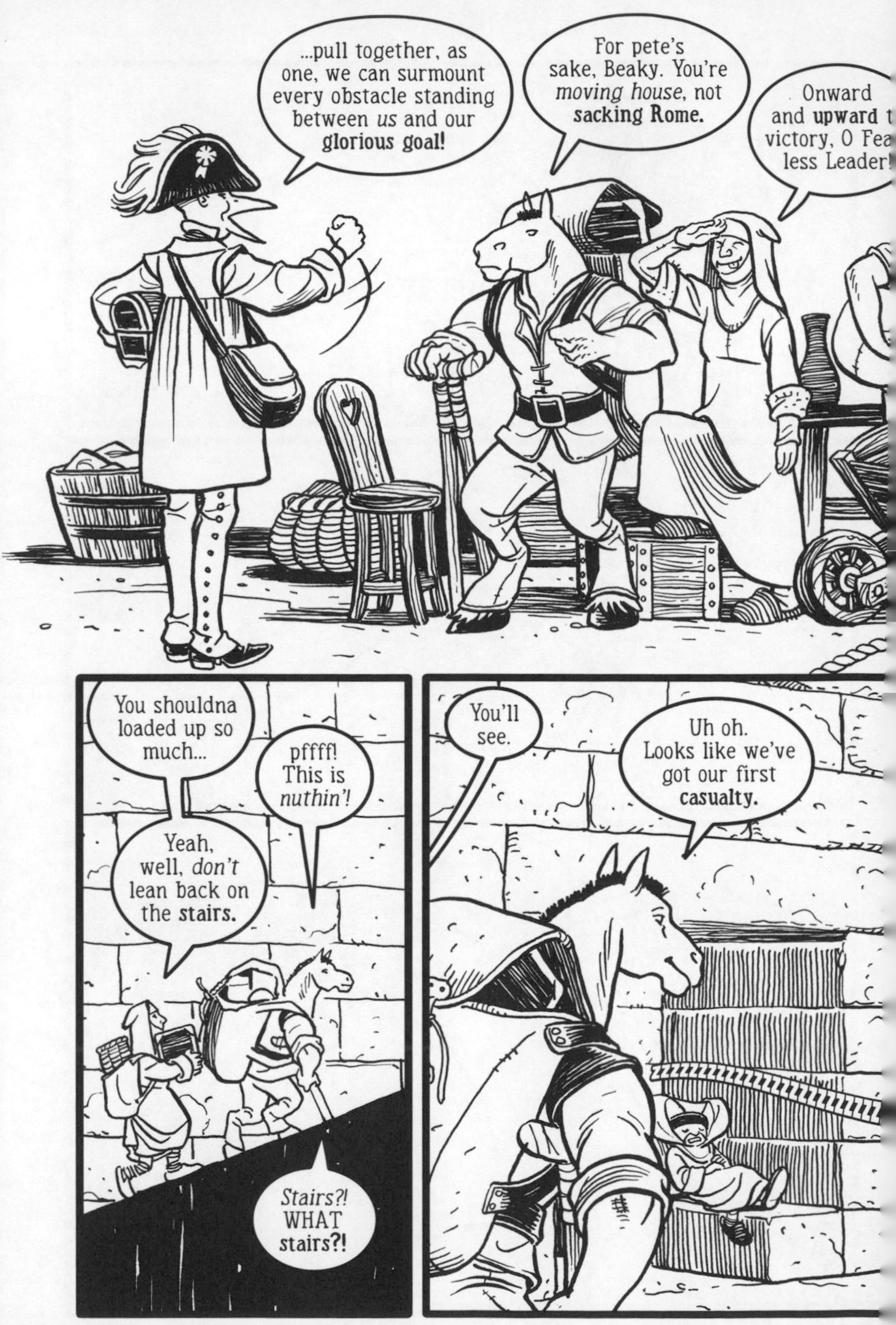
...pull together, as one, we can surmount every obstacle standing between *us* and our **glorious goal!**
For pete's sake, Beaky. You're *moving house*, not **sacking Rome.**
Onward and **upward** t victory, O Fea less Leader!
You shouldna loaded up so much...
pffff! This is *nuthin'!*
Yeah, well, *don't* lean back on the **stairs.**
Stairs?! WHAT **stairs?!**
You'll see.
Uh oh. Looks like we've got our first **casualty.**
zzzzzzzzzzzzzzzzzzzzzzzzzzz

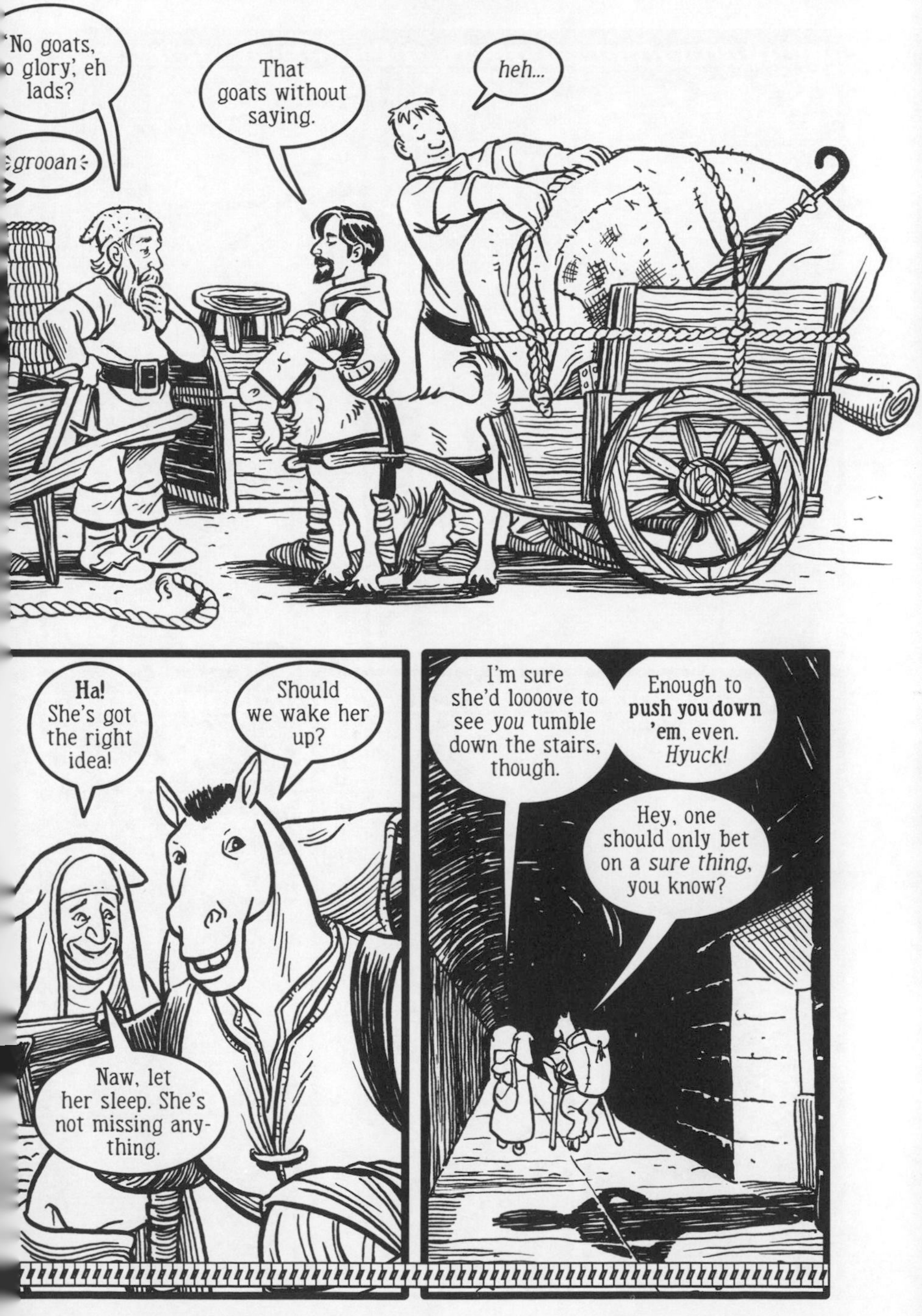
'No goats,
o glory,' eh
lads?
That
goats without
saying.
heh...
grooan
Ha!
She's got
the right
idea!
Should
we wake her
up?
Naw, let
her sleep. She's
not missing any-
thing.
I'm sure
she'd loooove to
see *you* tumble
down the stairs,
though.
Enough to
push you down
'em, even.
Hyuck!
Hey, one
should only bet
on a *sure thing*,
you know?

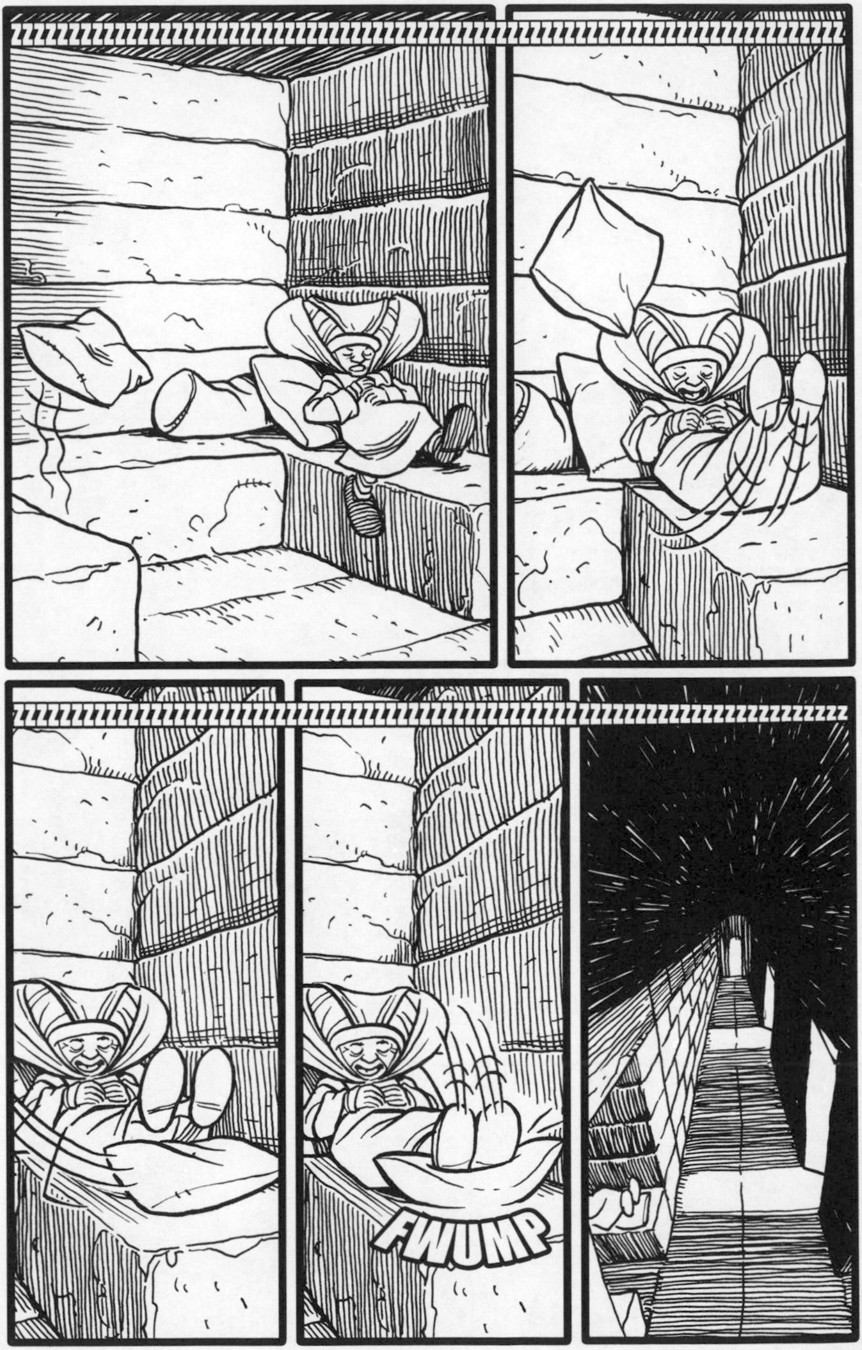
FWUMP

Chapter 14.

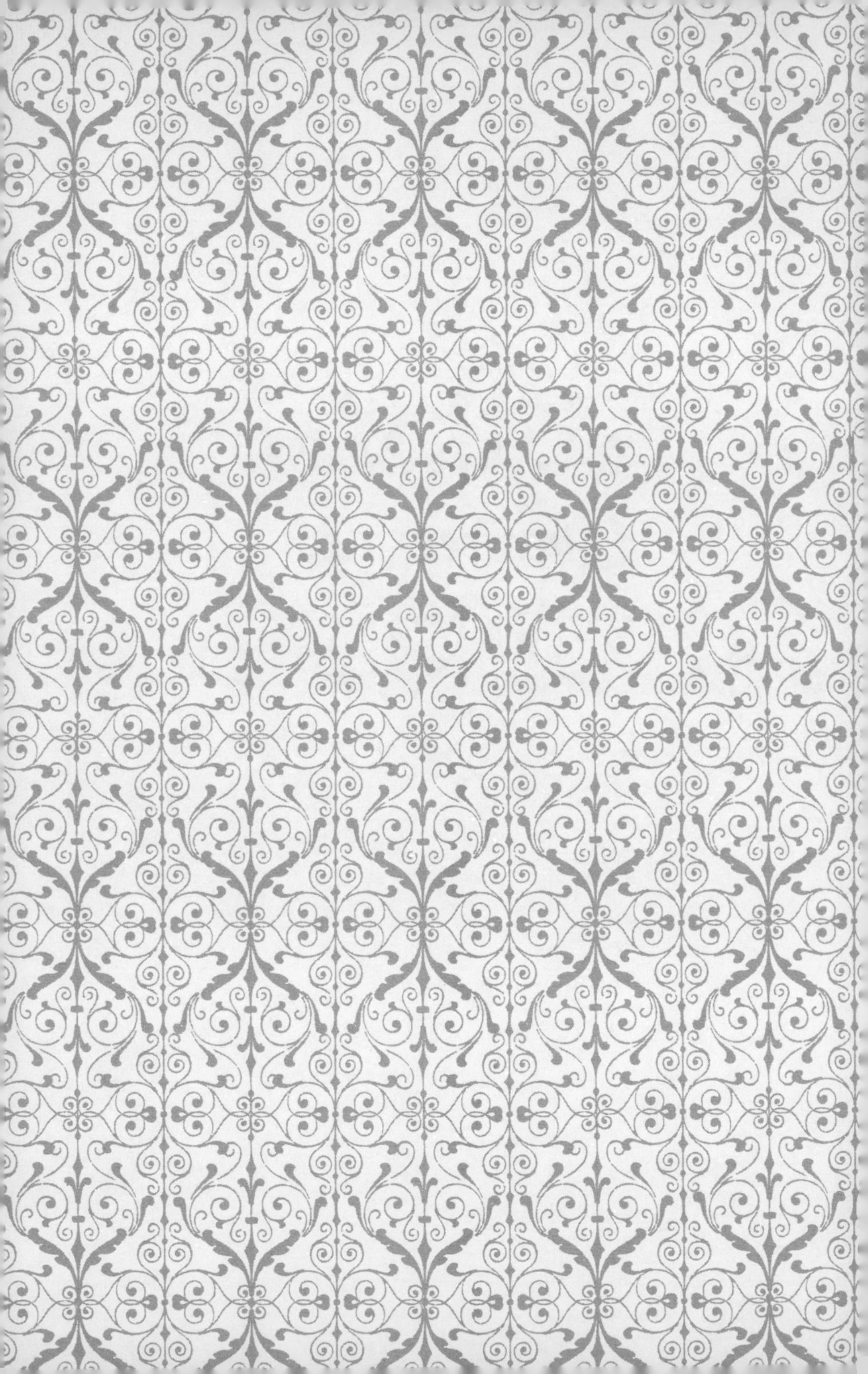

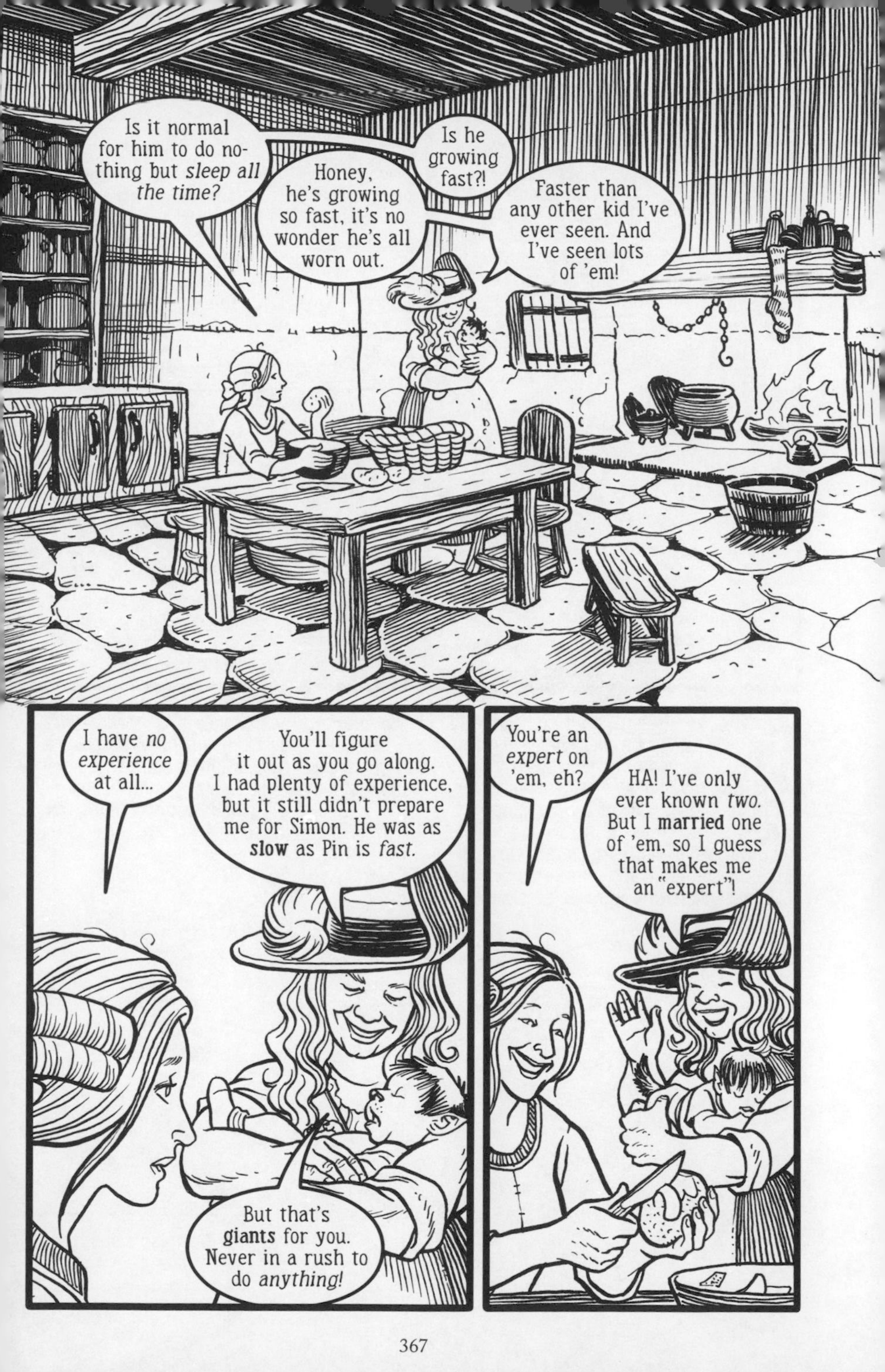
Is it normal for him to do nothing but *sleep all the time?*
Honey, he's growing so fast, it's no wonder he's all worn out.
Is he growing fast?!
Faster than any other kid I've ever seen. And I've seen lots of 'em!
I have *no experience* at all...
You'll figure it out as you go along. I had plenty of experience, but it still didn't prepare me for Simon. He was as **slow** as Pin is *fast.*
But that's **giants** for you. Never in a rush to do *anything!*
You're an *expert* on 'em, eh?
HA! I've only ever known *two.* But I **married** one of 'em, so I guess that makes me an "expert"!

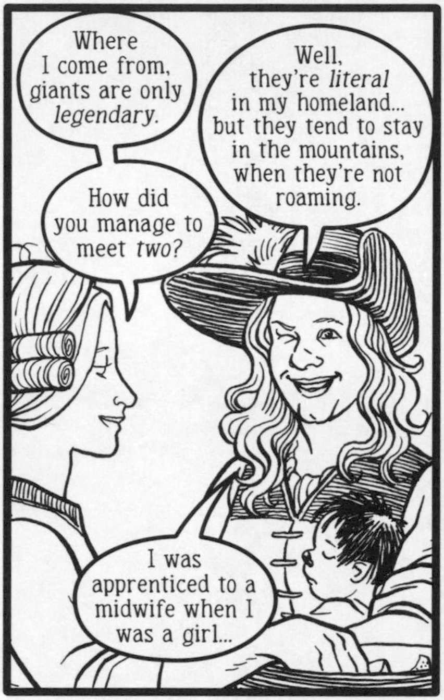
Where I come from, giants are only *legendary*.
Well, they're *literal* in my homeland... but they tend to stay in the mountains, when they're not roaming.
How did you manage to meet *two?*
I was apprenticed to a midwife when I was a girl...

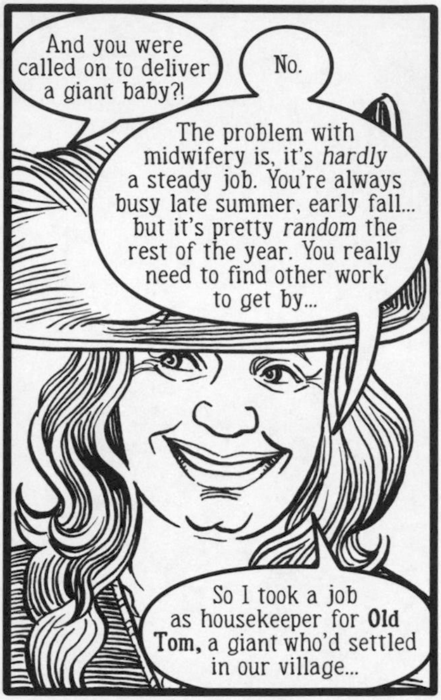
And you were called on to deliver a giant baby?!
No.
The problem with midwifery is, it's *hardly* a steady job. You're always busy late summer, early fall... but it's pretty *random* the rest of the year. You really need to find other work to get by...
So I took a job as housekeeper for **Old Tom,** a giant who'd settled in our village...

Tom was an oddball, as giants go, and a real oldtimer. He wouldn't eat meat of any kind; couldn't stand the thought of killing even the smallest creature. He'd had his fill of wandering the world...but instead of returning to the mountains, he built himself a tiny cottage on the edge of town and soon had the most fantastic garden ever seen.

He planted beanstocks that practically grew up to the sky--and blackberries as big as your fist, or bigger! Ears of corn that stood taller than any man in town... he had a real green thumb, that's for sure.

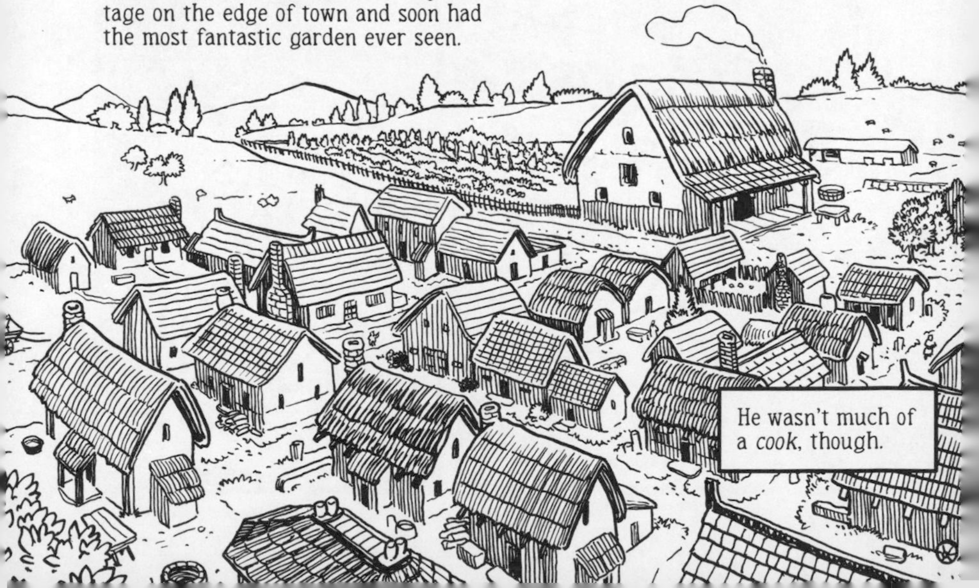
He wasn't much of a *cook*, though.

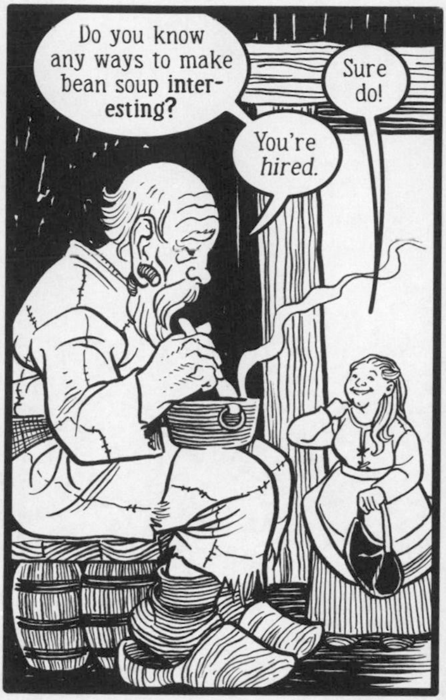
Do you know any ways to make bean soup **interesting?**
You're *hired.*
Sure do!

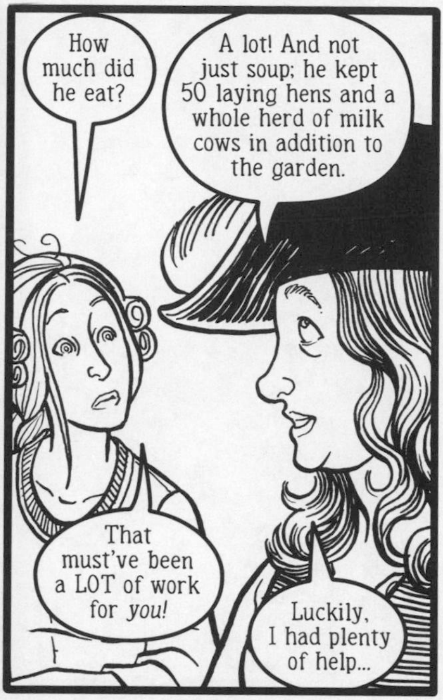
How much did he eat?
A lot! And not just soup; he kept 50 laying hens and a whole herd of milk cows in addition to the garden.
That must've been a LOT of work for *you!*
Luckily, I had plenty of help...

Children loved Tom, loved the garden. There was always a crowd of 'em around, willing to work for an armful of vegetables...or even just for the *fun* of it! Tom adored them all, and their stories and games. He always seemed a little awkward with the other villagers, though.

I guess when you'd lived as long, and pondered as much, as Old Tom had...a game of *hopscotch* could be more **profound** than village politics or gossip.

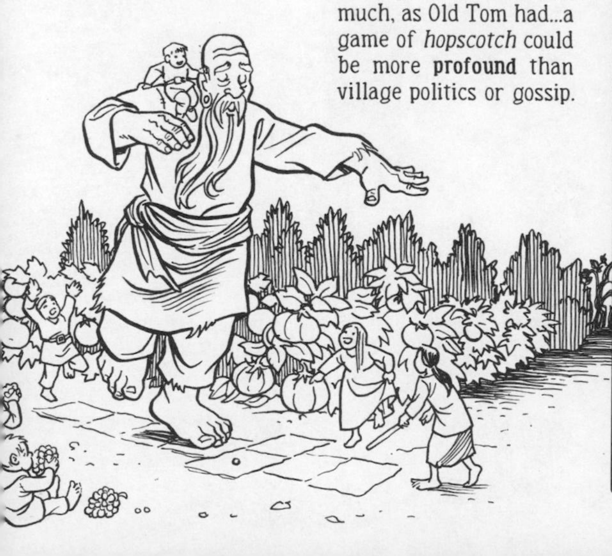

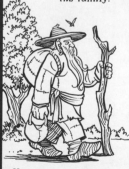

One day, out of the blue, he announced that he was taking a "little trip" to the mountains, to visit his family.

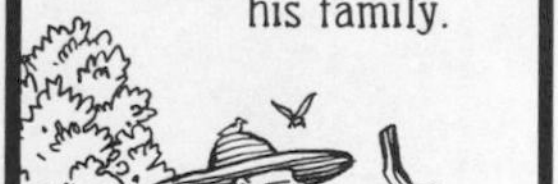

He was gone for *two whole months!* Well, that's Giants, for you. The kids and I kept busy pickling eggs and making cheese...

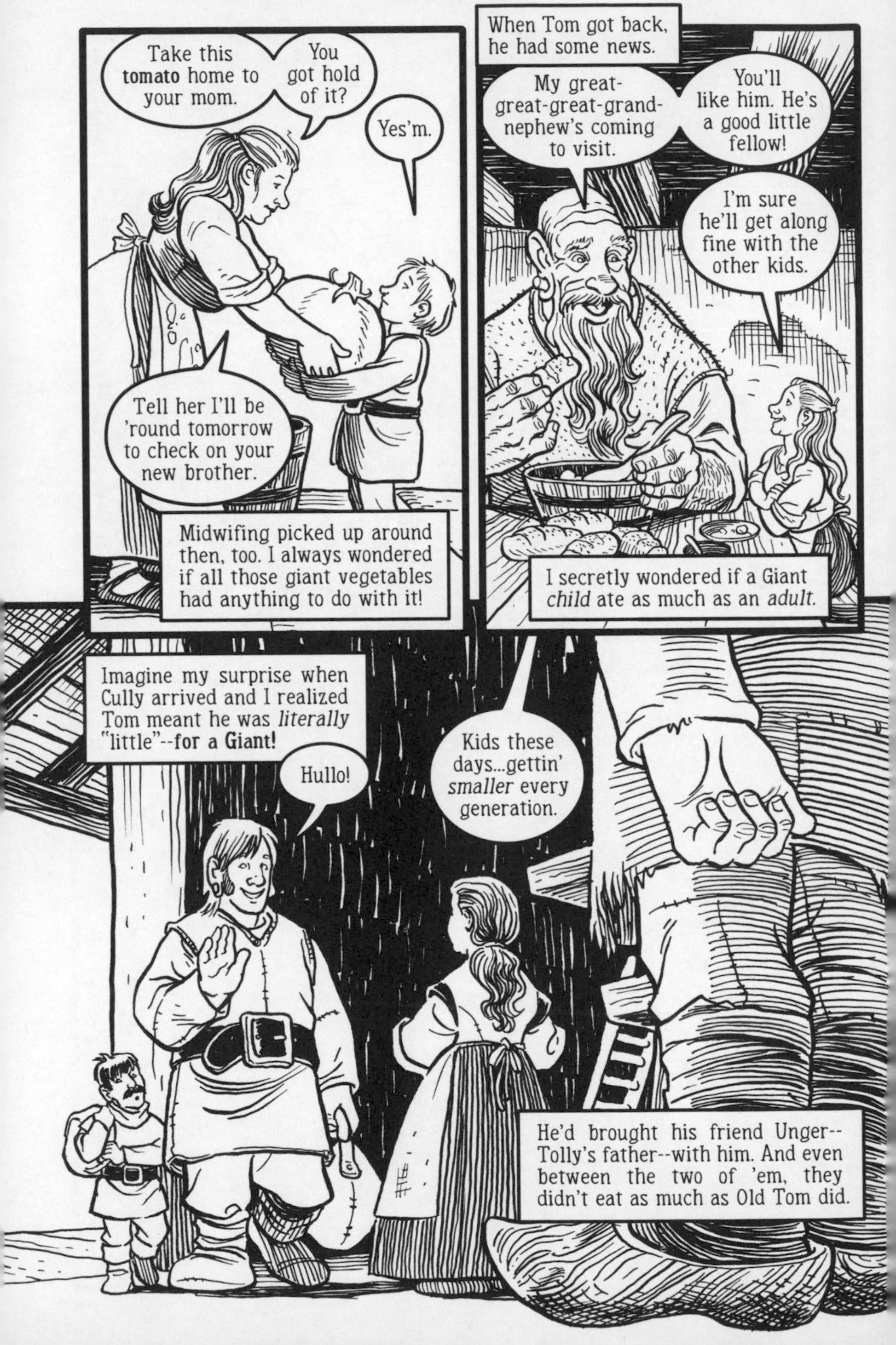
Take this **tomato** home to your mom.
You got hold of it?
Yes'm.
Tell her I'll be 'round tomorrow to check on your new brother.
Midwifing picked up around then, too. I always wondered if all those giant vegetables had anything to do with it!
When Tom got back, he had some news.
My great-great-great-grand-nephew's coming to visit.
You'll like him. He's a good little fellow!
I'm sure he'll get along fine with the other kids.
I secretly wondered if a Giant *child* ate as much as an *adult.*
Imagine my surprise when Cully arrived and I realized Tom meant he was *literally* "little"--**for a Giant!**
Hullo!
Kids these days...gettin' *smaller* every generation.
He'd brought his friend Unger--Tolly's father--with him. And even between the two of 'em, they didn't eat as much as Old Tom did.

Cully and I hit it off right away. He'd been roaming on his own for years before he met Unger. Unger traveled all over on "the King's business"-- well, you know what **that** means; he was a *spy*.

They told me all about their adventures together, and about Unger's funny brothers and his sweetheart Anika back home... we stayed up all night long talking and laughing. I hadn't had so much fun in years!

You know, people think Giants are stupid. They're not. They're **slow.** *Ponderous.* They'll still be pondering something long after *you've* forgotten it even happened...

Somehow, time just **stands still** for Giants. And you know what? If you get close enough to them, it stands still for you, too.

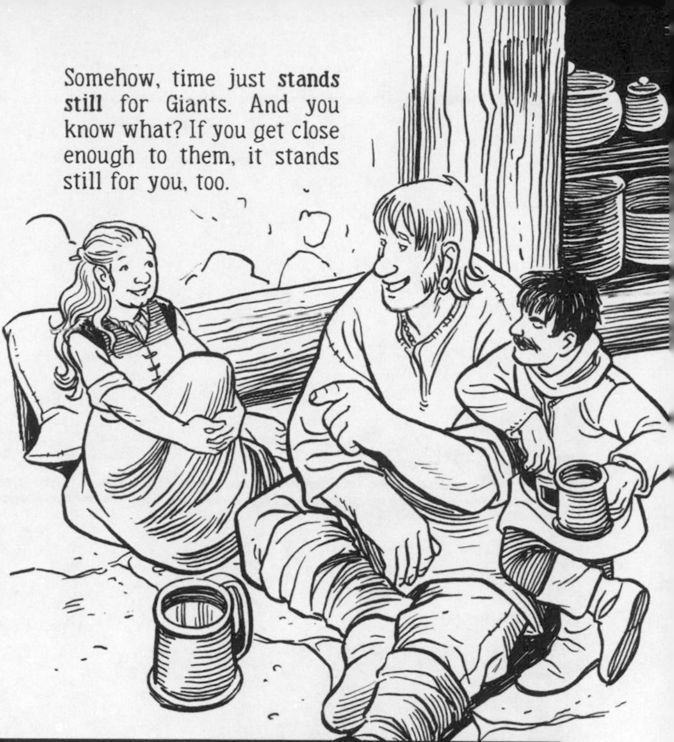

The kids loved them, of course. And I was happy to have the extra help!

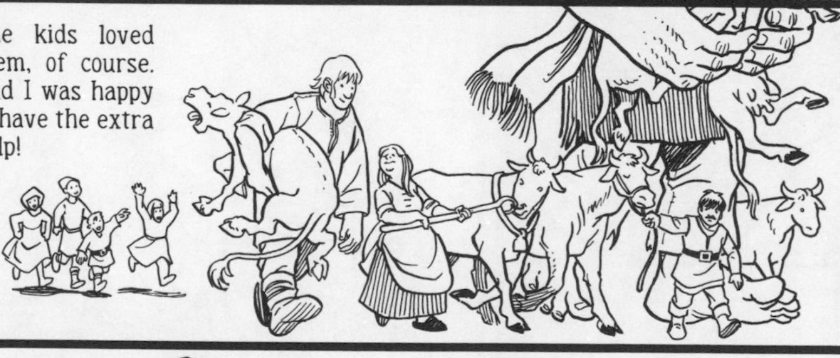

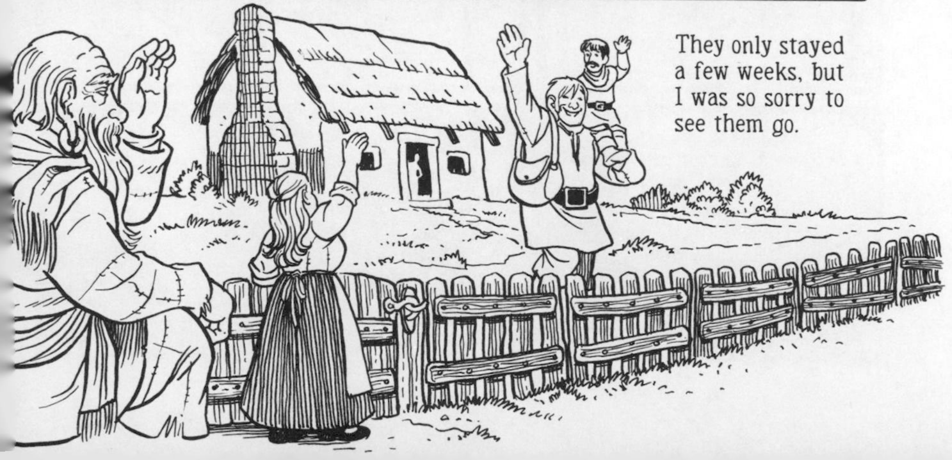

They only stayed a few weeks, but I was so sorry to see them go.

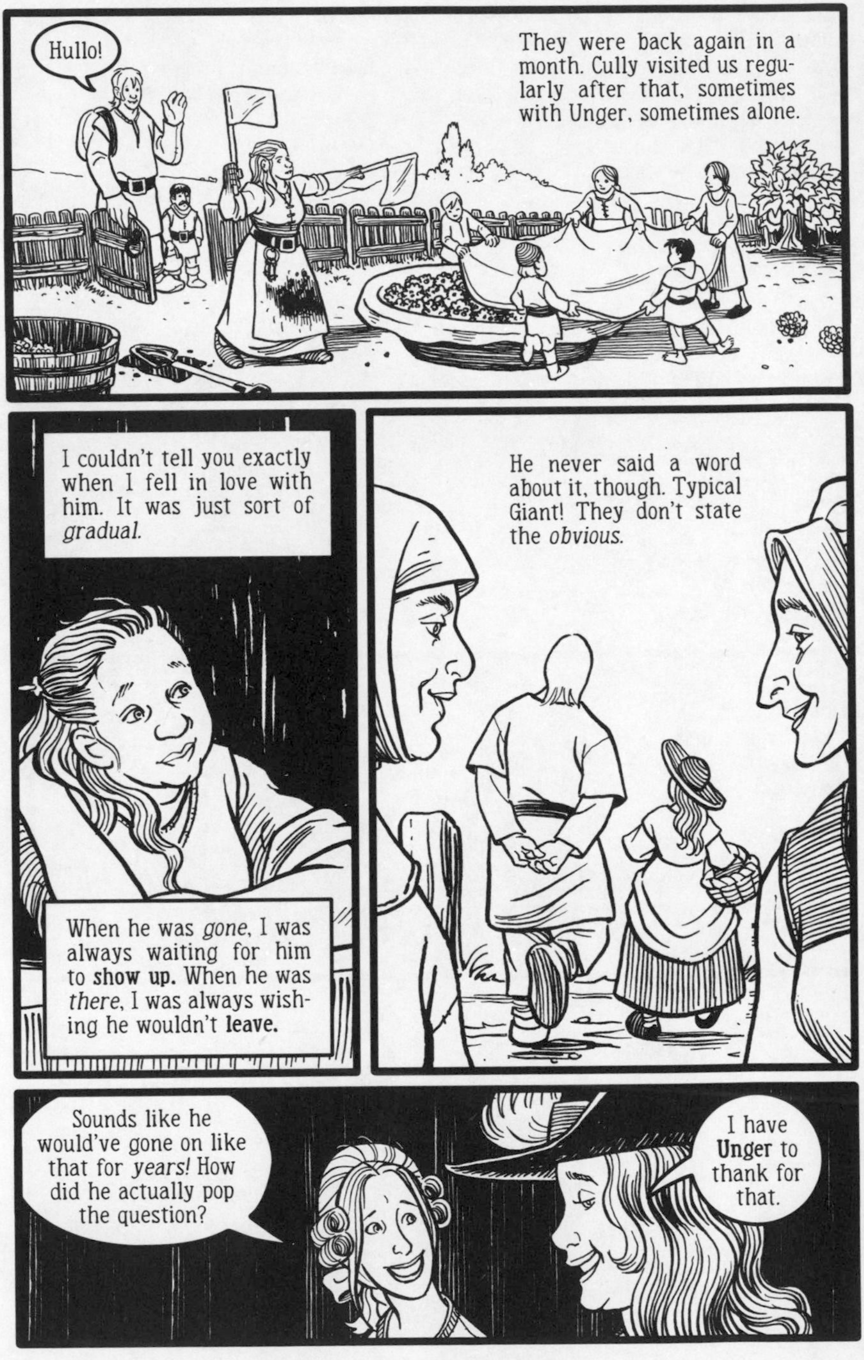
Hullo!
They were back again in a month. Cully visited us regularly after that, sometimes with Unger, sometimes alone.
I couldn't tell you exactly when I fell in love with him. It was just sort of *gradual.*
When he was *gone*, I was always waiting for him to **show up.** When he was *there*, I was always wishing he wouldn't **leave.**
He never said a word about it, though. Typical Giant! They don't state the *obvious.*
Sounds like he would've gone on like that for *years!* How did he actually pop the question?
I have **Unger** to thank for that.

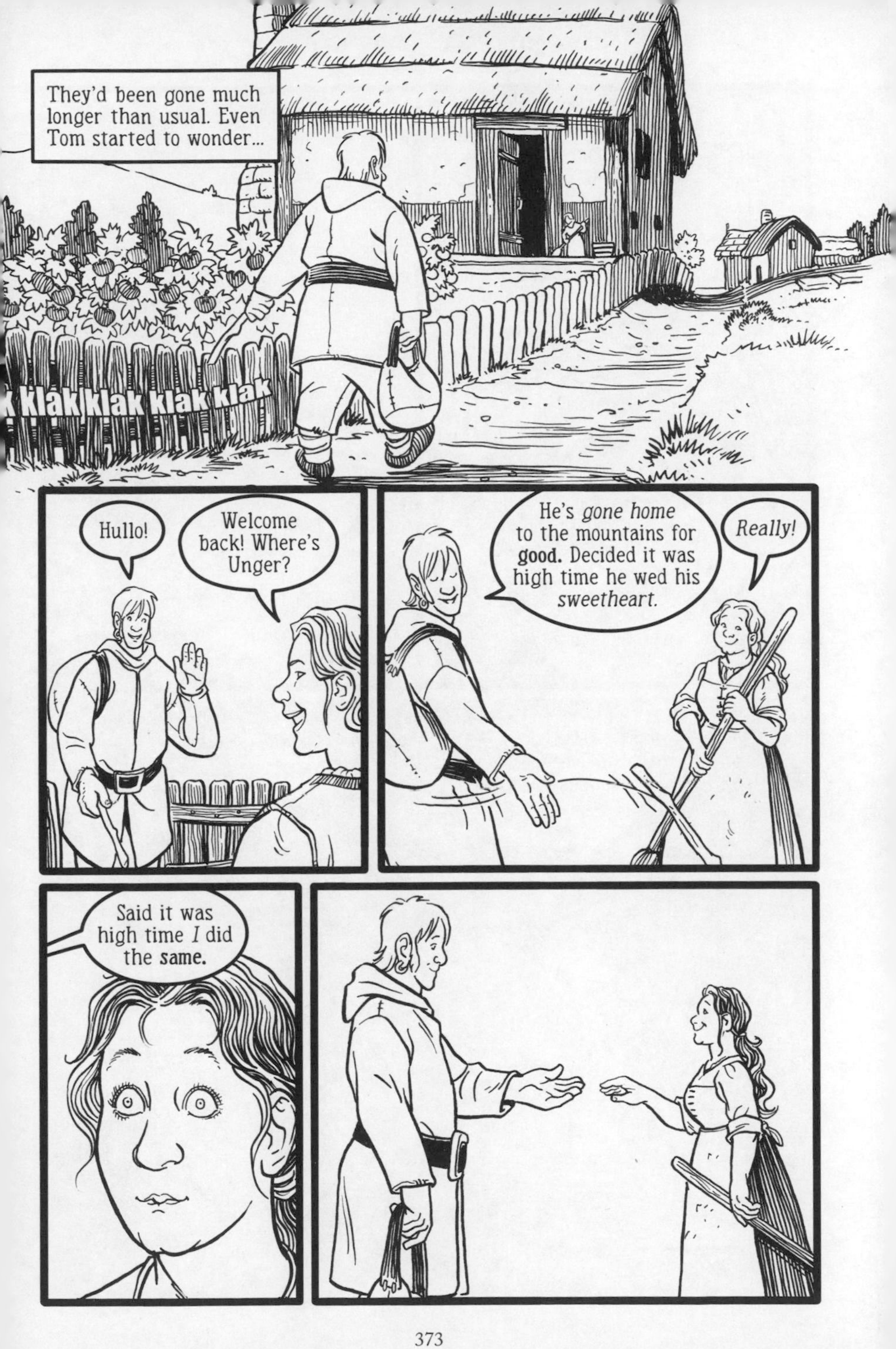
They'd been gone much longer than usual. Even Tom started to wonder...
klak klak klak klak
Hullo!
Welcome back! Where's Unger?
He's *gone home* to the mountains for **good.** Decided it was high time he wed his *sweetheart.*
Really!
Said it was high time *I* did the **same.**

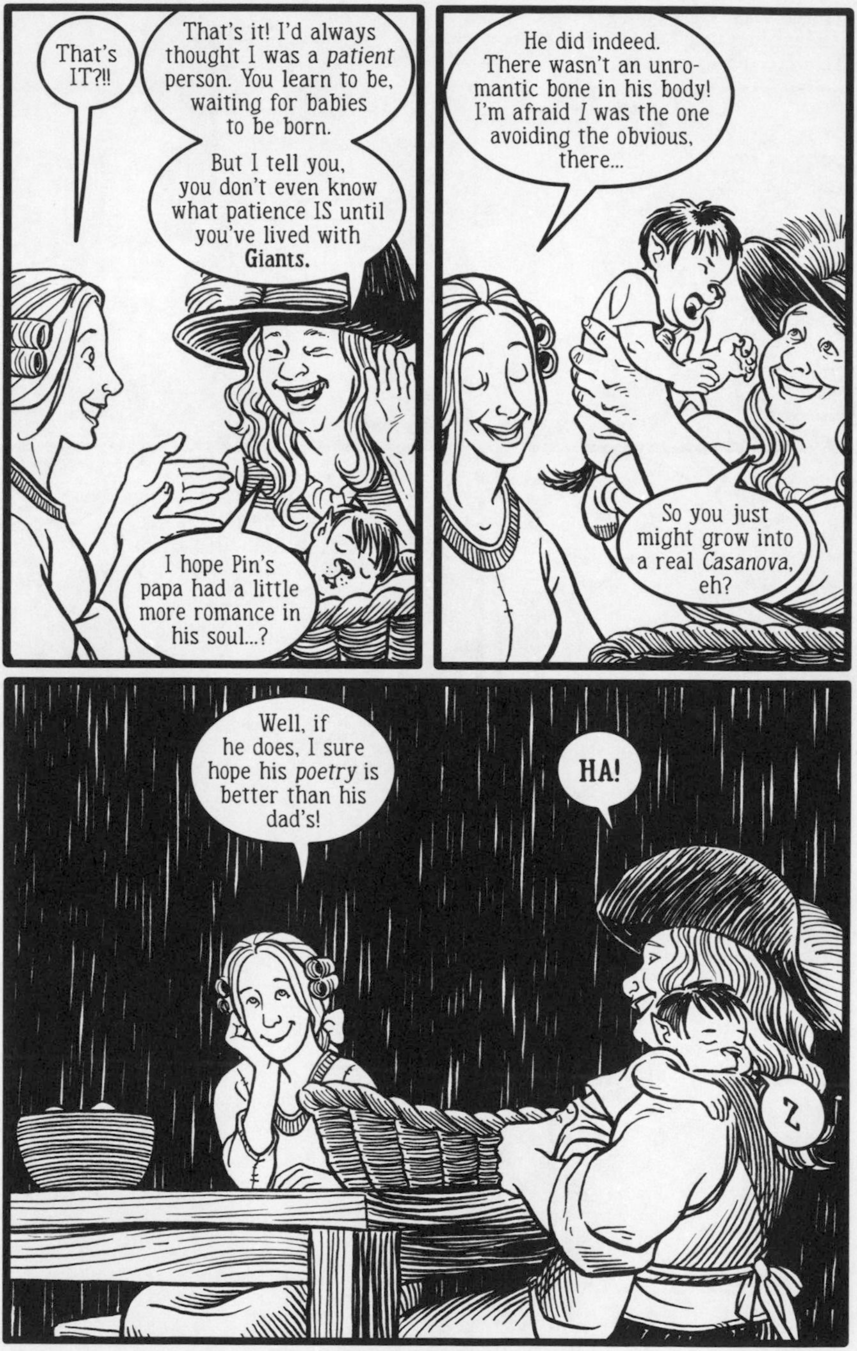
That's IT?!!
That's it! I'd always thought I was a *patient* person. You learn to be, waiting for babies to be born.
But I tell you, you don't even know what patience IS until you've lived with **Giants.**
I hope Pin's papa had a little more romance in his soul...?
He did indeed. There wasn't an unro-mantic bone in his body! I'm afraid *I* was the one avoiding the obvious, there...
So you just might grow into a real *Casanova*, eh?
Well, if he does, I sure hope his *poetry* is better than his dad's!
HA!
Z

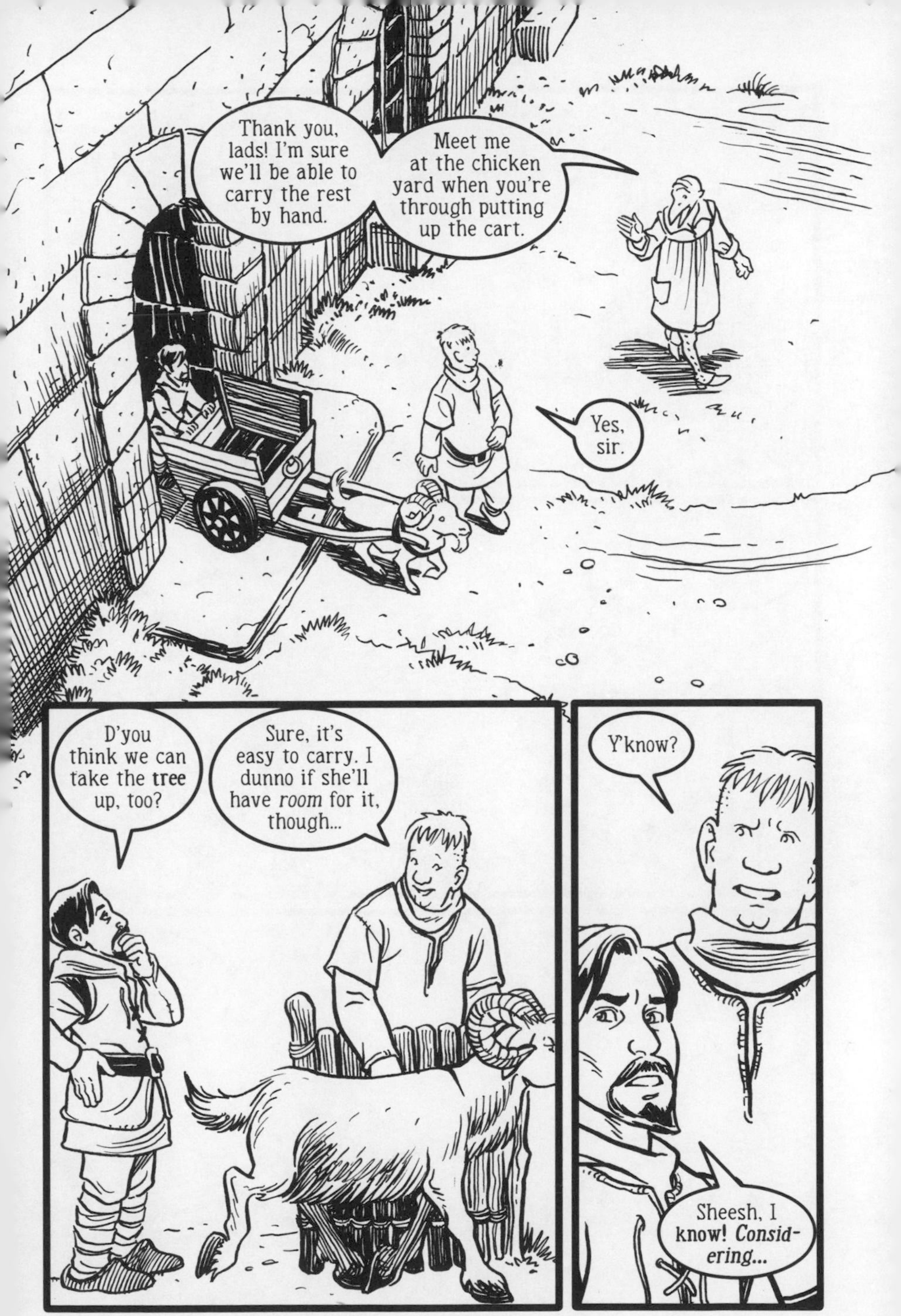
Thank you, lads! I'm sure we'll be able to carry the rest by hand.
Meet me at the chicken yard when you're through putting up the cart.
Yes, sir.
D'you think we can take the **tree** up, too?
Sure, it's easy to carry. I dunno if she'll have *room* for it, though...
Y'know?
Sheesh, I **know!** ***Consid-ering...***

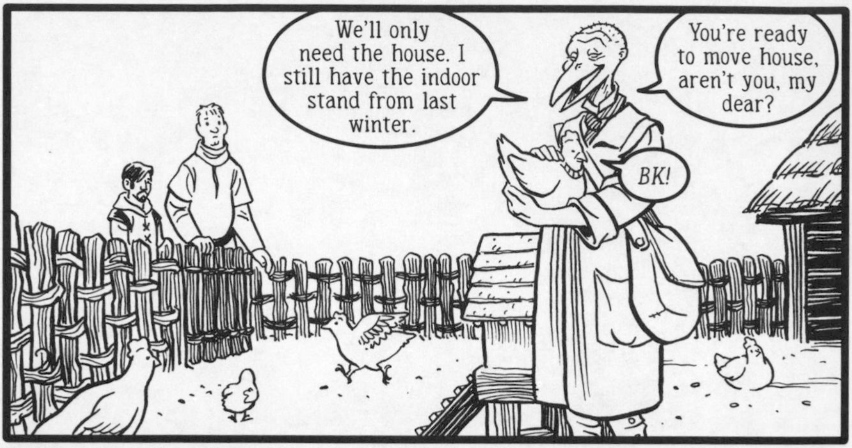
We'll only need the house. I still have the indoor stand from last winter.
You're ready to move house, aren't you, my dear?
BK!

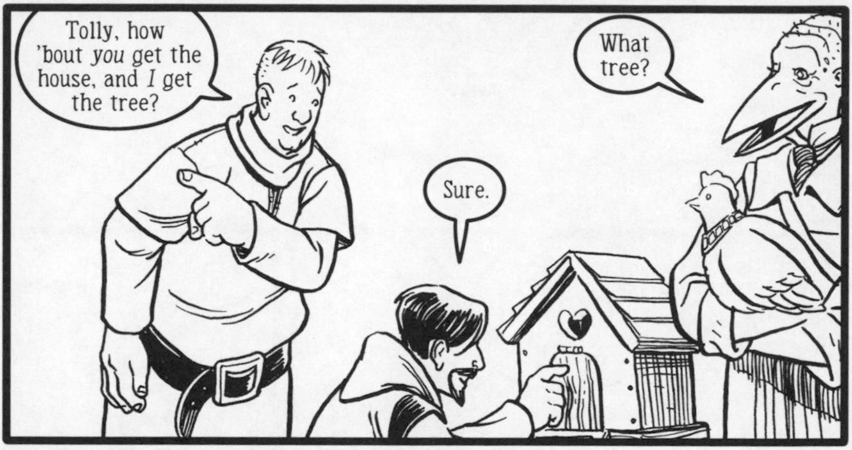
Tolly, how 'bout *you* get the house, and *I* get the tree?
What tree?
Sure.

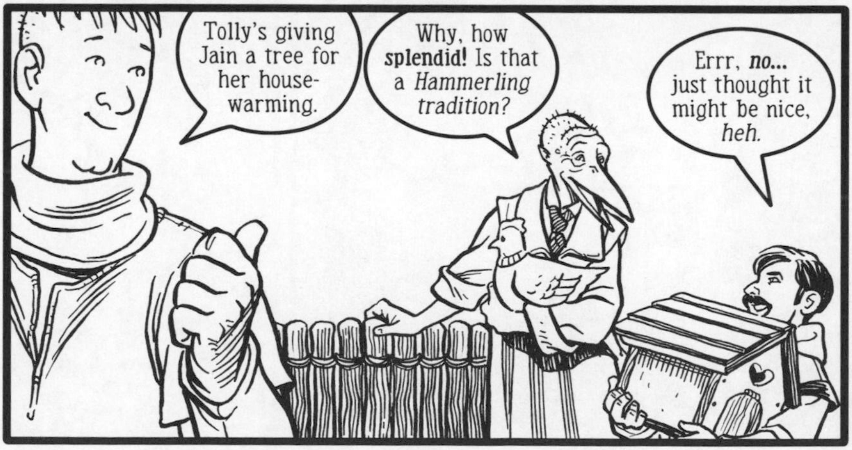
Tolly's giving Jain a tree for her house-warming.
Why, how **splendid!** Is that a *Hammerling tradition?*
Errr, **no...** just thought it might be nice, *heh.*

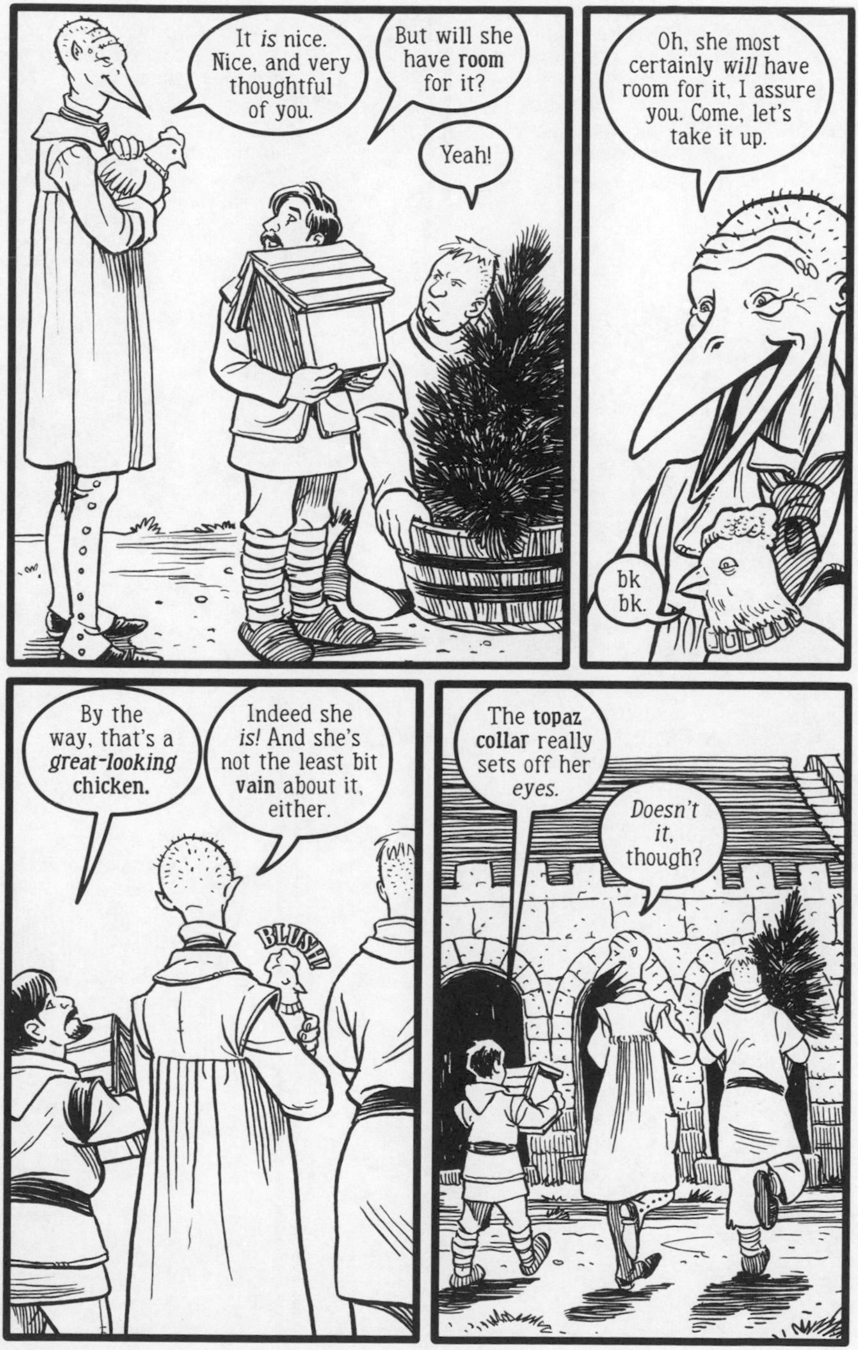
It *is* nice. Nice, and very thoughtful of you.
But will she have **room** for it?
Yeah!
Oh, she most certainly *will* have room for it, I assure you. Come, let's take it up.
bk bk.
By the way, that's a ***great-looking* chicken.**
Indeed she *is!* And she's not the least bit **vain** about it, either.
BLUSH!
The **topaz collar** really sets off her *eyes.*
Doesn't it, though?

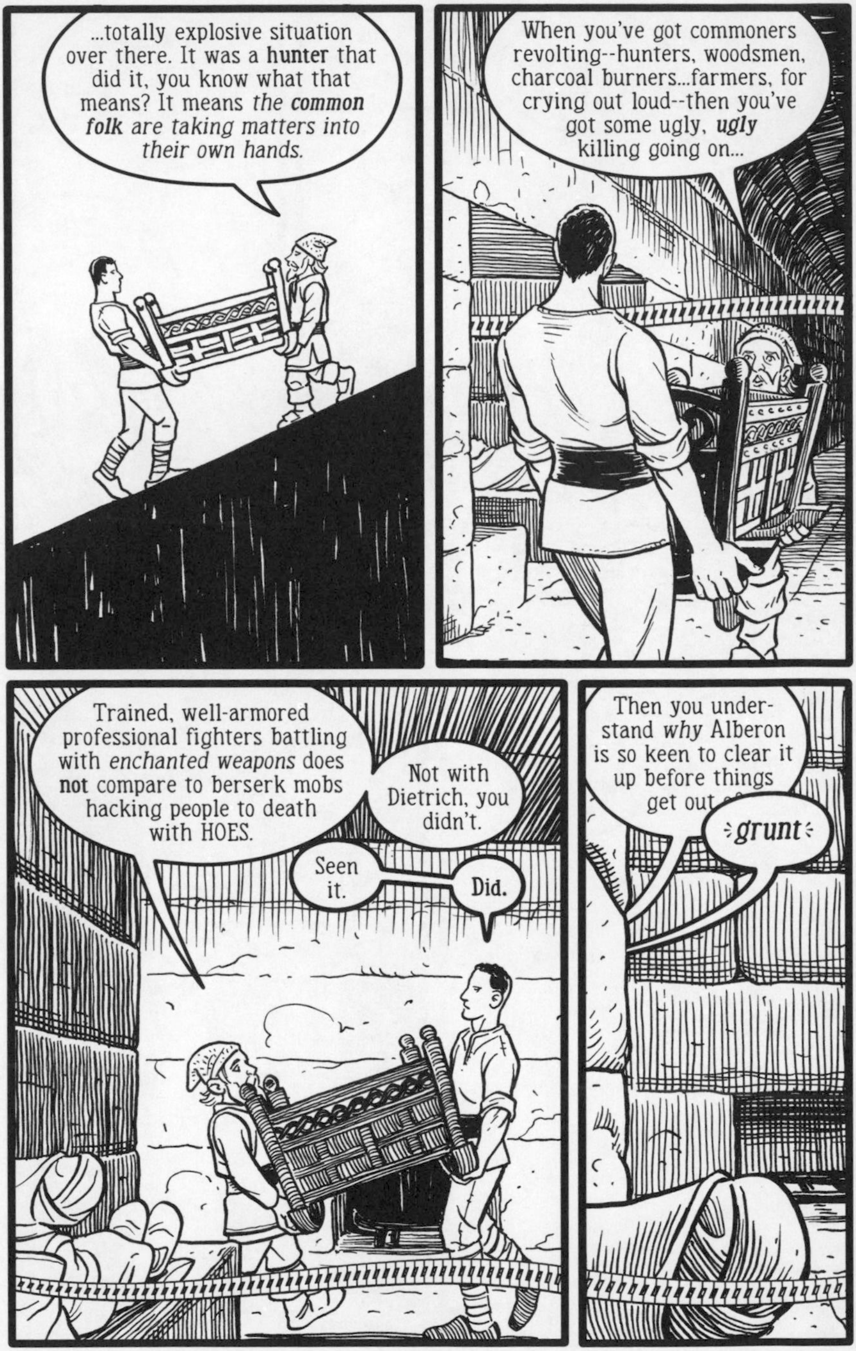
...totally explosive situation over there. It was a **hunter** that did it, you know what that means? It means *the **common folk** are taking matters into their own hands.*
When you've got commoners revolting--hunters, woodsmen, charcoal burners...farmers, for crying out loud--then you've got some ugly, ***ugly*** killing going on...
Trained, well-armored professional fighters battling with *enchanted weapons* does **not** compare to berserk mobs hacking people to death with HOES.
Not with Dietrich, you didn't.
Seen it.
Did.
Then you under-stand *why* Alberon is so keen to clear it up before things get out of
grunt

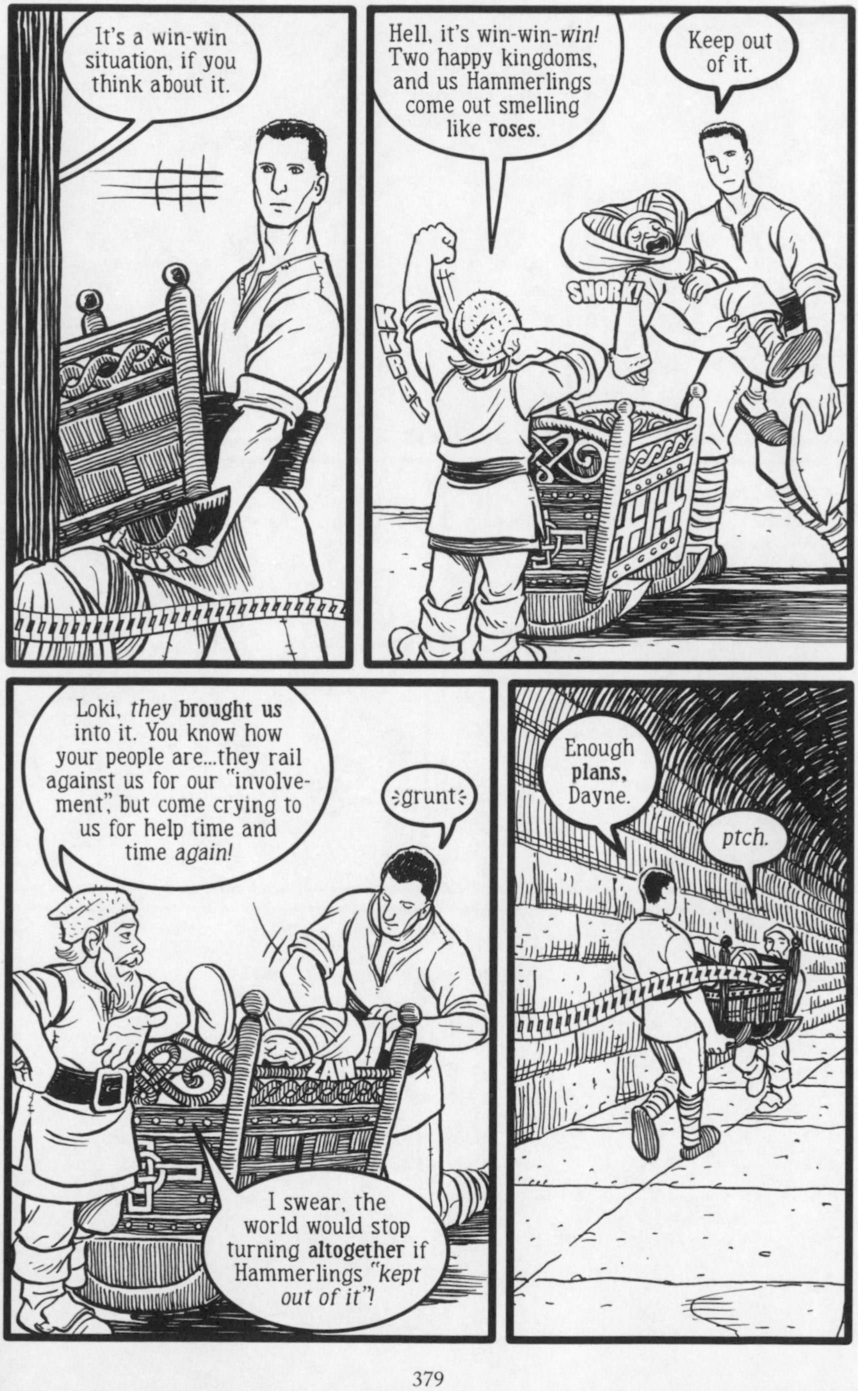
It's a win-win situation, if you think about it.
Hell, it's win-win-*win!* Two happy kingdoms, and us Hammerlings come out smelling like **roses**.
KKRAK
SNORK!
Keep out of it.
Loki, *they* **brought us** into it. You know how your people are...they rail against us for our "involvement", but come crying to us for help time and time *again!*
grunt
ZAW
I swear, the world would stop turning **altogether** if Hammerlings *"kept out of it"*!
Enough **plans,** Dayne.
ptch.

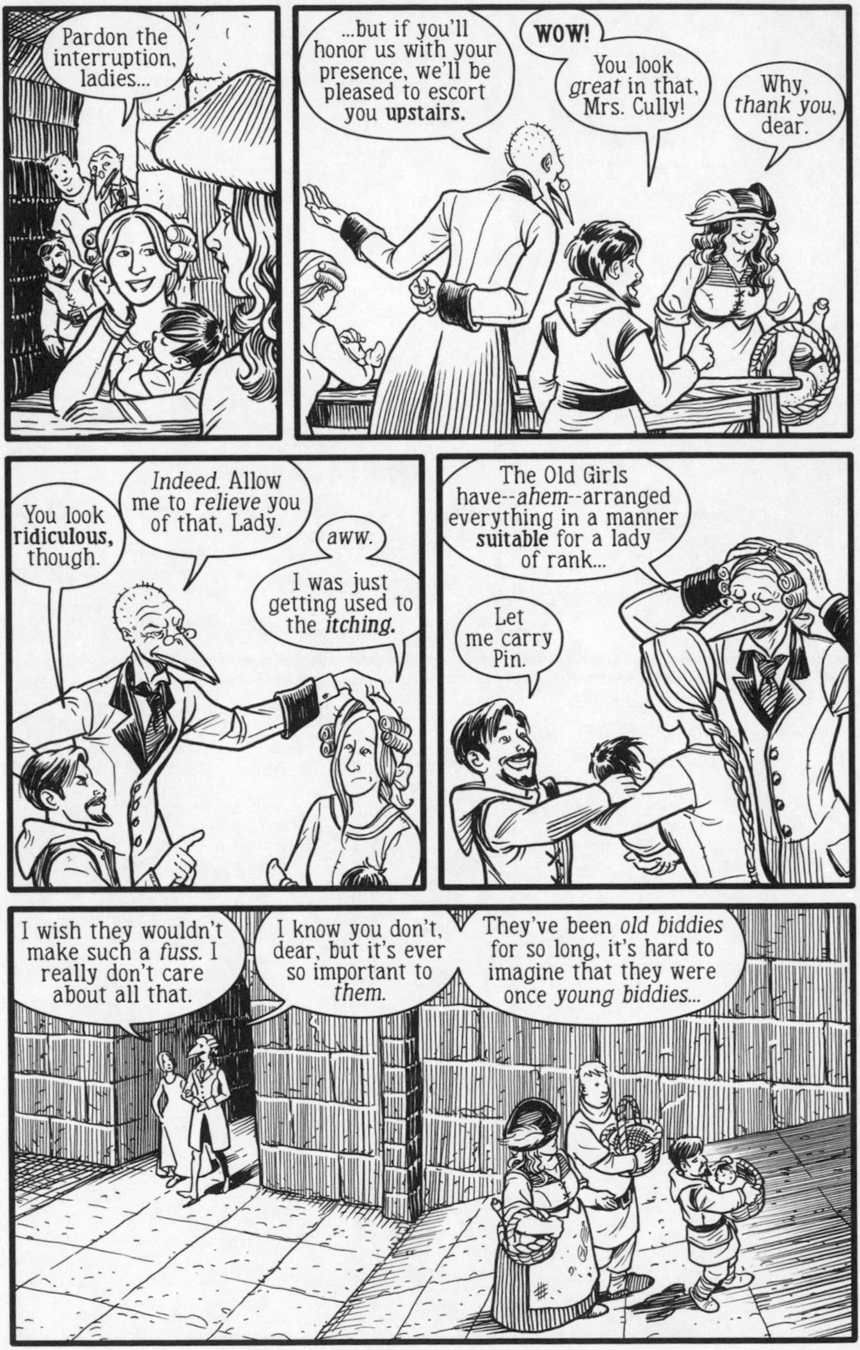
Pardon the interruption, ladies...
...but if you'll honor us with your presence, we'll be pleased to escort you **upstairs.**
WOW!
You look *great* in that, Mrs. Cully!
Why, *thank you*, dear.
You look **ridiculous,** though.
Indeed. Allow me to *relieve* you of that, Lady.
aww.
I was just getting used to the ***itching.***
The Old Girls have--*ahem*--arranged everything in a manner **suitable** for a lady of rank...
Let me carry Pin.
I wish they wouldn't make such a *fuss.* I really don't care about all that.
I know you don't, dear, but it's ever so important to *them.*
They've been *old biddies* for so long, it's hard to imagine that they were once *young biddies...*

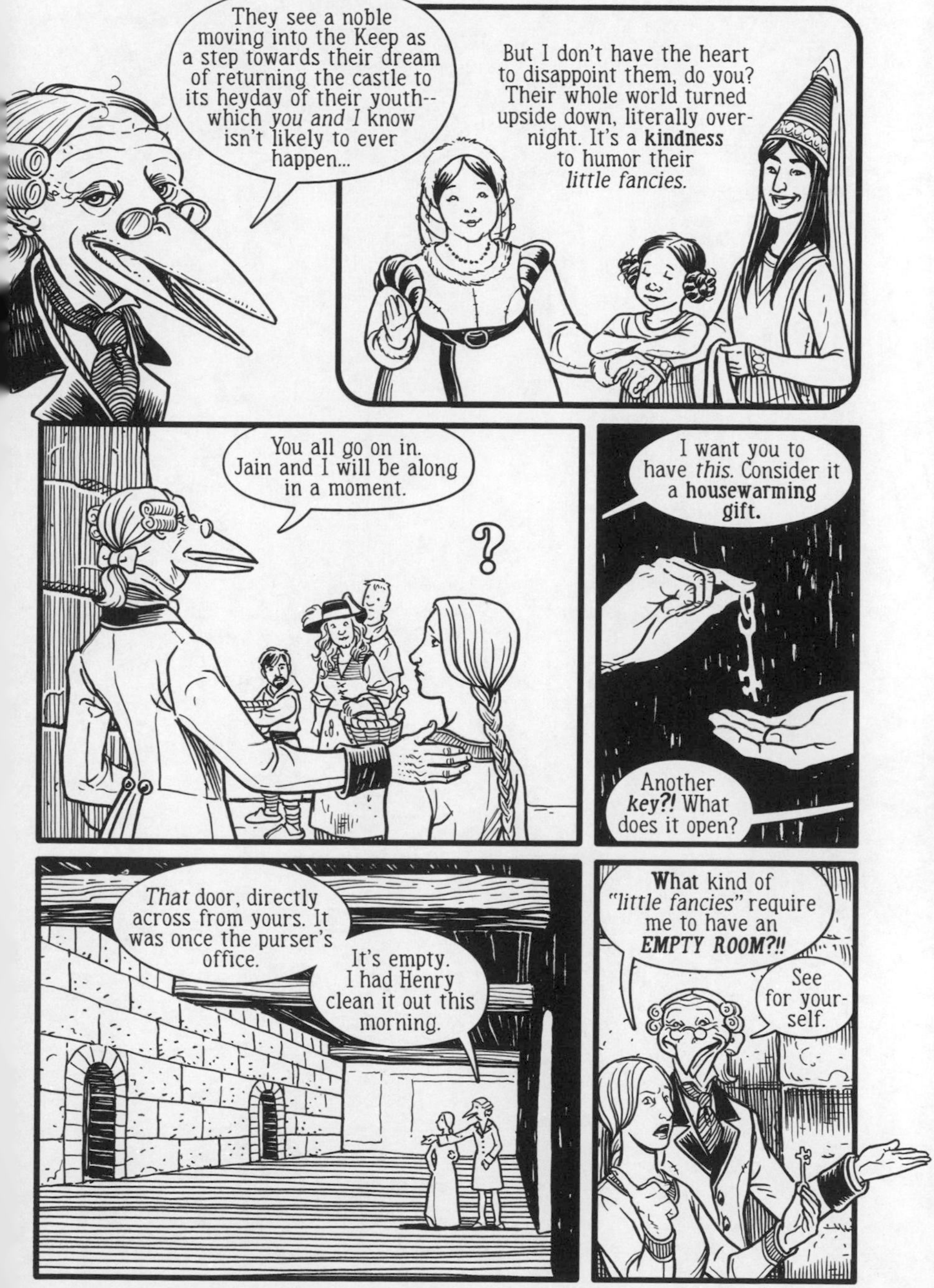
They see a noble moving into the Keep as a step towards their dream of returning the castle to its heyday of their youth-- which *you and I* know isn't likely to ever happen...
But I don't have the heart to disappoint them, do you? Their whole world turned upside down, literally over-night. It's a **kindness** to humor their *little fancies.*
You all go on in. Jain and I will be along in a moment.
?
I want you to have *this.* Consider it a **housewarming gift.**
Another ***key?!*** What does it open?
That door, directly across from yours. It was once the purser's office.
It's empty. I had Henry clean it out this morning.
What kind of *"little fancies"* require me to have an ***EMPTY ROOM?!!***
See for your-self.

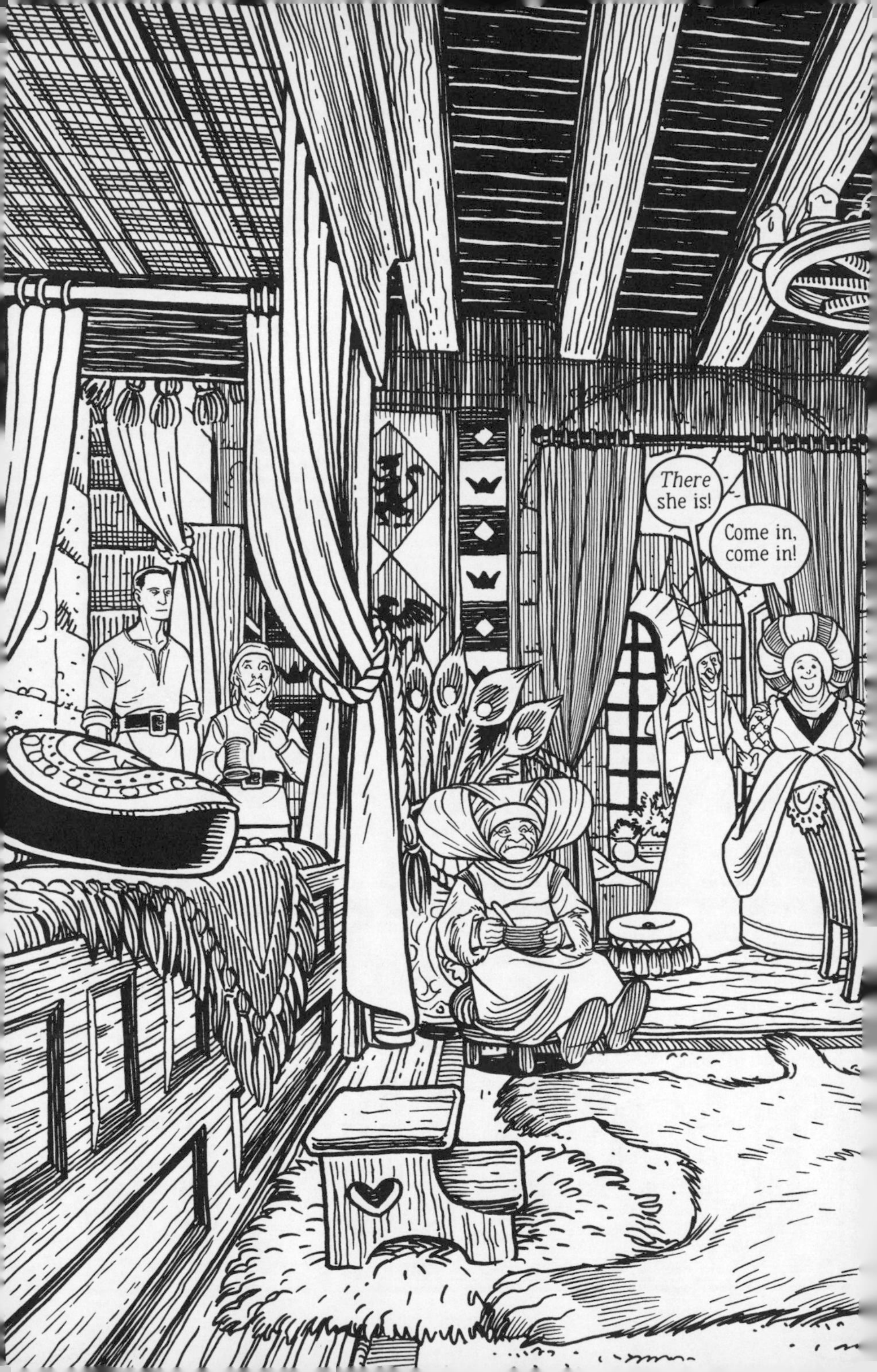
There she is!
Come in, come in!

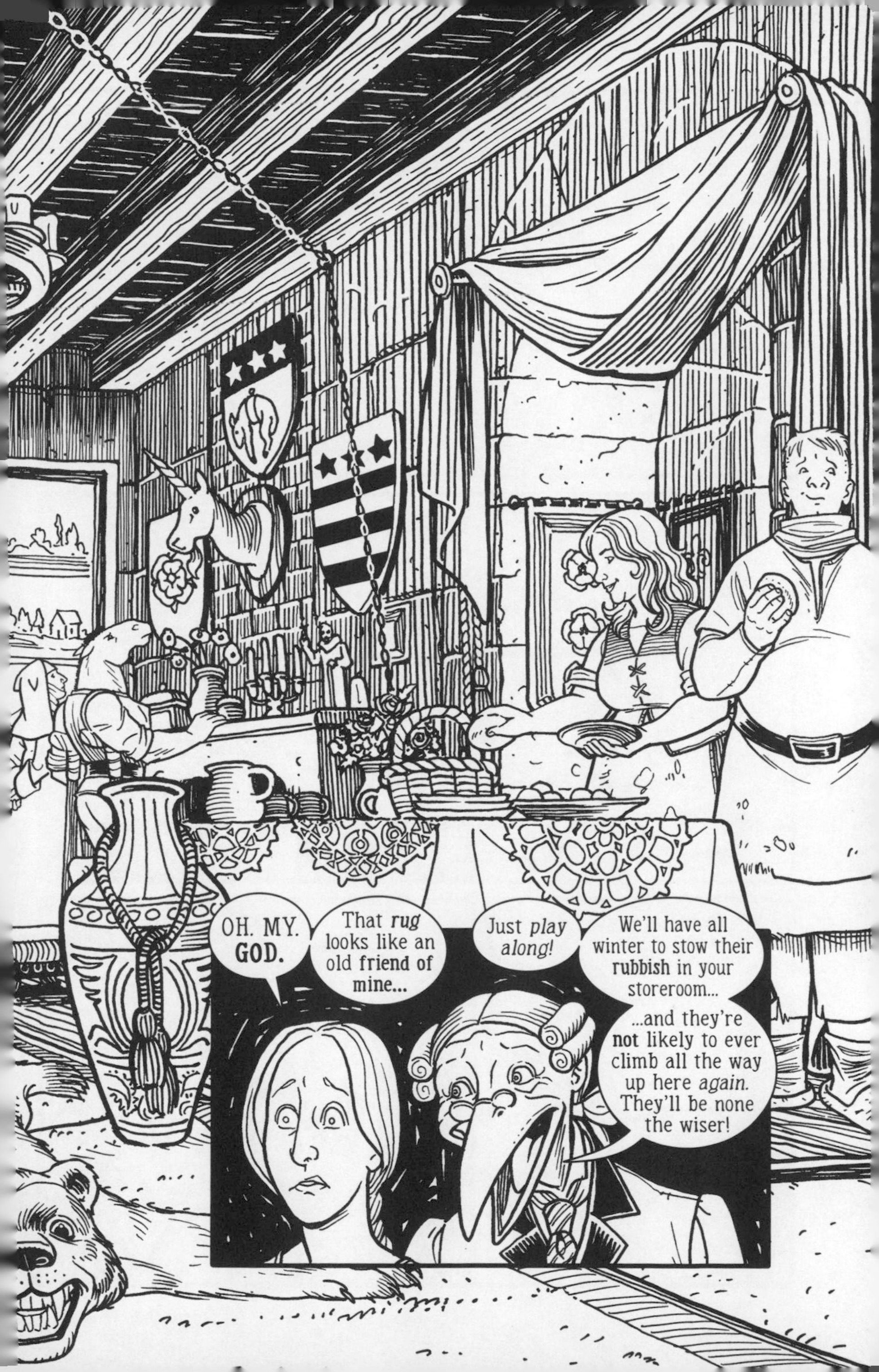
OH. MY. **GOD.**
That *rug* looks like an old **friend of mine...**
Just *play along!*
We'll have all winter to stow their **rubbish** in your storeroom...
...and they're **not** likely to ever climb all the way up here *again.* They'll be none the wiser!

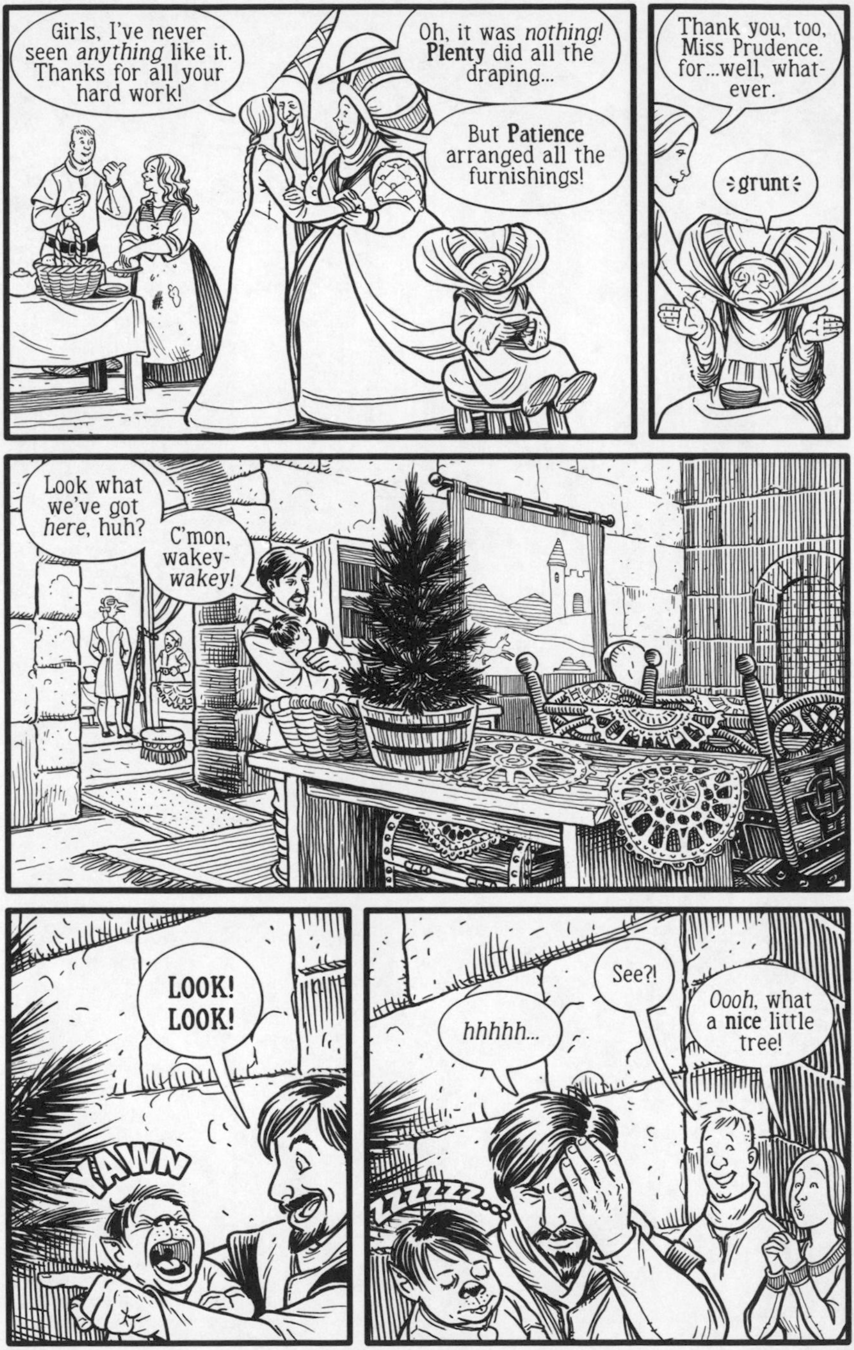
Girls, I've never seen *anything* like it. Thanks for all your hard work!
Oh, it was *nothing*! **Plenty** did all the draping...
But **Patience** arranged all the furnishings!
Thank you, too, Miss Prudence. for...well, whatever.
grunt
Look what we've got *here*, huh?
C'mon, wakey-*wakey*!
LOOK! LOOK!
YAWN
hhhhh...
See?!
Oooh, what a **nice** little tree!
ZZZZZZ

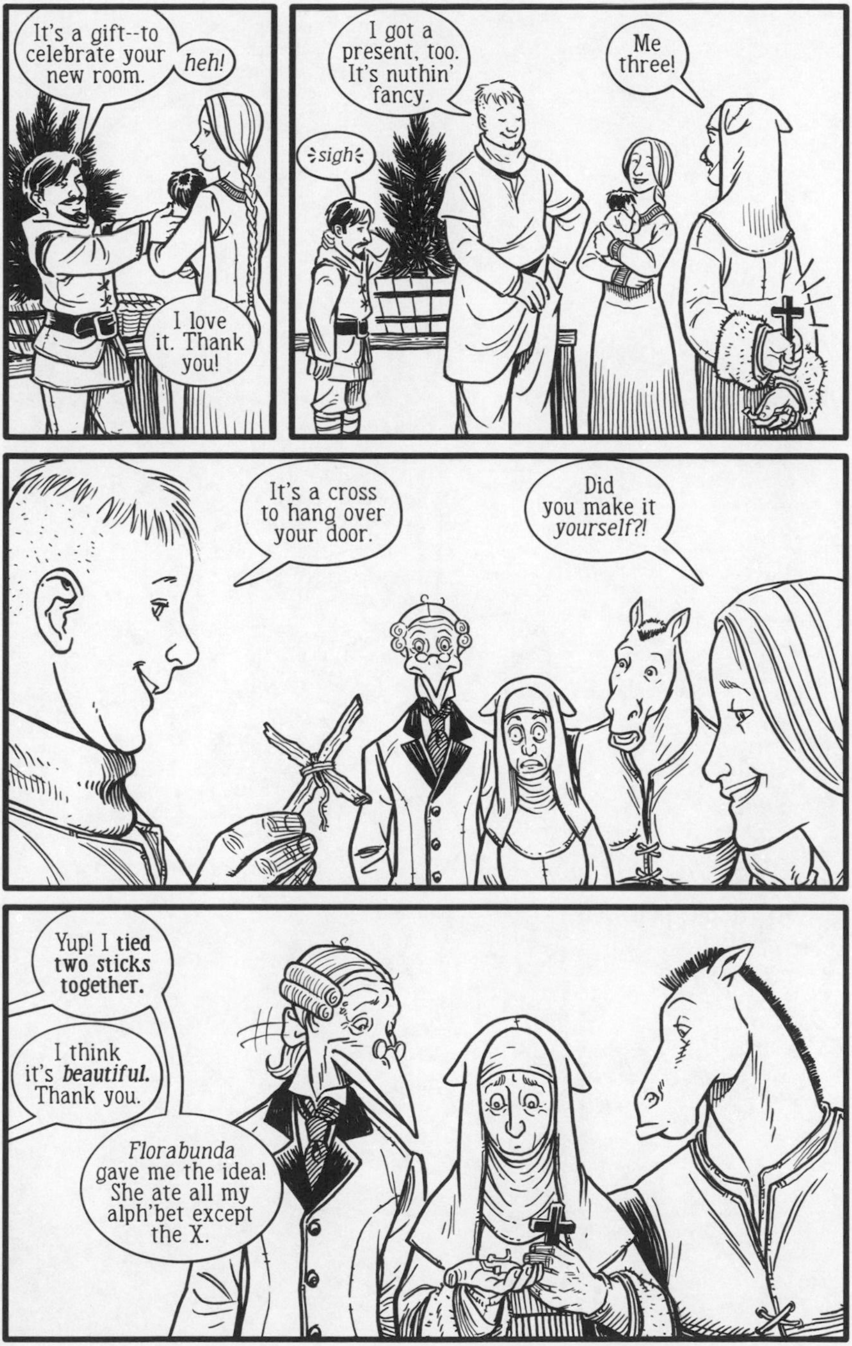
It's a gift--to celebrate your new room.
heh!
I love it. Thank you!
I got a present, too. It's nuthin' fancy.
sigh
Me three!
It's a cross to hang over your door.
Did you make it *yourself?!*
Yup! I **tied two sticks together.**
I think it's ***beautiful.*** Thank you.
Florabunda gave me the idea! She ate all my alph'bet except the X.

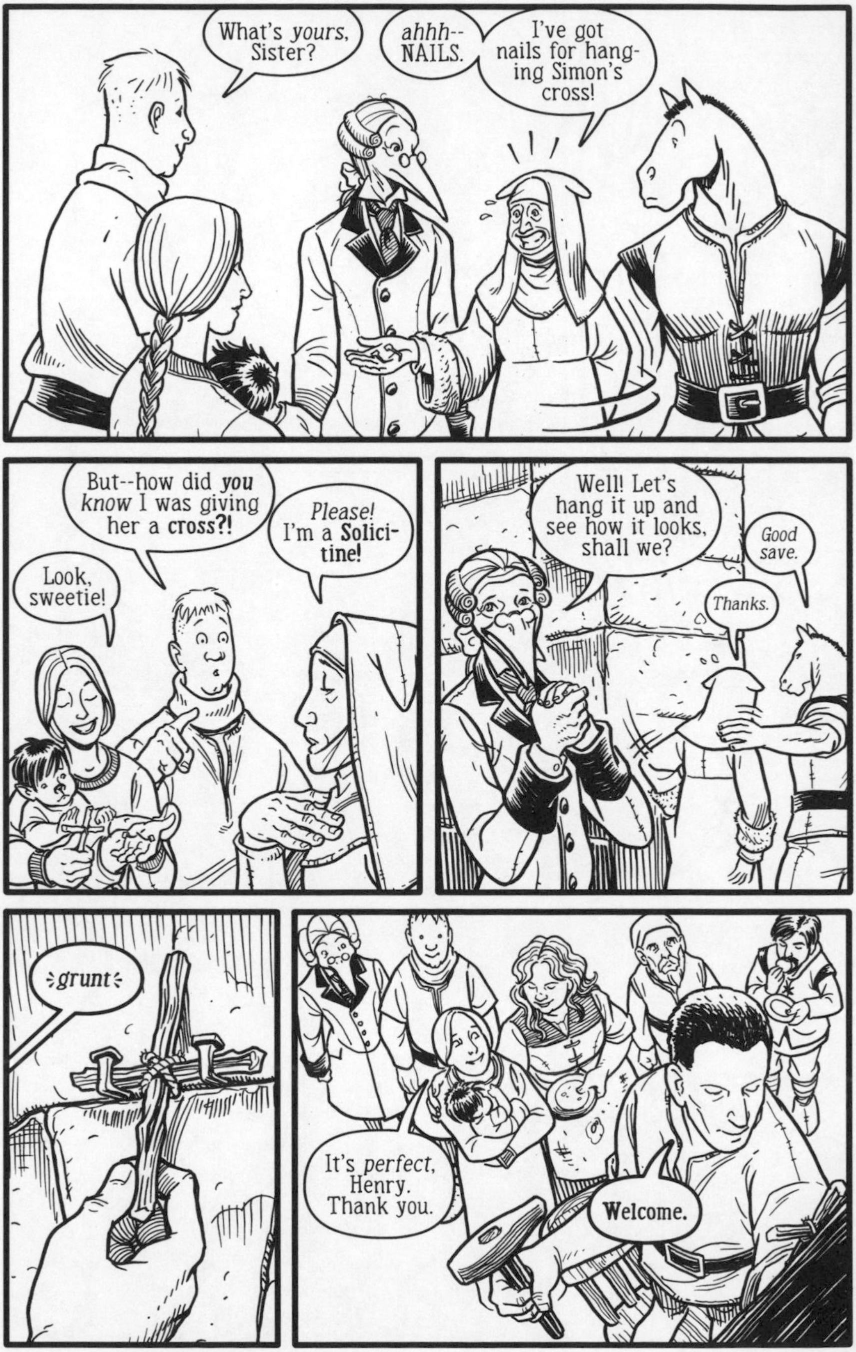
What's *yours*, Sister?
ahhh-- NAILS.
I've got nails for hang-ing Simon's cross!
But--how did **you** *know* I was giving her a **cross?!**
Please! I'm a **Solici-tine!**
Look, sweetie!
Well! Let's hang it up and see how it looks, shall we?
Good save.
Thanks.
grunt
It's *perfect*, Henry. Thank you.
Welcome.

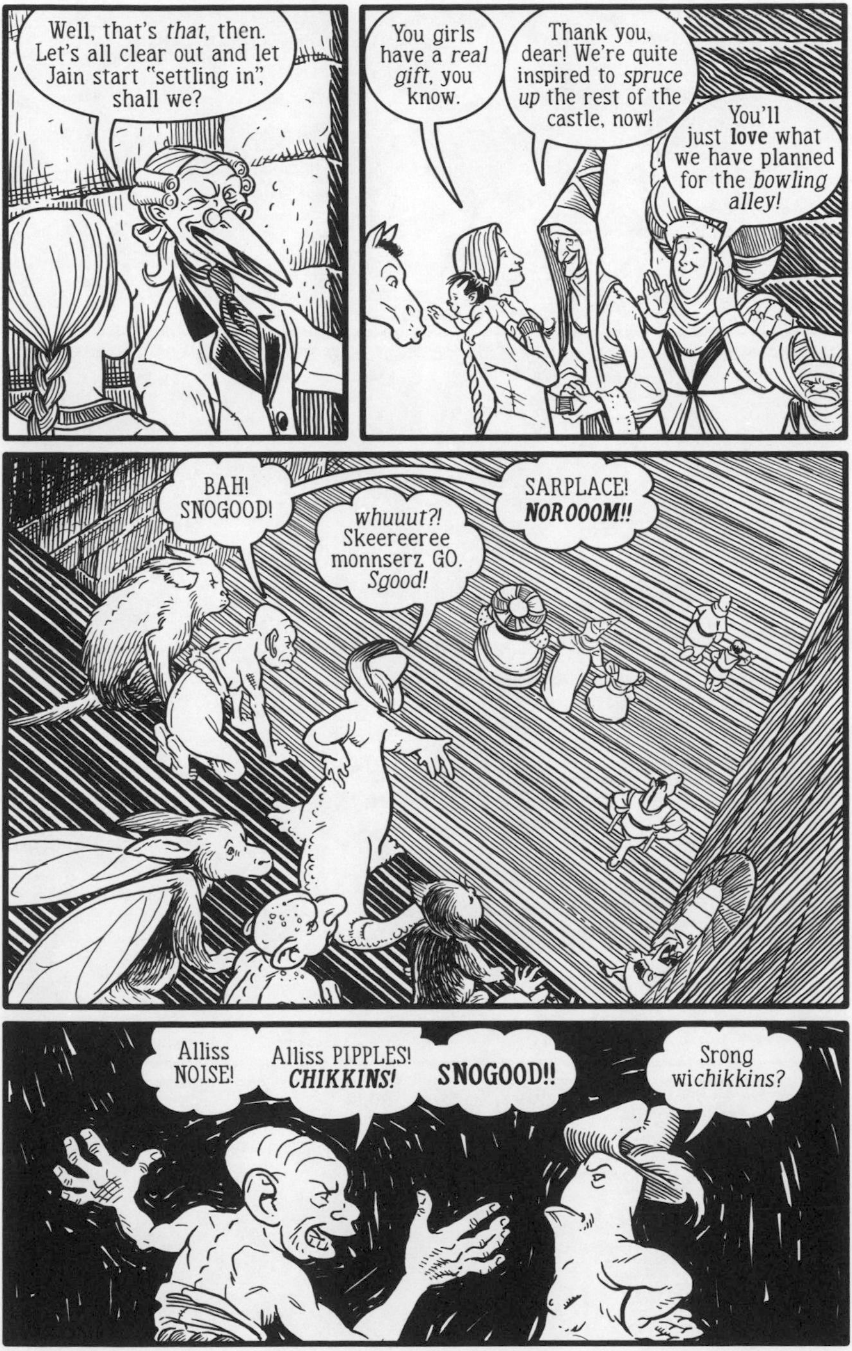
Well, that's *that*, then. Let's all clear out and let Jain start "settling in", shall we?
You girls have a *real gift*, you know.
Thank you, dear! We're quite inspired to *spruce up* the rest of the castle, now!
You'll just **love** what we have planned for the *bowling alley*!
BAH! SNOGOOD!
whuuut?! Skeereeree monnserz GO. *Sgood!*
SARPLACE! ***NOROOOM!!***
Alliss NOISE!
Alliss PIPPLES! ***CHIKKINS!***
SNOGOOD!!
Srong wi*chikkins?*

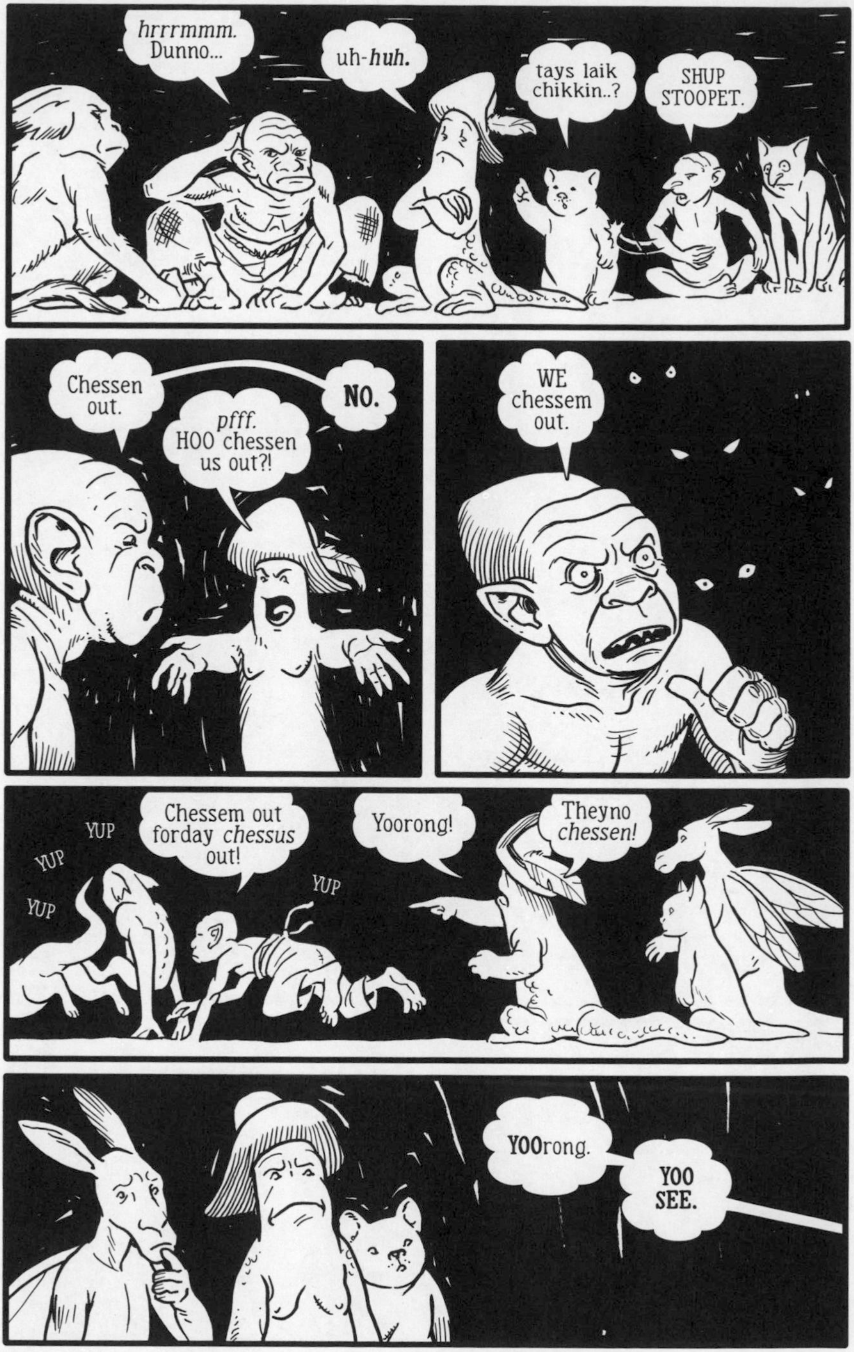
hrrrmmm. Dunno...
uh-huh.
tays laik chikkin..?
SHUP STOOPET.
Chessen out.
NO.
pfff. HOO chessen us out?!
WE chessem out.
YUP
YUP
YUP
Chessem out forday chessus out!
YUP
Yoorong!
Theyno chessen!
YOOrong.
YOO SEE.

Chapter 15.

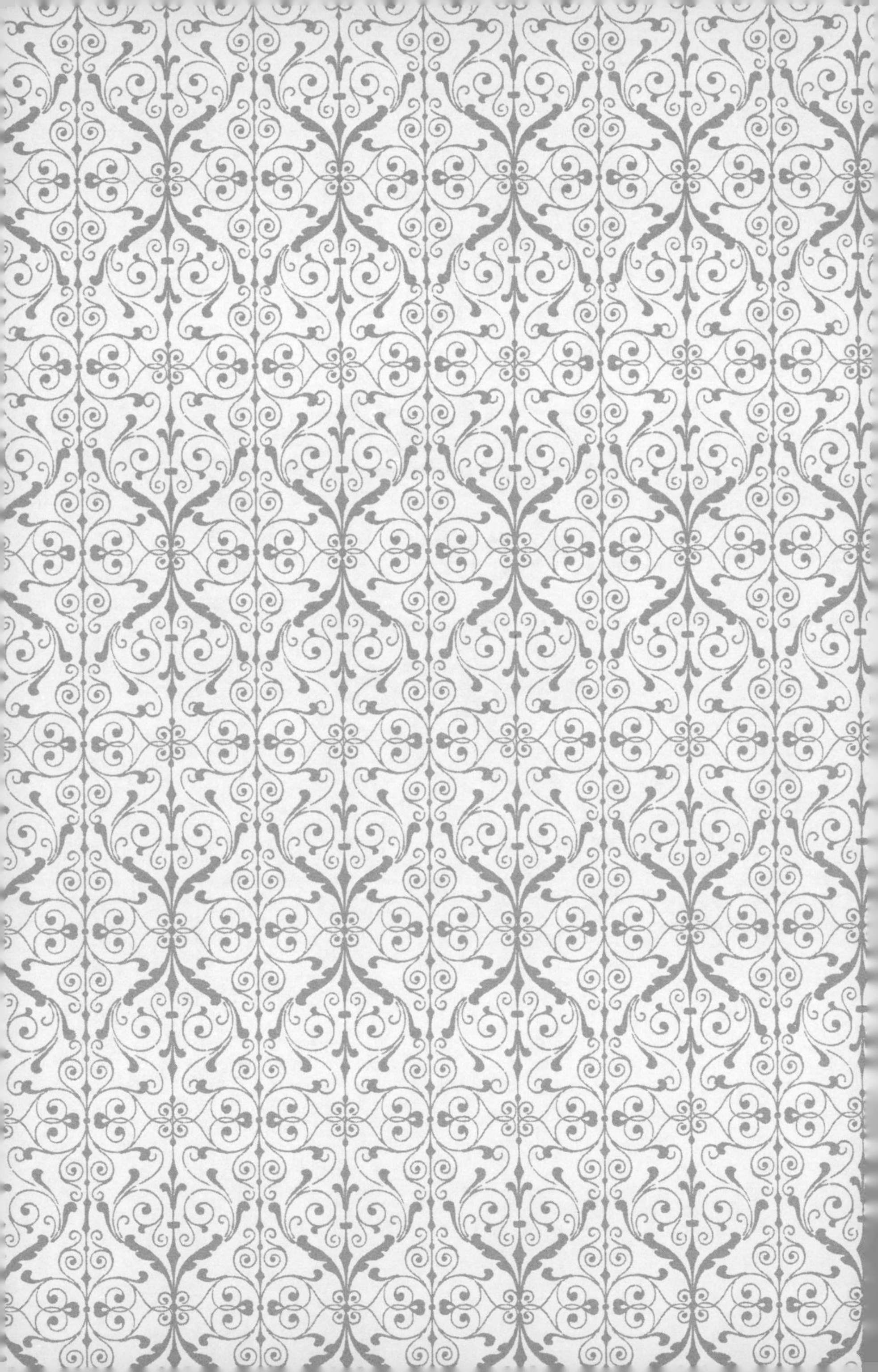

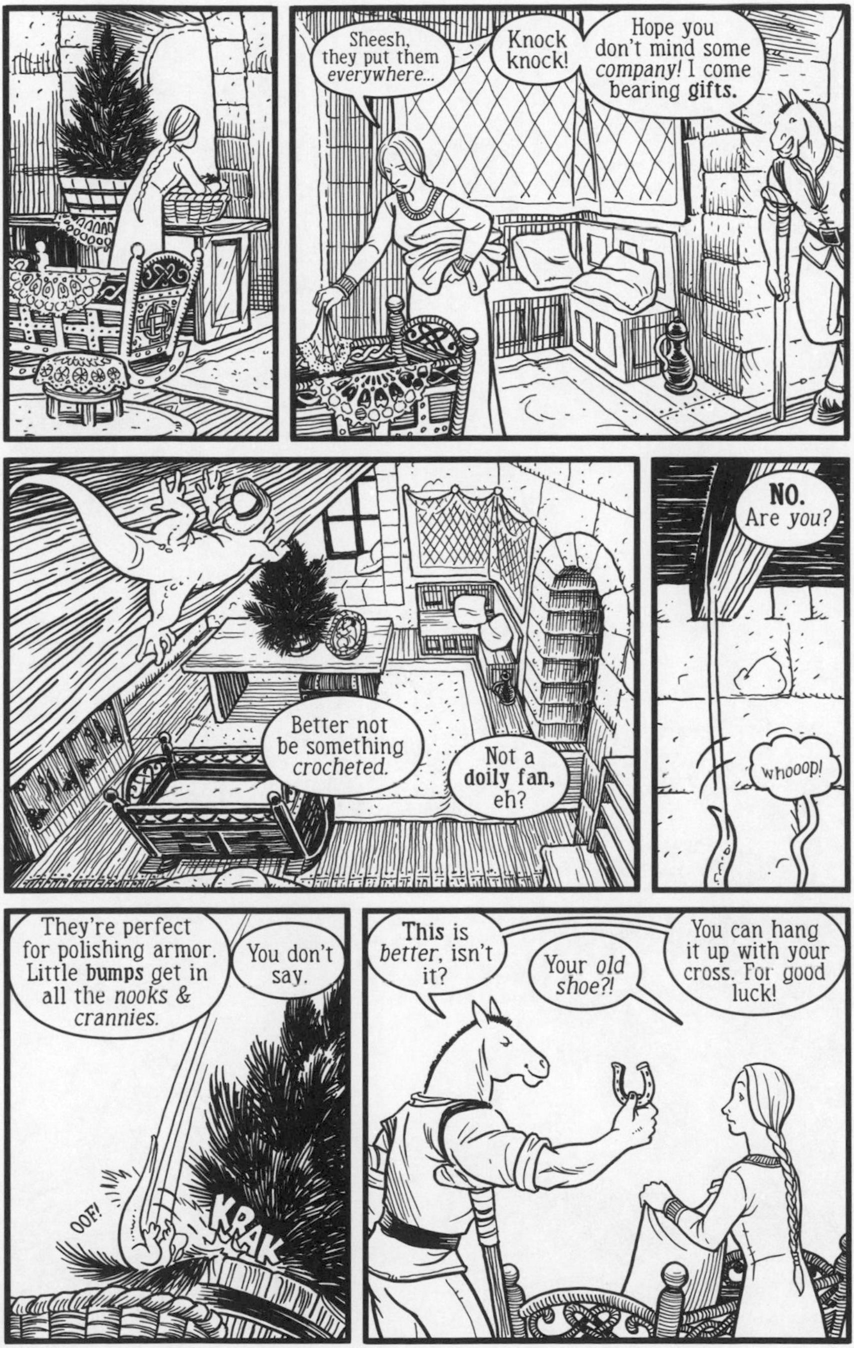
Sheesh, they put them everywhere...
Knock knock!
Hope you don't mind some company! I come bearing gifts.
Better not be something crocheted.
Not a doily fan, eh?
NO. Are you?
whooop!
They're perfect for polishing armor. Little bumps get in all the nooks & crannies.
You don't say.
OOF!
KRAK
This is better, isn't it?
Your old shoe?!
You can hang it up with your cross. For good luck!

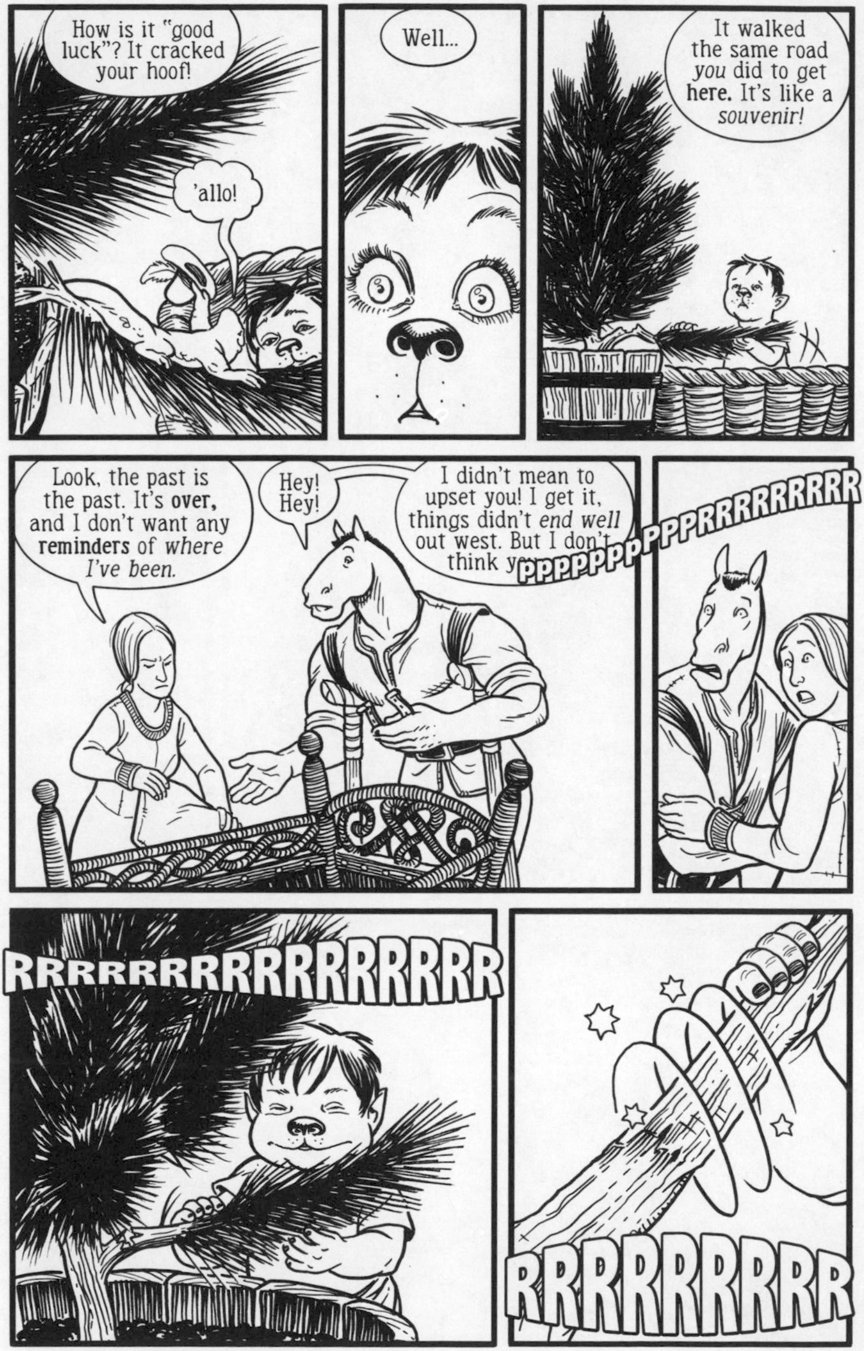
How is it "good luck"? It cracked your hoof!
'allo!
Well...
It walked the same road *you* did to get **here.** It's like a *souvenir!*
Look, the past is the past. It's **over,** and I don't want any **reminders** of *where I've been.*
Hey! Hey!
I didn't mean to upset you! I get it, things didn't *end well* out west. But I don't think y
PPPPPPPPPPPRRRRRRRRR
RRRRRRRRRRRRRRRR
RRRRRRRRR

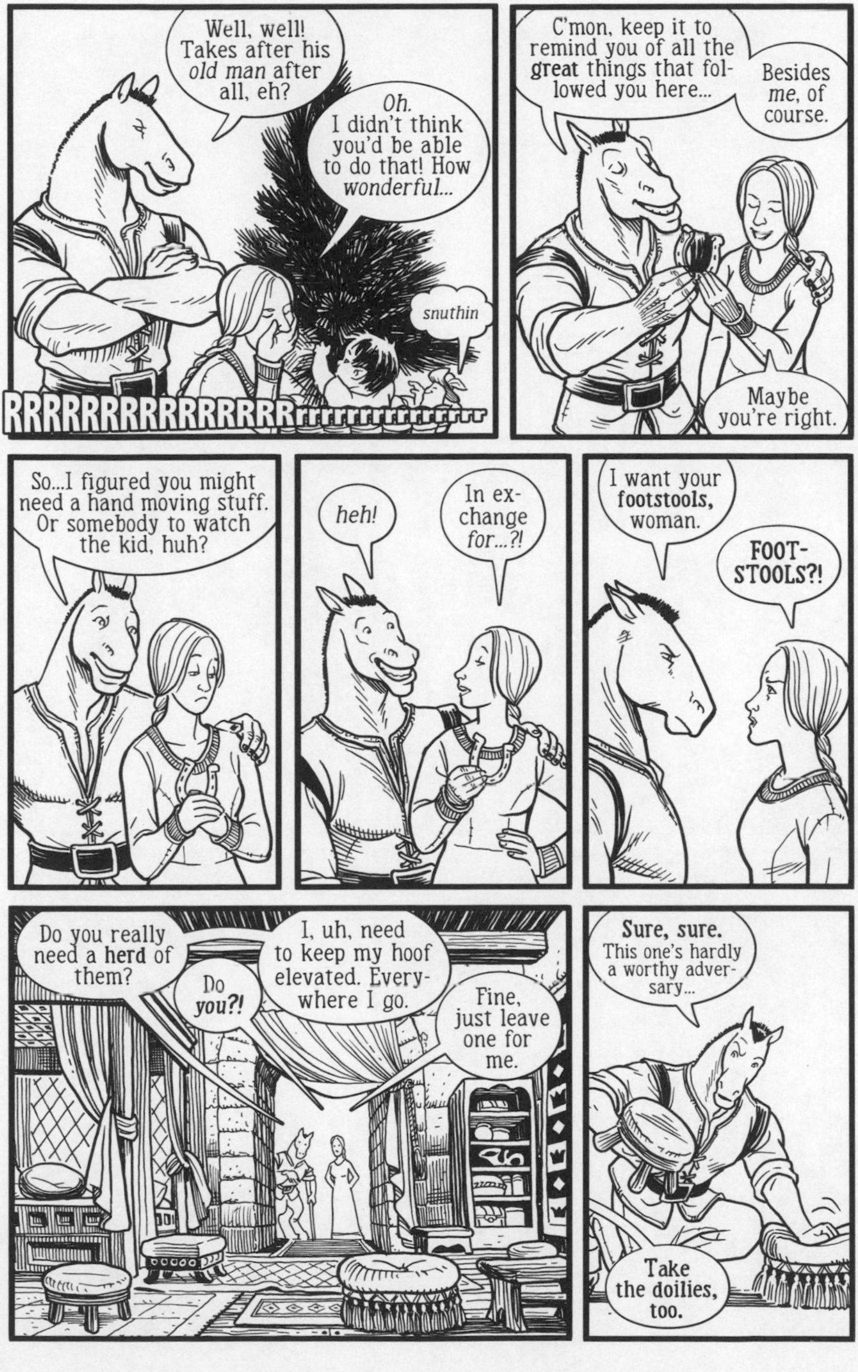
Well, well! Takes after his *old man* after all, eh?
Oh. I didn't think you'd be able to do that! How *wonderful...*
snuthin
RRRRRRRRRRRRRRRrrrrrrrrrrrrrrrr
C'mon, keep it to remind you of all the **great** things that followed you here...
Besides *me*, of course.
Maybe you're right.
So...I figured you might need a hand moving stuff. Or somebody to watch the kid, huh?
heh!
In exchange *for...?!*
I want your **footstools,** woman.
FOOT-STOOLS?!
Do you really need a **herd** of them?
Do *you?!*
I, uh, need to keep my hoof elevated. Everywhere I go.
Fine, just leave one for me.
Sure, sure. This one's hardly a worthy adversary...
Take the doilies, too.

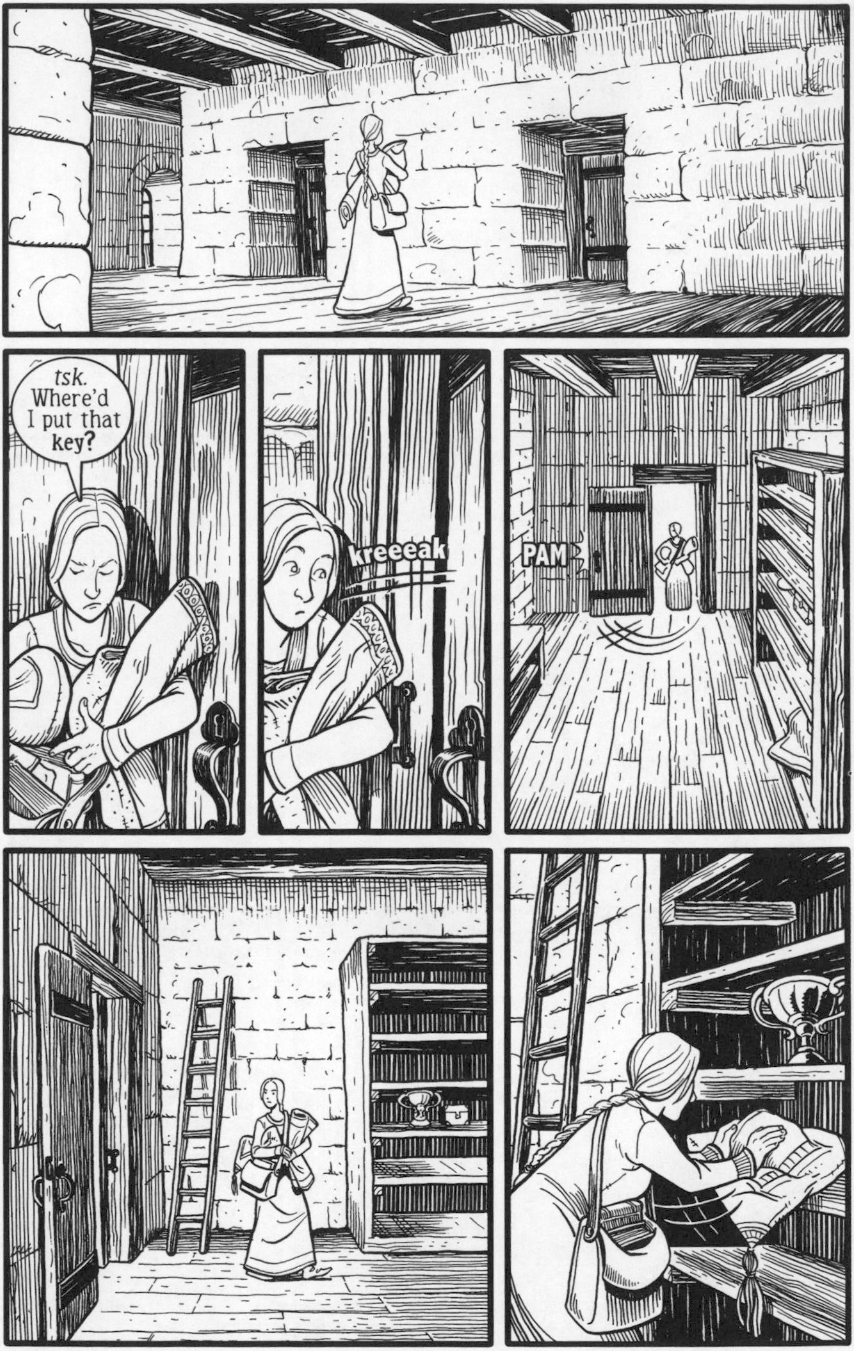
tsk. Where'd I put that key?
kreeeak
PAM

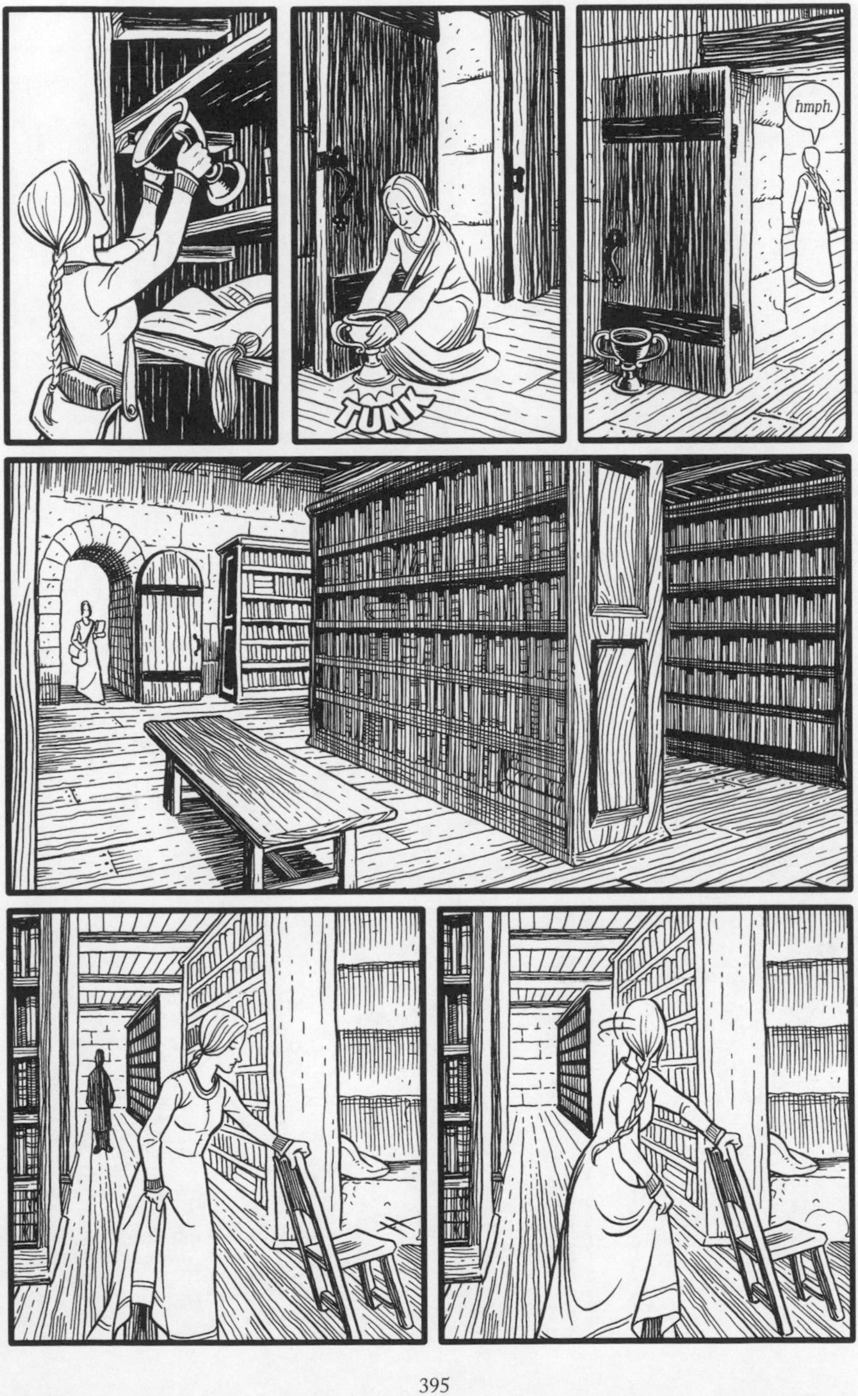
TUNK
hmph.

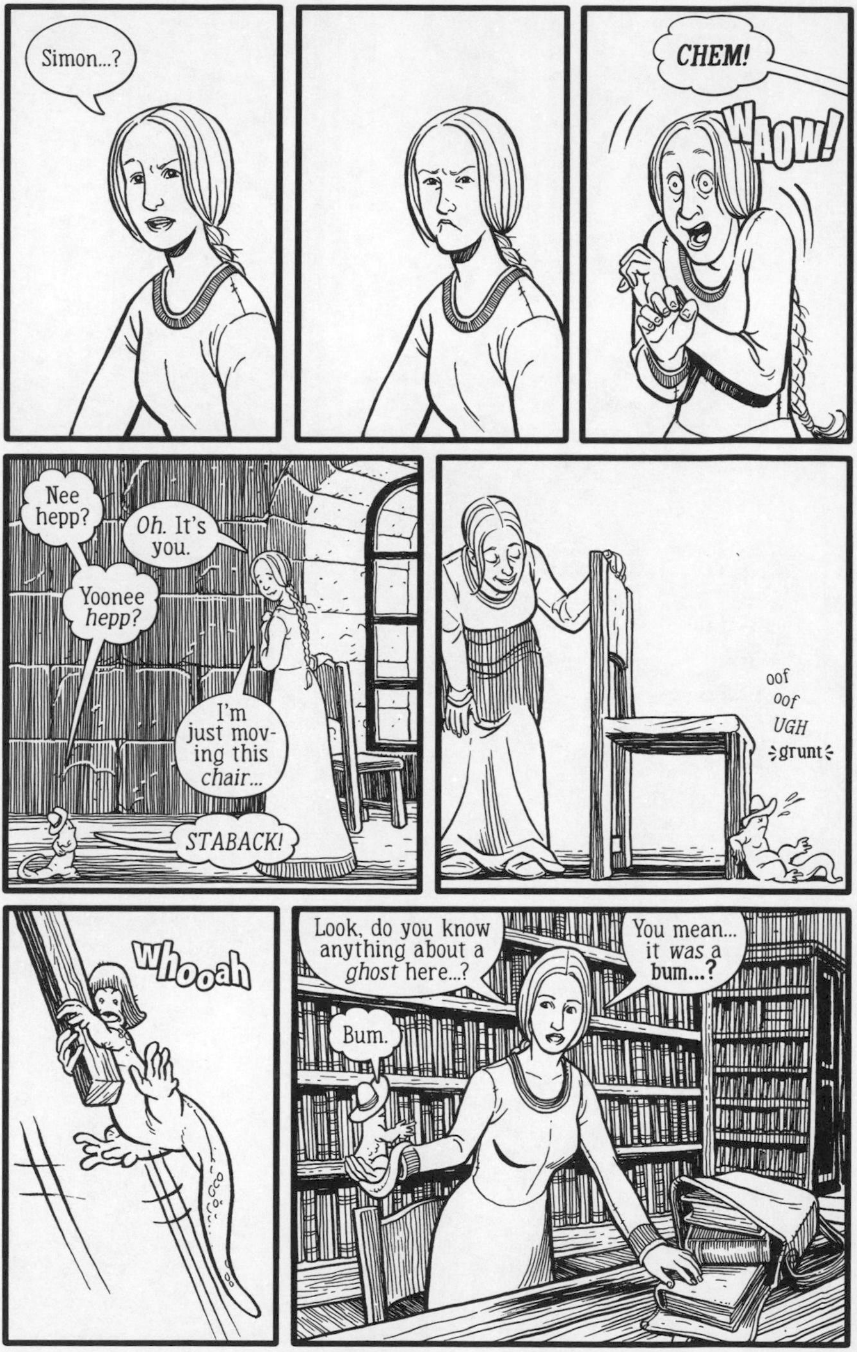
Simon...?
CHEM!
WAOW!
Nee hepp?
Oh. It's you.
Yoonee hepp?
I'm just moving this chair...
STABACK!
oof
oof
UGH
grunt
whooah
Look, do you know anything about a ghost here...?
You mean... it was a bum...?
Bum.

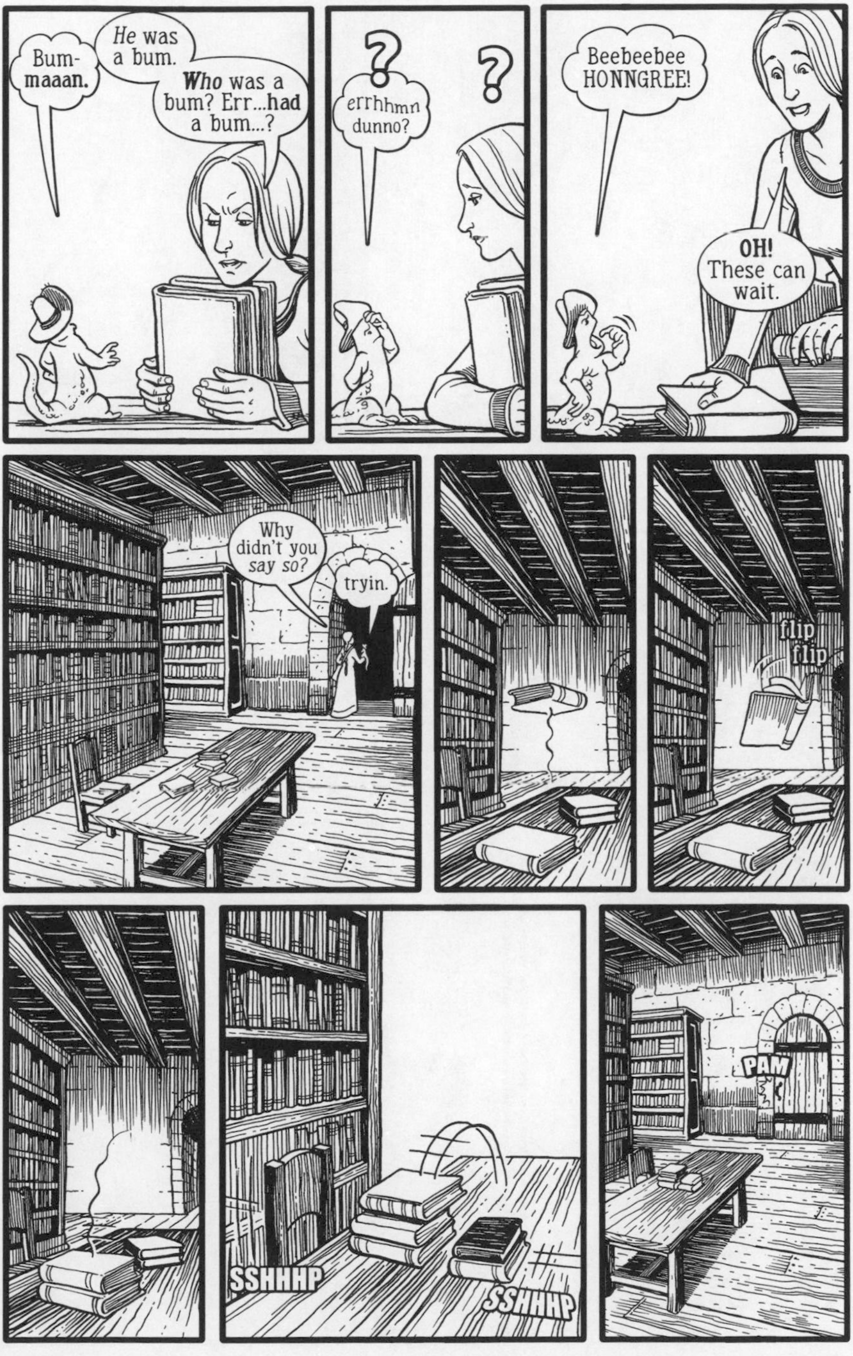
Bum-maaan.
He was a bum.
Who was a bum? Err...had a bum...?
?
errhhmn dunno?
?
Beebeebee HONNGREE!
OH! These can wait.
Why didn't you say so?
tryin.
flip flip
SSHHHP
SSHHHP
PAM

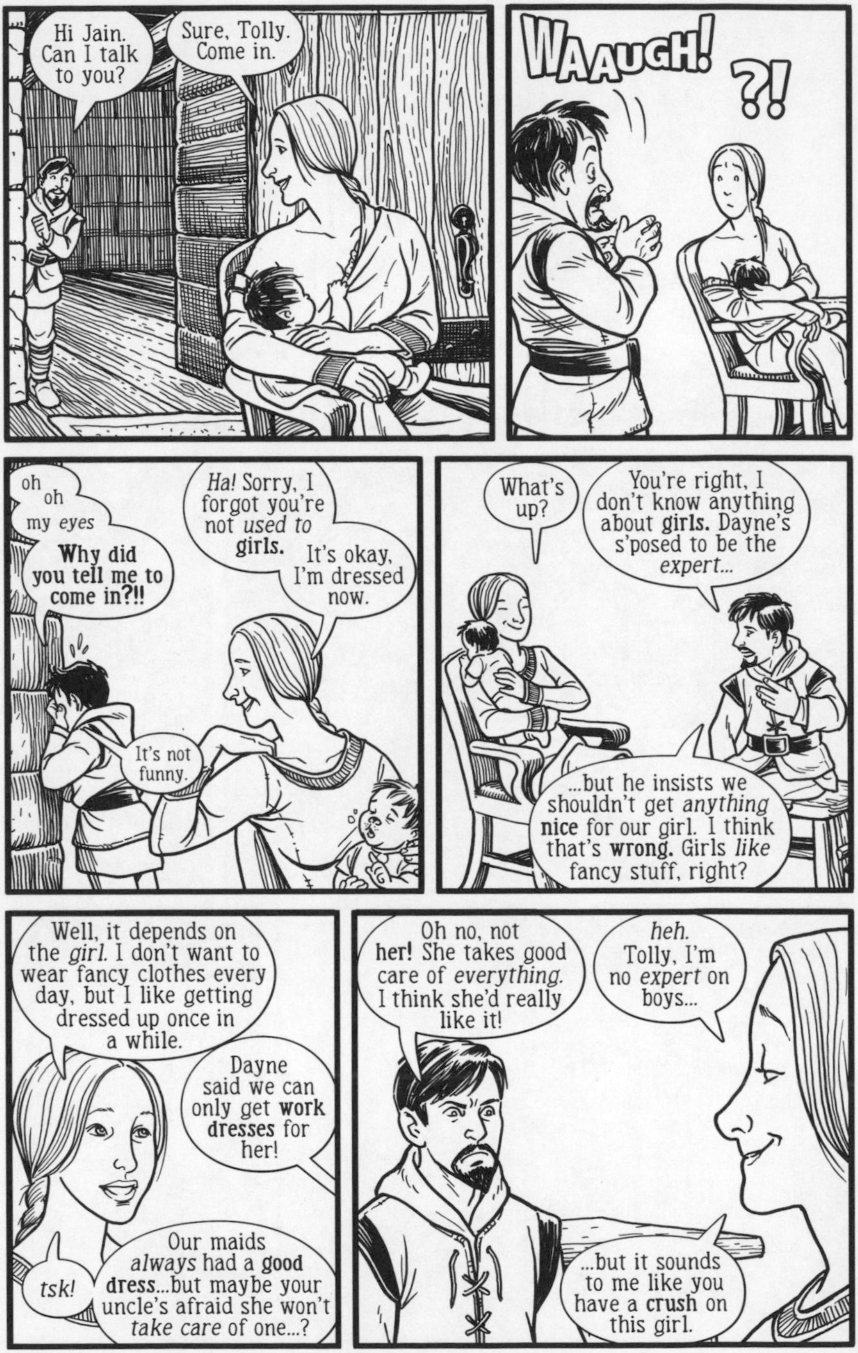
Hi Jain. Can I talk to you?
Sure, Tolly. Come in.
WAAUGH!
?!
oh oh my *eyes*
Why did you tell me to come in?!!
Ha! Sorry, I forgot you're not *used to* **girls.**
It's okay, I'm dressed now.
It's not funny.
What's up?
You're right, I don't know anything about **girls.** Dayne's s'posed to be the *expert...*
...but he insists we shouldn't get *anything* **nice** for our girl. I think that's **wrong.** Girls *like* fancy stuff, right?
Well, it depends on the *girl.* I don't want to wear fancy clothes every day, but I like getting dressed up once in a while.
Dayne said we can only get **work dresses** for her!
tsk!
Our maids *always* had a **good dress**...but maybe your uncle's afraid she won't *take care* of one...?
Oh no, not **her!** She takes good care of *everything.* I think she'd really like it!
heh. Tolly, I'm no *expert* on boys...
...but it sounds to me like you have a **crush** on this girl.

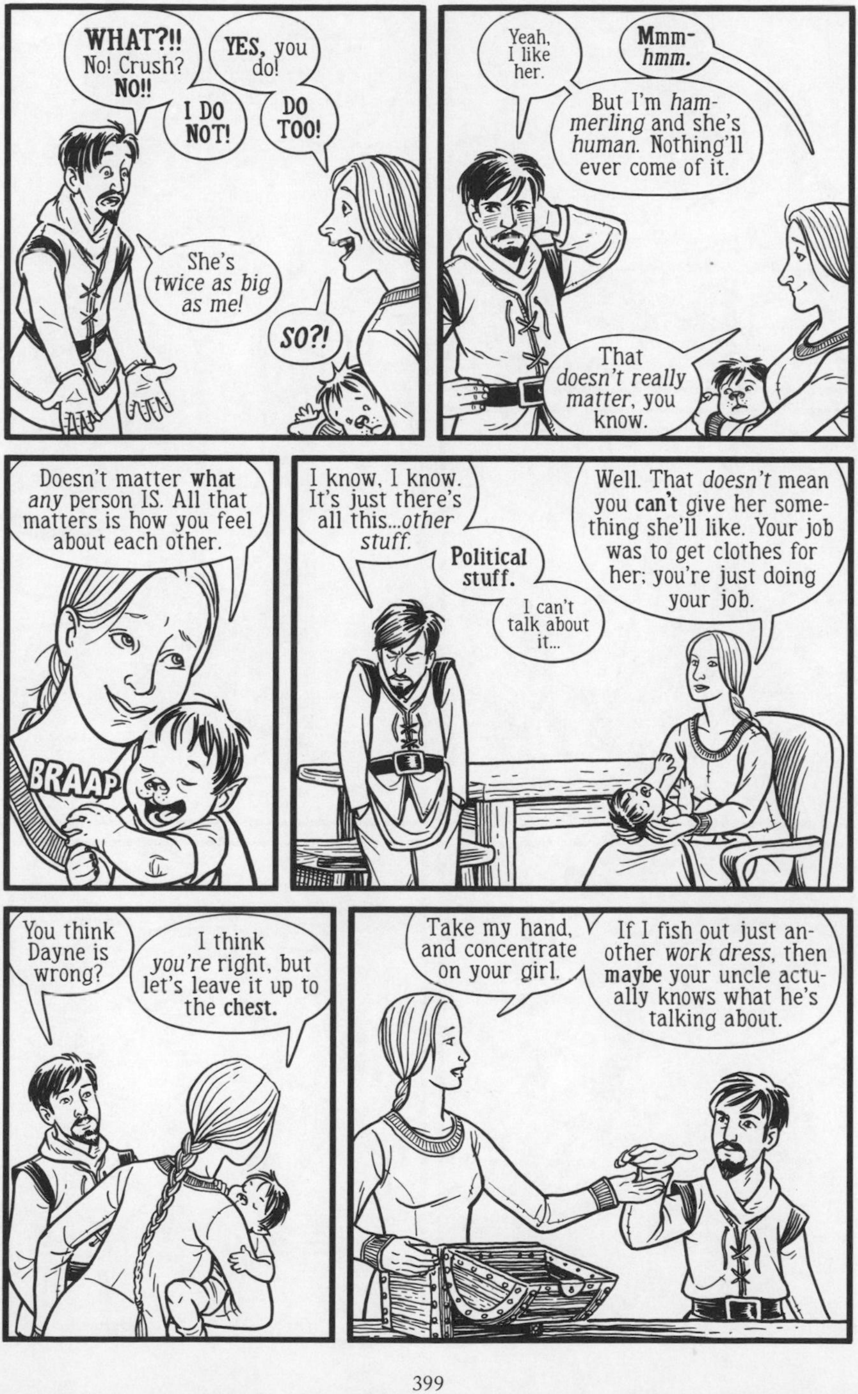
WHAT?!! No! Crush? NO!!
YES, you do!
I DO NOT!
DO TOO!
She's twice as big as me!
SO?!
Yeah, I like her.
Mmm-hmm.
But I'm hammerling and she's human. Nothing'll ever come of it.
That doesn't really matter, you know.
Doesn't matter what any person IS. All that matters is how you feel about each other.
BRAAP
I know, I know. It's just there's all this...other stuff.
Political stuff.
I can't talk about it...
Well. That doesn't mean you can't give her something she'll like. Your job was to get clothes for her; you're just doing your job.
You think Dayne is wrong?
I think you're right, but let's leave it up to the chest.
Take my hand, and concentrate on your girl.
If I fish out just another work dress, then maybe your uncle actually knows what he's talking about.

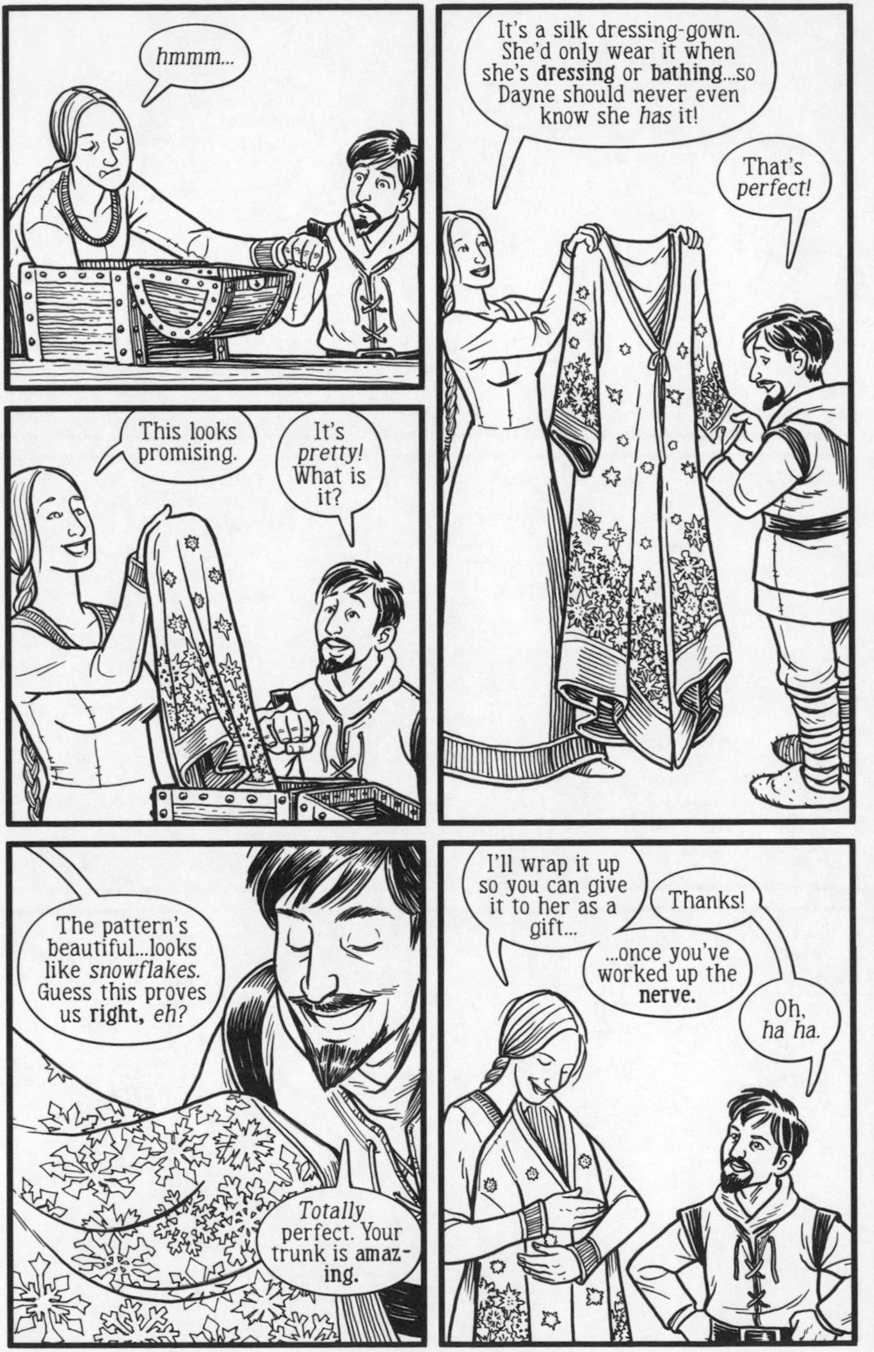
hmmm...
This looks promising.
It's *pretty!* What is it?
It's a silk dressing-gown. She'd only wear it when she's **dressing** or **bathing**...so Dayne should never even know she *has* it!
That's *perfect!*
The pattern's beautiful...looks like *snowflakes.* Guess this proves us **right,** *eh?*
Totally perfect. Your trunk is **amaz-ing.**
I'll wrap it up so you can give it to her as a gift...
Thanks!
...once you've worked up the **nerve.**
Oh, *ha ha.*

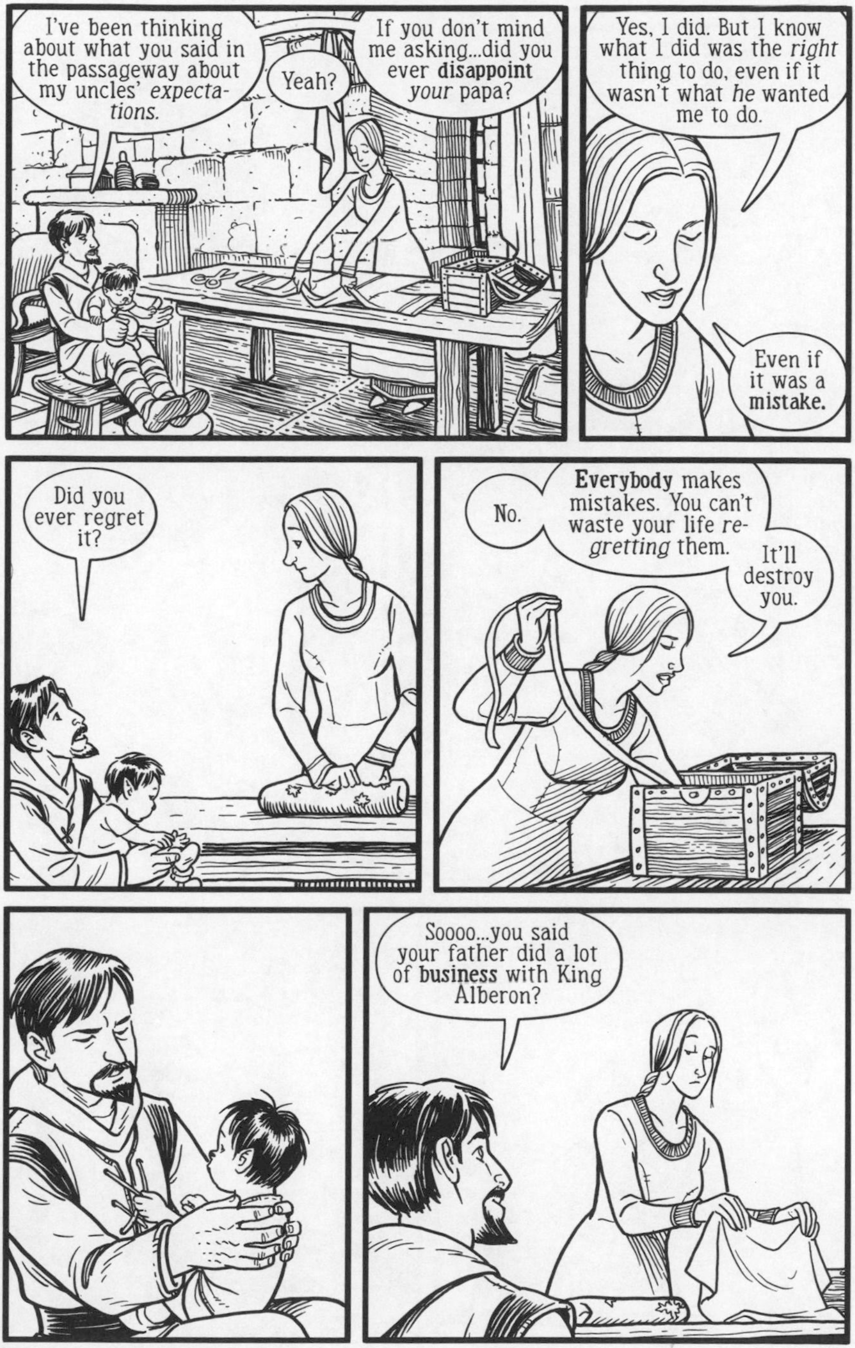
I've been thinking about what you said in the passageway about my uncles' *expectations.*
Yeah?
If you don't mind me asking...did you ever **disappoint** *your* papa?
Yes, I did. But I know what I did was the *right* thing to do, even if it wasn't what *he* wanted me to do.
Even if it was a **mistake.**
Did you ever regret it?
No.
Everybody makes mistakes. You can't waste your life *regretting* them.
It'll destroy you.
Sоooo...you said your father did a lot of **business** with King Alberon?

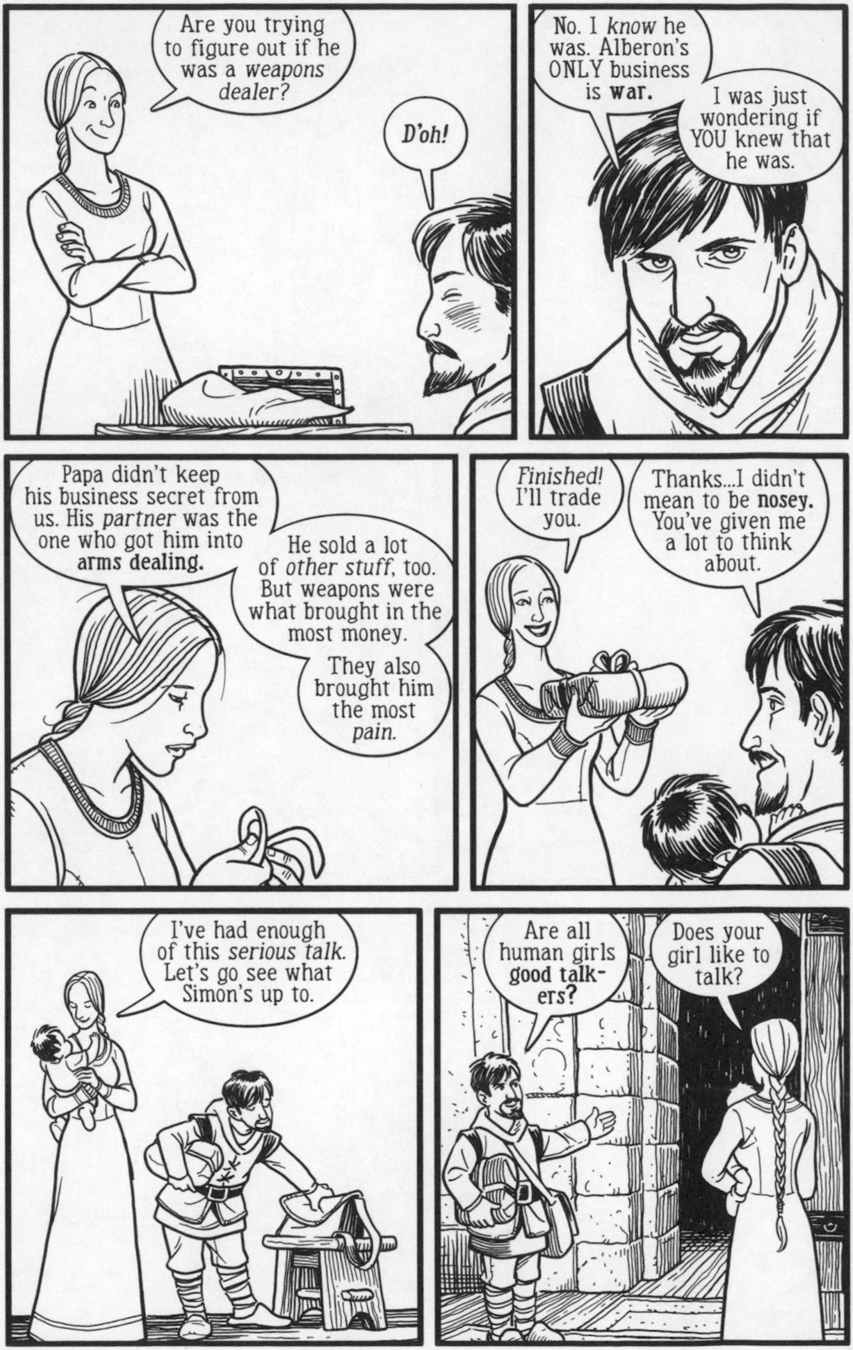
Are you trying to figure out if he was a *weapons dealer?*
D'oh!
No. I *know* he was. Alberon's ONLY business is **war.**
I was just wondering if YOU knew that he was.
Papa didn't keep his business secret from us. His *partner* was the one who got him into **arms dealing.**
He sold a lot of *other stuff*, too. But weapons were what brought in the most money.
They also brought him the most *pain.*
Finished! I'll trade you.
Thanks...I didn't mean to be **nosey.** You've given me a lot to think about.
I've had enough of this *serious talk.* Let's go see what Simon's up to.
Are all human girls **good talk-ers?**
Does your girl like to talk?

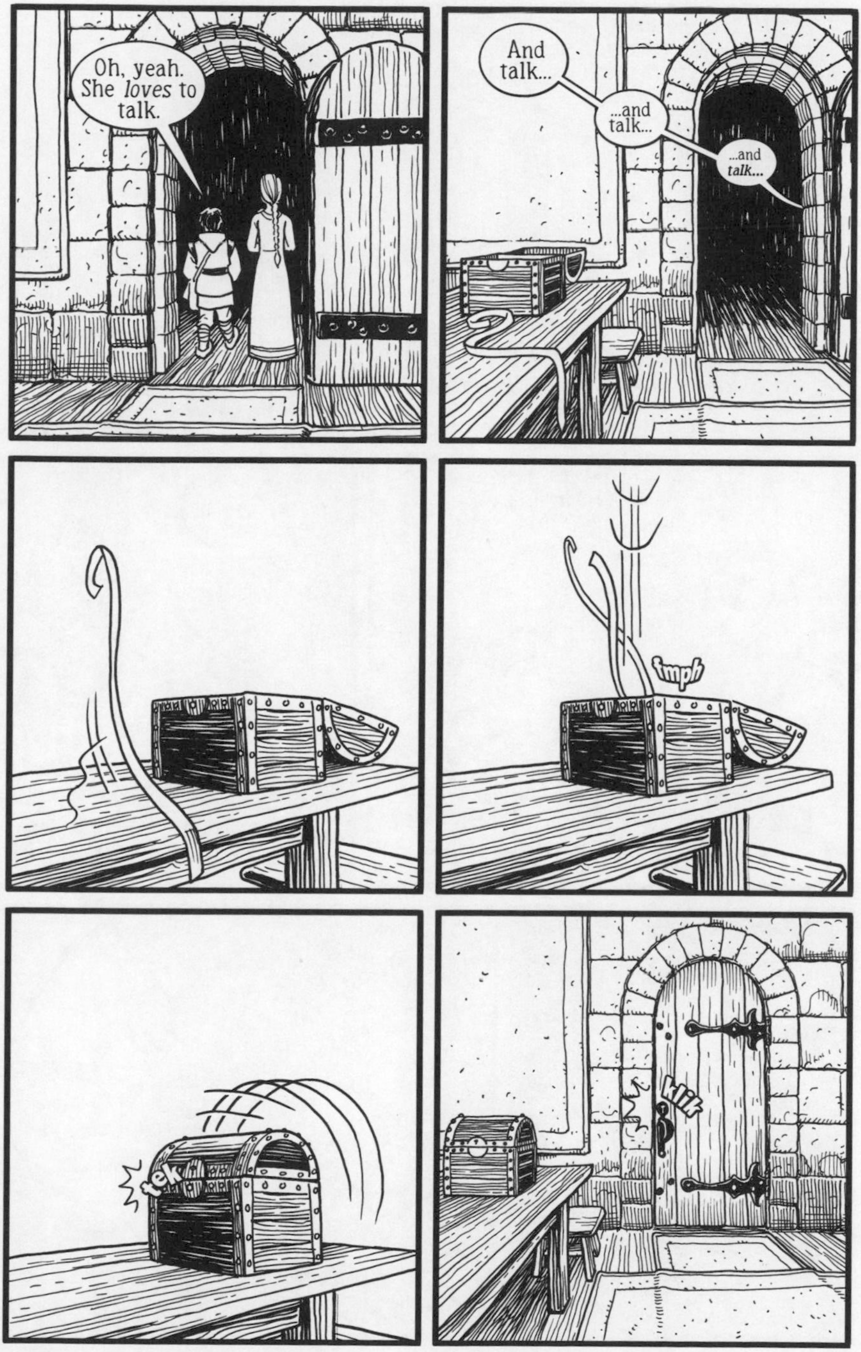
Oh, yeah. She *loves* to talk.
And talk...
...and talk...
...and *talk...*
fmph
tek
klik

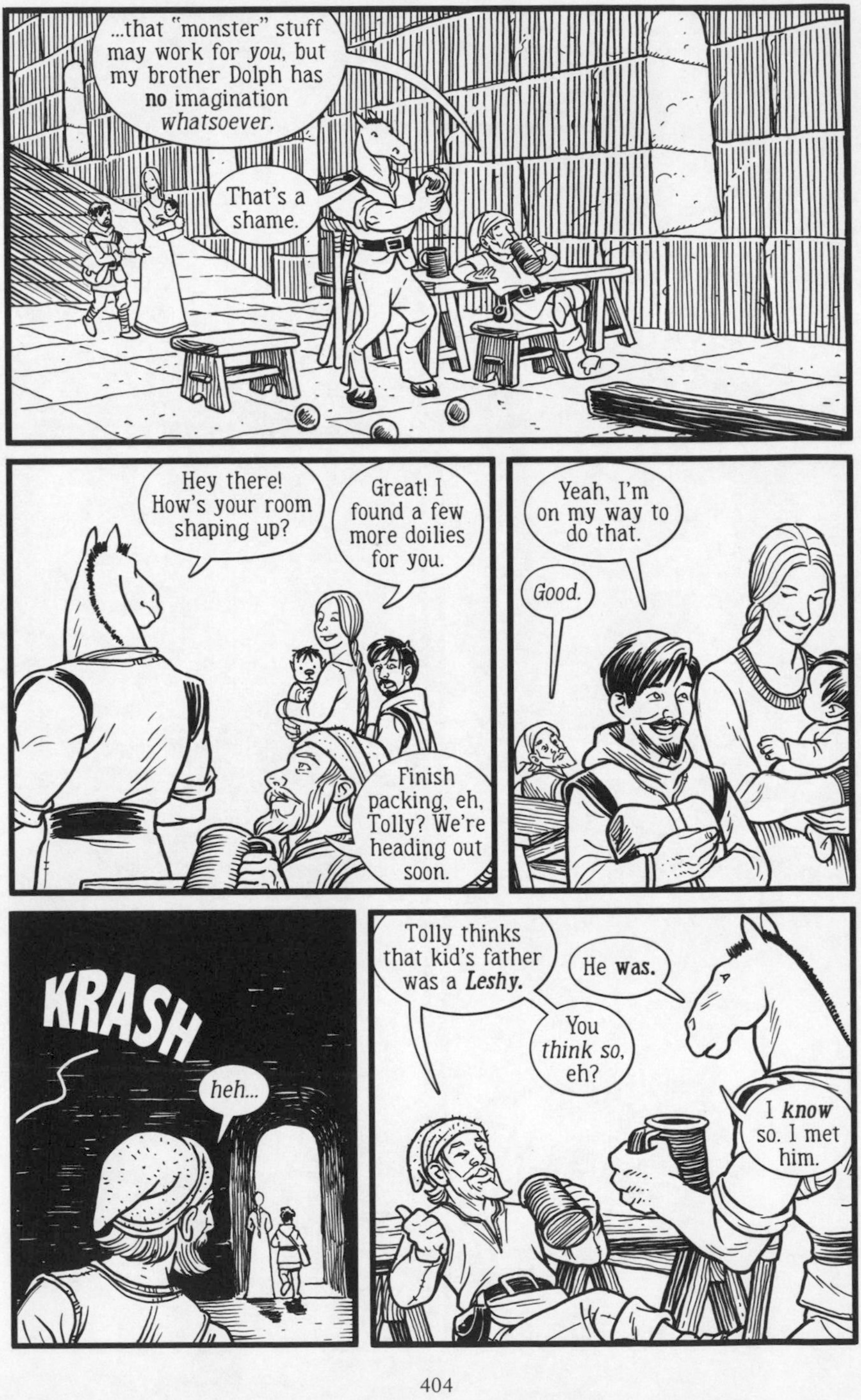
...that "monster" stuff may work for *you*, but my brother Dolph has **no** imagination *whatsoever.*
That's a shame.
Hey there! How's your room shaping up?
Great! I found a few more doilies for you.
Finish packing, eh, Tolly? We're heading out soon.
Yeah, I'm on my way to do that.
Good.
KRASH
heh...
Tolly thinks that kid's father was a ***Leshy.***
He **was.**
You *think so,* eh?
I ***know*** so. I met him.

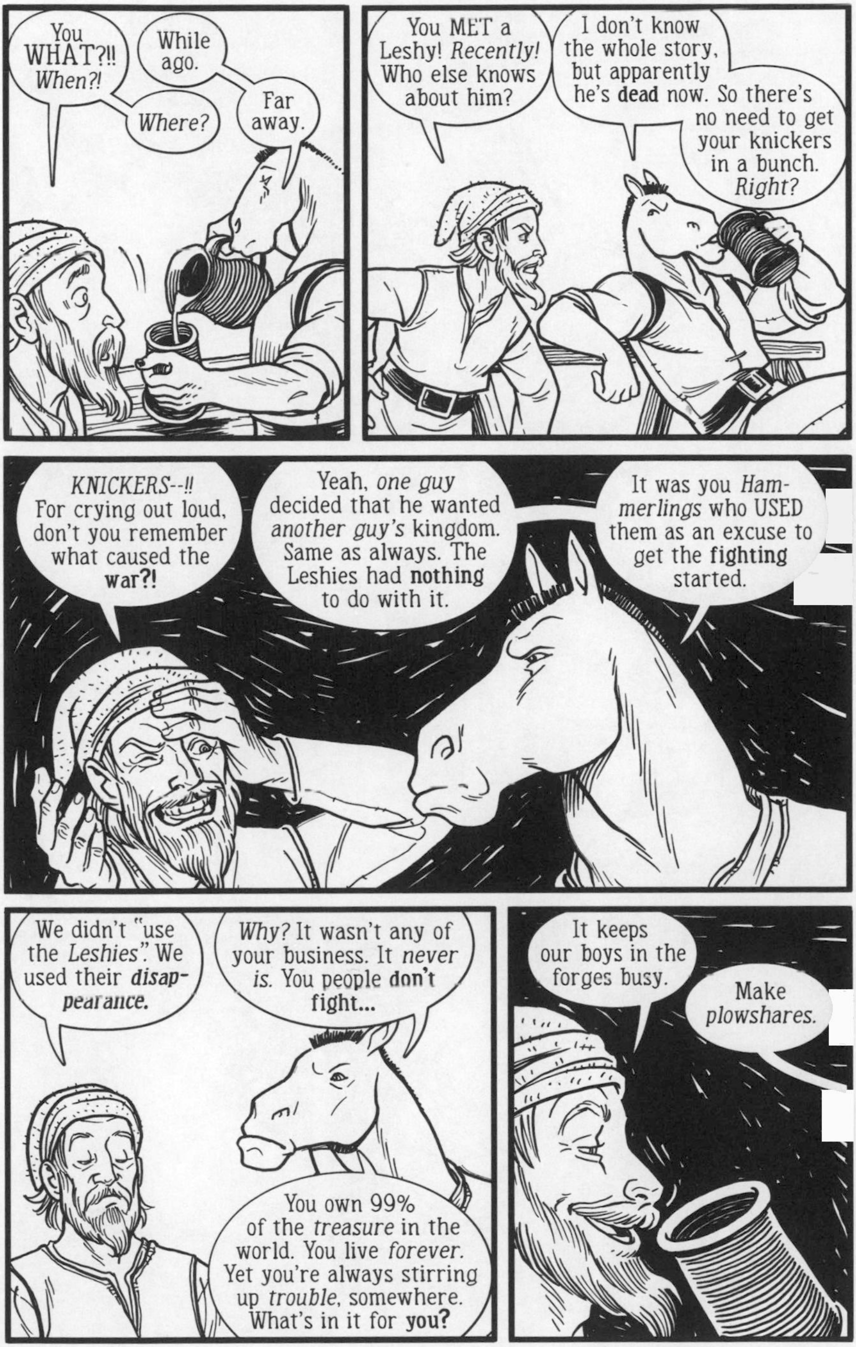
You WHAT?!! When?!
While ago.
Where?
Far away.
You MET a Leshy! Recently! Who else knows about him?
I don't know the whole story, but apparently he's dead now. So there's no need to get your knickers in a bunch. Right?
KNICKERS--!! For crying out loud, don't you remember what caused the war?!
Yeah, one guy decided that he wanted another guy's kingdom. Same as always. The Leshies had nothing to do with it.
It was you Hammerlings who USED them as an excuse to get the fighting started.
We didn't "use the Leshies". We used their disappearance.
Why? It wasn't any of your business. It never is. You people don't fight...
You own 99% of the treasure in the world. You live forever. Yet you're always stirring up trouble, somewhere. What's in it for you?
It keeps our boys in the forges busy.
Make plowshares.

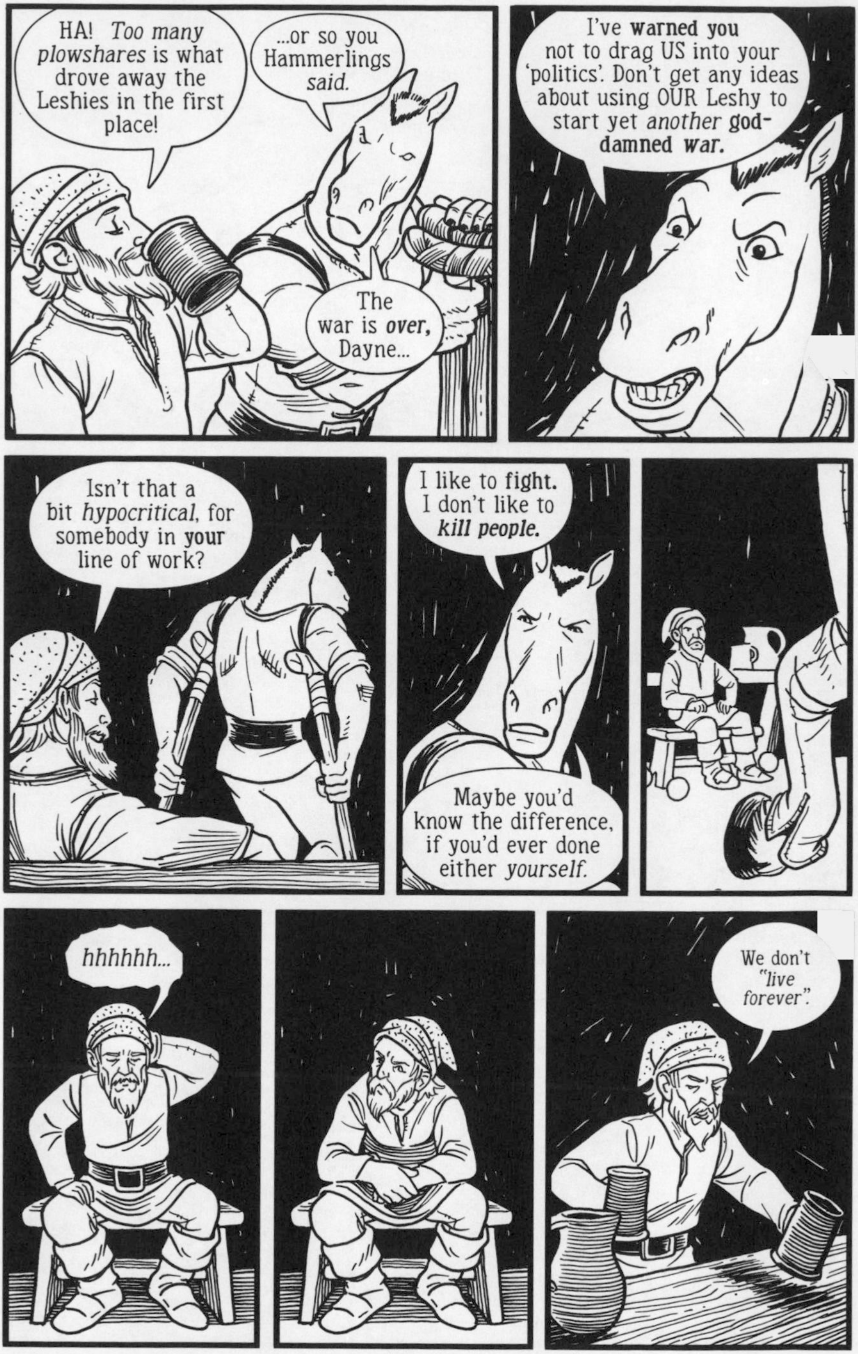
HA! *Too many plowshares* is what drove away the Leshies in the first place!
...or so you Hammerlings *said.*
The war is *over,* Dayne...
I've **warned you** not to drag US into your 'politics'. Don't get any ideas about using OUR Leshy to start yet *another* **god-damned war.**
Isn't that a bit *hypocritical*, for somebody in **your** line of work?
I like to **fight.** I don't like to ***kill people.***
Maybe you'd know the difference, if you'd ever done either *yourself.*
hhhhhh...
We don't *"live forever"*.

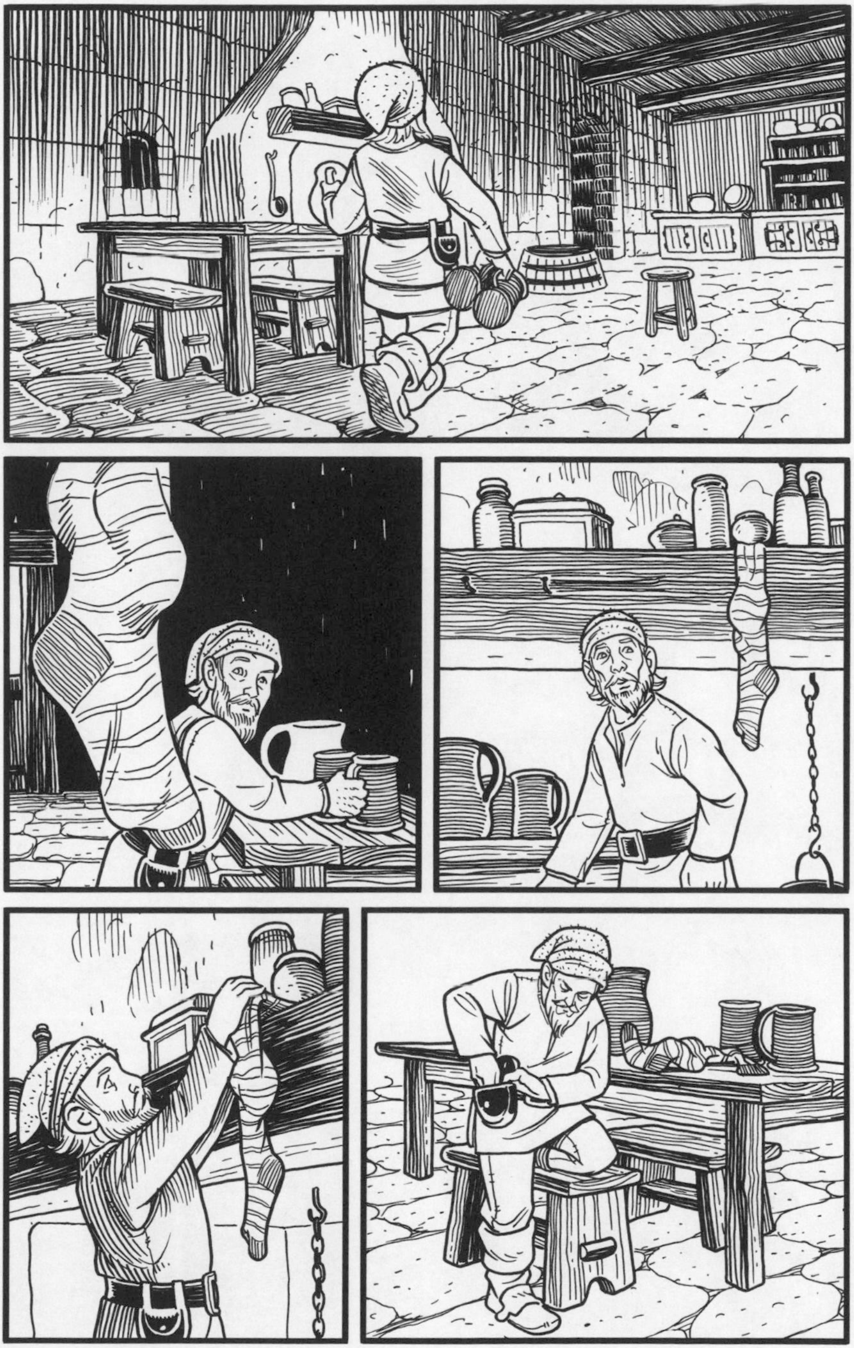

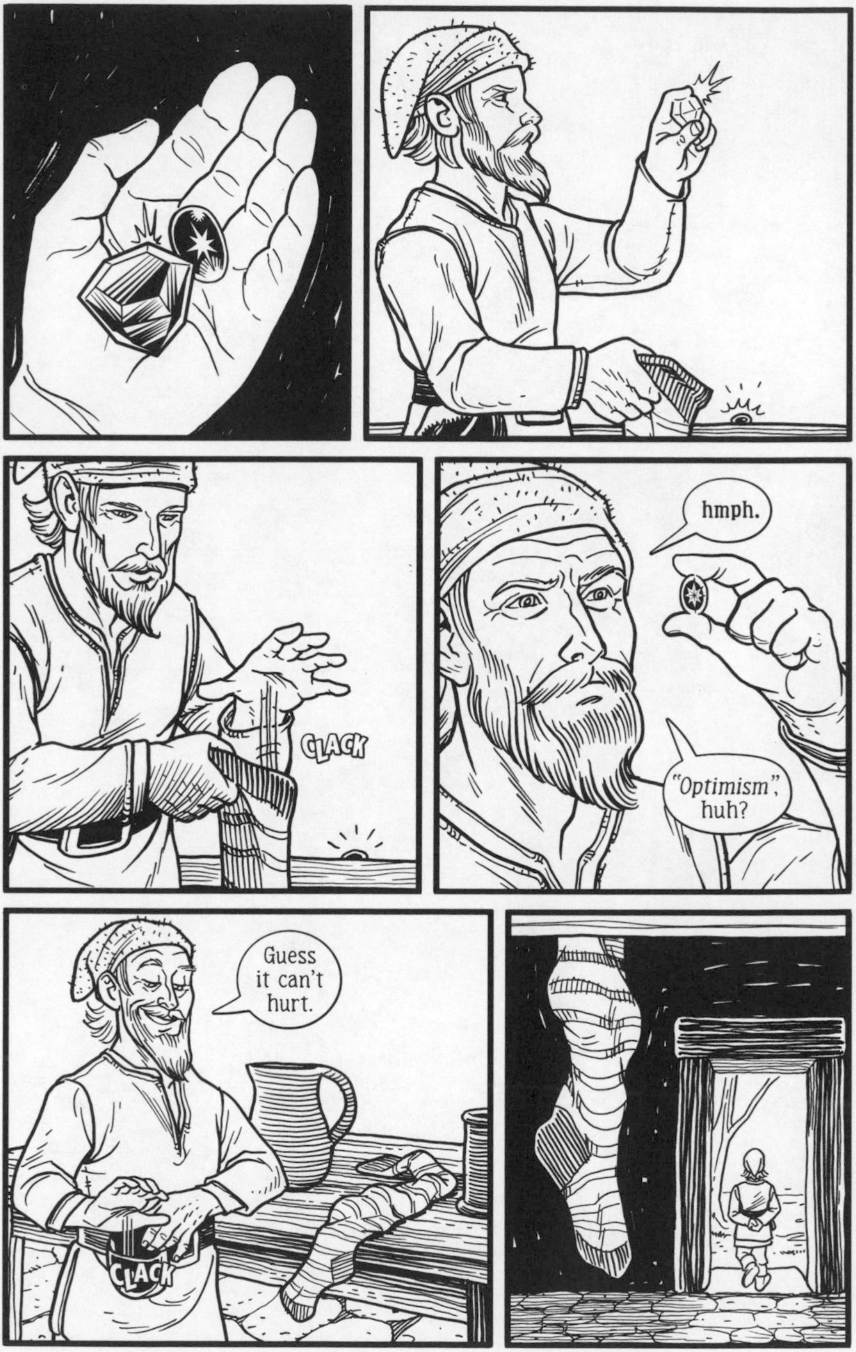
CLACK
hmph.
"Optimism", huh?
Guess it can't hurt.
CLACK

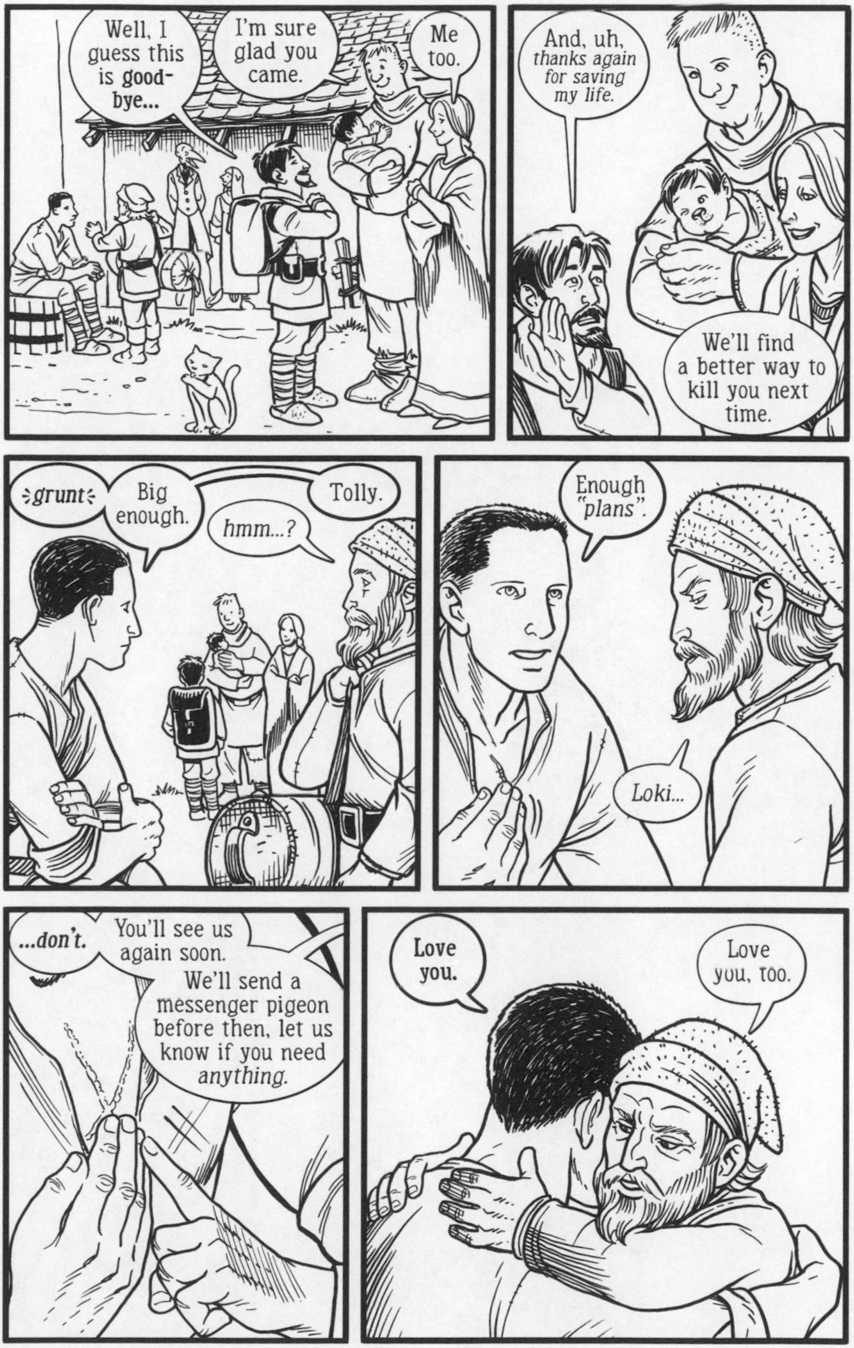
Well, I guess this is **good-bye...**
I'm sure glad you came.
Me too.
And, uh, *thanks again for saving my life.*
We'll find a better way to kill you next time.
grunt
Big enough.
Tolly.
hmm...?
Enough *"plans"*.
Loki...
...don't.
You'll see us again soon.
We'll send a messenger pigeon before then, let us know if you need *anything.*
Love you.
Love you, too.

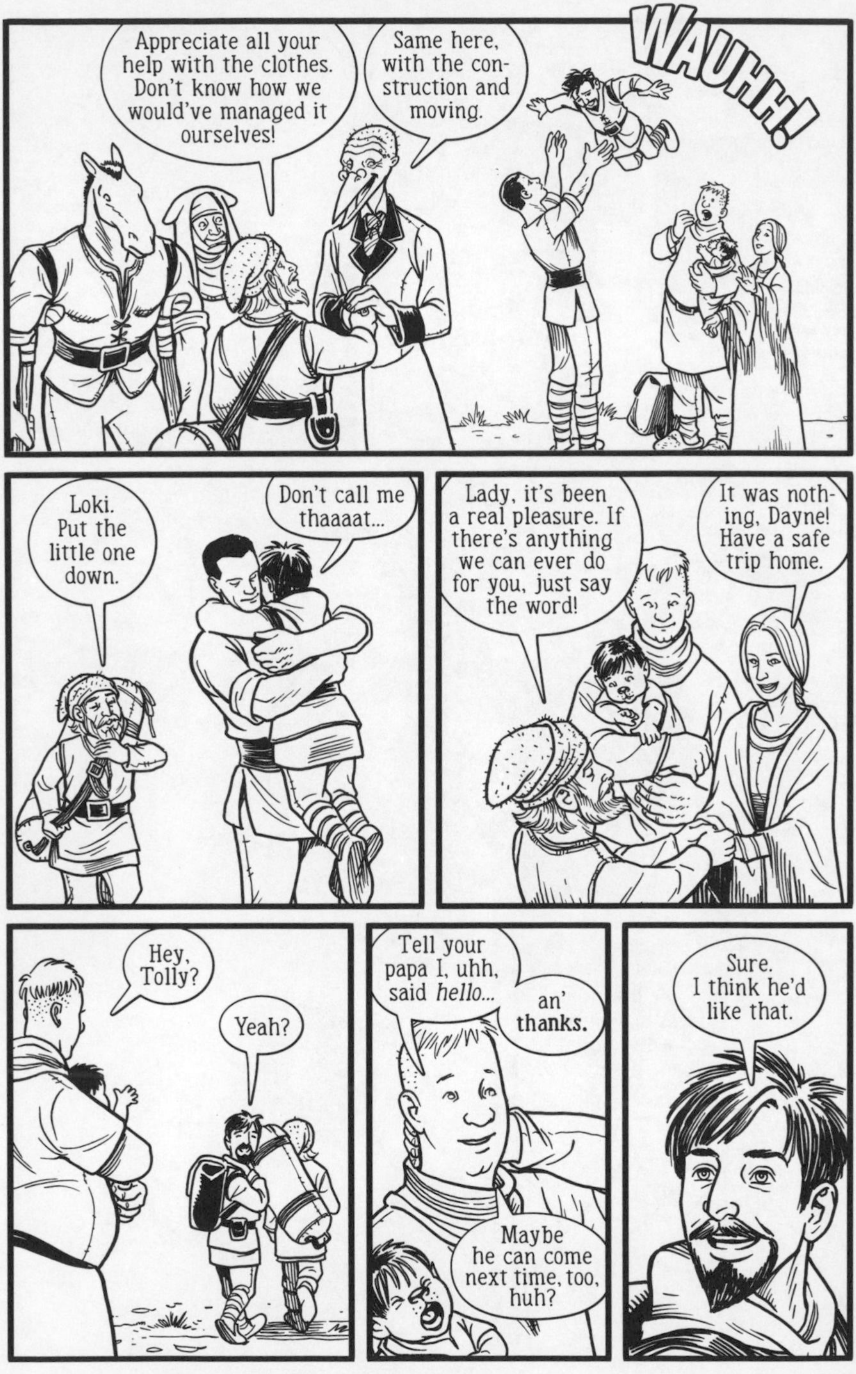
Appreciate all your help with the clothes. Don't know how we would've managed it ourselves!
Same here, with the construction and moving.
WAUHH!
Loki. Put the little one down.
Don't call me thaaaat...
Lady, it's been a real pleasure. If there's anything we can ever do for you, just say the word!
It was nothing, Dayne! Have a safe trip home.
Hey, Tolly?
Yeah?
Tell your papa I, uhh, said *hello...*
an' **thanks.**
Maybe he can come next time, too, huh?
Sure. I think he'd like that.

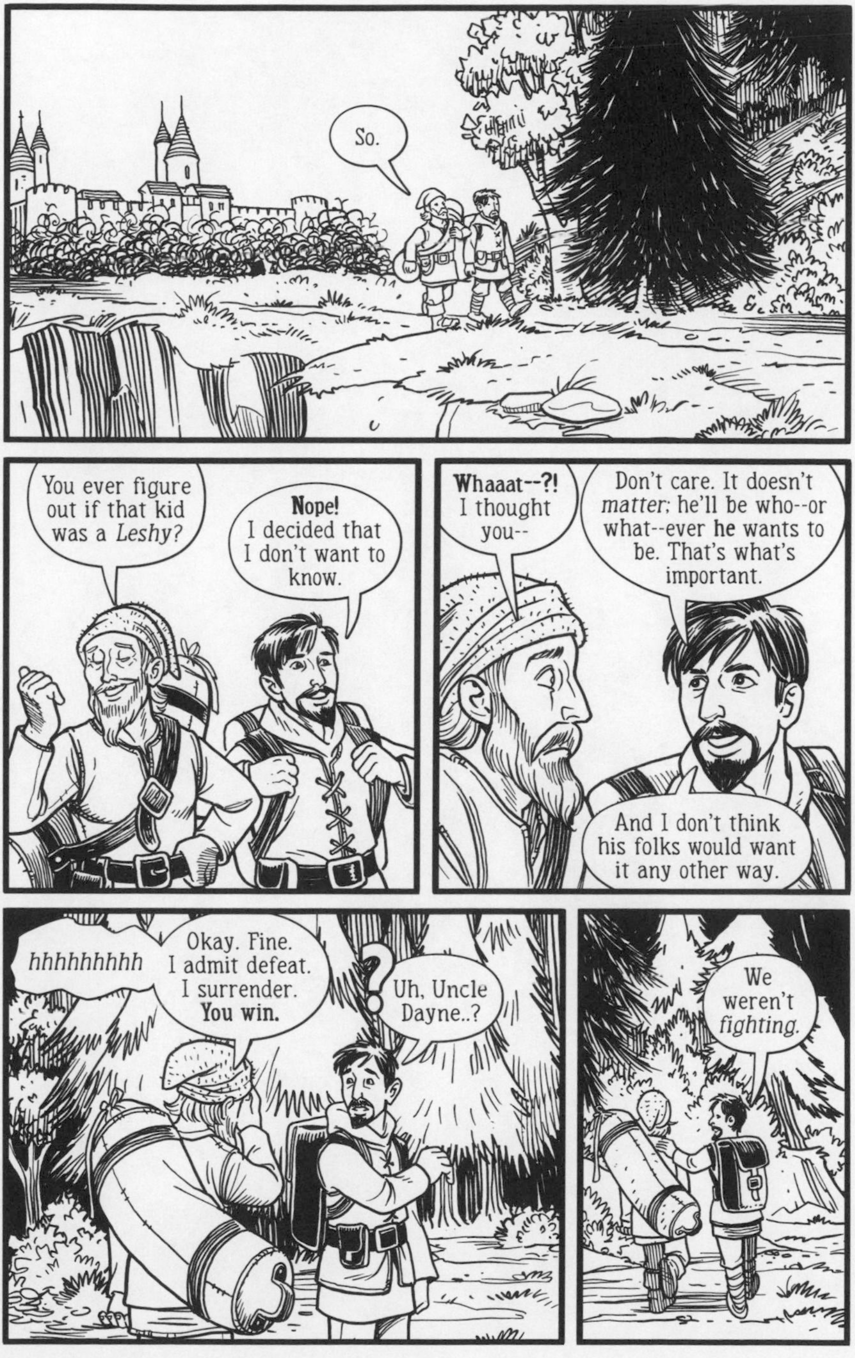
So.
You ever figure out if that kid was a *Leshy*?
Nope! I decided that I don't want to know.
Whaaat--?! I thought you--
Don't care. It doesn't *matter*; he'll be who--or what--ever **he** wants to be. That's what's important.
And I don't think his folks would want it any other way.
hhhhhhhhh
Okay. Fine. I admit defeat. I surrender. **You win.**
?
Uh, Uncle Dayne..?
We weren't *fighting.*

Chapter 16.

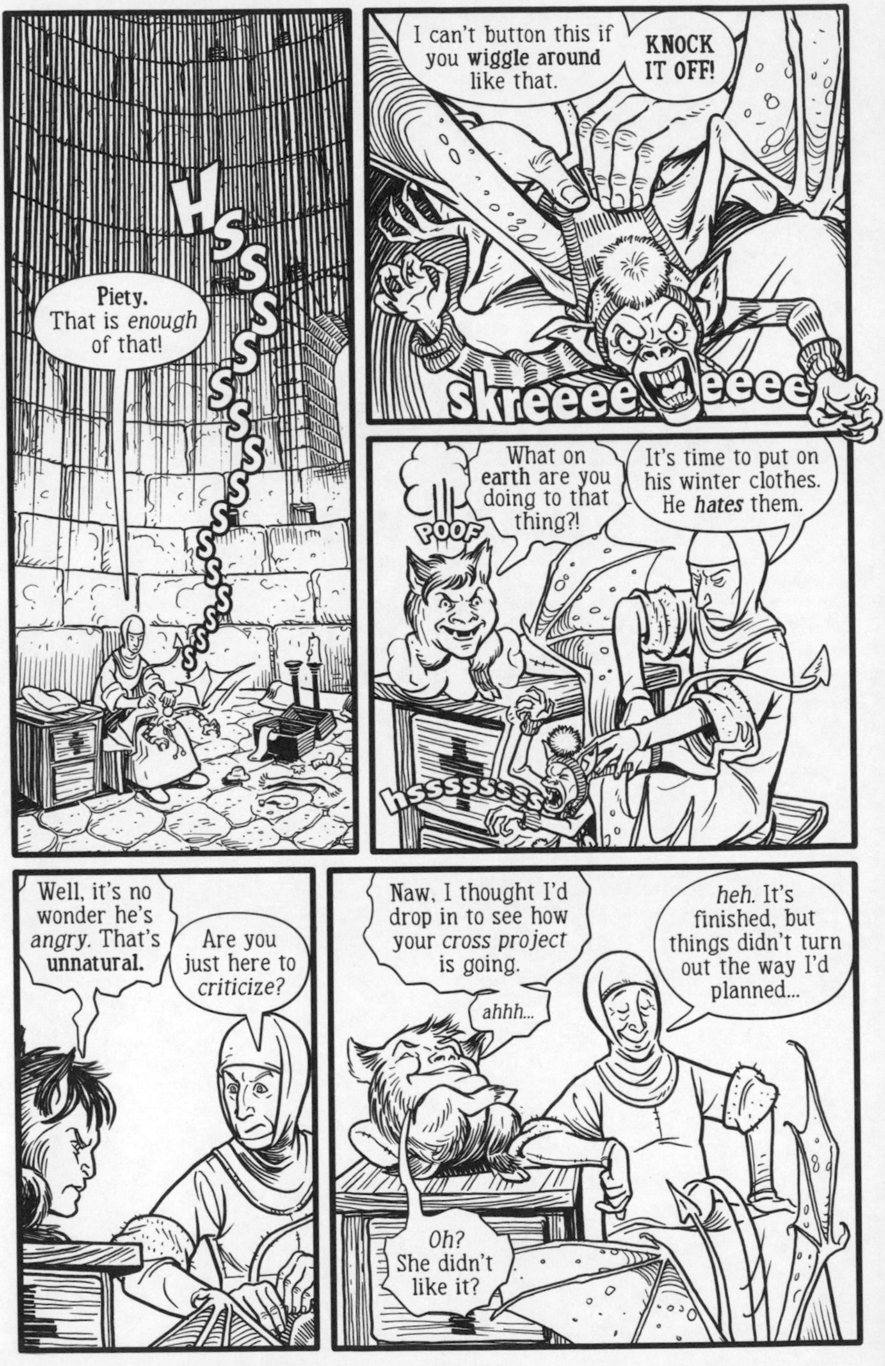
HSSSSSSSSSSSS
Piety. That is *enough* of that!
I can't button this if you **wiggle around** like that.
KNOCK IT OFF!
skreeeeeeee
What on **earth** are you doing to that thing?!
It's time to put on his winter clothes. He *hates* them.
POOF
hsssssssss
Well, it's no wonder he's *angry.* That's **unnatural.**
Are you just here to *criticize?*
Naw, I thought I'd drop in to see how your *cross project* is going.
heh. It's finished, but things didn't turn out the way I'd planned...
ahhh...
Oh? She didn't like it?

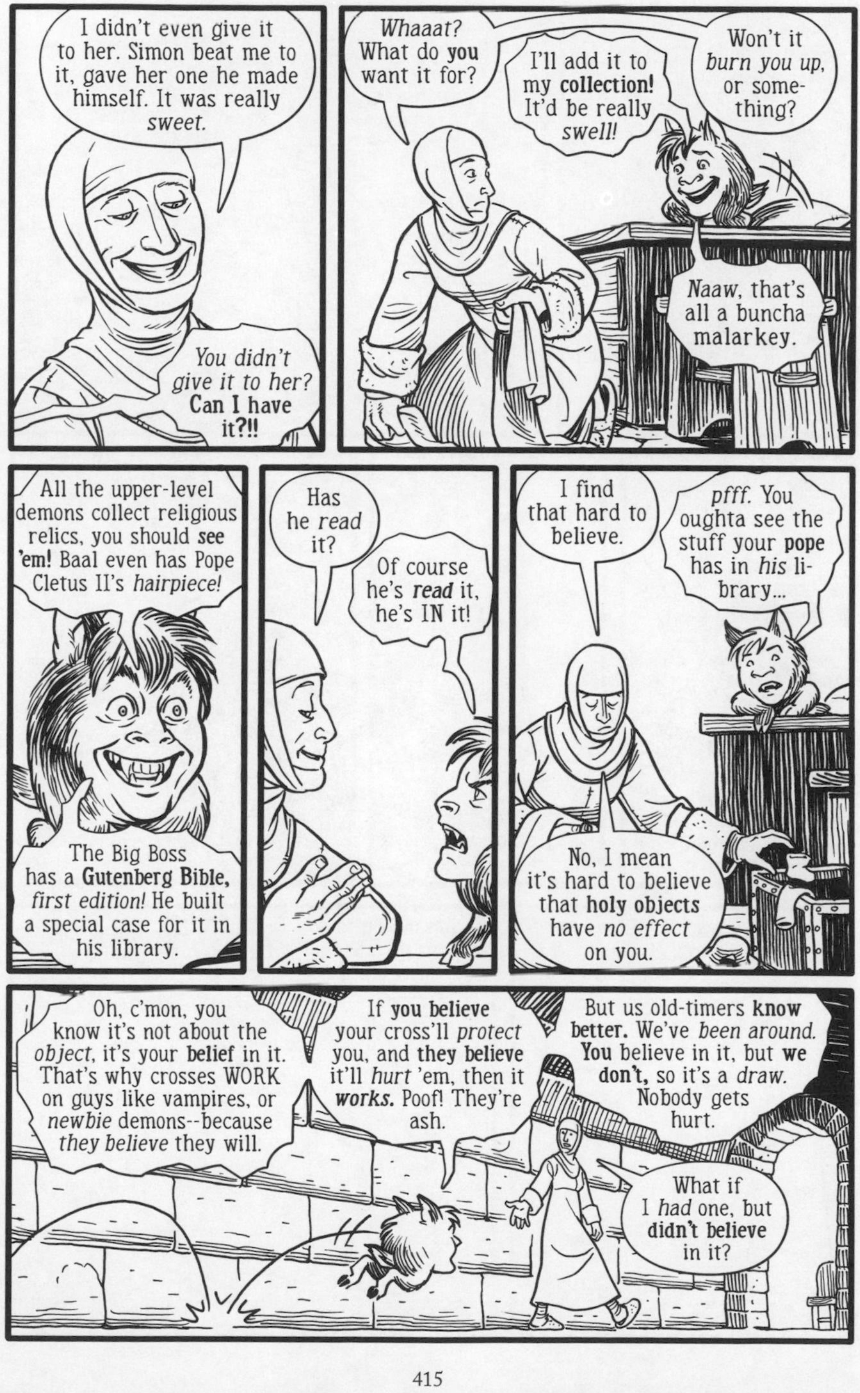
I didn't even give it to her. Simon beat me to it, gave her one he made himself. It was really *sweet.*
You didn't give it to her? **Can I have it?!!**
Whaaat? What do **you** want it for?
I'll add it to my **collection!** It'd be really *swell!*
Won't it *burn you up,* or something?
Naaw, that's all a buncha malarkey.
All the upper-level demons collect religious relics, you should **see 'em!** Baal even has Pope Cletus II's *hairpiece!*
The Big Boss has a **Gutenberg Bible,** *first edition!* He built a special case for it in his library.
Has he *read* it?
Of course he's ***read*** it, he's IN it!
I find that hard to believe.
pfff. You oughta see the stuff your **pope** has in *his* library...
No, I mean it's hard to believe that **holy objects** have *no effect* on you.
Oh, c'mon, you know it's not about the *object*, it's your **belief** in it. That's why crosses WORK on guys like vampires, or *newbie* demons--because *they believe* they will.
If **you believe** your cross'll *protect* you, and **they believe** it'll *hurt* 'em, then it ***works.*** Poof! They're ash.
But us old-timers **know better.** We've *been around.* **You** believe in it, but **we don't,** so it's a *draw.* Nobody gets hurt.
What if I *had* one, but **didn't believe** in it?

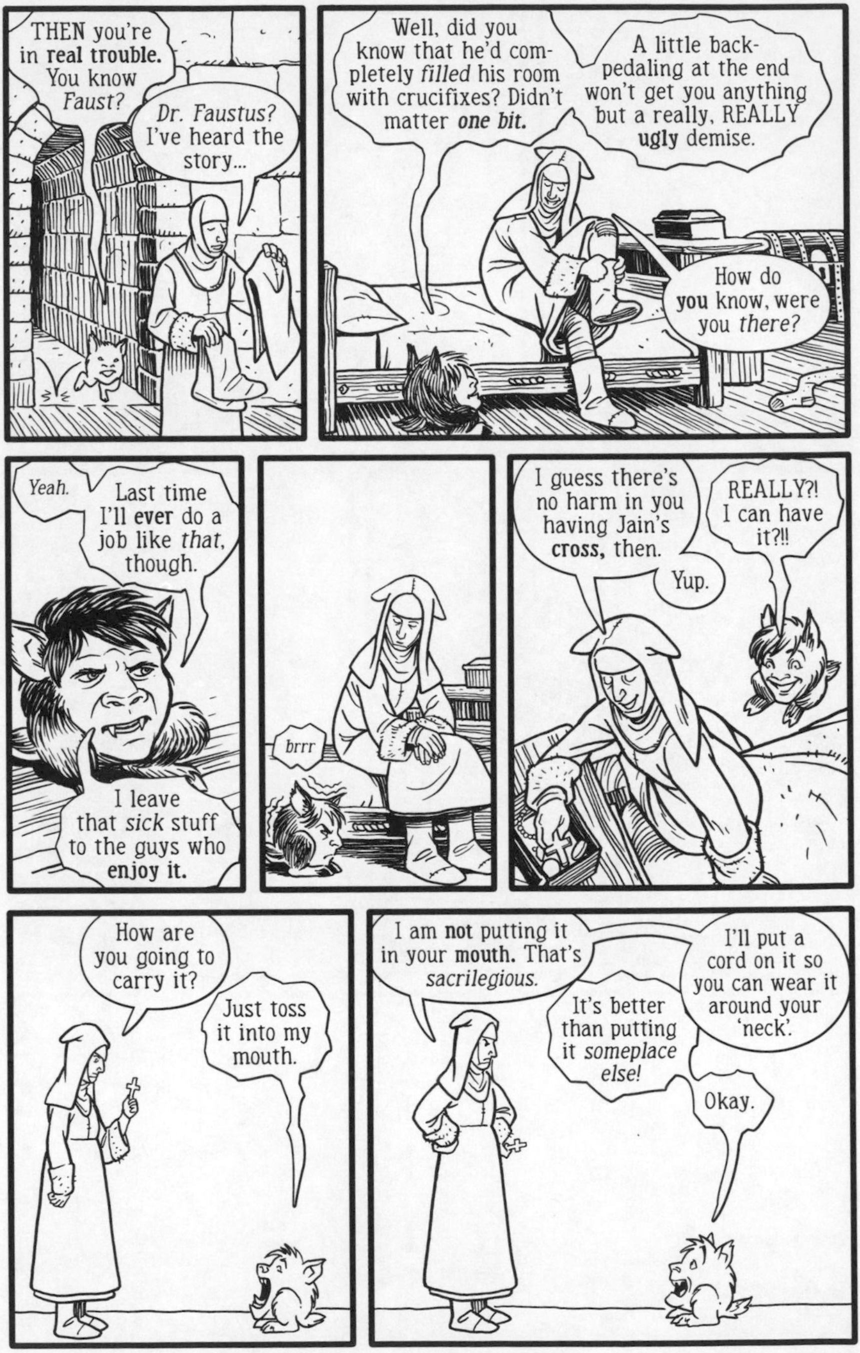
THEN you're in **real trouble.** You know *Faust?*
Dr. Faustus? I've heard the story...
Well, did you know that he'd completely *filled* his room with crucifixes? Didn't matter ***one bit.***
A little back-pedaling at the end won't get you anything but a really, REALLY **ugly** demise.
How do **you** know, were you *there?*
Yeah.
Last time I'll **ever** do a job like *that,* though.
I leave that *sick* stuff to the guys who **enjoy it.**
brrr
I guess there's no harm in you having Jain's **cross,** then.
Yup.
REALLY?! I can have it?!!
How are you going to carry it?
Just toss it into my mouth.
I am **not** putting it in your **mouth.** That's *sacrilegious.*
It's better than putting it *someplace else!*
I'll put a cord on it so you can wear it around your 'neck'.
Okay.

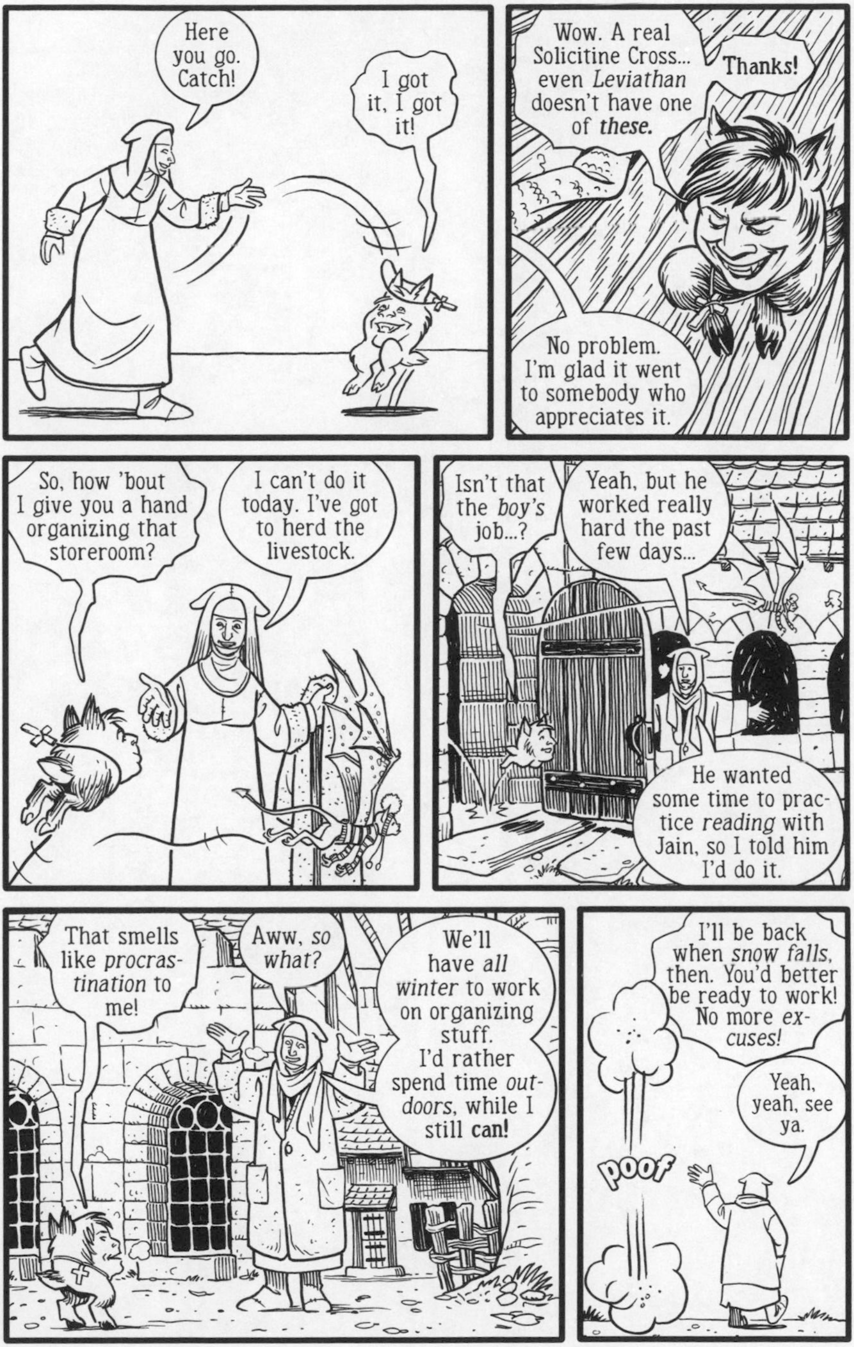
Here you go. Catch!
I got it, I got it!
Wow. A real Solicitine Cross... even *Leviathan* doesn't have one of ***these.***
Thanks!
No problem. I'm glad it went to somebody who appreciates it.
So, how 'bout I give you a hand organizing that storeroom?
I can't do it today. I've got to herd the livestock.
Isn't that the *boy's* job...?
Yeah, but he worked really hard the past few days...
He wanted some time to practice *reading* with Jain, so I told him I'd do it.
That smells like *procrastination* to me!
Aww, *so what?*
We'll have *all winter* to work on organizing stuff. I'd rather spend time *outdoors*, while I still **can!**
I'll be back when *snow falls*, then. You'd better be ready to work! No more *excuses!*
Yeah, yeah, see ya.
poof

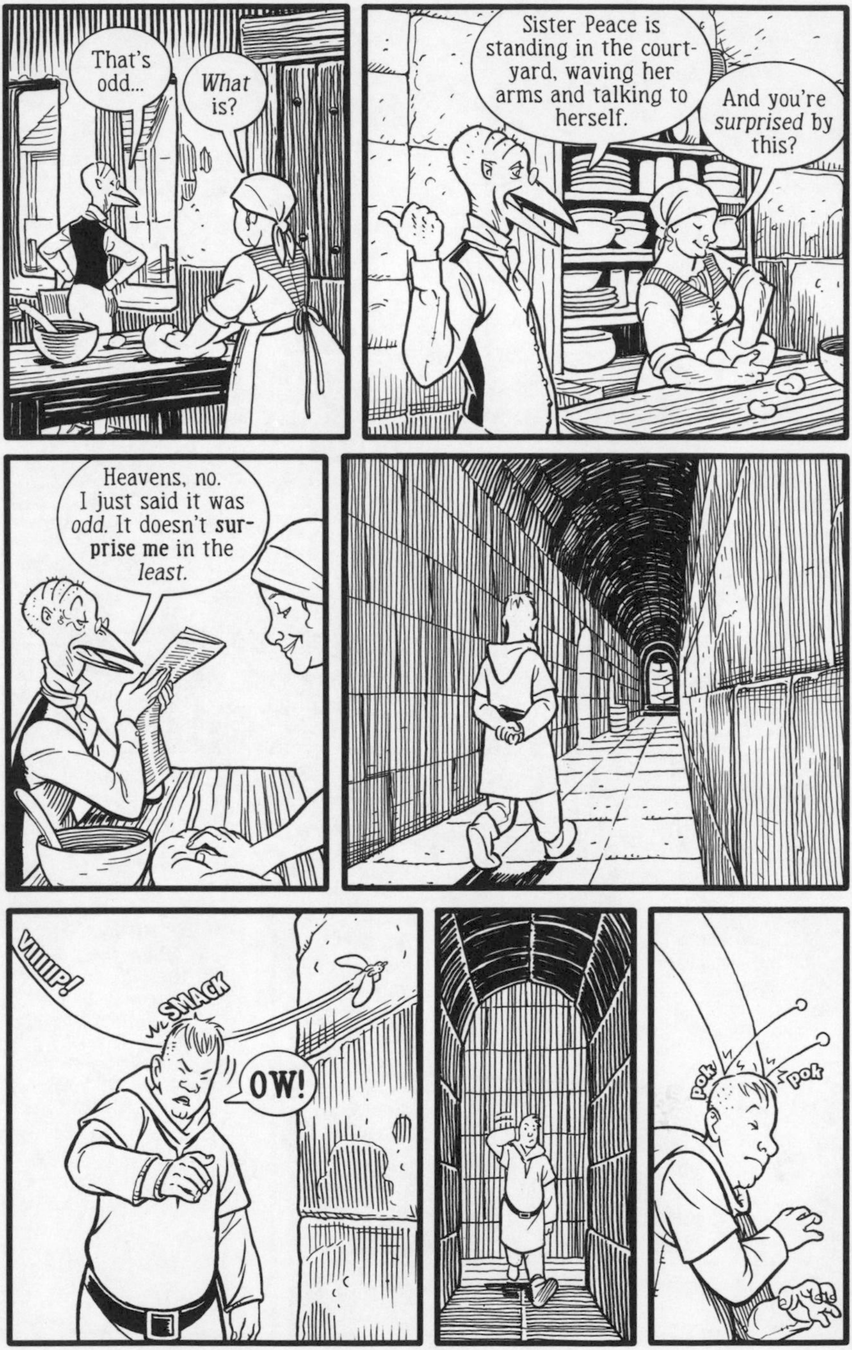
That's odd...
What is?
Sister Peace is standing in the court-yard, waving her arms and talking to herself.
And you're surprised by this?
Heavens, no. I just said it was odd. It doesn't surprise me in the least.
VIIIIP!
SMACK
OW!
pok
pok

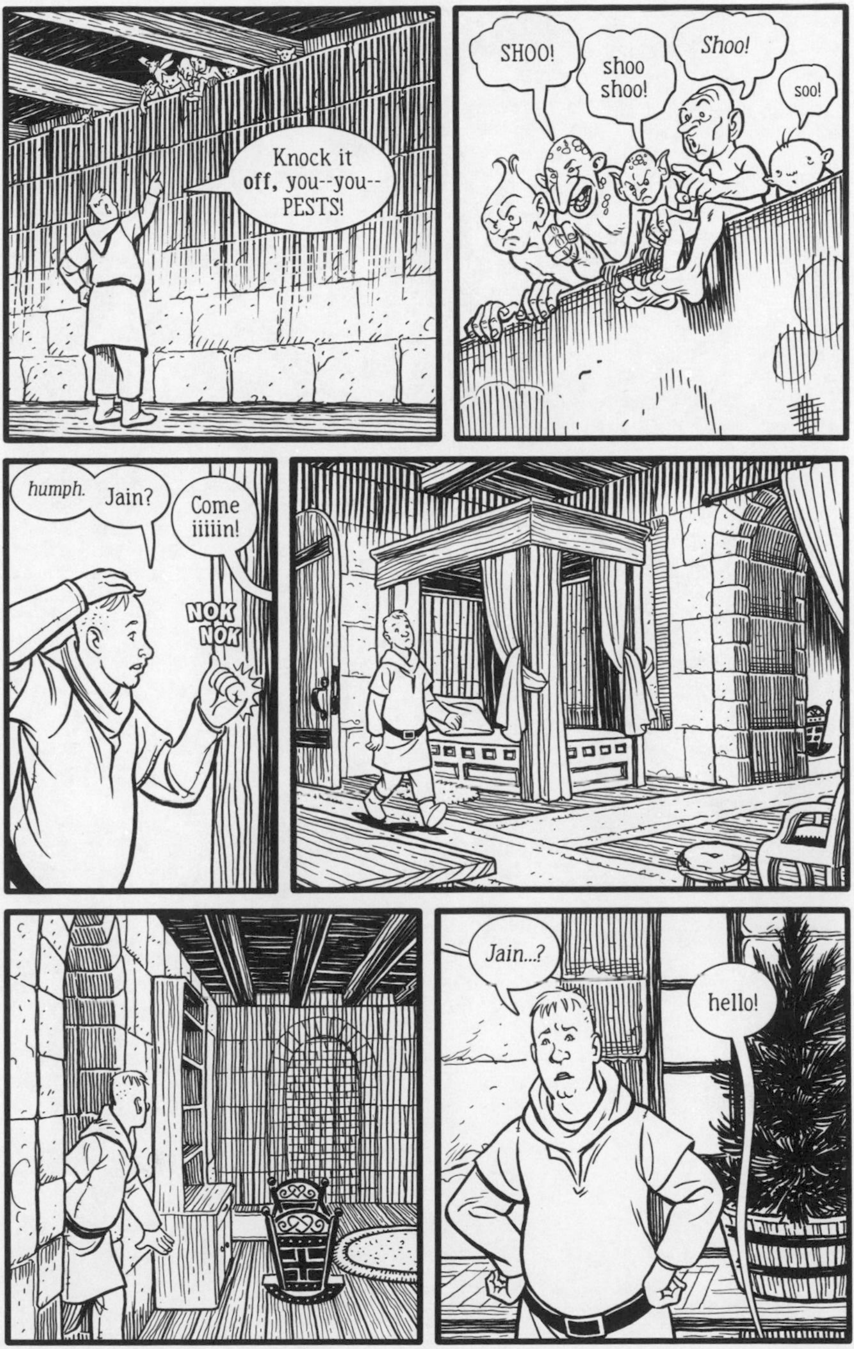
Knock it off, you--you--PESTS!
SHOO!
shoo shoo!
Shoo!
soo!
humph.
Jain?
Come iiiiin!
NOK NOK
Jain...?
hello!

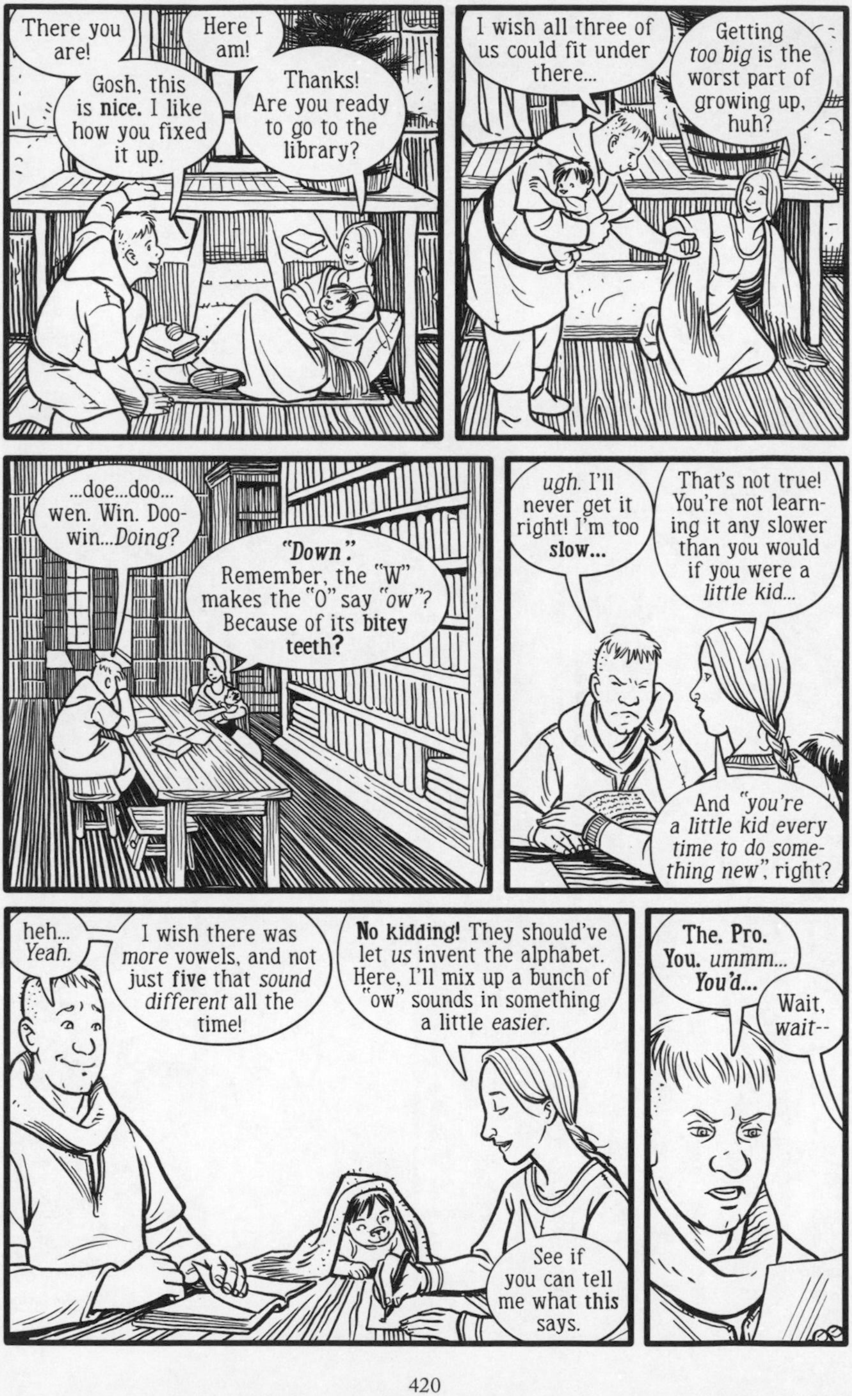
There you are!
Here I am!
Gosh, this is **nice.** I like how you fixed it up.
Thanks! Are you ready to go to the library?
I wish all three of us could fit under there...
Getting *too big* is the worst part of growing up, huh?
...doe...doo... wen. Win. Doo-win...*Doing*?
"Down." Remember, the "W" makes the "O" say *"ow"*? Because of its **bitey teeth?**
ugh. I'll never get it right! I'm too **slow...**
That's not true! You're not learning it any slower than you would if you were a *little kid...*
And *"you're a little kid every time to do something new"*, right?
heh... *Yeah.*
I wish there was *more* vowels, and not just **five** that *sound different* all the time!
No kidding! They should've let *us* invent the alphabet. Here, I'll mix up a bunch of "ow" sounds in something a little *easier.*
See if you can tell me what **this** says.
The. Pro. You. *ummm...* **You'd...**
Wait, *wait--*

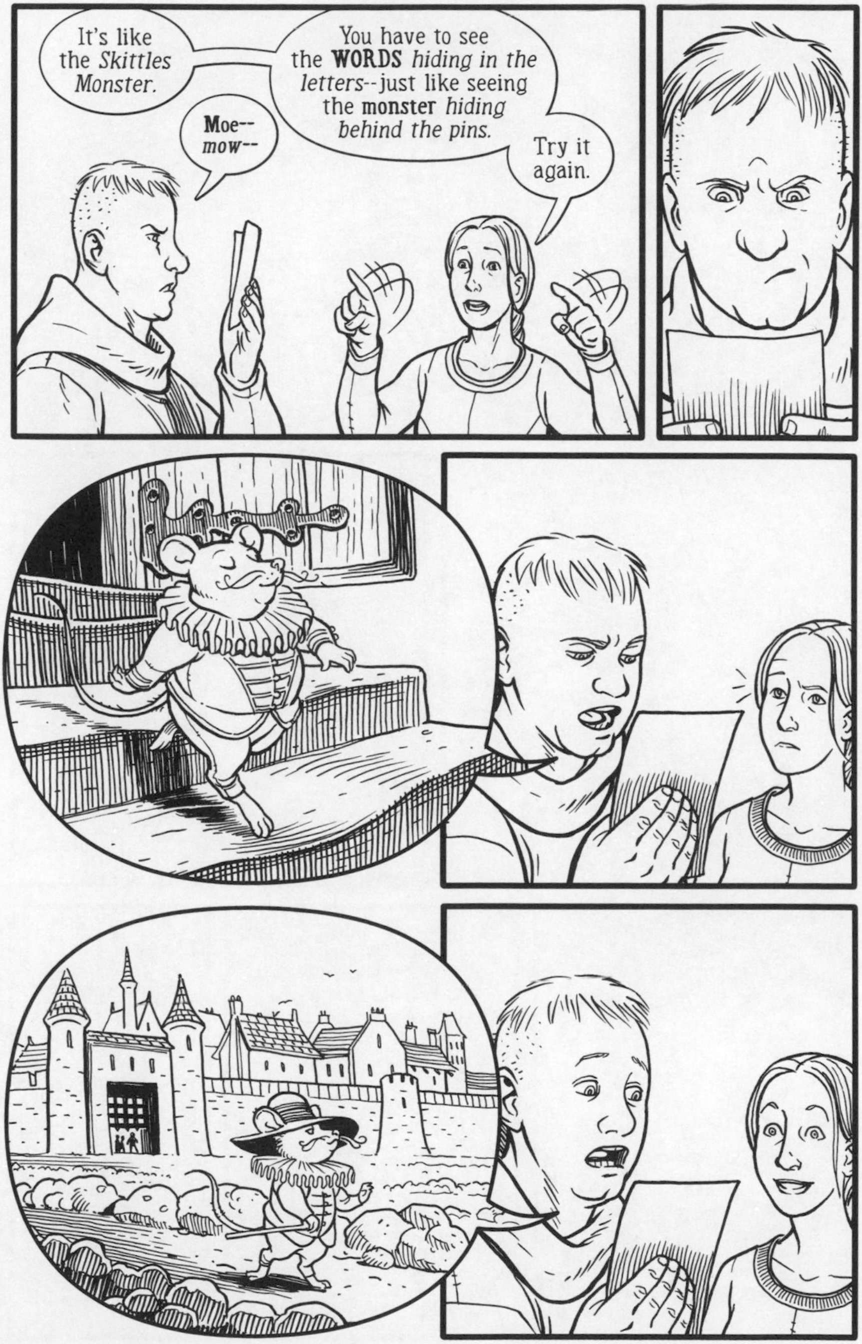
It's like the *Skittles Monster.*
You have to see the **WORDS** *hiding in the letters*--just like seeing the **monster** *hiding behind the pins.*
Moe-- *mow--*
Try it again.

"The proud mouse went out of the house and down the stairs, around the town and over the plowed field, to see the brown cow."

...

THAT'S IT!

"His face was almost entirely covered by hair. His beard resembled a piece of coarse felt, and his face was so dirty that cress could have sprouted there if one had sown the seeds."

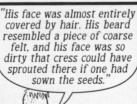

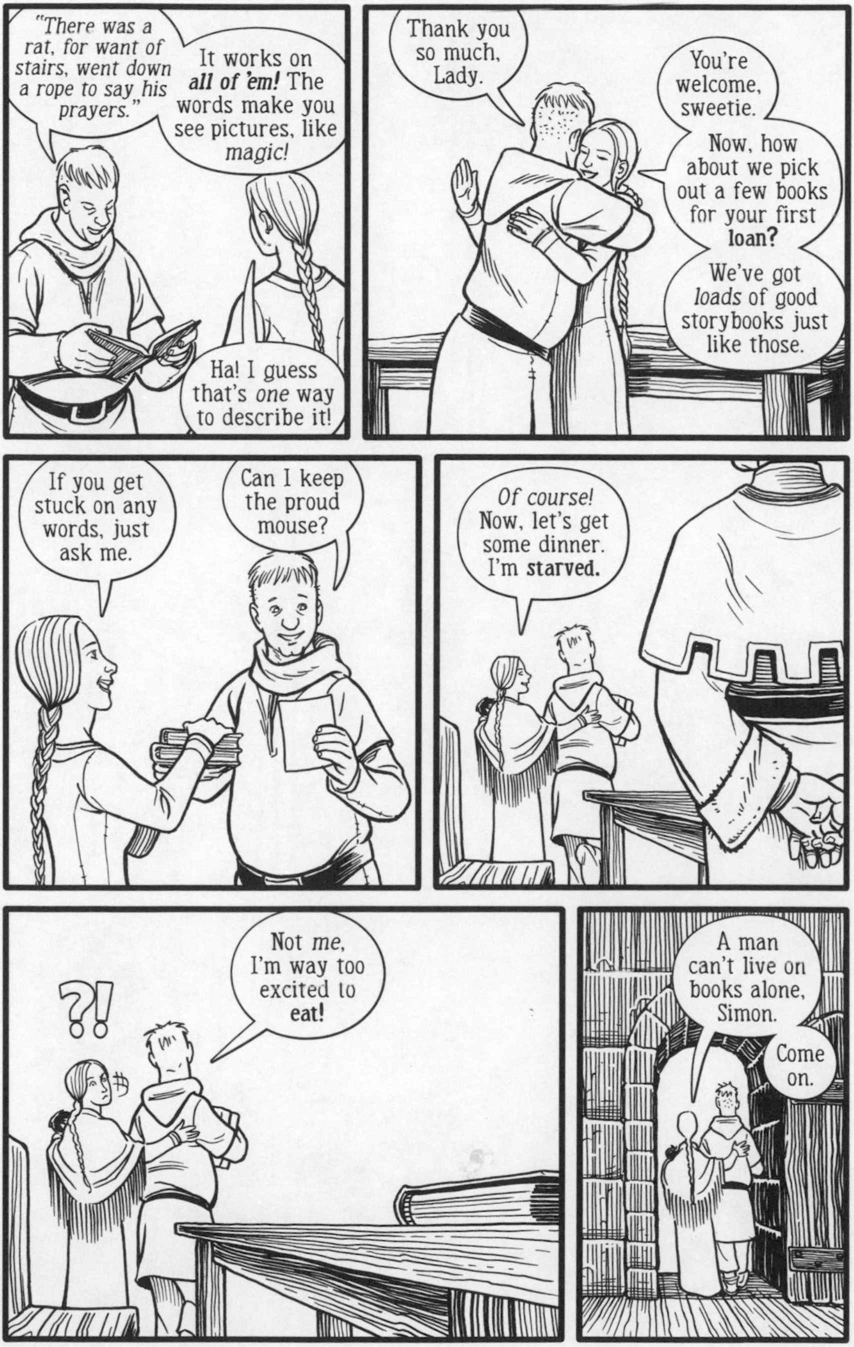
"There was a rat, for want of stairs, went down a rope to say his prayers."
It works on all of 'em! The words make you see pictures, like magic!
Ha! I guess that's one way to describe it!
Thank you so much, Lady.
You're welcome, sweetie.
Now, how about we pick out a few books for your first loan?
We've got loads of good storybooks just like those.
If you get stuck on any words, just ask me.
Can I keep the proud mouse?
Of course! Now, let's get some dinner. I'm starved.
Not me, I'm way too excited to eat!
?!
A man can't live on books alone, Simon.
Come on.

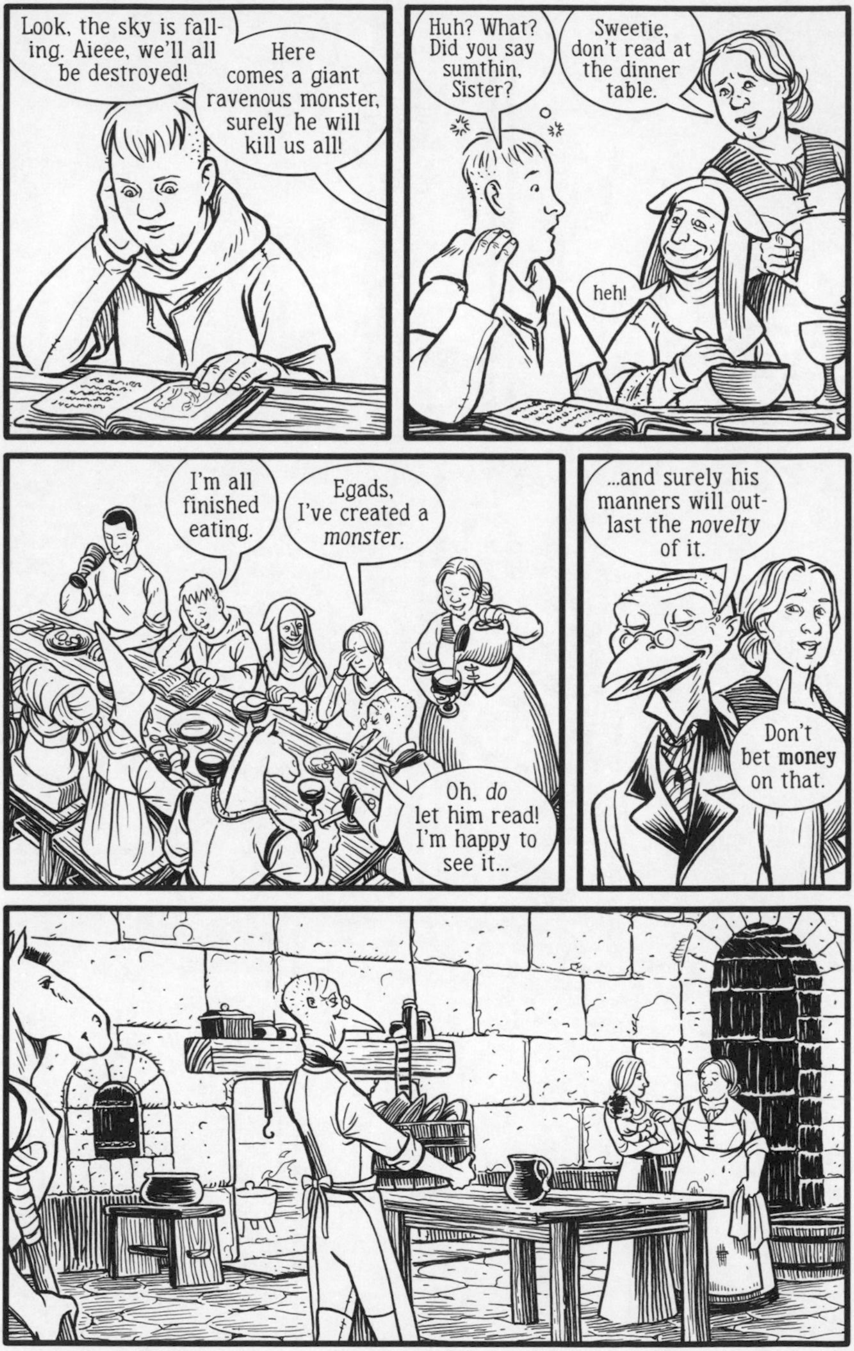
Look, the sky is falling. Aieee, we'll all be destroyed!
Here comes a giant ravenous monster, surely he will kill us all!
Huh? What? Did you say sumthin, Sister?
Sweetie, don't read at the dinner table.
heh!
I'm all finished eating.
Egads, I've created a *monster.*
Oh, *do* let him read! I'm happy to see it...
...and surely his manners will outlast the *novelty* of it.
Don't bet **money** on that.

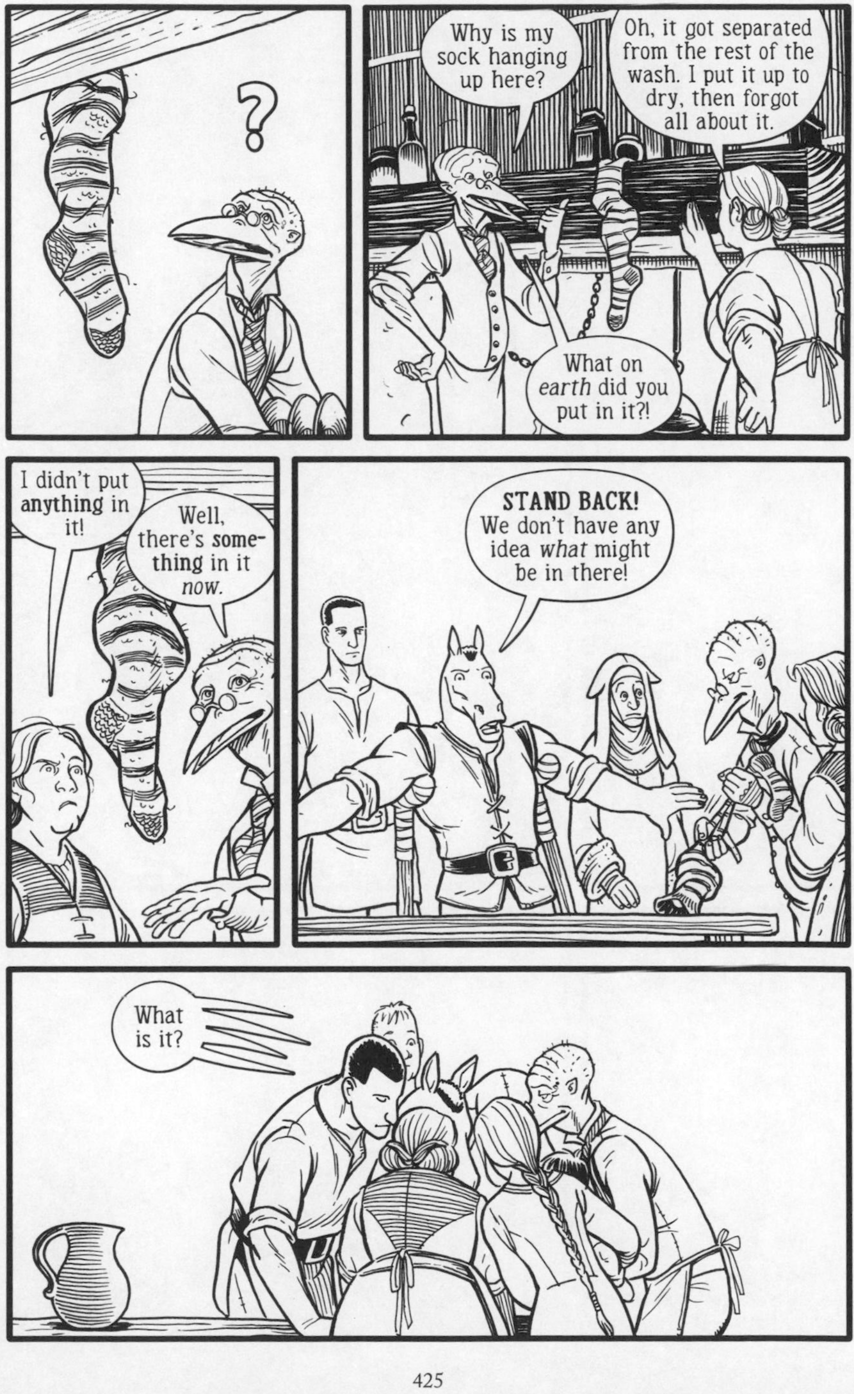
?
Why is my sock hanging up here?
Oh, it got separated from the rest of the wash. I put it up to dry, then forgot all about it.
What on *earth* did you put in it?!
I didn't put **anything** in it!
Well, there's **something** in it *now.*
STAND BACK! We don't have any idea *what* might be in there!
What is it?

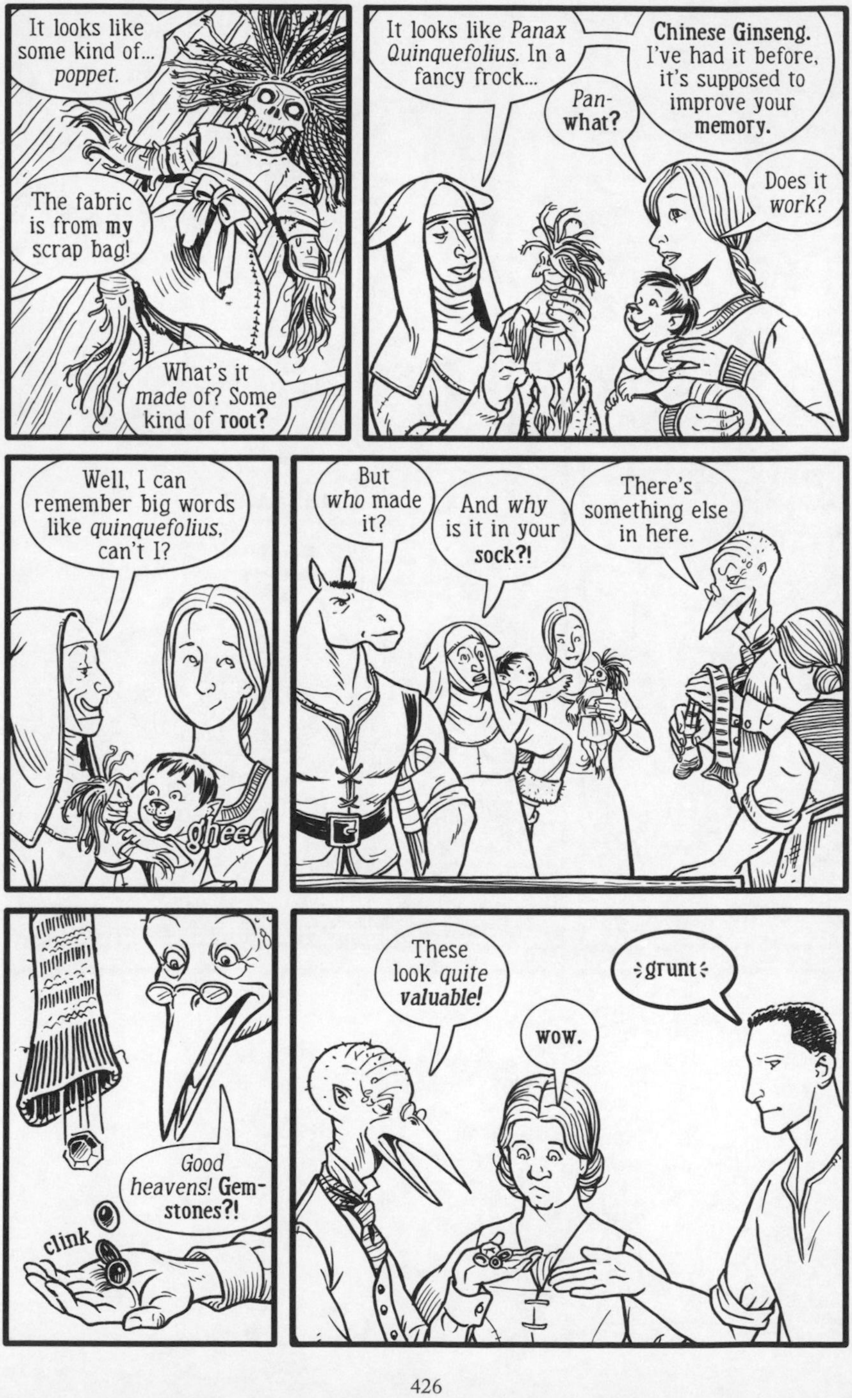
It looks like some kind of... *poppet.*
The fabric is from **my** scrap bag!
What's it *made* of? Some kind of **root?**
It looks like *Panax Quinquefolius.* In a fancy frock...
Pan- **what?**
Chinese Ginseng. I've had it before, it's supposed to improve your **memory.**
Does it *work?*
Well, I can remember big words like *quinquefolius,* can't I?
ghee!
But *who* made it?
And *why* is it in your **sock?!**
There's something else in here.
Good heavens! **Gem-stones?!**
clink
These look *quite* **valuable!**
WOW.
grunt

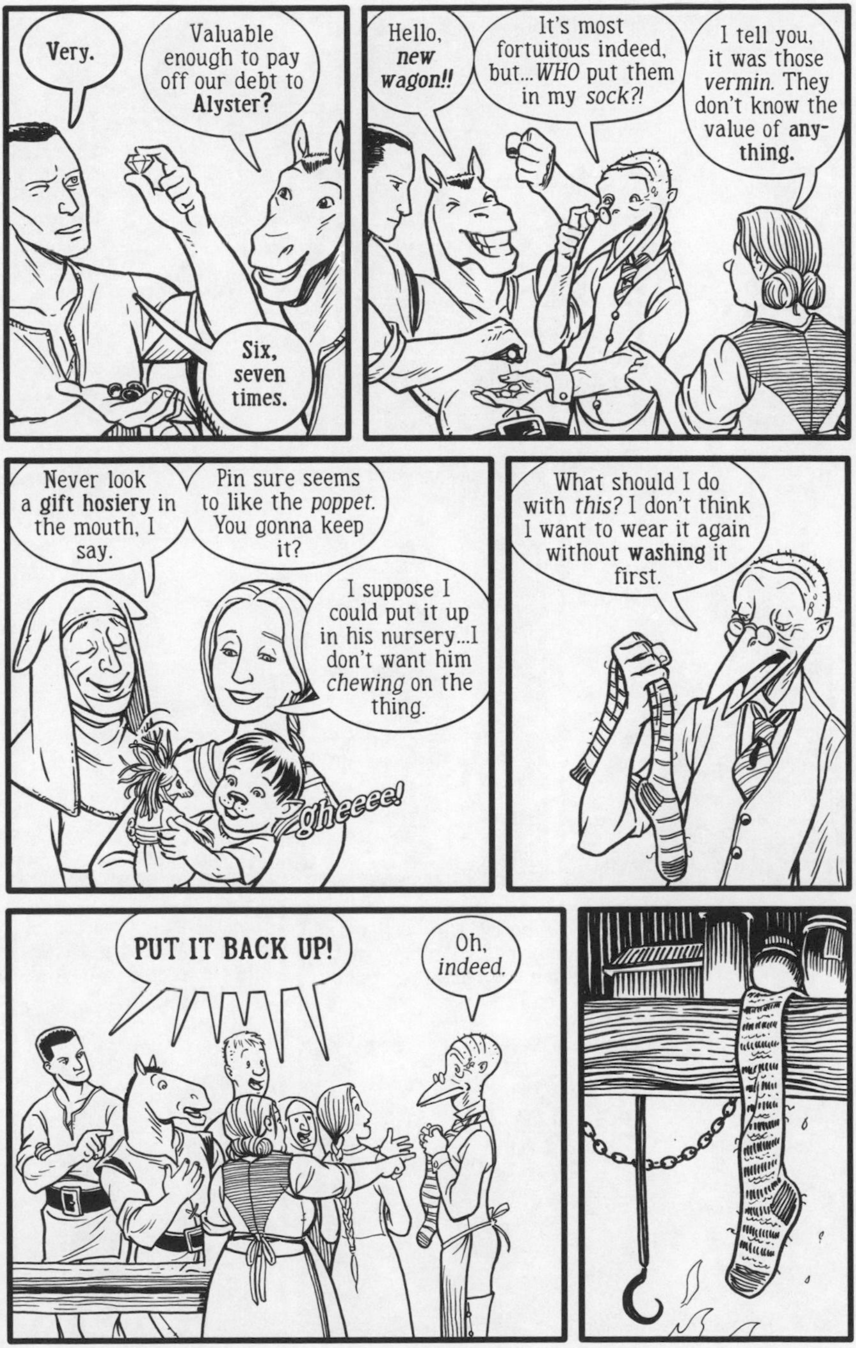
Very.
Valuable enough to pay off our debt to Alyster?
Six, seven times.
Hello, new wagon!!
It's most fortuitous indeed, but...WHO put them in my sock?!
I tell you, it was those vermin. They don't know the value of any-thing.
Never look a gift hosiery in the mouth, I say.
Pin sure seems to like the poppet. You gonna keep it?
I suppose I could put it up in his nursery...I don't want him chewing on the thing.
gheeeee!
What should I do with this? I don't think I want to wear it again without washing it first.
PUT IT BACK UP!
Oh, indeed.

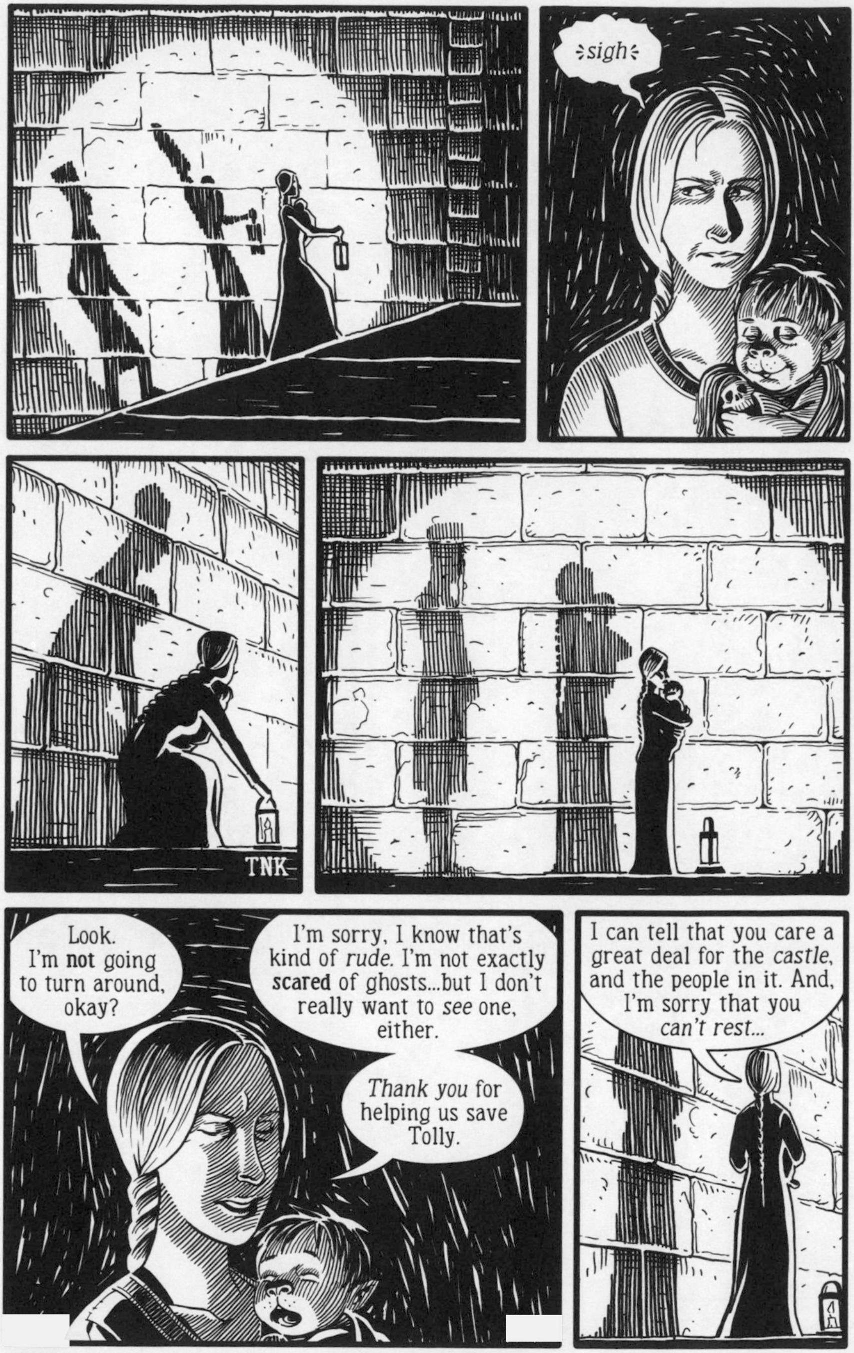
sigh
TNK
Look. I'm **not** going to turn around, okay?
I'm sorry, I know that's kind of *rude.* I'm not exactly **scared** of ghosts...but I don't really want to *see* one, either.
Thank you for helping us save Tolly.
I can tell that you care a great deal for the *castle,* and the people in it. And, I'm sorry that you *can't rest...*

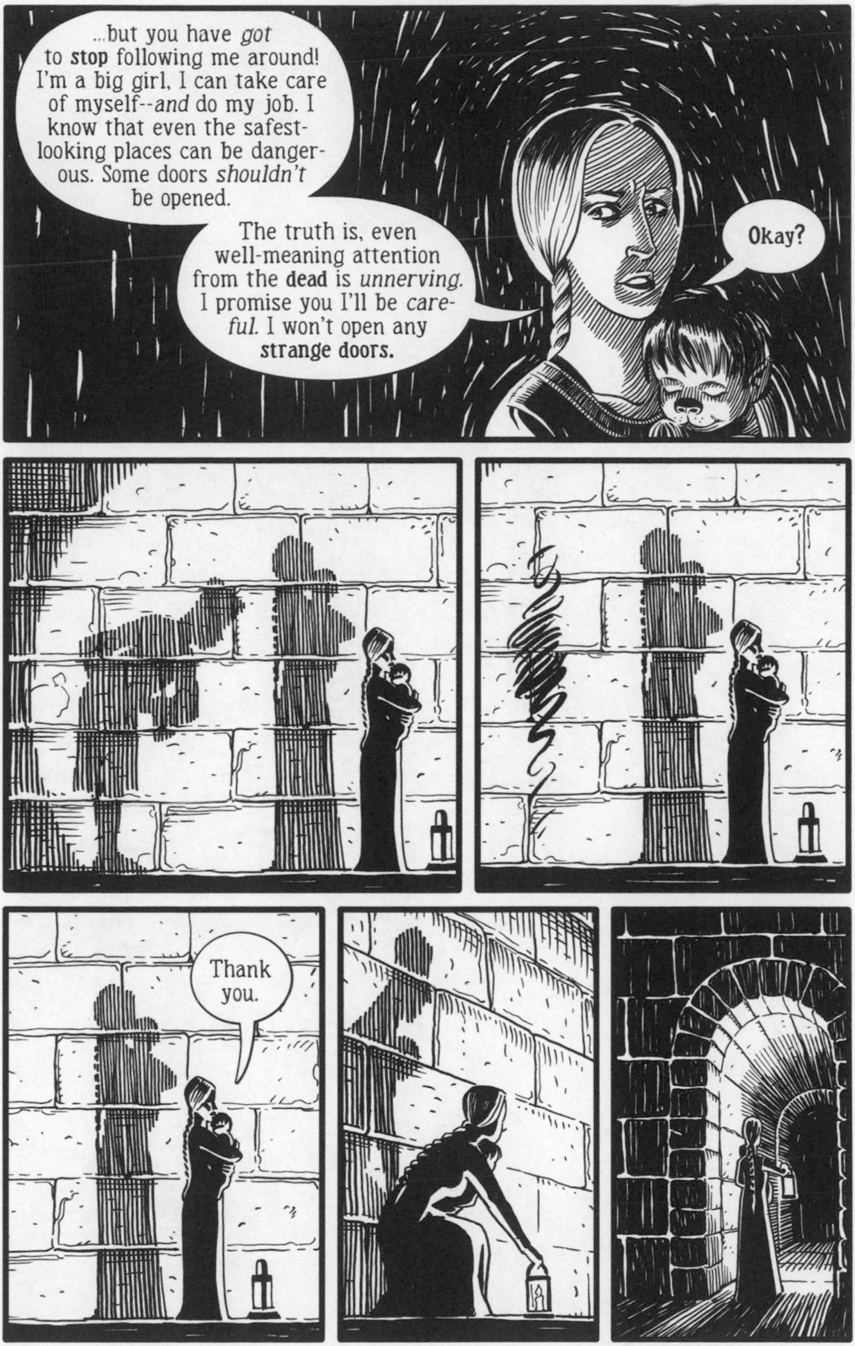
...but you have *got* to **stop** following me around! I'm a big girl, I can take care of myself--*and* do my job. I know that even the safest-looking places can be danger-ous. Some doors *shouldn't* be opened.
The truth is, even well-meaning attention from the **dead** is *unnerving.* I promise you I'll be *care-ful.* I won't open any **strange doors.**
Okay?
Thank you.

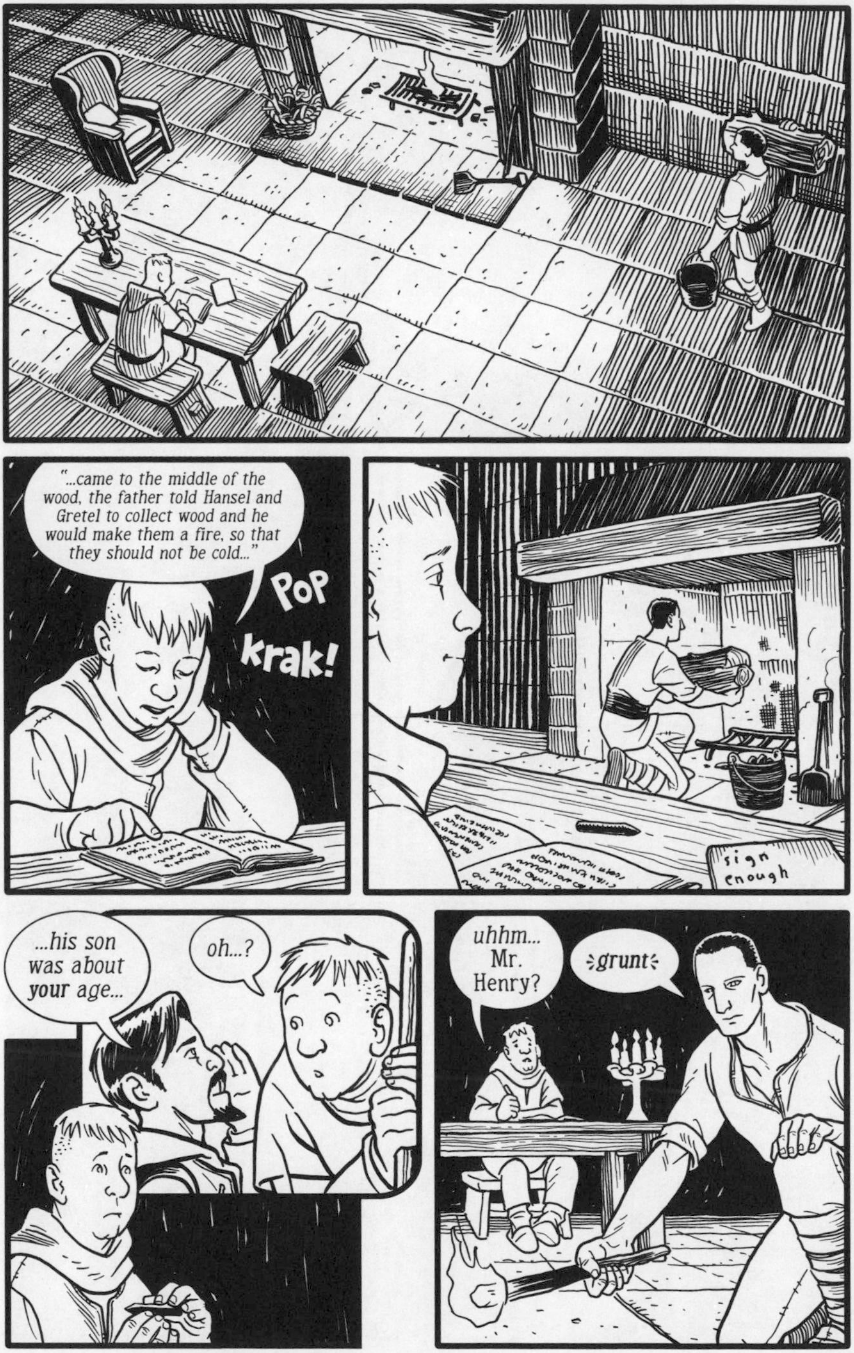
"...came to the middle of the wood, the father told Hansel and Gretel to collect wood and he would make them a fire, so that they should not be cold..."
POP
krak!
sign enough
...his son was about your age...
oh...?
uhhm... Mr. Henry?
grunt

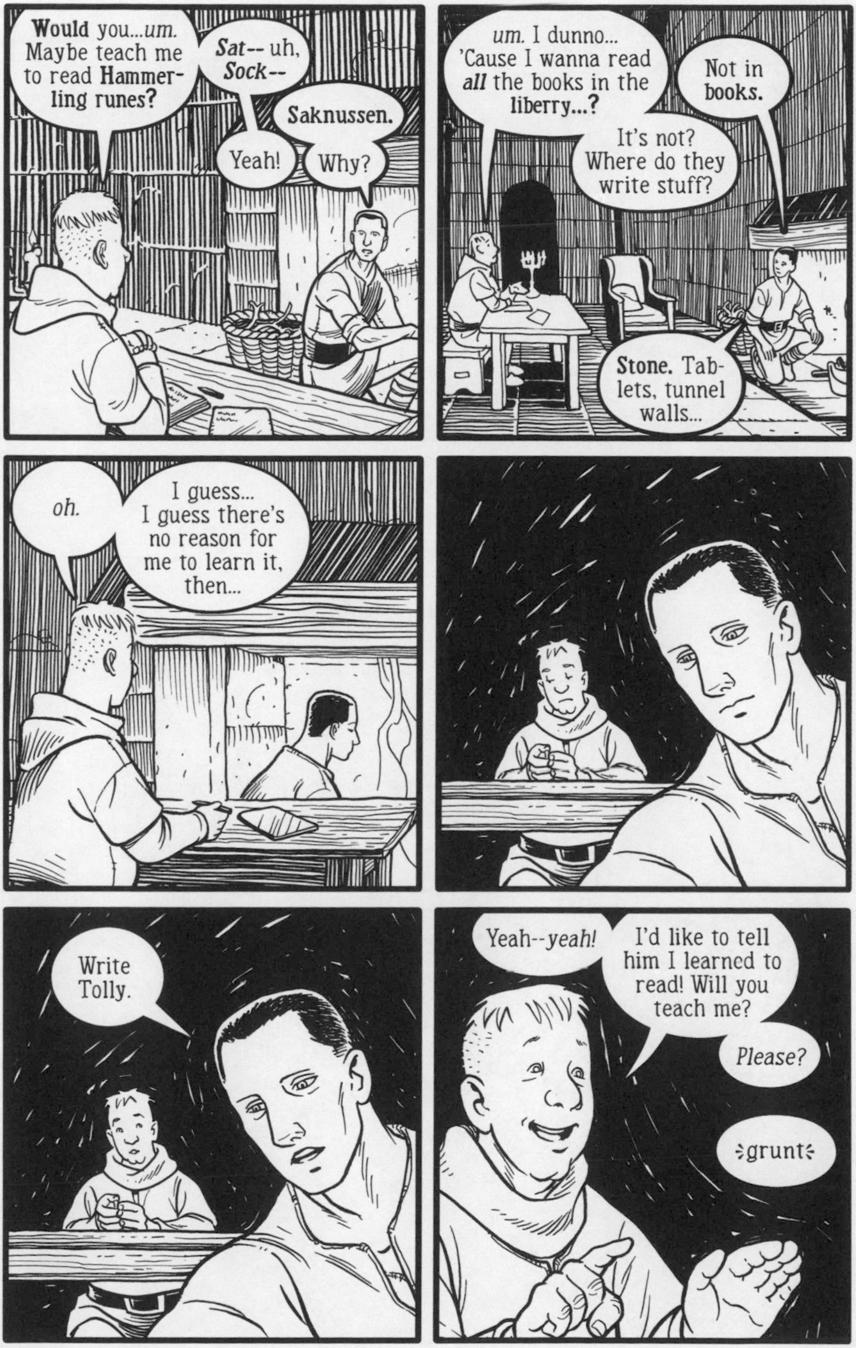
Would you...um. Maybe teach me to read Hammerling runes?
Sat-- uh, Sock--
Saknussen.
Yeah!
Why?
um. I dunno... 'Cause I wanna read all the books in the liberry...?
Not in books.
It's not? Where do they write stuff?
Stone. Tablets, tunnel walls...
oh.
I guess... I guess there's no reason for me to learn it, then...
Write Tolly.
Yeah--yeah!
I'd like to tell him I learned to read! Will you teach me?
Please?
grunt

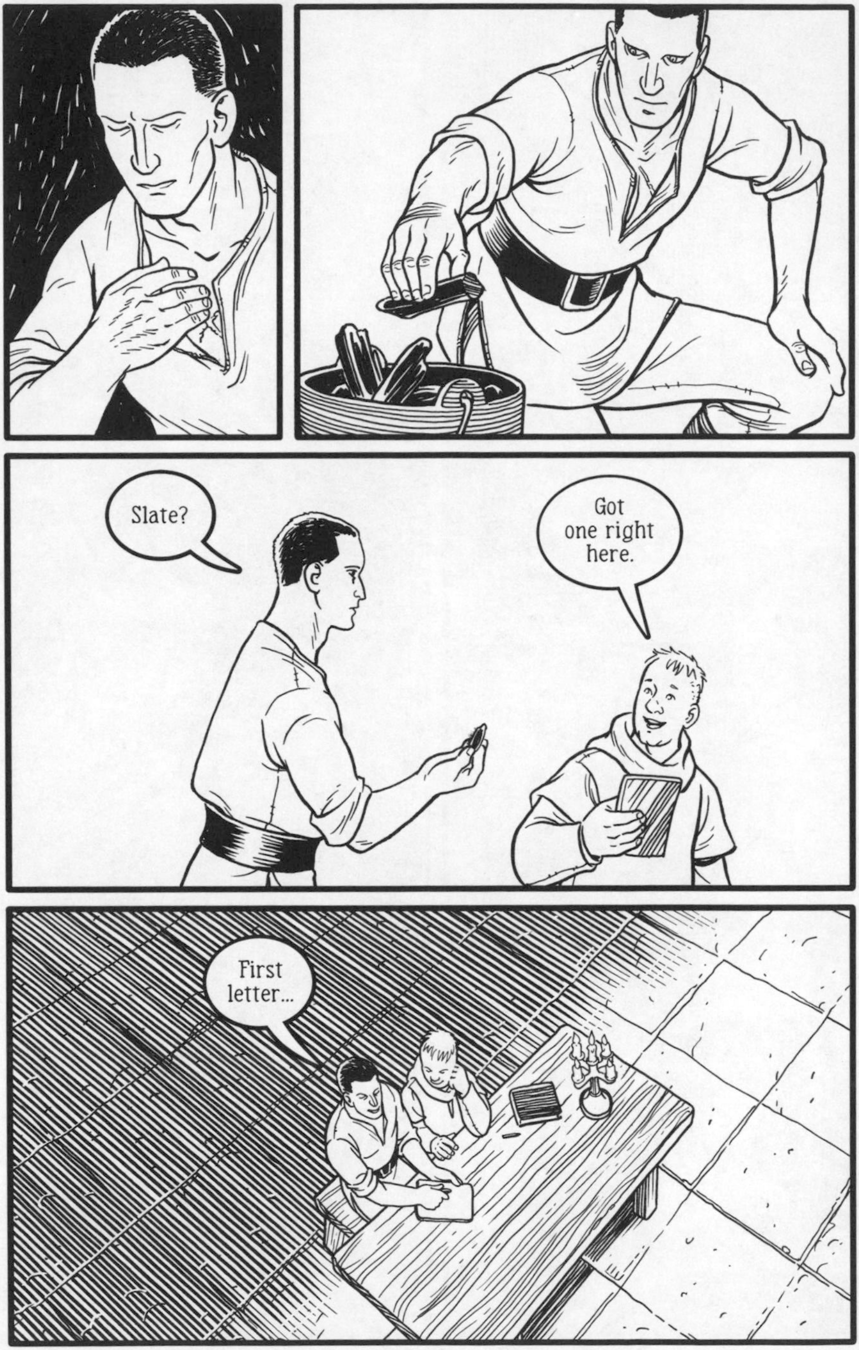
Slate?
Got one right here.
First letter...

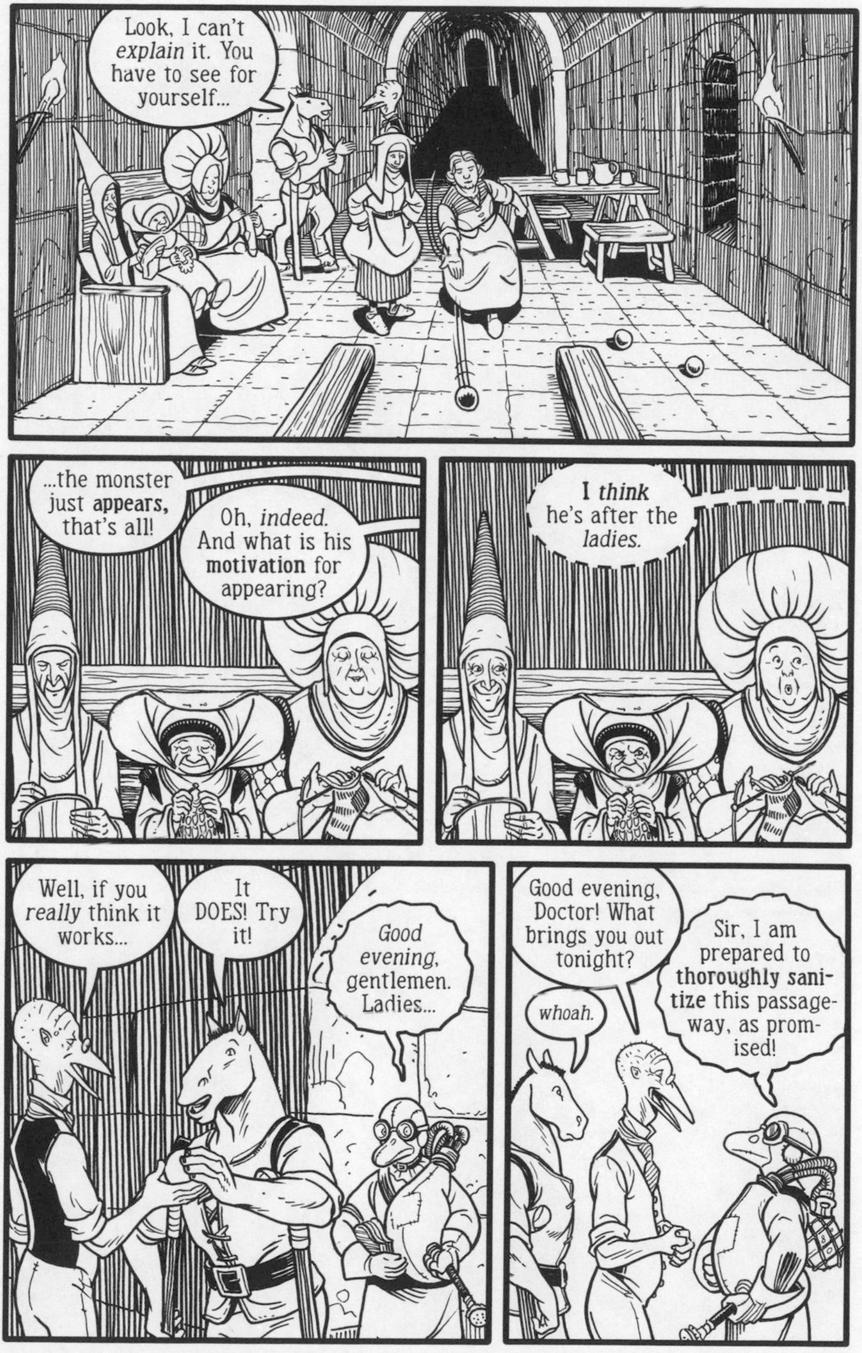
Look, I can't *explain* it. You have to see for yourself...
...the monster just **appears**, that's all!
Oh, *indeed*. And what is his **motivation** for appearing?
I *think* he's after the *ladies*.
Well, if you *really* think it works...
It DOES! Try it!
Good evening, gentlemen. Ladies...
Good evening, Doctor! What brings you out tonight?
whoah.
Sir, I am prepared to **thoroughly sanitize** this passageway, as promised!

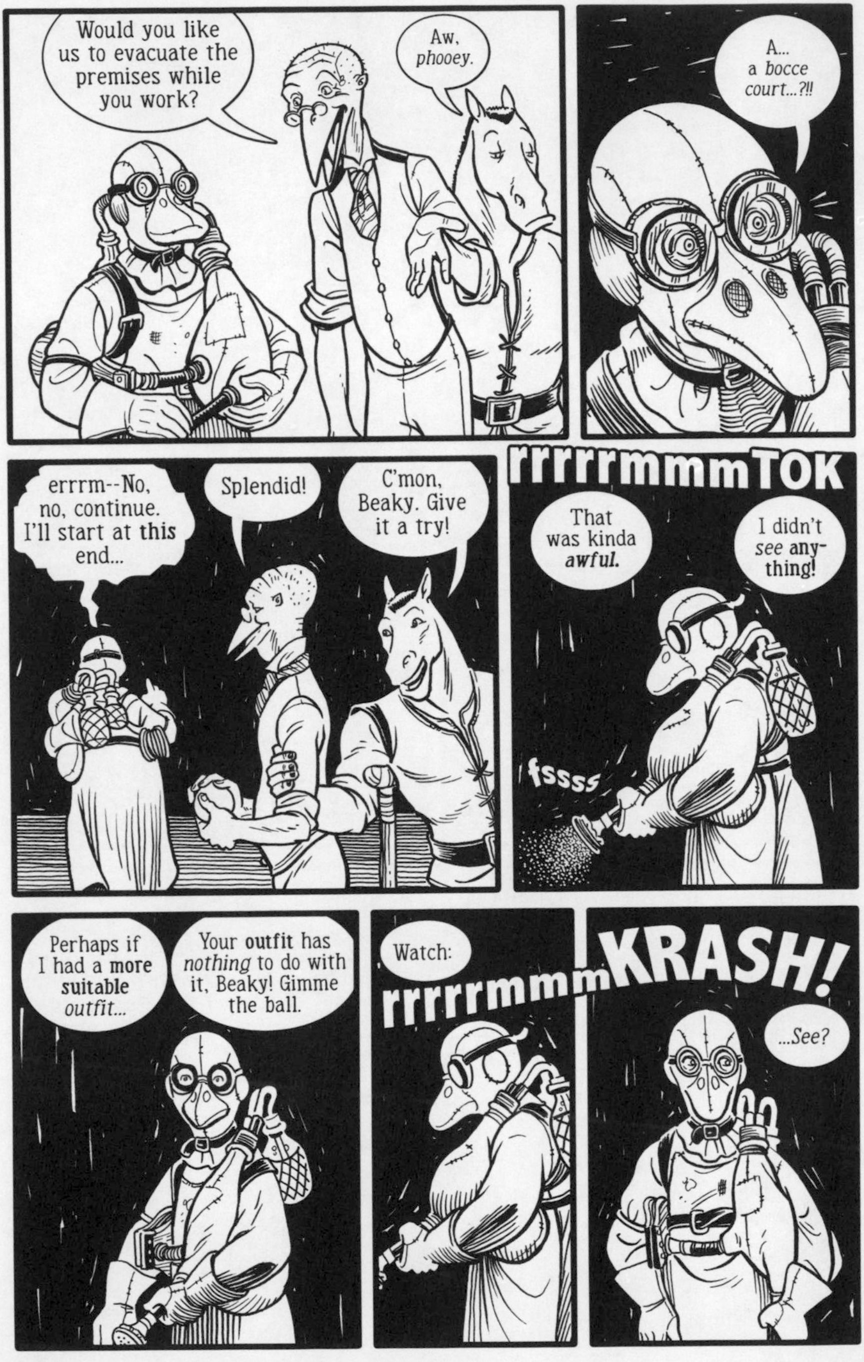
Would you like us to evacuate the premises while you work?
Aw, *phooey.*
A... a *bocce court*...?!!
errrm--No, no, continue. I'll start at **this** end...
Splendid!
C'mon, Beaky. Give it a try!
rrrrrmmmmTOK
That was kinda ***awful.***
I didn't *see* **any**-thing!
fssss
Perhaps if I had a **more suitable** *outfit...*
Your **outfit** has *nothing* to do with it, Beaky! Gimme the ball.
Watch:
rrrrrmmmmKRASH!
...See?

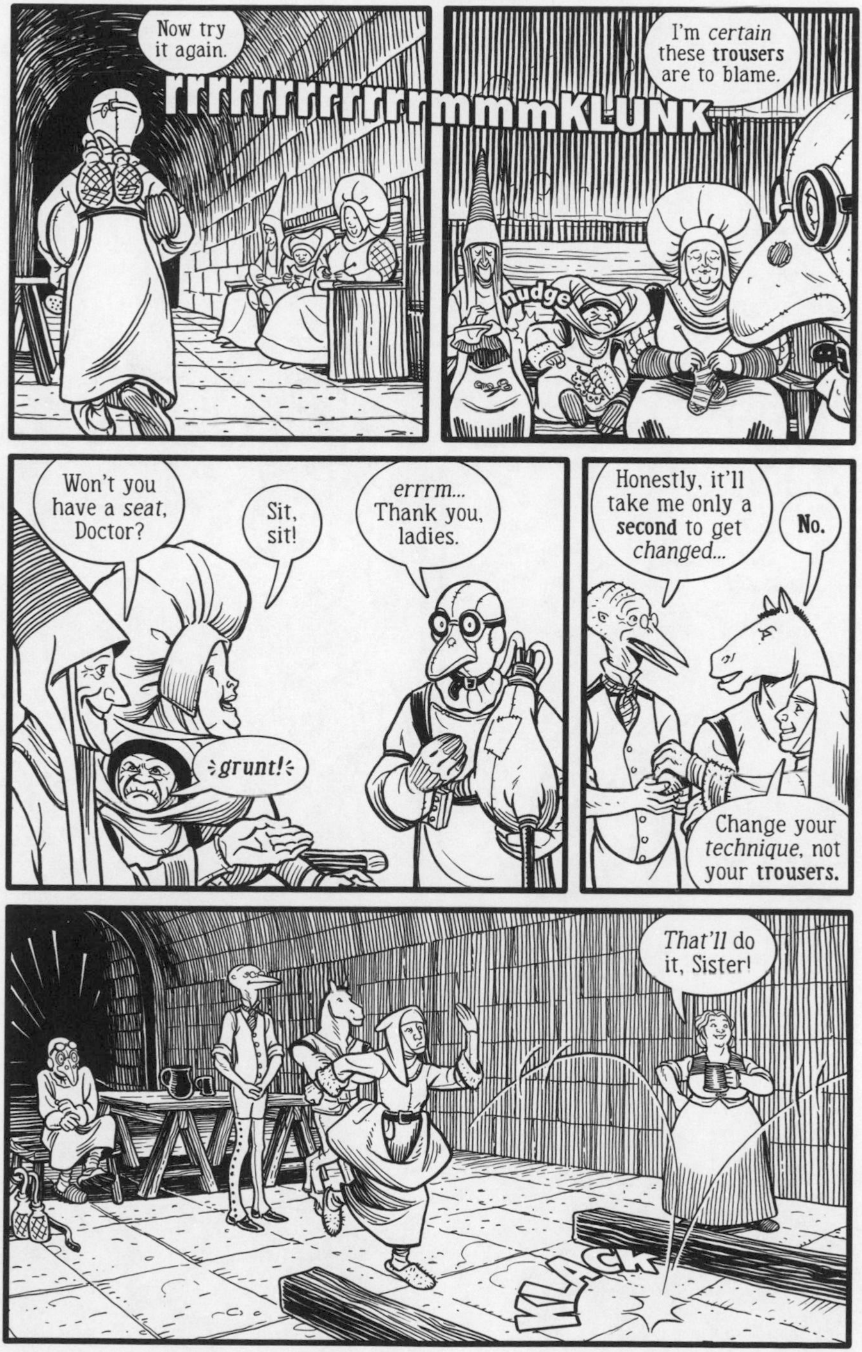
Now try it again.
rrrrrrrrrrrrrmmmmKLUNK
I'm *certain* these **trousers** are to blame.
nudge
Won't you have a *seat*, Doctor?
Sit, sit!
errrm... Thank you, ladies.
grunt!
Honestly, it'll take me only a **second** to get *changed...*
No.
Change your *technique*, not your **trousers.**
That'll do it, Sister!
KLACK

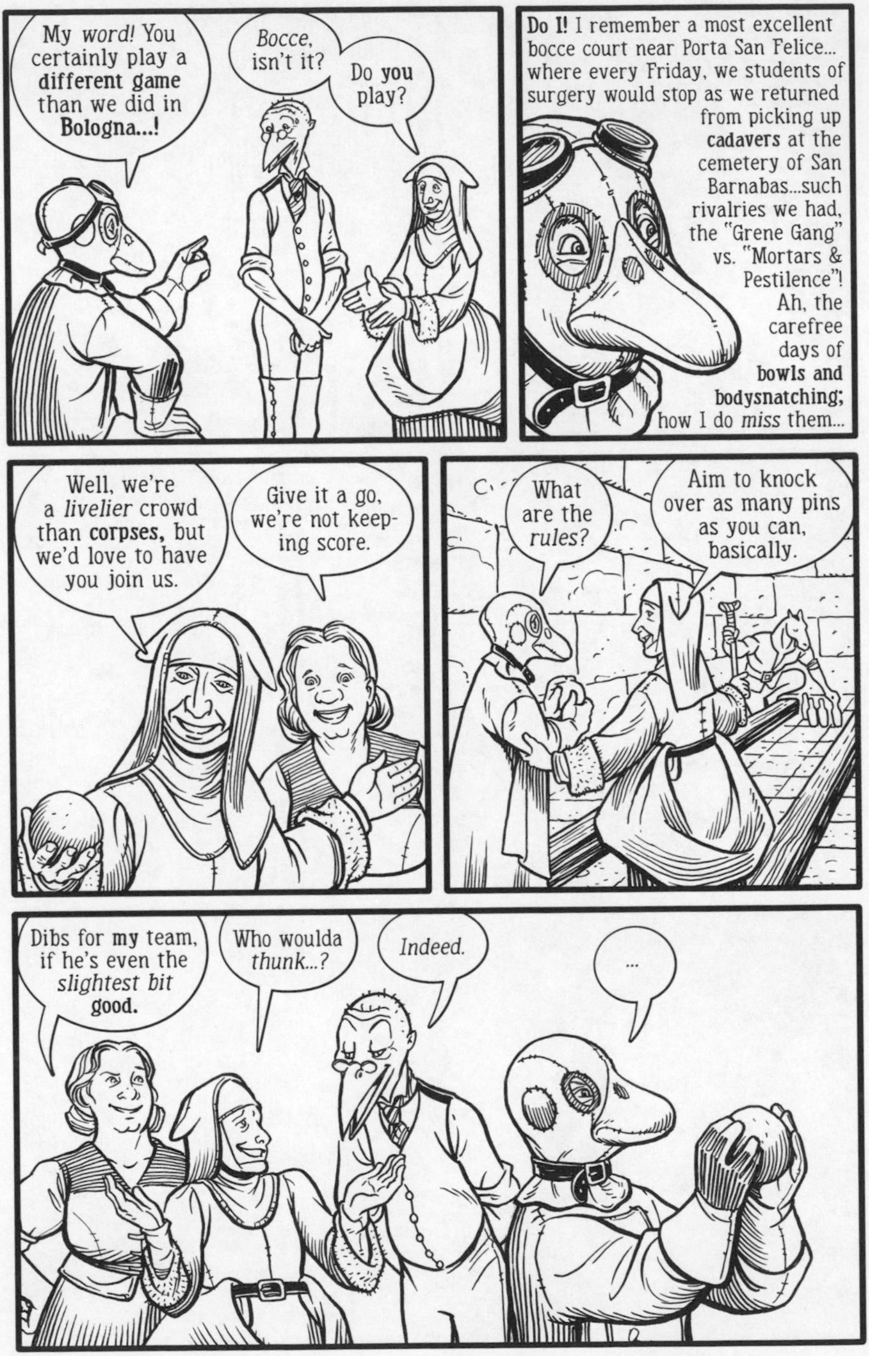
My *word!* You certainly play a **different game** than we did in **Bologna...!**
Bocce, isn't it?
Do **you** play?
Do I! I remember a most excellent bocce court near Porta San Felice... where every Friday, we students of surgery would stop as we returned from picking up **cadavers** at the cemetery of San Barnabas...such rivalries we had, the "Grene Gang" vs. "Mortars & Pestilence"! Ah, the carefree days of **bowls and bodysnatching;** how I do *miss* them...
Well, we're a *livelier* crowd than **corpses,** but we'd love to have you join us.
Give it a go, we're not keep-ing score.
What are the *rules?*
Aim to knock over as many pins as you can, basically.
Dibs for **my** team, if he's even the *slightest bit* **good.**
Who woulda *thunk...?*
Indeed.
...

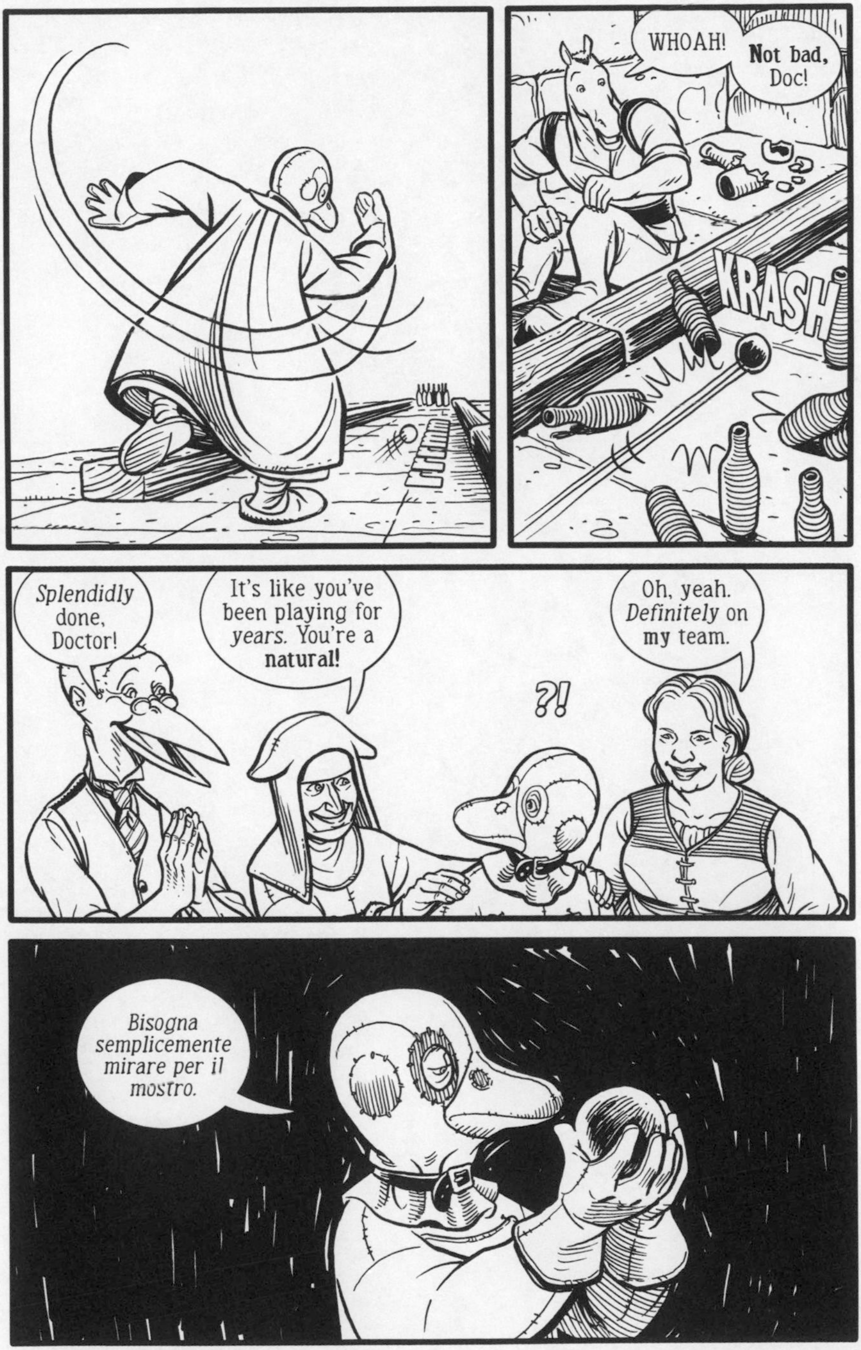
WHOAH!
Not bad, Doc!
KRASH
Splendidly done, Doctor!
It's like you've been playing for years. You're a natural!
?!
Oh, yeah. Definitely on my team.
Bisogna semplicemente mirare per il mostro.

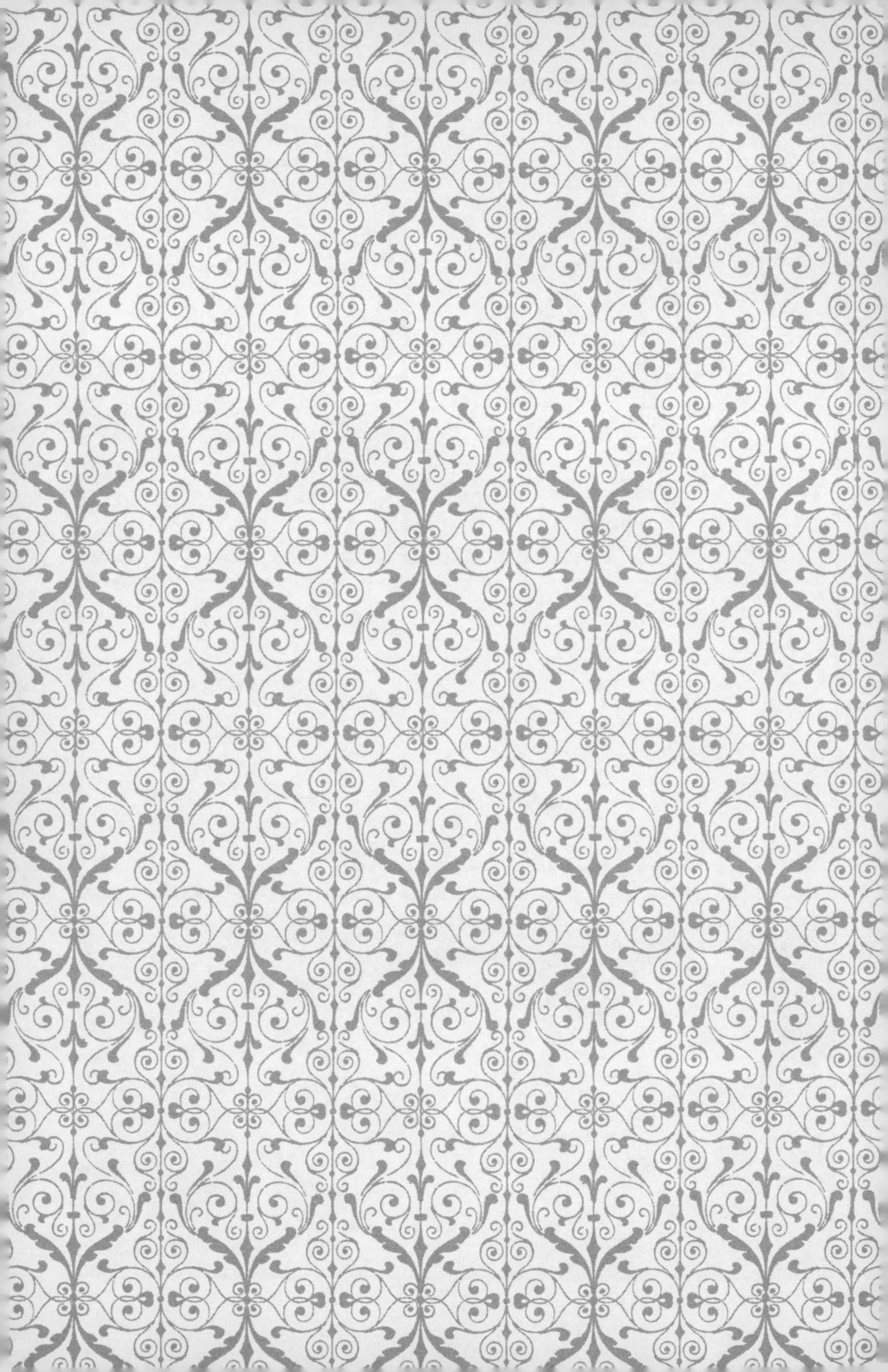

Chapter 17.

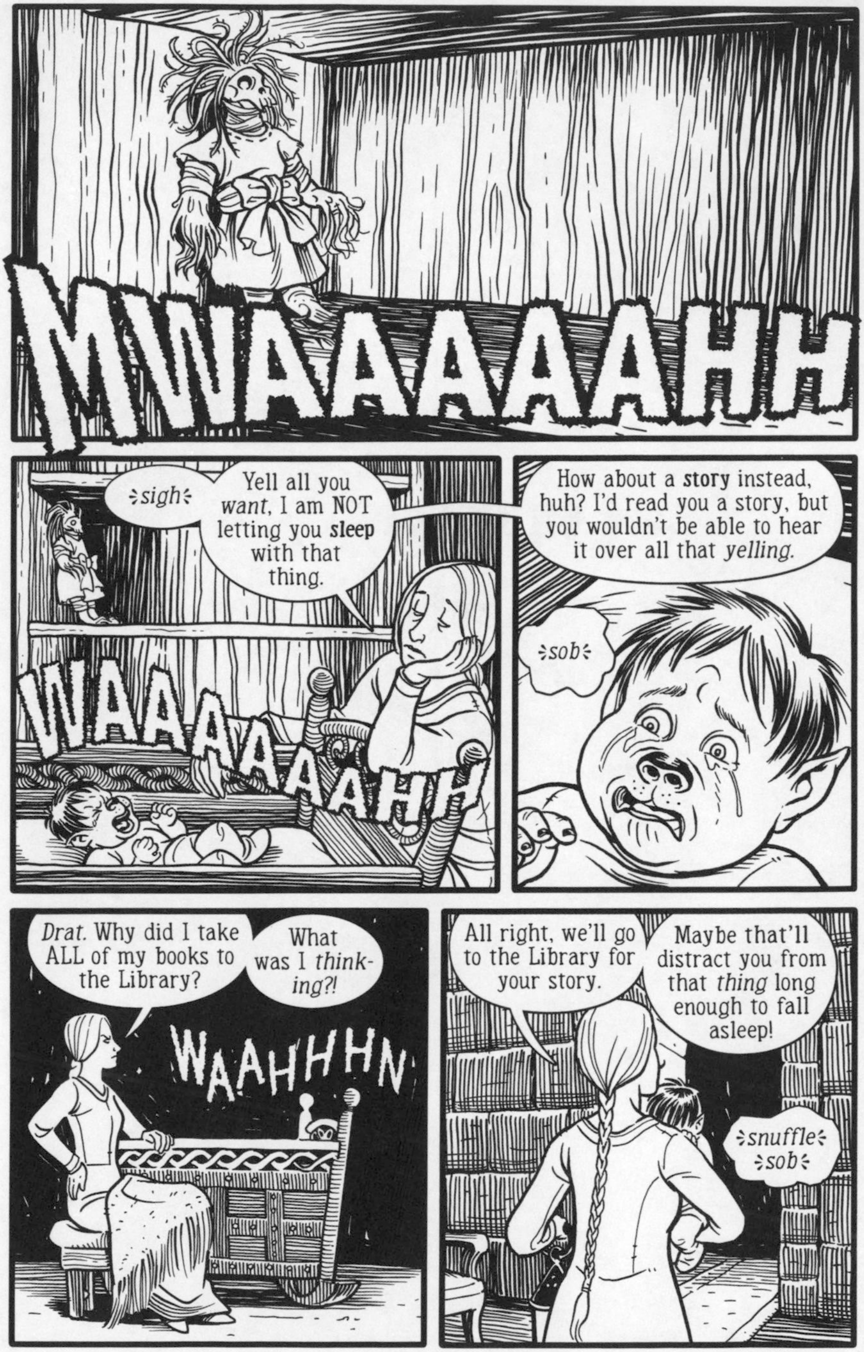
MWAAAAAAHH
sigh
Yell all you want, I am NOT letting you sleep with that thing.
WAAAAAAAAAHH
How about a story instead, huh? I'd read you a story, but you wouldn't be able to hear it over all that yelling.
sob
Drat. Why did I take ALL of my books to the Library?
What was I think-ing?!
WAAHHHN
All right, we'll go to the Library for your story.
Maybe that'll distract you from that thing long enough to fall asleep!
snuffle
sob

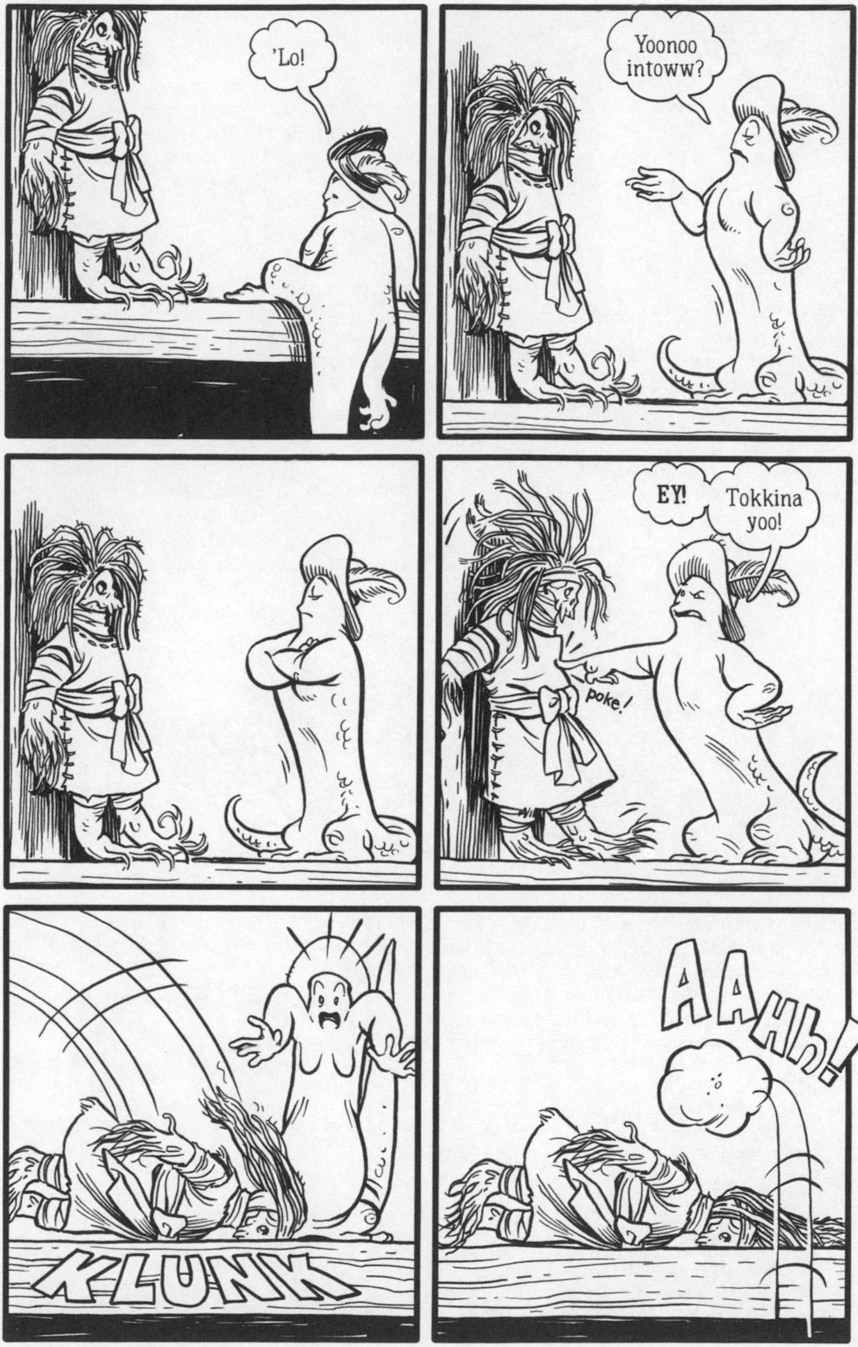
'Lo!
Yoonoo intoww?
EY!
Tokkina yoo!
poke!
KLUNK
AAHh!

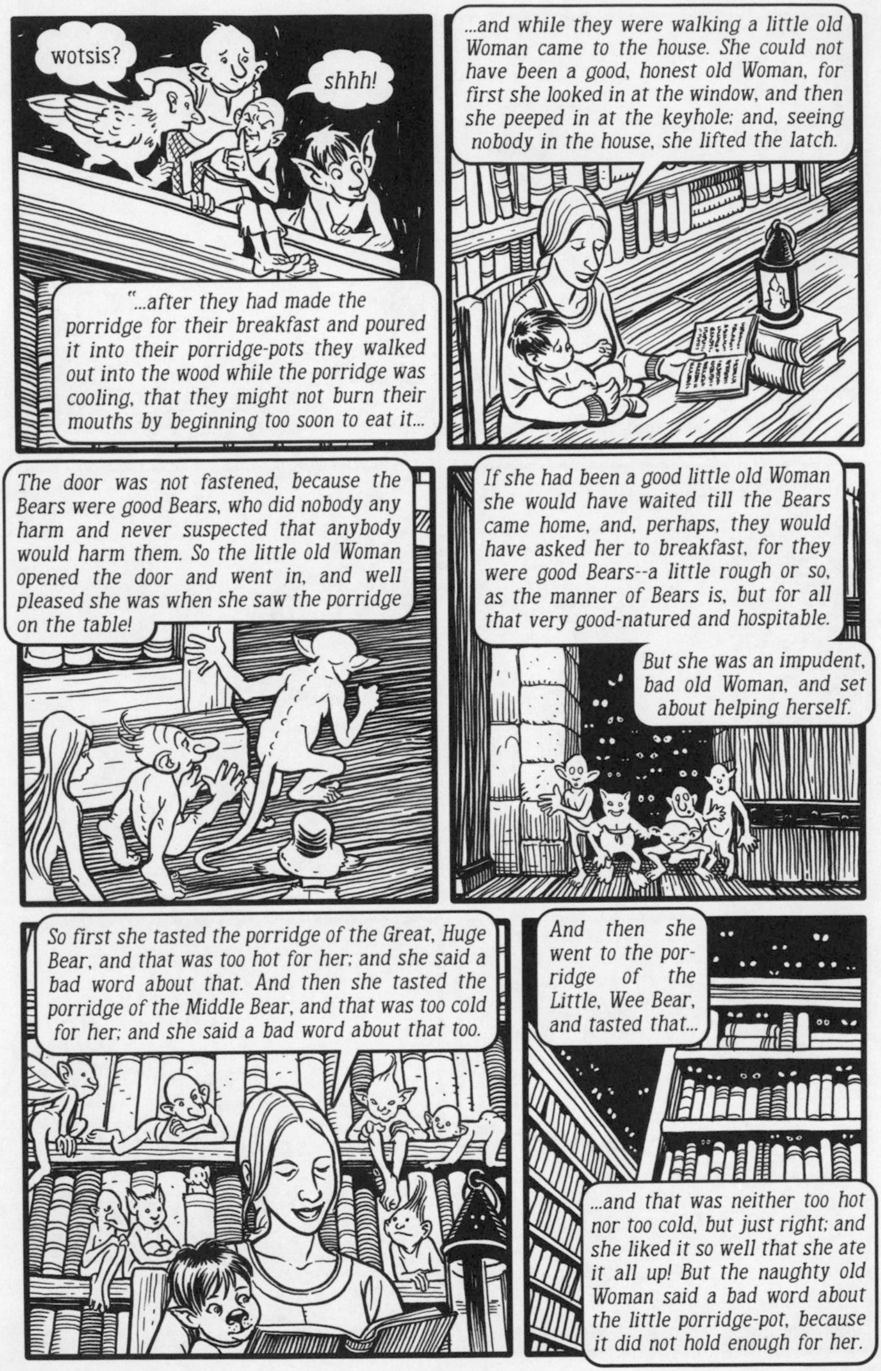
wotsis?
shhh!
"...after they had made the porridge for their breakfast and poured it into their porridge-pots they walked out into the wood while the porridge was cooling, that they might not burn their mouths by beginning too soon to eat it...
...and while they were walking a little old Woman came to the house. She could not have been a good, honest old Woman, for first she looked in at the window, and then she peeped in at the keyhole; and, seeing nobody in the house, she lifted the latch.
The door was not fastened, because the Bears were good Bears, who did nobody any harm and never suspected that anybody would harm them. So the little old Woman opened the door and went in, and well pleased she was when she saw the porridge on the table!
If she had been a good little old Woman she would have waited till the Bears came home, and, perhaps, they would have asked her to breakfast, for they were good Bears--a little rough or so, as the manner of Bears is, but for all that very good-natured and hospitable.
But she was an impudent, bad old Woman, and set about helping herself.
So first she tasted the porridge of the Great, Huge Bear, and that was too hot for her; and she said a bad word about that. And then she tasted the porridge of the Middle Bear, and that was too cold for her; and she said a bad word about that too.
And then she went to the porridge of the Little, Wee Bear, and tasted that...
...and that was neither too hot nor too cold, but just right; and she liked it so well that she ate it all up! But the naughty old Woman said a bad word about the little porridge-pot, because it did not hold enough for her.

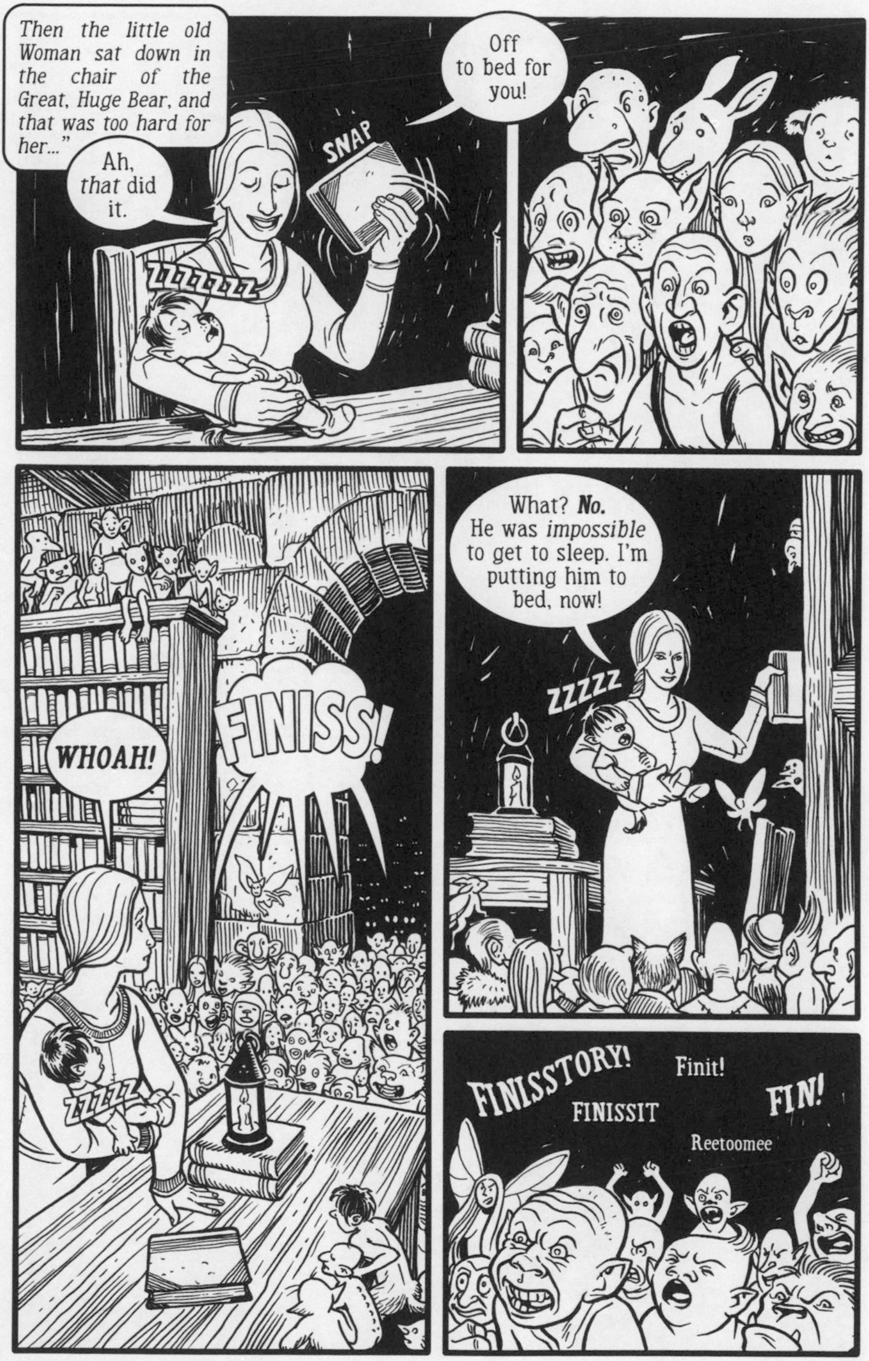
Then the little old Woman sat down in the chair of the Great, Huge Bear, and that was too hard for her..."
Ah, that did it.
SNAP
ZZZZZZZ
Off to bed for you!
WHOAH!
FINISS!
ZZZZZ
What? No. He was impossible to get to sleep. I'm putting him to bed, now!
ZZZZZ
FINISSTORY!
Finit!
FIN!
FINISSIT
Reetoomee

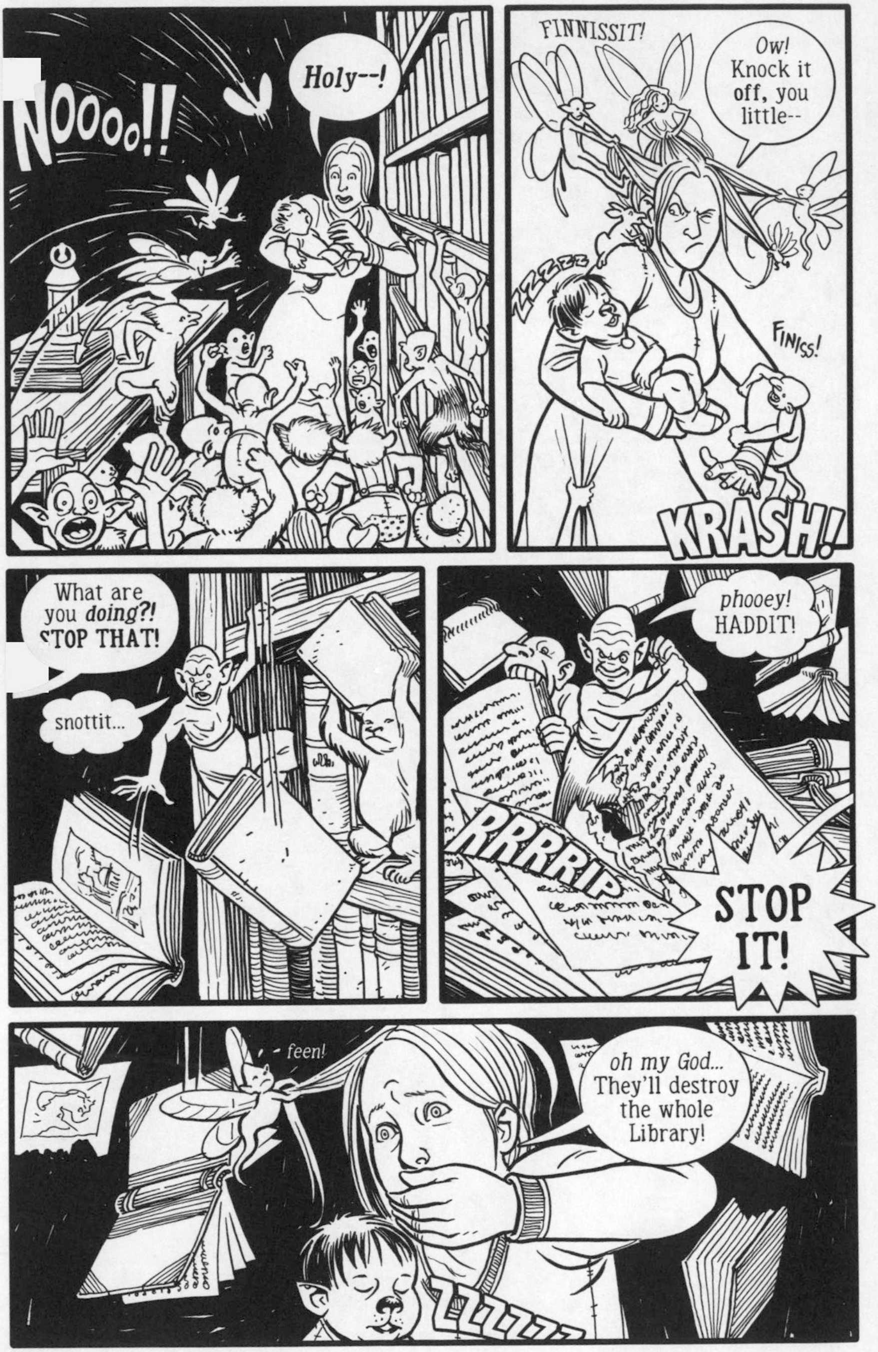
NOOOo!!
Holy--!
FINNISSIT!
Ow! Knock it off, you little--
ZZZZZZ
FINISS!
KRASH!
What are you *doing?!* STOP THAT!
snottit...
phooey! HADDIT!
RRRRRIP
STOP IT!
feen!
oh my God... They'll destroy the whole Library!
ZZZZZZZ

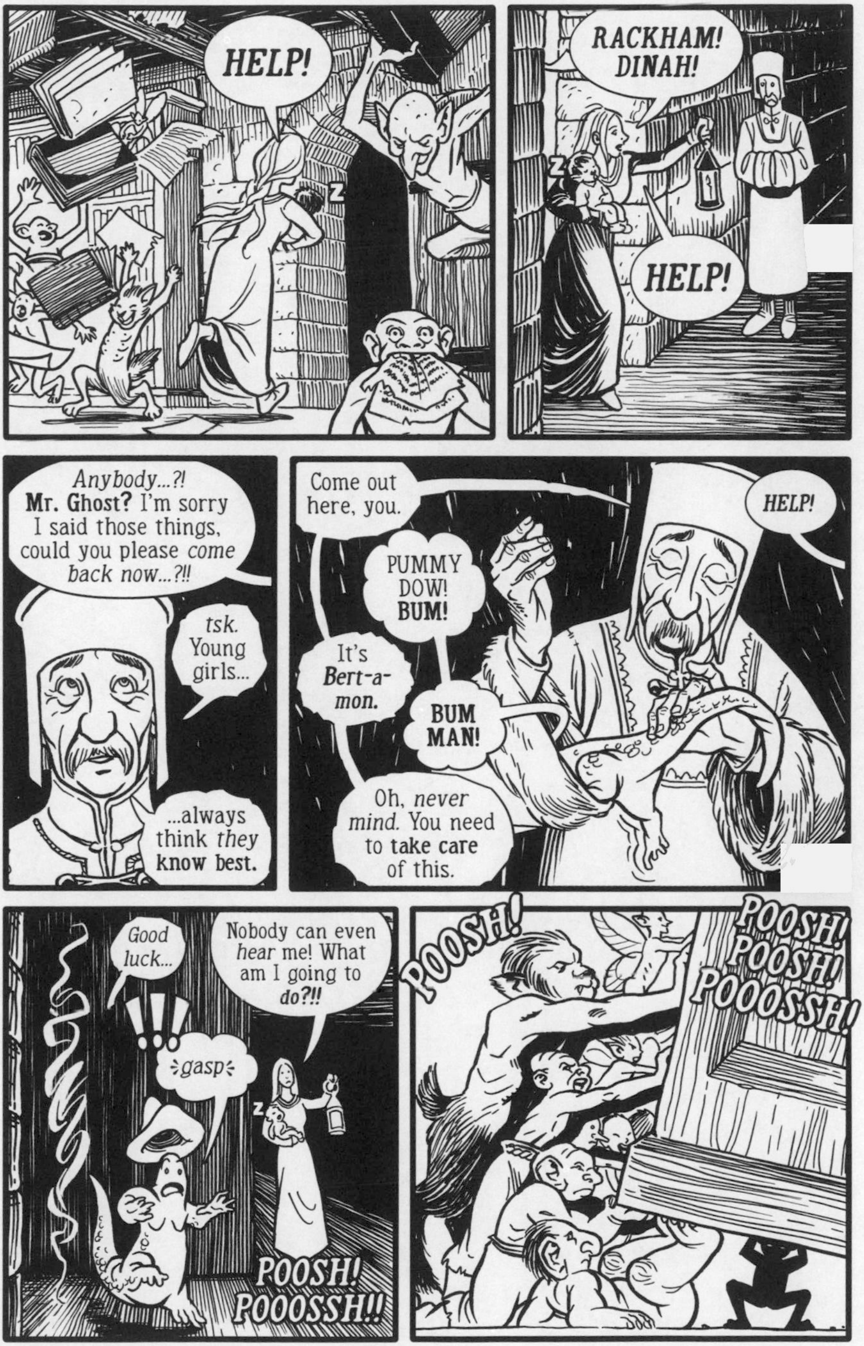
HELP!
RACKHAM! DINAH!
HELP!
Anybody...?! Mr. Ghost? I'm sorry I said those things, could you please come back now...?!!
tsk. Young girls...
...always think they know best.
Come out here, you.
HELP!
PUMMY DOW! BUM!
It's Bert-a-mon.
BUM MAN!
Oh, never mind. You need to take care of this.
Good luck...
Nobody can even hear me! What am I going to do?!!
!!!
gasp
POOSH! POOOSSH!!
POOSH!
POOSH! POOSH! POOOSSH!

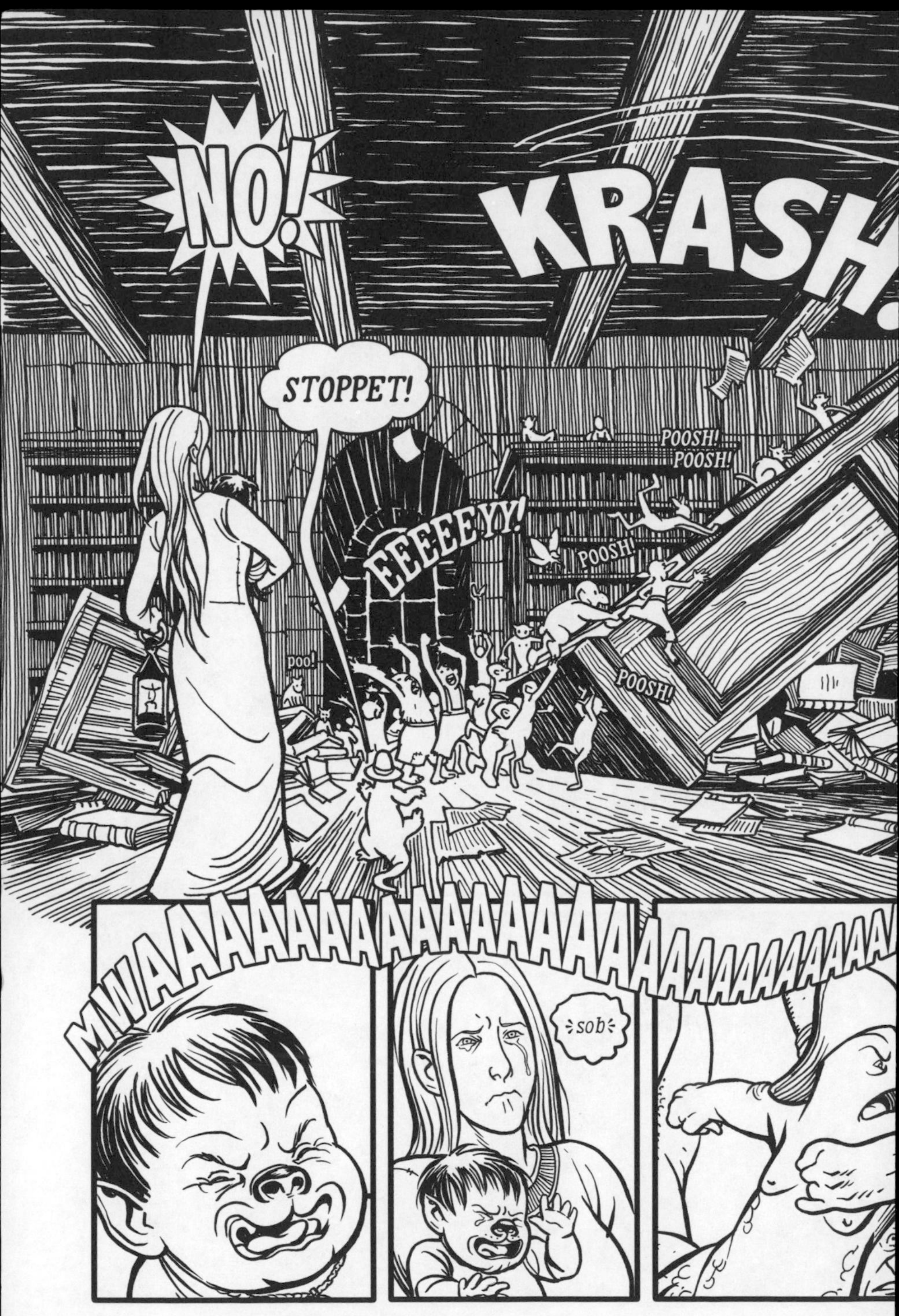
NO!
KRASH!
STOPPET!
POOSH!
POOSH!
EEEEEYY!
POOSH!
poo!
POOSH!
MWAAAAAAAAAAAAAAAAAAAAAAAAAAAAA
sob

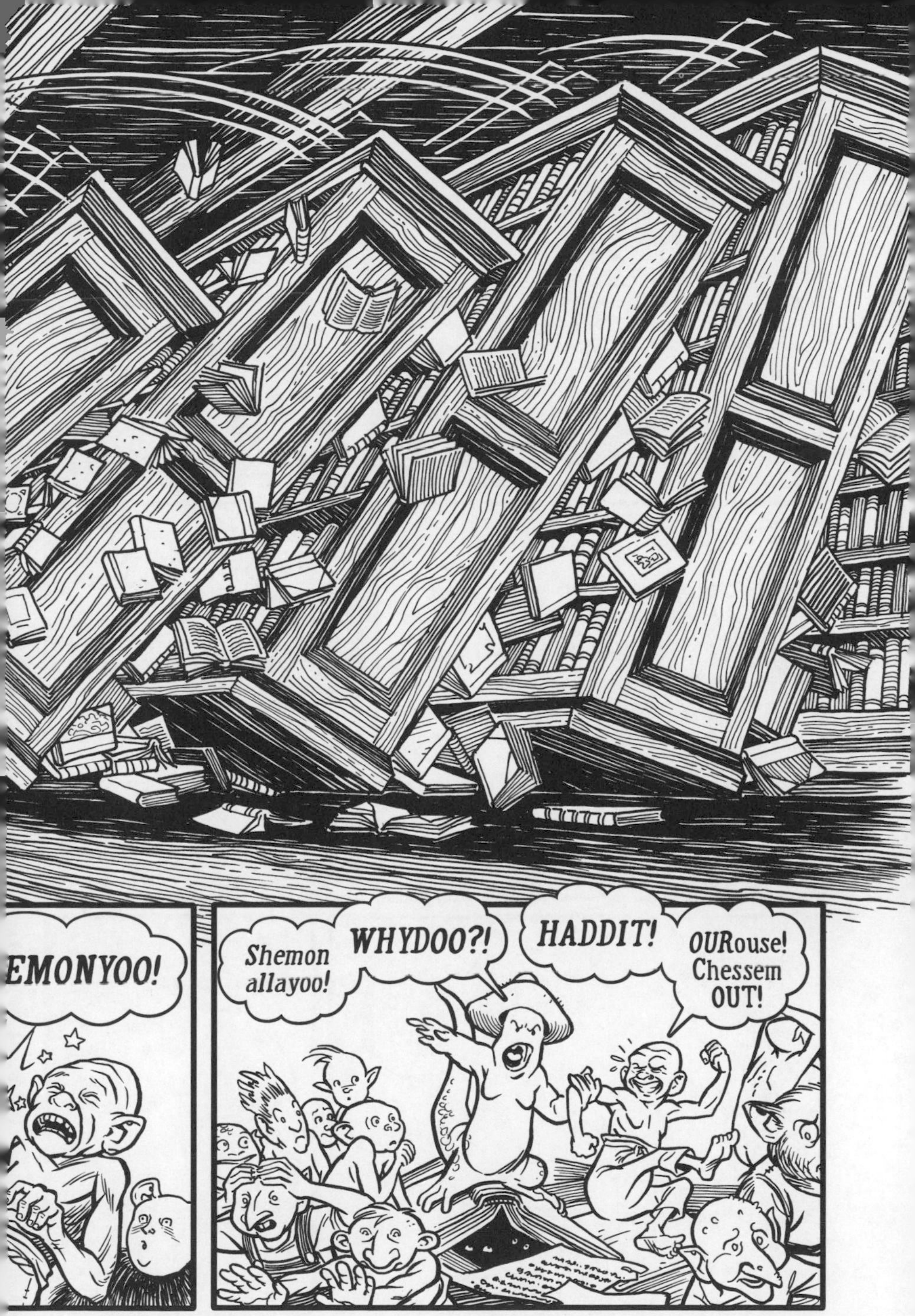
EMONYOO!
Shemon allayoo!
WHYDOO?!
HADDIT!
OURouse! Chessem OUT!

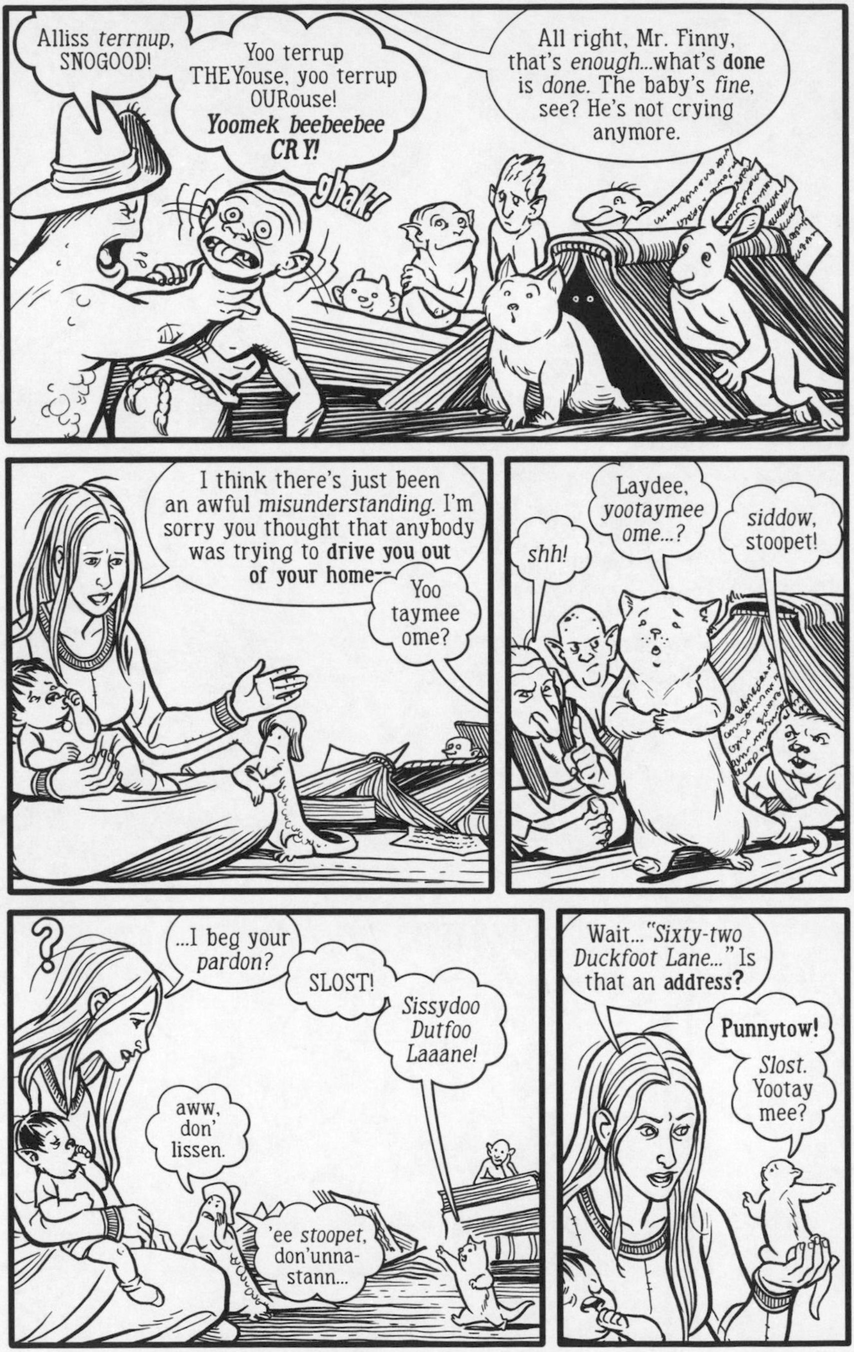
Alliss *terrnup*, SNOGOOD!
Yoo terrup THEYouse, yoo terrup OURouse! ***Yoomek beebeebee CRY!***
ghak!
All right, Mr. Finny, that's *enough*...what's **done** is *done*. The baby's *fine*, see? He's not crying anymore.
I think there's just been an awful *misunderstanding*. I'm sorry you thought that anybody was trying to **drive you out of your home--**
Yoo taymee ome?
shh!
Laydee, *yootaymee ome...?*
siddow, stoopet!
?
...I beg your *pardon?*
SLOST!
Sissydoo Dutfoo Laaane!
aww, don' lissen.
'ee *stoopet*, don'unna-stann...
Wait... "*Sixty-two Duckfoot Lane...*" Is that an **address?**
Punnytow!
Slost. Yootay mee?

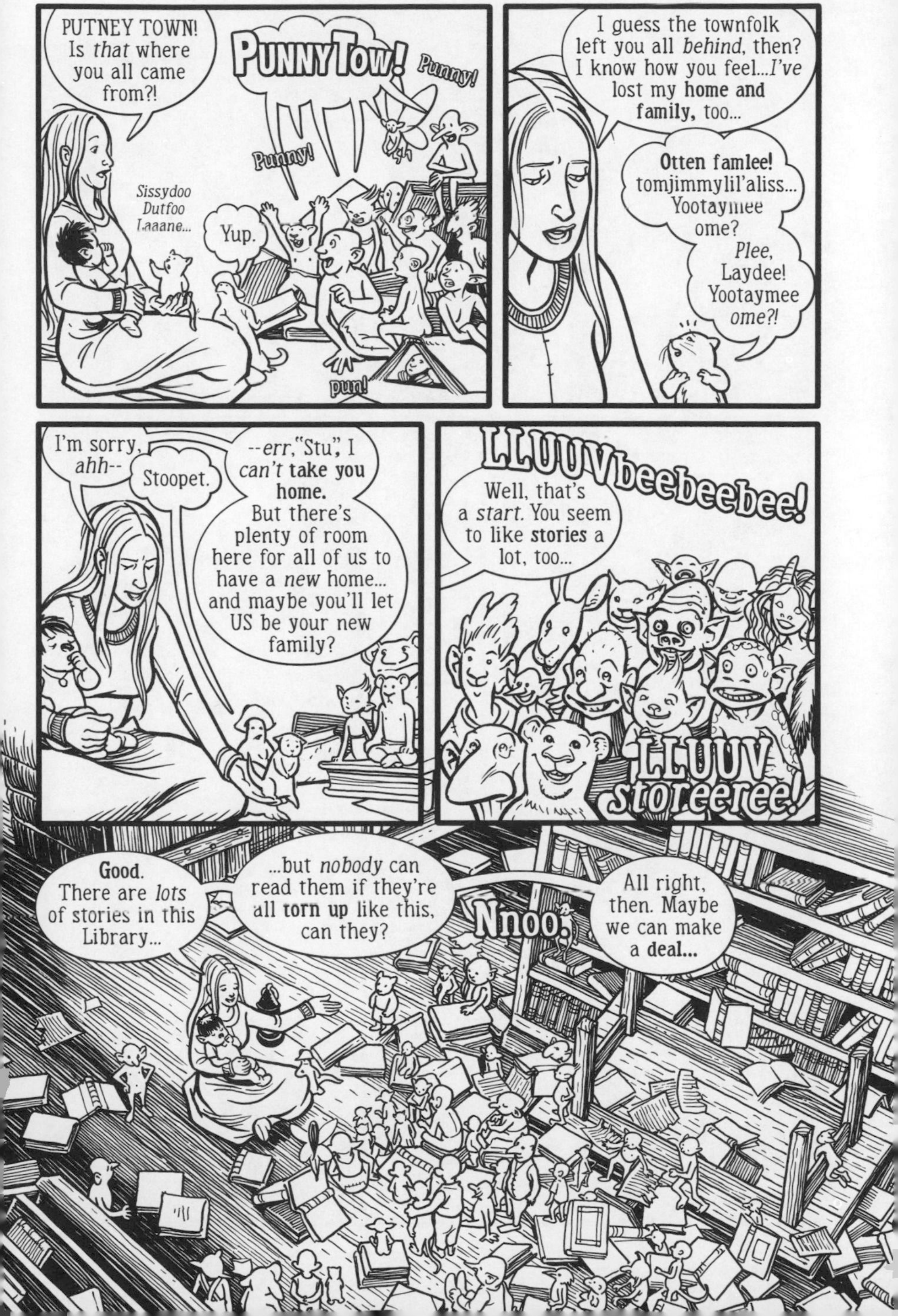
PUTNEY TOWN! Is *that* where you all came from?!
PUNNYTOW!
Punny!
Punny!
Sissydoo Dutfoo Laaane...
Yup.
pun!
I guess the townfolk left you all *behind*, then? I know how you feel...*I've* lost my **home and family,** too...
Otten famlee! tomjimmylil'aliss... Yootaymee ome? *Plee,* Laydee! Yootaymee *ome?!*
I'm sorry, *ahh*--
Stoopet.
--*err*,"Stu", I *can't* **take you home.** But there's plenty of room here for all of us to have a *new* home... and maybe you'll let US be your new family?
LLUUVbeebeebee!
Well, that's a *start*. You seem to like **stories** a lot, too...
LLUUV storeeree!
Good. There are *lots* of stories in this Library...
...but *nobody* can read them if they're all **torn up** like this, can they?
Nnoo.
All right, then. Maybe we can make a **deal...**

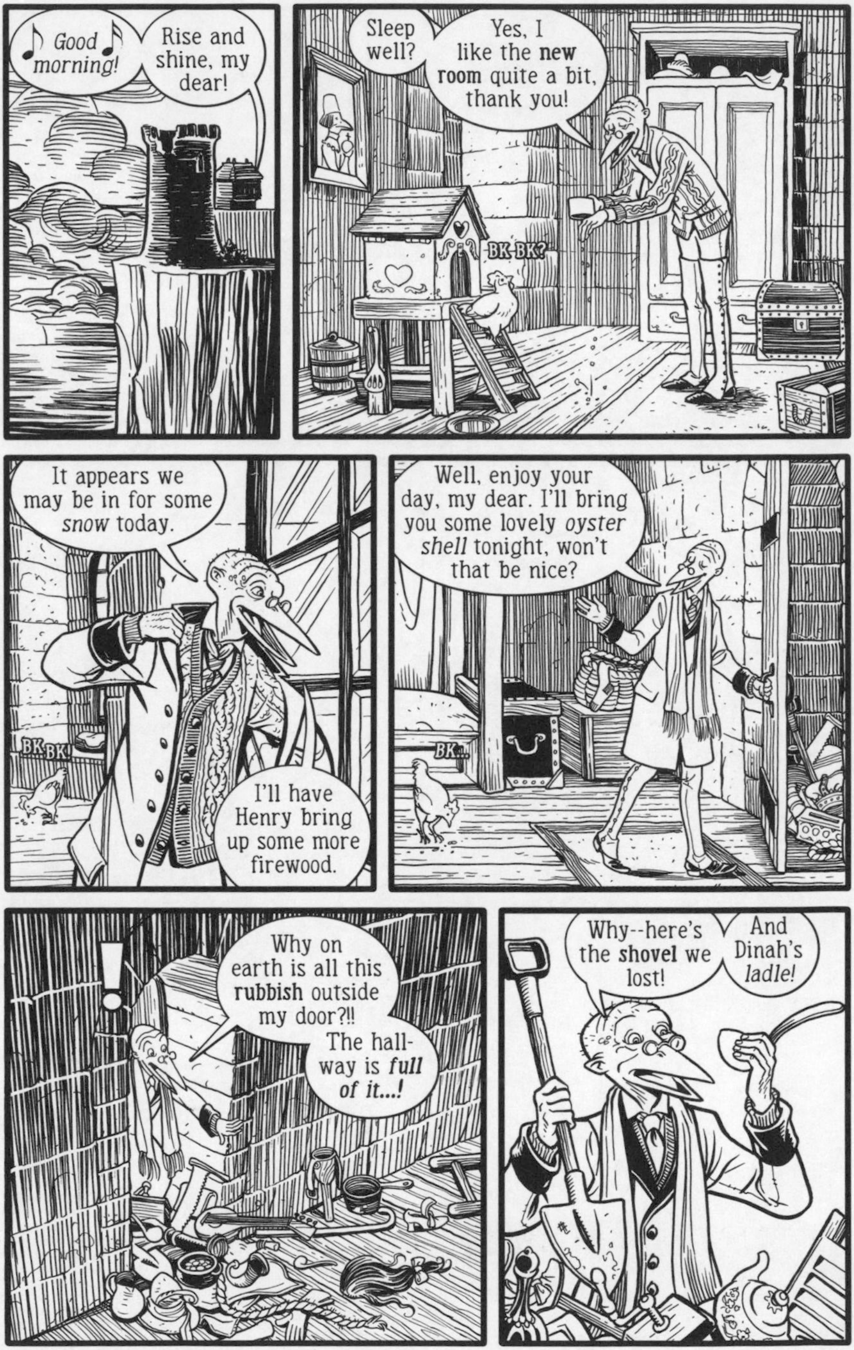
♪ Good ♪ morning!
Rise and shine, my dear!
Sleep well?
Yes, I like the **new room** quite a bit, thank you!
BK BK?
It appears we may be in for some *snow* today.
BK BK!
I'll have Henry bring up some more firewood.
Well, enjoy your day, my dear. I'll bring you some lovely *oyster shell* tonight, won't that be nice?
BK...
!
Why on earth is all this **rubbish** outside my door?!!
The hall-way is ***full of it...!***
Why--here's the **shovel** we lost!
And Dinah's *ladle!*

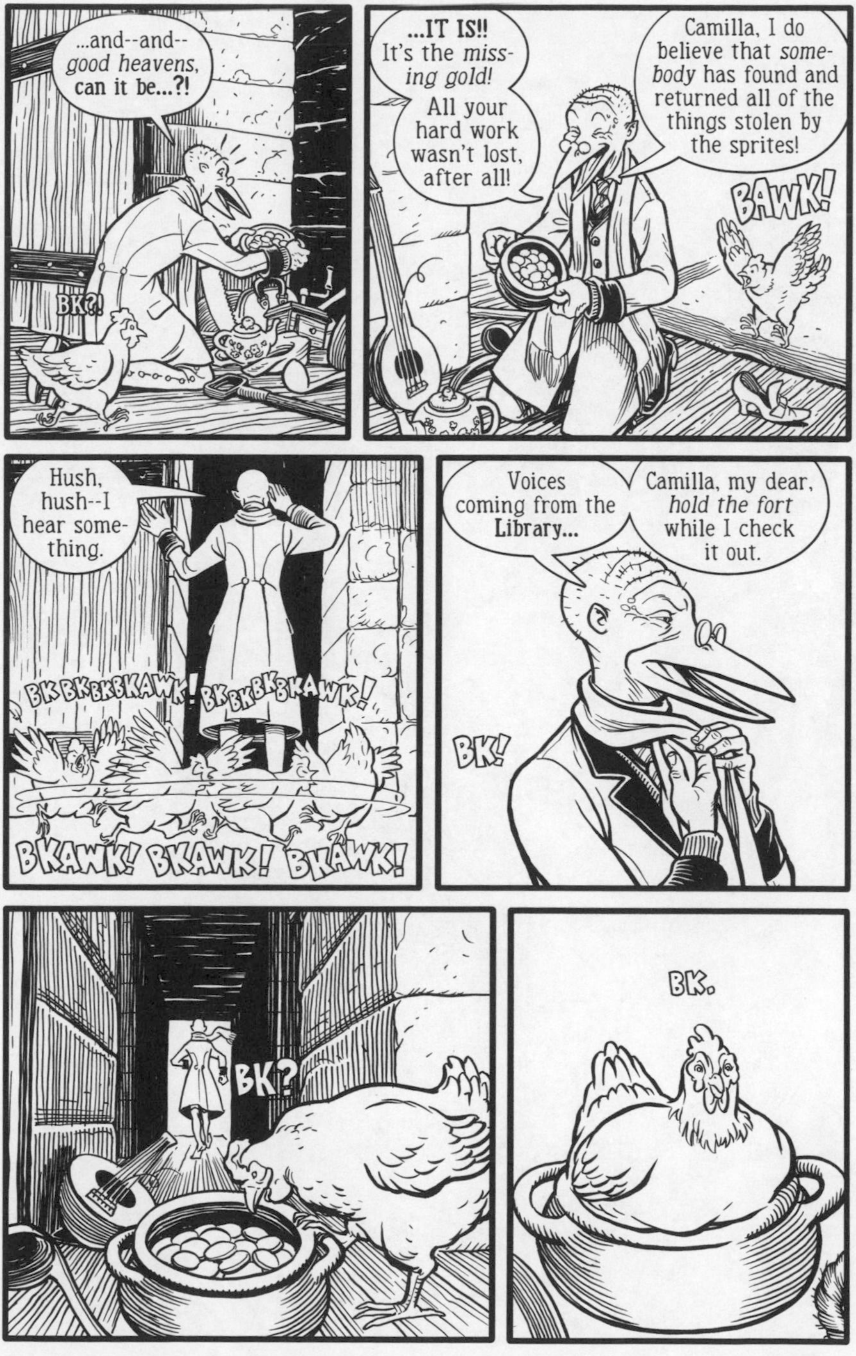
...and--and--
good heavens,
can it be...?!
BK?!
...IT IS!!
It's the *miss-ing gold!*
All your hard work wasn't lost, after all!
Camilla, I do believe that *some-body* has found and returned all of the things stolen by the sprites!
BAWK!
Hush, hush--I hear some-thing.
BKBKBKBKAWK! BKBKBKBKAWK!
BKAWK! BKAWK! BKAWK!
Voices coming from the **Library...**
Camilla, my dear, *hold the fort* while I check it out.
BK!
BK?
BK.

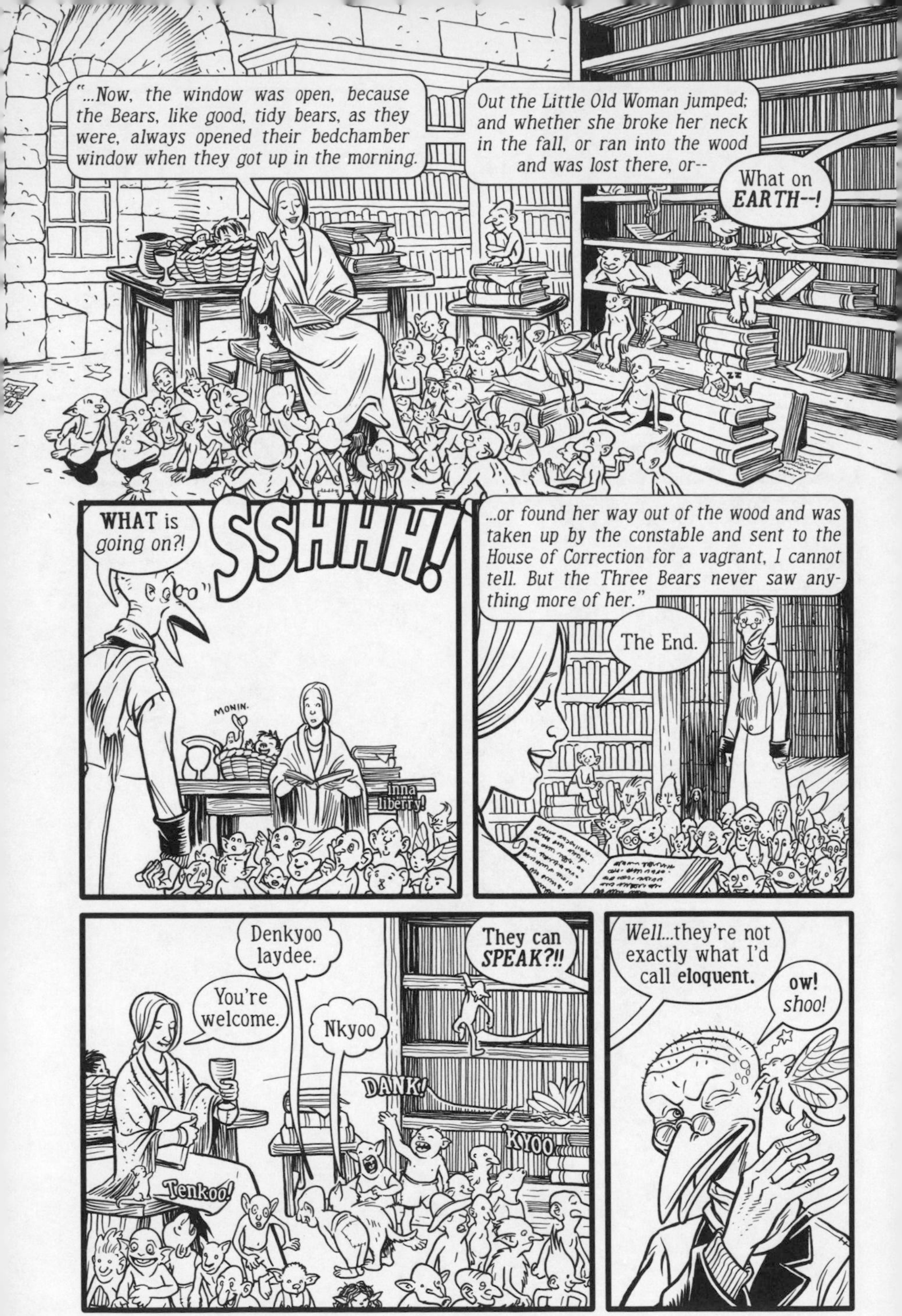
"...Now, the window was open, because the Bears, like good, tidy bears, as they were, always opened their bedchamber window when they got up in the morning.
Out the Little Old Woman jumped; and whether she broke her neck in the fall, or ran into the wood and was lost there, or--
What on EARTH--!
WHAT is going on?!
SSHHH!
MONIN.
inna liberry!
...or found her way out of the wood and was taken up by the constable and sent to the House of Correction for a vagrant, I cannot tell. But the Three Bears never saw anything more of her."
The End.
Denkyoo laydee.
You're welcome.
Nkyoo
They can SPEAK?!!
DANK!
'KYOO
Tenkoo!
Well...they're not exactly what I'd call eloquent.
ow! shoo!

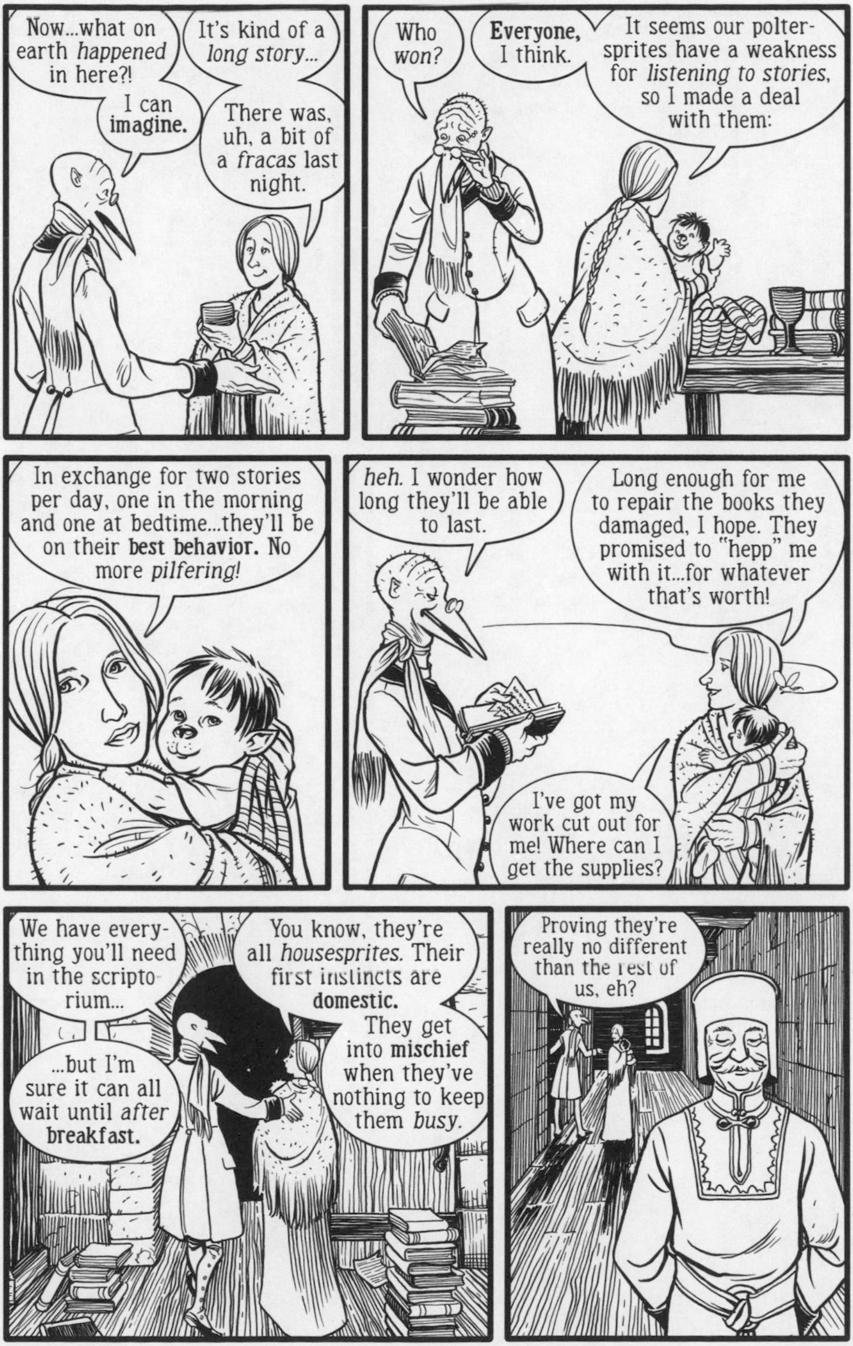
Now...what on earth *happened* in here?!
It's kind of a *long story*...
I can **imagine.**
There was, uh, a bit of a *fracas* last night.
Who *won?*
Everyone, I think.
It seems our polter-sprites have a weakness for *listening to stories*, so I made a deal with them:
In exchange for two stories per day, one in the morning and one at bedtime...they'll be on their **best behavior.** No more *pilfering!*
heh. I wonder how long they'll be able to last.
Long enough for me to repair the books they damaged, I hope. They promised to "hepp" me with it...for whatever that's worth!
I've got my work cut out for me! Where can I get the supplies?
We have every-thing you'll need in the scripto-rium...
...but I'm sure it can all wait until *after* **breakfast.**
You know, they're all *housesprites.* Their first instincts are **domestic.**
They get into **mischief** when they've nothing to keep them *busy.*
Proving they're really no different than the rest of us, eh?

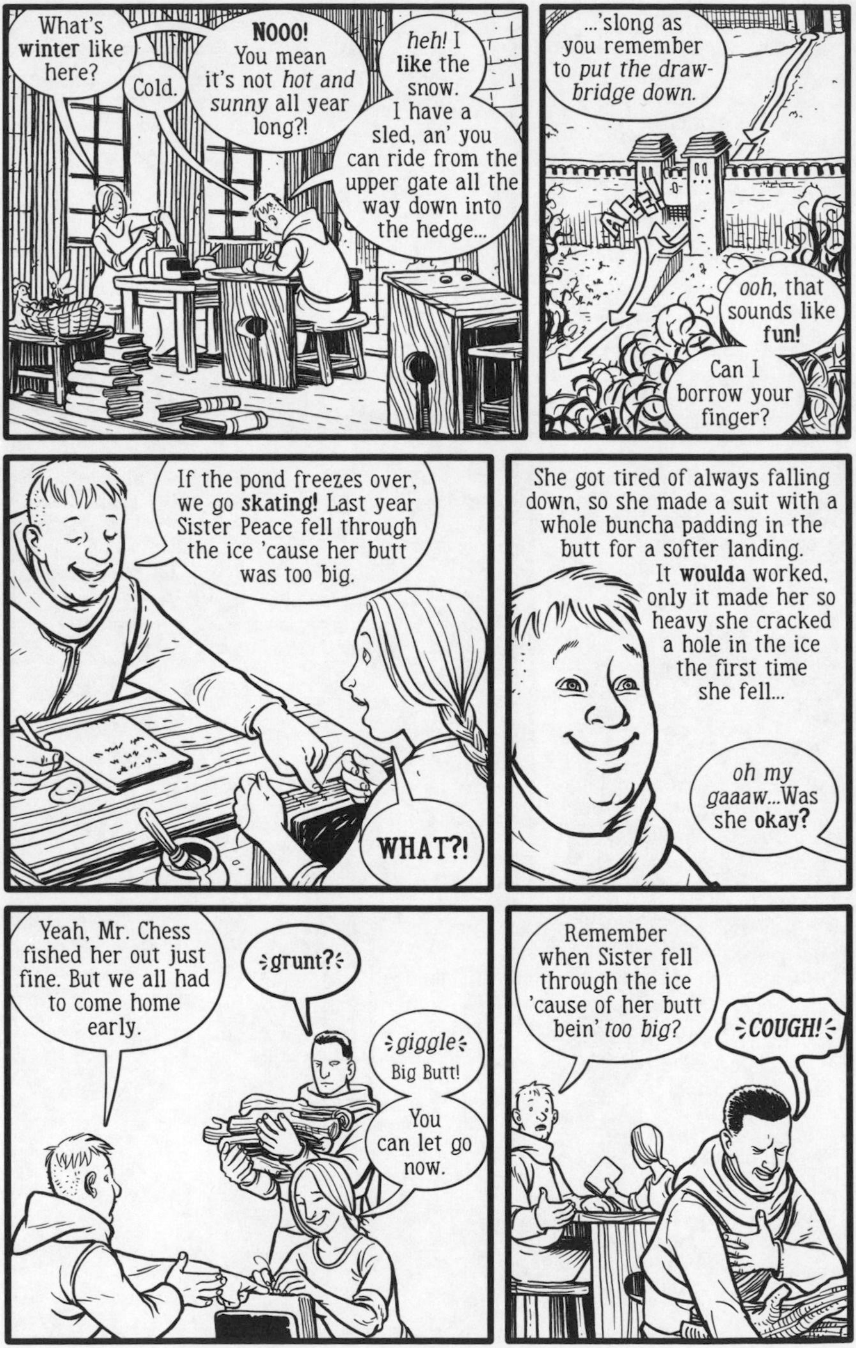
What's **winter** like here?
Cold.
NOOO! You mean it's not *hot and sunny* all year long?!
heh! I **like** the snow.
I have a sled, an' you can ride from the upper gate all the way down into the hedge...
...'slong as you remember to *put the draw-bridge down.*
AIEE!
ooh, that sounds like **fun!**
Can I borrow your finger?
If the pond freezes over, we go **skating!** Last year Sister Peace fell through the ice 'cause her butt was too big.
WHAT?!
She got tired of always falling down, so she made a suit with a whole buncha padding in the butt for a softer landing.
It **woulda** worked, only it made her so heavy she cracked a hole in the ice the first time she fell...
oh my gaaaw...Was she **okay?**
Yeah, Mr. Chess fished her out just fine. But we all had to come home early.
grunt?
giggle
Big Butt!
You can let go now.
Remember when Sister fell through the ice 'cause of her butt bein' *too big?*
COUGH!

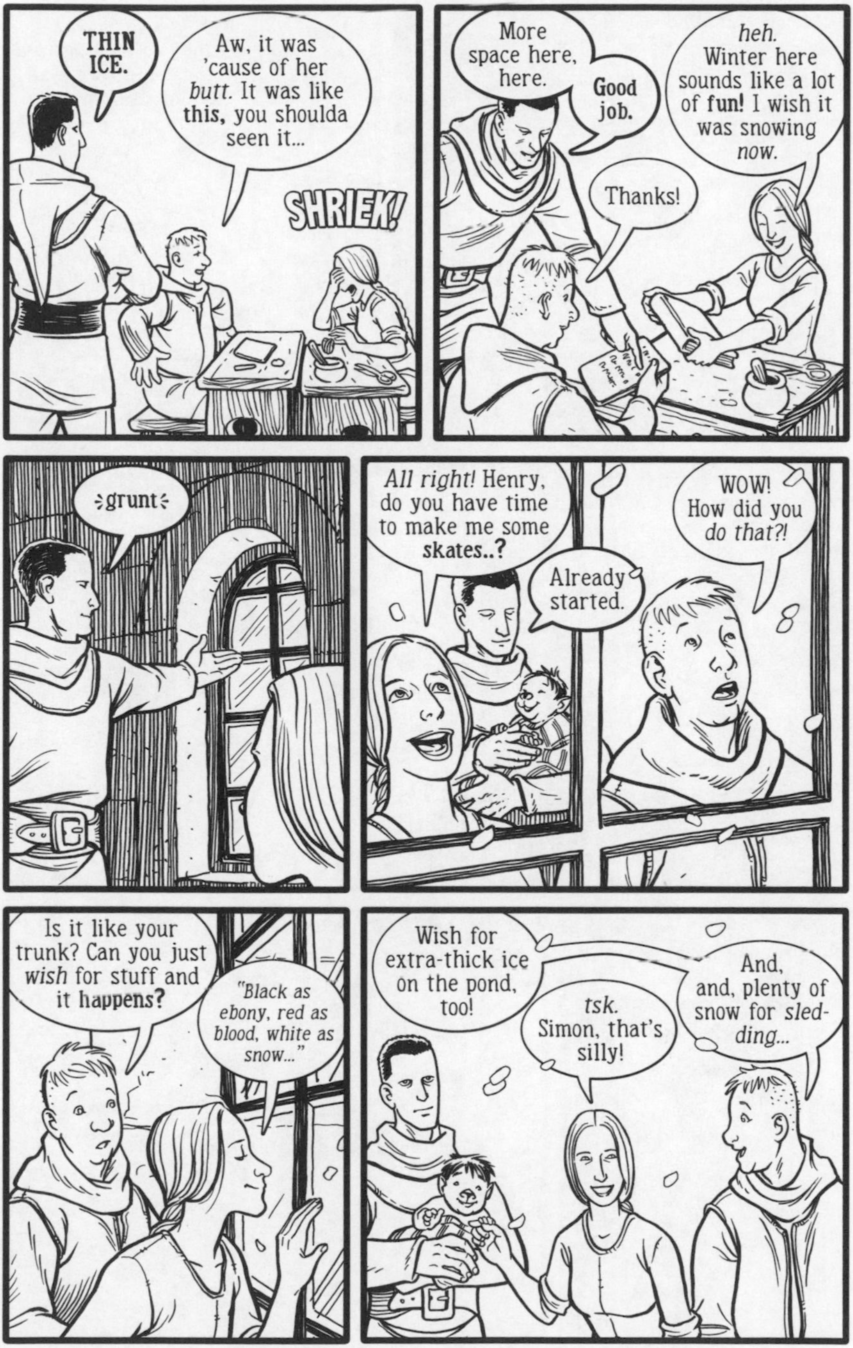
THIN ICE.
Aw, it was 'cause of her *butt.* It was like **this,** you shoulda seen it...
SHRIEK!
More space here, here.
Good job.
Thanks!
heh. Winter here sounds like a lot of **fun!** I wish it was snowing *now.*
grunt
All right! Henry, do you have time to make me some **skates..?**
Already started.
WOW! How did you *do that?!*
Is it like your trunk? Can you just *wish* for stuff and it **happens?**
"Black as ebony, red as blood, white as snow..."
Wish for extra-thick ice on the pond, too!
And, and, plenty of snow for *sled-ding...*
tsk. Simon, that's silly!

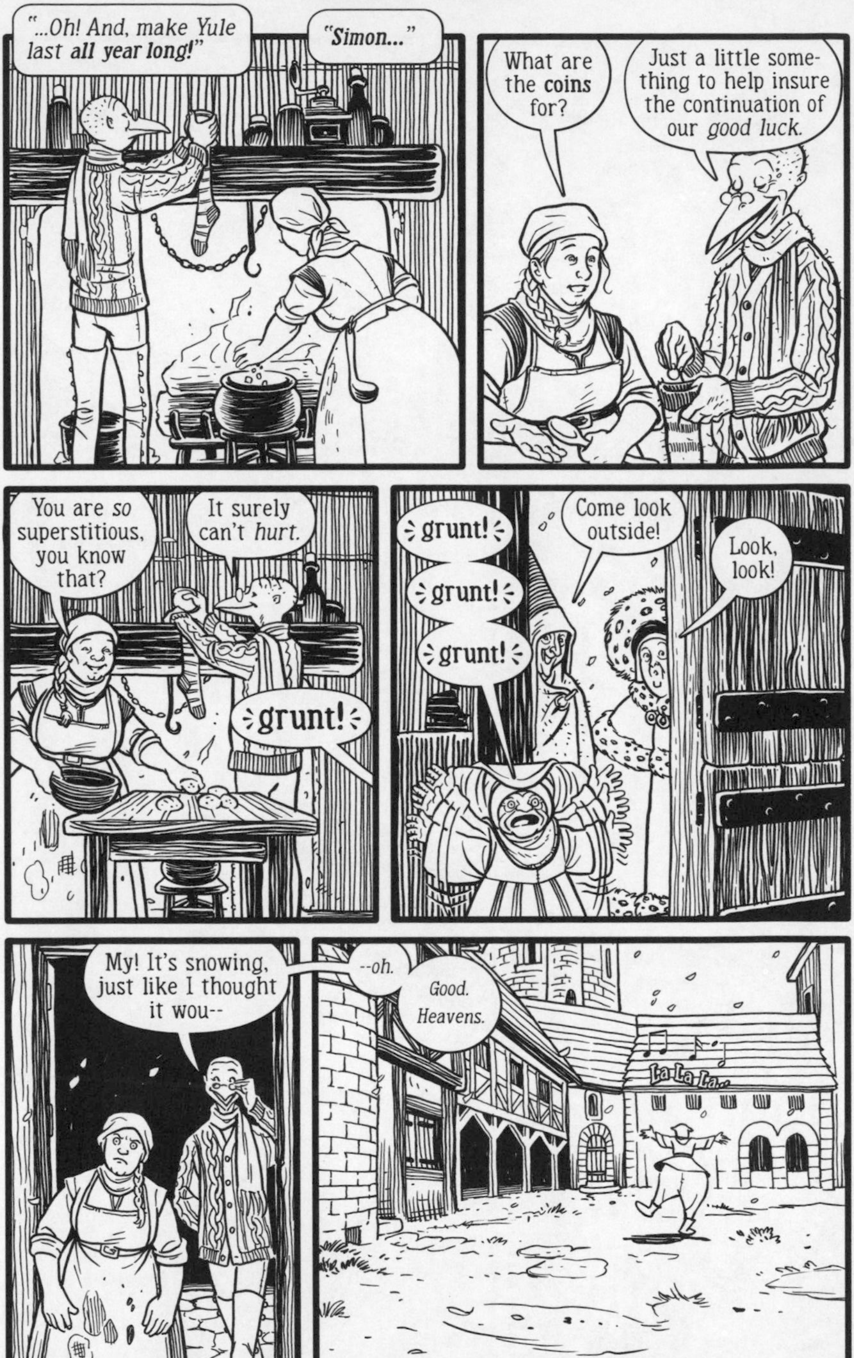
"...Oh! And, make Yule last all year long!"
"Simon..."
What are the coins for?
Just a little something to help insure the continuation of our good luck.
You are so superstitious, you know that?
It surely can't hurt.
grunt!
grunt!
grunt!
grunt!
Come look outside!
Look, look!
My! It's snowing, just like I thought it wou--
--oh.
Good. Heavens.
La La La..

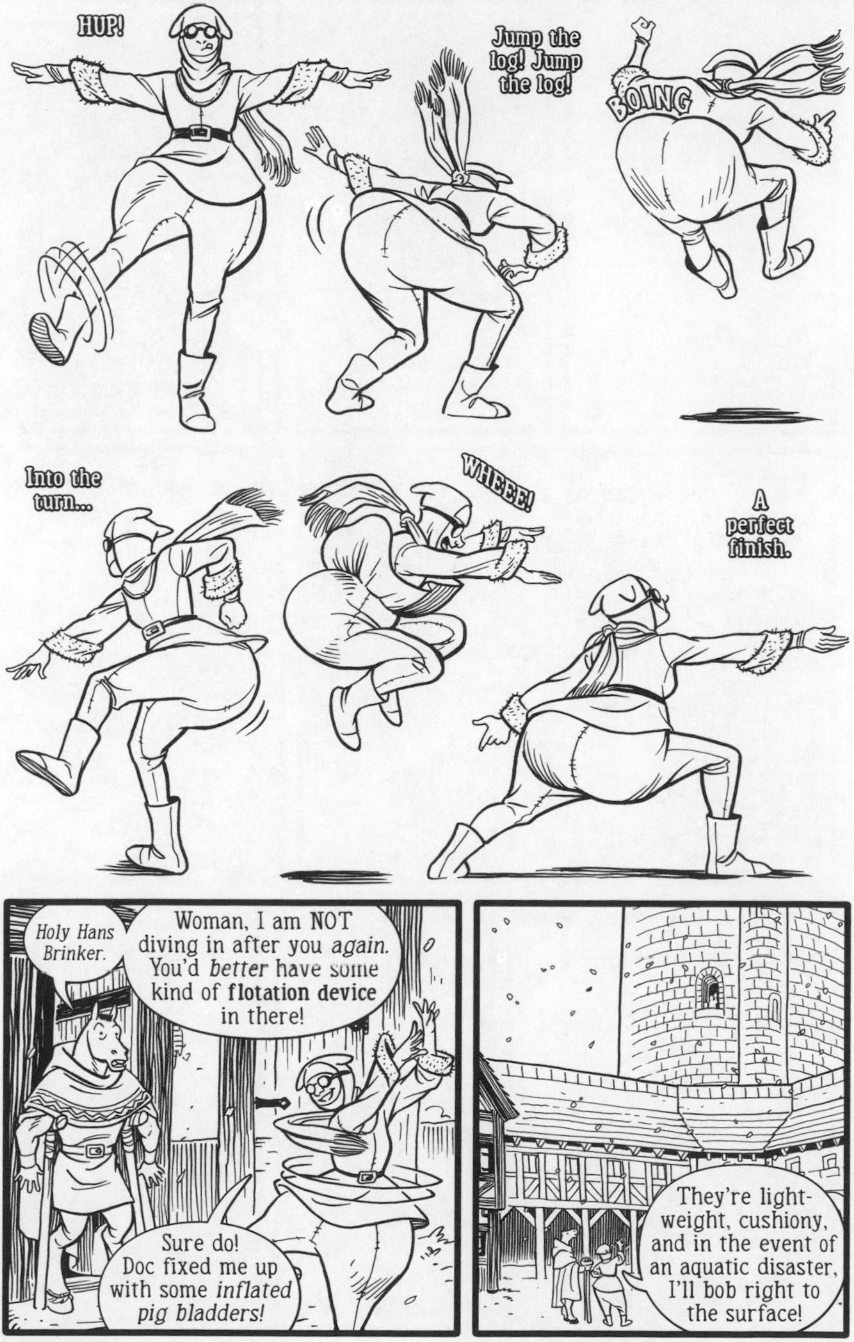
HUP!
Jump the log! Jump the log!
BOING
Into the turn...
WHEEE!
A perfect finish.
Holy Hans Brinker.
Woman, I am NOT diving in after you *again*. You'd *better* have some kind of **flotation device** in there!
Sure do! Doc fixed me up with some *inflated pig bladders!*
They're light-weight, cushiony, and in the event of an aquatic disaster, I'll bob right to the surface!

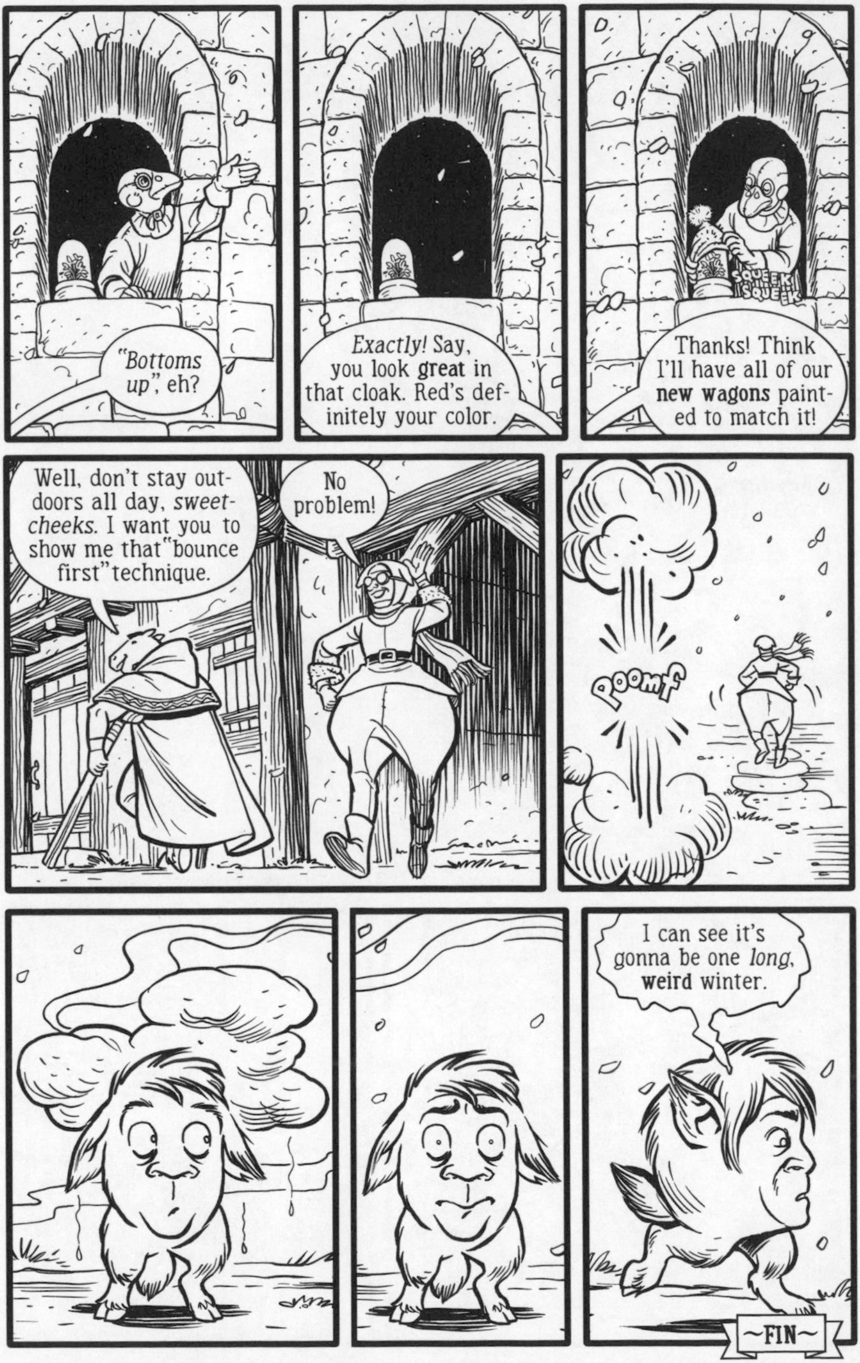
"Bottoms up", eh?
Exactly! Say, you look great in that cloak. Red's definitely your color.
SQUEEK SQUEEK
Thanks! Think I'll have all of our new wagons painted to match it!
Well, don't stay outdoors all day, sweetcheeks. I want you to show me that "bounce first" technique.
No problem!
POOMF
I can see it's gonna be one long, weird winter.
~FIN~

Epilogue.

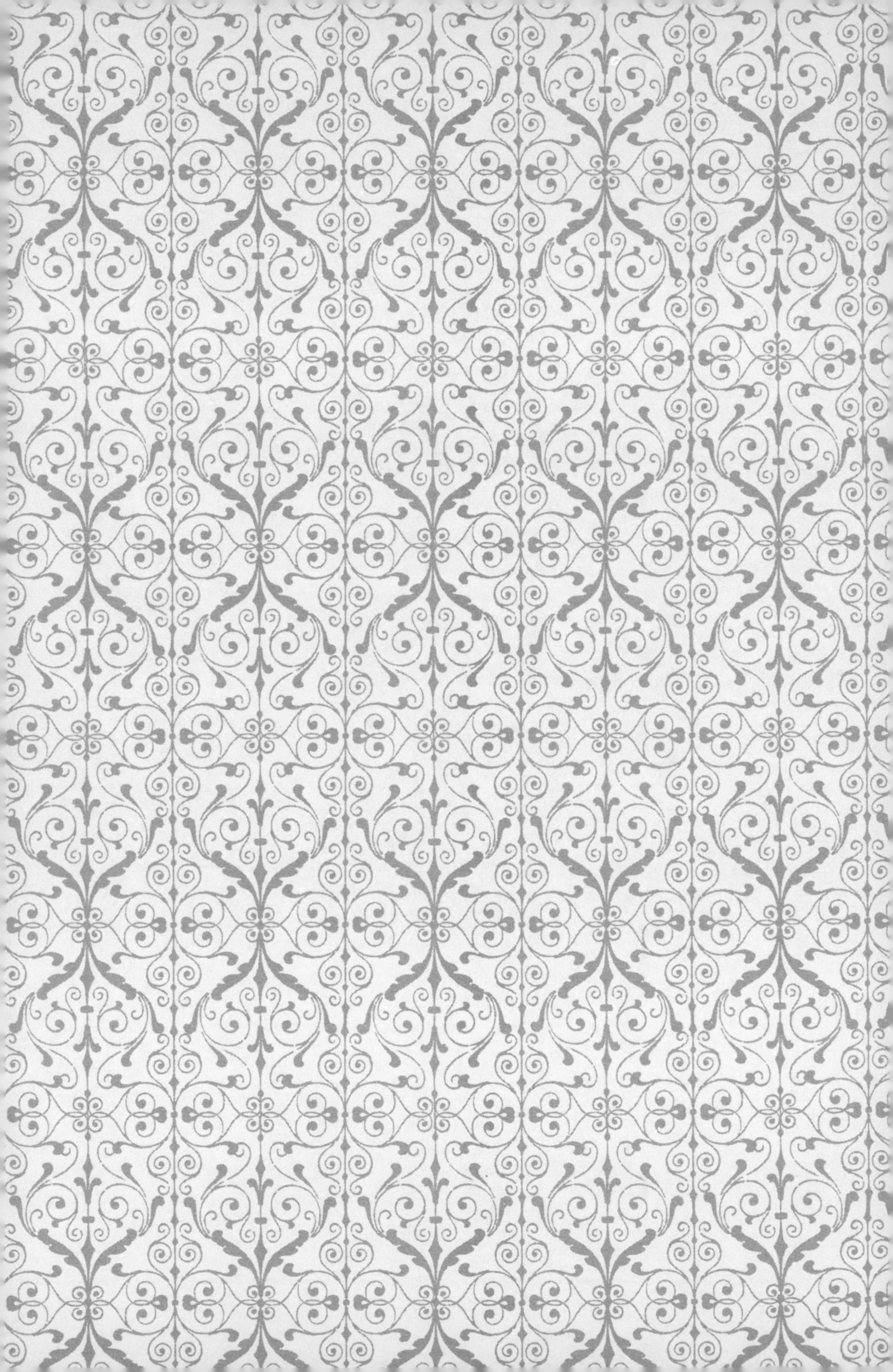

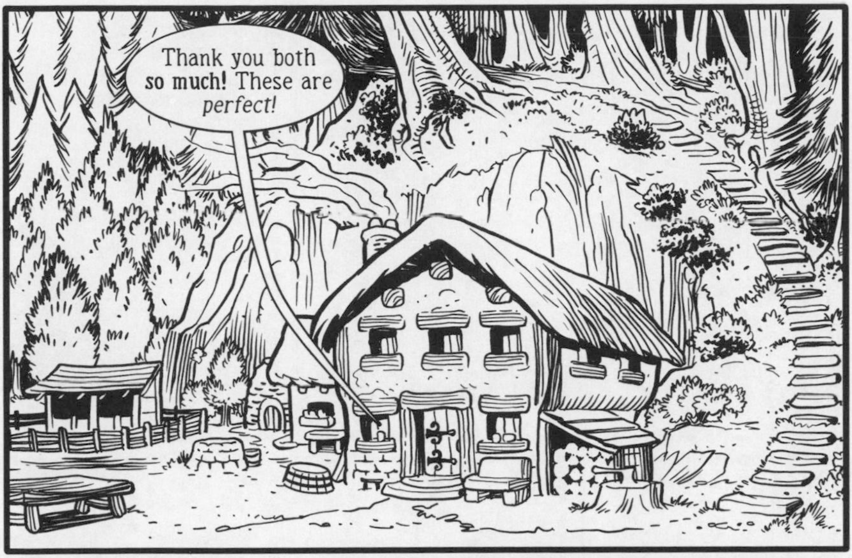
Thank you both **so much!** These are *perfect!*

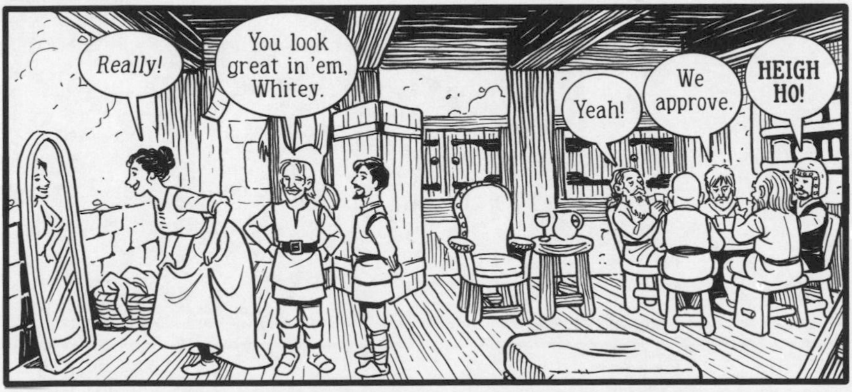
Really!
You look great in 'em, Whitey.
Yeah!
We approve.
HEIGH HO!

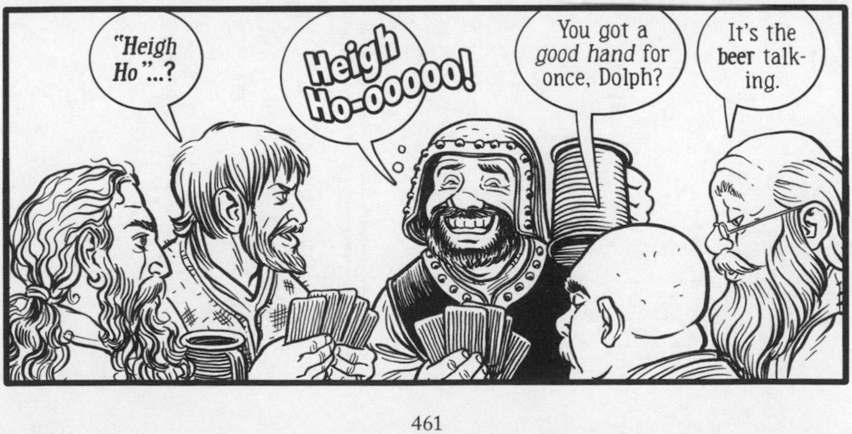
"Heigh Ho"...?
Heigh Ho-ooooo!
You got a *good hand* for once, Dolph?
It's the **beer** talk-ing.

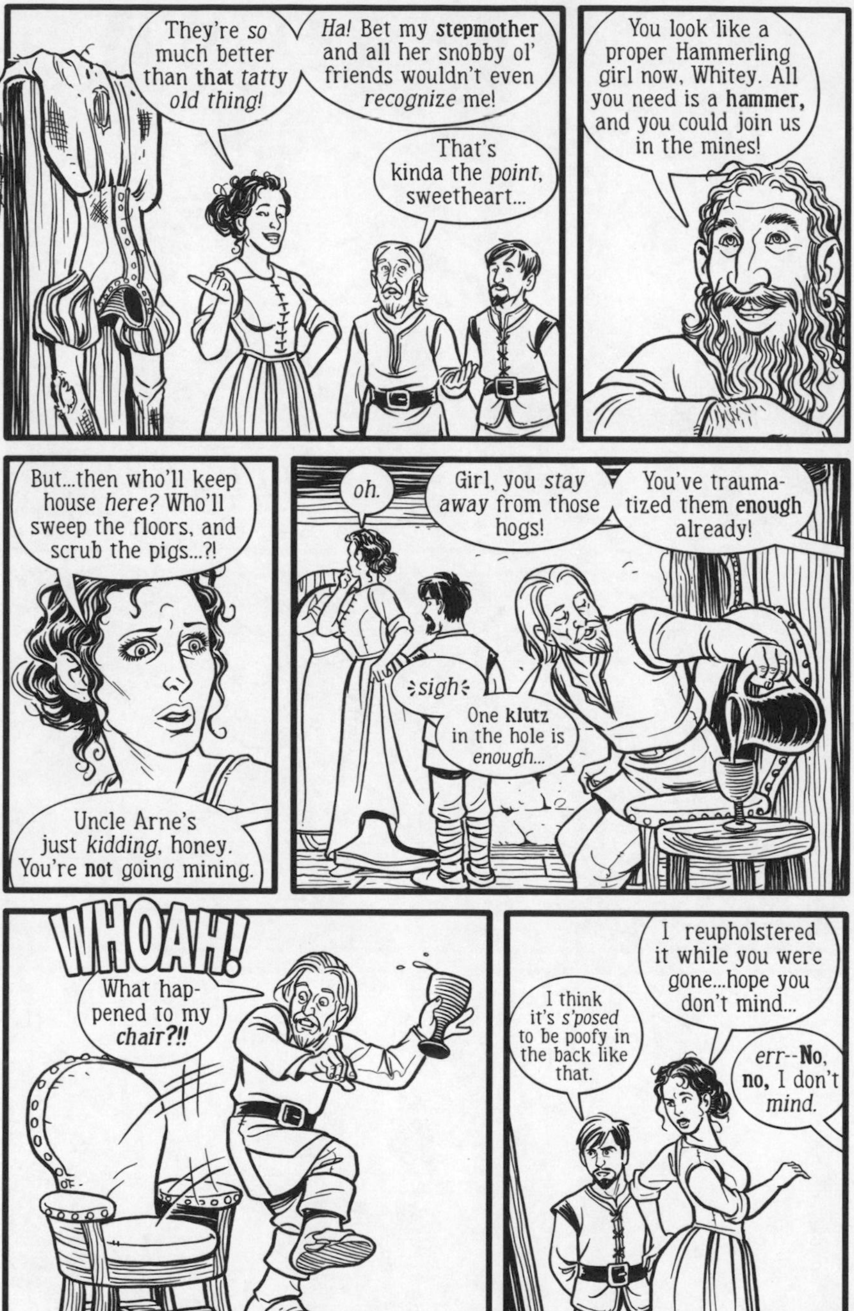
They're *so* much better than **that** *tatty old thing!*
Ha! Bet my **stepmother** and all her snobby ol' friends wouldn't even *recognize* me!
That's kinda the *point*, sweetheart...
You look like a proper Hammerling girl now, Whitey. All you need is a **hammer,** and you could join us in the mines!
But...then who'll keep house *here?* Who'll sweep the floors, and scrub the pigs...?!
Uncle Arne's just *kidding*, honey. You're **not** going mining.
oh.
Girl, you *stay away* from those hogs!
You've trauma-tized them **enough** already!
sigh
One **klutz** in the hole is *enough...*
WHOAH!
What hap-pened to my ***chair?!!***
I think it's *s'posed* to be poofy in the back like that.
I reupholstered it while you were gone...hope you don't mind...
err--**No, no,** I don't *mind.*

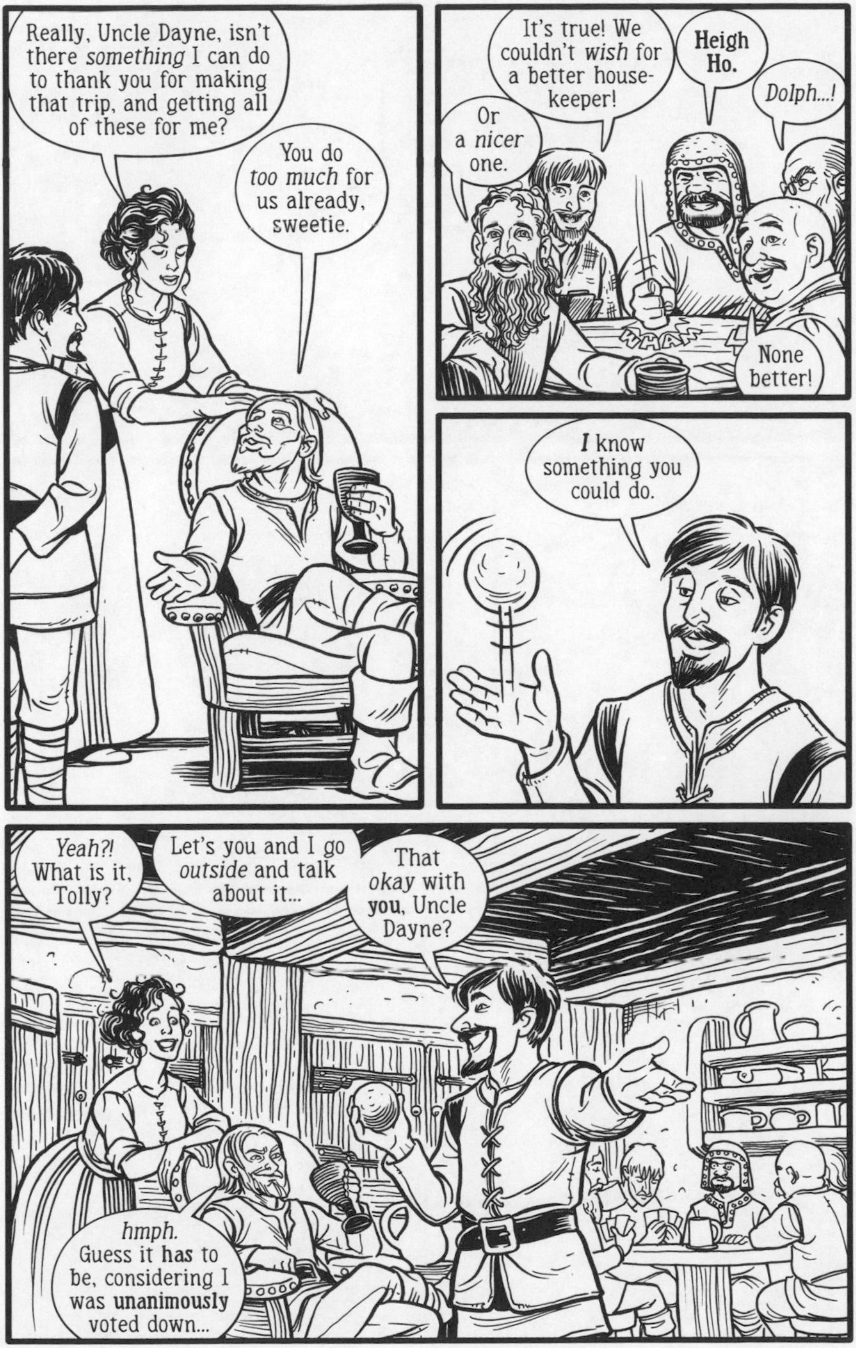
Really, Uncle Dayne, isn't there *something* I can do to thank you for making that trip, and getting all of these for me?
You do *too much* for us already, sweetie.
It's true! We couldn't *wish* for a better house-keeper!
Or a *nicer* one.
Heigh Ho.
Dolph...!
WHAM
None better!
I know something you could do.
Yeah?! What is it, Tolly?
Let's you and I go *outside* and talk about it...
That *okay* with **you**, Uncle Dayne?
hmph. Guess it **has** to be, considering I was **unanimously** voted down...

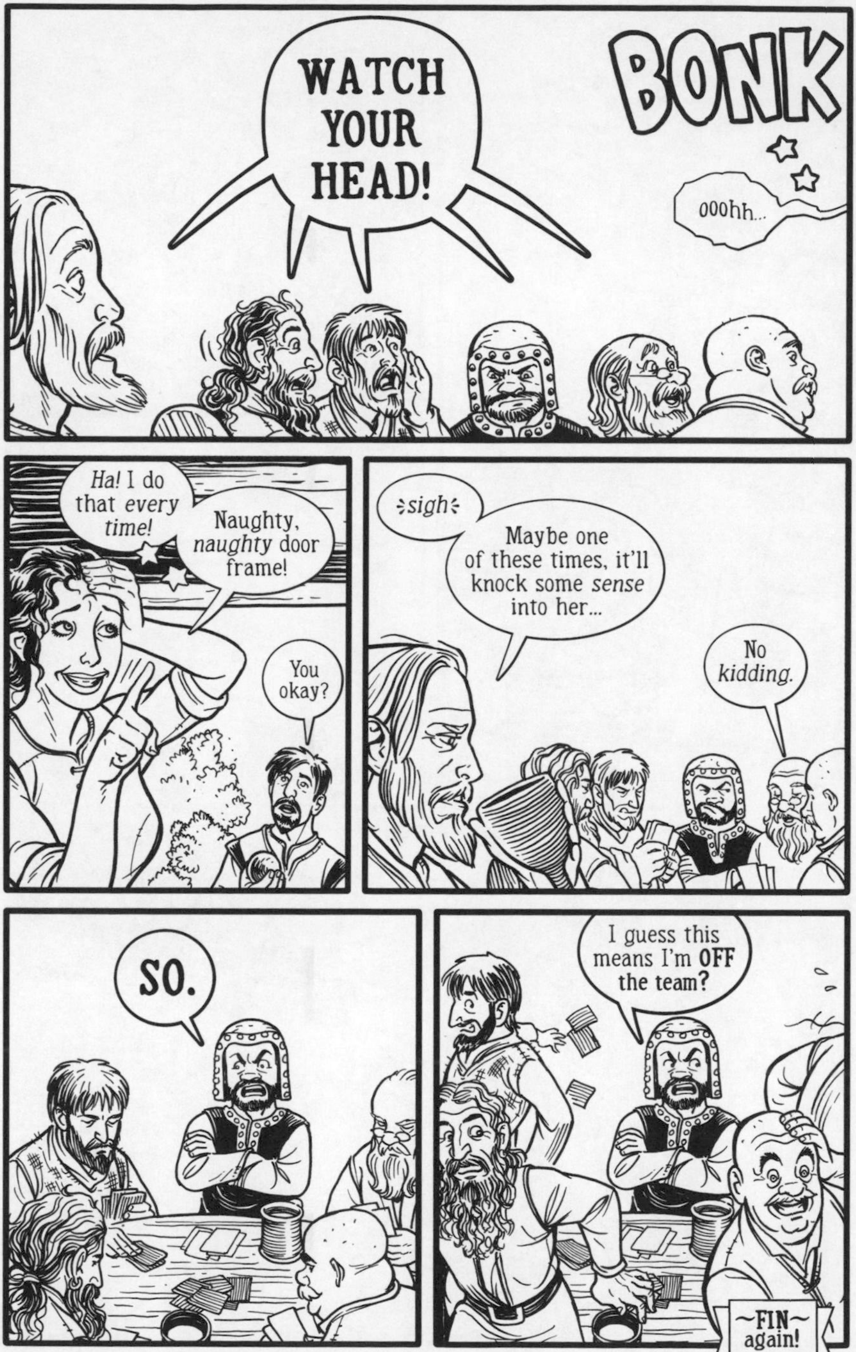
WATCH YOUR HEAD!
BONK
ooohh...
Ha! I do that *every time!*
Naughty, *naughty* door frame!
You okay?
sigh
Maybe one of these times, it'll knock some *sense* into her...
No *kidding*.
SO.
I guess this means I'm **OFF** the team?
~FIN~ again!

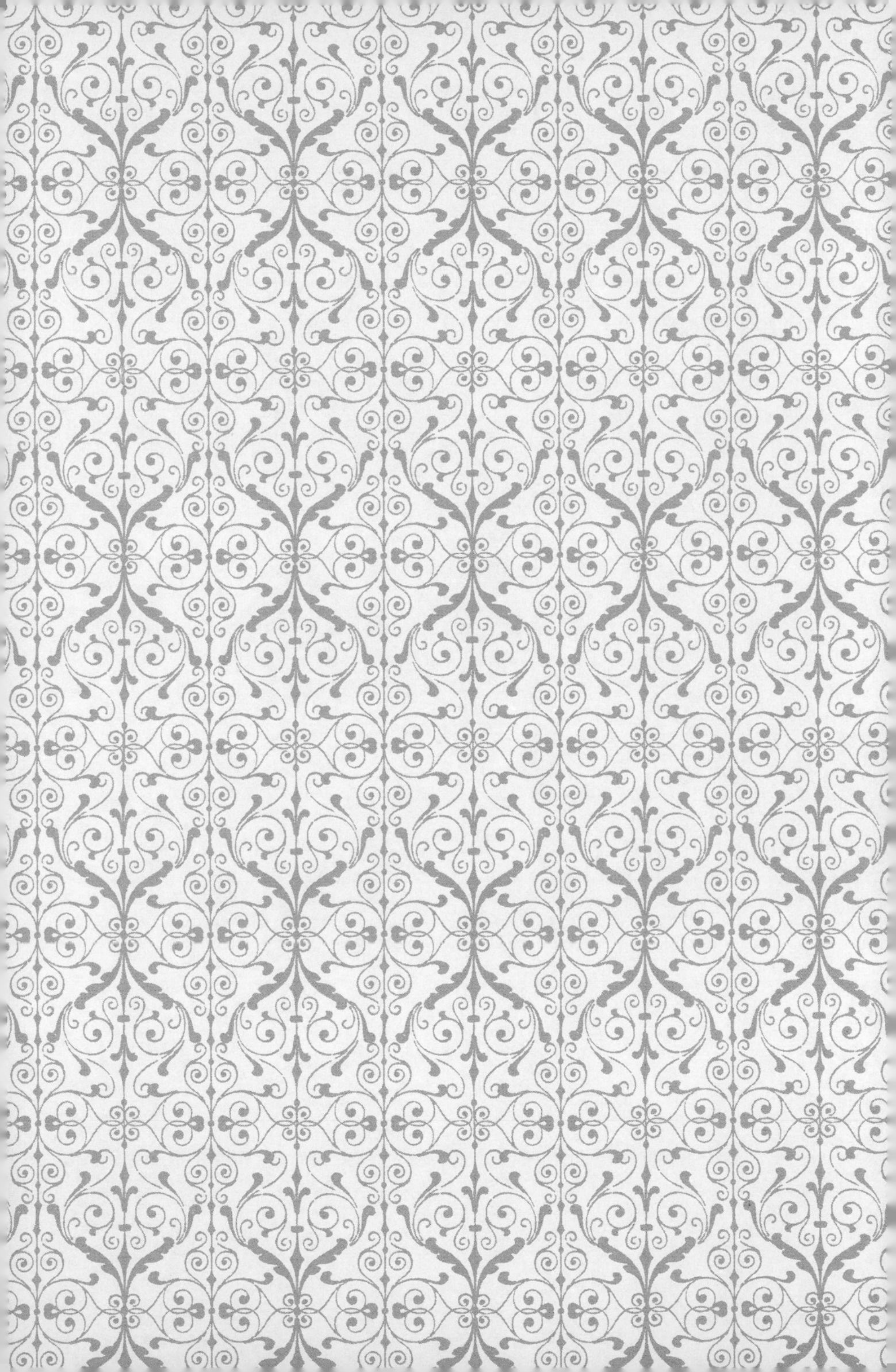

EDITED BY KIM THOMPSON.
GRAPHIC DESIGN BY ADAM GRANO.
PRODUCTION BY PRESTON WHITE.
ASSOCIATE PUBLISHER: ERIC REYNOLDS.
PUBLISHERS: GARY GROTH & KIM THOMPSON.

Castle Waiting is ™ & © Linda Medley.

Distributed in the U.S. by W.W. Norton and Company, Inc. (212-
354-5500); distributed to the U.S. comics market by Diamond
Comic Distributors (800-452-6642); distributed in Canada by
Canadian Manda Group (416-516-0911); distributed in the United
Kingdom by Turnaround Distribution (208-829-3009)

To receive a free catalogue of fine comics and books (including
Volume I of *Castle Waiting*) call 1-800-657-1100 or visit
fantagraphics.com

ISBN: 978-1-60699-633-1

First printing, February 2013. Printed in Singapore.